Jesus, Skepticism
& the Problem
of History

Jesus, Skepticism & the Problem of History

Criteria & Context in the Study of Christian Origins

DARRELL L. BOCK AND
J. ED KOMOSZEWSKI, EDITORS

ZONDERVAN ACADEMIC

Jesus, Skepticism, and the Problem of History
Copyright © 2019 by Darrell L. Bock and J. Ed Komoszewski

ISBN 978-0-310-53476-1 (softcover)

ISBN 978-0-310-53477-8 (ebook)

Requests for information should be addressed to:
Zondervan, 3900 Sparks Dr. SE, Grand Rapids, Michigan 49546

Cover design: Brand Navigation
Cover photography: Shutterstock, Dreamstime
Interior design: Kait Lamphere

Printed in the United States of America

19 20 21 22 23 24 25 26 27 28 29 /LSC/ 15 14 13 12 11 10 9 8 7 6 5 4 3 2 1

Contents

Foreword

N. T. WRIGHT

Raise the subject of Jesus and you are in for quite a conversation. Invite some scholars into the discussion and anything might happen. Add in the questions ancient historians want to raise—questions about archaeology, ancient artifacts, scrolls, and so on—and there's no knowing where you will get to.

The question of Jesus has been the talk of the town—among scholars and in the popular press—for well over two centuries now and shows no sign of slackening off. To understand what's going on, you need to know not just about the ancient sources but about philosophy, dogma, worldview issues, cultural prejudice, how to assess oral and written sources, and all the larger questions of what the ancient Jews were hoping for, what the ancient Romans were trying to do, and what the ancient Greeks thought about it all. You would need to do quite a lot of that just to understand one of the Roman emperors of the period (Titus, say, who led the army that destroyed Jerusalem in 70 CE). How much more when we are talking about a man whose birth marks the "turn of the eras" for today's world and whose followers to this day insist that he is not merely a powerful memory but a living and disturbing presence?

The present volume dives right into this conversation. The contributors discuss not only the theoretical issues (how we should have this conversation in the first place) but also several actual examples of what it all involves. There are helpful ways, and less helpful ways, of lining up the issues. This book teases out which are which. Some people today have serious doubts as to whether we can really have this historical conversation at all; well, the present authors have listened to these problems, and here address them head on. Some people today—anxious, perhaps, about the negative "results" of certain projects—think we can only talk about the human Jesus in a very limited way. Some worry that even raising the question about who Jesus really was, as a genuine human being of the first-century Middle-Eastern world, will upset the "ordinary believer." Will such questions do anyone any good? Those are fair issues to raise. But to toss out the whole process is to hide our heads in the sand. Mainstream Christianity has always insisted that Jesus was and is fully human, as well as fully divine. His full humanness invites us to understand him as a true figure of history. I have found that, whenever I engage in such work, fresh and sometimes surprising insight can emerge. As one fine scholar once put it, Christianity appeals to history, and to history it must go.

There is much in the present volume to stimulate further reflection about Jesus: who he was, who he is, how we can know, and what might follow as a result. It is important to address the valid questions and objections that have been raised, and these essays do just that. Many people in many contexts, including churches, seminaries, and universities, but going much wider, need help to understand how to address the subject and what happens when we do. The present collection is a good example of how to proceed and what is possible. It should provide a solid step forward in the ongoing conversations.

Tom Wright
Rt Revd Professor N T Wright DD FRSE
Research Professor of New Testament and Early Christianity,
University of St Andrews

Abbreviations

AB	Anchor Bible
ABD	*Anchor Bible Dictionary*. Edited by David Noel Freedman. 6 vols. New York: Doubleday, 1992
ABRL	Anchor Bible Reference Library
ANTC	Abingdon New Testament Commentaries
AsJT	*Asia Journal of Theology*
AUSS	*Andrews University Seminary Studies*
BAR	*Biblical Archaeology Review*
BBR	*Bulletin for Biblical Research*
BDAG	Danker, Frederick W., Walter Bauer, William F. Arndt, and F. Wilbur Gingrich. *Greek-English Lexicon of the New Testament and Other Early Christian Literature*. 3rd ed. Chicago: University of Chicago Press, 2000
BECNT	Baker Exegetical Commentary on the New Testament
BETL	Bibliotheca Ephemeridum Theologicarum Lovaniensium
BibInt	Biblical Interpretation Series
BMSSEC	Baylor-Mohr Siebeck Studies in Early Christianity
BNTC	Black's New Testament Commentaries
BPC	Biblical Performance Criticism
BZNW	Beihefte zur Zeitschrift für die neutestamentliche Wissenschaft
CBET	Contributions to Biblical Exegesis and Theology
CBQ	*Catholic Biblical Quarterly*
CurTM	*Currents in Theology and Mission*
CTSA Proceedings	Proceedings of the Catholic Theological Society of America
CW	*Classical World*
ECC	Eerdmans Critical Commentary
ECL	Early Christianity and Its Literature
EJL	Early Judaism and Its Literature

ETL	*Ephemerides Theologicae Lovanienses*
EvQ	*Evangelical Quarterly*
ExpTim	*Expository Times*
GFC	Geschichte des frühen Christentums
HBT	*Horizons in Biblical Theology*
HistTh	*History and Theory*
HTR	*Harvard Theological Review*
HvTSt	*Hervormde teologiese studies*
ICC	International Critical Commentary
IEJ	*Israel Exploration Journal*
IGNTP	The International Greek New Testament Project
JBL	*Journal of Biblical Literature*
JCDA	*Jesus, Criteria, and the Demise of Authenticity*
JCTCRS	Jewish and Christian Texts in Contexts and Related Studies
JETS	*Journal of the Evangelical Theological Society*
JGRChJ	*Journal of Greco-Roman Christianity and Judaism*
JQR	*Jewish Quarterly Review*
JRA	*Journal of Roman Archaeology*
JSHJ	*Journal for the Study of the Historical Jesus*
JSNT	*Journal for the Study of the New Testament*
JSNTSup	Journal for the Study of the New Testament Supplement Series
JSOTSup	Journal for the Study of the Old Testament Supplement Series
JTS	*Journal of Theological Studies*
LEC	Library of Early Christianity
LHBOTS	Library of Hebrew Bible/Old Testament Studies
LNTS	Library of New Testament Studies
NA^{28}	*Novum Testamentum Graece*, Nestle-Aland, 28th ed.
NCB	New Century Bible
Neot	*Neotestamentica*
NTS	*New Testament Studies*
NICNT	New International Commentary on the New Testament
NIGTC	New International Greek Testament Commentary
NovT	*Novum Testamentum*
NovTSup	Supplements to Novum Testamentum

NTL	New Testament Library
NTTS	New Testament Tools and Studies
NTTSD	New Testament Tools, Studies, and Documents
PHSC	Perspectives on Hebrew Scriptures and Its Contexts
PMMS	Palgrave Macmillan Memory Studies
PRSt	*Perspectives in Religious Studies*
QD	Quaestiones Disputatae
RBL	*Review of Biblical Literature*
RBS	Resources for Biblical Study
RCT	*Revista catalana de teologia*
SBLGNT	The Greek New Testament Society of Biblical Literature Edition
SBLDS	Society of Biblical Literature Dissertation Series
SBLSP	Society of Biblical Literature Seminar Papers
SBT	Studies in Biblical Theology
SemeiaSt	Semeia Studies
SHBC	Smyth & Helwys Bible Commentary
SNTSMS	Society for New Testament Studies Monograph Series
SP	Sacra Pagina
StBibLit	Studies in Biblical Literature
SymS	Symposium Series
TANZ	Texte und Arbeiten zum neutestamentlichen Zeitalter
TDNT	*Theological Dictionary of the New Testament*
TENTS	Texts and Editions for New Testament Study
THGNT	The Greek New Testament Tyndale House Edition
THNTC	Two Horizons New Testament Commentary
TSAJ	Texts and Studies in Ancient Judaism
TU	Texte und Untersuchungen
TynBul	*Tyndale Bulletin*
WBC	Word Biblical Commentary
WUNT	Wissenschaftliche Untersuchungen zum Neuen Testament
WW	*Word and World*
ZECNT	Zondervan Exegetical Commentary on the New Testament
ZNW	*Zeitschrift für die neutestamentliche Wissenschaft und die Kunde der älteren Kirche*
ZTK	*Zeitschrift für Theologie und Kirche*

Part One

. . .

The Value of New Testament Historical Studies

CHAPTER 1

The Historical Jesus and the Biblical Church: Why the Quest Matters

ROBERT M. BOWMAN JR. AND J. ED KOMOSZEWSKI

In a provocative essay, Scot McKnight argued that "historical Jesus studies are useless for the church."[1] McKnight's claim—which he did qualify in some important ways—invites Christian scholars to reflect on the significance of the quest of the historical Jesus for the church. How should the church view the modern, historical study of Jesus? What role, if any, should Christians play in historical Jesus studies, and what does the church stand to gain from participation?

THE REAL FIRST "QUEST"

Given that Jesus Christ is the founder and central figure of the Christian faith, the church obviously has legitimate concerns as to what people say about Jesus. The New Testament writers were well aware of a diversity of opinions about Jesus and reported in the Gospels on such diverse views, even during Jesus's own lifetime. Christ's question to the apostles, "Who do people say I am?" (Mark 8:27, cf. Matt 16:13; Luke 9:18) is as relevant today as it was in the first century.

In answer to this question, the disciples replied that at the time people identified Jesus as John the Baptist, Elijah, or perhaps one of the other prophets (Matt 16:14; Mark 8:28; Luke 9:19). These speculations were sparked by the reports of the exorcisms and miracles performed by Jesus and his disciples (Mark 6:12–15; Luke 9:7–8). The notion that Jesus was John the Baptist *redivivus* originated because Jesus's miracles became widely known not long after Herod Antipas had ordered John beheaded. Even Herod entertained this explanation (Matt 14:2; Mark 6:16–17; cf. Luke 9:9). The identification of Jesus as Elijah suggests that Jews at the time recognized that at least some of his miracles bore resemblances

---

1. Scot McKnight, "Why the Authentic Jesus Is of No Use for the Church," in *Jesus, Criteria, and the Demise of Authenticity*, ed. Chris Keith and Anthony Le Donne (London: T&T Clark, 2012), 176.

to miracles performed through Elijah. These two theories were closely related since John's own ministry marked him, if not as Elijah literally returned from the dead, as a kind of latter-day Elijah (Luke 1:17; cf. Mal. 4:5; see also John 1:20, 25), a view Matthew and Mark report Jesus himself affirmed (Matt 11:14; 17:10–13; Mark 9:11–13).

Of course, the idea that Jesus might have been John the Baptist would have been quickly dispelled, even before his final week in Jerusalem. It is certain that this explanation for the miracles of Jesus would have had no currency after his crucifixion. Nor does there seem to be any indication that the early church found it necessary to debunk suggestions that Jesus was the latter-day Elijah as they propagated the gospel. We can securely identify the *Sitz im Leben* of these "Jesus theories" as the Galilean ministry of Jesus.

The speculations that Jesus was John or Elijah were among the more complimentary theories about Jesus circulating during his itinerant ministry. All four Gospels report that Jesus's critics sometimes alleged that he was either demon possessed or in league with the devil (Matt 9:34; 10:25; 11:13; 12:24–28; Mark 3:22, 26; Luke 7:33; 11:15–20; John 7:20; 8:48–52; 10:20–21).[2] Here again, what people outside the circle of the disciples of Jesus were seeking to explain were the apparently undeniable reports of his impressive exorcisms and healings. Unlike the short-lived speculation that Jesus might have been a resurrected John, though, the theory that Jesus performed miracles by demonic power probably continued as a stock criticism of Jesus that the early Christian movement needed to answer. There is even evidence for this criticism centuries later in the Babylonian Talmud, which accused Jesus of "sorcery" (b. Sanh. 43a).[3]

Closely associated with the accusation of demonic activity or sorcery was the charge that Jesus was a blasphemer and a false prophet. The charge of blasphemy for making divine claims is found in all four Gospels (Matt 9:3; 26:65; Mark 2:7; 14:64; Luke 5:21; John 10:33).[4] Jesus's captors taunted him with challenges for him to "prophesy" (Matt 26:67–68; Mark 14:65; Luke 22:63–65), implying of course that he was a false prophet. The accusation that Jesus "was misleading the people" (Luke 23:2, 14) uses language that in Jewish parlance was an accusation

---

2. For a thoughtful analysis of why the opponents of Jesus made this accusation, see Dwight D. Sheets, "Jesus as Demon-Possessed," in *Who Do My Opponents Say I Am? An Investigation of the Accusations against Jesus,* ed. Scot McKnight and Joseph B. Modica, LNTS 327 (London: T & T Clark, 2008), 27–49.

3. On the Talmud's description of Jesus as independent of the early church, see Graham H. Twelftree, *Jesus the Miracle Worker: A Historical and Theological Study* (Downers Grove, IL: InterVarsity Press, 1999), 254–55.

4. See Darrell L. Bock, "Jesus as Blasphemer," in McKnight and Modica, *Who Do My Opponents Say I Am,* 76–94. Bock has written extensively on the subject.

of being a false prophet.[5] These numerous statements in the Gospels demonstrate that his Jewish critics viewed Jesus as a false prophet and magician or sorcerer—a purveyor of demonic power.[6]

All of these assessments of Jesus from outside the community of his followers had in common the acknowledgment that he was a miracle worker. As Barry Blackburn notes, "Scholars almost unanimously agree that this Galilean performed both cures and exorcisms, the success of which led both to a devoted following and opponents who charged him with sorcery."[7] People in the ancient world who did not believe in Jesus generally found the evidence for Jesus's miracles compelling but reinterpreted those miracles to fit with their cultural and religious assumptions. In the modern world people who do not believe in Jesus generally deny his miracles because they do not fit with their cultural and religious assumptions. What seemed most implausible about Jesus to many of the ancients was not that he did miracles but that he did so in ways that turned their cultural expectations upside down. What seems most implausible about Jesus to many moderns is not that he turned ancient cultural expectations upside down but that he did so in miraculous ways. Above all else, contemporary skeptics cannot abide a Jesus who turns *their* expectations upside down. Thus, the issue of plausibility is always with us but manifests itself in changing ways. The Christian church has always preached a Jesus who seems implausible to many.

ONE JESUS OR MANY?

The modern Quest that launched in the early years of the Enlightenment assumed, as did the church, that there had been one actual Jesus. For Hermann Samuel Reimarus, the eighteenth-century father of the Quest, the project had a simple, clear aim: to determine who Jesus really was and what he really did. Some 240 years later, scholarly thinking about Jesus has largely given up on the idea of knowing the truth about the actual Jesus. Instead, modern scholarship commonly distinguishes many different "Jesuses."

---

5. Joel B. Green, "The Death of Jesus," in *Handbook for the Study of the Historical Jesus*, 4 vols., ed. Tom Hólmen and Stanley E. Porter (Leiden: Brill, 2011), 3:2399.

6. Graham N. Stanton, "Jesus of Nazareth: A Magician and a False Prophet Who Deceived God's People?," in *Jesus and Gospel* (Cambridge: Cambridge University Press, 2004), 127–61.

7. Barry L. Blackburn, "The Miracles of Jesus," in *Studying the Historical Jesus: Evaluations of the State of Current Research*, ed. Bruce Chilton and Craig A. Evans, NTTS 19 (Leiden: Brill, 1998), 362, 392. See also Jostein Ådna, "The Encounter of Jesus with the Gerasene Demoniac," in *Authenticating the Activities of Jesus*, ed. Bruce Chilton and Craig A. Evans, NTTS 28 (Leiden: Brill, 2002), 279–302; Graham N. Stanton, *The Gospels and Jesus*, 2nd ed., Oxford Bible Series (Oxford: Oxford University Press, 2002), 235; Craig S. Keener, *Miracles: The Credibility of the New Testament Accounts*, 2 vols. (Grand Rapids: Baker Academic, 2011), 19, 23.

McKnight, for example, in his *Christianity Today* article on the subject distinguishes among the "Jewish Jesus" (the one Pilate crucified, "set in his Jewish context"), the "canonical Jesus" (the New Testament writings' interpretation of Jesus as "the agent of God's redemption"), the "orthodox Jesus" (the Second Person of the Trinity), and the "historical Jesus." Regarding the last of these, McKnight offers the following definition:

> The historical Jesus is the Jesus whom scholars have reconstructed on the basis of historical methods over against the canonical portraits of Jesus in the Gospels of our New Testament, and over against the orthodox Jesus of the church. The historical Jesus is more like the Jewish Jesus than the canonical Jesus or the orthodox Jesus.[8]

In the essay cited earlier, McKnight does more or less affirm the identity of the canonical and the orthodox Jesus. The Gospels *"have provided for us a depiction of Jesus (Son of God, Lord, Messiah, Son of Man, teacher, etc.), the creeds then developed that same Jesus into another set of meaningful categories (the divine-man), and that two stage depiction of Jesus is the church's Jesus."*[9]

Richard Soulen offers a similar analysis in his book *Defining Jesus: The Earthly, the Biblical, the Historical, and the Real Jesus, and How Not to Confuse Them.* As the subtitle suggests, Soulen also distinguishes four different kinds of Jesus. The "earthly Jesus" is synonymous with McKnight's "Jewish Jesus" (the known, certain facts about Jesus), the "biblical Jesus" is the same as McKnight's "canonical Jesus," the "historical Jesus" means the same thing as in McKnight, and the "real Jesus" means the Jesus subjectively experienced in the church.[10] In Soulen's analysis, McKnight's "orthodox Jesus" is left on the cutting-room floor. A fifth type, Jesus "as he actually was," is unknowable. The actual Jesus was unknown even to Jesus, because objective knowledge of oneself or of others is impossible for human beings. Only God knows who Jesus actually was.[11]

Of course, we do not know *everything* about Jesus as he actually was. The Gospels do not purport to give an exhaustive or comprehensive account of the life of Jesus. Rather, they claim to present accounts about Jesus based on eyewitness

---

8. Scot McKnight, "The Jesus We'll Never Know: Why Scholarly Attempts to Discover the 'Real' Jesus Have Failed. And Why That's a Good Thing," *Christianity Today* (April 9, 2010): 24.

9. McKnight, "Why the Authentic Jesus Is of No Use for the Church," 178, emphasis original.

10. Richard N. Soulen, *Defining Jesus: The Earthly, the Biblical, the Historical, and the Real Jesus, and How Not to Confuse Them* (Eugene, OR: Cascade Books, 2015), 9, 19–20, 76–79.

11. Soulen, *Defining Jesus*, 3–8. Similarly John P. Meier, "Basic Methodology in the Quest for the Historical Jesus," in Hólmen and Porter, *Handbook for the Study of the Historical Jesus*, 1:291–92.

testimonies of people who reported what they saw and heard (Luke 1:1–4; 24:48; John 15:27; 19:35; 20:30; 21:24; cf. Matt 26:13; Mark 14:9). John even makes a point of denying the possibility of giving an exhaustive account (John 21:25). Yet we can and do know *something* about Jesus as he actually was. The perspectival and partial nature of eyewitness testimony means that we do not know everything about Jesus, but it also assures us that what we know pertains to the actual Jesus "on the ground."

It is one thing to distinguish different aspects of what can be known about Jesus, but quite another to use such distinctions to make knowledge of the actual Jesus inaccessible. Against such analyses, the church must insist that there is really only one Jesus and that we have genuine knowledge about him. This means, on the one hand, that the church proclaims that its Jesus is the actual Jesus, the one who lived in history. As Lesslie Newbigin put it, "The long-running debate about the relationship between the Jesus of history and the Christ of faith is simply one manifestation of the illusion that has haunted our culture ever since the Enlightenment. There is only one Jesus, and there is only one history."[12] On the other hand, it means that the church is genuinely committed to making sure that what it proclaims and teaches about Jesus is faithful to what we can know about the actual Jesus. Thus, Michael Bird is right when he comments, "If Jesus is not to become the product of our own minds and aspirations we must vigilantly ensure that the Jesus of creeds, of worship, of faith, of scholarship, of liturgy, of devotion, of sermons and piety is the one and the same Jew who walked the plains of Palestine."[13] Thus, the church has a genuine interest in any intellectual or scholarly pursuit of knowledge that might shed some light on Jesus—refining or if necessary even correcting the way the church talks about Jesus.

THE EARTHLY JESUS IS THE CHURCH'S JESUS

As both McKnight and Soulen point out, and as most scholars in historical Jesus studies agree, we can be reasonably sure about quite a number of basic facts about the "earthly" or "Jewish" Jesus. Most generally, of course, we know that Jesus of Nazareth really existed. Against the popular atheist memes that Jesus never existed, supported by only a handful of writers with any academic

---

12. Lesslie Newbigin, *Foolishness to the Greeks: The Gospel and Western Culture* (Grand Rapids: Eerdmans, 1986), 61.

13. Michael Bird, "Shouldn't Evangelicals Participate in the 'Third Quest for the Historical Jesus'?" *Themelios* 29.2 (2004): 11 (5–14).

credibility,[14] the church is on absolutely solid historical ground in speaking of Jesus as an actual historical individual.[15] Beyond this rationally incontrovertible fact, a considerable number of specific facts about Jesus are so well supported historically as to be widely acknowledged by most scholars, whether Christian (of any stripe) or not:[16]

- Jesus was born about 6 to 4 BCE.
- He was a Galilean Jewish man.
- He grew up in Nazareth.
- His mother tongue was Aramaic (though he may also have known Hebrew and Greek).
- He was baptized by a wilderness prophet named John in the Jordan River shortly before John was arrested and executed by order of Herod Antipas, the tetrarch of Galilee.
- He conducted an itinerant ministry throughout Galilee and neighboring regions.
- He was followed by a group of disciples, both men and women.
- He taught about the kingdom of God.
- He often spoke in parables.
- He was reputed to be a wonder worker who cast out demons and healed people.

---

14. Robert M. Price, *The Christ-Myth Theory and Its Problems* (Austin, TX: American Atheist Press, 2011); and Richard Carrier, *On the Historicity of Jesus: Why We Might Have Reason for Doubt* (Sheffield: Sheffield Academic Press, 2014). Essays arguing different points of view are included in Thomas L. Thompson and Thomas S. Verenna, eds., *'Is This Not the Carpenter?' The Question of the Historicity of the Figure of Jesus*, Copenhagen International Seminar (Sheffield: Equinox, 2012; Durham: Acumen, 2013).

15. Especially relevant works on this point include Robert E. Van Voorst, *Jesus outside the New Testament: An Introduction to the Ancient Evidence* (Grand Rapids: Eerdmans, 2000); Paul Rhodes Eddy and Gregory A. Boyd, *The Jesus Legend: A Case for the Historical Reliability of the Synoptic Jesus Tradition* (Grand Rapids: Baker Academic, 2007); Bart D. Ehrman, *Did Jesus Exist? The Historical Argument for Jesus of Nazareth* (New York: HarperOne, 2012). See also the responses to Robert Price by Luke Timothy Johnson, James D. G. Dunn, and Darrell L. Bock in James K. Beilby and Paul R. Eddy, eds., *The Historical Jesus: Five Views* (Downers Grove, IL: InterVarsity Press, 2009), 89–103.

16. E.g., E. P. Sanders, *The Historical Figure of Jesus* (London: Penguin, 1993), 10–11; N. T. Wright, *Jesus and the Victory of God*, vol. 2 of *Christian Origins and the Question of God* (Minneapolis: Fortress, 1996), 147–48; Paula Fredriksen, *Jesus of Nazareth, King of the Jews: A Jewish Life and the Emergence of Christianity* (New York: Random House, 1999), 268; Amy-Jill Levine, "Introduction," in *The Historical Jesus in Context*, ed. Amy-Jill Levine, Dale C. Allison Jr., and John Dominic Crossan, Princeton Readings in Religions (Princeton: Princeton University Press, 2006), 4; Peter Pokorný, "Jesus Research as Feedback on His *Wirkungsgeschichte*," in Hólmen and Porter, *Handbook for the Study of the Historical Jesus*, 1:344–47; Soulen, *Defining Jesus*, 10–20. On Sanders's list, see also Mark Allan Powell, *Jesus as a Figure of History: How Modern Historians View the Man from Galilee* (Louisville: Westminster John Knox, 1998), 117; William R. Herzog II, *Prophet and Teacher: An Introduction to the Historical Jesus* (Louisville: Westminster John Knox, 2005), 1–3; Paul K. Moser, *Jesus and Philosophy: New Essays* (Cambridge: Cambridge University Press, 2008), 34–40.

- He showed and preached compassion to people whom Jews commonly regarded as unclean or wicked, such as lepers, tax collectors, prostitutes, and Romans.
- He engaged Pharisees in debate over matters pertaining to the Jewish Law (Torah).
- He went to Jerusalem at Passover the week of his death.
- He caused a disturbance in the temple in Jerusalem a few days before his arrest.
- He had a final meal with his inner circle of disciples that became the basis for the rite that Christians call the Last Supper (or Eucharist).
- He was arrested at the behest of the high priest in Jerusalem, the head of the Sanhedrin.
- He was crucified just outside Jerusalem by the order of Pontius Pilate, the prefect of Judea, in 30 or 33 CE.
- He was believed by his disciples to have appeared to them shortly after his death in experiences that convinced them that God had raised him from the dead.

This list leaves a number of highly controversial questions about Jesus still to be answered. Nevertheless, what can be known about Jesus with a high degree of confidence, apart from theological or ideological agendas, is perhaps surprisingly robust. Of course, there are people for whom some of these facts, or even the mere existence of Jesus, is inconvenient. Many contemporary atheists prefer to think that Jesus never existed. Most Muslims believe on dogmatic theological grounds that Jesus was not crucified and indeed that he never died—the traditional interpretation of the Qur'an (4:157–158).[17] Yet the church has "history"—that is, the facts—on its side in these matters.[18] The *onus probandi* falls on the side of those who dispute the church's understanding of Jesus with regard to these extremely well-evidenced facts.

To look at the situation from the other end, all of the generally accepted facts about Jesus are consistent with the church's beliefs about Jesus. That is, *there is not a single well-evidenced historical fact about Jesus that undermines the "orthodox" view of Jesus.* Nearly two and a half centuries of assiduous study, research, and discovery by archaeologists, historians, textual critics, and other scholars

---

17. See Todd Lawson, *The Crucifixion and the Qur'an: A Study in the History of Muslim Thought* (London: Oneworld, 2009).

18. A helpful collection of essays setting forth detailed arguments for most of these historical facts is Darrell L. Bock and Robert L. Webb, eds., *Key Events in the Life of the Historical Jesus: A Collaborative Exploration of Context and Coherence* (Grand Rapids: Eerdmans, 2010).

searching for an alternative Jesus have failed to turn up a scrap of evidence that contravenes what Christians have traditionally said about him.

Yes, occasionally someone claims to have uncovered such evidence. In the twenty-first century, perhaps the two most notorious such claims were those expressed in the sensationalistic novel *The Da Vinci Code*[19] and in the pseudo-archaeological media blitz concerning the so-called *Jesus Family Tomb*.[20] In both cases, legitimate scholars of historical Jesus studies, whether conservative Christian, theologically liberal Christian, or non-Christian, thoroughly and soundly refuted these claims.[21] The process of subjecting these claims to careful scrutiny not only refuted those claims but ended up shedding more light on Jesus's death and burial. The church should be grateful that so many scholars, including many who do not accept the church's faith in Jesus as the divine Savior of the world, were able to draw on a deep reservoir of knowledge about Jesus and his world to answer these popularized distortions of the facts. The Quest, for all its failings, has served the church well in cases like these.

The lack of any well-supported facts that contradict the biblical portrayals of Jesus in the Gospels accepted by the church is no minor matter. There are religions that advance highly revisionist theories about Jesus for which known facts are decidedly inconvenient. We have already mentioned the problem facing Muslim apologists in reconciling the claim of the Qur'an that Jesus never died with the historical evidence. A few religions of modern origin, perhaps most famously the Church of Christ, Scientist (i.e., Christian Science), also deny that

---

19. Dan Brown, *The Da Vinci Code* (New York: Doubleday, 2003).

20. James D. Tabor, *The Jesus Dynasty: The Hidden History of Jesus, His Royal Family, and the Birth of Christianity* (New York: Simon & Schuster, 2006); Simcha Jacobovici and Charles Pellegrino, *The Jesus Family Tomb: The Discovery, the Investigation, and the Evidence that Could Change History* (New York: HarperSanFrancisco, 2007); *The Lost Tomb of Jesus*, dir. Simcha Jacobovici, exec. prod. James Cameron (Discovery Channel, 2007; DVD, Port Washington, NY: Koch Vision, 2007); James D. Tabor and Simcha Jacobovici, *The Jesus Discovery: The New Archaeological Find that Reveals the Birth of Christianity* (New York: Simon & Schuster, 2012).

21. On *The Da Vinci Code*, see Darrell L. Bock, *Breaking the Da Vinci Code: Answers to the Questions Everyone's Asking* (Nashville: Thomas Nelson, 2004); Ben Witherington III, *The Gospel Code: Novel Claims about Jesus, Mary Magdalene, and Da Vinci* (Downers Grove, IL: InterVarsity Press, 2004); Bart D. Ehrman, *Truth and Fiction in* The Da Vinci Code: *A Historian Reveals What We Really Know about Jesus, Mary Magdalene, and Constantine* (New York: Oxford University Press, 2006); J. Ed Komoszewski, M. James Sawyer, and Daniel B. Wallace, *Reinventing Jesus: How Contemporary Skeptics Miss the Real Jesus and Mislead Popular Culture* (Grand Rapids: Kregel, 2006). On the "Jesus family tomb" issue, see Gary R. Habermas, *The Secret of the Talpiot Tomb: Unraveling the Mystery of the Jesus Family Tomb* (Nashville: Broadman & Holman, 2008); Charles L. Quarles, ed., *Buried Hope or Risen Savior: The Search for the Jesus Tomb* (Nashville: B&H Academic, 2008); James H. Charlesworth, ed., *The Tomb of Jesus and His Family? Exploring Ancient Jewish Tombs Near Jerusalem's Walls*, Fourth Princeton Symposium on Judaism and Christian Origins (Grand Rapids: Eerdmans, 2013); Craig A. Evans, *Jesus and the Remains of His Day: Studies in Jesus and the Evidence of Material Culture* (Peabody, MA: Hendrickson, 2015). The book edited by Charlesworth represents a broad cross-section of scholars from various disciplines as well as different perspectives on the historical Jesus.

Jesus died.[22] Yet perhaps the most certain fact known about Jesus is his death by crucifixion.[23]

THE CANONICAL JESUS IS THE ONLY JESUS WE HAVE

One commonality of the *Da Vinci Code* and *Jesus Family Tomb* theories was their appeal to noncanonical texts that supposedly provide support for a radically different view of Jesus. The most important of these texts, often called New Testament apocrypha or Christian apocrypha, are the various texts loosely designated the gnostic gospels.[24] Advocates of revisionist theories about Jesus do find support from a cadre of scholars that tout the apocryphal gospels, especially the gnostic texts, as evidence of alternative views of Jesus that the early church arbitrarily suppressed. Karen King, for example, asserts, "History, as we know, is written by the winners. In the case of early Christianity, this has meant that many voices in these debates were silenced through repression or neglect."[25] Elaine Pagels's 1979 book *The Gnostic Gospels*[26] laid down the basic narrative so often repeated in the mainstream media for the past four decades. Orthodox Christianity, according to this story, is merely one of many streams of Christian belief that flowed in the early centuries following the death of Jesus and was the one that happened to emerge politically victorious in the fourth century. The agenda set through this narrative has not been to add these texts to the canon of the New Testament but rather to call into question the whole idea of a canon. Most of the scholarly enthusiasm over the apocryphal gospels has not been about advocating the ideas those writings express but about exploiting them to undermine the church's understanding of Jesus as having any normative standing. In short, the value of the apocryphal gospels for many modern scholars is their utility in undermining the "canonical" Jesus.

Against this ever more common appeal to the apocryphal gospels against the

---

22. Mary Baker G. Eddy, *Science and Health, with Key to the Scriptures* (Boston: Christian Science Publishing, 1875), 42–46, 51. Eddy did not deny the crucifixion of Jesus, but she maintained that he did not actually die.

23. John Dominic Crossan, *Who Killed Jesus?* (New York: Harper, 1995), 5; Green, "Death of Jesus," 2383.

24. Various scholars have raised concerns about the terms *gnostic* and *Gnosticism*, e.g., Michael Allen Williams, *Rethinking "Gnosticism": An Argument for Dismantling a Dubious Category* (Princeton: Princeton University Press, 1996); Karen L. King, *What Is Gnosticism?* (Cambridge: Harvard University Press, 2003). Some of these concerns are a bit overblown; King, for example, also thinks that such "constructs" as *Judaism, Christianity,* or even *religion* are unhelpful (3).

25. Karen L. King, *The Gospel of Mary of Magdala: Jesus and the First Woman Apostle* (Santa Rosa, CA: Polebridge, 2003), 6–7.

26. Elaine Pagels, *The Gnostic Gospels* (New York: Vintage Books, 1979).

church's Jesus, the church need not assume *a priori* "that noncanonical gospels are less reliable historically simply because, for whatever reason, they did not find their way into the Christian canon."[27] Rather, the church's scholars quite properly use the tools of historical research to assess the value of those texts for our knowledge of what Jesus actually did and taught. What we find, in general, is that such texts are of extremely meager value for that purpose. No doubt, the apocryphal gospels shed significant light on different forms of Christianity in the second and third centuries. It is not exactly news that such different streams of Christian belief existed. The church fathers wrote voluminously about many of them. In this regard, we may be grateful for the discovery of the Nag Hammadi texts and other finds that have given us an inside look at some of these movements and enable us to understand their beliefs more accurately and even more charitably. At the same time, these discoveries have confirmed that the church got it right in privileging the texts about Jesus that became part of the formal canon of Scripture. There are at least two reasons for this stance.

First, the canonical Gospels are certainly earlier than most and likely earlier than all of the noncanonical gospels. Although there are some outliers, mainstream biblical scholarship dates the four New Testament Gospels to the first century, generally between the 60s and the 90s.[28] All of the noncanonical gospel texts, on the other hand, are generally dated to the second century or later. Bart Ehrman, for example, in his book *Lost Scriptures*, discusses the dates of seventeen gospels not included in the New Testament and dates none of them to the first century.[29] Elsewhere he admits that even though some of their contents may have sources going back to the first century, "the noncanonical Gospels are of greater importance for understanding the diversity of Christianity in the second and third and later centuries than for knowing about the writings of the earliest Christians."[30]

The noncanonical text most often suggested to originate from the first century is the Gospel of Thomas. It has been dated anywhere from the middle of the first century to the late second century, with a plurality favoring the view that it

---

27. This complaint is found in John S. Kloppenborg, "Sources, Methods and Discursive Locations in the Quest of the Historical Jesus," in Hólmen and Porter, *Handbook for the Study of the Historical Jesus*, 1:252.

28. E.g., David Noel Freedman, ed., *Anchor Bible Dictionary*, 6 vols. (New York: Doubleday, 1992); Michael D. Coogan, ed., *The Oxford Encyclopedia of the Books of the Bible* (Oxford: Oxford University Press, 2011); and Joel B. Green, Jeannine K. Brown, and Nicholas Perrin, eds., *Dictionary of Jesus and the Gospels*, 2nd ed. (Downers Grove, IL: InterVarsity Press, 2013); see also Bart D. Ehrman, *The New Testament: A Historical Introduction to the Early Christian Writings*, 6th ed. (New York: Oxford University Press, 2016), 100.

29. Bart D. Ehrman, *Lost Scriptures: Books That Did Not Make It into the New Testament* (New York: Oxford University Press, 2003), 7–89.

30. Ehrman, *New Testament*, 233.

was written in the middle third of the second century.[31] It is of course reasonable to posit earlier sources behind Thomas or any of the other noncanonical gospels, but the same thing can be said for the canonical Gospels, the sources of which must have been earlier still. Most scholars recognize that Thomas was either dependent on the Synoptic Gospels[32] or that it derived from a stream of tradition that overlapped the stream on which the Synoptics were dependent.[33] In either case, very little if any of the material in Thomas represents information about Jesus that originated earlier than the New Testament Gospels.

Second, the canonical Gospels are viable candidates for historical or factual information about Jesus, while the same simply cannot be said for the noncanonical gospels. Whatever precise genre classification one might prefer for the New Testament Gospels, they are certainly not myths (μῦθοι). Contrary to the "chronological snobbery" (as C. S. Lewis put it[34]) of some modern skeptics, Christians in the New Testament period were quite able to distinguish between myths and truth, and some early Christian writers insisted explicitly that their faith was based on the latter rather than the former (2 Tim 4:4; 2 Pet 1:16). As we have already seen, the canonical Gospels contain a great deal of information about the activities and teachings of Jesus that scholars have been able to confirm.

Justin Martyr, writing in the 150s, called the church's Gospels "memoirs" (ἀπομνημονεύματα) of the apostles (*1 Apol.* 66.3; 67.3; *Dial.* 100–107).[35] It is debatable whether the term was a technical term for a specific genre of writing, but it did indicate that Justin viewed the Gospels as preserving the recollections of eyewitnesses.[36] This description is very similar to Papias's statement decades earlier[37] that Mark's writing was based on what Peter "remembered"

---

31. See the survey of proposed dates in Simon Gathercole, *The Gospel of Thomas: Introduction and Commentary*, TENTS 11 (Leiden: Brill, 2014), 125–27. Some 13 of the 31 scholars he surveys favor the period 135–175 or so. Gathercole himself dates Thomas to the period ca. 135–200 (124).

32. A notable recent defense of this position is Mark Goodacre, *Thomas and the Gospels: The Case for Thomas's Familiarity with the Synoptics* (Grand Rapids: Eerdmans, 2012).

33. E.g., Stephen J. Patterson, "The Gospel of (Judas) Thomas and the Synoptic Problem," in *The Gospel of Thomas and Christian Origins: Essays on the Fifth Gospel*, Nag Hammadi and Manichaean Studies 84 (Leiden: Brill, 2013), 93–118.

34. C. S. Lewis, *Surprised by Joy: The Shape of My Early Life* (New York: HarperOne, 2017 [orig. publ. 1955]), 252–64, where Lewis confessed that prior to his conversion he was guilty of this error.

35. That Justin was referring to the canonical Gospels (including John) has been shown by Charles E. Hill, *Who Chose the Gospels? Probing the Great Gospel Conspiracy* (New York: Oxford University Press, 2010), 123–50.

36. Wally V. Cirafesi and Gregory P. Fewster, "Justin's Ἀπομνημονεύματα and Ancient Greco-Roman Memoirs," *Early Christianity* 7 (2016): 186–212.

37. Papias's work was at one time commonly dated ca. 125–140, but the trend over the past few decades has been to date it earlier, most likely ca. 95–110. See Robert W. Yarbrough, "The Date of Papias: A Reassessment," *JETS* 26 (1983): 181–91; Robert H. Gundry, *Matthew: A Commentary on His Handbook for a Mixed Church under Persecution*, 2nd ed. (Grand Rapids: Eerdmans, 1994), 610–11. A date of around 110 is favored also by Dennis R. MacDonald, *Two Shipwrecked Gospels: The Logoi of Jesus and Papias's Exposition*

(ἀπεμνημόνευσεν) what Christ had said or done (Eusebius, *Hist. eccl.* 3.39.15).[38] Charles Hill points out that Papias and Justin used two other significant terms in the same way: Papias stated that Peter did not present an "arrangement" (σύνταξις) of his recollections of Jesus, whereas Justin commented that the Gospel writers "arranged" (συντετάχθαι) their material; Papias said that Mark "followed" Peter, and Justin spoke of "the apostles and those who followed them," both using forms of the verb παρακολουθέω. This evidence seems sufficiently strong to conclude that more than likely Justin was dependent on Papias,[39] though it remains possible that Justin, without direct dependence on Papias, was utilizing a way of speaking about the Gospels that was already common in the early second century.[40] In either case, the understanding that the Gospels were remembrances or memoirs of the apostles regarding the words and deeds of Jesus is attested in Papias less than twenty years after most modern scholars think the Gospels had all been written. Craig Keener comments, "Their use of this term [memoirs] provides attestation that, from an early period, some saw the Gospels as a form of biography."[41]

Modern scholars rarely call the Gospels "memoirs" (other than when discussing Justin's use of the term), but many of them now accept the Greek term βίοι ("lives") as an appropriate term for classifying their genre. Richard Burridge's 1992 landmark study, for which the work of his professor Graham Stanton and others had prepared the way, has convinced most scholars working in Gospel studies today of this classification.[42] This genre is also labeled as ancient Greco-Roman biographies, with the qualifying adjectives distinguishing those ancient works from modern biographies written according to Western conventions or expectations. Prior to the recognition of the Gospels as ancient biographies,

of Logia about the Lord, ECL 8 (Atlanta: Society of Biblical Literature, 2012), 46–47. MacDonald goes on to date Luke-Acts later than Papias and to argue that Luke was dependent on Papias (47–48)!

38. That Papias meant what Peter remembered, not what Mark remembered, has been well argued by Richard Bauckham, *Jesus and the Eyewitnesses: The Gospels as Eyewitness Testimony*, 2nd ed. (Grand Rapids: Eerdmans, 2017), 211–12.

39. So Charles E. Hill, *The Johannine Corpus in the Early Church* (Oxford: Oxford University Press, 2004), 339–40; see also Michael J. Kok, *The Gospel on the Margins: The Reception of Mark in the Second Century* (Minneapolis: Fortress, 2015), 112–15.

40. E.g., Michael J. Kruger, *The Question of Canon: Challenging the Status Quo in the New Testament Debate* (Downers Grove, IL: IVP Academic, 2013), 184; Bauckham, *Jesus and the Eyewitnesses*, 212–13.

41. Craig S. Keener, *The Gospel of John: A Commentary*, 2 vols. (Grand Rapids: Baker Academic, 2012 [orig. 2003]), 1:5.

42. Richard A. Burridge, *What Are the Gospels? A Comparison with Graeco-Roman Biography*, SNTSMS 70 (Cambridge: Cambridge University Press, 1992), recently released in a twenty-fifth anniversary edition (Waco, TX: Word, 2018). Earlier works of importance include Graham N. Stanton, *Jesus of Nazareth in New Testament Preaching*, SNTSMS 27 (Cambridge: Cambridge University Press, 1974), 117–36; Charles H. Talbert, *What Is a Gospel? The Genre of the Canonical Gospels* (Philadelphia: Fortress, 1977); and David E. Aune, *The New Testament in Its Literary Environment*, ed. Wayne A. Meeks, LEC 8 (Philadelphia: Westminster, 1987), 47 (17–76).

many biblical scholars tended to assume a lack of interest by their authors in the "historical" Jesus or even in knowing anything factual about his life. That assumption is now more widely admitted not to have been credible, though the admissions are often grudging. Some scholars today prefer to describe one or more of the Gospels as ancient historiography or historical writing, but in the case of the Gospels there does not seem to be a sharp line between this genre and βίος.[43] Academic discussions about the genre of the Gospels are now largely focused not on deciding what that genre was, but on the significance of the βίοι genre for understanding the Gospels.[44]

Two cautions are in order regarding this classification of the canonical Gospels as βίοι. First, βίοι is a descriptive classification dependent on resemblances among texts, not a prescriptive category with rules by which the authors were bound. Keener has rightly cautioned that "identifying biographic genre does not allow us to impose a uniform genre-based grid on all ancient biographies or Gospels."[45] It is a mistake to infer from this genre classification that the Gospels should be expected to be like other βίοι in all respects, since *no* ancient "biography" was like all other such works in all respects. Scholars are busy proposing subcategories of βίοι to accommodate differences among works so classified, but it is in the very nature of literature that no systematic analysis of genre characteristics will ever be exhaustive or precise. One clearly important way in which the Gospels are different from typical ancient βίοι is their deep roots in the theological and literary heritage of the Jewish subculture.[46] Larry Hurtado's conclusion in his 1992 dictionary entry on the genre of the Gospels, published the same year as Burridge's book, still seems correct: "In very general terms, the Gospels can be likened to other examples of Greco-Roman popular biography, but they also form a distinctive group within that broad body of ancient writings."[47]

Second, identifying the Gospels as βίοι does not allow us to draw definitive

---

43. See Eve-Marie Becker, "Historiographical Literature in the New Testament Period (1st and 2nd Centuries CE)," in Hólmen and Porter, *Handbook for the Study of the Historical Jesus*, 2:1810–13.

44. Notable such works include Justin Marc Smith, *Why βίος? On the Relationship between Gospel Genre and Implied Audience*, LNTS 518 (London: T&T Clark, 2015); Craig S. Keener and Edward T. Wright, eds., *Biographies and Jesus: What Does It Mean for the Gospels to be Biographies?* (Lexington, KY: Emeth Press, 2016); Michael R. Licona, *Why Are There Differences in the Gospels? What We Can Learn from Ancient Biography*, foreword by Craig A. Evans (New York: Oxford University Press, 2017); Jean-Noël Aletti, *The Birth of the Gospels as Biographies: With Analyses of Two Challenging Pericopae*, Analecta Biblica Studia 10 (Rome: Gregorian University Press, 2017).

45. Craig Keener, "Ancient Biographies and the Gospels: Introduction," in *Biographies and Jesus*, ed. Keener and Wright, 2.

46. Michael F. Bird, *The Gospel of the Lord: How the Early Church Wrote the Story of Jesus* (Grand Rapids: Eerdmans, 2014), 270–71.

47. Larry W. Hurtado, "Gospel (Genre)," in *Dictionary of Jesus and the Gospels*, 1st ed., ed. Joel B. Green, Scot McKnight, and I. Howard Marshall (Downers Grove, IL: InterVarsity Press, 1992), 282 (full entry, 276–82).

conclusions about the historicity of their narratives. Greco-Roman biographies had somewhat varying purposes and were of varying quality as sources of historical information. As the view that the Gospels are βίοι has taken hold as the dominant position, Gospel scholars have sometimes appealed to different aspects of ancient Greco-Roman biographies as support for their varying opinions about the Gospels' historical value. Craig Blomberg, an evangelical scholar with a high view of the Gospels' historical value, has rightly warned, "concluding that the Gospels are biographical is not the same as deciding that everything in them actually happened. It makes it unlikely that they are largely fictitious, but some biographies in Jesus's world were poorly researched while others were well researched."[48] It would be a mistake to infer from the genre classification that certain elements in the Gospels must be historically accurate (because of the biographical interests of such works) or that they must not be historically accurate (because of the other sorts of purposes in other such works). We should certainly make close comparisons of the Gospels with Greco-Roman βίοι, as scholars are now doing, but with attention to how the Gospels are different from other such works as well as how they are similar to them.

Whether we categorize the Gospels as Greco-Roman memoirs, biographies, or some other similar genre designation, their intention to inform readers about the person of Jesus is clear both from their formal genre characteristics and from the considerable number of key factual claims they make about Jesus that historians can confirm. In contrast with the canonical Gospels, the extant apocryphal "gospels" do not at all qualify as memoirs, biographies, or historical writings about Jesus.[49] For the most part, they do not even *claim* to present historical information about Jesus. Most of them contain little or no narrative and virtually no references to specific events in the life of Jesus. The Gospel of Thomas is a collection of 114 largely unrelated sayings of Jesus, with barely any narrative framing at all. Stanton observed this difference years ago: "There is no trace of the opponents of Jesus, nor of the very varied types of people with whom Jesus associates in the canonical gospels, nor of the deeds of Jesus."[50] Most scholars classify Thomas as a collection of "wise sayings."[51] Karen King, among other scholars, classifies the Gospel of Mary as "a post-resurrection dialogue,"

---

48. Craig L. Blomberg, *The Historical Reliability of the New Testament: Countering the Challenges to Evangelical Christian Beliefs*, B&H Studies in Christian Apologetics (Nashville: B&H Academic, 2016), 27.

49. Some of the Jewish-Christian "gospels" may have been biographical in genre, but unfortunately no substantial copies of these works are extant; see Burridge, *What Are the Gospels*, 242; Smith, *Why βίος*, 16. Certainty about the genre of the Gospel of Peter is elusive because so much of the book is missing, but it does not appear to have been a βίος; cf. Smith, *Why βίος*, 123.

50. Stanton, *Jesus of Nazareth in New Testament Preaching*, 130.

51. Smith, *Why βίος*, 115.

moving from dialogues among the disciples to a dialogue between the Savior and Mary, before concluding with "dialogues between the soul and the Powers."[52]

The physical environment in which Jesus lived is virtually nonexistent in the ancient apocryphal gospels: in the four gospels named for Thomas, Peter, Mary, and Judas *combined* there are references to only three specific places (Jerusalem, Judea, and Joseph's Garden), compared to the dozens of locations named in the New Testament Gospels. To be fair, this is because the apocryphal gospels were not really intended to provide biographical information about Jesus. These texts feature supposed verbal exchanges between Jesus and a few of his disciples and little else, giving them relatively little grounding in the larger historical and cultural context.

Clarity about the genre or genres of the so-called apocryphal gospels has been hampered by designating them as "gospels." Jörg Frey has made the following important observation:

> In published collections of "New Testament Apocrypha," texts are usually grouped according to the genres of the writings of the New Testament: (a) gospels, (b) "apostolic" material (epistles and acts of different apostles), (c) apocalypses, and (possible as a further category, though not contained in the New Testament) (d) church orders. Such a distinction presupposes a clear idea about the genre "gospel."[53]

Going a step further, this classification of apocryphal texts presupposes that "gospel" *is* a genre, a common assumption for much of the twentieth century when these collections were being made. We now know this assumption was incorrect: the Gospels are not a genre unto themselves, *sui generis*, but are in form a type of ancient Greco-Roman βίοι. Categorizing the apocryphal writings into groups mimicking the arrangement of the New Testament canon has likely contributed to the mistaken impression that the apocryphal "Jesus books" are of the same genre as the canonical Gospels.

The different genres of the canonical and noncanonical texts about Jesus are part of the larger story of why the four Gospels became the foundation for the church's New Testament canon while the other texts did not. The so-called gnostic gospels generally took the form of self-described collections of "secret"

---

52. King, *Gospel of Mary of Magdala*, 30.

53. Jörg Frey, "Texts about Jesus: Non-Canonical Gospels and Related Literature," in *The Oxford Handbook of Early Christian Apocrypha*, ed. Tobias Nicklas and Joseph Verheyden (New York: Oxford University Press, 2015), 14.

or "hidden" sayings of Jesus, evidently because the four biographical texts about Jesus had already attained public acceptance and widespread use in the church. Examples of such texts include the Gospel of Thomas, the Gospel of Mary, the Apocryphon of John, the Dialogue of the Savior, the Sophia of Jesus Christ, the Gospel of Philip, and the Gospel of Judas. This is one of several lines of evidence showing that the four New Testament Gospels were the standard such texts early in the second century.[54]

Craig Evans has made the following wry comment: "When students ask me why certain Gospels were omitted from the canon of the New Testament and whether some of them ought to be included, I tell them to read these Gospels. They do, and that answers their questions."[55] The discovery and publication of the apocryphal gospels has provided an opportunity for the church to appreciate just how valuable the canonical Gospels really are as sources of information about Jesus. We may not be able to "prove" that everything in the New Testament Gospels took place, but at least they give us historically substantial, rich material that can be reasonably considered in seeking to learn something about Jesus of Nazareth. Charles Hill has rightly observed:

> It may be a well-guarded secret, but serious historians do not really believe that the teachings of the historical Jesus are better traced through the *Gospel of Judas*, the *Gospel of Mary*, the *Gospel of Philip*, or even the *Gospel of Thomas* than through Matthew, Mark, Luke, and John. Undoubtedly, some people in antiquity preferred the gnostic Gospels to the canonical ones, just as some do today. But the reasons for doing so, whatever they might have been and might be, do not justifiably include a better and truer access to the historical Jesus and his authentic Palestinian life situation.[56]

THE HISTORICAL JESUS IS THE REAL JESUS

What the church should think about "historical Jesus" studies depends primarily on what one understands the terms *history* and *historical* to mean. Joel Green points out that the English term *history* can mean the past itself, the "study" of the past, or "representation" (e.g., writing) of the past.[57] These are just three of

---

54. Charles E. Hill, "A Four-Gospel Canon in the Second Century? Artifact and Arti-fiction," *Early Christianity* 4.3 (2013): 310–34.
55. Craig A. Evans, *Fabricating Jesus: How Modern Scholars Distort the Gospels* (Downers Grove, IL: InterVarsity Press, 2006), 98–99.
56. Hill, *Who Chose the Gospels*, 234.
57. Joel B. Green, "Historicisms and Historiography," in *Dictionary of Jesus and the Gospels*, 2nd ed., 383.

many definitions available.[58] With regard to the term "the historical Jesus," we can distinguish two main definitions implied by Green's first and third definitions of *history*. By *historical Jesus* we could mean (1) Jesus as he actually was in the past; this definition would correspond to what Richard Soulen, quoted earlier, calls the "actual Jesus." On the other hand, by *historical Jesus* we could mean (2) any representation (in a book, film, etc.) that expresses who or what its author or creator understands Jesus to have been in the past. Green's second definition of *history* could apply to the historical Jesus in either definition, referring to the study of Jesus as he was in the past or to the study of representations of Jesus as their authors or creators understand him.

Now, with regard to our two main definitions, the first sense of historical Jesus has just one referent: Jesus as he actually was in the past. The second sense, however, has numerous referents, since there have been many representations made of Jesus as he was in the past.

Most scholars associated with "historical Jesus" studies insist on the second definition and reject the first. Acceptance of the distinction is practically a prerequisite for entrance into the guild. Likewise, the dominant assumption in this field is that the "historical Jesus" consisting of representations of Jesus never yields the actual Jesus of the past. John Meier states the matter epigrammatically: "The historical Jesus is not the real Jesus. The real Jesus is not the historical Jesus."[59]

One line of reasoning behind this sharp distinction is a general consideration that applies in all historical study. We never have enough information about an individual to produce a representation of that person as he or she actually was. We mentioned earlier Richard Soulen's assertion that a person cannot even know himself as he really is, let alone someone of the past. According to Meier, even the historical Richard Nixon merely overlaps with the real Richard Nixon, despite our having access to enough information to construct a "reasonably complete" representation of him. The situation is much worse with ancient figures because our information about them is so fragmentary. "With the exception of a relatively few great public figures, the 'real' persons of ancient history—be they Hillel and Shammai or Jesus and Simon Peter—are simply not accessible to us today by historical research and never will be."[60] As a result, the historical Jesus is not Jesus as he actually was but is "a modern abstraction and

---

58. Michael R. Licona, "Historians and Miracle Claims," *JSHJ* 12 (2014): 108, mentions having encountered sixteen definitions.

59. Meier, "Basic Methodology," 291.

60. Meier, "Basic Methodology," 294–95.

construct. . . . The historical Jesus may give us fragments of the 'real' person, but nothing more."[61]

On the basis of this understanding of the historical Jesus, scholars typically define the historical Jesus as the work of historians. Nearly half a century ago, Leander Keck asserted, "The historical Jesus is the historian's Jesus, not a Kantian *Ding an sich*." This statement has been echoed by various scholars, such as Dunn, who explicitly quotes Keck.[62] Marianne Meye Thompson, though not quoting Keck, also states, "The historical Jesus is the historian's Jesus."[63]

Notice the move that this assertion makes. Now the historical Jesus includes not every attempt to create a representation of Jesus but only those representations of Jesus produced by historians. This move may seem reasonable and innocent enough—historians do historical things—but implicit in this statement is that only certain kinds of representations qualify as "historical." What kinds are those? The standard answer is that the only qualified representations are those created according to the rules of the discipline of modern history, using "the scientific tools of modern research."[64] And those tools, we are informed, cannot consider the divine, the miraculous, or the claims of dogma and religion. In short, the "real" or "actual" Jesus, if he did anything miraculous or divine, if he was anything other than a regular human being, is by definition not "historical" because the historical excludes anything beyond the natural, anything specific to Christian faith. I. Howard Marshall, who was critical of this move, explained its implications with stark clarity: "The result is that the historian believes himself justified in writing a 'history' of Jesus in which the miraculous and supernatural do not appear in historical statements. The 'historical Jesus'—Jesus as he appears to the historian—is an ordinary man."[65]

Somebody call a philosopher.

C. Stephen Evans—an unusual philosopher who has written on historical Jesus studies—acknowledges "that the accounts given by historians about Jesus of Nazareth can never be completely certain or complete." Nevertheless, he finds the distinction between the real Jesus and the historical Jesus "unhelpful."[66]

---

61. Meier, "Basic Methodology," 296, 298.

62. James D. G. Dunn, *A New Perspective on Jesus: What the Quest for the Historical Jesus Missed* (Grand Rapids: Baker Academic, 2005), 29, citing Leander E. Keck, *A Future for the Historical Jesus* (Nashville: Abingdon Press, 1971), 20.

63. Marianne Meye Thompson, "The Historical Jesus and the Johannine Christ," in *Exploring the Gospel of John: In Honor of D. Moody Smith*, ed. R. Alan Culpepper and C. Clifton Black (Louisville: Westminster John Knox, 1996), 25.

64. Meier, "Basic Methodology," 296.

65. I. Howard Marshall, *I Believe in the Historical Jesus*, rev. ed. (Vancouver: Regent College, 2004), 59.

66. C. Stephen Evans, *The Historical Christ and the Jesus of Faith: The Incarnational Narrative as History* (Oxford: Clarendon, 1996), 8.

It "flies in the face of ordinary language, in which to say that an account given of some event is historical is not merely to say that it occurs in a narrative given by a modern historian, but that the event really occurred." Evans is prepared to speak of "the historians' Jesus" but prefers to distinguish this construct from "the historical Jesus" in order to avoid such confusion.[67] Likewise, N. T. Wright points out that it is still the case that most people assume that the terms history and historical refer to "past events"—what "actually happened"—and not merely to "what people write about past events."[68]

The problem with the distinction between the real and the historical is not merely a matter of its departure from the ordinary language used by most people. Equating the historical Jesus with the historian's Jesus implies that all accounts of Jesus by historians are "historical" while no accounts by non-historians qualify as such. As Evans points out, "If the 'historical Jesus' is simply an account given by a historian, then no account given by a historian can fail to be historical."[69] We could never deny that a particular historian's account of Jesus was historical no matter what errors it contained. One solution to this problem, of course, might be to maintain that an account qualifies as historical not just because it is presented by a historian but because it has been produced using "the scientific tools of modern research." Yet given the diversity of theories about Jesus constructed with these tools, it appears that either the tools are inadequate to the job or the ones wielding the tools do so with varying degrees of competency.

A related point is that if "historical" refers only to accounts of the past and not to the persons or events of the past, then we could never speak of an account as "historically inaccurate." Yet historians do this all the time, including scholars in historical Jesus studies. By "historically inaccurate" they mean "not what happened in the past."[70] Asserting that some things are "historical" in the sense that they actually happened while other things are not "historical" in that sense shows that we are all still using the term "historical" in this ordinary way.

It is not naïve, then, for someone to say that "the historical Jesus," meaning Jesus as he actually existed in the first century, did this or said that. Historians sometimes speak this way, though what they assert may be debatable. So, for example, Robert Miller has stated that the purpose of the Jesus Seminar is

---

67. Evans, *Historical Christ and the Jesus of Faith*, 8–9.

68. N. T. Wright, "Abandon Studying the Historical Jesus? No, We Need History," *Christianity Today* 54.4 (2010): 27.

69. Evans, *Historical Christ and the Jesus of Faith*, 9.

70. Meier comes close to making this point when he states that historians should not say that the Gospels do or do not depict "the historical Jesus," lest the distinction between the real Jesus and the historical Jesus be obscured. See Meier, "Basic Methodology," 298.

"clarifying what the historical Jesus said and did."[71] When Dale Allison opines, "Those who subscribe to Nicea should be anxious, for the historical Jesus did not think of himself what they think of him,"[72] he is making a claim about Jesus as he actually was in the past, not a claim about some modern historian's construct of Jesus. Indeed, Allison is claiming to know not only what Jesus didn't do or say but also what he didn't *think*. Even Meier, who argues at length for drawing a clear and consistent distinction between the real Jesus and the historical Jesus, forgets it as soon as he moves on to discussing which criteria "are helpful in reaching a decision about what material comes from the historical Jesus."[73]

Much historical Jesus scholarship looks suspiciously like a grand exercise in equivocation. We are told that the "real" or "actual" Jesus is inaccessible and unknowable, so that he must be distinguished from the "historical" Jesus, which is the modern historian's abstraction or hypothetical construct. At the same time, we are told by modern historians that "the historical Jesus" did or did not do certain things, that he taught one thing but not another, and so forth. The same concern must be raised regarding more simply worded assertions about what Jesus did or did not do or teach. If the real Jesus is really inaccessible and unknowable, then "historical Jesus" scholars should not be making such assertions as that "Jesus did not tell allegories, but did tell parables."[74]

Rather than get caught in such confusing (if not misleading) equivocation, we think it best to reclaim the expression "the historical Jesus" as properly referring to Jesus as he actually was in the past, in human history. The historical Jesus is not a different Jesus from the "real" or "actual" Jesus who lived and died in the first century. It does not much matter whether we refer to a modern representation about Jesus as a "historiographical Jesus" or a "historical reconstruction of Jesus" or a "historical portrait of Jesus." However, we should not use the term "the historical Jesus" to refer to such representations. There is one historical Jesus—the first-century man Jesus of Nazareth—and many historical representations about Jesus.

Once this semantic confusion has been dispelled, we are in a position to address the claim that historians cannot consider religious, miraculous, or divine elements as part of their study of the historical Jesus. As long as the historical Jesus is defined as the Jesus discernible by modern historical methods only and is distinguished from the actual, real Jesus of the past, the question of whether the

---

71. Robert J. Miller, *The Jesus Seminar and Its Critics* (Santa Rosa, CA: Polebridge, 1999), 22.

72. Dale C. Allison Jr., *The Historical Christ and the Theological Jesus* (Grand Rapids: Eerdmans, 2009), 89.

73. Meier, "Basic Methodology," 308; for additional examples see 319–23.

74. James M. Robinson, "The Gospel of the Historical Jesus," in Hólmen and Porter, *Handbook for the Study of the Historical Jesus*, 1:456.

historical Jesus actually performed miracles or rose from the dead can be set aside on a technicality, as it were. Some historians, including some who clearly believe that Jesus rose from the dead, maintain that this belief cannot be substantiated or even discussed historically because such events are by definition outside the bounds of what history can investigate. In our view, this is a disastrous concession that no Christian should ever make. In actuality, the concession would clear the field for critics of Christianity—historians or otherwise—to make their case against the church's Jesus unopposed. Evans warns:

> A look at the practices of historical critics, as well as theoretical accounts of what historical method involves, makes it evident that many scholars would claim that ordinary historical methods do require such a bias against the supernatural. If that is the case, then defending the historicity of the narrative using "ordinary" historical methods will necessarily be a losing battle. This raises the question as to whether the defenders of the narrative have essentially given away the contest by accepting the terms of the engagement of their opponents.[75]

The danger of conceding that the miraculous cannot be the subject of historical inquiry is that this methodological limitation in practice applies only to the believer, not to the skeptic. No historical argument is allowed if it concludes in favor of the miraculous, but historical arguments that call into question the miraculous are perfectly permissible. How this works may be illustrated from Bart Ehrman's book *How Jesus Became God.* Early in his treatment of the resurrection of Jesus, Ehrman assures his readers that bias against miracles is not a factor:

> The reason historians cannot prove or disprove whether God has performed a miracle in the past—such as raising Jesus from the dead—is *not* that historians are required to be secular humanists with an anti-supernaturalist bias. I want to stress this point because conservative Christian apologists, in order to score debating points, often claim that this is the case.[76]

Ehrman's explanation goes on for more than six pages, during which it becomes clear that the stricture from his perspective does not prevent the "historian" from denying the resurrection of Jesus, only from affirming it as

---

75. Evans, *Historical Christ and the Jesus of Faith*, 33.
76. Bart D. Ehrman, *How Jesus Became God: The Exaltation of a Jewish Preacher from Galilee* (New York: HarperOne, 2014), 143.

historical. Historians cannot conclude that Jesus rose from the dead because this statement presupposes theological beliefs that are specific to Christianity and not commonly shared by most or all people.[77] He then ties this claim explicitly to the conventional distinction between history and the past:

> History, for historians, is not the same as "the past." The past is everything that has happened before; history is what we can establish as having happened before, using historical forms of evidence. Historical evidence is not and cannot be based on religious and theological assumptions that some, but not all, of us share.[78]

Later, however, when Ehrman begins discussing the specific factual issues surrounding the resurrection of Jesus, his epistemological stance shifts even further. Ehrman briefly reviews various theories about what happened to the body of Jesus after his death: the disciples stole the body, the women went to the wrong tomb, or Jesus had only lost consciousness and not died. He then comments:

> I don't subscribe to any of these alternative views because I don't think we know what happened to the body of Jesus. But simply looking at the matter from a historical point of view, any of these views is more plausible than the claim that God raised Jesus physically from the dead. A resurrection would be a miracle and as such would defy all "probability." Otherwise, it wouldn't be a miracle. To say that an event that defies probability is more probable than something that is simply improbable is to fly in the face of anything that involves probability.[79]

In short, having claimed that his stance as a historian does not include any bias against miracles, Ehrman ends up asserting before the chapter is done that any explanation of the facts would be more historically plausible than a miracle. In the following chapter, Ehrman argues that the resurrection appearances should be understood as religious visions comparable to bereavement visions, perhaps precipitated by a combination of grief and guilt.[80] So maybe those "conservative Christian apologists" whom Ehrman mentioned had a point.

---

77. Ehrman, *How Jesus Became God*, 146–50.
78. Ehrman, *How Jesus Became God*, 150.
79. Ehrman, *How Jesus Became God*, 165.
80. Ehrman, *How Jesus Became God*, 193–204. Ehrman is careful to conclude that historians cannot prove whether the visions were "veridical" or not, but the force of his argument is at least to call their veridicality into doubt.

The technical term for the approach to history exemplified by Ehrman is *methodological naturalism*. The qualification "methodological" distinguishes this concept from ontological or metaphysical naturalism, which is the claim that the natural world or realm is all that exists. Methodological naturalism does not deny the existence of supernatural beings or of a transcendent world or realm, but it disallows them any role in the pursuit of scientific knowledge, including the physical and biological sciences as well as history and other human sciences (e.g., psychology, sociology, or anthropology). There are actually several different versions of methodological naturalism. Philosophers Paul Moser and David Yandell have defined the core idea as the position that "every legitimate method of acquiring knowledge consists of or is grounded in the hypothetically completed methods of the empirical sciences (that is, in natural methods)."[81]

Methodological naturalism has come under serious criticism in recent years, as has ontological naturalism.[82] It is far from a settled matter that scientists, let alone historians, must never entertain the question of supernatural activity or events. Once methodological naturalism becomes an inflexible rule from which no departure can be allowed, it becomes a dogma and is operationally indistinguishable from ontological naturalism. With regard to the study of the historical figure of Jesus, there is simply no reason why historians cannot investigate whether he performed miracles or rose from the dead. If Jesus did those things, then these were actions performed by a human being in particular places and at particular times in the past, and thus they occurred in history.

In a *tour de force* study, Craig Keener has shown that miracles—especially miraculous healings—have been reported throughout history across many cultures, including in the modern era. Keener discusses numerous documented examples from various parts of the world outside the West and in Western Christianity throughout church history. His catalogue of miracles concludes with a

---

81. Paul K. Moser and Keith Yandell, "Farewell to Philosophical Naturalism," in *Naturalism: A Critical Analysis*, ed. William Lane Craig and J. P. Moreland, Routledge Studies in Twentieth-Century Philosophy (London: Routledge, 2000), 9 (statement originally in italics).

82. In addition to the volume edited by Craig and Moreland, see especially Stewart Goetz and Charles Taliaferro, *Naturalism*, Interventions (Grand Rapids: Eerdmans, 2008); Bruce L. Gordon and William A. Dembski, eds., *The Nature of Nature: Examining the Role of Naturalism in Science* (Wilmington, DE: ISI Books, 2011); Alvin Plantinga, *Where the Conflict Really Lies: Science, Religion, and Naturalism* (Oxford: Oxford University Press, 2011); R. Scott Smith, *Naturalism and Our Knowledge of Reality: Testing Religious Truth-claims*, Ashgate New Critical Thinking in Religion, Theology, and Biblical Studies (London: Routledge, 2016 [orig. 2012]); Joseph B. Onyango Okello, *A History and Critique of Methodological Naturalism: The Philosophical Case for God's Design of Nature* (Eugene, OR: Wipf & Stock, 2016); Jonathan Bartlett and Eric Holloway, eds., *Naturalism and Its Alternatives in Scientific Methodologies*, Proceedings of the 2016 Conference on Alternatives to Methodological Naturalism (Broken Arrow, OK: Blyth Institute Press, 2016); and see the essays from varying perspectives in Kelly James Clark, ed., *The Blackwell Companion to Naturalism* (Malden, MA: John Wiley & Sons, 2016).

chapter on reports of healings of the blind and the lame, raisings of the dead, and nature miracles. Finally, Keener carefully engages possible non-supernatural explanations before defending the conclusion that at least many of the reports are best explained as actual miracles. Keener effectively argues that the types of miracles reported in the New Testament have numerous analogies from eyewitness testimonies of multitudes of people in both the past and present and so cannot be dismissed as incredible. "There therefore seems no reason, based on the principle of historical analogy, to deny that first-century eyewitnesses could have believed that they saw Jesus heal blind eyes, made paralytics walk, or raise the dead, all of which cures eyewitnesses also claim today."[83]

We agree with Ehrman that historical evidence cannot be based on theological assumptions specific to a particular religion. However, acknowledging that such events as naturally inexplicable healings take place in history does not presuppose a specific religious commitment or theological belief system. A particular miracle might entail or imply the validity of a theological claim, but that is not the same thing as the miracle assuming or presupposing a specific theological position. Drawing theological implications from a miraculous event, or interpreting a miracle as having a specific religious or theological meaning, is not itself a historical judgment even though it refers to the miracle as an event for which good historical evidence has been identified. Paul Eddy and Gregory Boyd propose an "open historical-critical method" in which the historian prefers natural explanations where they comport with the evidence but remains open to finding that an event was supernatural if the evidence supports it. Reaching such a conclusion does not assume a particular faith commitment and is to be distinguished from a theological explanation or interpretation of the event.

> The nature of the critical historiographical enterprise is such that it can never go beyond statements of probability, and its disciplinary parameters end before questions about the transcendent source and/or theological meaning of a plausibly supernatural occurrence can be answered.[84]

Similarly, Michael Licona has argued, "Historians can offer a positive verdict pertaining to the historicity of an event while leaving its cause undetermined. . . . If no natural explanation proves adequate and a supernatural one

---

83. Keener, *Miracles*, 2:761.
84. Eddy and Boyd, *Jesus Legend*, 88.

does, the historian can render a judgment on whether the event occurred but stops short of naming its cause."[85]

This "open historical-critical method" may be the best approach for the church's scholars to take in engaging the Quest. The method neither begs the question in favor of the church's understanding of Jesus nor closes the door to investigating the factual evidence pertaining to the most important and controversial aspects of the church's beliefs. It avoids the pitfall of divorcing the historical Jesus from the real Jesus, while acknowledging the valid distinction between the real Jesus of history and what we can know about him.

BACK TO JESUS

We must acknowledge that most scholars who purport to be studying the historical Jesus assume that the historical Jesus must be very different from the church's Jesus. It has been so from the beginning with Reimarus, who had argued that Jesus was a failed revolutionary. The driving purpose of such study has generally been understood to be to separate the wheat of a merely human historical Jesus from the chaff of the incarnate Christ. As Joachim Jeremias noted, "The whole scholarly activity, centered on the historical Jesus, represented an attempt to break loose from dogma. The battle cry was, 'Back to Jesus, the man from Nazareth!'"[86]

The church's proper response to this "quest" must of course be to disagree with the goal of finding a different Jesus. However, we would argue that it is a mistake to cede "the historical Jesus" to these questers. Christian scholars should not agree to the terms laid down by naturalists, but they can and should *engage the issues raised in the quest*—and thankfully, many are doing so.

Moreover, the church has its own quest: not to search for a Jesus of its own making, but to know the truth about Jesus and to represent him faithfully. Engaging the quest is important to the church not only in order to defend its beliefs about Jesus, but because the church is ever seeking a fuller, more accurate understanding of Jesus. The church's claim has never been that it knows everything about Jesus or that it knows him perfectly. We can and should learn even from those participants in the quest who do not share our views of Jesus but who often bring a wealth of information and insight into the contexts and meanings of specific elements in the accounts of Jesus in the church's Gospels.

---

85. Licona, "Historians and Miracle Claims," 122, 123.

86. Joachim Jeremias, "The Search for the Historical Jesus," in *Jesus and the Message of the New Testament*, ed. K. C. Hanson, Fortress Classics in Biblical Studies (Minneapolis: Fortress, 2002), 3. The observation has been made numerous times.

As N. T. Wright has put it, "Genuine historical study is necessary—not to construct a 'fifth gospel,' but rather to understand the four we already have."[87] Historical Jesus study pursued properly does not attempt to construct a "fifth Gospel," which liberals do with their selective reconstructions and fundamentalists have occasionally done with their forced harmonizations, by claiming, for example, that Peter denied Jesus six times.[88] Both extremes fail to allow each Gospel to speak on its own terms. Both are legitimate exercises taken to extremes: there is nothing wrong with trying to reconstruct what happened where our information is incomplete, or with harmonizing sources where reasonable harmonizations are possible.

The church's only interest is in following and believing in the historical Jesus—the real Jesus, the real man from Nazareth. The evidence shows that the Jesus of history was a real man who performed remarkable healings and exorcisms, who proclaimed that in him the kingdom of God had drawn near, who made various other astonishing claims for himself that his disciples came to understand were claims to deity, who died on a cross by the order of Pontius Pilate, and yes, who rose from the dead. There is no other Jesus.

---

87. Wright, "No, We Need History," 28.
88. Johnston M. Cheney, *The Life of Christ in Stereo* (Portland: Western Conservative Baptist Seminary Press, 1969), 190–92, 258; Harold Lindsell, *The Battle for the Bible* (Grand Rapids: Zondervan, 1976), 174–76.

CHAPTER 2

The Historical Jesus in Recent Evangelical Scholarship

CRAIG L. BLOMBERG AND DARLENE M. SEAL

B iblical scholarship tends to go in cycles, with flurries of activity in a particular area followed by quieter moments. Today is the day when Paul is in the limelight, with old, new, and newer perspectives and major, large tomes worth scrutinizing in detail flying off publishers' presses faster than even conscientious speed-readers can keep up with them. Study of the historical Jesus is lagging noticeably behind. Of course, it seems only fair. That topic took center stage during the twenty years from the mid-1980s to the mid-2000s, the heart of what has been called the Third Quest. The original quest of the historical Jesus was Albert Schweitzer's label for the (mostly German) studies of the nineteenth century, which he surveyed and then proceeded to debunk back at the beginning of the twentieth century. As a result, what ensued was what N. T. Wright labeled the period of "no quest," dominated by Rudolf Bultmann's skepticism of knowing much beyond the mere "thatness" of Jesus. Then, after World War II, came the new quest pioneered by several of Bultmann's former students, especially Günther Bornkamm, Ernst Käsemann, and James M. Robinson. It remained skeptical about significant portions of the Synoptic tradition but rehabilitated their main contours about what Jesus did and especially validated a raft of his sayings. Only from about 1980 onward, however, did a discrete third search for Jesus of Nazareth emerge, utilizing greater criteriological sophistication, interdisciplinary methodology, and extra-canonical sources. It asked holistic questions about cause and effect, studied the deeds of Jesus at least as much as the sayings and, most importantly, re-planted Jesus firmly in the Jewish soil in which he actually grew, ground that had regularly been lost in the midst of all of the anti-Semitism, especially in Europe, during the mid-twentieth century.[1]

---

1. See esp. Stephen Neill and Tom Wright, *The Interpretation of the New Testament 1861–1988*, 2nd ed. (Oxford: Oxford University Press, 1988), 112–46.

At least that's the way numerous people trying to sum up a century and a half of scholarship have boiled things down into manageable scope. History is never so neat and tidy, and phases of history tend to emerge more in the minds of historians as they try to systematize and make sense of it, communicating it to and making it interesting for others, than in the complexities and diversities of reality. Stanley Porter's detailed overview of the period covered by the three quests shows how there were numerous different approaches during each "phase," there never truly was a period of "no quest," and the generalizations about each quest are simply that—trends that get attention and characterize those periods of time slightly more than others but not to the degree that the overly abbreviated and simplified summaries might suggest.[2] Nevertheless, with these caveats in mind, what we aim to do in what follows is to sketch the broad contours of current historical Jesus scholarship, delineate evangelical contributions to it while giving attention to criticism and challenges faced by evangelical scholars, and finally to indicate some potential future directions that may bear fruit in historical Jesus research.

THE CURRENT STATE OF HISTORICAL JESUS RESEARCH

So where are we now? And where are evangelicals in the scholarly mix? The sweeping, oversimplified generalization to answer the first of these questions is that we are in a lull overall in the world of Jesus research. No works of the magnitude or influence of E. P. Sanders's *Jesus and Judaism* (1985),[3] Dominic Crossan's *The Historical Jesus* (1993),[4] N. T. Wright's *Jesus and the Victory of God* (1996),[5] or James D. G. Dunn's *Jesus Remembered* (2003)[6] have appeared in the last fifteen years. More voices than we previously heard are telling us that the Third Quest has played out its hand so that it is time to shuffle the cards and start a new game, as it were. On the fringes of biblical scholarship, the far left and the far right, we hear very odd messages. On the far left, among the atheists, people like Richard Carrier and Robert Price convince far too many gullible

---

2. Stanley E. Porter, *The Criteria of Authenticity in Historical-Jesus Research: Previous Discussion and New Proposals*, JSNTSup 191 (Sheffield: Sheffield Academic Press, 2000), 28–62. Cf. also F. Bermejo Rubio, "The Fiction of the 'Three Quests': An Argument for Dismantling a Dubious Historiographical Paradigm," *JSHJ* 7 (2009): 211–53.

3. E. P. Sanders, *Jesus and Judaism* (Philadelphia: Fortress, 1985).

4. John Dominic Crossan, *The Historical Jesus: The Life of a Mediterranean Jewish Peasant* (San Francisco: HarperSanFrancisco, 1991).

5. N. T. Wright, *Jesus and the Victory of God*, vol. 2 of *Christian Origins and the Question of God* (Minneapolis: Fortress, 1996).

6. James D. G. Dunn, *Jesus Remembered*, vol. 1 of *Christianity in the Making* (Grand Rapids: Eerdmans, 2003).

people that there really isn't any solid historical evidence for Jesus's existence at all.[7] Fortunately, bona fide biblical scholars like Bart Ehrman and Maurice Casey who have too often proved nemeses to evangelicals have enough integrity and knowledge to write entire monographs refuting such complete skepticism.[8]

On the far right appears F. David Farnell, taking after his mentor Robert Thomas and censuring any evangelical who would even participate in historical Jesus research as having capitulated to postmodernism, because apparently for him naive realism is the only acceptable epistemology, despite its inability to deliver the certainty of knowledge these scholars demand.[9] A good dose of critical realism is a much better solution. In other words, historical research on any topic can only ever deal with probabilities, but many probabilities are "beyond reasonable doubt" and we live by them every day. Someone who capitulates to Lessing's "ugly, broad ditch" that the accidental truths of history can never form the foundation for the necessary truths of reason, fails to realize that both fallen and finite human beings can never have 100 percent assurance about anything. Even an inerrant Scripture has to be interpreted by errant humans, though God-given revelation certainly gives us a significant advantage. Critical realism reminds us that we can achieve degrees of probability high enough to exceed the probabilities of the other options by enough of a gap that they merit our trust.[10]

In between these two extremes lies a broad spectrum of approaches. One can still find representatives of each of the various characterizations of Jesus that appeared in Ben Witherington's taxonomy over twenty years ago. Jesus may be an oriental guru, an itinerant Cynic philosopher, a uniquely spirit-infused miracle worker, an eschatological prophet, a stimulus for social change, a wise sage, or a marginalized Jewish messiah.[11] If we add in the perspective of freelance Muslim writer, Reza Aslan, we even have S. G. F. Brandon's Jesus as Zealot redux.[12]

---

7. Richard Carrier, *On the Historicity of Jesus: Why We Might Have Reason for Doubt* (Sheffield: Sheffield Phoenix, 2014); Robert M. Price, *Deconstructing Jesus* (Amherst, NY: Prometheus, 2000).

8. Bart D. Ehrman, *Did Jesus Exist? The Historical Argument for Jesus of Nazareth* (New York: HarperOne, 2012); Maurice Casey, *Jesus: Evidence and Argument or Mythicist Myths?* (New York: T&T Clark, 2014).

9. See his and several other chapters in F. David Farnell, ed., *Vital Issues in the Inerrancy Debate* (Eugene, OR: Wipf & Stock, 2015); cf. his and Thomas's chapters in Robert L. Thomas and F. David Farnell, eds., *The Jesus Crisis: The Inroads of Historical Criticism into Evangelical Scholarship* (Grand Rapids: Kregel, 1998).

10. For an excellent introduction, see Ben F. Meyer, *Reality and Illusion in New Testament Scholarship: A Primer in Critical Realist Hermeneutics* (Collegeville, MN: Michael Glazier, 1995). For application to the Jesus quest, see esp. Jonathan Bernier, *The Quest for the Historical Jesus after the Demise of Authenticity: Toward a Critical Realist Philosophy of History in Jesus Studies*, LNTS 540 (New York: T&T Clark, 2016).

11. Ben Witherington III, *The Jesus Quest: The Third Search for the Jew of Nazareth* (Downers Grove, IL: InterVarsity Press, 1995). The label "Oriental guru" is ours, but the concept is present in Witherington's set of chapter titles that form his taxonomy.

12. Reza Aslan, *Zealot: The Life and Times of Jesus of Nazareth* (New York: Random House, 2014). Cf. S. G. F. Brandon, *Jesus and the Zealots: A Study of the Political Factor in Primitive Christianity* (Manchester: University of Manchester Press, 1967).

Intriguingly, after repeated attempts to turn Jesus into a Pharisee, Essene, or even Zealot, to our knowledge he has yet to be depicted as a Sadducee.[13] Even that claim would make more sense than trying to say that Jesus never lived or that participating in the quest is a dangerous betrayal of one's faith. But it would be quite a stretch and utterly unpersuasive!

While proponents of all of Witherington's various characterizations can still be found, three loom noticeably larger than the rest: the eschatological prophet, the proponent of social change, and the marginalized Jewish messiah. Under the first of these headings, some like Amy-Jill Levine and André LaCocque try to make Jesus so Jewish that just about anything distinctive in the Gospels is eliminated as inauthentic.[14] This approach stands Bultmann's famous dissimilarity criterion[15] completely on its head, so that it becomes a similarity criterion. Instead of envisioning that what set Jesus apart from his contemporaries was least likely to have been invented by them, we now look for ways in which he can be shown to be thoroughly Jewish. Only what Jesus is reported to have said or done that is highly similar to early first-century Judaism in Israel becomes credible. Combine that with the flipside of the criterion of dissimilarity with emerging Christianity and you have Tom Holmén's continuum approach or double similarity criterion.[16] What was solidly a part of Jewish thinking and remained entrenched in emerging Christianity becomes that which is attributed to Jesus with greatest confidence. These scholars have commendably erased any trace of anti-Semitism from their portraits of Jesus, but we wonder whether Jesus would have ever had the influence he had if he were really as non-controversially Jewish as they claim. Nor are we left with any convincing reason for his crucifixion—one of those foundational facts attested to even by ancient non-Christian historians.[17]

The second approach relies on social-scientific analysis, both of the Gospel narratives and of the cultural dynamics most relevant to Jesus's Israel, to portray him as anti-imperial to one degree or another. Empire criticism has by now

---

13. For the more historically responsible works, see esp. for the Pharisee, Harvey Falk, *Jesus the Pharisee: A New Look at the Jewishness of Jesus* (New York: Paulist, 1985); for a close relationship with the Essenes, Bargil Pixner, *Paths of the Messiah: Messianic Sites in Galilee and Jerusalem: Jesus and Jewish Christianity in Light of Archaeological Discoveries* (San Francisco: Ignatius, 2010 [Germ. orig. 1991]).

14. Amy-Jill Levine, *The Misunderstood Jew: The Church and the Scandal of the Jewish Jesus* (San Francisco: HarperSanFrancisco, 2006); André LaCocque, *Jesus the Central Jew: His Times and His People* (Atlanta: SBL Press, 2015).

15. Rudolf Bultmann, *The History of the Synoptic Tradition*, rev. ed., trans. John Marsh (Oxford: Blackwell, 1963), 205.

16. See esp. Tom Holmén, ed., *Jesus in Continuum*, WUNT 289 (Tübingen: Mohr Siebeck, 2002). Cf. also Tom Holmén, ed., *Jesus from Judaism to Christianity: Continuum Approaches to the Historical Jesus*, LNTS 352 (New York: T&T Clark, 2007).

17. See John P. Meier, *The Roots of the Problem and the Person*, vol. 1 of *A Marginal Jew: Rethinking the Historical Jesus*, ABRL (New York: Doubleday, 1991), 177, and his "criterion of rejection and execution."

permeated studies of every New Testament book, and it is easy to succumb to one of two temptations: either to see implicit criticism of Roman rule lurking almost everywhere or to minimize the impact of the empire in just about every location except for the city of Rome itself. Richard Horsley is probably the most tireless champion of the first of these tendencies;[18] some evangelicals have veered more in the opposite direction, even if only by neglect.

The third cluster of studies proves the most promising. Sometimes it builds on Sanders's model of Jesus as prophet, sometimes it is willing to countenance the possibility that Jesus's symbolic actions pointed to a kind of messianic claim or consciousness, and occasionally it acknowledges that "divine identity" Christology emerged so early in the history of the Jesus movement that the only reasonable source for the disciples' belief in it must have been things that Jesus himself claimed fairly explicitly.[19] Witherington placed John Meier into the marginalized messiah category after the first two volumes of his magisterial work on the historical Jesus, in which he envisioned an "unpapal conclave" of a Jewish, Catholic, Protestant, and agnostic scholar cloistered in the basement of the Harvard Divinity School library until they could produce a consensus document, using the standard criteria of authenticity, of what Jesus most likely said and did. In recent volumes, Meier has added a Muslim scholar to his imaginary conclave. In each of the first four volumes, he promised that the next one would be his last, but in his fifth and most recent one he stopped making predictions. Having begun in 1991, one can only hope that he will live long enough to complete the project.[20] By his own admission, his fifth volume surprised him with his own findings; he now believes that only four parables of Jesus can be shown most likely to be authentic, even though for most Jesus researchers they provide the bedrock core of Jesus's teaching about the kingdom of God, the most central theme of his ministry.[21] Anyone who would now predict where Meier will finally land is therefore speculating prematurely.

Integral in supporting the studies that do see a messianic consciousness in the historical Jesus are the writings of Larry Hurtado and Richard Bauckham,

18. Perhaps most representative and extending the theme to all of Scripture is Richard A. Horsley, ed., *In the Shadow of Empire: Reclaiming the Bible as a History of Faithful Resistance* (Louisville: Westminster John Knox, 2008). Horsley himself nicely encapsulates his ideas on Jesus in his chapter, "Jesus and Empire," 75–96. For fuller details, see Richard A. Horsley, *Jesus and the Politics of Roman Palestine* (Columbia: University of South Carolina Press, 2014).

19. See esp. Andrew Ter Ern Loke, *The Origin of Divine Christology*, SNTSMS 169 (Cambridge: Cambridge University Press, 2017), and the studies he surveys.

20. John P. Meier, *A Marginal Jew: Rethinking the Historical Jesus*, 5 vols. ABRL (New York: Doubleday; New Haven: Yale University Press, 1991–2016).

21. John P. Meier, *Probing the Authenticity of the Parables*, vol. 5 of *A Marginal Jew: Rethinking the Historical Jesus*, ABRL (New Haven: Yale University Press, 2016).

though neither has written a historical Jesus volume *per se*.[22] Hurtado has repeatedly drawn attention to the partial parallels between the Gospels' portraits of Jesus and the depictions in Second Temple Judaism of God's Spirit, Torah, Wisdom, Logos or Word, and exalted patriarchs and archangels. With others, he has stressed that pre-70 CE Jewish monotheism was more varied than after the destruction of the temple in Jerusalem and allowed for a differentiated unity within the nature of God.[23] At least as important is his repeated demonstration of the "revolutionary" rather than evolutionary nature of early, high Christology, which occurs in every source we can locate as close to the time of the life of Christ as we choose to go.[24] Bauckham has stressed how Jesus-followers took a step that other Second Temple Jews never did, no matter how close they may have come to deifying other exalted figures or reifying more abstract concepts, when they included Jesus within the divine identity itself, yet without denying monotheism.[25]

One can also find some very large anthologies of historical Jesus research within the past decade that combine together disparate perspectives in a way that was much rarer a generation ago, showing both how more conservative scholarship has come of age and gained a measure of respect in the academy and how evangelicals themselves are more willing to interact with a broad spectrum of scholars and their work. Porter and Holmén's four-volume "handbook" (!) wins the prize both for quantity and price, while leaving almost no stone unturned and no topic unaddressed.[26] James Charlesworth and Petr Pokorný's two-volume anthology of Jesus research has about the same number of high quality contributions but without some of the less valuable entries that make Porter and Holmén double the length.[27]

A very encouraging development is the establishment of the *Journal for the Study of the Historical Jesus*, which issued its first volume in 2003. It has provided a forum for multiple critiques of and dialogue about some of the major or more recent contributions to the quest, like Wright's or Dunn's. It has also published

---

22. Unless one counts Richard Bauckham, *Jesus: A Very Short Introduction* (Oxford: Oxford University Press, 2011).

23. See esp. Larry W. Hurtado, *One God, One Lord: Early Christian Devotion and Ancient Jewish Monotheism*, 3rd ed. (New York: T&T Clark, 2015).

24. Larry W. Hurtado, "The Gospel of Mark: Evolutionary or Revolutionary Document?" JSNT 40 (1990): 15–32.

25. See esp. Richard Bauckham, *Jesus and the God of Israel: God Crucified and Other Studies on the New Testament's Christology of Divine Identity* (Grand Rapids: Eerdmans, 2008).

26. Tom Holmén and Stanley E. Porter, eds., *Handbook for the Study of the Historical Jesus*, 4 vols. (Leiden: Brill, 2011).

27. James H. Charlesworth and Petr Pokorný, eds., *Jesus Research*, 2 vols. (Grand Rapids: Eerdmans, 2007, 2014).

other thematically related fascicles on topics such as memory, orality, John the Baptist, and miracles, and also numerous stand-alone articles on individual passages, larger themes, and methodologies or criteria in historical Jesus research.[28] Even from its inception, the quality of the articles has matched that of the much better-known and longer-established journals in the fields of New Testament and biblical studies and sometimes exceeded it.

Of course if one proceeds to survey in detail the last ten-to-fifteen years of Jesus research, it becomes clear why attempts to subsume periods of time under one or even a handful of topics are inevitably doomed to fail. Developments proceed in numerous directions. For example, Dunn's *Jesus Remembered* propelled various other scholars to expand on the fairly obvious observation that has not been explicitly stated often enough: the most that historical and biographical works, including the Gospels, can do is give us events and figures as people remembered them.[29] A highly selective collection of information, anecdotes, and teachings are arranged as the historian or biographer desires, and in the ancient world this arrangement is often as much topical as chronological. The significance the author or compiler sees in the events is brought out by repetition, narrative asides, length of narration, sequence of arrangement, and numerous other literary and rhetorical features. Richard Bauckham's *Jesus and the Eyewitnesses*, now in a significantly updated and expanded edition, has supplied numerous reasons why "social memory"—the way things are remembered within groups of people who greatly value the memories of individuals or events they seek to preserve—makes it likely that the Gospel writers remembered Jesus quite well.[30]

On the other hand, too many critics point to modern tests of people's memories, which mislead or fail them, in order to cast doubts on how well the first-century tradents of the gospel tradition could have remembered Jesus.[31] The problem with such an approach is that memory is cultivated highly in oral cultures in ways that are almost non-existent in our modern print-driven societies. But, as Paul Foster has rightly pointed out, the most that discussion of social

---

28. The journal is published by E. J. Brill; sixteen consecutive volumes have appeared from 2003 to 2018 at the time of this printing.

29. For a balanced assessment of Dunn's approach and agenda, see esp. *Memories of Jesus: A Critical Appraisal of James D. G. Dunn's Jesus Remembered*, ed. Robert B. Stewart and Gary R. Habermas (Nashville: B&H Academic, 2010).

30. Richard Bauckham, *Jesus and the Eyewitnesses: The Gospels as Eyewitness Testimony*, 2nd ed. (Grand Rapids: Eerdmans, 2017), esp. 319–57.

31. E.g., April DeConick, "Human Memory and the Sayings of Jesus: Contemporary Experimental Exercises in the Transmission of Jesus Traditions," in *Jesus, the Voice, and the Text: Beyond the Oral and the Written Gospel*, ed. Tom Thatcher (Waco, TX: Baylor University Press, 2008), 135–79.

memory can accomplish is to create some expectations of careful preservation; it cannot authenticate any actual pericopae or themes within the Gospels.[32] Another group of Jesus researchers uses the refraction of light as an analogy for memory. What we have are refracted memories of Jesus, bent or skewed in a certain direction. But if we can recognize what those bents are and take them into account, we can still get back to probable authentic information about Jesus.[33] This approach forms something of a *via media* between using memory either to support or to challenge the Gospels' authenticity.

A different way to focus on how Jesus was remembered is to work backwards from effects to cause. N. T. Wright, already in *Jesus and the Victory of God*, just over twenty years ago and without appealing to social memory, creatively argued that a messianic consciousness must have been present already at the baptism of Jesus by John the Baptist. But he begins much later in Jesus's ministry with Jesus's confession at his trial before the Sanhedrin (Mark 14:62 pars.) and asks what must have provoked the high priest's question and Jesus's answer. Certainly the Gospels present Jesus's temple incident as a provocation and a catalyst for his arrest. But from E. P. Sanders onward the Third Quest has often viewed it also as a prediction of the temple's coming destruction rather than only an appeal for cultic reform. Either way, by enacting such a powerful "object lesson," who did Jesus think he was? Some fairly lofty self-understanding must be present. Continuing backward in history from that event, the so-called triumphal entry, with its conscious playing out of Zechariah 9:9, must have had a messianic meaning for Jesus. And in this way, Wright keeps going backward via cause and effect until he reaches Jesus's baptism.[34]

Jens Schröter, more recently, is not quite as optimistic as Wright about how much can be recovered. Yet he applies a somewhat similar strategy or criterion of necessary explanation to authenticate Jesus's encounters with John the Baptist, his call of the Twelve, the centrality of the kingdom for his message and ministry, his healing miracles and exorcisms, his messianic use of "Son of Man," his offer of purity for the impure, his arrest due to his actions against the temple, and his death by crucifixion.[35] Again, broader, holistic questions involving major

---

32. Paul Foster, "Memory, Orality, and the Fourth Gospel: Three Dead Ends in Historical-Jesus Research," *JSHJ* 10 (2012): 191–227, esp. 193–202.

33. Anthony Le Donne, *The Historiographical Jesus: Memory, Typology, and the Son of David* (Waco, TX: Baylor University Press, 2009), uses this approach to argue that the title "Son of David," most frequent in Matthew, may have been a church formulation to encapsulate for a Jewish-Christian audience the significance of Jesus's authentic claims to have authority over the temple.

34. Wright, *Jesus and the Victory of God*, 489–539.

35. Jens Schröter, *Jesus of Nazareth: Jew from Galilee, Savior of the World* (Waco, TX: Baylor University Press, 2014), esp. 85–199.

events in Jesus's life rather than just atomistic analysis of individual sayings are bearing fruit.

A very different kind of trend is the noticeable uptick in what has been called psychobiography. After decades of scholarly insistence that we not try to apply modern psychological insights to ancient people, especially those known only from highly selective and ideologically opinionated sources, there are now more sophisticated attempts that are gaining scholarly credibility, at least in some circles.[36] What, for example, might have been the effect on Jesus of growing up without a biological father? And the more others knew that Joseph was not that individual, the more Jesus would have been stereotyped and stigmatized as a *mamzer* (the Aramaic equivalent of bastard). Might those experiences account for how Jesus so emphasized God as Father?[37]

Of course, a majority of people who engage in Jesus research do not produce studies of his entire life. They are more likely to be interested in one particular phase, theme, or characteristic of his ministry. Study of the parables of Jesus proves perennially popular. One very recent work on the parables picks up on the growing recognition that they were indeed a kind of allegory (or at least analogy) and creates a helpful spectrum of just how allegorical a given parable was and the implications of each classification for Jesus's meaning.[38] On the other hand, the approach that takes a number of parables of Jesus as not depicting God's ways with humanity but lamenting the injustice of the all too real and merely human characters in the parables flies in the face of every known "king-parable" in the rabbinic tradition (which contains literally hundreds of them).[39] The way to account for master-figures in Jesus's parables doing somewhat unscrupulous things at times is to realize that they are not being likened to God *in every respect* and that often there is an implied *a fortiori* logic—from the lesser to the greater. If even a wicked human character would act a certain (positive) way under certain circumstances, how much more will God act in that same good fashion?[40]

Other historical Jesus studies focus on a particular phase of his life, such as his so-called withdrawal from Galilee. Controversy has long swirled around

---

36. See esp. the articles in the section on "Psychobiography: Jesus within His Contexts," in *Jesus Research: New Methodologies and Perceptions, The Second Princeton-Prague Symposium on Jesus Research Princeton 2007*, ed. James H. Charlesworth, Brian Rhea, and Petr Pokorný (Grand Rapids: Eerdmans, 2014), 399–466. Cf. also Bas van Os, *Psychological Analyses and the Historical Jesus* (New York: T&T Clark, 2011).

37. Andries van Aarde, *Fatherless in Galilee: Jesus as Child of God* (Harrisburg, PA: Trinity Press International, 2001).

38. Suk Kwan Wong, *Allegorical Spectrum of the Parables of Jesus* (Eugene, OR: Wipf & Stock, 2017).

39. For a classic recent example of this fallacy, see Elizabeth V. Dowling, *Taking Away the Pound: Women, Theology, and the Parable of the Pounds in the Gospel of Luke*, LNTS 324 (New York: T&T Clark, 2007).

40. See throughout Craig L. Blomberg, *Interpreting the Parables*, 2nd ed. (Downers Grove, IL: InterVarsity Press, 2012).

the question of whether the historical Jesus actually anticipated a gentile mission for his followers. Is this a foreshadowing of such a mission? Where did the seventy(-two) go whom Luke 10:1–20 says Jesus sent out later than and in addition to the Twelve (Mark 6:7–13 pars.), and were they presaging a sending of the disciples to the ends of the earth? The scales have tipped a little in the direction of acknowledging that this may be exactly what these passages indicate,[41] even if acceptance of the historicity of the Great Commission *per se* (Matt 28:19–20a), at least in the Trinitarian form in which it now exists, is still hard to find outside of explicitly evangelical circles.[42]

Another approach to historical Jesus studies is to focus on a particular theme. We have already mentioned the title Son of Man, Jesus's most characteristic and distinctive self-appellation. Despite Maurice Casey claiming to have found the definitive solution to the meaning of the label as non-titular and implying just a human being,[43] there seems to be a growing acceptance of the likelihood that Daniel 7:13 lies in the background *and* that in that passage there is a very exalted individual called a "son of man," and not just a corporate cipher for the saints of Israel. Yet the very ambiguity of this label allowed Jesus to invest his own significance into it, and the three main categories of his usage (earthly, heavenly, and suffering Son of Man sayings) may employ the title in slightly different ways.[44] Noticeably fewer scholars than in earlier eras continue to doubt the pre-Christian origin of the parables in 1 Enoch, which regularly refer to the Son of Man as a heavenly figure.[45] The probable pre-Christian origin of these parables makes it all the more likely that Jesus also could have used the designation in that titular sense.

These are just a few of the many possible examples that demonstrate why it is hard to characterize a period of time one is currently living in with the kinds of thematic labels historians may use years later. Who knows what will and won't have lasting value or influence? Who is to say which events in our own world will capture the interest of future researchers and writers to such a degree that they in turn will emphasize their effects and then look for trajectories backwards to their respective causes in our contemporary world? Where are we now, and where are evangelicals in the mix of historical Jesus research?

---

41. Esp. in light of Michael F. Bird, *Jesus and the Origin of the Gentile Mission*, LNTS 331 (New York: T&T Clark, 2007).

42. But within those circles, see now the argument of Loke, *Origin of Divine Identity Christology*, 174–80.

43. Maurice Casey, *The Solution to the 'Son of Man' Problem*, LNTS 343 (New York: T&T Clark, 2009).

44. See esp. Larry W. Hurtado and Paul L. Owen, eds., *'Who Is This Son of Man?' The Latest Scholarship on a Puzzling Expression of the Historical Jesus*, LNTS 390 (New York: T&T Clark, 2011).

45. See esp. Darrell L. Bock and James H. Charlesworth, eds., *Parables of Enoch: A Paradigm Shift*, JCTCRS 11 (New York: T&T Clark, 2013).

EVANGELICALS AND HISTORICAL JESUS STUDY

The short answer to where evangelicals are in the mix of Jesus research today is "almost everywhere." The proliferation of evangelicals in the academy means that there is hardly a discipline, subdiscipline, or sub-subdiscipline of New Testament, Gospels, or Jesus research in which committed, Bible-believing Christians have not published significant works at the highest levels of scholarship. One of the editors of this volume, Darrell Bock, has distinguished himself in numerous areas of historical Jesus studies. He has gained such credibility and cultivated such strong relationships with scholars across the theological and ideological spectra that even his critics often include and address his views.[46] The same is true of other leading evangelical Jesus researchers such as Craig Evans, Ben Witherington, and Michael Bird.[47] It is true also of leading evangelical specialists in subdisciplines, like Graham Twelftree with Jesus's miracles, Klyne Snodgrass with his parables, or Michael Licona on the resurrection.[48]

James Charlesworth, who is a member of the Institute of Biblical Research, a broadly evangelical society of biblical scholars, has itemized under twenty-seven different headings with varying degrees of probability what he believes we can know about the historical Jesus on historical grounds alone. He concludes that "we have obtained a vast amount of information about that Jew who ventured out from the hills of Nazareth, centered his ministry in Capernaum, went up to Jerusalem and the temple to worship, and eventually died on a wooden cross outside the western walls of Jerusalem." Charlesworth then adds that Jesus "urged all who heard him to be prepared for God's rule, which at times seemed incredibly close to those standing near him. He taught his followers habitually to pray [the so-called Lord's Prayer found at Luke 11:2–4]."[49]

Craig Keener goes even further in his lucid and amply endnoted *The*

---

46. Beginning in earnest with Darrell L. Bock, *Blasphemy and Exaltation in Judaism and the Final Examination of Jesus: A Philological-Historical Study of the Key Jewish Themes Impacting Mark 14:61–64,* WUNT 2/106 (Tübingen: Mohr Siebeck, 1998). This came on the heels of a major two-volume commentary on *Luke,* 2 vols. BECNT (Grand Rapids: Baker Academic, 1994, 1996), in which he discusses the historicity of each pericope in a distinct subsection of the commentary on that passage.

47. Of many books that could be listed, key works include Craig A. Evans, *Jesus and His Contemporaries: Comparative Studies* (Leiden: Brill, 2001); Ben Witherington III, *Jesus the Seer: The Progress of Prophecy* (Peabody, MA: Hendrickson, 1999); idem, *Jesus the Sage: The Pilgrimage of Wisdom* (Minneapolis: Fortress, 2000); Michael F. Bird, *Are You the One Who Is to Come? The Historical Jesus and the Messianic Question* (Grand Rapids: Baker, 2009).

48. See esp. Graham H. Twelftree, *Jesus the Exorcist: A Contribution to the Study of the Historical Jesus,* WUNT 2/54 (Tübingen: Mohr Siebeck, 1993); Graham H. Twelftree, *Jesus the Miracle-Worker* (Downers Grove, IL: InterVarsity Press, 1999); Klyne R. Snodgrass, *Stories with Intent: A Comprehensive Guide to the Parables of Jesus* (Grand Rapids: Eerdmans, 2008); Michael R. Licona, *The Resurrection of Jesus: A New Historiographical Approach* (Downers Grove, IL: InterVarsity Press, 2010).

49. James H. Charlesworth, *The Historical Jesus: An Essential Guide* (Nashville: Abingdon, 2008), 121.

Historical Jesus of the Gospels to treat in considerable detail Jesus's ethical teaching, his conflicts with other teachers, his prophetic words and actions, his self-understanding as more than an earthly Messiah, his confrontation with and provocation of the Jewish elite in Jerusalem, his arrest, his crucifixion as voluntary martyrdom, and his resurrection.[50] Keener's unparalleled mastery of the ancient Jewish and Greco-Roman primary sources, which he consistently cites in his works in far greater quantity than any other living scholar, adds tremendous credibility to his views.

Pride of place must nevertheless go to a collection of essays that is thoroughly evangelical, at least in a broad sense, and that applies greater methodological precision and consistency in analysis than any other recent work known to us. We are referring to Robert L. Webb and Darrell L. Bock's edited work, *Key Events in the Life of the Historical Jesus: A Collaborative Exploration of Context and Coherence*, which reflects the fruit of a decade of meetings of the Institute for Biblical Research's Historical Jesus Study Group.[51] As many of the eleven participants as were available gathered each year to vet drafts of one or two of the essays, spending several days together and going line-by-line through every chapter, discussing any possible ways to improve each study. All statements about specific Jewish or Greco-Roman backgrounds had to be buttressed by actual citations from ancient sources, personally confirmed by the scholars themselves. Second-hand quotations from other works of modern scholarship were not considered acceptable. The standard criteria of authenticity were applied to twelve key events,[52] and the authors were responsible for making the strongest but also the most honest case possible for both the authenticity and the meaning of each event. Each event had been selected from the outset on the conviction that other existing research already made the corroboration of historicity likely. If an argument seemed specious or was phrased in a way that went beyond what the evidence could fairly support, colleagues in the Study Group would invariably insist that the author rewrite that portion of the article.

Bock nicely sums up the results of the findings of the volume with respect to Jesus's overall identity and self-understanding. His words merit detailed quotation:

---

50. Craig S. Keener, *The Historical Jesus of the Gospels* (Grand Rapids: Eerdmans, 2009).

51. Darrell L. Bock and Robert L. Webb, eds., *Key Events in the Life of the Historical Jesus: A Collaborative Exploration of Context and Coherence*, WUNT 247 (Tübingen: Mohr Siebeck, 2009).

52. "Jesus' baptism by John," "exorcisms and the kingdom," "Jesus and the Twelve," "Jesus' table fellowship with sinners," "Jesus and the Synoptic Sabbath controversies," "Peter's declaration concerning Jesus' identity in Caesarea Philippi," "Jesus' royal entry into Jerusalem," "the temple incident," "the Last Supper," "blasphemy and the Jewish examination of Jesus," "the Roman examination and crucifixion of Jesus," and "Jesus' empty tomb and his appearance in Jerusalem" (Bock and Webb, *Key Events in the Life of the Historical Jesus*, vii–viii).

Summing up, the historical Jesus presented the kingdom of God and the opportunity for participation in it. Such participation involved a turning in repentance to reaffirm the covenantal responsibility God originally gave to Israel, something Jesus' participation in John the baptizer's baptism and the selection of the twelve introduced. Jesus' activity called for a restored people of God and a renewed relationship with God that was built upon his own authority. This new relationship, evidenced by the call to outsiders to come in, ultimately would reform the disciples' relationship to others, leading in directions of righteousness and reconciliation. With the privilege of being connected to God's rule came the rest of Jesus' teaching, which we have not sought to corroborate in our study. This teaching called for the pursuit of a challenging personal and societal righteousness that honored God, reconfigured our role as God's creatures, and served as a contrasting paradigm to the world about how to live. This trajectory appears to cohere with what we have established. By acting to show this decisive era's arrival, Jesus affirmed his central role in its coming, calling on people to believe in what God was doing through him and, in doing so, to follow him.[53]

Similar results had emerged from Martin Hengel and Anna Maria Schwemer's magisterial work in German, *Jesus und das Judentum*.[54] In fact, a remarkable cross section of historical Jesus monographs has been coming to comparable, if not identical conclusions about the numerous contours of the Jesus tradition that can be authenticated, especially from the Synoptic Gospels.[55] The contribution of *Key Events in the Life of the Historical Jesus* is not in suggesting that brand new areas of the Gospels' lives of Christ should be accepted as historical, but in establishing the historicity of the passages or themes the contributors had studied with a previously unparalleled methodological rigor.

Plans had been made from the outset to publish the volume of the findings of the IBR Study Group with Mohr Siebeck in Tübingen, Germany, with one of

---

53. Darrell L. Bock, "Key Events in the Life of the Historical Jesus: A Summary," in Bock and Webb, *Key Events in the Life of the Historical Jesus*, 825–53 (here 852).

54. Martin Hengel and Anna Maria Schwemer, eds., *Jesus und das Judentum*, GFC 1 (Tübingen: Mohr Siebeck, 2007).

55. In addition to works cited elsewhere in our essay, we could add Armand Puig i Tàrrech, *Jesus: A Biography* (Waco, TX: Baylor University Press, 2011); Gerald L. Borchert, *Jesus of Nazareth: Background, Witnesses, and Significance* (Macon, GA: Mercer University Press, 2011); Gerhard Lohfink, *Jesus of Nazareth: What He Wanted, Who He Was* (Collegeville, MN: Liturgical Press, 2012); Helen K. Bond, *The Historical Jesus: A Guide for the Perplexed* (New York: T&T Clark, 2012); Lee Martin McDonald, *The Story of Jesus in History and Faith: An Introduction* (Grand Rapids: Baker, 2013); Samuel Byrskog, Tom Holmén, and Matti Kankaanniemi, eds., *The Identity of Jesus: Nordic Voices*, WUNT 2/373 (Tübingen: Mohr Siebeck, 2014); José A. Pagola, *Jesus: An Historical Approximation*, rev. ed. (Miami, FL: Convivium, 2014); and others.

the two Wissenschaftliche Untersuchungen zum Neuen Testament series, which reflect the very highest levels of technical work and are among the world's most prestigious series of New Testament scholarship. But then, so that the volume would garner a wider audience, a paperback version with Eerdmans was slated to be published the year after the Mohr Siebeck volume. Finally, in 2012 Bock himself wrote a very short popularization of the work in his *Who Is Jesus? Linking the Historical Jesus with the Christ of Faith.*[56] Unfortunately, the word did not always get out as well as one might have hoped. Among some who did discover the volume, criticisms from either the left or the right may have forestalled at least some of the limelight that the book merited.

CRITICISM AND CHALLENGES OF EVANGELICAL HISTORICAL JESUS RESEARCH

The criticism leveled against the *Key Events in the Life of the Historical Jesus* volume will serve as a convenient case study to demonstrate the types of criticism that evangelical historical Jesus scholarship generally faces from both conservative and liberal ends of the spectrum. From the left wing, the main criticism that emerged against the IBR volume was that a society that has a confessional basis as its foundation for membership cannot possibly be expected to do dispassionate, reliable scholarship.[57] Put sharply, IBR is already committed to a high view of Scripture, so of course they are going to publish on those aspects of Jesus's life that they think can be well supported by historical methods alone. But where is the peer review or interaction with fellow scholars who take quite divergent positions? From the right wing, the mere engagement in historical-critical scholarship renders the product immediately suspicious.[58] By definition, not everything in the Gospels is going to be supported, and not everything that is supported will be supported with the same degree of confidence. At best, such an approach is of no value for the church; at worst it becomes dangerous because it can call people to question their faith. Talk about being caught between a rock and a hard place! On the one hand, the IBR work is viewed as too self-consciously Christian to be taken seriously as history; on the other hand, it is viewed as too self-consciously historical to be taken seriously as Christian.

---

56. Darrell L. Bock, *Who Is Jesus? Linking the Historical Jesus with the Christ of Faith* (New York: Howard Books, 2012).

57. E.g., Robert J. Miller, "Why It's Futile to Argue about the Historical Jesus: A Response to Bock, Keener, and Webb," *JSHJ* 9 (2011): 85–95.

58. E.g., throughout Barry Hofstetter, ed., *Basics of Biblical Criticism: Helpful or Harmful?* (Scotts Valley, CA: Create Space, 2012).

Both claims, on closer inspection, turn out to be vacuous. As Bultmann famously claimed, presuppositionless exegesis is impossible.[59] Every scholar has his or her functional non-negotiables, whether or not they have to affirm a confessional statement of faith in their school or place of worship. Every scholar has the challenge of being open to perspectives quite different from their own, and, quite frankly, in today's academy most evangelicals do this better than many of their left-wing counterparts, who seldom interact with positions outside their circle of like-minded scholars. Ironically, evangelicals have learned that they won't be taken seriously unless they interact with every major branch of scholarship and, even then, they aren't always given a fair hearing. More liberal scholars, on the other hand, can often avoid every position more conservative than their own and still gain a significant hearing.[60]

A different kind of criticism from the left wing is stranger. Dominic Crossan, for example, reflects a perspective, by no means unique to him, that suggests that one's objectivity in historical Jesus research depends on how many portions of the gospel tradition one winds up questioning.[61] In other words, if all one ever does is use the criteria of authenticity to support the historical trustworthiness of a passage, theme, or episode from the life of Christ, then one can't be using the tools properly. One shows lack of bias only by finding at least as many things to reject as unhistorical as are historical, and the more the better. Is there any other line of scholarly or critical inquiry where such a ridiculous approach would be countenanced? If a document is consistently historical (or consistently unhistorical), then that is what historians should label it, not that there must be a certain amount of material labeled unhistorical to make credible the verdict of the rest as historical.

At the other end of the theological spectrum, on the far right, the allegation is that at its best what historical Jesus research can accomplish is the verdict of *probable* authenticity of a certain *portion* of the gospel tradition. Christians, on the other hand, must declare with certainty that all of the Gospels, because they are part of the church's canonized, sacred Scripture, are reliable.[62] This too

59. Rudolf Bultmann, "Is Exegesis without Presuppositions Possible?," *Existence and Faith: Shorter Writings of Rudolf Bultmann*, ed. Schubert M. Ogden (London: Collins, 1961), 342–52.

60. As a classic example, see the two volumes produced by the Jesus Seminar: Robert W. Funk, Roy W. Hoover, and the Jesus Seminar, *The Five Gospels: The Search for the Authentic Words of Jesus* (New York: Macmillan, 1993); and Robert W. Funk and the Jesus Seminar, *The Acts of Jesus: The Search for the Authentic Deeds of Jesus* (New York: HarperCollins, 1998). A handful of evangelicals participated at the outset, with the number dwindling as proceedings unfolded. But nothing in the published results gives voice to their perspectives at all.

61. John Dominic Crossan, "Concluding Reflections: Reflections on a Debate," in *Will the Real Jesus Please Stand Up? A Debate between William Lane Craig and John Dominic Crossan*, ed. Paul Copan (Grand Rapids: Baker Academic, 1998), 154–55.

62. See throughout Norman L. Geisler and F. David Farnell, eds., *The Jesus Quest: The Danger from Within* (Maitland, FL: Xulon, 2014). Cf. F. David Farnell, "Three Searches for the 'Historical Jesus' but No

applies standards that no one would think of employing in any other arena of life and that, when employed in religious matters, don't deliver what their proponents desire anyway. Imagine a couple of hikers following a fairly clear trail through a mountain forest. Every now and then there are side paths, but they never seem as wide or free of obstacles as the main path. Fairly often, yellow marks on tree trunks near the correct path inform hikers that they are still going the right way. At any given point on the path, however, one of those marks may not be close enough to be in sight. Are the hikers paralyzed every time they come to a small, cluttered side path? Of course not; they stay on the main trail and eventually see another yellow mark on a tree trunk. Only if they were to go much further than they ever had previously without seeing such a mark and then observe that their trail was itself looking less and less like the main trail it had been all along, would they begin to suspect that they had unknowingly veered from their course.

The application to Jesus research is instructive. Enough details, especially from the Synoptic tradition, have been shown to be most probably authentic that when we have to return a verdict of *non liquet* (not clear)[63] for a variety of other details, we have no reason to be troubled. Since the vast majority of all evidence that might corroborate portions of ancient documents is forever lost to antiquity, it is unrealistic to expect historians to be able to authenticate large portions of those texts. In the case of the Synoptics, enough has been authenticated to give the benefit of the doubt to the text in those places where it cannot be tested.[64] One's faith does not have to rise and fall with every vagary of historical criticism. In fact, the only way to imagine that one has absolute certainty is to employ a deductive (rather than an inductive) form of reasoning that begins with divine inspiration of the canonical texts, moves to the premise that God cannot lie or deceive, and therefore deduces full inerrancy of the texts. But how does one postulate divine inspiration of the canonical texts in the first place? Either it is an unfalsifiable (and therefore unverifiable) "properly basic" truth that must just be posited, or one has to use historical arguments that the church made correct decisions in recognizing the God-breathed texts, which puts us right back into the realm of probabilities.[65]

The importance of evangelicals being involved in historical Jesus research is

---

Biblical Christ (Part 2): Evangelical Participation in the Search for the 'Historical Jesus,'" *Master's Seminary Journal* 24 (2013): 25–67.

63. The Latin expression Meier (*A Marginal Jew*, 5 vols.) likes to use when the criteria are inconclusive about a certain part of the gospel tradition.

64. Cf. esp. Craig L. Blomberg, *The Historical Reliability of the Gospels*, 2nd ed. (Downers Grove, IL: InterVarsity Press, 2007).

65. See further Craig L. Blomberg, *Can We Still Believe the Bible? An Evangelical Engagement with Contemporary Questions* (Grand Rapids: Brazos, 2014), 43–82 (on canon) and 119–45 (on inerrancy).

not so that they can substitute the inevitably truncated picture of what history can probably corroborate for the more full-orbed canonical portraits. A key reason for being involved is the apologetic value of the endeavor. At the very least, Jesus research can debunk the claims of the minimalists who say we can know very little about the life of Jesus of Nazareth (or the completely specious notion that he never existed). In a best-case scenario, it will convince some people that we can know quite a lot and that the portrait of the best historical Jesus works actually points in the direction of the divine Christ of the Scriptures. Norman Geisler has often asserted that no one ever becomes a believer through this kind of reasoning,[66] but this is a groundless assertion that is contradicted by the facts. One of us has personally met quite a few people, including former and current students as well as people at conferences and speaking engagements, who have expressed their thanks for many of us evangelicals engaged in Jesus research who have written works that were instrumental in their coming to the Lord. We have also met scholars on several continents who have told us that such works brought them back to faith when they were in serious doubt. For people like Farnell and Geisler to censure us for this kind of kingdom work is tragic, not least because it undermines the very evangelistic and apologetic causes they hold dear.

A second key reason for evangelical involvement is that historical Jesus research can highlight both what was dominant and what was distinctive about Jesus. Dominant items are things that are most likely going to be remembered and corroborated by independent sources (multiple attestation), and distinctive items will satisfy the various dissimilarity criteria. The person simply reading straight through all four Gospels or, like most Bible readers, reading each Gospel at different times with considerable intervals in between, is not as likely to pick up on these. In the first case, they will sense more multiple attestation than actually exists because they will probably not be looking for what characterizes Mark, Q, M, L, and John[67] but will be assuming that material that appears in parallel passages in Matthew, Mark, and Luke is multiply attested when in fact it represents only one independent source—Mark. In the second case, they are simply less likely to remember in detail the contents of what they read quite a bit earlier and not have as good a sense for what dominates the entire Synoptic tradition, whether based on only one independent source or several. As for what is distinctive, only detailed immersion in the historical-cultural backgrounds

---

66. One of us has heard him say this repeatedly at conferences and talks, including but not limited to the Evangelical Theological Society, in various places over the years.

67. Adopting the most common "four-source" solution to the Synoptic problem, first popularized by B. H. Streeter, *The Four Gospels: A Study of Origins* (London: Macmillan, 1924).

of Jesus's world will enable those judgment calls. But the same mindset that discourages participation in the larger arena of historical Jesus research often looks askance at spending too much time studying non-canonical texts from the ancient world,[68] without which one cannot get a good sense of what was distinctive about the Jesus of history.

A very different kind of challenge emerges from more moderate scholars nearer to the center of the spectrum. Perhaps the criteria of authenticity are all wrong, or largely wrong, and we need to replace them with different ones. Perhaps the approach to using criteria of any kind on individual portions of the gospel tradition is wrongheaded. In 2012, Chris Keith and Anthony Le Donne edited a book that threw down the gauntlet to those who would employ the standard criteria of authenticity.[69] A recurring refrain in the book was to refer back to two formative articles, each written by Morna Hooker in the 1970s. In fact, Hooker herself wrote the foreword for this volume.[70] Near the end of the period of the second (or, then, simply the "new") quest, Hooker had made important observations about the limitations of the criteria. The criterion of double dissimilarity (what is authentic in the Jesus tradition is that which is significantly dissimilar from both the Judaism of Jesus's day and the emphases of the emerging church) can demonstrate only what is distinctive, not necessarily what is characteristic of Jesus (unless at times what is distinctive is also dominant). Multiple attestation can be used positively much more reliably than it can be used negatively. In other words, the greater the number of independent sources that testify to something, the more likely it is, generally speaking, that the event actually happened. However, single attestation should not inherently cause suspicion; there could be any number of legitimate reasons why something may be preserved today in only one source that is nevertheless historical. The criterion of Palestinian environment remains at odds with the criterion of dissimilarity from Judaism. On the one hand, one asks for the element of the tradition to fit well into Jesus's world; on the other hand, to be noticeably distinct from it. Finally, the criterion of coherence, as useful as it may sound, is a derivative or secondary criterion, requiring a body of already well-authenticated material so that other things can be said to cohere with it.[71]

---

68. E.g., Robert L. Thomas, *Evangelical Hermeneutics: The New versus the Old* (Grand Rapids: Kregel, 2002), esp. 271–322.

69. Chris Keith and Anthony Le Donne, eds., *Jesus, Criteria, and the Demise of Authenticity* (New York: T&T Clark, 2012).

70. Morna D. Hooker, "Foreword: Forty Years On," in Keith and Le Donne, *Jesus, Criteria, and the Demise of Authenticity*, xiii–xvii.

71. Morna D. Hooker, "On Using the Wrong Tool," *Theology* 75 (1972): 570–81; Morna D. Hooker, "Christology and Methodology," *NTS* 17 (1970–71): 480–87.

When Hooker penned these critiques in the 1970s, she was aiming them largely at scholars more liberal than herself and thus more skeptical about the ability to reconstruct the exploits of the historical Jesus in any detail. Ironically, more moderate scholars are now using these same criticisms to reject evangelical attempts to engage in Jesus research. In a book review of Keith and Le Donne's volume, one of us pointed out that arguably the two best works of evangelical historical Jesus research in recent memory—Craig Keener's volume and the IBR anthology—were scarcely even taken into account.[72] In personal correspondence Keith replied that he hadn't even been aware of the IBR volume—a telling admission. Scot McKnight, one of the Keith and Le Donne book's contributors, who had previously written on the end and uselessness of the quests, noted that Keener's book had just arrived on his desk but that he hadn't had time to take it into account.

Intriguingly, one of the contributors to *Jesus, Criteria, and the Demise of Authenticity* was Dagmar Winter. The title of her essay was "Saving the Quest for Authenticity from the Criterion of Dissimilarity: History and Plausibility."[73] Clearly she was in a different camp than those who, like Keith and McKnight, wanted to give up on it altogether. Winter is best known for her book with Gerd Theissen, the title of which in English is translated as *The Quest for the Plausible Jesus: The Question of Criteria.*[74] Its title in German, however, is *Die Kriterienfrage in der Jesusforschung: Vom Differenzkriterium zum Plausibilitätskriterium* (The Question of Criteria in Jesus Research: From the Dissimilarity Criterion to the Plausibility Criterion).[75] Winter is not at all suggesting we abandon the Third Quest, or any quest. She is concerned that we need to take to heart the legitimate critiques of the standard criteria, which in fact the contributors to the IBR Jesus volume did. But she picks up on what Theissen first developed with Annette Merz in their historical Jesus book of the late 1990s and called the plausibility criterion.[76]

More specifically, the criterion of historical plausibility, as the translators of

---

72. Craig L. Blomberg, "Review of Chris Keith and Anthony Le Donne, eds., *Jesus, Criteria, and the Demise of Authenticity*," *Denver Journal* 16 (2013): n.p. Online: http://denverseminary.edu/resources/news-and-articles/jesus-criteria-and-the-demise-of-authenticity/.

73. Dagmar Winter, "Saving the Quest for Authenticity from the Criterion of Dissimilarity: History and Plausibility," in Keith and Le Donne, *Jesus, Criteria, and the Demise of Authenticity*, 115–31.

74. Gerd Theissen and Dagmar Winter, *The Quest for the Plausible Jesus: The Question of Criteria* (Louisville: Westminster John Knox, 2002).

75. Gerd Theissen and Dagmar Winter, *Die Kriterienfrage in der Jesusforschung: Vom Differenzkriterium zum Plausibilitätskriterium*, Novum Testamentum et Orbis Antiquus 34 (Göttingen: Vandenhoeck & Ruprecht, 1997).

76. Gerd Theissen and Annette Merz, *The Historical Jesus: A Comprehensive Guide* (Minneapolis: Fortress, 1998), 116–18.

the Theissen and Merz volume render it, contains four parts: under the category of "coherence and agreement" appear both "plausible coherence of influence" and "correspondence of context." Under "incoherence [or "distinctiveness"] and disagreement" come "plausible influence contrary to the tendency" and "individuality of context."[77] Quickly one realizes that this is the older double dissimilarity criterion combined with the newer continuum approach. N. T. Wright had already independently identified the same four-part approach as the criterion of double similarity and double dissimilarity.[78] In other words, if an element from the gospel tradition is conceivable in an early first-century Jewish context within Israel but at the same time has some distinctive twist that would not likely have been invented by conventional Judaism, and if at the same time it can be shown to have influenced subsequent Christianity but again not completely so that there is some unique element that a later Christian is not likely to have invented, then we have a very strong and powerful case for its authenticity.

Not surprisingly, Theissen and Merz's volume looks quite similar to the afore-mentioned "consensus" historical Jesus books in the contents from the Synoptics that it authenticates (see above). Such a similarity shows that even when scholars, at least in the Third Quest, were emphasizing dissimilarity, their other criteria were often validating what was characteristic, as well. Conversely, when scholars were preferring a continuum approach, they were not altogether abandoning the dissimilar. And since Winter's quest for a plausible Jesus is admitted as part of Keith and Le Donne's critique of the status quo, we do not have to speak of the demise of historical endeavors to establish authenticity. Of course, the historical Jesus will never be the real Jesus, but neither is the canonical Jesus. Both are just small subsets of everything Jesus was and did (John 21:25). Perhaps the language of "a plausible Jesus" is more appropriately modest and accurate in terms of what results than "the historical Jesus," in which case a change in terminology may be preferable to giving up on the endeavor altogether.

FUTURE PROSPECTS FOR HISTORICAL JESUS RESEARCH

If the quest is not dead but simply needs to take on different contours, what should those look like? One could easily envision a volume 2 to the IBR project, tackling another ten to twelve pericopae with perhaps slightly less solid cor-roborating evidence via the standard criteria of authenticity but with enough

---

77. Theissen and Merz, *Historical Jesus*, 118.
78. Wright, *Jesus and the Victory of God*, 131–33.

to make suggestive cases. One could take the areas that Theissen and Merz did not look at and do the same thing, only with their four-part criterion of historical plausibility. In all this discussion, nevertheless, nary a word has been uttered about the Gospel of John. The IBR project relied solely on multiply attested passages from the Synoptic Gospels. Wright in his historical Jesus book focused only on the Synoptics. Even more conservative evangelicals, such as Craig Keener and Darrell Bock, in their significant studies on the historical Jesus either bracket John or treat it separately from Matthew, Mark, and Luke.[79] All of this is of course intentional because of the thoroughgoing skepticism that historical Jesus scholars in general have had for more than 150 years now about the overall reliability of the Fourth Gospel. Why fight an uphill battle trying to convince less conservative scholars of a messianic Jesus in the Gospel of John if a credible case can be made from the material within the Synoptics?

As one looks toward the future, however, it is tempting to agree with those critics who allege that the Third Quest *has* played out its hand, but to agree for different reasons than they offer. It is not that the criteria are in as bad a shape as these critics claim; it is not that there is no reasonable consensus on anything. It is not that liberals are so skewed in their thinking that it is dangerous even to be involved in the same scholarly efforts they engage in, nor that conservatives are so confessionally hamstrung that they cannot approximate objectivity in their research. Rather, it is the almost total absence of the Gospel of John in all of these conversations. And yet for more than half a century now, what John A. T. Robinson in the late 1950s termed "the new look on John"[80] has been growing in adherents, in methodological precision, and in confidence that a significant minority of the unique details in the Fourth Gospel can be corroborated and included in a biography of Jesus *on historical grounds alone*, that is, without necessarily presupposing Christian faith.

The three volumes produced by the John, Jesus, and History Seminar of the Society of Biblical Literature and edited by Paul Anderson, Felix Just, and Tom Thatcher may best represent the *statis questionis* and just how far the "new look" has come.[81] A significant list of distinctive details from the Fourth Gospel passes one or more of the conventional criteria of authenticity with flying colors

---

79. Bock and Webb, *Key Events in the Life of the Historical Jesus*; Wright, *Jesus and the Victory of God*; Keener, *Historical Jesus of the Gospels*; Darrell L. Bock and Benjamin I. Simpson, *Jesus according to Scripture: Restoring the Portrait from the Gospels*, 2nd ed. (Grand Rapids: Baker, 2017).

80. John A. T. Robinson, "The New Look on the Fourth Gospel," *TU* 73 (1959): 338–50.

81. Paul N. Anderson, Felix Just, and Tom Thatcher, eds., *John, Jesus, and History*, 3 vols. (Atlanta: SBL Press, 2007–2016). Cf. also James H. Charlesworth, "The Historical Jesus in the Fourth Gospel: A Paradigm Shift?" *JSHJ* 8 (2010): 3–46; and Stanley E. Porter, *John, His Gospel, and Jesus: In Pursuit of the Johannine Voice* (Grand Rapids: Eerdmans, 2015).

and/or finds at least partial corroboration in extra-biblical evidence. The eight that Anderson particularly highlights are "Jesus' simultaneous ministry along-side John the Baptizer and the prolific availability of purifying power," "Jesus' cleansing of the temple as an inaugural prophetic sign," "Jesus' travel to and from Jerusalem and his multi-year ministry," "early events in the public ministry of Jesus" (John 2–4), "favourable receptions in Galilee among Samaritans, women and Gentiles," "Jesus' Judean ministry" with all its "archaeological realism," "the Last Supper as a common meal and its proper dating," and "Jesus' teaching about the way of the Spirit and the reign of truth."[82]

If one takes the double similarity and double dissimilarity criterion and applies it to John's Gospel, there is scarcely a pericope in which no elements at all satisfy this four-pronged test of historical plausibility.[83] Another, complementary approach is to return to the heyday of form and redaction criticism, strip off the most obviously redactional layers in each passage, and see what recurring themes remain in the cores of the passages left beneath. This approach need not imply that what is redactional is unhistorical, though obviously less conservative critics have often made that claim. Instead, as for John Meier, such situations should be labeled *non liquet*—we cannot *on historical grounds alone* render a verdict one way or the other. But what is not *demonstrably* redactional and especially what is demonstrably *not* redactional can then be scrutinized for patterns or repeated themes that may well represent what was most solidly affixed in the earliest tradition and therefore most likely to go back to the historical Jesus. Might any new items emerge that are not typically found in Jesus research that limits itself to the Synoptics? Or might certain emphases emerge that reflect themes present but not stressed as much in the Synoptics? Could these items and emphases improve our understanding of Jesus of Nazareth in any way?[84]

Paul Anderson has repeatedly called for a fourth quest of the historical Jesus that would aim to address these kinds of questions. Anderson would like to see the Synoptic and Johannine traditions be given equal parity as databases for examining who Jesus was and what he said and did.[85] The results might still draw

82. Cf. esp. Paul N. Anderson, *The Fourth Gospel and the Quest for Jesus: Modern Foundations Reconsidered*, LNTS 321 (New York: T&T Clark, 2008), 154–73.

83. See throughout Craig L. Blomberg, *The Historical Reliability of John's Gospel: Issues and Commentary* (Downers Grove, IL: InterVarsity Press, 2001).

84. For an example of how this might work, see Craig L. Blomberg, "The Historical Jesus from the Synoptics and the Fourth Gospel? Jesus the Purifier," *The Message of Jesus: John Dominic Crossan and Ben Witherington III in Dialogue*, ed. Robert B. Stewart (Minneapolis: Fortress, 2013), 163–79.

85. Anderson, *The Fourth Gospel and the Quest for Jesus*, 192; Paul N. Anderson, "Aspects of Historicity in the Fourth Gospel: Consensus and Convergences," in Anderson, Just, and Thatcher, *John, Jesus, and History*, 2:379–86.

more from the Synoptics than from John, but they would not be so uniformly and unilaterally dependent on just the Synoptics. Anderson himself has been working on such a project, but it remains to be seen if and when it will be published. There is certainly no reason for others to hold back from undertaking similar investigations.

Whether historians of the future will ever look back and describe a collection of studies as a fourth quest remains to be seen. If they do, it may not be because a groundswell of works including material from the Fourth Gospel has emerged, but perhaps for some other distinctives. It seems unlikely, however, that Jesus research will remain in the comparative lull that one senses at the moment. As Markus Bockmuehl has highlighted, even in those contexts that have become dominated by secularism and atheism, historians of the Western world (and, increasingly of the entire world) cannot explain major developments in civilization without taking into account the reception history of the Bible and especially the Gospels.[86] Jesus has been just too influential a figure over the last two millennia to envision it being otherwise. Truly educated people have to come to grips with him, whatever their conclusions may be.

As we study reception history, we often discover that people of previous generations had important insights into biblical studies that have been forgotten or at least minimized more recently. It is a myth to imagine that scholarship in the humanities always proceeds in an evolutionary fashion, with more recent developments inherently outstripping older ones. Even as the "theological interpretation of Scripture" is recovering the best of pre-critical exegesis,[87] New Testament research needs to be attuned to important yet often overlooked contributions of past generations. Perhaps they involve the abiding value of J. B. Lightfoot's nineteenth-century commentaries, especially on Paul,[88] or B. F. Westcott's still useful volume on John.[89] Maybe it will be learning again from Vincent Taylor's more conservative appropriation of form criticism in its heyday, when Bultmann and Dibelius were championing a more radical use.[90] In historical Jesus studies,

---

86. Markus Bockmuehl, *Seeing the Word: Refocusing New Testament Study*, Studies in Theological Interpretation (Grand Rapids: Baker Academic, 2006), 66–68.

87. For an excellent introduction, see Daniel J. Treier, *Introducing Theological Interpretation of Scripture: Recovering a Christian Practice* (Grand Rapids: Baker Academic, 2008).

88. Hence the recent publication of the rediscovered manuscripts of J. B. Lightfoot, *The Acts of the Apostles: A Newly Discovered Commentary*, ed. Ben Witherington III, Todd D. Still, and Jeanette M. Hagen (Downers Grove, IL: InterVarsity Press, 2014); and J. B. Lightfoot, *The Epistles of 2 Corinthians and 1 Peter: Newly Discovered Commentaries*, ed. Ben Witherington III, Todd D. Still, and Jeanette M. Hagen (Downers Grove, IL: InterVarsity Press, 2016).

89. B. F. Westcott, *The Gospel according to St. John* (London: John Murray, 1908).

90. Darlene M. Seal, "The Form Criticism of Vincent Taylor," in *Pillars in the History of Biblical Interpretation*, vol. 3, ed. Stanley E. Porter and Zachary K. Dawson (Eugene, OR: Pickwick, forthcoming).

it may involve following further in Dale Allison's footsteps to recover the best of Albert Schweitzer and the role of "consistent eschatology" in Jesus's thinking and actions.[91] If evangelicals continue with the momentum they have exhibited in recent decades, and succeed in throwing off the shackles with which the nay-sayers from right, left, and even center would chain them, the best days for historical Jesus research may be yet to come.

91. Dale C. Allison Jr., *Constructing Jesus: Memory, Imagination, and History* (Grand Rapids: Baker Academic, 2010), 31–220.

CHAPTER 3

Neglected Discontinuity between Early Form Criticism and the New Quest with Reference to the Last Supper

Michael B. Metts

This essay will point out some neglected aspects of discontinuity between early form criticism and New Questers. This is done to directly counter the arguments of certain critics of the criteria of authenticity (simply referred to as "criteria" from this point on), namely Chris Keith, who understand the criteria as too indebted to form criticism to prove useful. While Keith is correct in some of the methodological affirmations he predicates of New Quest criteriology, such predications are presented within an abbreviated context, partially eclipsing from view the larger context of historical Jesus questing taking place. In order to see clearly why the New Questers practiced the methodology they did, it is necessary to hear from them directly, not only about the challenges of form criticism but also about the challenges presented by earlier questing. Ernst Käsemann is primarily discussed, but input from Günther Bornkamm, James M. Robinson, and Norman Perrin is additionally provided. The essay attempts to focus on the Last Supper where possible, but where not possible, the pivotal events during Jesus's last week in Jerusalem are substituted. The Last Supper provides, then, a helpful kind of case study for the research presented.

INDEBTEDNESS

While Keith points out that Käsemann made an advance upon form criticism in that he sought "the historical figure of Jesus, rather than a prior state of the tradition," he maintains that Käsemann did so within an inherited form-critical understanding of Gospel prehistory.[1] In explaining how New Questers endeavored only to change the object of their inquiry rather than make "a break with form-critical methodology itself," he is less than fair.[2] Indebtedness is further seen in the New Quest's adoption of "the separation of the gospel tradition from early Christian theological interpretation."[3] With the collapse of form criticism and its understanding of Gospel prehistory, any methodology owing its logical apparatus in part to form-critical historiography also collapses.

There is no disagreement that form criticism is suffering on all fronts. Form criticism's foundations, which will be examined shortly, have long been seen as cracked and crumbling. The concern, rather, is to what extent the criteria are indebted to form criticism and therefore share in its failure. As will be demonstrated, it is possible to take a more generous reading of New Questers, and maintain a sufficient degree of *discontinuity* with form criticism, by understanding the work of New Questers as less reliant on their predecessors than Keith admits.[4] Certainly it can be agreed that insofar as New Questers have adopted specific principles of form criticism that have been demonstrably discredited, Keith's work provides present researchers with a helpful corrective. But, as will be demonstrated, the criteria of authenticity, specifically the criterion of dissimilarity, were actually purposed to correct fundamental misunderstandings in the historiography of not only certain form critics but also, importantly, First Quest historians.[5]

EARLY FORM CRITICISM

Form histories[6] were originally inclusive of oral tradition history, since their purpose was to demonstrate the prehistory of a certain Gospel text's

---

1. Chris Keith, "The Indebtedness of the Criteria Approach to Form Criticism and Recent Attempts to Rehabilitate the Search for an Authentic Jesus," in *Jesus, Criteria, and the Demise of Authenticity*, ed. Chris Keith and Anthony Le Donne (New York: T&T Clark, 2012), 25–48 (here 33).

2. Keith, "The Indebtedness of the Criteria Approach," 33. See also Benjamin I. Simpson, *Recent Research on the Historical Jesus*, Recent Research in Biblical Studies 6 (Sheffield: Sheffield Phoenix Press, 2014), 24.

3. Chris Keith, *Jesus Against the Scribal Elite: The Origins of the Conflict* (Grand Rapids: Baker Academic, 2014), 76; idem, "The Indebtedness of the Criteria Approach," 35–37.

4. Chris Keith, *Jesus' Literacy: Scribal Culture and the Teacher from Galilee*, LNTS 413 (London: T&T Clark, 2011), 30, argues that "the *entire enterprise* of criteria of authenticity is dependent upon a form-critical framework. For, the criteria approach *adopts wholesale* the form-critical conception of the development of the Jesus tradition and thus its method for getting 'behind' the text." (Emphasis added only to the second sentence.) Keith's essay, "Memory and Authenticity: Jesus Tradition and What Really Happened," *ZNW* 102 (2011): 155–77, is reprinted with modifications and expansions in *Jesus' Literacy*, so it will not be noted separately.

5. Keith neglects Käsemann's fashioning of dissimilarity as a response to the historical criticism of the First Quest. This neglect is likely due to his interests in portraying the criteria as exclusively indebted to a form-critical context. Keith, "The Indebtedness of the Criteria Approach," 25–48; idem, *Jesus Against the Scribal Elite*, 73–81; idem, *Jesus' Literacy*, 29–41.

6. While "form criticism" is often the given English translation of the German "Formgeschichte," "form

form[7]—not simply its literary categorization.[8] However, because of its historio-graphical ties to folkloristics, form criticism adopted now disproven traditioning laws which were in direct contradiction to the traditioning processes explicitly attested in the New Testament.[9] Whereas the New Testament attests eyewitnesses and teachers of its traditions,[10] and though the traditioning process has left a

history" would be a more accurate translation. The plural ("form histories") is used here only to specify the many works of form criticism used in Gospel research.

7. William Baird, *History of New Testament Research*, 3 vols. (Minneapolis: Fortress, 1992, 2003, 2013), 2:283, provides a direct quote from Rudolf Bultmann explaining the interest in oral tradition: "The purpose of Form Criticism is to study the history of the oral tradition behind the gospels." Werner H. Kelber, *The Oral and the Written Gospel: Hermeneutics of Speaking and Writing in the Synoptic Tradition, Mark, Paul, and Q* (Indianapolis: Indiana University Press, 1983), 18: "It remains the abiding achievement of form criticism to have focused attention on the predominantly oral nature of the bulk of the pre-canonical, synoptic tradition." Note also Christopher Tuckett, "Form Criticism," in *Jesus in Memory: Traditions in Oral and Scribal Perspectives*, ed. Werner H. Kelber and Samuel Byrskog (Waco, TX: Baylor University Press, 2009), 21–38 (here 29): "Both [Martin Dibelius and Bultmann] assumed, for example, that the tradition prior to the emergence of the earliest extant Gospel, Mark, was primarily oral tradition." Somewhat contrasting, Terence Mournet "The Jesus Tradition as Oral Tradition," in Kelber and Byrskog, *Jesus in Memory*, 45, notes that the oral character observations of Bultmann and Dibelius are only "lip service." While this is a fair assertion, the present focus is only to draw the connection with oral tradition, however tenuous the connection remained in practice.

8. Rudolf Bultmann declares at the outset of his seminal work, *The History of the Synoptic Tradition*, rev. ed., trans. John Marsh (Oxford: Blackwell, 1963; repr., Peabody, MA: Hendrickson, 1994), 3–4: "I am entirely in agreement with M. Dibelius when he maintains that form-criticism is not simply an exercise in aesthetics nor yet simply a process of description and classification; that is to say it does not consist of identifying the individual units of the tradition according to their aesthetic or other characteristics and placing them in their various categories. It is much rather '*to rediscover the origin and the history of the particular units and thereby to throw some light on the history of the tradition before it took literary form*'" (emphasis added). Darrell Bock summarizes form criticism with the following: "In short, form criticism, as originally formulated, is both descriptive and historical in its concerns" (Darrell L. Bock, "Form Criticism," in *Interpreting the New Testament: Essays on Methods and Issues*, ed. David Alan Black and David S. Dockery [Nashville: Broadman & Holman, 2001], 108). Also Terence C. Mournet, *Oral Tradition and Literary Dependence: Variability and Stability in the Synoptic Tradition and Q*, WUNT 2/195 (Tübingen: Mohr Siebeck, 2005), 56, writes: "Although the categorization of the various gospel traditions is one dimension of the form-critical process, it is not the sole or even primary purpose of the discipline. Through analysis and categorization, Dibelius hopes to '*explain the origin of the tradition about Jesus, and thus to penetrate into a period previous to that in which our Gospels and their written sources were recorded.*'" (Quoting Dibelius, *From Tradition to Gospel*). Mournet rightly notes that the work of both Bultmann and Dibelius were historically concerned both in purpose and design.

9. For one of the more influential studies discrediting form criticism's "laws of transmission," see E. P. Sanders, *The Tendencies of the Synoptic Tradition*, SNTSMS 9 (London: Cambridge University Press, 1969), 272. See John P. Meier, *The Roots of the Problem and the Person*, vol. 1 of *A Marginal Jew: Rethinking the Historical Jesus*, ABRL (New York: Doubleday, 1991), 182. Concerning the misuse of folkloristics by early form critics, specifically Bultmann who followed Herman Gunkel's understanding of the Grimm Brothers' traditioning, see Mournet, *Oral Tradition and Literary Dependency*, 5, 166–74. Paul Foster, "Memory, Orality, and the Fourth Gospel: Three Dead-Ends in Historical Jesus Research," *JSHJ* 10 (2012): 191–227 (here 204), critically explains that "Mournet wishes to hold onto the insights of the Grimm brothers that were used by the form critics, which led them to envisage an oral stage in the transmission process. However, he simultaneously rejects their accompanying conclusion that most traditions could not ultimately be traced back to the historical Jesus." Note also the thorough and careful discussion of Paul Rhodes Eddy and Gregory A. Boyd, *The Jesus Legend: A Case for the Historical Reliability of the Synoptic Jesus Tradition* (Grand Rapids: Baker Academic, 2007), 291–98. Lastly, Arland J. Hultgren, "Form Criticism and Jesus Research," in *Handbook for the Study of the Historical Jesus*, 4 vols., ed. Tom Holmén and Stanley E. Porter (Leiden: Brill, 2011), 1:649–71 (esp. 650–51 on its origins in folklore studies).

10. Notable is Richard Bauckham's emphasis on an observable "from the beginning" motif, characteristic of eyewitness testimony, seen in Luke 1:1–2; 3:23; 23:5; Acts 1:21–22; 10:36–42; and John 2:11; 15:26–27. The

clear impression throughout the New Testament,[11] form criticism ignored the significance of these attestations.[12] Instead, form criticism adopted folklorist principles, such as a lengthy period of tradition transmission, and one without any stabilizing influence acting on the tradition, such as specified, named tradents.[13] Bultmann, a leading form critic,

> understood the Jesus tradition to be a result of *Kleinliteratur*—unsophisticated traditions, created by the simple masses, responding to sociological needs

weightiest eyewitness testimonies belonged to those who were followers of Jesus *from the beginning*. See Richard Bauckham, *Jesus and the Eyewitnesses: The Gospels as Eyewitness Testimony*, 2nd ed. (Grand Rapids: Eerdmans, 2017), 114–54. Cf. Craig S. Keener, *Acts: An Exegetical Commentary*, vol. 1, *Introduction and 1:1—2:47* (Grand Rapids: Baker Academic, 2012), 185n161: "'From the beginning' appears in histories to claim the presence of eyewitnesses from the start." Concerning specified tradents, Eddy and Boyd, *The Jesus Legend*, 287, explain that "certain key individuals are singled out in the New Testament for their roles as faithful witnesses, teachers, and preservers of the Jesus tradition, for example Peter, James, and John, as well as James the brother of Jesus (e.g., Acts 1:15, 21–22; 2:14, 42 . . . 4:13, 19 . . . 5:15, 29; 8:14; 12:2; 1 Cor. 15:1–8; Gal. 2:9; Eph. 2:20)." (Two citations have been omitted.) They then summarize: "It is difficult to explain this common appeal to eyewitness testimony in the New Testament if it is not rooted in historical fact." James D. G. Dunn also speaks of "the prominence of teachers" in "Altering the Default Setting: Re-envisaging the Early Transmission of the Jesus Tradition," in *The Oral Gospel Tradition* (Grand Rapids: Eerdmans, 2013), 55n51, citing Acts 13:1; Rom 12:7; 1 Cor 12:28–29; Gal 6:6; Eph 4:11; Heb 5:12; James 3:1; Did. 13.2, 15.1–2.

11. Note Rom 6:17; 16:17; 1 Cor 11:2, 23–24; 15:3–8; Phil 4:9; 2 Thess 2:15; 2 Tim 3:14 and Jude 3, but see Michael F. Bird, *The Gospel of the Lord: How the Early Church Wrote the Story of Jesus* (Grand Rapids: Eerdmans, 2014), 88n58, for additional references. Bird also expertly notes the secondary research on Jesus traditions in Paul (26–27n15). Note also James D. G. Dunn, *Jesus Remembered*, vol. 1 of *Christianity in the Making* (Grand Rapids: Eerdmans, 2003), 182nn48, 49, for dozens of Jesus traditions associated with the epistolary literature of the New Testament. Concerning Jesus traditions reflected in James, see idem, *Beginning from Jerusalem*, vol. 2 of *Christianity in the Making* (Grand Rapids: Eerdmans, 2009), 1122–45, esp. 1132–36. Peter's knowledge of Jesus tradition is provided on 1147–66, esp. 1154. Concerning John, see idem, *Neither Jew nor Greek*, vol. 3 of *Christianity in the Making* (Grand Rapids: Eerdmans, 2015), 324–27, and idem, *Oral Gospel Tradition*, 138–63, and 164–95 (two essays previously published). Additionally, on James and the Jesus tradition, note Samuel Byrskog, *Story as History—History as Story: The Gospel Traditions in the Context of Ancient Oral History*, WUNT 123 (Tübingen: Mohr Siebeck, 2000), 167–76. An important study of New Testament traditioning history can be found further in the work of E. Earle Ellis, *The Making of the New Testament Documents*, BIS 39 (Leiden: Brill, 1999). Ellis expertly traces the traditions of the apostles (inclusive of Paul) directly to the Jesus traditions of the Gospels—and therefore to the earthly Jesus. His book is a direct response to the continued influence of both F. C. Baur and form criticism (1), which together understand the apostolic missions as existing in conflict, and understand the Jesus traditions and post-Easter traditions as incongruously related. An example of Ellis's handling of the traditioning process can be found in his discussion of the virtue and vice traditions "common to the Jacobean [James], Pauline, Petrine and Johannine missions," which share "an important link with Gospel traditions," namely Mark 7:21–23 (41). The basis of apostolic ethics, then, is the ethics of Jesus. The apostles "were involved in the formation and transmission of both gospel traditions *from the earthly Jesus* and of other traditions originating in the post-resurrection mission of the church" (45–46; emphasis added). The various apostolic "patterns of teaching" (Rom 6:17) are not seen as existing in conflict with one another but are in fact so mingled together as to warrant a mutual connection with the earthly Jesus and, therefore, the faithful transmission of his words and acts among his followers (53–237).

12. See Byrskog, *Story as History—History as Story*, 101–5. Also Alan Kirk, "Memory Theory and Jesus Research," in Hólmen and Porter, *Handbook for the Study of the Historical Jesus*, 1:809–42 (esp. subheading "Form Criticism and Memory," 809–15). Kirk explains the work of Bultmann as demonstrating a "programmatic disconnect between memory and the growing tradition" (810).

13. See Eddy and Boyd, *Jesus Legend*, 291–98. Cf. Bauckham, *Jesus and the Eyewitnesses*, 39–66 (for the significance of names associated with gospel traditions).

and operating under the same "law" as other folklore traditions. Bultmann's assessment of folk traditions led him to conclude that *ancient narrators do not give lengthy, unified accounts* but rather *create small, independent units of tradition* (the "forms" identified by form criticism). As these units of tradition are passed along, *they tend to be expanded*, with details being added.[14]

In essence, form criticism hypothesized that a Gospel text began as an isolated unit, known as a pericope, which was circulated independently of other traditions, and which had only a minimalist (if any) basis in the earthly Jesus's life.[15] At a certain point in its lengthy traditioning history, the "quite definite conditions and wants of life"[16] of the early Christian community altered the tradition with the end result that the pericope's meaning became something altogether different than what was meant in its original context.[17] In this fashion,

---

14. Eddy and Boyd, *Jesus Legend*, 240 (emphasis added).

15. Demonstrating the "'storied' nature of human knowing" and relating it to Jesus and his reception is one of N. T. Wright's significant contributions to New Testament studies: N. T. Wright, *The New Testament and the People of God*, vol. 1 of *Christian Origins and the Question of God* (Minneapolis: Fortress, 1992), 45, 109–20; idem, *Jesus and the Victory of God*, vol. 2 of *Christian Origins and the Question of God* (Minneapolis: Fortress, 1996), 137–44; idem, *Paul and the Faithfulness of God*, vol. 4 of *Christian Origins and the Question of God* (Minneapolis: Fortress, 2013), 24–47, 456–537, and 538–69. Wright has convincingly shown that people, specifically ancient Jews, do not find meaning in atomistic pericopae but in full narratives, and that such story-based thinking is intrinsic to the Jewish worldview. Dale C. Allison Jr., *Constructing Jesus: Memory, Imagination, and History* (Grand Rapids: Baker Academic, 2010), 405, points out the significance of 1 Cor 11:23–25 for Paul's knowledge of Jesus tradition "in a narrative context," evidenced by Paul's preface of ἐν τῇ νυκτὶ ᾗ παρεδίδετο ("in the night he [Jesus] was handed over"); see also Eric Eve, *Behind the Gospels: Understanding the Oral Tradition* (Minneapolis: Fortress, 2013), 165. Contrast Martin Dibelius, *From Tradition to Gospel*, trans. Bertram Lee Woolf, ed. William Barclay (London: Redwood, 1971), 178: "In the earliest period there was no connected narrative of the life, or at least of the work of Jesus, i.e. a narrative comparable to a literary biography or the legendary life of a saint."

16. Bultmann, *History of the Synoptic Tradition*, 4: "The proper understanding of form-criticism rests upon the judgement that the literature in which the life of a given community, even the primitive Christian community, has taken shape, springs out of quite definite conditions and wants of life from which grows up a quite definite style and quite specific forms and categories." This life situation is explained to be "influences at work in the life of the community." In his conclusion (368), Bultmann writes: "The motives that have led to its [the Gospel literature's] formation are plain. *The collection of the material of the tradition began in the primitive Palestinian Church.* Apologetic and polemic led to the collection and production of apophthegmatic sections." (Emphasis original). The premise of a hypothetical *Sitz im Leben* for gospel traditions is significantly informative of form criticism. And it invites the obvious question posed by Eddy and Boyd, *Jesus Legend*, 305: Why is there virtual silence in the Gospels concerning the early church's most pressing dilemmas, specifically the entrance and integration of gentiles into the church (with all of its related challenges)? Concerning Mark 7:19b, "(In saying this, Jesus declared all foods clean.)," Bauckham helpfully explains that rather than the early church demonstrating creativity with the traditions of Jesus to fit their own *Sitze im Leben*, Mark's interpretation is done "purely in an editorial aside" (*Jesus and the Eyewitnesses*, 605). "He does not modify the saying of Jesus itself."

17. Gerd Theissen and Annette Merz, *The Historical Jesus: A Comprehensive Guide* (Minneapolis: Fortress, 1996), 102, write: "In this view the primitive Christian tradition about Jesus owes its existence and its form exclusively to a 'preaching interest' oriented in the present." For fuller definitions of form criticism, see David E. Aune, "Form Criticism," in *The Blackwell Companion to the New Testament*, ed. David E. Aune (Chichester: Wiley-Blackwell, 2010), 140–55. Nicholas Perrin, "Form Criticism," in *Dictionary of Jesus and the Gospels*, 2nd ed. (Downers Grove, IL: InterVarsity Press, 2013), 288–94; Baird, *History of New Testament*

the traditions were dislocated from a *Sitz im Leben Jesu* and posited within a hypothetical *Sitz im Leben der Kirche*. Or, as Käsemann has pointed out: "the work of the Form Critics was designed to show that the message of Jesus as given to us by the Synoptists is, for the most part, not authentic but was minted by the faith of the primitive Christian community in its various stages."[18] Consequently, the Synoptic Gospels were observed to be collections of expanded accounts—even fabricated accounts—that demonstrated the needs of the early Christian communities over and against authentic[19] Jesus tradition.

For multiple reasons, however, form criticism has proven untenable, as classically formulated.[20] This is in large part a consequence of advancements made

---

Research, 2:269–87 (note the excellent bibliography provided on 2:514–18); Richard Bauckham, "The Gospels as Testimony to Jesus Christ: A Contemporary View of their Historical Value," in *Oxford Handbook of Christology*, ed. Francesca Aran Murphy and Troy A. Stefano (Oxford: Oxford University Press, 2015), 55–71 (here 58–9); Darrell L. Bock, *Studying the Historical Jesus: A Guide to Sources and Methods* (Grand Rapids: Baker Academic, 2002), 181–87; Tuckett, "Form Criticism," 21–38.

18. Ernst Käsemann, "The Problem of the Historical Jesus," in *Essays on New Testament Themes*, trans. S. J. Montague, SBT 41 (London: SCM, 1964), 15–47 (here 15). He continues: "Thus, from the fact that the genuine tradition about Jesus has only been transmitted to us embedded in the preaching of primitive Christianity and overlaid by it, the conclusion was drawn that the true bearer and moulder of the Gospel had been the Easter faith." Note the implications concerning the burden of proof also. Form criticism declares the Gospels as "not authentic" (15). This is the situation New Questers are addressing.

19. Although some postmodernist scholars have written critically against "authenticity" where it is understood in a positivist sense, it remains that few Jesus scholars presently writing use the term in this manner. Most notable scholars presently making methodological use of the criteria of authenticity in their research have explicitly likened their epistemological worth to probability. See e.g., Meier, *Marginal Jew*, 1:167–68: "Indeed, since in the quest for the historical Jesus almost anything is possible, the function of the criteria is to pass from the merely possible to the really probable, to inspect various probabilities, and to decide which candidate is most probable. Ordinarily the criteria cannot hope to do more." And at the close of chapter five: "As many a weary quester has remarked before, the use of the valid criteria is more an art than a science. . . . It can never be said too many times that such an art usually yields only varying degrees of probability, not absolute certainty." More recently in John P. Meier, *Probing the Authenticity of the Parables*, vol. 5 of *A Marginal Jew: Rethinking the Historical Jesus*, ABRL (New Haven: Yale University Press, 2016), 12 and n. 15, the criteria are said to be "rules for judging what comes from the historical Jesus" that "can hope to yield reliable results." Robert L. Webb, "The Historical Enterprise and Historical Jesus Research," in *Key Events in the Life of the Historical Jesus: A Collaborative Exploration of Context and Coherence*, ed. Darrell L. Bock and Robert L. Webb (Grand Rapids: Eerdmans, 2009), 56: "Thus, the purpose of the critical methods and criteria [of authenticity] are to ascertain the probability of whether or not—and to what extent—something stated in the written Gospels stage can be traced back to the events stage." Craig S. Keener, *The Historical Jesus of the Gospels* (Grand Rapids: Eerdmans, 2012), xxxiv: "The historical enterprise proceeds based on probabilities and works from a limited base of evidence; it is therefore limited in the claims it makes." Further, of the criterion of Palestinian environment, "Palestinian Jewish features need not guarantee that a saying must have inevitably originated with Jesus, but they do take us back to the earliest circle of witnesses for Jesus, greatly increasing the probability that the saying is authentic" (157). Concerning the positivist desire for "the exact words of Jesus" (*ipsissima verba Jesu*), or the imprecision of the "exact voice of Jesus" (*ipsissima vox Jesu*), Pitre proposes a helpful *via media* which avoids positivist certainty on the one hand, and a lack of definition on the other. He explains this as the *"substantia verba Jesu*—i.e., the substance of the words of Jesus" (Brant Pitre, *Jesus and the Last Supper* [Grand Rapids: Eerdmans, 2015], 47).

20. Six erroneous assumptions of form criticism are detailed by Eddy and Boyd in subheadings across 237–306: (1) The Assumption of a Purely Oral Period; (2) The Assumed Lack of a Coherent Narrative; (3) The Assumed Lack of Biographical Interest; (4) Limited Role of Eyewitnesses; (5) Assumed "Laws" of Oral and Written Traditions; (6) "Prophetic Inspiration" and Jesus Sayings. Bird, *The Gospel of the Lord*, 115–24, details four failings (they are subheadings also): (1) The Distinction between Palestinian and Hellenistic

in better understanding the socio-historical dynamics of first-century Palestine, namely, the recognition that it was, in Jesus's day, already Hellenized.[21] Since early form critics understood the traditioning process to have begun with an early, illiterate Palestinian oral tradition before terminating in a much later and inventive Hellenistic written tradition, their theories could not be espoused reliably in light of recent research.[22] The context of the earliest Christian communities included both Judaism and Hellenism mingled together, so that one culture could not be considered at the exclusion of the other.[23] The division between Palestinian and Hellenistic provenances also functioned as a procrustean bed for many Jesus traditions, specifically "cultic" traditions such as the Last Supper,[24] which were nearly always seen as secondary Hellenistic *nova*.[25]

Settings; (2) An Erroneous View of the Oral Tradition; (3) The Role of Christian Prophets Adding to the Dominical Tradition; and (4) The Link between Text Form and *Sitz im Leben*. Bauckham has reported the death of form criticism in *Jesus in the Eyewitnesses*, 240–9, which was confirmed in the second edition *nova* on pp. 590–615. One notable addition to the lists of failures that has not been mentioned in particular is Bultmannian form criticism's adoption of history-of-religions school premises.

21. Martin Hengel, *Judaism and Hellenism: Studies in Their Encounter in Palestine During the Early Hellenistic Period* (Philadelphia: Fortress, 1974; repr., Eugene, OR: Wipf & Stock, 2003), 104, writes the following when summarizing his findings: "On the whole, it emerges that Hellenism also gained ground as an intellectual power in Jewish Palestine early and tenaciously. From this perspective the usual distinction between Palestinian and Hellenistic Judaism needs to be corrected. Here it is not only used misleadingly as a designation of subject-matter and in a false contrast as a geographical concept, but tends to give a mistaken account of the new situation of Judaism in the Hellenistic period." Elsewhere Hengel notes the presence of "Greek-speaking Jewish Christians from 30/31 up to the time of Paul—indeed he himself [Paul] was one of them." Also: "The Aramaic-speaking primitive community in Jerusalem and the Greek-speaking Jewish-Christian community in Jerusalem, Caesarea, Damascus, Antioch, and Rome do not so much come one after another in time as stand side by side, so that it would also be possible in theory that traditions from the Greek-speaking 'primitive community' were also taken over by the Aramaic-speaking community" (Martin Hengel, "Christology and New Testament Chronology," in *Between Jesus and Paul: Studies in the Earliest History of Christianity* (Eugene, OR: Wipf & Stock, 2003), 37. See also Tuckett, "Form Criticism," 30.

22. Keith, *Jesus' Literacy*, 30–32, rightly acknowledges this point as one form-critical failure. But Käsemann, "Problem of the Historical Jesus," 36, anticipatingly writes: "The situation is made even more difficult by the fact that we cannot draw an exact line between Palestinian and Hellenistic Jewish Christianity, nor conversely, can we simply identify the two."

23. Cf. Bird, *Gospel of the Lord*, 44–45.

24. The Last Supper is endlessly portrayed in New Testament scholarship as an "institution narrative" or as "liturgical tradition." But Rudolf Pesch demonstrates that Mark 14:22–25 forms part of the pre-Markan passion composition, and is the "oldest account" of *the historical event* attested; he further explains that it "reflects accurately the historical Jesus' own understanding and interpretation of his death, i.e., as a vicarious sacrificial atoning death which is not in conflict with, but is the actual foundation of, Jesus' preaching of the kingdom of God, the renewal (by the apostles) of the saving mission to Israel, and its universal extension" (Robert J. Daly, "*Das Abendmahl und Jesu Todesverständnis*: Review," CBQ 43 [1981]: 308–10). Cf. Scot McKnight, *Jesus and His Death: Historiography, the Historical Jesus, and Atonement Theory* (Waco, TX: Baylor University Press, 2006), 262 with n10.

25. This was the result of the history-of-religions school's influence. See Dunn, *Beginning from Jerusalem*, 36–40, who notes that Wilhelm Heitmüller "posed the challenge [i.e., that early Christianity was influenced by other religions] most sharply in terms of the Pauline understanding of baptism and the Lord's Supper" (37). The Eucharist was said to reflect "the Dionysiac mystery cult." Cf. Bultmann, *History of the Synoptic Tradition*, 265 (explicitly relying on Heitmüller), and 369; Dibelius, *From Tradition to Gospel*, 189f. Despite advances, the notion of cult etiologies in the worship of the Pauline communities extended to future researchers. Though Käsemann, "Paul and Early Catholicism," in *New Testament Questions of Today*,

The dismissal of the Last Supper tradition in the life of the historical Jesus had a devastating effect on the scholarly understanding of the self-understanding of Jesus, his passion, and the significance of his death for Christians.[26] It is unsurprising then that many historical Jesus works since Bultmann have been negligent in their handling of the Last Supper. This neglect has rightly been pointed out by historical Jesus scholar Brant Pitre, who begins his recent study, *Jesus and the Last Supper*, stating as much.[27]

AN EXAMPLE OF RUDOLF BULTMANN'S FORMGESCHICHTE

An example of Bultmann's form-critical methodology can be seen in his treatment of the Last Supper tradition in Mark 14. Bultmann understands the actual pericope and any attested history originally behind Mark 14:22–25 as having been "displaced" by the Words of Institution tradition, now reported in its stead. This is a conclusion Bultmann asserts exegetically on account of the narrative lacking "any introduction of its own."[28] Mark adopts instead a "cult legend of the Hellenistic circles" associated with the Pauline mission, and it is this tradition that Mark has carefully and editorially inserted within his Gospel in order to gain "organic continuation" with Mark 14:12–16.[29] As he explains in *Jesus and the Word*, "The words concerning the Lord's supper are liturgical formulations from the Hellenistic celebration of the Eucharist, replacing an older account, of which traces still remain, especially in Luke."[30] The betrayal narrative of Mark 14:17–21 is reckoned a "separate unit of the tradition" also, since it "occurs in

---

trans. J. W. Montague (Philadelphia: Fortress, 1969), 246, does mention that Paul had to "battle against" the "distortion constantly." And elsewhere, citing 1 Cor 10:19ff., Käsemann, "The Pauline Doctrine of the Lord's Supper," in *Essays on New Testament Themes*, 108, writes: "The attempt to shed light on Paul's teaching on the Lord's Supper from its links with Hellenistic cult-meals has completely broken down, so far as the essential issues are concerned." It should also be mentioned that Third Questers have frequently pointed out Semitisms in the Last Supper account of Mark 14:22–25—firmly dislocating it from a Hellenistic provenance by using a criterion of authenticity. See e.g. Joachim Jeremias, *The Eucharistic Words of Jesus*, Study Edition (London: SCM, 1974), 173–84, who identifies no less than twenty-three Semitisms in the Last Supper account of Mark; also Maurice Casey, *Aramaic Sources of Mark's Gospel*, SNTSMS 102 (New York: Cambridge University Press, 1998), 219–52, who has reconstructed an entire Aramaic text underlying Mark's Last Supper account.

26. Note Rudolf Bultmann, "The Primitive Christian Kerygma and the Historical Jesus," in *The Historical Jesus and the Kerygmatic Christ: Essays on the New Quest for the Historical Jesus*, ed. Carl E. Braaten and Roy A. Harrisville (Nashville: Abingdon, 1964), 15–41 (here, 23): "The greatest embarrassment to the attempt to reconstruct a portrait of Jesus is the fact that we cannot know how Jesus understood his end, his death."

27. See Pitre, *Jesus and the Last Supper*, 14–21. Pitre points to Albert Schweitzer's reconstructed Jesus as the earliest catalyst of this neglect since the establishment of a covenant was not in keeping with Schweitzer's understanding of an imminent apocalypse.

28. Bultmann, *History of the Synoptic Tradition*, 265, 278.

29. Bultmann, *History of the Synoptic Tradition*, 265. The pericope "cannot have been an independent unit, but was composed for the sake of what followed" (278).

30. Rudolf Bultmann, *Jesus and the Word* (New York: Charles Scribner's Sons, 1958), 214.

Luke [22:21–23] in another place."[31] (Luke places the prophecy of Judas's betrayal after the Twelve partake of the Last Supper elements, while Mark places the prophecy before.) As additional evidence for his theory of the Supper's composition history, Bultmann identifies verse 26 also as editorial composition—with its mention of hymn singing, followed by an abrupt transition to the Mount of Olives—since it functions to bridge Peter's denial with the foregoing narrative.[32] The Passover preparation unit in Mark 14:12–16 is also seen as a fabrication, since it is "reminiscent of 1 Sam[uel] 10 where Samuel foretells whom Saul will meet on his way."[33] In sum, then, the constituent parts of the entire Last Supper tradition are dealt with accordingly: (1) The Passover preparation unit is considered a historical fabrication (verses 12–16); (2) the account of betrayal is considered unhistorical and "belongs to legend" (verses 17–21);[34] (3) the institution of the Lord's Supper is an etiological myth (verses 22–25); and (4) Peter's denial (verses 26–31), apart from verse 26 which is editorial and verse 28 which breaks the narrative sequence too crudely, is considered "an historical account but with legendary traits."[35] In short, Peter's desertion is taken as historical, and a meal of some sort is involved, though it is not a Paschal meal, nor with certainty a tradition arising from Jesus's last meal. "Thus the kerygma of Christ is cultic legend and the *Gospels are expanded cult legends*."[36] Elsewhere Bultmann flatly declares: "The Christ of the kerygma is not a historical figure which could enjoy continuity with the historical Jesus."[37] Within the work of Bultmann's form criticism, the Gospels are left, as can be seen, in shambles—solitary fragments that no longer, nor in any meaningful way, cohere.

Notably, for Bultmann's composition theory of a stratified Gospel prehistory to suffice, it necessitates, as in folkloristics, enough time for such significant

---

31. Bultmann, *History of the Synoptic Tradition*, 278.

32. Bultmann, *History of the Synoptic Tradition*, 278.

33. Bultmann, *History of the Synoptic Tradition*, 278, 264. The preparation pericope, Bultmann writes, is based on "a fairy-tale motif" (264).

34. Bultmann, *History of the Synoptic Tradition*, 264.

35. Bultmann, *History of the Synoptic Tradition*, 267.

36. Bultmann, *History of the Synoptic Tradition*, 370–71.

37. Bultmann, "The Primitive Christian Kerygma and the Historical Jesus," 18. Meier, *Marginal Jew*, 1:27, helpfully contextualizes Bultmann's expressed discontinuity in what is mostly existentialist historiography, noting Martin Heidegger and Martin Kähler: "Bultmann is one with Kähler in emphasizing the central Christian proclamation (kerygma) of Jesus' death and resurrection and in rejecting the historical Jesus as the basis or the content of the Christian faith." It should be noted, however, that despite Bultmann's desires, an existential hermeneutic of response to the Christ, or of an encounter with him, does nothing to achieve historical continuity between Jesus of Nazareth and the witness of the Gospels. Also, Stanley E. Porter, "A Dead End or a New Beginning? Examining the Criteria for Authenticity in Light of Albert Schweitzer," in *Jesus Research: An International Perspective, The First Princeton-Prague Symposium on Jesus Research*, ed. James H. Charlesworth and Petr Pokorný (Grand Rapids: Eerdmans, 2009), 16–35 (here, 17): "These scholars [inclusive of Bultmann] brought the widespread recognition that it was in fact impossible to write a life of Jesus."

developments to take place. But time is what the Jesus historian cannot afford. Unlike folklorists dealing with Homer, New Testament scholars are operating in a significantly smaller window of time, i.e., the time between Jesus and Mark's Gospel, but with an important and often neglected check on the Last Supper tradition in Paul, roughly reducing the window of time by a decade. Further, we might ask: Where were all the disciples while undirected changes were taking place to the Jesus traditions? For one New Testament scholar, they must have been translated immediately to heaven after his resurrection![38]

Discernable from Bultmann's radically skeptical[39] *History of the Synoptic Tradition* is his manner of dividing the material between Palestinian and Hellenistic Christian provenances, his denial of continuity between Jesus and kerygma, and his folkloristic indebted traditioning theories.

ERNST KÄSEMANN AND THE NEW QUEST[40]

Despite the influence of Bultmann, several New Questers of the 1950s and 1960s disagreed emphatically regarding the possibility of knowledge of the historical Jesus.[41] Publication after publication on the historical Jesus followed as New Questers began to pay more and careful attention to the neglected historicity of the Gospels.[42] Käsemann, a student of Bultmann, prompted the New Quest

---

38. Vincent Taylor, *The Formation of the Gospel Tradition* (London: Macmillan, 1933), 41.

39. I regard methodological doubt of a historical account that places the burden of proof on that account as overly skeptical. Several scholars have also seen the work of Bultmann as too radical in its severing of Jesus from the kerygma. See esp. James M. Robinson, *A New Quest for the Historical Jesus*, SBT 25 (London: SCM, 1959), 85–92. Stanley E. Porter, *The Criteria for Authenticity in Historical-Jesus Research: Previous Discussion and New Proposals*, JSNTSup 191 (Sheffield: Sheffield Academic Press, 2000), 45, writes: "This model [Jesus as an eschatological prophet] apparently dominated German depictions of Jesus for the first half of the twentieth century. The results of such an orientation were found in the work of scholars such as Bultmann, who were highly skeptical of attempts to find the historical Jesus in documents produced by Christian faith." Cf. Gerd Theissen and Dagmar Winter, *The Quest for the Plausible Jesus: The Question of Criteria* (Louisville: Westminster John Knox, 2002), 105. More recently, Aune, "Form Criticism," 144, organizes discussion of the *Sitze im Leben* search by form critics under the heading "Early Christian Creativity and the Historical Skepticism of Form Critics." And Simpson, *Recent Research on the Historical Jesus*, 18, writes: "A number of Bultmann's students launched the New Quest, or Second Quest, in reaction to the skepticism of their teacher."

40. That is, a "New Quest" as opposed to the preceding "No Quest" period associated with Bultmann. That Bultmann—but not his students—is associated with a No Quest period for historical Jesus research already invites suspicion over the idea of historiographical/methodological continuity between him and his students. However, it should be noted that the No Quest period was, more or less, only a mood in German-speaking scholarship and does not function as an accurate definition of the period since Jesus questing continued, particularly in English-speaking scholarship. Cf. Porter, *Criteria of Authenticity in Historical-Jesus Research*, 45.

41. Cf. Alexander J. M. Wedderburn, *Jesus and the Historians*, WUNT 269 (Tübingen: Mohr Siebeck, 2010), 81: The movement, begun by Bultmann's students, "reacted to what it perceived as Bultmann's negative attitude towads the possibility, legitimacy and value of historical knowledge of Jesus."

42. In addition to the New Quest works cited below, additional post-Bultmannian Jesus research is

by declaring that a historical Jesus could be corroborated through a careful handling of the Gospels, using the right criteria and using criteria rightly. While Käsemann considered the Gospels to have been colored by the faith of the early Christian communities, it remains, importantly, that he regarded authentic history as still attested within these traditions. Where Bultmann understood firm discontinuity to be bridged only by means of an existential encounter,[43] Käsemann affirmed a continuity that could be meaningfully bridged through carefully applying specific criteria.[44] As a result, New Questers both pioneered and implemented specific criteria, the "criteria of authenticity," in order to critically substantiate genuine Jesus traditions. This was done in an effort to counter the idea that Jesus had been lost beneath later kerygmatic traditions. On the contrary, genuine Jesus traditions were a part of them. Historical Jesus scholars Theissen and Winter importantly explain that "for the 'New Quest' (J. Robinson) *the issue of the continuity between the historical Jesus and the Jesus Christ of post-Easter faith stood at the center of the discussion.*"[45]

It is the governing conviction of New Questers that Jesus cannot be separated from the significance attributed to him in the Gospels.[46] It was the *Leben Jesu* historians who largely posited a historical Jesus apart from the kerygma. It was Bultmann who asserted encounter with a bare kerygmatic Christ apart from the Nazarene's historicity. But it was Käsemann, and other New Questers, who affirmed kerygmatic history—or history within the kerygma.[47] Jesus cannot

---

carefully catalogued by Craig Evans, *Life of Jesus Research: An Annotated Bibliography*, JSNTSup 13 (Leiden: Brill, 1996), 27–109, 127–46. See further, Baird, *History of New Testament Research*, 3:129–91.

43. Bultmann, "The Primitive Christian Kerygma and the Historical Jesus," 18: "The Christ of the kerygma is not a historical figure which could enjoy continuity with the historical Jesus." And (30): "The Christ of the kerygma has, as it were, displaced the historical Jesus and authoritatively addresses the hearer—every hearer." Further (31): "It rests upon encounter, in so far as it keeps itself open to the possibilities of self-understanding which history offers us as the possibilities of one's own self-understanding."

44. Käsemann, "Blind Alleys in the 'Jesus of History' Controversy," in *New Testament Questions for Today*, 23–65 (here 47): "It may be readily conceded that the kerygma has preserved some essential traits of the earthly Jesus." Baird, *History of New Testament Research*, 3:136, writes, "The current return to the quest was encouraged, according to Käsemann, by the recognition that the Synoptic Gospels contain more reliable tradition than had been supposed, and that the kerygma included facts and presupposed a *continuity* with the historical tradition of Jesus" (emphasis added). Further (137, emphasis added): "Käsemann wants . . . to demonstrate the material *continuity* between the historical Jesus and the kerygma."

45. Theissen and Winter, *Quest for the Plausible Jesus*, 2 (emphasis added). See Käsemann, "Problem of the Historical Jesus," 15–47; idem, "Blind Alleys in the 'Jesus of History' Controversy," 23–65; Baird, *History of New Testament Research*, 3:136–38.

46. Cf. Günther Bornkamm, *Jesus of Nazareth* (New York: Harper & Brothers, 1960), 21: "Our task, then, is to seek the history in the Kerygma of the Gospels, and in this history to seek the Kerygma."

47. For Keith, perhaps on account of his postmodernist influence, interpreted history does not seem to provide access to the historical Jesus. Contrastingly, for Käsemann, the presence of "historification in our Gospels" (the German reads *Historisierung*) is the problem intended by his essay title: "The Problem of the Historical [*historischen*] Jesus." If the kerygma is only interpretation, what is the historian to do with the historical? Contrast also the thought of Jonathan Bernier, *The Quest for the Historical Jesus after the Demise of Authenticity: Toward a Critical Realist of Philosophy of History in Jesus Studies*, LNTS 540 (New York:

be de-theologized—or demythologized—with the result that he approximates nothing in early Christian proclamation; if New Questers can be regarded as having a central methodological axiom, it would be this:[48] Kerygmatic history is still history. Or, as New Testament scholar James D. G. Dunn writes: "a history, of course, seen from the standpoint of faith, but the history of Jesus nonetheless."[49]

Although Keith states that it is the concern of Käsemann and other New Questers to "extricate" Gospel history from its "theological framework," [50] Käsemann actually seeks to re-introduce the importance of theology through wedding the historical Jesus with the kerygma. He puts beyond doubt the certain weddedness of history with kerygma when he writes:

> The heart of our problem lies here: the exalted Lord has almost entirely swallowed up the image of the earthly Lord and yet the community maintains the identity of the exalted Lord with the earthly. The solution of this problem cannot, however, if our findings are right, be approached with any hope of success along the line of supposed historical *bruta facta* but only along the line of the connection and tension between the preaching of Jesus and that of his community. The question of the historical Jesus is, in its legitimate form, the question of the continuity of the Gospel within the discontinuity of the times and within the variation of the kerygma.[51]

T&T Clark, 2016), 28, who writes: "The fatal impasse that ultimately undid the criteria approach lay precisely in its efforts to exclude the subjective, thus reducing it to its empirical component. . . . Those who now declare that we cannot know anything about Jesus are primarily disillusioned empiricists . . ." Apart from assuming the demise of the criteria, which is not substantiated in his treatment (cf. pp. 1–2n3), Bernier works with the assumption that criteriologists intend the criteria as historicist tools in a positivist sense. But this would be a relapse back into the First Quest, which sought a historical Jesus by means of *bruta facta*.

48. Käsemann, "Blind Alleys in the 'Jesus of History' Controversy," 36, "I simply do not understand the extraordinarily radical antithesis of historical and material continuity between Jesus and the primitive Christian preaching which permeates his whole essay; indeed, our ways probably begin to diverge here at the very outset." Further (47): "It may readily be conceded that the kerygma has preserved some essential traits of the earthly Jesus." For Bornkamm, *Jesus of Nazareth*, 20, the subject connection is nigh "indissoluble." Tellingly, in each instance throughout *Jesus, Criteria, and the Demise of Authenticity* where the historiographical developments from Bultmann to Käsemann are within view or explicitly discussed (pp. 12, 36, 54, 115, 121, 129), the departure of Käsemann and other New Questers from Bultmann's historiography is noticeably absent. Rather, the contributors portray Käsemann in each instance as actually carrying forward what Bultmann started without additional clarification. Refreshingly, Michael Bird has recently stated the contrast with careful accuracy: "Ernst Käsemann, in a direct and deliberate critique of his mentor Rudolf Bultmann, argued that the early church never lost interest in the life of Jesus as being properly basic to its faith" (Bird, *Gospel of the Lord*, 24).

49. James D. G. Dunn, *Jesus Remembered*, vol. 1 of *Christianity in the Making* (Grand Rapids: Eerdmans, 2003), 79.

50. Keith, "Indebtedness of the Criteria Approach," 36.

51. Käsemann, "Problem of the Historical Jesus," 46.

KÄSEMANN AND DISSIMILARITY

Since form criticism very much perpetuated the methodological doubt seen in the *Leben Jesu* histories, Käsemann's criteriology is rightly regarded as a response to both approaches.[52] Note how Käsemann describes the previous two centuries of Gospels scholarship in Germany:

> Anyone who tries to upset this verdict [that the road of Liberalism in reconstructing a "life-story" of Jesus was a vain one] is seeking to rob us of the fruit and the meaning of all our research of the last two centuries and to conjure up once again the painful story of historical criticism, which would then have to be repeated in an even more drastic form. He is also failing to understand that the discovery of historical facts and their causal nexus is not necessarily of help to us in our own historical situation but that these must be interpreted before their relevance and their challenge can be made plain. Mere history is petrified history, whose historical significance cannot be brought to light simply by verifying the facts and handing them on. On the contrary, the passing on of the *bruta facta* can, as such, directly obstruct a proper understanding of it.[53]

Demonstrating his acceptance of the burden of historical proof, a burden demanded by previous questing,[54] Käsemann writes that "the obligation now

---

52. See Simpson, *Recent Research on the Historical Jesus*, 18: "He [Käsemann] criticized his teacher's work on two points. First, he argued that the dialectic theologians, who reacted to the liberalism of the First Quest by retreating from historical research, made the same mistake of the First Quest in reverse, by abandoning history in favor of theology." Simpson explains that Bultmann and the dialectic theologians abandoned history in favor of theology while First Questers made the opposite error in abandoning theology in favor of history. Dunn, *Jesus Remembered*, also characterizes the quests this way with his chapter titles "Flight from Dogma" and "Flight from History." Cf. Werner H. Kelber, "Rethinking the Oral-Scribal Transmission/ Performance of the Jesus Tradition," in *Jesus Research: New Methodologies and Perceptions, The Second Princeton-Prague Symposium on Jesus Research Princeton 2007*, ed. James H. Charlesworth, Brian Rhea, and Petr Pokorný (Grand Rapids: Eerdmans, 2014), 500–530 (here, 501): "Deeply lodged in the immense labors of the various quests was, and is, the conflict between theology and history, modernity's version of the medieval contest of faith versus reason."
53. Käsemann, "Problem of the Historical Jesus," 23–24.
54. Against Chris Keith, "Die Evangelien als 'kerygmatische Erzählungen' über Jesus und die 'Kriterien' in der Jesusforschung," in *Jesus Handbuch*, ed. Jens Schröter and Christine Jacobi (Tübingen: Mohr Siebeck, 2017), 86–98 (here 87): "Diese Position kehrt die Perspektive gegenüber einer älteren Sichtweise geradezu um, wie sie beispielsweise im 'Leben Jesu' von David Friedrich Strauß in der zweiten Auflage aus den 1830er Jahren erkennbar wird, wo Kriterien für den Erweis des unhistorischen Charakters von Teilen der Jesusüberlieferung entwickelt wurden." But historical criticism had already made the reversal. In a very important sense, the quest for the historical Jesus is itself based upon the skeptical premise that the Gospels are unreliable. Note Ben F. Meyer, *The Aims of Jesus*, Princeton Theological Monograph Series 48 (Eugene, OR: Pickwick, 2002), 29: "What makes Reimarus significant is that he conceived the history of Jesus as an unknown that remained to be known." Wedderburn shared similar sentiment (*Jesus and the Historians,*

laid upon us is to investigate and make credible not the possible unauthenticity of the individual unit of material but, on the contrary, its genuineness."[55] In the face of historical criticism and Bultmannian skepticism, "radical criticism" is necessary to achieve authenticity by newer Jesus historians.[56]

It is with this recognition, then, that the sensibility of the criterion of dissimilarity may be introduced. Wherever methodological doubt exists concerning the historical Jesus or whether some saying or event attributed to him was the invention of the early church, a doubt that continues to persist in Jesus studies,[57]

161–64). See also Bornkamm, *Jesus of Nazareth*, 20: "The critical exegete and historian is therefore *obliged*, in questions concerning the history of the tradition, to speak of 'authentic' or 'inauthentic' words of Jesus and thus to distinguish words of the historical Jesus from 'creations by the Church'" (emphasis added). Also, Robinson, *New Quest for the Historical Jesus*, 38: "In the nineteenth century the burden of proof lay upon the scholar who saw theological interpolations in historical sources; in the twentieth century the burden of proof lies upon the scholar who sees objective factual source material in the primitive Church's book of common worship. The result is obvious: the burden of proof has shifted over to the person who maintains the possibility of the quest." (Käsemann, therefore, inherits the burden since he maintains the possibility of Jesus questing after his twentieth-century predecessors.) See also, Porter, *Criteria for Authenticity in Historical-Jesus Research*, 65: "As a result of the scepticism engendered in some circles by those typically identified as part of the 'no quest' period (and who were at the heart of developing form criticism), the burden was placed upon those who wished to distinguish tradition and its development within the early Church from the purported authentic words of Jesus." Theissen and Winter, *Quest for the Plausible Jesus*, 128, explain that "the tradition in general is considered untrustworthy" for Käsemann, again, on account of earlier questing. And most recently, Bauckham, *Jesus and the Eyewitnesses*, 611 (2nd ed.), writes, "It is worth noting that this criterion [dissimilarity] was not borrowered from the ordinary methods of historical enquiry, but invented for this situation in which the sources had already been virtually disqualified as reliable sources for history."

55. Käsemann, "Problem of the Historical Jesus," 34.

56. Käsemann, "Problem of the Historical Jesus," 35; idem, "Blind Alleys in the 'Jesus of History' Controversy," 35–65. Tom Holmén, "Authenticity Criteria," in *The Routledge Encyclopedia of the Historical Jesus*, ed. Craig A. Evans (New York: Routledge, 2010), 43–54 (here 43): "A reason for the increase of the awareness at this point was that the revived interest in the historical figure of Jesus now had to face the skepticism about the historical reliability of the Gospels that mainly in the wake of form criticism had rather widely landed in scholarship." See further Theissen and Winter, *Quest for the Plausible Jesus*, 2, 113, who also note the skepticism of form criticism. Section 2.2 (95–112) is titled: "The Critical Method of Dialectical Theology and the Skepticism of Form Criticism." Theissen and Winter frequently observe the discordance between earlier form criticism and subsequent questers.

57. See Paula Fredriksen, *From Jesus to Christ*, 2nd ed. (New Haven: Yale University Press, 2000), 97: "The intuition of earlier scholars was sound: 'What really happened' during Jesus' ministry is not recoverable from the evangelical descriptions of what happened. But by examining these descriptions in light of our knowledge of Jesus' historical context, we can establish with reasonable security what *possibly* happened, what *probably* happened, and what *could not have possibly* happened." I. Howard Marshall, "The Last Supper," in Bock and Webb, *Key Events in the Life of the Historical Jesus*, 481–588, notes both Marcus Borg and John W. Riggs (481–83). Borg writes from the position of skepticism and with specific reference to the Last Supper: "It is difficult to make any historical judgment about the details of the 'last supper,' including the words actually spoken by Jesus, simply because the remembrance and celebration of it were so central in the worship of the early church. Thus the details of the story have been affected by the liturgical practice of the early church" (Marcus Borg, *Jesus: A New Vision: Spirit, Culture, and the Life of Discipleship* [San Francisco: Harper & Row, 1987], 187–88). And more caustically, Riggs writes: "That which eventually became the sacrament which is variously called the Lord's Supper, Holy Communion, the Eucharist and the mass does not have its origins in any putative last supper that Jesus shared with his disciples. There was no last supper of Jesus such as that which is portrayed in Paul's letter to Corinth or in the gospels . . . . The passion narratives of the gospels, which include the last supper scenes, are ecclesial compositions" (John W. Riggs, "The Sacred Food of Didache 9–10 and Second-Century Ecclesiologies," in *The Didache in Context: Essays on Its Text, History, and Transmission*, ed. Clayton N. Jefford, NovTSup 77 [Leiden: Brill, 1995], 257).

dissimilarity from such invention provides the critical historian a means of nego-
tiating such skepticism. Corroborating this contention, Theissen and Winter
offer the following explanation of Käsemannian dissimilarity:

> Käsemann pointed out what in his view was *the current deficit in life-of-Jesus*
> *research*, on the one hand, *and in Bultmann's theology*, on the other. With
> the Bultmannian concept of the kerygma as his point of departure, he is
> concerned with the dual anchor points of the kerygma: *the Easter faith, on the*
> *one hand* (here he sees a deficit in the life-of-Jesus theology and a correct, though
> one-sided, new starting point by Bultmann), and *the proclamation of Jesus*
> [or teachings of Jesus], *on the other hand* (here he sees a deficit in Bultmann's
> *approach* and a correct approach in the life-of-Jesus theology, which appealed
> one-sidedly to the teaching of Jesus).[58]

Käsemann's criterion of dissimilarity, then, intends to address "the painful story of historical criticism," or the First Quest, on the one hand, with its
modernist-positivist desire for "historical facts and their causal nexus" absent of
theological meaning,[59] and, on the other hand, to address Bultmann's "radical"
model of form criticism that "leaves us in a lurch" since it is strictly "concerned
with the *Sitz im Leben*" of the early church and not the life of the historical
Jesus.[60] Recognizing these two poles that Käsemannian criteriology intends to
negotiate is critical for understanding the necessity of the criteria—and it is to
Keith's detriment that his arguments neglect the historical-critical polemic of
Käsemannian criteriology.

It should be carefully affirmed that while the criterion of dissimilarity was the
tool Käsemann and others used for demonstrating authentic Jesus tradition, the
greater scope of historiography it operated within is one of historical continuity.[61]
New Questers intentionally employed this criterion as a means of bridging Jesus
and the kerygma or demonstrating how the two could in fact be continuous.

---

58. Theissen and Winter, *Quest for the Plausible Jesus*, 114 (emphasis added).

59. Käsemann, "Problem of the Historical Jesus," 23.

60. Käsemann, "Problem of the Historical Jesus," 35. Note also (25): "Primitive Christianity is obviously
of the opinion that the earthly Jesus cannot be understood otherwise than from the far side of Easter, that
is, in his majesty as Lord of the community and that, conversely, *the event of Easter cannot be adequately*
comprehended if it is looked at apart from the earthly Jesus."

61. Note Jürgen Becker, "The Search for Jesus' Special Profile," in Hólmen and Porter, *Handbook for*
the Study of the Historical Jesus, 1:57–89 (here 85): "[C]riteria are helpful when they keep in mind both
the original conditions of an historical phenomenon and its later consequences. Jesus is perceived as an
historical person only where he is interpreted in view of his religious, cultural, and social home and also in
view of the impact he made on history. And both these contexts are marked by continuity and innovation.
We cannot integrate Jesus totally into Christianity and make his Jewish roots a matter of indifference; nor
can we interpret Jesus exclusively in a Jewish context and strip him of the impact he made on history."

In this regard, their methodology is *not entirely unlike* Tom Holmén's hermeneutic of dissimilarity within the continuum of Judaism—Jesus—Christianity.[62]

In light of this analysis, then, it is difficult to see Käsemann as still affirming the form-critical historiography of Bultmann in a meaningful way or to interpret Käsemann's historiography as locked in methodological one-to-one correspondence with form criticism, while at the same time appreciating the ways in which he advances Jesus research. The criteriology adopted by New Questers is better thought of as a critique of previous approaches rather than as an advancement of, or an unreflecting adoption of, form criticism. Käsemann provides a rallying cry for future Jesus historians, and he directly challenged the reigning scholarship of his day. He writes excitedly about the developments following Bultmann's skepticism. He states:

> A case is being made out with particular vigour for the reliability, if not of the whole of the Passion and Easter tradition of the Gospels, at least of the most primitive elements in it. In both cases, the concern is to counteract any drastic separation, or even antithesis, of kerygma or tradition.[63]

GÜNTHER BORNKAMM

Günther Bornkamm, another pupil of Bultmann's, was the first New Quest scholar to produce a full treatment of the historical Jesus. At the outset of his

---

62. See Tom Holmén, ed., *Jesus in Continuum*, WUNT 2/289 (Tübingen: Mohr Siebeck, 2012), 3–9: "dissimilarity in the continuum" (9). But note Holmén's important essays critical of dissimilarity and other criteria: Holmén, "Doubts about Dissimilarity: Reconstructing the Main Criterion of Jesus of History Research," in *Authenticating the Words of Jesus*, ed. Bruce Chilton and Craig A. Evans, NTTS 28.1 (Leiden: Brill, 1999), 47–80; idem, "Seven Theses on the So-Called Criteria of Authenticity of Historical Jesus Research," *RCT* 33 (2008): 343–76. In his essay, "Doubts about Dissimilarity," Holmén, noting Ben F. Meyer and Morna D. Hooker, explains the criterion of dissimilarity as demanding that Jesus be dissimilar from his Jewish context (52–56; esp. 55). But is it the case that the criterion of dissimilarity, specifically dissimilarity to Judaism, be understood so strictly? As will be shown, New Questers such as Norman Perrin did not seek to employ the criterion in a manner that divorced Jesus from Judaism. Rather, while interpreting Jesus within his Jewish context, they sought that material that set him apart as a Jewish individual. It remains, however, that Holmén's "Doubts about Dissimilarity" essay is full of valuable corrections for dissimilarity, including: (1) Dissimilarity does not act as a test of inauthenticity, i.e., it cannot excise tradition that fails to accord with it. There is, in effect, no criterion of similarity/inauthenticity such that if a tradition fails to pass authenticity, it would thereby prove unhistorical or inauthentic. (2) By subjecting the criterion of coherence to dissimilarity, the atomization of Jesus tradition is necessarily entailed. This is due to John Meier and others who understand coherence as only applicable to the unimpeached material remaining after primary criteria operate. (Or more simply put, by understanding coherence as a secondary criterion.) But it should be noted that not all scholars accept coherence as a secondary criterion. Notable in this regard is Pitre, a former student of John Meier, who departs from Meier on this point. See Brant Pitre, *Jesus, the Tribulation, and the End of the Exile: Restoration Eschatology and the Origin of the Atonement*, WUNT 2/204 (Tübingen: Mohr Siebeck, 2005), 27.

63. Käsemann, "Problem of the Historical Jesus," 17.

volume, *Jesus of Nazareth*, he makes it clear that he is following the lead of Käsemann, which can be seen in the way that he details history's weddedness to the kerygma:

> In another respect also, *faith's interest in pre-Easter history must be made clear.* The following question could be posed concerning the post-Easter Church which lived in the assurance of the presence of the risen Christ and in the hope of his speedy return: Did not the Church fall into strange anachronism? *She made herself contemporary with her earthly pre-Easter Lord. She made herself contemporary with the Pharisees and high priests* of long ago. *She made herself contemporary with the first hearers of Jesus* who heard his message of the coming of God's kingdom; *with the disciples* who followed after him; *with the sick* whom he healed; *with the tax collectors and sinners* with whom he sat down at table.[64]

Here Bornkamm, in agreement with Käsemann, reflects on the pre-Easter historical element in the Gospels as a problem for questers—one positively understood—and one that merits an answer.[65] How is the historian to regard the pre-Easter historical element that is mingled so inextricably with the kerygma of the Gospels, if the Gospels *only* reflect their authors' *Sitze im Leben*? For Bornkamm, the resulting portrait of Jesus is somewhat complicated due to this mingling, but nonetheless still traceable. Jesus's journey to Jerusalem and his declarations of suffering and vindication are taken as historical. Luke 13:31–33 is considered to hold an authentic kernel in its description of Jesus's desire to proceed to Jerusalem as other prophets had; as Bornkamm explains, Jesus's likely intention here is to take his prophetic message of the coming kingdom of God to the city of God.[66]

Though he posits the existence of post-Easter legendary developments within Jesus's passion narrative, he nevertheless affirms the broad historicity of the

---

64. Bornkamm, *Jesus of Nazareth*, 23 (emphasis added). Cf. Käsemann, "Problem of the Historical Jesus," 30–34. See too Baird, *History of New Testament Research*, 3:159; on 3:163 he writes: "Bornkamm affirms the *continuity* between the historical Jesus and the Christ of the post-Easter faith" (emphasis added).

65. Bornkamm, *Jesus of Nazareth*, 22, notes that "it cannot be seriously maintained that the Gospels and their tradition do not allow enquiry after the historical Jesus. Not only do they allow, they demand this effort." Käsemann, "Problem of the Historical Jesus," 22, also notes the historical legitimacy of pre-Easter gospel traditions as problematic for Old Quest Jesus studies, which posited strong discontinuity between pre-and post-Easter Jesuses. Käsemann, "Blind Alleys in the 'Jesus of History' Controversy," 23: "The 'new question' only merits being called 'new' because the theological relevance of the historical element has become, to a quite unprecedented extent, an acute and decisive problem which no one has really succeeded in mastering."

66. Bornkamm, *Jesus of Nazareth*, 154–55.

passion. And he affirms it as uniquely historical with respect to the earlier narratives of the Gospels, specifically on account of "the fullness of detail and the connection of events."[67] Put another way, Bornkamm regards the historicity here, though still not uncomplicated by post-Easter reflections, as uniquely authentic because of the shared details and chronological agreement among the Gospels.

Concerning the Last Supper specifically, "the texts do reveal for certain" that "Jesus celebrates the Supper with his disciples in the expectation of the approaching kingdom of God."[68] Though denying the final meal of Jesus as paschal in nature, Bornkamm even goes on to affirm a degree of authenticity of the Words of Institution. He takes the bread and wine references as historically authentic, though they are said to be couched in later liturgical development.[69] The developments from Bultmann's sundering of history from kerygma are positively telling. Bornkamm breaks through the cult etiology barrier to the historicity of the Last Supper adopted by Bultmann from the latter's history-of-religions predecessors.

JAMES M. ROBINSON

Yet a third student of Bultmann, the first to designate the New Quest as such, was James M. Robinson. Robinson did not mince words when he explained the New Quest as a self-conscious critique of Bultmann:

> The German repudiation of the quest of the historical Jesus at the opening of the century found its definitive crystallization in the scholarship of Rudolf Bultmann. *His form-critical research tended to confirm the view that such a quest is impossible,* and his existential theology carried through the thesis that such a quest is illegitimate. Therefore *it is not surprising that the critical restudy of his position by his pupils should begin here.*[70]

Citing Käsemann's initial response as the first indication, Robinson points out how the students of Bultmann were primarily concerned with the kerygma's continuity with the historical Jesus, since Bultmann had presented significant

---

67. Bornkamm, *Jesus of Nazareth*, 154–55.
68. Bornkamm, *Jesus of Nazareth*, 160.
69. Bornkamm, *Jesus of Nazareth*, 161.
70. Robinson, *New Quest for the Historical Jesus*, 12 (emphasis added). Cf. Baird, *History of New Testament Research*, 3:168–79.

challenges to such continuity.[71] No less significant was Bornkamm's book *Jesus of Nazareth* discussed above, which was the first book written among Bultmann's students on the historical Jesus, and which was concerned also with the question of continuity.[72] The task of New Questers, then, was to demonstrate that the Jesus of history and the early Christian kerygma were historically related in a meaningful, even genuine way—that is, "if we do not wish ultimately to find ourselves committed to a mythological Lord."[73]

Throughout his carefully argued book, Robinson explains that demonstrating continuity is the task, not just of Bultmann's students but of any scholar who might seek to authenticate Jesus as a meaningful historical figure for Christian faith:

> For how can the indispensable historicity of Jesus be affirmed, while at the same time maintaining the irrelevance of what a historical encounter with him would mean, once this has become a real possibility due to the rise of modern historiography? Such a position cannot fail to lead to the conclusion that the Jesus of the kerygma could equally well be only a myth, for one has in fact declared the meaning of his historical person irrelevant.[74]

What Robinson seeks to demonstrate in his final chapter is that both kerygma and history, together, are necessary ingredients for Jesus questing. If there is only kerygma, then researchers are operating with "a significant formal deficiency: it [the kerygma] sees Jesus only in terms determined by the Christian encounter, and thus obscures formally the concreteness of his historical reality."[75] The opposite error, Robinson states, would be to follow in the "illegitimacy of the original quest," which assumed that un-interpreted history could demonstrate Jesus "undialectically, unparadoxically, unoffensively" as Lord, when it can only

---

71. Robinson, *New Quest for the Historical Jesus*, 14; citing Käsemann, "The Problem of the Historical Jesus."

72. Robinson, *New Quest for the Historical Jesus*, 16.

73. Robinson, *New Quest for the Historical Jesus*, 13. Bornkamm also laid out in chapter three of *Jesus of Nazareth*, according to Robinson (16), an "attempt to describe the human *impression* Jesus made upon people in a way clearly suggestive of the meaning Jesus has for faith, as if a human contact with Jesus were—at least potentially—an encounter with the *kerygma*." Somewhat interesting is Robinson's word "impression," which in context functions as a sort of bridge between Jesus and the faith of his first followers. This is not unlike Dunn's own methodological use of "impact" in *Jesus Remembered*, 329, which likewise functions as a bridge between the historical Jesus and apostolic teaching. Robinson seems to anticipate present discussion of "impact" and "memory." Concerning memory, he writes that early Christians "responded to [their] situation by intuitively explicating their memory until they found in it the *kerygma*, i.e., by 'kerygmatizing' their memory" (Robinson, *New Quest for the Historical Jesus*, 86). Scholars, such as Byrskog who focuses on autopsy, have recognized the importance of a narrativizing component in the telling of history (*Story as History—History as Story*, 222–23).

74. Robinson, *New Quest for the Historical Jesus*, 88; cf. 85–92.

75. Robinson, *New Quest for the Historical Jesus*, 86.

observe "Jesus 'born of a woman, born under the law.'"[76] (Robinson refers here to historical criticism and history as *bruta facta*.)

It is important to stop and note once again that the historiographical task following Bultmann significantly shifted, specifically given Bultmann's unique challenges to Jesus questers in understanding Jesus to have been eclipsed entirely by early Christian preaching. And with this shift in task came a shift in methodology. In pointing to the criteriology of Käsemann and other New Questers, Robinson writes:

> For a new and promising point of departure has been worked out by precisely those scholars who are most acutely aware of the difficulties of the previous quest. As a matter of fact this new development is recognized in its full significance only when one observes that it forms a central thrust in a second, "post-Bultmannian" phase of post-war German theology.[77]

NORMAN PERRIN

Another scholar closely associated with the New Quest is Norman Perrin. Perrin, who studied at the German University of Göttingen for his doctorate, described the post-Bultmannian developments as follows:

> The issues which were taken up most immediately and most vigorously in the subsequent discussion were, rather, those of the question of the continuity between the Christ of the kerygma and the historical Jesus, and of the significance of an existentialist view of history in connection with the "problem of the historical Jesus."[78]

Perrin also explains the significance of Käsemann's essay, "The Problem of the Historical Jesus," as follows:

> In his essay, "Das Problem des historischen Jesus," he sounded a warning about the danger of a position in which there was not a real and material continuity between the historical Jesus and the kerygmatic Christ: the danger

---

76. Robinson, *New Quest for the Historical Jesus*, 86–87 (a reference to Gal 4:4).
77. Robinson, *New Quest for the Historical Jesus*, 10. Later (14), Robinson notes that Bornkamm's "divergences [from Bultmann] express the newly awakened concern for the message and conduct of Jesus in their relation to the *kerygma*."
78. Norman Perrin, *Rediscovering the Teaching of Jesus* (New York: Harper & Row, 1976), 226.

of falling into Docetism, or of having faith degenerate into a mere mysticism or moralism.[79]

Notable here is Perrin's understanding of New Questers as affirming a historical Jesus who exists in continuity with early Christian proclamation. This is, again, a theological turn that was taken in order to advance upon previous questers who had sought methodologically to differentiate Jesus from the kerygma.

Perrin additionally noted that, like Käsemann, he accepted the burden of proof in Jesus questing. Perrin explicitly states that "if we are to ascribe a saying to Jesus, *and accept the burden of proof laid upon us*, we must be able to show that the saying comes neither from the church nor from ancient Judaism."[80] And further corroborating the arguments of this present essay, Perrin carefully explains what he intends by the criterion of dissimilarity from Judaism:

> The earliest form of a saying we can reach may be regarded as authentic if it can be shown to be dissimilar to *characteristic* emphases both of ancient Judaism and of the early Church . . . [81]

He continues:

> The teaching of Jesus was set in the context of ancient Judaism, and *in many respects that teaching must have been variations on themes from the religious life of ancient Judaism. But if we are to seek that which is most characteristic of Jesus,* it will be found not in the teachings which he shares with his contemporaries, but in *the things wherein he differs from them.*[82]

Evident from these two quotes by Perrin is his concern to illumine, or accentuate, Jesus's teaching against the background of his contemporaries and the more common, or characteristic, practices of Judaism. The idea is to recognize how

---

79. Perrin, *Rediscovering the Teaching of Jesus*, 226. Perrin makes explicit his support for the continuity concern of New Questers on p. 234.

80. Perrin, *Rediscovering the Teaching of Jesus*, 39.

81. Perrin, *Rediscovering the Teaching of Jesus*, 39 (emphasis added). By emphasizing a contrast with the characteristic practices of Judaism, Perrin's criteriology proves somewhat innocuous to objections concerning the need for exhaustive knowledge of Jesus's Jewish context, and to charges of distancing Jesus from Judaism. Note Porter, *Criteria of Authenticity in Historical Jesus Research*, 74 and n22; Dunn, *Jesus Remembered*, 82–83, citing Morna Hooker, "Christology and Methodology," *NTS* 17 (1970): 480–87; also Hooker, "On Using the Wrong Tool," *Theology* 75 (1972): 570–81.

82. Perrin, *Rediscovering the Teaching of Jesus*, 39 (emphasis added).

Jesus's teachings stand out within his context—not what makes Jesus opposed to the religion of Judaism.[83] While the criterion could lend itself hazardously to anti-Jewish prejudices and accommodate egregious agendas, it does not appear that the New Questers cited in the present essay were concerned with such aims.[84] Perrin cites Joachim Jeremias's work on Jesus's formulaic use of "Amen, I say to you" as an example of dissimilarity. While the saying is "a feature of the teaching style of Jesus," it is common to Judaism as well. Dissimilarity is seen in the unique manner that Jesus employs the phrase, as an introduction to teaching, rather than, more commonly, a conclusion.[85] Again, Perrin's dissimilarity is not of the sort that envisions Jesus against Judaism, but more a sincere effort to identify Jesus's uniqueness within his continuity with Judaism.

CONCLUDING THOUGHTS

The foregoing analysis is not intended to adopt the New Quest's vision of the historical Jesus, nor an antiquated adoption of its criteriology outside of recent advances. Nor has it attempted to discredit all of Keith's concerns about criteria, or revive the spirit of Second Questers. It is, however, intended to observe more carefully the points of discontinuity between the New Quest and what came before it. Bultmann himself understood this, and explicitly responded to his students in his essay "The Primitive Christian Kerygma and the Historical Jesus."[86] While it is easy from our own historical vantage point to identify continuity between Bultmann and the continued influence of form criticism in the work of New Questers, Käsemann's theological turn was taken seriously in his day.[87] While Bultmannian form criticism had nigh established as dogma

---

83. See the helpful analysis by Theissen and Winter, *Quest for the Plausible Jesus*, 131. The goal of dissimilarity in Perrin's thought is to reveal "what is distinctive in Judaism or the church." Theissen and Winter cite here from Perrin's *What is Redaction Criticism?* (Philadelphia: Fortress, 1969), 71.

84. See Dagmar Winter's noted research in "Saving the Quest for Authenticity from the Criterion of Dissimilarity: History and Plausibility," in Keith and Le Donne, *Jesus, Criteria, and the Demise of Authenticity*, 120n16. Meier, *Marginal Jew*, 5:15, continues to affirm the criterion: "While I agree that we should be very suspicious of a historical Jesus who is strikingly discontinuous from the Judaism of his time and place, there are cases where the question of discontinuity from Jewish views of the time legitimately—indeed, even necessarily—arises as one sifts the Jesus tradition for a historical core."

85. Perrin, *Rediscovering the Teaching of Jesus*, 38.

86. Bultmann, "Primitive Christian Kerygma and the Historical Jesus," 15: "Today the situation is reversed. The emphasis lies on elaborating the unity of the historical Jesus and the Christ of the kerygma." And pp. 20–21: "There are two types of attempts at going beyond the 'that' and at demonstrating the continuity between the historical Jesus and the kerygma as a material agreement." (With Käsemann's work explicitly cited.) Bultmann is arguing against his former students' attempt to maintain historical continuity. See Baird, *History of New Testament Research*, 3:124–25n155.

87. Note the importance posited by Stephen Neill and Tom Wright, *The Interpretation of the New Testament, 1861–1986* (Oxford: Oxford University Press, 2003), 288–91.

the declaration that the historical Jesus was meaningless for the kerygma,[88] Bultmann's students boldly asserted Jesus as a historical person, accessible to the critical historian both through and in continuity with the kerygma. [89] New Testament scholar Richard Bauckham presents the transition from early form criticism to the criteria of authenticity as follows:

> *Those who looked at it theologically* were not so sure as Bultmann that Christian faith needed to know nothing about the Jesus who lived in Palestine except that he existed. *But the form critical view of the way the Gospel traditions reached the Gospels hindered a new quest.* Because the tradition was supposed to be oriented to the present and unconcerned with the preservation of Jesus traditions, anything of historical value would have survived in spite of the tendencies of the tradition. So extremely rigorous criteria were needed to identify "authentic" material. [. . .]. This was the situation that the "criteria of authenticity" were designed to meet.[90]

It should be clear that it is no longer permissible to speak of New Quest historiography outside of the explicitly stated historical concerns of New Questers for continuity. Even in the case of the criterion of dissimilarity, historians continue to labor for continuity with early Christian teachings and continuity with known Jewish practices. This careful focal point has been blurred by recent critics who aim to explain New Quest historiography only in terms of an erroneous view of dissimilarity or who otherwise prove a vacuous contextual understanding as to how dissimilarity was methodologically tuned to include a specific nuance for continuity.

In closing this discussion, a few summarizing points are in order. First, while early form criticism was concerned with both the historicity of gospel tradition and the tradition's oral character in its more primitive stages, such concerns were worked out in the now discredited folklorist-influenced theories of tradition transmission. Second, Bultmann's form criticism was overly skeptical of gospel

---

88. Neill and Wright observe that the impossibility of Jesus questing handed down by Bultmann was "regarded as almost canonical for a quarter of a century" (*Interpretation of the New Testament*, 291).

89. Reginald Fuller further sought to advance upon the idea of continuity between the historical Jesus and the kerygma. At the outset of his work *The Foundations of New Testament Christology*, he explicitly states it as his goal to affirm such a Jesus: "As we shall see, he had his own self-understanding. But the church's Christology never consisted in simply repeating that self-understanding—although, as we shall seek to show, *there is a direct line of continuity between Jesus' self-understanding and the church's christological interpretation* of him" (Reginald H. Fuller, *The Foundations of New Testament Christology* [New York: Scribner's, 1965], 15 [emphasis added]).

90. Bauckham, "Gospels as Testimony to Jesus Christ," 58 (emphasis added).

traditions, and this can be observed in his historiography of methodological doubt. In the work of Bultmann, the historical Jesus becomes unnecessary for Christian teaching, a simple datum only presupposed by but not meaningfully essential to kerygmatic proclamation. In docetic fashion, Bultmann claimed that there was no possibility of Jesus questing despite envisaging the existence of a primitive oral tradition that potentially pointed to him. Third, beginning with Käsemann, the New Quest sought in a fundamental manner to change course from Bultmann, specifically by seeking a Jesus in continuity with the Gospels. New Questers should not be seen as maintaining the same program of form criticism. A fair amount of research was provided validating this claim. Much of recent discussion over the criteria of authenticity would be served better by appreciating the discontinuity between Bultmann and his students. Relatedly, despite Keith's interest in portraying the criteria as wholly dependent upon a form-critical framework, it was observed in Käsemann's programmatic essay that his corrective criteriology is informed by a second pole, that of First Quest histories. Recognizing this is important, since it proves troublesome for Keith's indebtedness claim.

Fourth and lastly, the logic of Perrin's dissimilarity criterion is clear: If a tradition cannot be attributed to a presumed inventive early church, and it can be shown to have continuity with Jesus's Jewish context—but also an identifiable uniqueness—then such traditions are likely from Jesus and are, as in the words of Käsemann, "more or less safe ground" regarding authenticity. As long as there exists skepticism over the Gospels' historicity, and irrespective of form criticism's failure, there remains an abiding, even welcoming, place for the criteria of authenticity. The criterion of dissimilarity aids sensibly in establishing a reliable portrait of the historical Jesus *specifically where* skepticism abounds concerning the early Christians as preservers of Jesus tradition.

Part Two

■ ■ ■

The Gospels and the
Historical Jesus

CHAPTER 4

Textual Criticism and the Criterion of Embarrassment

DANIEL B. WALLACE

INTRODUCTION

Almost a half century ago, like a lone voice crying in the wilderness, Morna Hooker protested the validity of the criteria of authenticity in her article, "Christology and Methodology."[1] She expanded this a year later in "On Using the Wrong Tool."[2] Here, she lays out one of the fundamental objections to the optimistic use of these criteria, namely, that it masks its prejudices with an air of objectivity: "Any attempt at reconstructing what lies behind our gospels is highly speculative, and will in large measure reflect our own presuppositions about the material."[3]

The notion that presuppositions govern methods is nothing new. Hooker's insight echoes what Catholic modernist George Tyrrell had claimed about Adolf von Harnack's reconstruction of the life of Jesus: "The Christ that Harnack sees, looking back through nineteen centuries of Catholic darkness, is only the reflection of a Liberal Protestant face, seen at the bottom of a deep well."[4]

Perhaps the most extreme example of such prejudices can be found in Germany in the first half of the twentieth century. The criterion of dissimilarity was reinforced by the anti-Semitism that found its apex in the Nazi state. In 1899, Houston Stewart Chamberlain published his highly influential *Die Grundlagen*

---

1. Morna D. Hooker, "Christology and Methodology," *NTS* 17 (1970–71): 480–87. She laments that her "criticisms were dismissed or ignored by scholars who were wedded to the use of such criteria" (idem, "Foreword: Forty Years On," in *Jesus, Criteria, and the Demise of Authenticity*, ed. Chris Keith and Anthony Le Donne [London: T&T Clark, 2012], xiii).
2. Morna D. Hooker, "On Using the Wrong Tool," *Theology* 75 (1972): 570–81.
3. Hooker, "On Using the Wrong Tool," 580.
4. George Tyrrell, *Christianity at the Cross-roads* (London: Longmans, 1909), 44.

des neunzehnten Jahrhunderts, a racist work that claimed, *inter alia*, that Jesus was not a Jew.[5] As nonsensical as this viewpoint was, it nevertheless gained some traction within German higher criticism. Walter Grundmann, a card-carrying Nazi and assistant to Gerhard Kittel on the *Theologisches Wörterbuch*, took up the same stance; Paul Fiebig and Gerhard Kittel were also some of the more outspoken anti-Judaic voices in the ranks of NT scholars in this period of history.

According to Maurice Casey, the "no quest" lull (between Schweitzer's *Quest of the Historical Jesus*[6] and Käsemann's "Das Problem des historischen Jesus"[7]) was, in reality, the "phase of the quest as the most crucial because it is the most illuminating."[8] Casey argues that the tentacles of the Nazi mindset reached far beyond World War II when he speaks of the "*social function* of the work of Bultmann and others": "The *effect* of their radical criticism was to ensure that out from under the synoptic Gospels there could never crawl a Jewish man."[9] This is implicit in his views on the Jesus Seminar, which is "going off the rails altogether"[10] because it presents a non-Jewish Jesus.[11] Not all see the anti-Semitic attitude in Germany as quite so influential on NT scholarship,[12] but it does seem to be the case that part of the impulse for the criterion of dissimilarity, as practiced by more than a few scholars, is a subconscious distancing of Jesus from Judaism because of certain cultural values.[13]

---

5. Houston Stewart Chamberlain, *Die Grundlagen des neunzehnten Jahrhunderts*, 2 vols. (Munich: Bruckmann, 1899).

6. Albert Schweitzer, *The Quest of the Historical Jesus: A Critical Study of Its Progress from Reimarus to Wrede* (London: Black, 1910), the English translation of Schweitzer's quest-ending book first published in 1906.

7. Ernst Käsemann, "Das Problem des historischen Jesus," a lecture delivered in 1953 and published the next year (*ZTK* 51 [1954]: 125–53).

8. Maurice Casey, "Where Wright is Wrong: A Critical Review of N. T. Wright's *Jesus and the Victory of God*," *JSNT* 69 (1998): 95–103 (here 96).

9. Maurice Casey, *Jesus of Nazareth: An Independent Historian's Account of His Life and Teaching* (London: T&T Clark, 2010), 11. His section, *The Nazi Period* (4–9), argues that during the so-called "no quest" period there was a strongly Germanic focus on the uniqueness of Jesus, in particular his distinction from anything Jewish.

10. Casey, "Where Wright Is Wrong," 97. Although he does not mention the Jesus Seminar in this place, he sets the table for his agenda when he lambastes the Jesus Seminar at the beginning of his article, noting that Wright's book is "infinitely better than anything to emerge from the American Jesus Seminar" (ibid., 95).

11. Casey, *Jesus of Nazareth*, 18–22. Here he also criticizes John Dominic Crossan for succumbing to the social environment in which Crossan finds himself, resulting in a Jesus who "does not emerge as a plausible first-century Jewish leader" (20).

12. For a historical overview of this influence, see Peter M. Head, "The Nazi Quest for an Aryan Jesus," *JSHJ* 2.1 (2004): 55–89. Though Head judiciously avoids the *post hoc propter hoc* fallacy, he nevertheless perceptively submits, "One way in which Grundmann is paradigmatic for the whole Quest would be that he exhibits in an outstanding manner the way in which assumptions and biases arising from the scholar's own social and religious setting do shape and *can* determine the outcome of any investigation into the historical Jesus" (88).

13. In this regard, E. P. Sanders's contribution to our understanding of the historical Jesus can hardly be overestimated. As Casey notes concerning Sanders's overall agenda seen in *Jesus and Judaism*, *The Historical Figure of Jesus*, and *Paul and Palestinian Judaism*, "one of Sanders's first tasks was to demolish Christian prejudices about Judaism" (Casey, *Jesus of Nazareth*, 15).

As Tyrrell did a century ago, another Catholic scholar, Francis Schüssler Fiorenza, has argued that the quest for Jesus is often skewed by anti-Catholic bias: "When I began graduate studies, it was commonly accepted in New Testament studies that in addition to multiple attestation by independent sources, a saying probably went back to the historical Jesus if its origin could be traced neither to Judaism nor to the early Church. . . . What does this rule mean? It means quite simply: if one can show that a statement is at the very same time both anti-Jewish and anti-Roman Catholic, then, behold, *ecco*, one has shown it to be an authentic saying of Jesus."[14]

The prejudices are not only anti-Semitic and anti-Catholic. Theissen and Merz note that even in the popular mind Jesus is fashioned in the interpreter's image, in which they see him as "the great brother," "the forerunner of socialism," an existentialist, a "Galilean artist who had the art of living," the hero of those who oppose institutionalized religion.[15] Even in the scholarly imagination, he is a cynic philosopher, friend of all mankind, political troublemaker, a mistaken apocalyptic visionary, empathetic rabbi, the Messiah, God incarnate. These views are all conditioned—at least to some degree—by the prejudices and pre-suppositions of the exegete.[16]

It is this state of affairs that has caused a small but growing cadre of academics to line up with Hooker and jettison the legitimacy of the authenticity touch-stones altogether. Most notably, we see this attitude in the 2012 multi-author volume, *Jesus, Criteria, and the Demise of Authenticity*, which includes essays by such luminaries as Dale Allison, Scot McKnight, Morna Hooker, and Mark Goodacre. Several others, including Helen Bond and Stanley Porter, have also raised their voices against the historicity tests of the third quest. This chapter focuses on just one criterion that has hardly been jostled in the debates, and how it relates to the text of the Gospels.

---

14. Francis Schüssler Fiorenza, "The Jesus of Piety and the Historical Jesus," *CTSA Proceedings* 49 (1994): 95 (whole article, 90–99). His equating of the "early Church" with Roman Catholicism, however, is a curious anachronism. See also Anthony Le Donne, "The Rise of the Quest for an Authentic Jesus: An Introduction to the Crumbling Foundations of Jesus Research," in Keith and Le Donne, *Jesus, Criteria, and the Demise of Authenticity*, 3–21 (here 7): "In order to establish Jesus as the great originator of Christianity (really, as the archetype of German Protestantism) it was necessary to establish his original teachings." Note, too, Allison's point: "It is our expectations that largely determine how we use the criteria. We can always find parallels when we need them to exclude material, and we can always find differences when we want to authenticate material. Tools do not dictate how they are used; the hands that hold them do that" (Dale C. Allison Jr., "It Don't Come Easy: A History of Disillusionment," in Keith and Le Donne, *Jesus, Criteria, and the Demise of Authenticity*, 186–99, here 197).

15. Gerd Theissen and Annette Merz, *The Historical Jesus: A Comprehensive Guide* (Minneapolis: Fortress, 1998), 2.

16. Even Bultmann himself admitted that presuppositionless exegesis is not possible. Rudolf Bultmann, "Is Exegesis Without Presuppositions Possible?," in *Existence and Faith: Shorter Writings of Rudolf Bultmann* (New York: Meridian, 1960), 289–96.

THE CRITERION OF EMBARRASSMENT

On a continuum of disillusion with the authenticity principles, the criterion of dissimilarity gets pummeled the most. Much of this is due to the cultural baggage of some of the practitioners, as noted above. But it is also because all this criterion can produce is an *eccentric* Jesus. If the man from Nazareth had been completely unlike the Judaism of his day and unlike the early Christ-followers, he would have been an extreme outlier who had neither learned from his roots nor impacted his devotees. No wonder liberal Protestantism gravitated toward this imaginary iconoclast! But in that first-century milieu, such a Jesus simply would not have been understood.

On the other end of the spectrum, the embarrassment yardstick has received minimal criticism. This criterion, in the words of John P. Meier,

> focuses on actions or sayings of Jesus that would have embarrassed or created difficulty for the early Church. The point of the criterion is that the early Church would hardly have gone out of its way to create material that only embarrassed its creator or weakened its position in arguments with opponents. Rather, embarrassing material coming from Jesus would naturally be either suppressed or softened in later stages of the Gospel tradition, and often such progressive suppression or softening can be traced through the Four Gospels.[17]

Meier has laid out some of the most detailed analysis and defense of the criteria for authenticity to date.[18] And first on his list of primary criteria is *embarrassment*.[19] Significantly, this touchstone is neither critiqued nor even mentioned in Hooker's two influential articles, nor in her "Forty Years On" foreword to *Jesus, Criteria, and the Demise of Authenticity*. Furthermore, in her commentary on Mark, Hooker even implies that later Gospels were embarrassed by the baptism

---

17. John P. Meier, *The Roots of the Problem and the Person*, vol. 1 of *A Marginal Jew: Rethinking the Historical Jesus*, ABRL (New York: Doubleday, 1991), 168.

18. Meier, *Roots of the Problem and the Person*, 167–95.

19. The criterion of embarrassment is also found prominently on other lists, such as those by Robert H. Stein, "The 'Criteria' for Authenticity," in *Studies of History and Tradition in the Four Gospels*, vol. 1 of *Gospel Perspectives*, ed. R. T. France and David Wenham (Sheffield: JSOT Press, 1980), calling it "*Divergent Patterns from the Redaction*," 247; Craig A. Evans, "Authenticity Criteria in Life of Jesus Research," *Christian Scholars Review* 19 (1989): 18–19 ("Tradition Contrary to Editorial Tendency"); Theissen and Merz, *Historical Jesus*, 117, labeling it "the criterion of 'resistance to the tradition'"; Bruce J. Malina, "Criteria for Assessing the Authentic Words of Jesus: Some Specifications," *Authenticating the Words of Jesus*, ed. Bruce Chilton and Craig A. Evans (Leiden: Brill, 2002), 27–28; Darrell L. Bock and Robert L. Webb, eds., *Key Events in the Life of the Historical Jesus: A Collaborative Exploration of Context and Coherence* (Grand Rapids: Eerdmans, 2009), passim; Casey, *Jesus of Nazareth*, 104–105.

of Jesus, later scribes were embarrassed by the anger of Jesus, and later Christians were embarrassed by Jesus's equating Peter with Satan.[20] Thus, even Hooker sees a place for embarrassment as a historical criterion. In Allison's article, "How to Marginalize the Traditional Criteria of Authenticity," he offers his critique of the embarrassment index in only one and a half pages.[21] Stanley Porter gives a more sustained treatment,[22] but he errs in claiming, without qualification, that "this criterion is a specific form of the criterion of double dissimilarity."[23] In reality, even though there is some overlap between these two authenticity principles, embarrassment is often *against* dissimilarity. How is an angry Jesus out of sorts with Second Temple Judaism, or a Jesus who is baptized by John alienated from the repentant remnant awaiting the kingdom of God? Even Anthony Le Donne, one of the editors of *Jesus, Criteria, and the Demise of Authenticity*, found this criterion not only valid but "among the stronger arguments."[24]

ARGUMENTS AGAINST EMBARRASSMENT

Arguments from Matthean Priority

Cases against the embarrassment canon have come from other corners, too. Those who hold to the Griesbach hypothesis tone down the difficult passages in Mark in relation to their parallels in Matthew. William Farmer, the leading twentieth-century advocate of Griesbach, interacted at length with "the Abbott-Streeter Linguistic Argument for Markan Priority."[25] Almost all of the passages discussed here would fit the criterion of embarrassment (though it was not called this at the time).[26] Of course, because he embraced Matthean priority, he could not see Mark's pericopae as somehow embarrassing to a "later" Matthew.

---

20. Morna D. Hooker, *The Gospel According to Saint Mark*, BNTC (Peabody, MA: Hendrickson, 1997), 44, 79–80, 207.

21. Dale C. Allison Jr., "How to Marginalize the Traditional Criteria of Authenticity," in *Handbook for the Study of the Historical Jesus*, 4 vols., ed. Tom Holmén and Stanley E. Porter (Leiden: Brill, 2011), 1:5–7 (whole essay, 1:3–30).

22. Stanley E. Porter, *The Criteria for Authenticity in Historical-Jesus Research: Previous Discussion and New Proposals*, JSNTSup 191 (London: T&T Clark, 2000), 106–10.

23. Porter, *Criteria for Authenticity in Historical-Jesus Research*, 110. Tom Holmén offers some rationale for combining the two criteria (Tom Holmén, "Doubts about Double Dissimilarity: Restructuring the Main Criterion of Jesus-of-History Research," in Chilton and Evans, *Authenticating the Words of Jesus*, 75–76). But see Fernando Bermejo-Rubio, "Changing Methods, Disturbing Material: Should the Criterion of Embarrassment be Dismissed in Jesus Research?," *Revue des études juives* 175 (2016): 1–25 (here 5–6).

24. Anthony Le Donne, *The Historiographical Jesus: Memory, Typology, and the Son of David* (Waco, TX: Baylor University Press, 2009), 89.

25. William R. Farmer, *The Synoptic Problem: A Critical Analysis* (Macon, GA: Mercer, 1976), 159–69, referring to Edwin A. Abbott and Burnett Hillman Streeter.

26. Farmer discusses, in order, Mark 6:5; 1:32, 34; 3:20; 10:35; 15:44; 3:15; 8:24; 11:21; and 16:4, and the parallels in Matthew and Luke. Only Mark 15:44 and 16:4 would not be examples of embarrassment as far as the criterion is defined.

The dismissal of this criterion for Griesbach followers is systemic. But are the arguments convincing?

Consider Farmer's treatment of Mark 6:5. He compares this text ("he *could* not do any miracle there, except . . ." [οὐκ ἐδύνατο ἐκεῖ ποιῆσαι οὐδεμίαν δύναμιν, εἰ μή]) with Matthew 13:58 ("he *did* not do many miracles there" [οὐκ ἐποίησεν ἐκεῖ δυνάμεις πολλάς]), claiming that Jesus's *inability* in Mark[27] is really no different from his *inactivity* in Matthew. Luke omits the statement altogether. Farmer concludes, "the passage offers no clear indication that Luke has 'excised' or that Matthew has 'toned down' a phrase in Mark which might cause offense or suggest difficulties . . ."[28] An argument from silence about Luke is one thing, but his claim against Matthew toning down Mark's statement rings hollow.

Along the same lines, Farmer explains the differences in Mark 1:32, 34 where Jesus healed *many* of the sick who were brought to him, with Matthew 8:16 where he healed *all* (so also Luke 4:40). Farmer claims that the "many" in Mark 1:34 are a *part* of "the whole city" in v. 33 and does not have as its "immediate antecedent" the "all" in v. 32.[29] Though possible, this understanding is unlikely because of the repetition of "who were sick" (vv. 32, 34) with the single alteration being "all" vs. "many": ἔφερον πρὸς αὐτὸν πάντας τοὺς κακῶς ἔχοντας ("they began bringing *all* who were sick" [v. 32]), followed by ἐθεράπευσεν πολλοὺς κακῶς ἔχοντας ("he healed *many* who were sick" [v. 34]).[30] There remains this significant difference in the two healing accounts in Mark and Matthew that cannot be reconciled in this manner. Whether the "many" is meant to equal the "all" will be handled later, but here we simply point out that Matthew 8:16 and Luke 4:40 reword the text so as to leave no doubt that all were healed.

The double problem of the healing of the blind man in Mark 8:22–26 is particularly vexing for Farmer. First, Luke and Matthew omit this healing story *and* the healing of the deaf man in chapter 7—the *only* two healings in Mark omitted by *both* Matthew and Luke, which, not coincidentally, are the only two healings in the Synoptics that involve spittle. The other problem is that in the second pericope Jesus's expectoration into the face of the blind man was not entirely successful, requiring a second touch. Farmer dismisses this by linking the Mark 7 healing with that in Mark 8: since the earlier healing was a single act, this could not be the reason why Matthew and Luke chose to omit *both* of these stories. So this leaves just the use of spittle to be accounted for. Farmer then asks,

---

27. Yet Mark's statement is emphasized by his double negative (οὐκ . . . οὐδεμίαν).

28. Farmer, *Synoptic Problem*, 160.

29. Farmer, *Synoptic Problem*, 162.

30. See later discussion.

"Did both Matthew and Luke have an aversion to the use of saliva in healing stories about Jesus? There is no reason to think so, for so far as is known such stories were not regarded as offensive *in any sense*."[31]

This is simply not the case, especially when it involved an unanticipated volley into the visage. After canvassing the uses of spittle in the Jewish world of late antiquity, Sarah Bourgeois notes that the Hebrew Bible, Mishnah, Dead Sea Scrolls, and the Talmud reveal disgust, even abhorrence, at expectoration in general, and view spitting on another person as an act of shaming and disrespect.[32] It is not until the Talmud that we see saliva mentioned somewhat frequently in a therapeutic manner. Expanding the scope to also include Greco-Roman literature, Bourgeois finds *no real parallels to Mark 8*, even in later therapeutic texts.[33] It is hardly the case, therefore, that the use of spittle and the manner of delivery would not be regarded as offensive. The healing of the blind man in Mark thus stands solidly as an instance of embarrassment for the readers of his day and apparently for the other evangelists as well.

Peter Head's Christological Argument

On different grounds, Peter Head diminishes the difficulties of many passages in Mark that deal with Christology. He argues for *Markan* priority, but his approach is to downplay the differences between the Synoptics, especially contending that Matthew was *not* embarrassed by Mark's Christology—a Christology that focuses more on Jesus's emotions, inability, and ignorance than does

---

31. Farmer, *Synoptic Problem*, 167 (emphasis added).

32. Sarah L. Bourgeois, "Mark 8:22–26: Jesus and the Use of Spittle in a Two-Stage Healing" (ThM thesis, Dallas Theological Seminary, 1999).

33. Bourgeois, "Mark 8:22–26." The second chapter, "The Use of Spittle in the Ancient World" (7–33), examines Egyptian, Greco-Roman, and Jewish literature from the thirteenth century BCE down through the Amoraic era. Regarding the Jewish materials, Num 12:14 alludes to the disgrace that a father might bring upon his wayward daughter by befouling her face with his spit. Job speaks of the scorn heaped on him when people spit in his face (17:6; 30:10). The Mishnah demands a large fine of four hundred zuz when one man's spittle lands on another (m. B. Qam. 8.6). Members of the Sanhedrin condemned Jesus with fists and spit to the face (Mark 14:65).

In chapter 3 (34–52), Bourgeois examines all potential parallels. Two are of note. The one parallel that Farmer claims is "*especially*" relevant is that of Vespasian healing a blind man with his spittle (recorded by Tacitus, *Hist.* 4.81 and Suetonius, *Ves.* 7.2–3). See Bourgeois, "Mark 8:22–26," 38–41, where she discerns several differences, including Vespasian's initial resistance to the use of his saliva, the magical overtones of the passage, and the lack of expectoration. All this renders the so-called parallel unconvincing.

Among Jewish sources, y. Sotah 1.4 in the Palestinian Talmud is frequently enlisted. It tells the story of a wife suspected of acting inappropriately with a rabbi. Her husband instructs her to spit in the rabbi's face before she may return home. Through an elaborate scheme, the rabbi's *public* reputation remains unsullied and the marriage is salvaged because the woman spits in his face as though she were doing a magic charm. The parallels are superficial. As Bourgeois notes, "In reality, the woman's act of spitting is viewed by the rabbi, the woman, the rabbi's disciples, and the husband as a way of humiliating the rabbi. The fact that the rabbi could make the act of spitting appear to be a magical healing enabled him to avoid public disgrace" (Bourgeois, "Mark 8:22–26," 43–44).

Matthew's. Head's essential approach is constructive, and he views Matthew as "a developer rather than a corrector of Mark."[34] He concludes that *"the 'traditional' christological argument for Markan priority is fatally flawed."*[35] Though the reviews have been positive overall, both Moule and Tuckett see Head's approach as "somewhat 'overhyped' and exaggerated" and that Head's conclusion about the fatal flaw in traditional arguments for Markan priority "goes far beyond what the nature of the evidence will allow."[36]

One of Head's complaints is that the arguments in exegetical literature for Markan priority on the basis of Jesus's emotions "exhibit a common weakness in simply listing the relevant passages, without any critical discussion."[37] But he commits this same error in his handling of Matthew 24:36; he mentions it half a dozen times but nowhere does he offer a detailed treatment of this verse, nor even discuss its textual problem.[38]

To be sure, although source criticism is helpful in identifying the oldest literary strata for the Gospels, this is not the same as claiming historicity.[39] Determining which Gospel was the source for the others does not necessarily imply its historical accuracy. But the argument from embarrassment may do just that since the embarrassing feature in a given pericope is either out of sync with the evangelist's redactional agenda or is altered by a later author. Embarrassment is often the residue of a well-established tradition that makes its way into the written text. Head, however, rejects this as a legitimate criterion,[40] weakening his argument for Markan priority and potentially setting aside evidence of genuine historical data in the earliest stratum.

Rafael Rodriguez's Critique

What at first blush appears to be one of the most sustained arguments against the canon of embarrassment is Rafael Rodriguez's "The Embarrassing Truth about Jesus: The Criterion of Embarrassment and the Failure of Historical Authenticity."[41] The first half of his chapter defines the criterion and offers a

---

34. Peter M. Head, *Christology and the Synoptic Problem: An Argument for Markan Priority*, SNTMS 94 (Cambridge: Cambridge University Press, 1997), i.

35. Head, *Christology and the Synoptic Problem*, 259 (emphasis original).

36. C. M. Tuckett, "Review of Peter Head, *Christology and the Synoptic Problem*," *NovT* 41 (1999): 396. C. F. D. Moule asks whether Head "give[s] too little weight to the assumptions of the Oxford Seminar" and opines, "it still seems a plausible assumption that successive redactors should tend (however dangerously docetic it may be) to show Christ as in full control of circumstances and without weakness or ignorance" ("Review of Peter Head, *Christology and the Synoptic Problem*," *JTS* 49 [1998]: 741).

37. Head, *Christology and the Synoptic Problem*, 100.

38. We will return to this passage later.

39. Head, *Christology and the Synoptic Problem*, 46.

40. Head, *Christology and the Synoptic Problem*, 117, 120.

41. Rafael Rodriguez, "The Embarrassing Truth about Jesus: The Criterion of Embarrassment and the

few key examples that scholars have detected in the Gospels.[42] This is followed by *Why the Criterion of Embarrassment Cannot Deliver Authenticity*. After what appear to be palpably weak arguments offered by other scholars,[43] Rodriguez admits, "In the end, I am not persuaded by any of these revisionist reconstructions."[44] The section was just a teaser, it seems, culminating in Rodriguez's own very brief take on why these gospel narratives were not embarrassing.[45] The final section before the conclusion, *The Embarrassing Truth about Our Criterion*, is almost as short.[46] Here, there is more stylistic flair than substantive reasoning. To find the author's arguments against the criterion requires careful sifting of the entire chapter. These arguments are addressed in the next section ("Counterarguments"). In Rodriguez's conclusion we see his overarching critique of the embarrassment benchmark: "Historians of Jesus never should have turned to isolating historical data apart from the larger historical representations of which those data are a part . . ."[47] There is some validity to this argument, which this essay hopes to address—at least in part.

COUNTERARGUMENTS ON BEHALF OF THE EMBARRASSMENT CRITERION

Bermejo-Rubio's Counterarguments

Recently, the embarrassment principle has received a thorough defense in Fernando Bermejo-Rubio's article, "Changing Methods, Disturbing Material."[48] He addresses the various criticisms against this criterion with penetrating acuity.[49]

First, even assuming the demise of form criticism as a legitimate enterprise, "the criterion of embarrassment seems to be independent, both historically and logically, from any particular approach."[50] Thus, many of the arguments against

---

Failure of Historical Authenticity," in Keith and Le Donne, *Jesus, Criteria, and the Demise of Authenticity,* 132–51.

42. After an introduction (Rodriguez, "Embarrassing Truth about Jesus," 132–33), these two sections comprise almost eight pages (134–41).

43. Rodriguez, "Embarrassing Truth about Jesus," 141–44. This section focuses on Jesus's baptism, the Pharisees' accusation of Jesus as being demon-possessed, and the portrayal of the disciples. Rodriguez discusses the treatments on these motifs/events by Leif Vaage, William Arnal (Jesus's baptism), Michael Humphries (demon possession), Theodore Weeden, and Werner Kelber (disciples' portrayal).

44. Rodriguez, "Embarrassing Truth about Jesus," 145.

45. Rodriguez, "Embarrassing Truth about Jesus," 145–46, one and a quarter pages long.

46. Rodriguez, "Embarrassing Truth about Jesus," 146–48, less than two pages.

47. Rodriguez, "Embarrassing Truth about Jesus," 149.

48. Bermejo-Rubio, "Changing Methods, Disturbing Material," 1–25.

49. Bermejo-Rubio, "Changing Methods, Disturbing Material," 4–9. Throughout the article, Bermejo-Rubio deals in particular with Rodriguez's writings.

50. Bermejo-Rubio, "Changing Methods, Disturbing Material," 4. The argument is on 4–5.

the criteria of authenticity become irrelevant when it comes to embarrassment. (Bermejo-Rubio also makes the case that although it has been argued that embarrassment is simply a subset of dissimilarity, the two, though often overlapping, are not identical.)[51]

Second, to the objection that the difficult material was surely not *that* difficult or else it would have been expunged from the record, he reasons that it is likely that many of these pericopae were either too well known or "had such a pedigree" that they could not be athetized. In some cases, such a story might be "consciously included for apologetic purposes, in order to neutralize it and thereby counter anti-Christian polemics."[52]

Third, Bermejo-Rubio adds a "complementary" point: "The fact that an element is included in a text does not mean that it coheres well with that text. Narrative inclusion does not imply logical integration."[53]

The Enigmatic Jesus as a Counterargument

As we have noted, Hooker, Tyrrell, Casey, Fiorenza, Allison, and a host of others have contended that much of the work done in authenticity studies depends to a large degree on the presuppositions of the scholar. But, as we have argued, the embarrassment criterion is much less susceptible to this criticism. This is because the difficulty in the text is often a difficulty for the very presuppositions the scholar embraces.

One final piece of evidence on behalf of embarrassment goes back to the earliest layers of the tradition. As even the Jesus Seminar would recognize, Jesus was often intentionally ambiguous, enigmatic, and provocative in his teaching, frequently using hyperbole, paradox, and even antinomy in his discourses. He created cognitive dissonance in his followers at every turn. His parables certainly reveal this, as he himself said they would (Matt 13:10–15). In Mark especially the disciples are often scratching their heads in ignorance, fear, or disbelief as they try to grasp what this Galilean carpenter is about.[54] Mark is not alone; this

---

51. Bermejo-Rubio, "Changing Methods, Disturbing Material," 5–6.
52. Bermejo-Rubio, "Changing Methods, Disturbing Material," 7.
53. Bermejo-Rubio, "Changing Methods, Disturbing Material," 7. He offers a final argument, but this is more related to the *effect* on the reader than on authorial intentions: "embarrassing material is virtually neutralized within a captivating narrative framework" (8). In essence, Bermejo-Rubio argues that *quite a bit* of historical material slips through, almost unconsciously, because it is part of the warp and woof of the historical tradition. This in fact is the major thrust of his article, and he focuses on the possibility of "the hypothesis of a nationalistic Jesus [who] somehow involved in anti-Roman activities manages to make best sense of the paradoxical presence of all that compromising material . . ." (20). The author seems to be resurrecting a modified version of S. G. F. Brandon's political theory in his *Jesus and the Zealots: A Study of the Political Factor in Primitive Christianity* (New York: Scribner's, 1968) and idem, *The Trial of Jesus of Nazareth* (New York: Stein & Day, 1968).
54. See Mark 4:41; 5:31; 6:48–52; 7:17–18; 8:14–21, 31–33; 9:5–6, 9–10, 30–32; 10:13–16, 23–27; 14:3–9.

theme plays out again and again in the other Synoptics too.[55] John's Gospel is no different in this regard.[56] And the lack of understanding of many dominical sayings tacitly reveals not only embarrassment on the disciples' part but also difficulties for the early church as believers tried to get a bead on the Nazarene. Several of these texts seem to have made ancient scribes uncomfortable as well. Such a portrait is not in isolated pericopae (the main objection to the criterion of embarrassment raised by Rodriguez) but is part of "the larger historical representations"[57] of Jesus in all four Gospels.

EMBARRASSMENT AND TEXTUAL CRITICISM

It is our contention that early scribes were occasionally embarrassed at material in the Gospels to the extent that they altered the text.[58] And their embarrassment in the least comports with the view that the later evangelists were indeed somewhat embarrassed by—or at a minimum found difficult—some of what they read in Mark. In other words, the pattern we see with Luke's and especially Matthew's tweaking of Mark is mirrored to some extent in the textual variants. What the scribes do with their texts does not *necessarily* suggest that their exemplar text involved something historical. But it does show *a pattern of reaction to the material that is on a continuum with the evangelists.* As such, it underscores the legitimacy of the criterion of embarrassment for Jesus studies.

---

55. E.g., Matt 8:27; 14:25–33; 15:15–20; 16:5–12, 21–23; 17:1–8; 18:1–5; 19:9–12, 23–26; 26:6–13; Luke 2:41–51; 5:4–11; 7:18–23; 8:24–25, 45–46; 9:32–34, 43–45, 51–56; 18:31–34; 24:13–35, 36–42.

56. John 2:18–22; 4:31–34; 6:16–21, 60–65; 9:1–3; 11:11–16, 38–44; 12:12–16; 13:5–11; 14:1–7, 8–11; 16:16–19, 25–33; 20:8–9, 11–16.

57. Rodriguez, "Embarrassing Truth about Jesus," 149.

58. Up until recently, textual criticism was treated only occasionally and haphazardly in authenticity studies. This changed at the end of the twentieth century when Stanley E. Porter and Matthew Brook O'Donnell published "The Implications of Textual Variants for Authenticating the Words of Jesus," in *Authenticating the Words of Jesus*, ed. Bruce Chilton and Craig A. Evans, NTTS 28.1 (Leiden: Brill, 1999), 97–133. They were apparently the first to systematically incorporate text-critical evidence in their treatment of authenticity criteria. (See also Stanley E. Porter's chapter, "The Criterion of Greek Textual Variance," in *Criteria of Authenticity in Historical-Jesus Research: Previous Discussion and New Proposals* [London: T&T Clark, 2000], 181–209.) Porter and O'Donnell dealt with variants as part of multiple attestation, arguing not only for authenticity but even *ipsissima verba* of a few dominical sayings in Greek. In the second volume edited by Chilton and Evans on authenticating the historical Jesus, Porter and O'Donnell addressed the acts of Jesus in relation to textual criticism: "The Implications of Textual Variants for Authenticating the Activities of Jesus," in *Authenticating the Activities of Jesus*, ed. Bruce Chilton and Craig A. Evans, NTTS 28.2 (Leiden: Brill, 1999), 121–51. Rather than working under the umbrella of multiple attestation, this chapter takes a different tack than Porter's (and O'Donnell's) other two essays. Further, its focus is on establishing the original *texts* of the Gospels rather than on showing the link between textual criticism and *historical* authenticity: "In our study, we have refrained from concluding for each of the examples above whether the action depicted is or is not authentic, but have instead tried to develop criteria in relation to textual variants that need to be taken into account in future Historical Jesus research" (Porter and O'Donnell, "Authenticating the Activities of Jesus," 143). The criterion of embarrassment is not addressed except in one passage (Mark 9:2 and parallels; pp. 140–42).

We will focus on three basic categories regarding scribal alterations under the broad rubric of *embarrassment/difficulty*: (1) dissimilarity between the Gospels, (2) difficult dominical sayings, and (3) potentially embarrassing dominical acts and historicity (including the wording of certain narratives).[59]

Dissimilarity between the Gospels

The ancient copyists had a strong tendency to harmonize passages between Synoptic Gospels. This is especially true of the "Western" and Byzantine scribes, but even the Alexandrians[60] did not always resist the temptation of making the evangelists say the same thing.[61] Von Soden attributed most gospel harmonizations to the influence of Tatian's *Diatessaron*.[62] Scholars in the last century have rejected this as the primary source of harmonizations, but such variants

---

59. Whether the sayings and narrative of Mark's Gospel were truly embarrassing to Matthew is at times difficult to assess. The shifts between the two often seem to reveal differences in the overarching purpose of each. Matthew's Gospel is pedagogical, while Mark's is dialogical. Matthew is instructing his readership about who Jesus is, often with an apologetic approach. Mark seems to assume that the readers already embrace Jesus, but he wants his readers to truly own their faith and to deepen it. Where Mark raises questions, Matthew gives answers. The subtleties and challenges in Mark's Gospel tend to be altered or omitted in Matthew.

Space does not permit to offer anything but one brief example, as this is outside the specific scope of this article. Matthew's revision of Mark's baptism is often claimed as an instance in which Matthew felt embarrassed by John's baptism of Jesus, since John came explicitly to baptize "for the forgiveness of sins" (Mark 1:4). Some even hint that Mark's version of the account might not have caused difficulties for the earliest Christ-followers, presumably because the notion of Jesus's sinlessness was a later development. But such views seem to overlook the subtle ways in which Mark himself distinguishes Jesus from the others whom John baptized. When Mark 1:5 and 1:9 are compared, six parallels emerge: (1) people/Jesus (2) come (3) from a specified location (4) to be baptized (5) in the Jordan River (6) by John. Yet, there is a missing element in v. 9 whose absence implicitly elevates Jesus above the repentant remnant: "confessing their sins." In the very text in which Jesus is first introduced into the narrative of the Gospel, Mark gives us a clue of his stylistic art: he will give hints and tips, but perhaps not much explicit information, about who Jesus was and what he came to do. *Mark expects his readers to work at understanding his meaning.* (Similarly, Ernest Best, *Mark: The Gospel as Story* [Edinburgh: T&T Clark, 1983], argues that frequently Mark does not give "an explicit account of a conclusion where this is already known to his readers" [73]). If Mark is writing to a group of Christians who are facing persecution, it makes good sense that he would write his Gospel this way, for these early readers needed to own their understanding of Jesus rather than depend merely on creedal confessions.

60. We are using the terms "*Western,*" *Byzantine, Caesarean,* and *Alexandrian* for convenience, recognizing that whether text-types exist has been debated in recent years. See David C. Parker, *An Introduction to the New Testament Manuscripts and Their Texts* (Cambridge: Cambridge University Press, 2008), 165–74, 286–301, 305–8; Eldon J. Epp, "Textual Clusters: Their Past and Future in New Testament Textual Criticism," in *The Text of the New Testament in Contemporary Research: Essays on the Status Quaestionis,* 2nd ed., ed. Bart D. Ehrman and Michael W. Holmes, NTTSD 42 (Leiden: Brill, 2013), 519–77. But even Epp concludes that "clusters function much as 'text types have since Westcott-Hort, though with the recognition that now definitions are necessarily less rigid, manuscripts are more numerous, and their interrelationships are much more complex" ("Textual Clusters," 570).

61. See Willem Franciscus Wisselink, *Assimilation as a Criterion for the Establishment of the Text: A Comparative Study on the Basis of Passages from Matthew, Mark and Luke* (Kampen: Kok, 1989).

62. Hermann Freiherr von Soden, *Die Schriften des Neuen Testaments in ihrer ältesten erreichbaren Textgestalt* (Göttingen: Vandenhoeck & Ruprecht, 1911), vol. 1, Heft 2, 1639–46, §380 ("Bedeutung des Textes des Diatessaron für die Textkritik") and passim.

are nevertheless ubiquitous among the manuscripts.[63] This even occurs when no real or even apparent discrepancy existed between the Gospels. Examples can be found on any page of Aland's *Synopsis Quattuor Evangeliorum*.

Many of these harmonizations could perhaps be described as responses on the part of the scribes to perceived *micro-aggressions*. The exemplar that is changed may be treated—consciously or subconsciously—as an error on the part of the exemplar's scribe. Significantly, Mark is changed by the copyists proportionately more often than Matthew,[64] while Matthew is changed the least.[65] The tendency toward conformity to Matthew's Gospel by scribes of Mark seems to be an implicit argument for a general scribal embarrassment about Mark's narrative and the Markan Jesus. At the same time, the statistics are not as overwhelming as many two-source advocates have claimed.[66] The direction of the harmonization is not just manuscripts of Mark harmonizing to Matthew.[67]

---

63. See Gordon D. Fee, "Modern Textual Criticism and the Synoptic Problem: On the Problem of Harmonization in the Gospels," in *Studies in the Theory and Method of New Testament Textual Criticism*, Eldon J. Epp and Gordon D. Fee (Grand Rapids: Eerdmans, 1993), 174–82. A quick check of the NA[28] apparatus for Mark reveals that over one hundred Gospel parallels are listed among the variants (indicated by "*p*)"), which indicates a potential reason for scribal alteration. See Mark 1:7, 10, 20, 23, 24, 32, 39, 40, 41, 44; 2:7, 9, 16, 19, 22 (3x), 26; 3:3, 4, 5, 8, 15, 32; 4:3, 10, 24; 5:1, 22, 36; 6:3, 7, 14, 26, 29, 38, 43, 44, 53; 7:6, 24; 8:8, 11, 16, 17, 19, 20, 29, 34, 36 (2x); 9:2, 12, 19, 28, 40; 10:1, 19, 25, 28, 31, 34, 40, 47, 48; 11:3, 7, 8, 9, 17, 29; 12:15, 19, 23, 30, 36; 13:6, 23, 27; 14:9, 21, 22, 24, 25, 30, 38, 41, 45, 47, 62, 65, 72; 15:3, 15, 17, 19, 20, 23, 24, 26, 34, 36, 40. The Nestle-Aland apparatus of course leaves out many parallels and sometimes includes dubious ones that are only seen as parallels in certain manuscripts. But overall it is a useful guide for giving a ballpark figure on this phenomenon.

64. Fee, "Problem of Harmonization," 175. Fee claims that Mark is altered by scribes more than Luke as well, but the statistics do not seem to bear this out. The NA[28] apparatus for Luke reveals well over two hundred Gospel parallels listed by "*p*)": Luke 3:8, 16 (2x), 17, 19; 4:1, 2, 3, 5 (2x), 8, 12, 31, 34, 35, 37, 38, 40; 5:10–11, 12, 13, 14, 19, 21 (2x), 22, 24 (3x), 27 (2x), 28, 33 (2x), 34, 38 (2x), 39; 6:2, 5, 6, 7, 9 (2x), 10, 11, 14 (2x), 20, 29 (2x), 37, 38, 42 (2x), 48, 49 (2x); 7:2, 7 (2x), 9, 19, 22, 28, 35; 8:5, 8, 14, 19, 26, 29 (2x), 31, 37, 44, 45 (2x), 48, 50, 51, 54; 9:10, 12, 13, 14, 17, 19, 22, 23 (2x), 25 (2x), 27 (2x), 28, 30, 33, 34, 35, 39, 45, 49, 50 (2x); 10:3, 6, 14, 23, 24; 11:2 (3x), 3 (2x), 4 (3x), 11, 13, 14, 15, 18, 24, 25, 29 (2x), 30 (2x), 34 (2x), 35–36, 39, 42, 43, 44, 49 (2x), 51 (2x); 12:1, 2 (2x), 7 (2x), 10, 11, 22, 24, 25, 27, 29, 31, 34, 39, 43, 44, 59; 13:24, 25, 35 (2x); 14:24, 27; 17:2, 3, 6, 21, 33, 34, 35; 18:15, 20, 21, 22, 25 (2x), 32, 35, 37, 39; 19:11, 17, 25, 26, 27, 31, 38, 45; 20:4, 5, 10, 23 (2x), 24, 27 (2x), 29, 30, 32, 33 (2x), 43, 47; 21:2, 7, 8, 10, 26, 36; 22:4, 14, 19–20, 47, 48, 54, 55, 64; 23:1, 16, 21, 34, 37, 38 (2x), 53, 55. Proportionately, the manuscripts of Luke collectively harmonize this Gospel to the others the most often.

65. A cursory look at the NA[28] apparatus of Matthew reveals almost one hundred Gospel parallels listed by "*p*)": Matt 3:10; 4:6, 18, 19; 5:25, 29, 32, 44; 6:24; 7:2; 8:9, 10, 13, 15, 23, 28, 29, 31; 9:6, 12 (2x), 13, 14, 15 (2x), 17 (2x), 24, 27; 10:4; 11:2, 8, 19, 21; 12:1; 13:4, 9, 13, 34, 44; 14:14, 15 (2x), 22; 15:1, 27, 36 (2x), 37, 38; 16:4 (2x), 13, 21, 23; 17:9, 20, 23 (2x); 19:9 (2x), 16, 17, 20; 20:19, 22, 23 (3x), 30, 31; 21:1, 3, 9, 13; 22:27; 23:19; 24:7, 17, 29, 31, 41; 25:27; 26:7, 9 (2x), 26, 27, 28, 29, 39 (2x), 55, 73; 27:42, 46; 28:8. In light of the comparative size of Matthew and Mark, as well as the hundreds of instances of Q between Luke and Matthew, it seems fair to say that proportionately Matthew is harmonized less than Mark.

66. Fee, for example, speaks of "far more variants that could be attributed to harmonization" among the manuscripts of Mark than Matthew ("Problem of Harmonization," 175). Statistically, they are virtually identical, but proportionately Mark's scribes do harmonize more, though hardly "far more." Bart D. Ehrman, *The Orthodox Corruption of Scripture: The Effect of Early Christological Controversies on the Text of the New Testament*, updated ed. (Oxford: Oxford University Press, 2011), overstates the situation when he speaks of scribal changes from Matthew to Mark as "a relatively rare phenomenon" (108).

67. Statistics *alone* really prove nothing regarding embarrassment, since the reasons for scribal alterations

Nevertheless, the tendency to harmonize was so strong that such textual variants often become an argument for *single attestation* regarding authenticity. That is, when copyists changed the text to conform it to another Gospel, the base text that they changed offers single attestation. The changes made become, in a sense, multiple attestation, which are, because of this, judged to be another step removed from historicity.

The scribes may have been far more familiar with the wording in one Gospel while copying another; the result of harmonizations in many such instances is likely to be subconscious. The more egregious the differences, the more likely the changes were conscious. One might even hypothesize that simple *dissimilarity* especially may have been the catalyst for the copyists to subconsciously alter some passages, while *embarrassment* moved them to consciously revise others.

Dominical Sayings

Our examination of the material will necessarily be selective. But these are suggestive of a much larger phenomenon. Six passages (or groups of passages) will be treated here. The first four demonstrate that copyists sometimes saw such difficulties in the text that they changed the wording, a tactic in line with Matthew and Luke in their use of Mark. The fifth example also illustrates this, but here scribes faced two competing impulses: the desire for harmonization vs. the temptation to modify embarrassing utterances. The final passage has often been used to prove proto-orthodox corruption of the NT, and thus it belongs in this section. However, I will argue that Mark's text was tweaked by *Matthew* rather than by the ancient scribes; it thus serves as a counterexample.[68]

1. Mark 2:26

In the pericope of the plucking of grain, Jesus responds to the Pharisees' accusation that his disciples were doing work that was forbidden on the Sabbath.[69] In Mark's Gospel he asks, "Have you never read what David did when he was in need and was hungry, along with those with him? How he entered the house of God when Abiathar was high priest and ate the sacred bread—which is not lawful [for anyone] to eat except the priests—and he also gave it to those who were with him?" Except for a few stylistic changes between Mark 2:26 and

---

are variegated. But as we will see, many of these changes do indeed seem to be due to embarrassment or perceived discrepancies in the text.

68. In what follows, translations of Scripture are the author's own unless otherwise noted.

69. m. Sabb. 7.2 speaks of the thirty-nine kinds of work that are prohibited, including reaping, threshing, and winnowing—all of which Jesus's disciples did when they plucked heads of grain, rubbed them in their hands, blew off the chaff, and ate them.

its parallels in Matthew 12:4 and Luke 6:4, the only difference is the omission of Mark's "when Abiathar was high priest" (ἐπὶ Ἀβιαθὰρ ἀρχιερέως) by both Matthew and Luke. An examination of the OT passage alluded to (1 Sam 21:1–7) reveals why they omitted this line, namely, Abiathar was *not* high priest when this incident occurred. Ahimelech is the high priest mentioned in the passage; Abiathar, his son, would later become the high priest.

Several solutions to this problem have been suggested:

1. Text-critical: the text is wrong and needs to be emended;
2. Hermeneutical: our interpretation is wrong and needs to be altered;
3. Dominical: Jesus is wrong (or intentionally midrashic);
4. Source-critical: Mark's source (Peter?) is wrong (or intentionally midrashic);
5. Mark is wrong (or intentionally midrashic).

What concerns us here is the text-critical solution. There are two basic alterations in the ancient witnesses: D W 271 it sy^s and a few others omit ἐπὶ Ἀβιαθὰρ ἀρχιερέως, no doubt in conformity to the parallels in Matthew and Luke. This is almost strictly a "Western" reading. The ancient witnesses A C Θ Π Σ Φ 074 1 131 209 *f*^1, 13 and many others add τοῦ before ἀρχιερέως, which more naturally bears the meaning "in [the days] of Abiathar the high priest" or "in [the passage] about Abiathar the high priest," suggesting a more general timeframe. This reading has a mixture of some Byzantine, Caesarean, and even secondary Alexandrian support. Neither reading has compelling external evidence (though it is early in both instances), and both are evidently motivated by scribal piety toward the text. The reading ἐπὶ Ἀβιαθὰρ ἀρχιερέως is clearly superior, almost certainly gives rise to the others, and is obviously authentic. It is of course possible that both the later evangelists and the scribes saw only a potential misunderstanding on the part of the reader and considered Mark's wording to be ambiguous. But it matters little if they saw the exemplar's wording as a historical blunder or simply capable of misunderstanding; what seems to drive their emendation is a desire to make sure that the text did not contain an inaccurate historical reference on the lips of Jesus. Difficulty with the autographic wording thus also suggests that ἐπὶ Ἀβιαθὰρ ἀρχιερέως may well be close to *ipsissima verba* (whether uttered in Greek or Aramaic).

2. MATTHEW 5:22

In the Sermon on the Mount we read of a particularly harsh condemnation by Jesus of those who are angry with others in the community of faith: "Everyone who is angry with his brother will be subject to judgment" (πᾶς ὁ ὀργιζόμενος τῷ ἀδελφῷ αὐτοῦ ἔνοχος ἔσται τῇ κρίσει). The majority of manuscripts read εἰκῇ ("without cause") after τῷ ἀδελφῷ αὐτοῦ. This insertion has support from ℵ² D L W Θ 0233 *f*[1, 13] 33 𝔐 it sy co Ir[lat] Or[mss] Cyp Cyr. The reading is widespread and early, found in "Western," Caesarean, Byzantine, and even Alexandrian witnesses. For the most part, the best Alexandrian and some other witnesses (𝔓[64] ℵ* B 1424[mg] aur vg Or Hier[mss]) lack it. The external evidence overall favors the exclusion of the adverb.[70] An intentional change would likely arise from the desire to qualify ὀργιζόμενος, especially in light of the absolute tone of Jesus's words.

If εἰκῇ is a scribally motivated reading that crept into the text at a very early date, why is there no restriction added in the manuscripts to the last two clauses of verse 22? There we read, "Whoever says to his brother, 'Raka,' will be liable to the council. Whoever says, 'Fool,' will be liable to the hell of fire."[71] The thrice-mentioned ἔνοχος (to judgment, the council, and hell) may well be, as Jeremias puts it, "three expressions for the death penalty in a kind of crescendo."[72] If so, then the anger "without cause" is the source of the exclamations "Raka!" and "Fool!" While εἰκῇ makes good practical sense in this context, and is almost certainly a true interpretation of Jesus's meaning (cf. Mark 1:41 [*v.l.*]; 3:5; 10:41), it has the earmarks of being a motivated reading. The dominical saying, therefore, most likely was put in more absolute terms that many scribes were not comfortable leaving alone.

3. "After Three Days" (Mark 8:31; 9:31; 10:34)

In Jesus's predictions of his resurrection in Mark's version, three times he says that he will rise from the dead "after three days" (μετὰ τρεῖς ἡμέρας in Mark 8:31; 9:31; 10:34). And every time scribes changed the text to "on the third day."

The first prophecy is in the pericope about the Messianic disclosure near Caesarea Philippi. The parallels to Mark 8:31 in Matthew 16:21 and Luke 9:22 have "on the third day" (τῇ τρίτῃ ἡμέρᾳ). In Mark 8:31 several witnesses have τῇ τρίτῃ ἡμέρᾳ in place of μετὰ τρεῖς ἡμέρας, a reading evidently motivated by a desire for conformity to the other Gospels and a desire to conform to the more precise historical record (so W 33[vid] *f*[1, 13]).

The second prediction occurs in Mark 9:31, with parallels in Matthew 17:23 and Luke 9:44. Luke does not mention the resurrection here, but Matthew does,

---

70. There is a remote possibility that εἰκῇ could have been accidentally omitted from these witnesses by way of homoioarcton (the next word, ἔνοχος, begins with the same letter).

71. Several witnesses repeat "to his brother" (L Θ *f*[1, 13] 700 it[ffl] sy[s, c] bo Cyp) to the last clause, due to assimilation to τῷ ἀδελφῷ αὐτοῦ in the first two clauses.

72. J. Jeremias, "ῥακά," *TDNT* 6:975.

speaking of it as "on the third day." The Markan defectors this time are far more numerous and significant: A C³ K N W Γ Θ $f^{1, 13}$ 28 565 700 1241 1424 (2542) 𝔐 aur f l vg sy all read τῇ τρίτῃ ἡμέρᾳ. The conformity to the Matthean "on the third day" is the reading of the Byzantine, Caesarean, and a few "Western" witnesses.

In Mark 10:34, the third prediction of the passion and resurrection, the witnesses that change "after three days" to "on the third day" are virtually identical to those in 9:31 (A K N W Γ Θ $f^{1, 13}$ 28 565 700 1241 1424 2542 𝔐 aur f l vg sy Or).[73] The parallel in Matthew 20:19 reads τῇ τρίτῃ ἡμέρᾳ; Luke 18:33 has τῇ ἡμέρᾳ τῇ τρίτῃ. We see then that in every verse in Mark that speaks of Jesus's resurrection as occurring "after three days," a large contingent of witnesses conform the text to the Matthean and Lukan parallels.

On the other hand, a few witnesses, mostly of the "Western" variety, have the reading "after three days" in Matthew 16:21 (D it bo), Matthew 17:23 (D it sy^s bo), Luke 9:22 (D it Mcion), and Luke 18:33 (it^l). In Luke 24:46 only the Persian Diatessaron has "after three days." There are no variants to "on the third day" in either Matthew 20:19 or Luke 24:7. Thus, of the seven prophecies in Matthew and Luke, five have variants reading "after three days." But only three of them are attested by any Greek witness at all, each instance being just Codex Bezae. The remaining two have but a single non-Greek witness in support.

In sum, the Lord's predictions about his resurrection in Mark always speak of it as "after three days" (Mark 8:31; 9:31; 10:34), while in Matthew and Luke it is always "on the third day" (Matt 16:21; 17:23; 20:19; Luke 9:22; 18:33; 24:7, 46).[74] Every instance of "after three days" in Mark is changed to "on the third day" by Matthew and Luke. The scribes were simply following the evangelists' lead. All of the prophecies in Mark are changed by several and significant witnesses. The evidence, though not completely uniform, strongly suggests that the scribal changes to these Markan dominical prophecies are due to difficulty with the λόγια Ἰησοῦ vis-à-vis the resurrection accounts. But such changes imply that the Lord predicted his resurrection as occurring "after three days."[75]

---

73. The only difference is that instead of the third corrector of Ephraemi Rescriptus Origen adds his weight to this reading.

74. The only time we see the resurrection referred to as occurring "after three days" in Matthew is in 27:63 where it is not a direct dominical saying (i.e., Jewish leaders reported to the Sanhedrin what Jesus had said). Luke 24:7 is the angelic reminder of Jesus's words to the women; as such, we might expect it to conform to the Lukan Jesus's predictions.

75. See Harold W. Hoehner, *Chronological Aspects of the Life of Christ* (Grand Rapids: Zondervan, 1977), for evidence that "after three days" was an inclusive phrase and was naturally to be taken to mean after *parts* of three days. As Hoehner puts it, in the OT and rabbinic literature, "a part of a day is equivalent to the whole day" (72; whole discussion on 71–74). In light of this, the reasons for Matthew and Luke changing the wording may be due more to a potential *misunderstanding by the readers* than to any desire to correct the

4. JOHN 4:17

In the fourth chapter of the Fourth Gospel Jesus encounters a Samaritan woman at Jacob's well. In the encounter, after the woman asks Jesus for the "living water" he says, "Go, call your husband, and come here" (v. 16). The woman responds with a formally correct statement: "I have no husband" (v. 17), to which Jesus declares, "Correctly you have said, 'I have no husband,' for you have had five husbands and the one whom you now have is not your husband. This you said truthfully" (vv. 17b–18).

But there is more to this encounter. The woman's three-word response is οὐκ ἔχω ἄνδρα. In affirming this response, the Lord reverses the word order, putting the emphasis on the man, "Correctly you have said, 'A *husband* I don't have'" (ἄνδρα οὐκ ἔχω). This is then followed by the disclosure that she has had five husbands and is now living with a man who is not her husband.

Jesus's restatement of the woman's response, introduced by ὅτι and put in the first person, is an instance of direct discourse. But precisely because he did not quote her exactly, a few scribes had some problems with this. So as not to impugn Jesus's recollection of what she had just said, they followed two strategies. First, they altered the *woman's* speech to conform to Jesus's. Thus, ℵ C* D L 1241 j r¹ render the woman's response as ἄνδρα οὐκ ἔχω. That her words were changed instead of the Lord's is somewhat unusual in terms of which texts get harmonized. Within the same context, it is typically the second expression that is conformed to the first. Here it is the other way around, most likely for pious reasons. Second, some of these same witnesses altered Jesus's direct discourse to indirect, changing the verb in his answer to the second person ἔχεις (ℵ D it vg^mss), but still retaining the same word order as most manuscripts have here (ἄνδρα οὐκ ἔχεις). Far less significant but still worthy of mention: two twelfth-century minuscules and two fifth-century Old Latin manuscripts change Jesus's word order to conform to the woman's. The evidence is laid out as follows:

All of the witnesses that change either the woman's utterance or Jesus's or both do so to conform the two statements to each other. There was evidently some discomfort over Jesus misquoting the woman's words. The emphasis he places on ἄνδρα is but a foreshadowing of his disclosure about her past and present state. Yet a few scribes seem to have been oblivious to the tensions in this exchange and John's narrative artistry, showing concern only for matching the parallel assertions.

The larger question about how this scribal embarrassment relates to an

---

wording of the prophecy. Later scribes would most likely not have the same understanding of the Jewish idiom; for them, the changes would have been made for the sake of accuracy.

authentic dominical saying is beyond the scope of this essay. But this pericope, like John's Gospel in general, is based on at least a "historical core."[76] Nevertheless, the Fourth Gospel is hardly the first place one would go in search of *ipsissima verba*, so what can we affirm? Just the probability that Jesus underscored that the woman was living with a man unlawfully and that he said it in a way that was more emphatic than her initial affirmation.

John 4:17a	Nestle-Aland[28]	ℵ C* D L 1241 j rˡ
Samaritan woman's answer	οὐκ ἔχω ἄνδρα	ἄνδρα οὐκ ἔχω

John 4:17b	Nestle-Aland[28]	ℵ D it vgᵐˢˢ	1217 1355 b e
Jesus's response	ἄνδρα οὐκ ἔχω	ἄνδρα οὐκ ἔχεις	οὐκ ἔχω ἄνδρα

5. MARK 10:17–18

In the pericope about the rich (young) ruler, a man earnestly inquires about his own destiny, asking, "Good teacher, what must I do to inherit eternal life?" (v. 17). Jesus responds with seeming incredulity, "Why do you call me good? No one is good except God alone" (v. 18). The parallel in Matthew 19:16–17 makes a few key alterations: the evangelist removes "good" from "teacher," making the adjective stand alone as "good [thing]," and he changes "Why do you call me good?" to "Why do you ask me *about* the good?" (Mark's διδάσκαλε ἀγαθέ, τί ποιήσω ἵνα ζωὴν αἰώνιον κληρονομήσω; . . . τί με λέγεις ἀγαθόν; thus becomes διδάσκαλε, τί ἀγαθὸν ποιήσω ἵνα σχῶ ζωὴν αἰώνιον; . . . τί με ἐρωτᾷς περὶ τοῦ ἀγαθοῦ; in Matthew). Matthew has effectively lessened suspicions about the deity of Christ that Mark's wording might have raised.

We may well expect some copyists to amend Mark's phrasing, but in this instance the scribes modified *Matthew's* dialogue to conform to Mark's: διδάσκαλε ἀγαθέ (Matt 19:16) is read by C E F G H K M S U W Y Γ Δ Θ *f*¹³ 33 565 579 700 1241 1424 𝔐 lat sy sa mae boᵖᵗ Ju Orᵖᵗ et al.; τί με λέγεις ἀγαθόν (Matt 19:17) is found in C K W (Γ) (Δ) *f*¹³ 33 565 579 1241 1424* 𝔐 f q syᵖˑʰ sa boᵐˢ et al. Why would so many and such diverse manuscripts alter Matthew's wording here? Most likely it is due to the parallel in Luke saying essentially the same thing as

---

76. Craig S. Keener, *The Gospel of John: A Commentary*, vol. 1 (Peabody, MA: Hendrickson, 2003), 587. See his introductory treatment of historicity in John (40–47), which includes mention of a growing list of scholars who argue that though John is decidedly a theological treatise, it has a strong historical framework. The list includes B. F. Westcott, C. H. Dodd, W. F. Albright, Raymond Brown, James Charlesworth, D. A. Carson, Leon Morris, David Wenham, Craig Blomberg, Thomas D. Lea, Francis J. Moloney, Claudia J. Setzer.

Mark (the ruler calls Jesus "good teacher"; Jesus responds with "Why do you call me good?" [Luke 18:18–19]). With two Gospels already having this wording, the impulse to modify just one Gospel for harmonization's sake was stronger than the impulse to alter the expressions of two Gospels for theological reasons.[77] In this instance, the scribal concern for harmonization trumped concerns over an ambiguous Christology, since two of the Synoptics already presented this ambiguous exchange. We see here therefore two competing principles that various scribes followed: harmonization vs. alteration due to some difficulty. Though frequently, if not usually, these two principles were not in conflict, in this instance they were and harmonization won out for the Byzantine, "Western," some Caesarean, and even a few Alexandrian witnesses.

6. MATTHEW 24:36

One of the most difficult dominical sayings is found in the heart of the Olivet Discourse. In Matthew's version, Jesus says, "Now concerning that day and hour no one knows [it], neither the angels of heaven, *nor the Son* [οὐδὲ ὁ υἱός], except the Father alone." The phrase "nor the Son," however, is textually uncertain. The phrase οὐδὲ ὁ υἱός in the parallel passage, Mark 13:32, however, is firmly established.[78] Luke omits the verse entirely.

Did scribes delete this phrase from the text of Matthew or did Matthew athetize it as he reworked the Markan Olivet Discourse for his own purposes? The majority of New Testament scholars today would argue that οὐδὲ ὁ υἱός is authentic in Matthew 24:36 and that the omission was born out of pious scribal motives to safeguard the omniscience of Christ.[79] If so, then this might be a good illustration of scribal alteration due to embarrassment. It is, in fact, the central proof text in Bart Ehrman's *magnum opus*, *Orthodox Corruption of Scripture*, as well as in several of his other writings, in which he argues that proto-orthodox scribes significantly revised the New Testament for theological reasons.[80]

---

77. Matthew's wording is harmonized to Mark's in approximately 30 percent of the more significant parallels. See Charles Powell, "The Textual Problem of οὐδὲ ὁ υἱός in Matthew 24:36" (paper presented at the annual meeting of the Evangelical Theological Society, Colorado Springs, CO, November 2001), 5, 15–19. Powell discusses 61 of the more significant parallels between Matthew and Mark, and notes that 18 of them involve scribal corrections of Matthew toward Mark (29.5 percent). This high of a percentage is often overlooked in Synoptic studies, as we mentioned earlier (see note 66).

78. Only one tenth-century Greek MS (Codex X) and one late Vulgate MS delete the expression.

79. See Daniel B. Wallace, "The Son's Ignorance in Matthew 24:36: An Exercise in Textual and Redaction Criticism," in *Studies on the Text of the New Testament and Early Christianity: Essays in Honour of Michael W. Holmes*, ed. Daniel Gurtner, Paul Foster, and Juan Hernández, NTTSD 50 (Leiden: Brill, 2015), 182–86, for a brief history of the discussion of this textual problem.

80. See Bart D. Ehrman, *The Orthodox Corruption of Scripture: The Effect of Early Christological Controversies on the Text of the New Testament* (New York: Oxford University Press, 1993), 91–96; idem, *Misquoting Jesus: The Story Behind Who Changed the Bible and Why* (New York: HarperCollins, 2007), 95,

I will argue instead that Matthew expunged the phrase but altered Mark's text in another fashion so that it essentially says the same thing. This treatment is a brief summary of my chapter, "The Son's Ignorance in Matthew 24:36: An Exercise in Textual and Redaction Criticism," published in a *Festschrift* for Michael Holmes.[81]

The evidence is of three sorts: external, internal, and redactional. As for the external evidence, although the omission is more weakly attested,[82] it has sufficient backing to be a viable candidate for representing the autographic wording.[83]

The textual problem ultimately needs to be decided by internal evidence.[84] Nearly a half century ago, Metzger's *Textual Commentary on the Greek New Testament* laid out this evidence succinctly. This turned the tide of scholarly opinion into unqualified acceptance of οὐδὲ ὁ υἱός.[85] Metzger put forth two basic arguments for the longer reading from the realms of grammar and theology: "The omission of the words because of the doctrinal difficulty they present is more probable than their addition by assimilation to Mk 13.32. Furthermore, the presence of μόνος and the cast of the sentence as a whole (οὐδὲ ... οὐδέ ... belong together as a parenthesis ...) suggest the originality of the phrase."[86] In defense of the shorter reading, we will first address these arguments, then offer evidence from redaction criticism.

The case from grammar is not nearly as strong as Metzger and those who have followed him insinuate. In fact, it is against the longer reading. In Metzger's view, the expression οὐδὲ οἱ ἄγγελοι is the first part of correlative conjunctive phrases, with οὐδὲ ὁ υἱός following. Metzger's *suggestion* (as he calls it) has become *certainty* for some scholars who turn one grammatical possibility into an inviolable principle. For example, Bart Ehrman has asserted that "the phrase οὐδὲ ὁ υἱός ... is ... *necessary* on internal grounds."[87] But are the correlative conjunctions really a grammatical necessity? Put simply: Does *neither* demand a *nor*?

It is evident to anyone with a minimal grasp of ancient Greek that οὐδέ is often used correlatively, but also that it can be used alone in the sense of

---

110, 204, 209, 223n19, 224n16; idem, "Text and Transmission: The Historical Significance of the 'Altered' Text," in *Studies in the Textual Criticism of the New Testament*, NTTS 33 (Leiden: Brill, 2006), 333.

81. Wallace, "Son's Ignorance," 182–209.

82. The omission is the reading of א¹ (or א²ᵃ) L W 33 892 1241 *f*¹ 𝔐 g¹ l vg sy co Ath Did^{mss} Phoebadius Ambr^{mss} Bas Gregory Hier^{mss}; the addition is found in א*,² B D Θ *f*¹³ it Diatessaron^{arm} Ir^{lat} Or Hier^{mss} Chr.

83. For discussion, see Wallace, "Son's Ignorance," 188–91, 192–99.

84. The discussion on internal evidence summarizes Wallace, "Son's Ignorance," 199–205.

85. Wallace, "Son's Ignorance," 185.

86. Bruce M. Metzger, *A Textual Commentary on the Greek New Testament*, 2nd ed. (New York: United Bible Societies, 1994), 52.

87. Ehrman, *Orthodox Corruption*, 92 (italics added). See also Daniel J. Harrington, *The Gospel of Matthew*, SP 1 (Collegeville, MN: Liturgical Press, 1991), 342.

"not even." In Matthew 24:36 without οὐδὲ ὁ υἱός the text reads naturally enough: "But concerning that day and hour no one knows it—*not even* the angels in heaven—except the Father alone." Altogether, Matthew has twenty-seven instances of οὐδέ. The *only* other paired occasion (i.e., besides its possibility in our passage) is in Matthew 12:19. Yet even here, it is not the evangelist's wording; he is quoting Isaiah 42:2.[88] The single οὐδέ, then, is completely in line with Matthew's style seen everywhere else in his Gospel. In other words, intrinsic probability is *uniformly* on the side of a single οὐδέ in Matthew 24:36. The paired οὐδέ, treated by itself, makes sense in the passage, but it is wholly at odds with intrinsic evidence.

The argument from theology is also invalid. The issues here are complex, involving controversies within the early church, a growing canon consciousness, the beginnings of the codex, and patristic citations of this passage. I summarized the evidence elsewhere:

> The idea that proto-orthodox scribes changed the text of Matthew in the late second to third century in reaction to Adoptionism lacks sufficient evidence. If the scribes were following the leads of their theological mentors, then the lack of any tension over this passage by second and third century Fathers suggests that the omission of "nor the Son" was not a reaction to Adoptionism. Some other time and some other reason needs to account for the omission. And many of the same scribes who omitted "nor the Son" in Matthew wrote it out in Mark in the same codex. This is strong evidence that doctrinal agendas were not driving early orthodox scribal activity concerning Matt 24:36. And even later scribes, to the extent that they were influenced by the Fathers, would be generally faithful to record the text, leaving the theological tensions to the preachers and theologians to sort out.[89]

Third is the argument from redaction. It is well known that where Mark's Christology raises questions, Matthew's gives answers. The reasons for such revisions are often assumed to be out of concern that Mark's Christology was defective and not in keeping with the church's high view of Christ in the late first century. But, as Moule has pointed out, "it still seems a plausible assumption that successive redactors should tend (however dangerously docetic it may be)

---

88. Cf. Matt 5:15; 6:15, 20, 26 (2x), 28–29; 7:18; 9:17; 10:24; 11:27; 12:4, 19; 13:13; 16:9–10; 21:27, 32; 22:46; 23:13; 2:21, 36; 25:13, 45; 27:14. Apart from our target text, only in 12:9 do we see οὐδέ functioning correlatively.

89. Wallace, "Son's Ignorance," 205. Full discussion of internal evidence on pp. 201–5.

to show Christ as in full control of circumstances and without weakness or ignorance."[90] We have already, in the course of this paper, discussed several passages that demonstrate Mark's more primitive Christology.[91] An examination of all the parallels between Matthew and Mark reveals that Matthew never seems to display a lower Christology when it comes to Jesus's holiness, volition, power, knowledge, emotions, the disciples' derived authority from Jesus, or worship of Jesus—unless Matthew 24:36 is the *lone* exception.[92]

How would it be the lone exception? By adding "nor the Son," this verse is almost verbatim what Jesus says in Mark 13:32 *except* in one significant point: Matthew *adds* μόνος to "except the Father," thus doubly underscoring the Father's exclusive knowledge of the time of these eschatological events. Without the μόνος, Matthew's Christology would be identical to Mark's in this place. By omitting οὐδὲ ὁ υἱός but adding μόνος to his revision of Mark, Matthew's Jesus is implicitly stating what Mark's Jesus explicitly says. The μόνος preserves Matthew's high Christology without altering the basic point the Markan Jesus is making. Only the *omission* of "nor the Son" in Matthew 24:36 reflects Matthew's editorial strategy, while adding it is contrary to all that we know of his Christological redactions.

To sum up: Although most exegetes today would argue that early copyists excised "nor the Son" from Matthew 24:36, an examination of the internal evidence and redactional motifs paints a different picture. It is Matthew rather than the scribes who eliminates the phrase while adding μόνος to the Father's knowledge. This textual problem thus serves as a counter-example to scribal changes motivated by a desire to remove difficulties in the text. As such, however, it draws attention to Matthew's propensity to soften such dominical sayings, yet without altering their basic substance.

Dominical Acts and Historicity

Our examination of this material will, much like the dominical sayings above, be selective rather than exhaustive. This section is broader than the acts of Jesus. It also includes the evangelists' narratives and editorial comments as well as statements by others in the text. Six passages will be briefly examined here. They all show that scribes occasionally saw difficulties in the text that may have prompted them to alter the wording.

---

90. Moule, "Review of Peter Head, *Christology and the Synoptic Problem*," 741.
91. See the section *"Arguments from Matthean Priority."*
92. See Wallace, "Son's Ignorance," 205–8.

1. MATTHEW 27:9–10

The final prophecy that belongs to Matthew's fulfillment motif is in Matthew 27:9–10: "Then what was spoken by Jeremiah the prophet was fulfilled: *'They took the thirty silver coins, the price of the one whose price had been set by the people of Israel, and they gave them for the potter's field, as the Lord commanded me'*" (NET). But this introductory formula is "fraught with difficulties."[93] Chief among them is that v. 9 is apparently a loose quotation from Zechariah 11:13. Scholars have dealt with this problem with a variety of approaches,[94] some of which speak more of the ingenuity of the scholar than the substance of the evidence. What concerns us here, however, is not whether the evangelist misattributed the prophecy to the wrong seer, but that some scribes thought that at least their exemplar erred. Three variants arise due to this difficulty: Some witnesses read Ζαχαρίου here instead of Ἰερεμίου (22 syr[hmg] arm[mss]); several others pass over the name and read simply "by the prophet" (διὰ τοῦ προφήτου; Φ 33 157 1579 it[a, b] vg[ms] syr[s, p] bo[ms] Aug[mss]); and two other manuscripts attribute the prophecy to Isaiah (21 it[l]).[95] The reason for "Isaiah" here may be that since he was the most prominent of the prophets, it could be a metonymy similar to "Psalms" representing the Old Testament poetical books in Luke 24:44. This seems to happen in a few other places among the NT manuscripts.[96]

None of the variants commends itself as authentic; "Jeremiah" is certainly the harder reading and is, in fact, attested by the great majority of manuscripts. But the fact that there are three variant readings to Matthew's wording, all of them apparently attempting to remedy a difficulty, argues once again that scribal practices are on a continuum with the later evangelists' handling of Mark. What Matthew and Luke (and even some Markan copyists) did with Mark's "Abiathar" is what several scribes did with Matthew's "Jeremiah." If one falls under the embarrassment canon, so does the other.

2. MARK 1:34

In Mark 1 the evangelist portrays the first group of healing miracles of Jesus as occurring immediately after the Lord cured Peter's mother-in-law (Mark 1:31). The evangelist then narrates, "When evening came, after sunset, they began

---

93. Donald A. Hagner, *Matthew 14–28*, WBC 33B (Dallas: Word, 1995), 813.

94. For a succinct summary of the views, see Hagner, *Matthew 14–28*, 815.

95. See Metzger, *Textual Commentary*, 55, for other witnesses.

96. Metzger lists Matt 1:22; 2:5; 13:35; 21:4; and Acts 7:48 as examples of this (*Textual Commentary*, 27). Matt 1:22 does not really fit this pattern, since the quotation in v. 23 is from Isa 7:14 (thus, the motive for some scribes to insert "Isaiah" here is not simply because "it is the name of the best known prophet" [*Textual Commentary*, 27]). Possibly Mark 1:2 is an instance as well, though there "Isaiah" is likely authentic.

bringing to him all who were sick and demon-possessed" (v. 32). We then learn that "he healed many who were sick with various diseases and drove out many demons" (v. 34). Many exegetes have argued that the two groups are identical, based on the Semitic use of "many" frequently having the same force as "all."[97] This interpretation is most likely correct, though a few scholars disagree.[98] However, Matthew reverses the order of the "all" and the "many" (8:16), so that the antecedent is inclusive, implying that everyone who came to Jesus was healed.

Codex Cantabrigiensis changes the text of Mark 1:34 so that it conceptually agrees with Matthew 8:16 and Luke 4:40. Instead of ἐθεράπευσεν πολλοὺς κακῶς ἔχοντας ποικίλαις νόσοις ("he healed many who had various diseases"), D reads simply ἐθεράπευσεν αὐτούς ("he healed them"). The scribe (or the *Vorlage*'s scribe) seems to be following the same basic strategy of the later evangelists. The reason for this scribal change, however, can hardly be to remove a Semitism; rather, it is most likely that the copyist thought that "many" implied that the Lord did not heal all,[99] thus impugning the power and authority of Jesus.[100]

3. MARK 1:41

In recent years, an unusual variant reading has shown up in the text of modern translations and at least one Greek NT.[101] Of the extant Greek manuscripts for Mark 1:41, all but one have σπλαγχνισθείς: "And moved with compassion [σπλαγχνισθείς], he stretched out his hand and touched him and said to him, 'I am willing; be cleansed!" Codex D, the most erratic of all New Testament manuscripts, though representing in general a very early text, here has ὀργισθείς ("becoming angry"). The NIV 2011, which follows the reading of D, renders this verse, "Jesus was indignant. He reached out his hand and touched the man. 'I am willing,' he said. 'Be clean!'" The original NIV (1984) read "Filled with compassion, Jesus reached out his hand and touched the man. 'I am willing,' he said. 'Be clean!'" Like the NIV 2011, a few other modern versions translate ὀργισθείς. A major stimulus for this change seems to be a chapter in Gerald

---

97. Apparently an interpretation first suggested by Joachim Jeremias, *Die Abendmahlsworte Jesu* (Göttingen: Vandenhoeck & Ruprecht, 1935), 68–69 (English translation, *The Eucharistic Words of Jesus*, based on the third edition and the author's added notes [Minneapolis: Fortress, 1977], 179–82). Jeremias supplies more examples of the equation of "the many" with "all" in the NT (J. Jeremias, "πολλοί," *TDNT* 6:540–42).

98. See especially Rudolf Pesch, *Das Markusevangelium*, part 1 (Freiburg im Breisgau: Herder, 1980), 134–35.

99. It is scarcely possible that this fifth-century copyist was aware of the Semitic idiom. For Matthew and Luke, the revision of Mark is due to eliminating an ambiguity; for Bezae, Mark's wording is probably a cause of embarrassment.

100. Likewise, for the next clause, instead of "he cast out many demons" (δαιμόνια πολλὰ ἐξέβαλεν) D, along with ff², alters the wording and omits the "many" (τοὺς δαιμόνια ἔχοντας ἐξέβαλεν αὐτὰ ἀπ' αὐτῶν).

101. E.g., REB, CEB, ERV, SBLGNT.

Hawthorne's *Festschrift* by Bart Ehrman, entitled "A Leper in the Hands of an Angry Jesus."[102] A spate of articles and one dissertation have been published on the variant in Mark 1:41, many in response to Ehrman's essay.[103]

Bezae is not the only witness to have this reading, though it is the only Greek witness. There are three Old Latin witnesses to this variant in addition to the Latin text of the bilingual Bezae (d): t[a, ff2, rl]. Perhaps most significantly, Ephraem's *Commentary on the Diatessaron*, which is probably our best witness to what Tatian's mid-second-century *Diatessaron* actually read, speaks on more than one occasion of this pericope, referring to *both* compassion and anger in the commentary as though these were in the triple tradition of this Synoptic pericope (Mark 1:41; Matt 8:3; Luke 5:13).[104] Still, this is paltry evidence for the "angry" reading.

The internal evidence for ὀργισθείς fares much better. Commentaries on Mark have almost routinely adopted it because it is obviously a much harder reading[105] and in the parallels both Matthew and Luke have neither ὀργισθείς nor σπλαγχνισθείς here. The simplest explanation for this omission is that their copies of Mark read ὀργισθείς.[106] Elsewhere, they both follow the strategy of

---

102. Bart D. Ehrman, "A Leper in the Hands of an Angry Jesus," in *New Testament Greek and Exegesis: Essays in Honor of Gerald F. Hawthorne*, ed. Amy M. Donaldson and Timothy B. Sailors (Grand Rapids: Eerdmans, 2003), 77–98. The REB was not influenced by Ehrman's essay, as it was published fourteen years prior.

103. See, e.g., Kirsopp Lake, "ΕΜΒΡΙΜΗΣΑΜΕΝΟΣ and ΟΡΓΙΣΘΕΙΣ, Mark 1,40–43," *HTR* 16 (1923): 197–98; Mark Proctor, "The 'Western' Text of Mark 1:41: The Case for the Angry Jesus" (PhD diss., Baylor University, 1999); Jeff Cate, "The Unemotional Jesus in Manuscript 1358," *The Folio: Bulletin of the Ancient Biblical Manuscript Center* 28.2 (Fall 2011): 1; Peter J. Williams, "An Examination of Ehrman's Case for ὀργισθείς in Mark 1:41," *NovT* 53 (2011): 1–12; Tjitze Baarda, "Mk 1:41: ὀργισθείς; A Reading attested for Mar Ephraem, the Diatessaron, or Tatian," *ZNW* 103 (2012): 291–95; Jean-Claude Haelewyck, "The Healing of a Leper (Mark 1:40–45): A Textual Commentary," *ETL* 89 (2013): 15–36; Joel E. Lisboa and Thomas R. Shepherd, "Comparative Narrative Analysis as a Tool in Determining the *Lectio Difficilior* in Mark 1:40–45—A Narrative Analysis of Codices Bezae, Vaticanus, and Washingtonianus," *Neot* 49.1 (2015): 75–89; Cristian Piazzetta and Wilson Paroschi, "Jesus and the Leper: A Text-critical Study of Mark 1:41 (Jesus e o Leproso: Um Estudo Crítico-Textual de Marcos 1:41)," *Kerygma: Revista de Teologia do Unasp* 12.1 (2016): 45–60; Peter E. Lorenz, "Counting Witnesses for the Angry Jesus in Mark 1:41," *TynBul* 67.2 (2016): 183–216.

104. Lorenz, "Counting Witnesses," 204, argues that "the simpler hypothesis is to understand the commentator's conflated reference to Jesus' anger and compassion not as referring to any reading at all . . ." It is not clear why this would be the simpler explanation, since even those who advocate ὀργισθείς would certainly admit that σπλαγχνισθείς was in circulation in the mid-second century. On the other hand, Baarda makes two significant points: first, Mark 1:41 is "not the only case in which Ephraem shows awareness of a deviant reading in the separate Gospels"; and second, Ephraem had some difficulty in explaining the wrath of Jesus; this confirms the idea that this wording was actually found in the [Diatessaron]" (Baarda, "Mk 1:41: ὀργισθείς," 294).

105. As is seen in the variety of explanations for it.

106. E.g., Ernst Lohmeyer, *Das Evangelium des Markus*, 11th Auflage; MeyerK (Göttingen: Vandenhoeck & Ruprecht, 1951), 44–46; Vincent Taylor, *The Gospel according to St. Mark: The Greek Text with Introduction, Notes, and Indexes*, 2nd ed. (London: Macmillan, 1966), 187; C. E. B. Cranfield, *The Gospel according to Saint Mark: An Introduction and Commentary*, 3rd ed. (Cambridge: Cambridge University Press, 1977), 92; Pesch, *Markusevangelium*, 1.144; Robert A. Guelich, *Mark 1–8:26*, WBC (Dallas: Word 1989), 72, 74; Hooker, *Mark*, 79; Robert H. Stein, *Mark*, BECNT (Grand Rapids: Baker, 2008), 105–6, 110–11; Joel Marcus, *Mark 1–8: A New Translation with Introduction and Commentary*, AB 27 (New York: Doubleday, 2000), 205–6; James R. Edwards, *The Gospel according to Mark* (Grand Rapids: Eerdmans, 2002), 70; R. T. France, *The Gospel*

omitting potentially embarrassing Markan material,[107] rendering this a live option in this place.

If the reading of D reflects the original wording in Mark 1:41, then here is an instance in which scribes were evidently embarrassed by the reading, turning Jesus's anger into compassion. That both participles have the same ending (-ισθεις), as well as similar rounded letters in majuscule script prior to this ending, might indeed be the basis for the substitution.[108] Nevertheless, no general consensus has been reached over this textual problem, which renders it only a possible illustration of scribal embarrassment.

4. MARK 5:1

The well-known exorcism of the Gerasene demoniac(s) is found in Mark 5:1–20; Matthew 8:28–34; and Luke 8:26–39. Mark gives the most detailed and vivid narrative of this incident. Almost equally well known are the discrepancies over where this miracle occurred. In NA[28] the place is "the region of the Gerasenes" (τὴν χώραν τῶν Γερασηνῶν) in Mark 5:1 and Luke 8:26, and "the region of the Gadarenes" (τὴν χώραν τῶν Γαδαρηνῶν) in Matthew 8:28. Because of these differences, scribal alterations abound. In Mark 5:1, A C K *f*[13] 𝔐 sy[p, h] have Γαδαρηνῶν, conforming Mark's wording to Matthew's. Several other witnesses have Γεργεσηνῶν here (א[2] L Δ Θ *f*[1] 28 33 565 579 700 892 1241 1424 2542 bo). At Matthew 8:28, a few witnesses change the text to Γερασηνῶν in conformity with Mark and Luke, while several others read Γεργεσηνῶν (א[2] K L W *f*[1, 13] 565 579 700 892* 1424 𝔐 bo Epiph[mss]). And in Luke, Γαδαρηνῶν is found in A K W Γ Δ Ψ *f*[13] 565 700[c] 892 1424 2542 𝔐 sy), while Γεργεσηνῶν is the reading of א L Θ Ξ *f*[1] 33 579 700[c] 1241 Epiph. These variants and their main witnesses can be seen in the table below.[109]

---

of Mark: A Commentary on the Greek Text, NIGTC (Grand Rapids: Eerdmans, 2002), 115. Recent exegetes who adopt σπλαγχνισθείς as the authentic reading here include Robert H. Gundry, *Mark: A Commentary on His Apology for the Cross* (Grand Rapids: Eerdmans, 1993), 102, and Adela Yarbro Collins, *Mark: A Commentary*, Hermeneia (Minneapolis: Fortress, 2007), 177.

107. See the earlier treatments of Mark 2:26 and the two healing miracles in Mark involving spittle.

108. Williams sees this as a distinct possibility ("Examination of Ehrman's Case"), but he regards the ὀργισθείς as coming from σπλαγχνισθείς and specifically as occurring accidentally (6–9). This seems to be a bit of a stretch, and it does not explain how ὀργισθείς could have found its way into Bezae without being corrected by the διορθωτής. As Parker has likely demonstrated, at least *fifteen correctors* at various times had a hand in changing the text of Cantabrigiensis, producing over 150 corrections to Mark alone (David C. Parker, *Codex Bezae: An Early Christian Manuscript and Its Text* [Cambridge: Cambridge University Press, 1992], 48–49, 124). Yet ὀργισθείς is left untouched.

109. Metzger, *Textual Commentary*, 18, has a similar list (with several notable differences), but the witnesses are based on UBS[4]; the above list is based on NA[28]. SBLGNT refers to *The Greek New Testament: SBL Edition*, ed. Michael W. Holmes (Atlanta: SBL, 2010); THGNT is *The Greek New Testament*, produced at Tyndale House, Cambridge; ed. Dirk Jongkind, Peter J. Williams, Peter M. Head, and Patrick James (Cambridge: Cambridge University Press, 2017).

	Γερασηνῶν	Γαδαρηνῶν	Γεργεσηνῶν
Mark 5:1	ℵ* B D latt sa; NA²⁸, SBLGNT, THGNT	A C K f¹³ 𝔐 syᵖ˒ʰ	ℵ² L (W) Δ Θ f¹ 28 33 565 579 700 892 1241 1424 2542 syˢ˒ʰᵐᵍ bo
Matthew 8:28	892ᶜ latt syʰᵐᵍ sa mae	(ℵ*) B C (Δ) Θ syˢ˒ ᵖ˒ʰ Epiph; NA²⁸, SBLGNT, THGNT	ℵ² K L W f¹˒¹³ 565 579 700 892* 1424 𝔐 bo Epiphᵐˢˢ
Luke 8:26	𝔓⁷⁵ B D latt syʰᵐᵍ (sa); NA²⁸, SBLGNT, THGNT	A K W Γ Δ Ψ f¹³ 565 700ᶜ 892 1424 2542 𝔐 sy	ℵ L Θ Ξ f¹ 33 579 700* 1241 (bo) Epiph

A few observations can be made about these variants. First, only the Latin tradition (Itala and Vulgate) and the Sahidic harmonize all the passages to read *Gerasenes*. No Greek manuscripts harmonize all three texts with this reading. Second, *Gadarenes* is found in all three Gospels only in the Peshitta and Harklean Syriac version. Again, no Greek witnesses support the triple tradition. Third, *Gergesenes* has the most consistent support in all three pericopae and is the only one with Greek manuscripts behind it in the triple tradition (L, family 1, 565, 579, 700, Bohairic).

The geographical problems are implicit in these competing variants. Of the three readings, *Gergesa* is most likely the right location for this exorcism (the only region close to the Sea of Galilee and with a steep bank [κρημνός in Mark 5:13]) but it is almost surely a secondary reading in all the Synoptics.[110] As Tjitze Baarda articulated, this variant is quite possibly due to a conjecture made by Origen, a reading that then made its way into several manuscripts.[111] The other two cities (Gerasa and Gadara) were part of the Decapolis, gentile cities east of Tiberias. Both were southeast from the Sea of Galilee, Gadara five miles and Gerasa more than thirty miles. Neither one could reasonably accommodate a herd of swine rushing to the sea. "Skeptics have made sport of the pigs running the great distance from Gerasa (or even from Gadara . . .), across steep ravines and wadis before plunging into the lake."[112] Gergesa, however, if it is the same

---

110. Gundry, *Mark*, 255–57, argues for the authenticity of Γεργεσηνῶν, offering a decent discussion of why this site is the true location, but a much less convincing argument for the authenticity of the reading.

111. See Tjitze Baarda, "Gadarenes, Gerasenes, Gergesenes and the 'Diatessaron' Traditions," in *Neotestamentica et Semitica: Studies in Honour of Matthew Black*, ed. E. Earle Ellis and Max Wilcox (Edinburgh: T&T Clark, 1969), 181–97.

112. Edwards, *Mark*, 153.

as the modern Kursi,[113] was very near the shore with a steep bank. Origen's conjecture, therefore, could possibly be based on actual evidence.

That the text in all three Gospels has such variants suggests that the scribes were dealing with a geographical difficulty. The issues are beyond the scope of this essay, but they seem to reveal some embarrassment on the part of these copyists.

5. LUKE 23:45

During the last three hours of Jesus's suffering on the cross, "darkness came over the whole land" (Luke 23:44), "when the sun's light failed" (τοῦ ἡλίου ἐκλιπόντος [v. 45]). The problem with this translation, however, is that ἐκλείπω, when collocated with "sun" or "moon" was a technical term meaning "to eclipse."[114] But a solar eclipse is astronomically impossible in this instance since Jesus's death occurred at Passover, when the moon was full; an eclipse (either solar or lunar) can only happen during a new moon. Further, no eclipse has ever lasted more than a few minutes, yet this one is said to have spanned three hours.[115] What exactly Luke means (whether some physical occurrence of darkness or a symbolic portent of Jesus's death) is beyond the scope of this essay.[116] What concerns us, however, is that many ancient scribes apparently found the evangelist's statement troubling.

The variants fall into three groups: (1) some form of ἐκλείπω ("to eclipse") describing the event, (2) some form of σκοτίζω ("to darken"), or (3) omission of the sun's darkening.[117] The NA[28] has the aorist genitive absolute construction τοῦ ἡλίου ἐκλιπόντος, supported by 𝔓[75*] א (B) C[*vid] L 070 579 (597) (1005) (1012) (2372) sa bo (Cyr) Or.[118] The reading ἐσκοτίσθη ὁ ἥλιος ("the sun was darkened") is found in the majority of witnesses (A C[3] D K Q W Γ Δ Θ Ψ *f*[1, 13] 28 157 180 205 349 565 700 892 1006 1010 1071 1241 1292 1342 1424 1505 𝔐 lat sy[(h)] Mcion[E vid] Or[lat mss]). Codex 33 omits the entire clause. Some form of ἐκλείπω's participle has

---

113. Though Cranfield suggests that "Mark wrote 'Gerasenes' with reference to a town by the lake (whose name may be preserved Kersa or Koursi on the eastern shore), but that readers mistook this for a reference to the well-known Gerasa" (*Mark*, 176).

114. BDAG, s.v. ἐκλείπω 3 ("Luke's diction is standard for description of an eclipse"); LSJ, s.v. ἐκλείπω II ("intr., of the Sun or Moon, *suffer eclipse*"). The verb ἐκλείπω can simply mean *fail, give out, be gone, depart, die out, be inferior*, but when describing the sun or moon it takes on the technical sense of *to eclipse*.

115. The NASA website features a page entitled, "Ten Millennium Catalog of Long Solar Eclipses" (https://eclipse.gsfc.nasa.gov/SEcatmax/SEcatmax.html), giving data for the longest solar eclipses between 4000 BCE and 6000 CE. The longest total eclipse will occur on July 16, 2186, and last 7 minutes 29 seconds. The longest annular eclipse occurred on December 7, 150 CE, lasting 12 minutes 24 seconds.

116. See Raymond E. Brown, *The Death of the Messiah: From Gethsemane to the Grave*, vol. 2, ABRL (New York: Doubleday, 1994), 2:1038–43, for a detailed discussion on the problem.

117. Including patristic citations, *The New Testament in Greek: The Gospel According to St. Luke*, Part Two: Chapters 13–24, ed. by the American and British Committees of the IGNTP (Oxford: Clarendon, 1987), records at least fifteen different readings, with seven having no Greek manuscript support.

118. The manuscripts in parentheses have the present participle ἐκλείποντος.

solid Alexandrian support, while the easier reading ἐσκοτίσθη is supported by Byzantine, "Western," and Caesarean witnesses. The internal evidence, however, is so strongly in favor of the "eclipsed" reading that it is most likely authentic. It is difficult to account for ἐκλιπόντος if ἐσκοτίσθη is original. This suggests that scribes, too, felt the awkwardness of Luke's word choice and adjusted the expression to speak of a general darkness.

6. JOHN 8:57

In a hostile dialogue between Jesus and the religious leaders in the temple, the Lord claims that Abraham rejoiced to see "my day" and when he saw it, he was glad (John 8:56). The Jews then responded contemptuously: "You are not yet fifty years old yet you have seen Abraham?" (v. 57). To the modern reader the apparent assessment of Jesus's age seems odd. Irenaeus dealt with the difficulty by claiming that Jesus must have been at least in his forties at the time of this exchange; he thought that Jesus's ministry extended more than two decades![119] The heated response, however, almost certainly was focusing on Jesus's youth vis-à-vis his obvious authoritative manner.[120] The scribe of one ninth-century codex, however, had both a better sense of chronology than Irenaeus and a somewhat liberated sense of his or her own role: the majuscule codex Λ (039) has σαράκοντα ("forty") instead of πεντήκοντα ("fifty") here.[121] It may be that the scribe thought that some exemplar in the ancestry of Λ had this reading since the abbreviation for *fifty* in Greek was N̄ while *forty* was M̄. Thus, although πεντήκοντα and σαράκοντα are not sufficiently alike for an accidental change, M̄ and N̄ are. The scribe of 039 most likely was thinking only that an error had crept into the transmissional line rather than that it was in the original text of John 8:57.

These six illustrations carry different levels of conviction, due in large part to questions as to what was the *prior* text that was being changed. But the earlier text in the first, second, and fifth examples is indisputable. And in each instance some later scribes seemed to have difficulty with the wording and revised it to what they considered appropriate.

Scribal Conservatism

We have looked at several passages in which scribes seemed to have altered the text that they were copying because of some difficulty or embarrassment

---

119. Irenaeus, *Haer.* 2.22.
120. Keener, *John*, 1:769, gives both Jewish and Greco-Roman sources that imply a certain age threshold one must normally meet for certain roles of authority.
121. This is in the first hand of the manuscript; it was corrected to πεντήκοντα.

they encountered. Some of these examples of scribal revision were supported by remarkably few witnesses. We must not think that the scribes were systematically and radically changing the text. For the most part, they did not feel the freedom to adjust the wording to fit their own agendas. In fact, the great majority of scribes had no agenda at all, apart from making a faithful copy. In this respect, they were unlike the evangelists, whose redactional fingerprints can be seen everywhere.[122] Matthew especially was far more systematic than any scribe in modifying Mark's Gospel to fit his themes and motifs. And yet, as Head notes, Matthew was "a developer rather than a corrector of Mark"[123]—at least in general.

Wisse makes a similar point about scribal conservatism: "The claims of extensive ideological redaction of the Gospels and other early Christian literature run counter to all of the textual evidence."[124] Kurt and Barbara Aland likewise speak of "how rarely significant variants occur."[125] At the end of their chapter on scribal errors, Metzger and Ehrman conclude:

> Lest the foregoing examples of alterations should give the impression that scribes were altogether willful and capricious in transmitting ancient copies of the New Testament, it ought to be noted that other evidence points to the careful and painstaking work on the part of many faithful copyists. . . .
>
> Even in incidental details one observes the faithfulness of scribes. . . . These examples of dogged fidelity on the part of scribes could be multiplied and serve to counterbalance, to some extent, the impression that this chapter may otherwise make upon the beginner in New Testament textual criticism.[126]

CONCLUSION

In this essay, we have laid out a pattern of reaction to the exemplar text that scribes were copying—a pattern that is on a continuum with the later evangelists.

---

122. Frederik Wisse, "The Nature and Purpose of Redactional Changes in Early Christian Texts: The Canonical Gospels," in *Gospel Traditions in the Second Century: Origins, Recensions, Text, and Transmission*, ed. William L. Peterson (Notre Dame, IN: University of Notre Dame Press, 1989), 42–43, discusses several differences between the scribes and the evangelists in handling the text of Mark's Gospel.

123. Head, *Christology and the Synoptic Problem*, i.

124. Wisse, "Redactional Changes," 52–53.

125. Kurt Aland and Barbara Aland, *The Text of the New Testament: An Introduction to the Critical Editions and to the Theory and Practice of Modern Textual Criticism*, 2nd ed. (Grand Rapids: Eerdmans; Leiden: Brill, 1989), 28.

126. Bruce M. Metzger and Bart D. Ehrman, *The Text of the New Testament: Its Transmission, Corruption, and Restoration*, 4th ed. (Oxford: Oxford University Press, 2005), 271.

Yet these scribes were not as systematic nor as motif driven as Matthew and Luke. However, they sometimes altered the wording because it was almost surely embarrassing or at least problematic for them, and adjustments therefore were needed. If the text was occasionally embarrassing or troublesome for the scribes, it must have been embarrassing or troublesome for the evangelists. These variant readings, therefore, constitute evidence that the criterion of embarrassment is a valid tool in the search for historical authenticity in the Jesus traditions.

CHAPTER 5

Collective Memory and the Reliability of the Gospel Traditions

ROBERT MCIVER

I n this chapter a case will be made that the traditions found in the Gospels should be considered products of collective memory. We will explore the implications that this conclusion has for the accuracy with which the traditions preserve the teachings and activities of Jesus. This shall be done by looking at four significant processes in the formation, preservation and transmission of the memories of Jesus over the thirty to sixty years between the events of his earthly ministry and the writing of the Gospels. The processes considered are as follows: (1) the formation of the initial memories of eyewitnesses; (2) the formation of the earliest collective memories of Jesus; (3) the survival of eyewitnesses up to the period in which the Gospels were written; (4) the retention of memories of Jesus over thirty to sixty-year periods. As each of these is considered in turn, attention will be given to the factors that influence the reliability of memory during that process.

THE FORMATION OF THE INITIAL MEMORIES OF EYEWITNESSES OF JESUS

Evaluations of the Contribution of Eyewitness Memories to the Gospel Traditions

Very few would attempt to deny that Jesus lived in Palestine, gathered followers, came into conflict with the Jewish authorities, was crucified, and that subsequently a movement arose in which people claimed he was a teacher and miracle worker.[1] Events in Jesus's life and ministry were of a nature that would

---

1. Among those few who would argue against the possibility that Jesus did, in fact, live in Palestine, taught, healed, and was crucified, is Robert M. Price, who says, "For me the Christ of faith has all the more importance since I think it most probable that there was never any other" (Price, "Jesus at the Vanishing

have left vivid memories in the minds of those who witnessed them. They would have been moments of great personal significance, moments they would have reflected on as they decided whether or not to become followers of Jesus.[2] Any part of the gospel traditions that is an accurate account of what happened during the life of Jesus relies on events and sayings having been accurately remembered. But how accurate is human memory? Can it be relied upon? Does it persist for a long time? Can the events found in human memory be reliably passed from one individual to another?

Assessments of how much credence should be attributed to the contribution made by eyewitnesses to the traditions about Jesus vary considerably. Richard Bauckham finds the incorporation of eyewitness testimony into the gospel traditions and the eyewitnesses continued availability right up to the time that the Gospels were written to be strong evidence that the gospel accounts are accurate, the accuracy of the transmission of Jesus teaching being enhanced by memorization of the traditions by the disciples and other early followers of Jesus. "Memorization," Bauckham claims, is a means of preserving the tradition "faithfully with a minimum of change."[3]

Judith C. S. Redman protests strongly against Bauckham's too quick endorsement of the preservative powers of human memory.[4] She points out that psychological research has led to the identification of many factors that can change eyewitnesses' memory of an event. She notes that (i) facets of another individual's report may be unconsciously incorporated into eyewitnesses' memory of that event; (ii) witnesses tend to avoid conflicting with reports from others and usually choose a culturally appropriate version of the event; (iii) post-event information can influence what elements of an event are retained in memory;

Point," *The Historical Jesus: Five Views*, eds. James K. Beilby and Paul Rhodes Eddy [Downers Grove, IL: IVP Academic, 2009], 56). See the "Response to Robert M. Price" by John Dominic Crossan (ibid., 86), who suggests a list of facts that almost nobody denies to be true of Jesus. Nor does this exhaust what Crossan considers to be able to be known about Jesus. See also Crossan, *The Historical Jesus: The Life of a Mediterranean Jewish Peasant* (San Francisco: HarperSanFrancisco, 1991), and idem, *The Birth of Christianity: Discovering What Happened in the Years Immediately after the Execution of Jesus* (San Francisco: HarperSanFrancisco, 1998). A position of outright skepticism concerning the existence of Jesus, such as that advocated by Price, is held by a very small number of academics.

2. David Pillemer considers memories of personal trauma, flashbulb memories, memories of critical incidents, and moments of insight to be but varieties of a phenomenon he describes as a "personal event memory." Such events evoke a strong emotional response and are likely to form memories of the personal circumstances occurring at the time of the formation of the memory, together with vivid sensory memories, which enable the re-living of the event in the imagination (David Pillemer, *Momentous Events, Vivid Memories* [Cambridge, MA: Harvard University Press, 1998]).

3. Richard Bauckham, *Jesus and the Eyewitnesses: The Gospels as Eyewitness Testimony* (Grand Rapids: Eerdmans, 2006), 305.

4. Judith C. S. Redman, "How Accurate Are Eyewitnesses? Bauckham and the Eyewitnesses in the Light of Psychological Research," *JBL* 129 (2010): 177–97.

(iv) eyewitnesses guess some elements of their report, and over time these guesses become treated as part of the original memory; (v) errors become frozen into memories; and, most importantly, (vi) while group memories are more stable than individual memories, group memories incorporate from a very early time the mistakes made by individual eyewitnesses; and furthermore, (vii) these group memories will be further shaped by theological considerations within the community. These and other considerations led Redman to conclude, "The continued presence in Christian communities of eyewitnesses to Jesus' ministry until the time when these events were recorded is a guarantee only of the community's agreed version, not of the exact details of the event itself." Her overall view of what can be known of Jesus and his teachings appears to be quite negative. She concludes, "In other words, it seems likely that the answer to the question How much can we reliably know about the Jesus of history from the Gospels in the light of Bauckhams work? is still 'not much.'"[5]

Redman raises some very important issues regarding the accuracy of eyewitnesses, including the very real possibility that false memories may have been incorporated into the eyewitnesses' memories of Jesus's ministry. Research into false memories has enabled an assessment to be made of the potential impact such memory frailties might have had on the Jesus traditions.

False Memories and Bias

Psychologists have been studying qualities of human memory since the beginning of the discipline.[6] The specific issue of the reliability of eyewitness memories was considered as early as 1908 in the collection of essays, *On the Witness Stand*, by Hugo Münsterberg, and much research has been devoted to the topic in the years since that time.[7] Particular attention has been given to the study of the circumstances in which a false memory can be generated in eyewitnesses,

---

5. Redman, "How Accurate Are Eyewitnesses?," 193, 197.

6. Many consider that the origins of experimental psychology should be traced to the work of Herman Ebbinghaus, in which he experimented on his own memory retention. His findings were published as *Über das Gedächtnis* (Leipzig: Duncker and Humblot, 1885); translated into English by 1913, and published as *Memory: A Contribution to Experimental Psychology* (New York: Dover, 1964).

7. For example, Renate Volbert and Max Steller, "Is this Testimony Truthful, Fabricated, or Based on False Memory? Credibility Assessment 25 Years after Steller and Köhnken (1989)," *European Psychologist* 19 (2014): 207–20. See also the summary of consensus in Saul M. Kassin, V. Anne Tubb, Harmon M. Hosch, and Amina Memon, "On the 'General Acceptance' of Eyewitness Testimony Research: A New Survey of the Experts," *American Psychologist* 56 (2001): 405–16 (see esp. tables 1 and 5). In addition see the summary comments of Gary L. Wells, Roy S. Malpass, R. C. L. Lindsay, Ronald P. Fisher, John W. Turtle, Solomon M. Fulero, "From the Lab to the Police Station: A Successful Application of Eyewitness Research," *American Psychologist* 55 (2000): 581–98; Gary L. Wells and Elizabeth A. Olson, "Eyewitness Testimony," *Annual Review of Psychology* 54 (2003): 277–94; Elizabeth F. Loftus, "Memory in Canadian Courts of Law," *Canadian Psychology* 44 (2003): 207–12; Elizabeth F. Loftus and Katherine Ketcham, *Witness for the Defense: The Accused, the Eyewitness, and the Expert Who Puts Memory on Trial* (New York: St. Martin's, 1991).

and many experiments have been designed to demonstrate the processes by which false memories might be generated and communicated to others.

A widely used method of generating false memories in psychology laboratories is the Deese, Roediger, and McDermott False Memory Procedure (DRM).[8] Roediger and McDermott discovered that if experimental participants were asked to recall the following list of words, "bed, rest, awake, tired, dream, wake, snooze, blanket, doze, slumber, snore, nap, peace, yawn, drowsy," that the word "sleep" would be "remembered" as frequently as any of the words in the middle of the list. This should not be surprising, given that the word "sleep" has strong associations with all the other words in the list, and memory retrieval is a reconstructive process. Roediger and McDermott published several lists of words with strong associations that have been used by a great number of other researchers investigating memory. The DRM procedure has been found to be a very robust method of generating false memories under a wide variety of circumstances.[9] Yet one must note what kind of an error it is to include "sleep" in a list comprised of "bed, rest, dream," etc. It is true that "sleep" is not part of the list. But it is *consistent* with the list. While many participants remember "sleep" being part of the list, nobody remembers completely unrelated words such as "whale" or "microwave." "Sleep" is a mistake, but one that is consistent with what was actually on the list. In making sense of the world around it, human memory makes associations between linked things. One could question whether "sleep" is a *false* memory, or just memory working in its usual way as it endeavors to bring out the underlying meaning of experiences.

---

8. Henry L. Roediger III and Kathleen B. McDermott, "Creating False Memories: Remembering Words Not Presented in Lists," *Journal of Experimental Psychology: Learning, Memory & Cognition* 21 (1995): 803–14. Cf. also the analysis of 55 fifteen-word lists with their associated critical items, together with figures for backward associative strength, and forward associative strengths, in Henry L. Roediger III, Jason M. Watson, Kathleen B. McDermott, and David Gallo, "Factors that Determine False Recall: A Multiple Regression Analysis," *Psychonomic Bulletin & Review* 8 (2001): 385–407, esp. 399–407.

9. For example: Luciano Grüdtner Buratto, Carlos Falcão de Azevedo Gomes, Thiago da Silva Prusokowski, and Lilian Milnitsky Stein, "Inter-Item Associations for the Brazilian Version of the Deese/Roediger-McDermott Paradigm," *Psicologia: Reflexão e Crítica* 26 (2013): 367–75; Joanna Ulatowska and Justyna Olszewska, "Creating Associative Memory Distortions—A Polish Adaption of the DRM Paradigm," *Polish Psychological Bulletin* 44 (2013): 449–56; Mark J. Huff, Jennifer H. Coane, Keith A. Hutchison, Elisabeth B. Grasser, and Jessica E. Blais, "Interpolated Task Effects on Direct and Mediated False Recognition: Effects of Initial Recall, Recognition, and the Ironic Effect of Guessing," *Journal of Experimental Psychology: Learning, Memory, and Cognition* 38 (2012): 1720–30; Lauren M. Knott, Emma Threadgold, and Mark L. Howe, "Negative Mood State Impairs False Memory Priming When Problem-Solving," *Journal of Cognitive Psychology* 26 (2014): 580–87; Ederaldo José Lopes and Ricardo Basso Garcia, "On the Possibility of Using Reaction Time to Study False Memories," *Psychology & Neuroscience* 7 (2014): 393–97. See also the long list of experimental conditions which have been investigated in John G. Seamon, Madeleine S. Goodkind, Adam D. Dumey, Ester Dick, Marla S. Aufseeser, Sarah E. Strickland, Jeffrey R. Woulfin, and Nicholas S. Fung, "'If I Didn't Write It, Why Would I Remember It?' Effects of Encoding, Attention, and Practice on Accurate and False Memory," *Memory and Cognition* 31 (2003): 445–57.

Redman mentions that "facets of another individual's report may be uncon-sciously incorporated into eyewitnesses' memory of that event." This has indeed been verified experimentally and is often described as the social contagion of memory.[10] For example, Mark J. Huff, Sara D. Davis and Michelle L. Meade report an experiment in which they showed participants six photographs of com-mon household scenes sequentially on a screen for fifteen seconds each. Each photograph was preceded by a heading: "The Toolbox," "The Bathroom," "The Kitchen," "The Bedroom," "The Closet," and "The Desk." In a fictitious recall test, participants were asked to remember items they had seen in the photographs on two separate occasions. First, after completing a filler task, they were given six pages with the respective headings, "The Toolbox," etc., and given two minutes for each of them to write down as many of the items in each picture as possible. Next—the part of the experiment that simulated social interaction—participants were told that an additional purpose of the experiment was to see how much pleas-antness affected whether a particular item was remembered. They were then given five sets of responses that they were informed were answers from other participants and invited to identify those items on the answers that were pleasant, a process that ensured attention was given to each of the items. Some of the participants saw "answers from other participants" that were seeded with contagion items, some whose presence might be highly expected, others less so, according to an experi-mental protocol (e.g., some participants saw lists of remembered objects from the kitchen scene that included "toaster" and "napkins," items absent from the photo). When asked a second time to recall what had been seen in the photographs, many of the participants "recalled" the items that had been added as contagion items to the "answers from other participants." This was true of both the control group, who had not had the contagion items on any list that they had seen (i.e., were self-generated), and the experimental group who had. Noteworthy, though, is that the incidence of contagion items was significantly higher (statistically) in the group that had been shown lists with the contagion items on them.[11]

Huff, David, and Meade based their experimental protocol on earlier experi-ments by Henry L. Roediger III, Michelle L. Meade, and Erik T. Bergman, who had used a similar set of six photographs, but used a confederate of the researchers to act

10. For example, Jonathan Koppel, Dana Wohl, Robert Meksin, and William Hirst, "The Effect of Listening to Others Remember on Subsequent Memory: The Roles of Expertise and Trust in Socially Shared Retrieval-Induced Forgetting and Social Contagion," *Social Cognition* 32 (2014): 148–80; Aileen Oeberst and Julienne Seidemann, "Will Your Words Become Mine? Underlying Processes and Cowitness Intimacy in the Memory Conformity Paradigm," *Canadian Journal of Experimental Psychology / Revue canadienne de psychologie expérimentale* 68 (2014): 84–96.

11. Mark J. Huff, Sara D. Davis, and Michelle L. Meade, "The Effects of Initial Testing on False Recall and False Recognition in the Social Contagion of Memory Paradigm," *Memory and Cognition* 41 (2013): 820–31.

the role of experimental participant.[12] The confederate and one other participant took turns at remembering items from the photographs, during which process the confederate would introduce a high-expectancy and low-expectancy contagion item. When later asked to recall items from the photographs, even the control group who had not been provided with the contagion item occasionally reported high-expectancy contagion items (e.g., a toaster in the kitchen scene). But the group who had been in a social situation where a contagion item was suggested recalled them with a statistically significant higher frequency than the control group.

What is to be made of this "social contagion" of memory? Strictly speaking, "remembering" a contagion item that was not in the original photograph is a memory error. But while some incorrectly remembered a "toaster" as part of the kitchen scene, nobody remembered a "hippopotamus" as being in the kitchen scene. Once again, "false memories" have been generated, but they are in fact memories that are consistent with what was actually present. The "false memory" is generated as part of the human brain's ability to make sense of its environment by linking together similar items that are usually found together.

Other experimental protocols have been used to generate false memories,[13] but they almost all share a common trait: false memories may be induced, but they are memories that are consistent with the stimulus. Social contagion may introduce a false memory, but that false memory is, to a degree, consistent with what actually is being remembered.

Redman also raises the issue of bias when she says that post-event information can influence which elements of an event are retained in memory. A key element of the process she mentions is that of *hindsight bias*, which might be defined as the change between how one estimated the likelihood of a certain outcome before the event had occurred and how in hindsight one remembers what one considered to be the likelihood of a particular outcome after the outcome is known.[14] Hindsight bias has been studied in such diverse contexts as an auditor's judgment of whether or not a company would survive after one year, investor behavior, age, the law courts, history, and sporting events.[15] It should be noted,

12. Henry L. Roediger III, Michelle L. Meade, and Erik T. Bergman, "Social Contagion of Memory," *Psychonomic Bulletin & Review* 8 (2001): 365–71; Michelle L. Meade and Henry L. Roediger III, "Explorations in the Social Contagion of Memory," *Memory & Cognition* 30 (2002): 995–1009.

13. A number of these are described in Robert K. McIver, *Memory, Jesus, and the Synoptic Gospels* (Atlanta: Society of Biblical Literature, 2011), 60–70. See also idem, "Eyewitnesses as Guarantors of the Accuracy of the Gospel Traditions in the Light of Psychological Research," *JBL* 131 (2012): 530–33.

14. Alisha Coolin, Edgar Erdfielder, Daniel M. Bernstein, Allen E. Thornton, Wendy Loken Thornton, "Explaining Individual Differences in Cognitive Processes Underlying Hindsight Bias," *Psychonomic Bulletin & Review* 22 (2015): 328–48; Matúš Konečný and Viera Bačová, "Hindsight Bias and Its Reversal: What Will Time Reveal?" *Studia Psychologica* 454 (2012): 251–58.

15. Kim L. Anderson, "The Effects of Hindsight Bias on Experienced and Inexperienced Auditors'

however, that even though the significance attached to memories of the past is adjusted to account for subsequent events, this process does not introduce memories of things that did not happen. They are still based on real events.

Accuracy of Eyewitness Memory

The brain's attempts to derive meaning, significance, and causation from memories of past events allows the incorporation of elements of bias, and even memories of things that were not actually seen or heard by the eyewitness. Hindsight bias and suggestibility are but two of what Daniel Schacter has described as *The Seven Sins of Memory*.[16] Even so, memory should not be dismissed as arbitrary. It is capable of remarkable feats of recall, as is illustrated in one of the very few studies of eyewitness memory that has been able to make use of police interviews of an actual crime.

In an attempted robbery of a gun store in Burnaby, Vancouver, Canada, a robber with a handgun held up a gun store. He tied up the owner, picked up several weapons, and left. The owner managed to release himself rather quickly and rushed outside, hoping at least to get a description of the getaway car. Once outside, he surprised the thief, who was still loading the stolen merchandise into his car. The gun store owner and thief exchanged shots, leaving the thief dead and the owner of the gun store injured. The police interviewed available witnesses, and a decision was made to not prosecute the owner of the gun store. Researchers are not usually able to approach witnesses directly, and quite rightly so, given the possibility of introducing bias into memories. But because this case was not going to prosecution, John C. Yuille and Judith L. Cutshall were given access to the records of the police interviews and crime-scene photos. In addition, they were given permission to contact the witnesses, which they were able to do three months after the crime. From the photos and other evidential data, Yuille and Cutshall were able to determine a number of factual matters that could

Relevance Ratings of Adverse Factors Versus Mitigating Factors," *Journal of Business & Economics Research* 12 (2014): 199–208; Rasoul Sadi, Hassan Ghalibaf Asl, Mohammad Reza Rostami, Aryan Gholipour, and Fattaneh Gholipour, "Behavioral Finance: The Explanation of Investors' Personality and Perceptual Biases Effects on Financial Decisions," *International Journal of Economics and Finance* 3 (2011): 234–41; Julia Groß and Ute J. Bayen, "Adult Age Differences in Hindsight Bias: The Role of Recall Ability," *Psychology and Aging* 30 (2015): 253–58; Merrie Jo Stallard and Debra L. Worthington, "Reducing the Hindsight Bias Utilizing Attorney Closing Arguments," *Law and Human Behavior* 22 (1998): 671–83; Baruch Fischhoff, "Hindsight ≠ Foresight: The Effect of Outcome Knowledge on Judgment Under Uncertainty," *Journal of Experimental Psychology: Human Perception and Performance* 1 (1975): 288–99; Jennifer M. Bonds-Raacke, Lakeysha S. Freyer, Sandra D. Nicks, and Rena T. Durr, "Hindsight Bias Demonstrated in the Prediction of a Sporting Event," *The Journal of Social Psychology* 141 (2001): 349–52.

16. Daniel L. Schacter, *The Seven Sins of Memory: How the Mind Forgets and Remembers* (Boston: Houghton Mifflin, 2001). Schacter lists the seven sins of memory as transience, absent-mindedness, blocking, misattribution, suggestibility, bias, and persistence (pp. 1–11 and *passim*).

be tested in the police interviews and in the follow-up interviews. They set up rather strict criteria for considering a memory accurate and discovered that, on average, witnesses were entirely accurate in 80 percent of the details that they recounted of the crime, at least up to three months after the event.[17] All the witnesses remembered the gist of what had taken place.

How should this result be judged? Is it lamentable that eyewitnesses were only 80 percent accurate in the details they remembered? Or should we celebrate that they were only 20 percent erroneous? What should not be overlooked, however, is that even the 20 percent of incorrect details were consistent with what actually happened. The core of the memory was preserved, even if some of the details were not entirely accurate.

Accuracy of Memories of Individual Eyewitnesses of Jesus

The memories of the initial eyewitnesses to Jesus's activities during his earthly ministry would have been subject to the same vicissitudes that beset all human memory. Their memories would have been partial, largely composed of individual actions or sayings, and subject to the intrusion of false memories. If it is legitimate to apply the results of Yuille and Cutshall's research to the recollections of those who were eyewitnesses of Jesus's activities, one might expect their memories to have been accurate in 80 percent of the details. From the point of view of reliability, one would wish that the memories of the eyewitnesses of Jesus would be 100 percent accurate in what they remembered. What is of significance, though, is that the 20 percent of the details that are not remembered accurately are nevertheless *consistent* with what was said and done. The gist of Jesus's sayings as well as the general trend of his actions and activities would have been preserved. These memories would be framed by the cultural expectations and life experiences of the witnesses, but they would retain the essence of what happened, particularly when added to the memories of other eyewitnesses, as the various groups who knew Jesus formed a collective memory of him.

FORMATION OF INITIAL COLLECTIVE MEMORIES OF JESUS

Some of the experiments just recounted have revealed the influence a group can have on an individual's memory of events as a collective memory of an event is formed. Collective memory may be described as follows:

---

17. John C. Yuille and Judith L. Cutshall, "A Case Study of Eyewitness Memory of a Crime," *Journal of Applied Psychology* 71 (1986): 291–301.

Collective memory is an elusive concept that suggests that groups and nations have sets of common memories that contribute to the group's self-understanding and identity. Naturally, these memories have no independent existence outside the memories of individuals, be they in the group or not. Nevertheless, such memories are "collective" in the sense that they are common to all the individuals that form the group. These collective memories can also represent the esoteric knowledge that provides the theoretical basis for the professional conduct of groups such as judges, doctors, and priests.[18]

The Social Circumstances of First-Century Palestine and the Formation of Collective Memory

That memories of Jesus, his teaching, and his activities would become part of the collective memory of those amongst whom he lived is inevitable, particularly given the social circumstances in which he lived. Archaeology has revealed much about the physical layout of Nazareth, Capernaum, and Jerusalem, the towns and city most associated with Jesus in the gospel accounts.

Jesus's public ministry was centered on Capernaum (Matt 4:13; Mark 2:1). In the first century, Capernaum was a small fishing village on the northern shores of the Sea of Galilee, about six to ten hectares in extent. It had a population of between six hundred and one thousand five hundred people and interesting things that were done and said would have circulated with great freedom, particularly given the living conditions. Many of the inhabitants of the small village would meet regularly at the synagogue (Mark 1:21; Luke 4:16), but the village had no theatre or public forums.[19] It seems almost trivial to point out that modern methods of home entertainment such as reading, radio, and television were not available. Furthermore, what lighting was available after dark would have been provided by fires and very inefficient lamps. Thus, most of the evenings would have been spent engaged in talk of one kind or another. Stories of interesting events would have circulated, and stories of particular significance to the group

---

18. McIver, *Memory, Jesus, and the Synoptic Gospels*, 82–83; see also further discussion pp. 81–94. Most modern uses of the concept of collective memory can be traced back to the French sociologist Maurice Halbwachs, who began to use the term in 1925. Read today, Halbwachs's work (e.g., Maurice Halbwachs, *On Collective Memory* [Chicago: University of Chicago Press, 1992]) is a fascinating mixture of very useful insights and rather idiosyncratic arguments, and assessments of Halbwachs's writings on the topic range from an enthusiastic, if selective, account of those parts of his general theory subsequently found to have been useful (e.g., Patrick H. Hutton, *History as an Art of Memory* [Hanover, VT: University Press of New England, 1993], 73–90) to a discrediting of his work by a hostile concentration of those parts of his arguments that few take seriously (e.g., Noa Gedi and Yigal Elam, "Collective Memory—What Is It?," *History and Memory* 8 [1996]: 30–50).

19. Jonathan L. Reed, *Archaeology and the Galilean Jesus* (Harrisburg, PA: Trinity, 2000), 139–69; Robert K. McIver, "The Archaeology of Galilee," in *The Content and Setting of the Gospel Tradition*, ed. Mark Harding and Alanna Nobbs (Grand Rapids: Eerdmans, 2010), 9–12.

sharing them would have been repeated often. What Jesus said and did would have been the topic of many conversations, and each social group at Capernaum would have developed a "collective memory" of him and his doings, particularly those groups that modeled their own behavior and beliefs on his teachings.

Apart from the birth narratives, few stories in the gospel accounts relate to Nazareth. But given that the town was much smaller than Capernaum,[20] it is again inevitable that everybody who lived there would have known him well. First-century Jerusalem was much larger than either Nazareth or Capernaum. At the time of Jesus, it is estimated that the population was between forty thousand and eighty thousand,[21] the higher number reached in 66 CE, just prior to the Jewish revolt. The numbers of those in Jerusalem at the time of Jesus's crucifixion would have swelled considerably by pilgrims visiting the city for Passover. Yet, even though he spent but a small part of his ministry there, few in the city would have been unaware of his activities around the temple and the circumstances of his death. The Roman authorities, as was their wont, took care to parade him past as many of those in the city as possible on the way to his death, and the place of crucifixion was chosen so that many would be aware of the fate of those who rebelled against Rome (Mark 15:21–22; Luke 23:26–33; John 19:16–17). These events would have been part of the collective memory of most who lived in Jerusalem. In particular, it would have been the topic of extended conversation by those who considered themselves to be his followers. Many groups in Jerusalem would have formed strong collective memories of Jesus's death from such conversations.

The Twelve Disciples

One group would have had a particularly strong and relatively well-defined collective memory of Jesus's teachings: the twelve men who were known as his inner group of disciples. These men spent much time with Jesus during his ministry and, shortly before the events that culminated in his crucifixion, were given a task which would have required them to formulate and commit to memory a coherent body of teaching.

Jesus was known as a teacher (Matt 7:28–29; Mark 4:38; 5:34; 9:17; John 6:59, etc.).[22] As such, he would have followed the practice of all teachers found in the

---

20. Robert K. McIver, "First-Century Nazareth," in *Glaube und Zukunftsgestaltung: Festschrift zum hundertjährigen Bestehen der Theologischen Hochschule Friedensau: Aufsätze zu Theologie, Sozialwissenschaften und Musik,* ed. Bernhard Oestreich, Horst Rolly, and Wolfgang Kabus (Frankfurt am Main: Peter Lang, 1999), 139–59; Willibald Bösen, *Galiläa: Lebensraum und Wirkungsfeld Jesu* (Freiburg: Herder, 1998), 97–110.

21. Magen Broshi, "Estimating the Population of Ancient Jerusalem," *BAR* 4 (1978): 10–15.

22. "The church today, so diverse in all of its expressions, likely converges around the theological

ancient Near East—he would have taught his disciples to memorize his teaching.[23] The term *memorizing* has a different meaning for modern readers from that which it probably had for ancient teachers and students. Verbatim memorization of longer texts is only possible with the ability to reference a written text.[24] It is known that the poems of Homer were memorized verbatim on the basis of the written text that existed in the Greco-Roman period.[25] But for oral material, such as that memorized by the Rabbis and their students—and no doubt Jesus and his disciples—a saying or parable would have been considered sufficiently memorized if the disciple was able to repeat its core meaning. Some types of material lend themselves to verbatim or near-verbatim memorization. These include short aphorisms, particularly those aphorisms of two or more lines that have strong thematic parallels between the lines. It is perhaps significant that much of Jesus's teaching material preserved in the Synoptic Gospels comes in the form of easily memorized aphorisms or parables, which convey their meaning with a coherent story and a punchline, often expressed in an aphorism.

The gospel accounts record that as Jesus was making his way to Jerusalem, he sent his disciples ahead of him to share his teachings in the villages he was about to enter (Matt 10:5–8; Mark 6:7; Luke 9:1–6; 10:1). By this stage of his public ministry, Jesus had been instructing his disciples for some time and one would expect that the disciples would have been well prepared to share the fundamental tenets Jesus had been teaching them. Their having to teach on their own would have provided additional impetus for the disciples to establish Jesus's teachings quite firmly in their own memories.[26] As they taught, they would have continuously rehearsed the things they had learned.

---

confession of Jesus as Lord and Savior. . . . Yet there are only three occurrences of the title Savior, referring to Jesus, in the four Gospels (Luke 1:69 [lit., "a horn of salvation"], 2:11; John 4:42). Yet they speak frequently of Jesus as Lord and rabbi. Jesus is addressed as Lord no fewer than 83 times, and as rabbi or teacher 56 times. (The next most frequently used title for Jesus is the enigmatic Son of Man, found no fewer than 37 times.)" So Stephen D. Jones, *Rabbi Jesus: Learning from the Master Teacher* (Macon, GA: Peake Road, 1997), 1.

23. Rainer Riesner, "Jesus as Preacher and Teacher," in *Jesus and the Oral Gospel Tradition*, ed. Henry Wansbrough (Sheffield: JSOT Press, 1991), 186–87. Education, both in the Greco-Roman context and within Judaism, relied heavily on memorization. As it developed among the Greeks, "Basic education relies heavily on memory and recitation, limits attendance to those who can pay, offers strictly restricted instruction in writing, and defines grammar in terms of the sounds of the spoken language" (Tony M. Lentz, *Orality and Literacy in Ancient Greece* [Carbondale: Southern Illinois University Press, 1989], 56). For the place of memorization in Jewish education one can profitably consult Birger Gerhardsson, *Memory & Manuscript: Oral Tradition and Written Transmission in Rabbinic Judaism and Early Christianity* with *Tradition & Transmission in Early Christianity* (Grand Rapids: Eerdmans, 1998).

24. Ian M. L. Hunter, "Lengthy Verbatim Recall: The Role of Text," in *Progress in the Psychology of Language*, ed. Andrew W. Ellis, vol. 1 (London: Lawrence Erlbaum Associates, 1985), 207–35. Hunter carefully defines lengthy verbatim recall as "complete word-for-word fidelity of a sequence of 50 words or longer" (p. 207). By doing so, he excludes proverbs and stock phrases.

25. Lentz, *Orality and Literacy*, 35–45, esp. 42.

26. Heinz Schürmann, "Die vorösterlichen Anfänge der Logientradition," in *Der historische Jesus und*

The Synoptic Gospels record more than just the aphorisms and parables of Jesus, however. It is difficult to imagine Jesus teaching his disciples about his own miracles and his other deeds recorded in the Gospels. One can only speculate as to when the disciples started to recount the stories about Jesus. Some of the miracle stories of Jesus's ministry could well have formed part of what the twelve disciples shared in their teachings prior to the events of Easter. They are likely to have been repeated often by Jesus's followers when they began to recognize themselves as a group of fellow travelers linked by their joint understanding of the importance of Jesus in their lives. Furthermore, the events surrounding the crucifixion and resurrection of Jesus must have been the topic of many conversations among both Jesus's followers and his enemies. In this manner, many versions of collective memory concerning Jesus would have developed among different groups. Although travel was arduous, many did travel in the ancient world, and the book of Acts recounts some of those early Christians who travelled widely—Peter, Paul, Barnabas, Timothy, and others. As Christians met during their travels, they would have inevitably discussed their memories and understanding of Jesus. In doing so, the various collective memories of Jesus would have taken shape, and common themes would have emerged.

The Survival of Eyewitnesses until the Gospels Were Written

The New Testament emphasizes the importance of eyewitnesses as guarantors of the Christian traditions in several places (Luke 1:2; Acts 1:8, 22; 2:32; 3:15; 5:32; 10:39; 1 Pet 5:1; 2 Pet 1:16). Researchers have shown that there is a qualitative difference between the memories of eyewitnesses of events that occurred in the distant past and those who learned about an event that they had not witnessed.[27] Thus, the presence of eyewitnesses at the time the Gospels were written acted as a stabilizer of the traditions included in them. Yet, given the likely date the Gospels were written, how likely is it that eyewitnesses were still alive?

Dating the writing of the Gospels is problematic. Aside from the fact that Luke-Acts must have been written after Paul's arrival in Rome sometime in 59 CE,[28] there is very little hard evidence which allows an accurate dating of

---

der kerygmatische Christus, ed. Helmut Ristow and Karl Matthiae (Berlin: Evangelische Verlagsanstalt, 1960), 361–69. Cf. Rainer Riesner, *Jesus als Lehrer: eine Untersuchung zum Ursprung der Evangelien-Überlieferung*, WUNT 2/7 (Tübingen: Mohr, 1981), 453–75, 500–501; idem, "Jesus as Preacher and Teacher," 197–201.

27. See, for example, Dorthe Berntsen and Dorthe K. Thomsen, "Personal Memories for Remote Historical Events: Accuracy and Clarity of Flashbulb Memories Related to World War II," *Journal of Experimental Psychology: General* 134 (2005): 242–57.

28. Udo Schnelle gives 59 CE as the date for Paul's arrival in Rome, *Einleitung in das Neue Testament*, 4th ed. (Göttingen: Vandenhoeck & Ruprecht, 2002], 45), and other possible dates are canvassed in Rainer Riesner, *Paul's Early Period: Chronology, Mission Strategy, Theology* (Grand Rapids: Eerdmans, 1998), 3–28.

the writing of any of the Gospels. Such evidence that exists leads most scholars to posit a gap of between thirty and sixty years between the time of Jesus's death and the writing of the Gospels.[29]

Given that the average life expectancy at birth in the Roman Empire was approximately 23 years, at first sight it might appear that all eyewitnesses would have been long dead only thirty years later. But the demographics of populations comparable to those of the first century Roman Empire reveal that while life expectancy at birth might have only been 23, this average is much influenced by high infant mortality rates. It appears likely that at the time of the Roman Empire only 51 percent of people lived to the age of 10, but those who did lived an additional 38 years, on average, resulting in an average lifespan of 48 years for the population as a whole. Some particularly robust and lucky individuals lived into their 70s (about 8 percent of the population) and a very few into their 80s (1.6 percent).[30] Admittedly, 1.6 percent is a very small part of the population, but some did live to reach 80 years of age and older.

If one takes into account the age profile of the population, and the likely number of those who were eyewitnesses of Jesus's ministry in Capernaum and Galilee, and of his death and resurrection in Jerusalem, it is possible to estimate the number of surviving eyewitnesses at various intervals after the death and resurrection of Jesus. The estimates are given in Table 1.[31]

---

29. In his monograph, *Redating the New Testament* (London: SCM, 1976), 352, John A. T. Robinson proposed dates as early as "40–60+" CE for Matthew, 45–60 CE for Mark, "57–60+" CE for the Gospel of Luke, and similar dates have been suggested by John Wenham (*Redating Matthew, Mark and Luke: A Fresh Assault on the Synoptic Problem* [London: Hodder & Stoughton, 1991], xxv, 223–44) and Bo Reicke (*The Roots of the Synoptic Gospels* [Philadelphia: Fortress, 1986], 174–80). Reicke explicitly dates Luke to around 60 CE (p. 180). Robertson, Wenham, and Reicke represent some of the earliest dating that has been seriously proposed, but nevertheless, even by their dating, there is a period of 10 to 35 years between the events of the life of Jesus and the writing of the Gospels. Most who work with the Synoptic Gospels, however, tend to use dates closer to those suggested by Werner Georg Kümmel in his *Introduction to the New Testament* (London: SCM, 1975), 98, 120, 151, 246, of between 64 and 70 CE for Mark, 80 and 100 CE for Matthew, 70 and 90 CE for Luke, and 90 and 100 CE for John); or those suggested by Schnelle, of shortly before or after 70 CE for Mark, about 90 CE for Matthew and Luke, and between 100 and 110 CE for John (*Einleitung in das Neue Testament*, 244, 266, 288).

30. On the challenges of using the existing evidence to formulate and understand the demographics of the population of the Roman Empire and associated life expectancies, see McIver, *Memory, Jesus, and the Synoptic Gospels*, 189–202; Walter Scheidel, *Measuring Sex, Age and Death in the Roman Empire: Explorations in Ancient Demography*, JRA Supplementary Series (Ann Arbor, MI: Journal of Roman Archaeology, 1996); and idem, "Progress and Problems in Roman Demography," in *Debating Roman Demography*, ed. Walter Scheidel (Leiden: Brill, 2001), 1–81. See also Jonathan L. Reed, "Instability in Jesus' Galilee: A Demographic Perspective," *JBL* 129 (2010): 343–65. The figures cited in the text reflect Coale-Demeny West Model, level 3 (female), from Ansley J. Coale and Paul Demeny, *Regional Model Life Tables and Stable Populations*, 2nd ed. (New York: Academic Press, 1983).

31. A number of estimates and approximations have had to be used to arrive at the figures in Table 1. For example, archaeologists have been able to estimate the number of inhabitants in Capernaum and Jerusalem at the time of Jesus (see comments on population sizes in 2(a) in main text). The first approximation that has been used in Table 1 is that only those 15 years of age and older are likely to have formed clear memories of

TABLE 1: *Surviving Eyewitnesses of Jesus at Later Time Periods*
According to the Coale-Demeny West Model, for Level 3 Females

	Capernaum	Large Crowds	Jerusalem	Subtotals
Yr 0	1,005	10,000	51,750	62,755
Yr +5	847	8,636	44,692	54,175
Yr +10	701	7,356	38,069	46,126
Yr + 15	573	6,174	31,952	38,700
Yr + 20	466	5,094	26,360	31,919
Yr + 25	374	4,117	21,307	25,799
Yr + 30	294	3,244	16,787	20,326
Yr + 35	224	2,469	12,775	15,467
Yr + 40	162	1,786	9,243	11,191
Yr + 45	110	1,208	6,250	7,568
Yr + 50	67	740	3,830	4,637
Yr + 55	36	399	2,067	2,502
Yr + 60	16	177	918	1,111

As may be seen from Table 1, conservative estimates reveal that of the approximately 60,000 eyewitnesses of Jesus's ministry, death, or resurrection who were aged 15 years or older, at least 20,000 would likely have been alive 30 years later, and over 1,000 up to 60 years later. Thus, it might be reasonably concluded that living eyewitnesses would have been able to contribute to the traditions that formed the basis of the Gospels and that their continued presence in the communities out of which the Gospels arose would have served to ensure

---

Jesus of the type that would survive for 30 or more years. The Coale-Demeny West Model level 3 life tables were then used to estimate the number of those in Capernaum and Jerusalem who were aged at least 15 years in about 30 CE. The loosest approximation in the table is the number in the large crowds that followed Jesus for parts of his ministry (e.g. Matt 4:25; 5:11; 20:29; Mark 4:1; Luke 7:12; 14:25–26; John 6:2). The number 10,000 was chosen arbitrarily, in part because of the mention of 5,000 men besides women and children on one occasion where crowds were present (Matt 14:21; Mark 6:44; Luke 9:14; John 6:10). The numbers in the various crowds that followed Jesus could well have been much higher, but conservative estimates have been used in the table. From the beginning, the life table has been used to estimate the number of survivors of each age. It should be noted that, while exact numbers are given in the table (so that the process of iteration does not add to much additional error), in reality these are but poor estimates of the numbers of survivors. The estimates are likely on the low side.

that what was said about Jesus corresponded to their actual memories of him—memories that corresponded to what Jesus had actually done and said.

THE RETENTION OF MEMORIES OF JESUS FOR PERIODS OF THIRTY TO SIXTY YEARS

What Happens to Individual Human Memory over Thirty to Sixty Years?

It appears that a number of eyewitnesses of Jesus and his activities were still alive when the Gospels were written, but given the nature of human memory, we might ask: How much would they have remembered of Jesus? And how accurate would that memory have been?

A great volume of published research investigating human memory appears each year, but most of it reports research on memory intervals that are of a very short duration—seconds, minutes, hours, days—and not the thirty-plus years that elapsed between the ministry of Jesus and the writing of the Gospels. This should not be surprising, given the methodological challenges of studying memory over long periods of time. Nevertheless, some experiments trace what happens to human memory over longer periods of time.

Willem A. Wagenaar, for example, studied his own memory over a period of six years.[32] While this is not a period in excess of thirty years, when combined with information that will be reported later, his experiment provides a way to estimate what happens to memories of events over longer periods of time. For a period of six years, at the end of each day, Wagenaar filled out one or two pre-printed forms headed with a random number. On each form he recorded one event that, based on the categories who/what/where/when, were "at the time of recording, unique and fully distinguishable from all other things that happened before" (p. 229). He also wrote down a question about a critical detail that, if answered correctly, would provide evidence that he was actually remembering the event rather than something like it. In his article he gave a sample of a filled-in form, which had the following information: random number: 3329; who: Leonardo da Vinci; what: I went to see his "last supper"; where: in a church in

---

32. Willem A. Wagenaar, "My Memory: A Study of Autobiographic Memory over Six Years," *Cognitive Psychology* 18 (1986): 225–52. Wagenaar was able to benefit from earlier studies, such as Marigold Linton, "Memory for Real World Events," in *Explorations in Cognition*, ed. Donald A. Norman and David E. Rumelhart (San Francisco: Freeman, 1975), 376–404; idem, "Real World Memory after Six Years: An in vivo Study of Very long Term Memory," in *Practical Aspects of Memory*, ed. M. M. Gruneberg, P. E. Morris, and R. N. Sykes (London: Academic Press, 1978), 69–76; and Richard T. White, "Memory for Personal Events," *Human Learning* 1 (1982): 171–83. Linton's study of her own autobiographical memory extended over a period of six years, while White's study extended for seventeen months.

Milano; when: Saturday, September 10, 1983; salience: 1/month; involvement: nothing; pleasantness: pleasant; question about a critical detail: Who was with me?; answer: Beth Loftus and Jim Reason. Waganaar then had somebody else turn his forms into a series of questions and tried to identify an incident on the basis of one or more of the cues. The cue most likely to produce a memory was "what," the cue least likely to produce a memory was "when." He discovered that after thinking about the four cues and answering the question relating to the critical detail, his longer-term memory of events showed a decay rate somewhat similar to the decay rate of his shorter-term memories. After six months he was able to remember over 90 percent of events. His memories decayed from that point, but over time showed less and less decay. After five years he was still able to recall just under 40 percent of the incidents he had noted.[33]

Harry P. Bahrick devised an experiment that traced human memory for languages over a period of fifty years.[34] He compensated for the impossibility of following the same group of individuals over this time period by using a large sample. In that sample were individuals who had studied Spanish at school and/ or university and who had subsequently done little with the language. Bahrick discovered that over the first three to five years after cessation of studies, the loss of language followed a pattern not dissimilar to that of Wagenaar's memory for events in his life. Indeed, this loss was so severe that those who had not studied Spanish for an extended length of time or who had poor grades in their language classes had lost all of their knowledge of Spanish. But after three years, those who had studied longer and who had good grades essentially kept the same competency levels for the next thirty years, after which time there was a gradual decay.[35]

These results tend to lead to the conclusion that the first three to five years after the death and resurrection of Jesus would have been critical to the preservation of memories about him. Those memories that were retained for this length of time would have been available up to the time period in which it is likely the Gospels were written. If Wagenaar's experiment is any guide, approximately 40 percent of the deeds and sayings of Jesus could potentially have been remembered during the time the Gospels were written.

---

33. Wagenaar, "My Memory," figure 3.

34. Harry P. Bahrick, "Semantic Memory Content in Permastore: Fifty Years of Memory for Spanish Learned in School," *Journal of Experimental Psychology: General* 113 (1984): 1–29; see also idem, "Long Term Maintenance of Knowledge," in *The Oxford Handbook of Memory*, ed. Endel Tulving and Fergus I. M. Craik (Oxford: University Press, 2000), 247–362, in which Bahrick outlines not only his own research on the maintenance of long-term knowledge, but other relevant research.

35. See figure 2.6 in Bahrick, "Spanish in Permastore," 22–23.

RELIABILITY

How "Reliable" is Collective Memory?

So far it has been argued that there would have been a significant pool of eyewitnesses to the life of Jesus when the Gospels were written thirty or more years after his death and that there is evidence that a substantial percentage of memories of Jesus could have survived for this length of time. Many of these memories would likely have been held within groups as collective memories, especially within groups of Jesus's followers.

The collective memory of the past is often fiercely contested because of the importance it plays in the present group identity.[36] The past is remembered precisely because of its relevance to the present, and those who have a different viewpoint regarding what the present identity of a group should be often argue it in terms of how their view best fits the past.[37] Because of the pressure brought to bear on collective memory, it is clear that collective memory is not necessarily a dispassionate and accurate rendition of the past. Yet examination of how the past has been shaped in collective memory shows that there are limits to the malleability of collective memory. This may be illustrated in the realm of politics and nation building.[38]

Roy F. Baumeister and Stephen Hastings have examined the kinds of changes that have taken place in collective memory.[39] In some cases, there is selective omission of disagreeable facts in collective memories of heroes of the past or in events of national significance in the past.[40] They give as an example the

---

36. "The past, anthropologist Arjun Appadurai has suggested, is a 'scarce resource,' and conflict over its ownership is recurrent . . . Contest, conflict, controversy—these are the hallmark of studies of collective memory" (Michael Schudson, "Dynamics of Distortion in Collective Memory," in *Memory Distortion: How Minds, Brains, and Societies Reconstruct the Past*, ed. Daniel L. Schacter [Cambridge: Harvard University, 1995], 361).

37. "Memory selects and distorts in the service of present interests [a process Schudson describes as "Instrumentalization"] . . . Examples of instrumentalization are legion. Indeed, the problem may be to find cases of cultural memory that cannot be readily understood as the triumph of present interests over truth" (Schudson, "Dynamics of Distortion in Collective Memory," 351).

38. Alin Coman, Adam D. Brown, Jonathan Koppel, and William Hirst, "Collective Memory from a Psychological Perspective," *International Journal of Politics, Culture, and Society*, 22 (2009): 125–141, begin their article by highlighting that, despite the burgeoning study of collective memory, and the importance of memory to the discipline of psychology, relatively little research on the phenomenon has taken place within the discipline. In their article they trace those experiments that deal with social interaction and mechanisms of remembering and forgetting in groups. Their point is well made. The most useful studies about the malleability of collective memory have been done in the disciplines of history and politics.

39. Roy F. Baumeister and Stephen Hastings, "Distortions of Collective Memory: How Groups Flatter and Deceive Themselves," in *Collective Memory of Political Events: Social Psychological Perspectives*, ed. James W. Pennebaker, Dario Paez, and Bernard Rimé (Mahwah, NJ: Erlbaum, 1997), 282.

40. Rafi Nets-Zehngut documents what might be considered to be an example of selective omission in collective memory (he uses the term, "collective amnesia"), when he notes that between 1948 and 1967 there are only two documents from the records of the Israeli army that mention the Palestinian exodus in

absence in collective memory of the pro-slavery actions and speeches of Thomas Jefferson, one of the significant contributors to the American Declaration of Independence, which states that "all men are created equal." Another change cited by Baumeister and Hastings is that of exaggeration and embellishment. They cite several examples, such as the exaggeration of the war efforts in World War II of the British and American armies when compared to the much greater numbers of troops involved in the battles in Russia. Other strategies they document include connecting one event to other events, blaming the enemy, blaming circumstances, and contextual framing. These are but some of the means by which collective memories are transmuted to fit the needs of the present.

One of the strategies that Baumeister and Hastings canvas is outright fabrication. While they find the occasional use of outright fabrication in the shaping of collective memory,[41] they conclude:

> Still, it seems that by and large outright fabrication of collective memory is rare. The implication may be that collective memories are constrained by the facts. Facts may be deleted, altered, shaded, reinterpreted, exaggerated, and placed in favorable contexts, but wholesale fabrication seems to lie beyond what most groups can accomplish. Presumably, a thorough historical search would eventually uncover an example or two of fabrication, but these would be extreme exceptions. Fabrication is thus not one of the standard techniques of altering collective memory for self-serving ends.[42]

This conclusion fits that of the substantive two-volume analysis of the collective memory of Abraham Lincoln by Barry Schwartz.[43] He demonstrates that Abraham Lincoln has indeed been remade in collective memory to fit the needs of contemporary society. This has been done by ignoring those parts of his writings and actions that do not fit today's memories of him and by emphasizing those aspects that do. Yet Schwarz concludes, "The remaking of

relation to the war of independence of 1948 ("The Israeli Army's Official Memory of the 1948 Palestinian Exodus, 1949–2004," *War in History* 22 [2015]: 211–34, esp. 228–29).

41. Baumeister and Hastings, "Distortions of Collective Memory," cite one example, that of Betsy Ross being asked by George Washington to create a new flag for the new nation (the United States of America). This is, in fact, a story "invented in 1876 by some of her descendants in order to create a tourist attraction in Philadelphia" (p. 281).

42. Baumeister and Hastings, "Distortions of Collective Memory," 282.

43. Barry Schwartz, *Abraham Lincoln and the Forge of National Memory* (Chicago: University of Chicago Press, 2000), and idem, *Abraham Lincoln in the Post-Heroic Era: History and Memory in Late Twentieth-Century America* (Chicago: University of Chicago Press, 2008). See also his comments on George Washington in, idem, "Social Change and Collective Memory: The Democratization of George Washington," *American Sociological Review* 56 (1991): 221–36.

Abraham Lincoln, although based on some invention and much exaggeration, is nonetheless constrained by the historical record."[44]

One must conclude, then, that while collective memory is always shaped to meet the needs of the present by such processes as selective omission of irrelevant or inconvenient data and the emphasis of those traits that best fit the needs of the present, there is a basic historic kernel that is almost impossible to erase. When recalling the life of an individual, the important characteristics of that individual are preserved.

Reliability of the Gospel Accounts

If anything in the gospel accounts of Jesus sayings and activities is historically reliable, it will have been preserved in fallible human memory for periods of thirty or more years. So far in this chapter several "moments" in the transmission of such memories have been considered, and research and other evidence has been cited that allow an assessment to be made of the accuracy of the memories that would have been formed and preserved at each of these stages.

Those that knew and saw Jesus during his earthly ministry would have formed vivid memories of him.[45] Such memories are not immune from the usual vicissitudes normally attached to human memory: transience, bias, and openness to suggestion. In fact, the investigation of eyewitness memories by Yuille and Cutshall cited earlier in this chapter reveals that eyewitness memories are only 80 percent accurate in recalling details. Yet this does not mean that these memories are worthless. The 20 percent of memories that are inaccurate are nonetheless consistent with the gist of what happened. Likewise, other research showed that while it was possible to create errors in memory in the laboratory, almost all of these errors were consistent with what was actually there in the original stimulus. Thus, one can conclude with some confidence that while the earliest followers of Jesus were forming their personal memories of him, it is more than likely that, although some details were incorrect, what they did remember would have been highly consistent with what Jesus actually did and said. These memories

---

44. Schwartz, *Abraham Lincoln in the Post-Heroic Era*, 234. Schwartz insists, one must "appreciate the limits of Lincoln's reconstructability." "'To make a good symbol to help us think and feel,'" we must start "'with an actual personality which more or less meets this need,' and we improve it by omitting the inessential and adding 'whatever is necessary to round out the ideal' . . . The 'actual personality' that we start with . . . limits the range of things the collective memory can do. . . . From the initial conception of Lincoln as a man of the people we know that later generations subtracted little; they only superimposed new traits" (Schwartz *Abraham Lincoln and the Forge of National Memory*, 104; Schwartz is citing the words of Charles Horton Cooley).

45. In his book, *Momentous Events, Vivid Memories* (Cambridge: Harvard University Press, 1998), David Pillemer describes the vivid memories that individuals form of significant events in their lives as "personal-event memories."

were shaped further in the process of forming collective memories about Jesus. The collective memory of the eleven surviving apostles of Jesus is a special case, given their close association with Jesus over an extended period of time. Their memories of Jesus would have been particularly strong and resilient, given that they had been taught by Jesus in a manner recognizable to their own generation (i.e., by memorizing what Jesus was teaching them), and by having their memories consolidated as they were sent out to preach and teach about Jesus while he was still alive.

Despite the lower life expectancy of those living in the Roman Empire compared to most modern populations, during the period in which the Gospels were likely to have been written there would still have been a substantial number of living eyewitnesses to his ministry. It has been shown in research by others that such memories are of a measurably higher quality than those based only on hearsay. The results of other research also suggests that not everything that was known about Jesus would have survived the thirty or more years over which this was retained in human memories. Yet a significant proportion would have been available to the Gospel writers.

In summary, the argument of this chapter is that the Gospels are in large part a product of a process that developed and preserved collective memories of Jesus's activities and teaching. Collective memories are selective in that they are shaped to fit the present needs of those that use them. It is important to note, however, that while collective memories are selective, what is selected is likely to be based on memories of actual events. Furthermore, while such memories may incorporate inaccurate details, even the inaccuracies are most likely to be consistent with what Jesus did and said. In other words, like the substance of other collective memories, the gist of the gospel traditions is reliable and provides a sound general picture of Jesus's sayings and doings.

CHAPTER 6

The Historicity of the Early Oral Jesus Tradition: Reflections on the "Reliability Wars"

PAUL RHODES EDDY

J esus was an itinerant Jewish teacher who proclaimed the kingdom of God in both word and deed, *but not in script*. This observation explains both the importance of the oral Jesus tradition within the early church (visible in statements from Paul to Papius and beyond) and the relevance of orality and memory studies for Jesus scholarship today. Given that other essays in this volume engage contemporary memory studies, this essay will be devoted to the orality/oral tradition side of things.[1]

Before proceeding, two preliminary words. First, it is important to be clear about what can be gleaned by the Jesus/Gospels scholar from the study of orality/oral tradition. One thing we shouldn't expect is anything like a precise recovery of the early oral Jesus tradition itself. In a recent article, Paul Foster concludes that the use of both orality and memory studies within Jesus research are "dead-ends," with one of his chief complaints being "there is no direct access to an oral layer of the Jesus tradition"; it is "unretrievable and inaccessible."[2] True enough. But, contrary to Foster, this isn't a mark against these fields. There are other gifts that orality studies have to offer. For example, a growing number of scholars are making use of media- and performance-critical studies in their investigation of the Gospels.[3] Additionally, this field has a direct bearing upon the contested

---

1. The reflections offered in this essay are informed by my prior work in this area. See Paul Rhodes Eddy and Gregory A. Boyd, *The Jesus Legend: A Case for the Historical Reliability of the Synoptic Jesus Tradition* (Grand Rapids: Baker Academic, 2007), chs. 6–10; Paul Rhodes Eddy, "Orality and Oral Transmission," in *Dictionary of Jesus and the Gospels*, 2nd ed., ed. Joel B. Green, Jeannine K. Brown, and Nicholas Perrin (Downers Grove, IL: InterVarsity Press, 2013), 641–50.

2. Paul Foster, "Memory, Orality, and the Fourth Gospel: Three Dead-Ends in Historical Jesus Research," *JSHJ* 10 (2012): 191–227 (206, 207; see also 211).

3. A number of key works in this area have been recently published by Wipf & Stock/Cascade in their Biblical Performance Criticism series.

question of the historical reliability of the early oral Jesus tradition, an area of intense debate within what Zeba Crook has dubbed "the reliability wars."[4] Now, to be clear, there is no way to prove at a very specific and concrete level whether the early oral Jesus tradition was reliable or not, since there is no way to dependably reconstruct this tradition. However, what we can do is: (1) gain an understanding of the various dynamics, genres, and models associated with oral transmission cross-culturally, (2) in light of these findings, analyze the data and dynamics of the written Jesus tradition found in the Gospels (and beyond), and finally (3) based on these prior considerations, draw plausible conclusions as to the likely nature of the early oral Jesus tradition—including its historical reliability. That we are, at best, left with generalities and probabilities should not bother us, since probabilities are what any field of historiography trades in, given the inherent limitations of historical method itself.[5]

Second, it is worth stopping to acknowledge that there is more at stake in the "reliability wars" than historical curiosity. Historical Jesus studies—along with the historical-critical method that gave birth to it—were forged within the context of modern European Christendom and its discontents. Behind particular historical decisions are historical methods and the philosophies of historiography that ground them. And behind those are comprehensive—and competing—religio-philosophical worldviews. And lest one think that it is only the traditionalist-conservative who brings an extra-historical agenda to the table, Helmut Koester reminds us otherwise:

> [The historical-critical method] was designed as a hermeneutical tool for the liberation from conservative prejudice and from the power of ecclesiastical and political institutions. Those who fear that the historical-critical method threatens their control over the religious orientation and theological judgment of their constituencies are absolutely correct.[6]

Annette Teffeteller has observed that "the discussion of orality has been burdened with more than its share of ideological baggage."[7] Her observation

---

4. Zeba Crook, "Collective Memory Distortion and the Quest for the Historical Jesus," *JSHJ* 11 (2013): 53–76 (76).

5. The probabilistic nature of historical claims poses no problem to Christian faith, once the notion of faith is properly understood in its covenantal context. For a helpful reflection on faith and history, see N. T. Wright, *The New Testament and the People of God*, vol. 1 of *Christian Origins and the Question of God* (Minneapolis: Fortress, 1992), 93–96.

6. Helmut Koester, "Epilogue: Current Issues in New Testament Scholarship," in *The Future of Early Christianity: Essays in Honor of Helmut Koester*, ed. B. A. Pearson (Minneapolis: Fortress, 1991), 474.

7. Annette Teffeteller, "Orality and the Politics of Scholarship," in *Politics of Orality*, ed. C. Cooper (Boston: Brill, 2007), 67–86 (67).

is certainly applicable to its use within Jesus/Gospels scholarship today. Now, this recognition in and of itself should not hamper a robust academic pursuit for the historical. But it does mean that we must be cognizant that we cannot neatly separate debates about the interpretation of historical evidence from philosophical debates about historiography and, further still, metaphysics itself.[8]

THE TWO TRAJECTORIES: A BRIEF SURVEY

Among scholars who have explored the question of the historical reliability of the early oral Jesus tradition, two basic trajectories of approach have emerged: one that is generally optimistic about its reliability and, conversely, one that is generally pessimistic.[9] Scholars within each of these trajectories agree that the dynamics at play within an orally dominant culture lead to both stability and variation—both fixity and flexibility—within a tradition. Disagreement arises as each trajectory imagines and articulates *the nature of and balance between* stability and variation within oral traditional contexts generally, and within the early Jesus tradition in particular.

The purpose of this essay is twofold. First, a brief survey of these two trajectories will be offered. Second, a set of considerations drawn from contemporary orality/oral tradition studies will be summarized, which, taken together, suggest that the optimistic trajectory should be taken seriously—more seriously than it is in many quarters of Jesus studies today.

The Pessimistic Trajectory

A primary anchor of the pessimistic trajectory throughout much of twentieth century New Testament (NT) scholarship can be found in Rudolph Bultmann's form-critical enterprise.[10] Bultmann's model is characterized by a set of assumptions about the early Jesus movement, including: (1) Its relative disinterest both in the biographical details of Jesus's life and in careful preservation of eyewitness reminiscences about Jesus. (2) The absence of a lengthy, orally based narrative framework of Jesus's life prior to its presumed *de novo* creation in the writing of Mark's Gospel. (3) A tendency to creatively fabricate sayings of, and stories about, Jesus, when present needs of the post-Easter community called for it.[11]

---

8. Boyd and I have explored some of these issues in *Jesus Legend*, esp. ch 1.

9. I am using this "two trajectories" model for heuristic purposes. Various perspectives on this issue fall along a broad continuum, of course.

10. Bultmann, *The History of the Synoptic Tradition*, rev. ed., trans. John Marsh (Oxford: Blackwell, 1963 [Germ. ed. 1921]).

11. E.g., Bultmann, *History of the Synoptic Tradition*, 127, 245, 322, 372.

These convictions fostered a highly skeptical view of the historical reliability of both the Gospels themselves and the oral Jesus tradition that lay behind them.

As more recent, orally sensitive critics have pointed out, the methods and presuppositions of Bultmann's model of oral tradition are, for the most part, deeply indebted to *written* texts, highly *literate* assumptions, and significantly limited data regarding the nature of oral transmission itself. Ironically, at the very time that NT studies was settling into the text-based Bultmannian paradigm, Milman Parry and Albert Lord were initiating the modern discipline of fieldwork-based orality studies through their ground-breaking work in Serbo-Croatia. Their work eventually served as a chief catalyst for an interdisciplinary revolution in the 1960s, commonly known as the "turn to orality." From classical studies to anthropology to linguistics, scholars such as Marshall McLuhan, Jack Goody, Eric Havelock, and Walter Ong pushed the orality-literacy conversation to new depths.[12]

The turn to orality had very little impact upon Jesus/Gospels research for more than a decade. It was Werner Kelber—a profoundly influential figure within the pessimistic trajectory—who in 1983 provided the first extensive exploration of the early Jesus tradition in light of the revolution in orality studies.[13] Kelber's thought was informed by the work of Parry and Lord, Havelock, Goody, and, especially, Walter Ong. Whatever criticisms one might have of Kelber's book, there is no question that it provided NT scholarship with a great gift by introducing the key insights from interdisciplinary orality studies while calling attention to the post-Gutenberg, highly literate media bias of NT studies itself.

This gift notwithstanding, Kelber's work could not help but reflect some of the characteristic weaknesses of the then-current state of orality scholarship. First, Kelber adopted a "Great Divide" mentality by casting the categories of "oral" and "written" as mutually exclusive and generally antagonistic.[14] Taking a cue from the polarization in Ong's work, Kelber identified the "oral" with all things beautiful (i.e., freedom, reality, creative potential, and even "life" itself), while the "written" was cast as absence, illusion, suppression, and, inevitably, "death."[15] Today, this characterization is widely recognized as an ideological

---

12. For a helpful history, see Khosrow Jahandarie, *Spoken and Written Discourse: A Multi-Disciplinary Perspective*, Contemporary Studies in International Political Communication 1 (Stamford, CT: Ablex, 1999).

13. Werner H. Kelber, *The Oral and the Written Gospel: The Hermeneutics of Speaking and Writing in the Synoptic Tradition, Mark, Paul, and Q* (Philadelphia: Fortress, 1983).

14. The Great Divide approach has been widely disavowed in the field, and most scholars are now wary of falling into its more obvious forms. For an early critique, see Ruth Finnegan, "Literacy versus Non-Literacy: The Great Divide? Some Comments on the Significance of Literature in Non-Literate Cultures," in *Modes of Thought: Essays on Thinking in Western and Non-Western Societies*, ed. Robin Horton and Ruth Finnegan (London: Faber and Faber, 1973), 112–44.

15. Kelber, *Oral and the Written Gospel*, 158, 185.

construct based upon an empirically false generalization and an unhelpful romanticizing of the "oral."

But it is another related dimension of Kelber's book that placed him squarely within the pessimistic trajectory. According to Kelber, the oral is by nature fleeting, vanishing, destined to "the steep price of oblivion."[16] Kelber asserts that oral speech does not lend itself well to such qualities as permanence, fixity, or "verbatim memorization," which he portrays as "the retarded language of robot minds."[17] And so, despite its important role of awakening NT studies to the world of orality, Kelber's book unfortunately served to tie an orally sensitive approach to a strongly skeptical view of the stability and reliably of oral transmission. While Kelber's more recent work on orality has been significantly developed and nuanced, it nonetheless continues to overemphasize the malleable, unstable nature of the early oral Jesus tradition.[18]

In line with Bultmann and Kelber, scholars working within the pessimistic trajectory highlight the fluidity, malleability, and distortion of oral transmission. Interestingly, this privileging of variability over stability can be traced back to the headwaters of contemporary orality studies. Although Parry and Lord both claimed that oral tradition is, by definition, a complex mixture of a broadly stable tradition and it's always creatively improvised oral performances, flexibility, fluidity, and variation came to be seen as the chief characteristics of oral tradition. In Lord's words: "The most distinctive characteristic of [oral] poetry is its fluidity of text."[19] A chief reason for this emphasis was Lord's conviction—one that he tended to generalize to all forms of orality—that oral tradition is never composed prior to, but always *in the midst of*, the performance itself.[20] This conviction led to a tendency to see the oral and the memorized/highly stable as inherently incompatible.

Lord's sentiment has permeated many sectors of orality studies today. It is not surprising, then, to see a range of Jesus scholars from Kelber onward painting the early oral Jesus tradition as historically unreliable due, in no small part, to the inherently unstable nature of oral tradition itself. For example, Robert Funk of the Jesus Seminar compared the dynamics of the early oral Jesus tradition to the contemporary telling and retelling of a joke, or to the growth of urban

---

16. Kelber, *Oral and the Written Gospel*, 19.

17. Kelber, *Oral and the Written Gospel*, 27–28.

18. E.g., Werner Kelber, "The Case of the Gospels: Memory's Desire and the Limits of Historical Criticism," *Oral Tradition* 17 (2002): 55–86.

19. A. B. Lord, "Oral Poetry," in *Encyclopedia of Poetry and Poetics*, ed. Alex Preminger (Princeton: Princeton University Press, 1965), 591.

20. Albert Lord, *The Singer of Tales* (Cambridge: Harvard University Press, 1960), 13.

legends such as the presence of UFOs at Roswell.[21] Similarly, Bart Ehrman likens the fickle nature of ancient oral tradition to what happens when we play the "telephone game" today.[22] And John Dominic Crossan does nothing to hide his contempt for the idea of highly stable, memorized tradition when he writes: "Jesus left behind him thinkers not memorizers, disciples not reciters, people not parrots."[23]

The Optimistic Trajectory

For those within the optimistic trajectory, while flexibility and variation are commonly recognized as key dynamics of oral tradition, the qualities of stability and continuity over time—qualities that naturally lead to a more optimistic appraisal of its historical capacities—are given significant attention.

The first robustly optimistic alternative to the Butlmannian model came in 1961 with the publication of Birger Gerhardsson's *Memory and Manuscript*.[24] Gerhardsson proposed that the process of oral transmission exemplified by the "school" dynamic of Rabbinic Judaism provided the best comparative model by which to understand the transmission dynamics of the early oral Jesus tradition. Fundamental to this thesis is the conviction that strict memorization of tradition within the context of a teacher-disciple relationship allowed for subsequent situation-specific use of that tradition in a flexible manner. Gerhardsson's model directly challenged a number of the reigning assumptions of the Bultmannian paradigm. For example, eyewitness disciples formed a natural link between Jesus and the Gospels by way of memorized, flexibly employed oral tradition.

Reactions to Gerhardsson's model were strong and polarized. A number of scholars appropriated his model as a way of demonstrating the stability and reliability of the Jesus tradition. Critics, however, quickly charged Gerhardsson with "anachronism," claiming that he was illegitimately projecting a later rabbinic phenomenon back onto the pre-70 CE Jesus movement.[25] A second criticism of Gerhardsson's model was that it simply did not fit the variations of the tradition

---

21. Robert W. Funk, Roy W. Hoover, and the Jesus Seminar, *The Five Gospels: The Search for the Authentic Words of Jesus* (New York: Macmillan, 1993), 27; Robert W. Funk and the Jesus Seminar, *The Acts of Jesus: The Search for the Authentic Deeds of Jesus* (New York: HarperCollins, 1998), 5–6.

22. Bart Ehrman, *Jesus, Interrupted: Revealing the Hidden Contradictions in the Bible (and Why We Don't Know about Them)* (New York: HarperOne, 2010), 146–47.

23. John Dominic Crossan, *The Historical Jesus: The Life of a Mediterranean Jewish Peasant* (San Francisco: HarperSanFrancisco, 1991), xxxi.

24. Birger Gerhardsson, *Memory and Manuscript: Oral Tradition and Written Transmission in Rabbinic Judaism and Early Christianity* (Uppsala: Gleerup, 1961).

25. E.g., Morton Smith, "A Comparison of Early Christian and Early Rabbinic Tradition," *JBL* 82 (1963): 169–76.

visible within the Gospels themselves.[26] In later publications, Gerhardsson responded to his critics by both clarifying and nuancing his model.[27]

For over two decades now, the work of Kenneth Bailey has served as a prime example of a post-Gerhardsson model within the optimistic trajectory.[28] Bailey's insights are largely expressed as anecdotes gleaned from his personal experiences of oral transmission within contemporary Middle Eastern village life. He situated his own model of oral tradition as a third mediating alternative—positioned between Bultmann's "informal uncontrolled," and Gerhardsson's "formal controlled," models—namely that of an "informal controlled" approach. Key to the informal control is the regular gathering of the community for the purposes of re-telling and preserving the shared tradition (known in Arabic as a *haflat samar*), including the verbal correction of a speaker in the midst of performance whenever the shared communal norms of faithful re-telling are violated. Bailey proposes that the balance of stability and flexibility found in the Synoptic Gospels generally reflects what one would expect within this model.[29] Importantly, Bailey recognizes that different degrees of stability and flexibility will attach to different oral genres. Viewed through the lens of this model, we should expect a significant degree of continuity and stability over time for the early sacred Jesus tradition. The essence of Bailey's model has been adopted by several scholars within the more optimistic trajectory, including N. T. Wright and James Dunn.[30]

Another key figure within the optimistic trajectory is Richard Bauckham, who offers a model proposing a strong line of continuity from Jesus to the Gospels via authoritative eyewitness testimony.[31] When it comes to comparing his proposal with other models of oral tradition, Bauckham presents his thesis as an example of formal controlled oral tradition—and in this sense, similar to Gerhardsson's—and yet one that allows for a significant degree of flexibility.[32] Reactions to Bauckham's model have ranged widely, and Bauckham in turn has

---

26. Gerhardsson (*Memory and Manuscript*, 96–7, 146–48, 176–79, 334–35), however, maintained from the beginning that his model can account for this variation by stipulating that, once memorized, the tradition can be creatively and flexibly deployed for a variety of purposes.

27. E.g., Birger Gerhardsson, *The Gospel Tradition* (Lund: Gleerup, 1986); idem, *The Reliability of the Gospel Tradition* (Peabody, MA: Hendrickson, 2001).

28. See Kenneth E. Bailey, "Informal Controlled Oral Tradition and the Synoptic Gospels," *AsJT* 5 (1991): 34–54; idem, "Middle Eastern Oral Tradition and the Synoptic Gospels," *ExpTim* 106 (1995): 363–67.

29. Bailey, "Informal Controlled," 51.

30. N. T. Wright, *Jesus and the Victory of God*, vol. 2 of *Christian Origins and the Question of God* (Minneapolis: Fortress, 1996), 133–36; James D. G. Dunn, *Jesus Remembered*, vol. 1 of *Christianity in the Making* (Grand Rapids: Eerdmans, 2003), 205–10; idem, "Kenneth Bailey's Theory of Oral Tradition: Critiquing Theodore Weeden's Critique," *JSHJ* 7 (2009): 44–62.

31. Richard Bauckham, *Jesus and the Eyewitnesses: The Gospels as Eyewitness Testimony* (Grand Rapids: Eerdmans, 2006).

32. Bauckham, *Jesus and the Eyewitnesses*, 257–60.

offered thoughtful rejoinders.[33] While there certainly are differences between the models of Bailey, Dunn, and Bauckham, with others I am impressed by the broad commonalities they share.[34]

CONSIDERATIONS IN SUPPORT OF THE OPTIMISTIC TRAJECTORY

The remainder of this essay will be devoted to summarizing several considerations that have arisen from within contemporary studies of orality/oral tradition that serve to support the optimistic trajectory. First, a few words of ground-clearing and context-setting are in order.

Two Preliminary Issues: Oral Tradition, Genre Specificity, and the Temptation of Hasty/False Generalizations

A number of orality scholars have emphasized the complexity and variability of oral transmission, even to the point of raising questions about a single, clear definition of "oral tradition."[35] And yet, one finds hasty and/or demonstrably false generalizations being made about "oral tradition" on a regular basis. This tendency can be traced right back to the fountainhead of contemporary oral tradition studies: the Parry-Lord theory. Lord and many of his advocates quickly universalized the essence of his oral-formulaic theory—and the Serbo-Croatian model on which it was based—to virtually *all* forms of oral tradition.[36] Other scholars, however, have resisted the allure of hasty generalizations, emphasiz-

---

33. E.g., the group of response essays in *Journal for the Study of the Historical Jesus* 6 (2008); for his rejoinders see Richard Bauckham, "In Response to My Respondents: *Jesus and the Eyewitnesses* in Review," *JSHJ* 6 (2008): 225–53.

34. E.g., James D. G. Dunn, "Eyewitnesses and the Oral Jesus Tradition," *JSHJ* 6 (2008): 85–105 (89).

35. E.g., Ruth Finnegan, "'Oral Tradition': Weasel Words or Transdisciplinary Door to Multiplexity?," *Oral Tradition* 18 (2003): 84–86; David Williams Cohen, "The Undefining of Oral Tradition," *Ethnohistory* 36 (1989): 9–18; David Henige, "Oral, but Oral What? The Nomenclatures of Orality and their Implications," *Oral Tradition* 3 (1988): 229–38.

36. E.g., Lord ("Oral Poetry," 591) states that lack of memorization, "fluidity of text" and "the absence of a single fixed text" characterize "the technique of [oral] composition . . . no matter which genre of verse is in question." Now, in light of the wide-ranging cross-cultural evidence, we know composition *prior to* performance—and thus the conscious goal of memorization of an original oral text for later performance—is a common feature of various oral genres (especially historical and religious) in a wide variety of cultures. E.g., see Knud Rasmussen, *The Netsilik Eskimo: Social Life and Spiritual Culture*, trans. W. E. Calvert (New York: AMS, 1976), 320, 517–19; Steven Feld, "Wept Thoughts: The Voicing of Kaluli Memories," in *South Pacific Oral Traditions*, ed. Ruth Finnegan and Margaret Orbell (Bloomington: Indiana University Press, 1995), 96–8; John Brockington, "The Textualization of the Sanskrit Epics," in *Textualization of Oral Epics*, ed. Lauri Honko, Trends in Linguistics Studies and Monographs 128 (New York: de Gruyter, 2000), 193–215 (here 209–11); Saad Abdullah Sowayan, *Nabati Poetry: The Oral Poetry of Arabia* (Berkeley: University of California Press, 1985), esp. 93–100, 110–22, 186–7, 198–202; Edward R. Haymes, "Oral Theory and Medieval German Poetry," *Oral Tradition* 18 (2003): 258–60; B. W. Andrzejewski and I. M. Lewis, *Somali Poetry: An Introduction* (Oxford: Clarendon, 1964), 45–46; Eric Rutledge, "Orality and Textual Variation in the *Heike*

ing instead the diversity of phenomena associated with oral tradition. Ruth Finnegan, for example, has consistently expressed her "long-lasting doubts over generalized conclusions about oral forms," while highlighting *the specific* with regard to oral tradition—e.g., specific cultures, performance arenas, and genres.[37] According to Finnegan, we can no longer make simple appeals to "generalized concepts like 'literacy' or 'orality.'" Instead, we must recognize "diverse literacies and oralities" with all of their "multifarious specificities."[38]

One point of specificity is particularly germane to the concerns of this essay: that of *genre*. Fieldwork studies have demonstrated the cross-cultural common-place within orally dominant contexts of making an important distinction between narrative genres regarded as *true* (e.g., as relating actual events of the past) and those regarded as *fictional*.[39] For example, Ruth Finnegan herself has noted this distinction in contexts ranging from various African cultures to the South Pacific Islands.[40] Related to this phenomenon is the cross-cultural tendency to treat certain oral genres—i.e., religious, ritualistic, and historical traditions central to a community's sense of identity—with greater care than other genres, including the imposition of more stringent constraints upon variation and flexibility.[41]

Such distinctions are directly pertinent to the early Jesus tradition, which, as the Gospels reveal, intended to convey actual happenings in the life of Jesus. Unfortunately, this sort of distinction has been largely neglected within much of the last one hundred years of Jesus research due to the oral genre insensitivity that characterized the form-critical work of Bultmann and his followers (i.e., Bultmann drew conclusions about oral tradition generally from folklore/entertainment genres). Adopting hasty/false generalizations regarding oral tradition remains a constant hazard. But there are things we can do to curb this tendency, including basing our more general conclusions about oral transmission upon a

---

Monogatari," in *Heike biwa: katari to ongaku*, ed. Kamisango Yuko (Kusakabe-shi: Hitsuji Shobo, 1993), 349, 357–9.

37. Ruth Finnegan, *The Oral and Beyond: Doing Things with Words in Africa* (Chicago: University of Chicago Press, 2007), 185. Similarly, from earlier in her career, see Ruth Finnegan, "A Note on Oral Tradition and Historical Evidence," *HistTh* 9 (1970): 195–201; idem, *Literacy and Orality: Studies in the Technology of Communication* (New York: Blackwell, 1988), 108–9.

38. Finnegan, *The Oral and Beyond*, 185.

39. E.g., Judith Huntsman, "Fiction, Fact, and Imagination: A Tokelau Narrative," *Oral Tradition* 5 (1990): 283–315.

40. See respectively, Ruth Finnegan, *Oral Literature in Africa* (Nairobi: Oxford University Press, 1976), 363–73; idem, "Introduction, or Why the Comparativist Should Take Account of the South Pacific," *Oral Tradition* 5 (1990): 159–84 (171–72).

41. E.g., Finnegan, *Literacy and Orality*, 99–101, 108n15, 109; Joel Kuipers, *Power in Performance: The Creation of Textual Authority in Weyewa Ritual Speech* (Philadelphia: University of Pennsylvania Press, 1990); Sowayan, *Nabati Poetry*, 123–24.

range of cross-cultural/genre field studies, and articulating our claims in properly qualified terms.

Oral Tradition, Oral History, and the Question of Time Span

Another consideration involves the common observation that, all things being equal, the longer the time span between an oral account and its originating event, the greater the likelihood of historical distortion. For example, scholars have frequently distinguished between three chronological moments with regard to history in oral traditions: the remote past, the recent past, and in between these, the middle (or gap) period.[42] It has been observed that oral traditions about the recent past—i.e., within a generation or two of the originating event—regularly lack the cosmological, mythological, and purely sociologically motivated elements of traditions that characterize traditions about the remote past. They are often based upon personal remembrances and tend to provide historically based causal connections between events.[43] It is not uncommon within traditions about the recent past that "[r]andom historical events are remembered because they happened to known individuals."[44] This distinction has led some scholars to call for a clear distinction between *oral history* and *oral tradition*, where the former is defined as oral transmissions "about events and situations which are contemporary, that is, which occurred during the lifetime of the informants."[45] *Oral tradition*, in turn, is defined as oral material that has been "transmitted over several generations."[46]

These questions are, of course, directly relevant to our analysis of the early oral Jesus tradition. As a number of Jesus scholars have pointed out, given the relatively short period of time between Jesus and the writing of the Gospels, technically speaking we are in the realm not of *oral tradition per se*, but rather of *oral history*.[47] In this light, considerations of the historical value of the oral

---

42. E.g., J. C. Miller, "Introduction: Listening for the African Past," in *The African Past Speaks: Essays on Oral Tradition and History*, ed. J. C. Miller (Hamden, CT: Archon, 1980), 35–39; John Tosh with Seán Lang, *The Pursuit of History: Aims, Methods and New Directions in the Study of Modern History*, 4th ed. (London: Longman, 2006), 332.

43. Miller, "Introduction: Listening for the African Past," 22; R. G. Willis, *On Historical Reconstruction from Oral Traditional Sources* (Chicago: Northwestern University Press, 1976), 15.

44. Thomas Spear, *Kenya's Past: An Introduction to Historical Method in Africa* (London: Longman, 1981), 47.

45. Vansina, *Oral Tradition as History*, 12. Clear recognition of the importance of this distinction for historical reconstruction is as ancient as Thucydides. Jan Assmann's category of "communicative memory," with its time span of up to one hundred years, correlates with Vansina's oral history category. See Jan Assmann, "Introduction: What is Cultural Memory?," *Religion and Cultural Memory: Ten Studies*, trans. Rodney Livingstone (Stanford, CA: Stanford University Press, 2006), 24.

46. Henige, "Oral, but Oral What?" 232. See also Vansina, *Oral Tradition as History*, 12–13, 27–28; Tosh and Lang, *Pursuit of History*, 310.

47. E. P. Sanders and Margaret Davies, *Studying the Synoptic Gospels* (Philadelphia, PA: Trinity, 1989),

transmission of relatively recent events become crucial. As it turns out, a broad range of studies—spanning from ancient Greece, to nineteenth-century Serbo-Croatia, to contemporary Africa, and beyond—have concluded that the oral transmission of relatively recent events (i.e., within roughly eighty to one hundred fifty years of the originating event) encoded within an *intentionally historical genre* tend to be generally reliable in nature.[48] Related to this is a distinction, highlighted by Jan Assmann, between *communicative memory* and *cultural memory*, where the former is anchored in the living memory of those within a generation or so of the originating event(s).[49] General considerations such as these do not, of course, insure the reliability of any particular instance of oral transmission. But they should inform our horizon of expectations, our methodological approaches, and our considerations in locating the historical burden of proof.[50]

Four Common, Cross-Cultural Phenomena and Implications for the Early Oral Jesus Tradition

While the threat of hasty/false generalizations is an ever-present one, it is also the case that certain features and dynamics of oral tradition/transmission have been documented in a broad, cross-cultural fashion, allowing us to extrapolate more safely. We will now turn to four of these areas, each of which has implications for our consideration of the general reliability of the early oral Jesus tradition.

TRADITIONAL REFERENTIALITY: THE FUNCTIONING OF TRADITION WITHIN ORAL TRADITION

More than anyone else working in the realm of contemporary oral tradition studies, John Miles Foley has revolutionized our understanding of how oral

---

143; Wright, *New Testament and the People of God*, 423–24. The emphasis of Bauckham on the role of eyewitnesses in the transmission of the early Jesus tradition aligns with this nod to oral history. In the context of this distinction, it is important to remember that the personal reminiscences of oral history can quickly assume a stylized form of articulation for easier memorization and communication.

48. Wolfgang Kullmann, "Homer and Historical Memory," in *Signs of Orality: The Oral Tradition and Its Influence in the Greek and Roman World*, ed. E. Anne MacKay (Boston: Brill, 1999), 95–113 (96–99); B. A. Stolz, "Historicity in the Serbo-Croatian Heroic Epic: Salih Ugljanin's 'Grcki rat,'" *Slavic and Eastern European Journal* 11 (1967): 423–32 (423); Jan Vansina, "Afterthoughts on the Historiography of Oral Tradition," in *African Historiographies: What History for Which Africa?*, ed. Bogumil Jewsiewicki and David Newbury, African Modernization and Development 12 (Beverly Hills, CA: Sage, 1986), 105–10 (109–10); Tosh and Lang, *Pursuit of History*, 332. Markus Bockmuehl has emphasized this phenomenon of "living memory" in relation to the Jesus tradition. See Markus Bockmuehl, *Seeing the Word: Refocusing New Testament Study*, Studies in Theological Interpretation (Grand Rapids: Baker Academic, 2006), 170–72, 178–87.

49. Assmann, "Introduction: What is Cultural Memory?," 3–30.

50. The issue of burden of proof in historical research is a contested one. Boyd and I have offered suggestions in *Jesus Legend*, 364–71.

tradition—or, more broadly, what Foley calls traditional "verbal art"—actually functions.[51] Space will allow only a brief summary of some of Foley's key insights. To begin, Foley observes that, within an orally dominant cultural context, while the performance (whether oral or written) is the "enabling event," *the tradition itself* is the "enabling referent."[52] That is to say, unlike the modern, post-Gutenberg context with our comparatively autonomous texts, any particular articulation of oral tradition within orally dominant cultures fundamentally depends upon both the wider pool of communally shared tradition and a knowledgeable audience steeped within that tradition. Within such a context, due to the limiting factors associated with any single performance, most of what is important *is not explicitly stated.* Here, Foley emphasizes the importance of *metonymy*—i.e., a "mode of signification wherein the part stands for the whole."[53] In an oral/aural traditional context, metonymy is "the fundamental principle" of efficient and effective communication.[54] It is within this light that Foley warns us of the modern, text-centric tendency to treat orally oriented instances of verbal art in an anachronistic fashion.[55] Thus, in order to understand the workings of oral tradition, Foley calls for a deep appreciation of the phenomenon of *traditional referentiality* and its inherent communicative economy, wherein dense, idiomatic expression is the assumption and "only the properly prepared audience is equipped to understand."[56] More specifically, "[t]raditional referentiality enables an extremely economical transaction of meaning, with the modest, concrete part standing for a more complex whole. *Pars pro toto* is the fundamental principle."[57]

---

51. Anyone working within the field of oral tradition/verbal art today is well served by immersing themselves in Foley's corpus. Key works include: John Miles Foley, *Immanent Art: From Structure to Meaning in Traditional Oral Epic* (Bloomington: Indiana University Press, 1991); idem, *The Singer of Tales in Performance* (Bloomington: Indiana University Press, 1995); idem, *How to Read an Oral Poem* (Urbana: University of Illinois Press, 2002). Foley has also offered the field of biblical studies a great gift by serving for many years as a willing dialogue partner. See e.g., John Miles Foley, "Words in Tradition, Words in Text: A Response," *Semeia* 65 (1995): 169–80; idem, "Memory in Oral Tradition," in *Performing the Gospel: Orality, Memory, and Mark*, ed. Richard A. Horsley, Jonathan A. Draper, and John Miles Foley (Minneapolis: Fortress, 2006), 83–96.

52. John Miles Foley, "What's in a Sign?," in MacKay, *Signs of Orality*, 1–27 (see 11); idem, *Singer of Tales in Performance*, 28. Homeric scholar Egbert Bakker's helpful notion of the "activation" of tradition fits nicely with Foley's thesis. See Egbert J. Bakker, "Activation and Preservation: The Interdependence of Text and Performance in an Oral Tradition," *Oral Tradition* 8 (1993): 5–20.

53. Foley, *Immanent Art*, 7. See also John Miles Foley, "Selection as *pars pro toto*: The Role of Metonymy in Epic Performance and Tradition," in *The Kalevala and the World's Traditional Epics*, ed. Lauri Honko (Helsinki: Finnish Literature Society, 2002), 106–27.

54. Foley, "What's in a Sign?," 11. This phenomenon appears to be ubiquitous within orally oriented contexts.

55. Foley, "What's in a Sign?," 9–10.

56. Foley, "What's in a Sign?," 7.

57. Foley, "What's in a Sign?," 11.

All of this is to say that, in order for an oral tradition to even function within an ancient, orally oriented context, such as that of the early Jesus movement, *a conserving impulse was absolutely essential.* Seen in this light, the virtually constant emphasis on flexibility, fluidity, and variation (alongside the occasional perfunctory nod to stability) that tends to characterize portrayals of oral tradition within the pessimistic trajectory—a widespread, interdisciplinary phenomenon, by the way, that characterizes orality scholarship far beyond the field of biblical studies—should strike us as strangely imbalanced and inappropriate.[58] Yes, flexibility, fluidity, and variation play a significant role within the verbal dynamics of orally dominant cultures. But such dynamics are only sensibly enacted within the conserving conceptual parameters of a stable, communally shared tradition that functions as the "enabling referent," the permanent anchor of each and every one of its own performative variations. It is *the enabling power of the stability of tradition*—a *necessary precondition* for any of its flexible variations—that is given its due recognition within the optimistic trajectory, even as it suffers a general downgrading, if not outright neglect, within the pessimistic trajectory.

Long Oral Narratives

Foley's theory of tradition sheds light on another important issue: namely, the question of the existence and dynamics of long oral narratives. Twentieth-century form criticism fueled the notion that oral narratives were, by nature, short, independent units of tradition, which means that the longer narrative frameworks found within the Gospels represented later-written fabrications. Working from this sort of assumption, for example, Robert Funk concludes that "the syntagmatic thread of the gospels . . . is mostly fictive. It is a fiction of the ancient storyteller."[59] For years, many within the wider field of oral traditional studies held that long oral narratives simply didn't—couldn't—exist. And then something of a revolution occurred. A wide range of cross-cultural fieldwork has

---

58. This point alone deserves its own essay. Several disciplinary streams of influence combined in the twentieth century to champion the "turn to performance," and with this turn came something of a philosophical-aesthetic antipathy toward things fixed/stable/static/structured/distanced—in short, objectified. In the field of orality studies, while the "stable" had to be acknowledged simply on an empirical basis, it was the "flexible" and "fluid" that enamored post-1960s scholarship (with a prior shot in the arm supplied by Lord himself). This deep-seated ideological bias is rarely grappled with by Jesus scholars who import orality studies into their discipline. It doesn't help that far too few address this issue head-on in the wider field of orality studies. But some, like Ruth Finnegan, do (e.g., *Oral and Beyond*, 192–96). And when she does, she rightly points toward the important work of the British cultural anthropologist, Karin Barber, as supplying a well-needed corrective to the field. See Karin Barber, "Text and Performance in Africa," *Oral Tradition* 20 (2005): 264–77; and esp. idem, *The Anthropology of Texts, Persons and Publics* (New York: Cambridge University Press, 2007), 67–102. Barber ("Text and Performance in Africa," 268) reminds us that "constituting [oral] text as object-like is the condition of possibility of a poetics of fluidity."

59. Robert W. Funk, "On Distinguishing Historical from Fictive Narrative," *Forum* 9 (1993): 179–213 (188).

now shown that long oral narratives are common, and that they are capable of far more than many modern scholars had ever imagined.

A key figure in this revolution was the Finnish scholar of folklore, Lauri Honko. In his groundbreaking fieldwork among the Tulu people of South India, Honko focused on the Siri epic, a long oral epic performed by illiterate tradents and (in its transcribed form) composed of 15,683 lines, almost the exact length of the Iliad.[60] Similar to other orally dominant cultures, the Tulu had rarely performed the Siri epic in its entirety. But upon Honko's request they did so—a feat that takes six to seven days to complete. Honko notes that, while he and many other folklorists were trained to believe that long epics were exclusively a product of "written culture," this assumption has now been "shattered" and "obliterated."[61] Contemporary fieldwork has "brought to light numerous long oral epics in the living traditions of Central Asia, India, Africa, and Oceania, for example. The existence of genuine long oral epics can no longer be denied."[62] In Honko's words, this realization represents nothing short of a "paradigm shift" in the field of folkloristics.[63]

It turns out that individual oral performances are frequently dependent upon a lengthy narrative plotline composed of various smaller sub-units. Honko has observed that these long oral narratives are implicitly known by the community audience (at least in terms of the overarching plotline), are rarely performed in totality (unless, of course, a visiting anthropologist asks for a demonstration), and typically include several very popular sub-narrative sections that are performed more often than others.[64] Moreover, the degree of detail in which the meta-narrative's segments are played out varies considerably, depending largely on the particular performance situation (i.e., audience composition, time constraints, purpose, etc.). It is at this point that Honko's concept of a "mental text" has proven to be fruitful.[65] The long narrative schematic itself functions as something of a mental text within the mind of the performer, one that is "edited" for each particular performance. There is also a significant degree of flexibility in terms of the placement, order, and length of the smaller units of the narrative tradition in any given performance.[66]

---

60. Lauri Honko, *Textualizing the Siri Epic* (Helsinki: Academia Scientiarum Fennica, 1998), 11.

61. Honko, *Textualizing the Siri Epic*, 18.

62. Lauri Honko, "Introduction: Oral and Semiliterary Epics," in *The Epic: Oral and Written*, ed. L. Honko, J. Handoo, and J. M. Foley (Mysore, India: Central Institute of Indian Languages, 1998), 9.

63. Lauri Honko, "Text as Process and Practice: The Textualization of Oral Epics," in Honko, *Textualization of Oral Epics*, 3–54 (here 3–4).

64. Honko, *Textualizing the Siri Epic*, 193–94.

65. Honko, *Textualizing the Siri Epic*, 92–99.

66. As Honko ("Introduction: Oral and Semiliterary Epics," 14) notes, the phenomenon of *multiforms*

In light of these findings, it is possible to fruitfully reimagine certain features of the early Jesus narrative traditions: e.g., the implicit, communally shared knowledge of the gospel metanarrative plotline by which to make sense of the many individually recounted sub-units of tradition; the passion narrative as one of the more popular and often told sub-narratives. Thorleif Boman was one of the first to apply insights on longer oral narratives to the oral Jesus tradition, pointing out that, contrary to classical form-critical theory, orally recounted historical narratives do not emerge out of independently circulating units of prior tradition.[67] More recently, Jens Schröter, working with Paul Ricoeur's findings on narrative and representation, has suggested that the narrative framework of the gospel tradition (he uses Mark as a case study) has no less claim to historicity than the individual sayings of Jesus.[68] All things considered, there is good reason to conclude that the lengthy written narratives of the Gospels—and, intriguingly, perhaps even the Q material—are rooted in a prior oral narrative matrix of Jesus's life.[69]

Strong Tradition Bearers

Another important line of consideration is bound up with the phenomenon that John Niles has identified as the "strong tradition bearer"—i.e., recognition that, commonly, it is the gifted, communally acknowledged individual tradent(s) who functions as the primary custodian of tradition within an orally dominant community.[70] This phenomenon has also been highlighted in David Rubin's impressive study, *Memory in Oral Tradition*, when he discusses the important role of "expertise in remembering."[71] The context to this issue involves the now-defunct idea, one tied to Romantic literary theory, of "an ideal folk community—an undifferentiated company of rustics, each of whom contributes equally to the processes of oral tradition."[72] If this idea sounds familiar, it should.

---

enables performers to either expand to well over one hundred lines—or condense to as little as two lines—the same sub-narrative component, depending on the constraints of each performance.

67. Thorleif Boman, *Die Jesus-Überlieferung im Lichte der neueren Volkskunde* (Göttingen: Vandenhoeck & Ruprecht, 1967), 21–31.

68. Jens Schröter, "Von der Historizität der Evangelien: Ein Beitrag zur gegenwärtigen Diskussion um den historischen Jesus," in *Der historische Jesus: Tendenzen und Perspektiven der gegenwärtigen Forschung*, ed. Jens Schröter and Ralph Brucker, BZNW 114 (Berlin: de Gruyter, 2002), 163–212.

69. On the theory that narrative elements of the Q material were embedded in a prior "narrative-kerygmatic framework," see Stephen Hultgren, *Narrative Elements in the Double Tradition: A Study of Their Place within the Framework of the Gospel Narratives*, BZNW 113 (New York: de Gruyter, 2002), 311–25 (310).

70. John D. Niles, *Homo Narrans: The Poetics and Anthropology of Oral Literature* (Philadelphia: University of Pennsylvania Press, 1999), 173–93.

71. David Rubin, *Memory in Oral Tradition: The Cognitive Psychology of Epic, Ballads, and Counting-out Rhymes* (New York: Oxford University Press, 1995), 167–70.

72. Niles, *Homo Narrans*, 174.

It informed the early form-critical enterprise that, in turn, profoundly shaped subsequent Jesus/Gospels studies. It took decades of data from cross-cultural fieldwork in the twentieth century before a definitive shift in the field took place. Niles explains:

> In any region where oral narratives have been collected systematically, certain performers stand out for their large repertory and authoritative style . . . Collectors often seek out and record these outstanding tradition-bearers for the same reasons that other people like to listen to them: they perform whole songs and stories, not just fragments, and they perform them with verve and authority. Having a good voice never hurts, but it is not their voice but their command of a large body of traditional lore that makes them stand out from others.[73]

Niles notes that among the important natural gifts required to be a strong tradition bearer is an unusually retentive memory, one that enables the individual tradent to "absorb whole narratives and internalize them when other people hear them and forget them."[74] And while many contemporary folklorists and anthropologists tend to focus on the creative capacities of oral performers, Niles provides balance by noting that, typically, the strong tradition bearer is "confident enough to power a tradition and yet affectionate enough, in regard to their sources, to want to steer the tradition along familiar lines."[75] This quality of faithfulness to the tradition is vastly more important when one is dealing with what the community perceives to be historically rooted and/or community-defining narrative, as opposed to entertainment-oriented folktales (a point neglected in far too many studies of oral transmission, including post-Bultmannian form criticism).

In considering the early Jesus tradition in light of the strong tradition-bearer phenomenon, one notices the importance placed upon both *tradition* and *teachers*. For example, Paul's letters reflect a deep concern with passing on established traditions (e.g., 1 Cor 11:2, 23; 15:1–3; Gal 1:9; Phil 4:9; Col 2:6–7; 1 Thess 4:1; 2 Thess 2:15; 3:6). Indeed, as Robert Stein notes, for Paul

> Such traditions were to be "held" on to (I Cor. 15:1–2; 2 Thess. 2:15); life was to be lived "in accord" with the tradition (2 Thess. 3:6; cf. Phil. 4:9), for the

---

73. Niles, *Homo Narrans*, 174. See also Finnegan, *Oral and Beyond*, 184–85.
74. Niles, *Homo Narrans*, 185.
75. Niles, *Homo Narrans*, 180.

result of this would be salvation (I Cor. 15:1–2), whereas its rejection meant damnation (Gal 1:9). The reason for this view was that this tradition had God himself as its ultimate source (I Cor. 11:23).[76]

In accordance with this emphasis on divinely grounded tradition, the early Jesus movement stressed the importance of *teachers* (e.g., Acts 13:1; Rom 12:7; 1 Cor 12:28–29; Eph 4:11; Heb 5:12; James 3:1; *Didache* 15:1–2). Undoubtedly influenced by the example of Jesus's own teaching ministry and his call to intentional discipleship, teachers had a central role within the early church and appear to have been the first funded ministers (Gal 6:6; 1 Tim 5:17–18; *Didache* 13:2).[77] In a predominantly oral community such as the early church, the primary function of these teachers would have been to faithfully transmit, interpret, and apply the early Christian traditions.[78] Jan Vansina notes that certain recognized tradents function as a sort of "walking reference library" of community traditions, and we have every reason to believe that Jesus's immediate disciples would have played a similar role as the primary custodial tradents within the earliest Christian community.[79]

THE CRITICAL ROLE OF THE ACTIVE TRADITIONAL AUDIENCE

This leads to a final area of consideration. As we have just seen, the custodial role of the strong tradition bearer within orally dominant cultures is crucial. That being said, there is compelling, cross-cultural evidence suggesting that the wider community also shares a sense of responsibility for the tradition's preservation.[80]

---

76. Robert H. Stein, *The Synoptic Problem: An Introduction* (Grand Rapids: Baker, 1987), 191.

77. Samuel Byrskog, "The Transmission of the Jesus Tradition: Old and New Insights," *Early Christianity* 1 (2010): 441–68 (esp. 442–46); Craig S. Keener, "Assumptions in Historical-Jesus Research: Using Ancient Biographies and Disciples' Traditioning as a Control," *JSHJ* 9 (2011): 26–58 (39–53).

78. Dunn, *Jesus Remembered*, 176.

79. Vansina, *Oral Tradition as History* (Madison: University of Wisconsin Press, 1985), 37. Bauckham, Byrskog, and Dunn provide distinct models—with much common ground—of how this would have taken place.

80. As mentioned above, this phenomenon—in the form of the *haflat samar*—plays a key role in Bailey's model of oral tradition. The most powerful critique of Bailey's model to date has come from Theodore J. Weeden Sr., "Kenneth Bailey's Theory of Oral Tradition: A Theory Contested by Its Evidence," *JSHJ* 7 (2009): 3–43. Weeden compares the oral anecdotes told to Bailey by Egyptian Christians about their community's founder, the nineteenth-century missionary John Hogg, with details of the same stories taken from a biography of Hogg written by his daughter: Rena Hogg, *A Master-Builder on the Nile* (New York: Revell, 1914). (I am grateful to Weeden for sending me a copy of this book and for several rounds of correspondence on the Bailey thesis in 2006 while working on *Jesus Legend*.) A number of these comparisons turn up discrepancies that lead Weeden to reject Bailey's model. Space considerations prevent much of an engagement with Weeden's critique here. Suffice it to say that his careful investigative work has posed troubling questions for some of Bailey's particular examples. Nonetheless, the fact that the broad phenomenon of the custodial role of the audience is so widely reported in cross-cultural field studies (on which, see below) confirms that this phenomenon itself is securely documented far beyond Bailey's proposal. And, more importantly, Bailey himself clearly admits that his examples are not based on carefully documented fieldwork but rather on anecdotes and his own personal impressions. Thus, while Weeden's critique is relevant to, even problematic

In an article exploring the complex dynamics of oral tradition, Bruce Rosenberg observes: "*Empowered to criticize*, oral/aural audiences are genuinely part of the performance, creatively, and not merely passively."[81] Especially with regard to certain oral genres—e.g., religious, ritualistic, and historical tradition central to a community's sense of identity—the traditional audience tends to share responsibility for its preservation. For example, if an oral tradent misrepresents the tradition—sometimes in even relatively minor ways—members of the audience frequently offer vocal protest and correction in the midst of performance. Hence, while the oral performer is entrusted with the creative expression of traditional material, the communal audience's shared knowledge of the wider tradition functions as a counterbalancing authority within each specific performance. Again, this conclusion emerges from a wide range of cross-cultural fieldwork.[82] David Rubin—arguably the premier contemporary researcher of the role of memory in oral tradition—explains:

> [A]n audience knowledgeable in a tradition is a strong conservative force that keeps the [tradent] within traditional bounds by voicing its approval, by offering alternative versions it thinks are preferred, or even by providing corrections.[83]

Based on her own fieldwork in the African context, Finnegan similarly notes that audience members commonly

> break into the performance with additions, queries, or even criticisms. This is common not only in the typical and expected case of story-telling but even in such formalized situations as that of the complex Yoruba *ijala* chants. . . . [I]f one thinks the performer has made a mistake he cuts in with such words as

> > I beg to differ; that is not correct.
> > You have deviated from the path of accuracy. . . .

---

for, several of Bailey's specific cases, it in no way calls into question the well-documented, cross-cultural array of similar phenomena. For a defense of Bailey's basic model against Weeden's critique, see Dunn, "Kenneth Bailey's Theory of Oral Tradition: Critiquing Theodore Weeden's Critique."

81. Bruce A. Rosenberg, "The Complexity of Oral Tradition," *Oral Tradition* 2 (1987): 73–90 (86; emphasis added).

82. E.g., Andrzejewski and Lewis, *Somali Poetry*, 46; Foley, *Immanent Art*, 45; Honko, *Textualizing the Siri Epic*, 197; Sowayan, *Nabati Poetry*, 111; Charles L. Briggs, *Competence in Performance: The Creativity of Tradition in Mexicano Verbal Art* (Philadelphia: University of Pennsylvania Press, 1988), 354; William Shiell, *Delivering from Memory: The Effect of Performance on the Early Christian Audience* (Eugene, OR: Pickwick, 2011), 25–28.

83. Rubin, *Memory and Oral Tradition*, 135.

The possibility of both clarification and challenge from members of the audience and their effect on the performance is indeed one of the main distinctions between oral and written literary pieces.[84]

If the early Jesus movement was typical of other orally dominant cultures in this regard—and we have no reason to think otherwise—then all members of the community would have had a stake in, and thus to some degree a responsibility for, preserving the essential elements of the original Jesus tradition. In his study of the early Christian audience within the performance arena, William Shiell emphasizes that the audience would have played an active role as it "asks questions, corrects material, provides feedback, debates each other, or interrupts."[85] Perhaps this dynamic lies behind Paul's injunction for believers to "test" prophecies and teachings (1 Cor 14:29; 1 Thess 5:19–22). In any case, the customary responsibility orally dominant communities generally assume regarding traditional material with religious/historical import offers further evidence for the optimistic side of the ledger in the reliability debate.

---

84. Finnegan, *Oral Literature in Africa*, 11.
85. Shiell, *Delivering from Memory*, 25.

CHAPTER 7

Reconstructing the Historical Pharisees: Does Matthew's Gospel Have Anything to Contribute?

JEANNINE K. BROWN

Drawing on Matthew for reconstruction of the historical Pharisees may feel less than intuitive to Gospels scholars. It is more common to see Matthew's portrait of the Pharisees enlisted for an exploration of Matthew's own polemic context read back into the first *Sitz im Leben*. Günter Stemberger is illustrative in this regard, summing up the hermeneutical issues succinctly:

> In general, [in Matthew] the Pharisees are the regular, ever-present, principal enemies of Jesus. . . . The sketchy use of the Pharisees in this portrait scarcely permits itself to be evaluated for a historical reconstruction extending beyond the facts known from Mark and Q. It is rather of interest for a picture of the enemy of the Christian community that Matthew represents.[1]

The assumption that Matthew provides little historically credible evidence for understanding the Pharisees is heightened by the differing portrait of the Pharisees in Luke-Acts, in which this character group performs a more varied role. For example, in Luke some Pharisees warn Jesus about Herod's plot against him (Luke 13:31); and in Acts the author identifies some of the early believers

---

1. Günter Stemberger, *Jewish Contemporaries of Jesus: Pharisees, Sadducees, Essenes*, trans. Allan W. Mahnke (Minneapolis: Fortress, 1995), 28. See also Saldarini, who speaks of Matthew "reading the late first century situation back into the life of Jesus on a grand scale" (Anthony J. Saldarini, *Pharisees, Scribes, and Sadducees in Palestinian Society: A Sociological Approach*, rev. ed. [Grand Rapids: Eerdmans, 2001], 173). Hakola draws on social identity theory to suggest that Matthew's portrait of the Pharisees arises from the ambiguous role of the Torah within Matthew's community (Raimo Hakola, "Pharisees as Others in the New Testament," in *Others and the Construction of Early Christian Identities*, ed. Raimo Hakola, Nina Nikki, and Ulla Tervahauta, Publications of the Finnish Exegetical Society 106 [Helsinki: The Finnish Exegetical Society, 2013], 13–65).

in Jesus as Pharisees (Acts 15:5) and portrays Pharisaic scribes among the Sanhedrin as sympathetic to Paul (Acts 23:9). Accordingly, Reidar Hvalvik suggests
that the portrait of the Pharisees in Luke-Acts "[i]mmediately . . . seems more
historically trustworthy than the picture found in Matthew, Mark, and John."[2]

Finally, Matthew's portrait of Pharisees comes to an intense climax in chapter 23, where Jesus proclaims seven woes against them. Anthony Saldarini proposes that the "list is so polemical and the Pharisees and scribes so identified with
one another that little reliable historical information can be gleaned from it."[3]

Given this set of scholarly appraisals, it might seem foolhardy to wade into
the waters and attempt an assessment of Matthew's contribution for the historical
Pharisees. Yet I believe something may be gained by taking another look at the
question, especially as there continues to be a lack of consensus regarding the
historical Pharisees in the pre-70 CE Jewish world.[4]

METHOD OF APPROACH

There are various ways to analyze what in Matthew might correspond to the
historical realities of Pharisees during the time of Jesus's life and ministry. Traditional criteria of authenticity, especially that of multiple attestation, will tend
toward a minimalist portrait given the paucity of sources about the pre-70 CE
Pharisees and the lack of extant materials produced by the group itself.[5] So
although a helpful starting point, isolating traditions that overlap among discreet
sources will not be adequate for a comprehensive approach to the topic.

N. T. Wright (and others) has suggested and developed a more maximal
approach, which reviews the sources on the Pharisees and attempts to fit these
into a larger schema or story that can then be assessed for its coherence and plausibility.[6] Martin Pickup describes his own method in it this way: "Any data drawn

---

2. Reidar Hvalvik, "Paul as a Jewish Believer—according to the Book of Acts," in *Jewish Believers in Jesus: The Early Centuries*, ed. Oskar Skarsaune and Reidar Hvalvik (Grand Rapids: Baker Academic, 2017), 149.

3. Saldarini, *Pharisees, Scribes, and Sadducees*, 165.

4. In a fairly recent volume on the historical Pharisees, Green offers this sobering conclusion: "The sources about [Pharisees] reinforce one another, when they do at all, only at the most general level. This means that our historical description of the Pharisees must come from discrete, uncorroborated materials, which, by their very nature, do not constrain speculation" (William Scott Green, "What Do We Really Know about the Pharisees, and How Do We Know It?," in *In Quest of the Historical Pharisees*, ed. Jacob Neusner and Bruce Chilton [Waco, TX: Baylor University Press, 2007], 423).

5. We could add to these limitations uncertainty related to source relationships among the Gospels that "impedes any historical inquiry about the Pharisees" (Martin Pickup, "Matthew's and Mark's Pharisees," in Neusner and Chilton, *In Quest of the Historical Pharisees*, 68. In my analysis, I will be assuming the two-source hypothesis, although my work does not for the most part necessitate that theory.

6. N. T. Wright, *The New Testament and the People of God*, vol. 1 of *Christian Origins and the Question of God* (Minneapolis: Fortress, 1992), 181–203. On his critical realist theory, Wright explains, "It acknowledges that all knowledge of realities external to oneself takes place within the framework of a worldview, of which

from a gospel document for purposes of performing historical reconstruction on the Pharisees must be interpreted with regard for the entire picture of the Pharisees that the document presents."[7] In what follows, I will attempt this more maximal (and narrative) method, especially as my task is to assess Matthew's discreet portrait of the Pharisees for its (level of) historicity. In other words, my task is not the larger goal of reconstructing the historical Pharisees. Instead, I will be assessing what from the portrait of the Pharisees in the First Gospel rests on fairly solid historical moorings; i.e., what Matthew might offer any such reconstruction.

In this particular endeavor, my own narrative work on Matthew can contribute to the task since it has been focused on producing a coherent reading of Matthew's Gospel, including a coherent picture of its various characters and character groups.[8] Various parts of a narrative sketch of the Matthean Pharisees will then be assessed in relation to other potential sources for the historical Pharisees, including other New Testament books (e.g., Mark, Luke-Acts), Josephus, rabbinic materials, and the Dead Sea Scrolls. The emphasis throughout the chapter will be on the contribution of Matthew's portrait for a historical understanding of Pharisees in the early part of the first century CE.

WHAT MATTHEW MIGHT CONTRIBUTE TO THE HISTORICAL RECONSTRUCTION OF THE PHARISEES

Relationship between Jesus and the Pharisees in Matthew

An obvious place to start for answering the question of what Matthew offers to a historical reconstruction of Pharisees is their relationship with Jesus as portrayed by the evangelist. Other than the disciples and crowds, Matthew's Jesus has the most interaction with this group (often paired with "scribes"). While it is easy to see that Matthew emphasizes and heightens the conflict between Jesus and the Pharisees in comparison to Mark (and Luke), the source of this conflict, as Matthew portrays it, offers points of affinity with rabbinic material that likely finds its origins in the pre-70 CE Jewish context.

According to Matthew, conflict between Jesus and Pharisees centers on interpretation and application of the Torah. We see this already in the first major discourse—the Sermon on the Mount, where Matthew brings together teachings

---

stories form an essential part. And it sets up as hypotheses various stories about the world in general or bits of it in particular and tests them by seeing what sort of 'fit' they have with the stories already in place" (45).

7. Pickup, "Matthew's and Mark's Pharisees," 110.

8. See Jeannine K. Brown and Kyle Roberts, *Matthew*, THNTC (Grand Rapids: Eerdmans, 2018); Jeannine K. Brown, *Matthew*, Teach the Text Commentary Series (Grand Rapids: Baker, 2015).

of Jesus around the topics of kingdom, Torah, and discipleship (Matt 5:1–7:29). In the thematic statement for the body of the Sermon (5:17–20), Jesus speaks of his aim to fulfill the law and the prophets (5:17) and warns against setting aside "one of the least of these commands" (5:19). He then calls for a "righteousness" or "covenant loyalty" (δικαιοσύνη, *dikaiosynē*) that "exceeds that of the scribes and the Pharisees" for entering God's kingdom (5:20).[9] The rest of this section of the Sermon (the "Antitheses"; 5:21–48) expounds on this "greater *dikaiosynē*" through comparisons between six Old Testament teachings and Jesus's extension of each of these toward an even higher ethic.[10]

Yet quite a few of the subsequent accounts of the conflict between Jesus and the Pharisees about the Torah focus quite particularly on concerns related to purity and meals. This set of concerns is corroborated by rabbinic material that illumines Pharisees in the pre-70 CE context and so provides a fruitful area for reconstruction of historical Pharisees.

Pharisees and Jesus vis à vis Purity Aims and Practices

Matthew sketches a portrait of Jesus and Pharisees in conflict over purity aims and practices. This conflict focuses specifically on Jesus's eating practices, questions of tithing, and prioritization of such considerations, each of which I will address in turn. To begin, however, we can examine a text that provides a summary critique of Jesus toward Pharisees related to (and infused with language of) purity that speaks to the value of integrity (Matt 23:25–28):

> How dire it will be for you, scribes and Pharisees, you hypocrites! For you clean [καθαρίζω, *katharizō*] the outside of the cup and dish, but inside they are full of greed and self-indulgence. You blind Pharisee, first clean the inside of the cup so that the outside might also be clean [καθαρός, *katharos*]. How dire it will be for you, scribes and Pharisees, you hypocrites! For you are like whitewashed tombs that appear beautiful on the outside but on the inside are full of the bones of the dead and of everything unclean [ἀκαθαρσία, *akatharsia*]. In the same way, on the outside you appear righteous to others, but on the inside you are full of hypocrisy and lawlessness.

---

9. Translations of Matthew in this chapter are my own; see Brown and Roberts, *Matthew*. Outside of Matthew, the NIV is used unless otherwise indicated.

10. Pickup helpfully frames these six comparisons as cases of misapplication of Torah: "We should understand the six examples Jesus gives as six cases of Torah instruction from the scribes and Pharisees—all of which are applied in ways that result in an inadequate level of righteousness. . . . The problem is that the scribes and Pharisees put these precepts of Scripture into practice as if the precept expressed the limit of moral consideration rather than its starting point" ("Matthew's and Mark's Pharisees," 100–101). Pickup is addressing here Matthew's portrait of the Pharisees and not yet assessing its historical import.

The images used by Jesus—vessels for eating and tombs—have strong purity associations, and so "[r]itual defilement is clearly in mind."[11] As Pickup argues, "Jesus' contrast between outward and inward purity makes no sense unless the washing of these eating vessels was a real practice."[12] Matthew 23:24 has already introduced purity concerns by drawing on images of unclean creatures—a gnat and a camel (cf. Lev 11:4, 20–23). Jesus continues in this vein and uses images associated with ritual purity as a metaphor for the person who should be clean both inside and out.[13] This call for integrity (and repudiation of hypocrisy) is thematic across the Gospel (e.g., Matt 5:8, 21–48; 6:1–18, 22–24; 15:1–20; 23:13–35). These two "woes" pointed toward Pharisees (see below for discussion of the vitriol of Matt 23) highlight a key critique the Matthean Jesus levels at Pharisees: their concern for purity does not go deep enough.

At two points in Jesus's Galilean ministry,[14] Matthew narrates conflict between Pharisees and Jesus related to his (or his disciples') eating practices, which signal purity concerns. In the first pericope (Matt 9:9–13), Pharisees are upset that Jesus "eat[s] with tax collectors and sinners," a reference to a meal Jesus attends at the home of Matthew, a tax collector. Jesus responds by communicating that his mission is to sinners (rather than to the righteous). This pericope provides a window into Pharisaic concerns over lax eating habits.

The issue seems to be Jesus's practice of eating with those who were lax in Torah observance, therefore becoming the source of ritual contamination to Jews who were maintaining a more exacting level of purity. The historical Pharisees seem to have been concerned with this greater level of purity adherence. As Jacob Neusner concludes from his review of the rabbinic evidence, Pharisees were "ordinary people eating meals at home in conditions that are analogous to conditions required of priests in the Temple or in their homes."[15] Amy-Jill Levine frames their likely aims and practices in this way:

---

11. John Nolland, *The Gospel of Matthew: A Commentary on the Greek Text*, NIGTC (Grand Rapids: Eerdmans, 2005), 941. See pp. 938–41 and notes for rabbinic points of connection regarding purity.

12. Pickup, "Matthew's and Mark's Pharisees," 83n38. Strange, analyzing the archaeological record, illumines a broad distribution of artifacts associated with purity, which "suggests that some major group led the way in preserving the traditions of purity outside the Temple" (James F. Strange, "Archaeology and the Pharisees," in Neusner and Chilton, *In Quest of the Historical Pharisees*, 251).

13. R. T. France, *The Gospel of Matthew*, NICNT (Grand Rapids: Eerdmans, 2007), 874 and n42.

14. Mark and Luke place the Pharisees primarily in Galilee (though see Mark 12:13 and Luke 19:39). Matthew expands their role with a number of references to their presence in Jerusalem (n. 65 below). While Josephus locates Pharisees (exclusively) in Jerusalem, their absence from Galilee in his writings cannot be read as an argument against Pharisaic activity there, since "Josephus was not interested in village life" (Saldarini, *Pharisees, Scribes, and Sadducees*, 173), and since he does not show sustained interest in Pharisees, i.e., what we have in Josephus about the Pharisees is fairly incidental (Steve Mason, "Josephus' Pharisees: The Narratives," in Neusner and Chilton, *In Quest of the Historical Pharisees*, 37).

15. Jacob Neusner, "The Debate with E. P. Sanders since 1970," in Neusner and Chilton, *In Quest of the Historical Pharisees*, 404. Note Neusner's language "analogous" (vs. identical); Wright addresses the

The Pharisees may well have been engaged in directing the practices of Temple purity to the home, such that the household table mirrors the Temple altar, and those at the Table eat with the same status as the priests serving in Jerusalem. Thus the Pharisees would be particularly concerned that their food be properly tithed, and that they not be in states of ritual impurity.[16]

In this reconstruction, Jesus's meal behavior as recorded in Matthew 9 would have raised concerns for Pharisees. And as Matthew will later highlight, Jesus had earned a reputation for such behavior, being known as "a glutton and a drunkard, a friend of tax collectors and sinners" (Matt 11:19).

This combination of themes—eating habits and care regarding those with whom one eats—suggests concern related to "secondary pollution," which involved having physical contact with "something touched by a person or thing in an unclean state."[17] While Pharisees exhibited such concern for secondary pollution, Matthew, in these texts, implies that Jesus did not.[18] This does not mean, however, that Jesus himself was lax in his observance of purity laws. Matthew's portrait of Jesus shows no sign of any disregard for purity practices related to primary contaminants legislated in the Torah. For example, Matthew's Jesus exhorts a man he has healed of a skin disease to pursue the purification requirements stipulated in the Torah (Matt 8:1–4; cf. Lev 14:1–32). As I note elsewhere, this exhortation "suggests a view of the Matthean Jesus as reflexively attentive to the Torah's purity regulations."[19] And it would have been common-place for Jesus to incur ritual impurity, as all Jews would have, and then proceed to follow Torah regulations for becoming ritually clean. As David de Silva offers, "being an observant Jew . . . did not mean avoiding all uncleanness but rather knowing when he or she had incurred pollution so as to attend to its purification at once."[20]

---

importance of nuance in this regard in his statement that "Pharisaic purity is *of a different degree within the same scale* as that which applied to those working in the Temple" (author's emphasis; Wright, *New Testament and the People of God*, 187n109).

16. Amy-Jill Levine, "Discharging Responsibility: Matthean Jesus, Biblical Law, Hemorrhaging Woman," in *Treasures New and Old: Recent Contributions to Matthean Studies*, ed. David R. Bauer and Mark Allan Powell, SymS 1 (Atlanta: SBL Press, 1996), 388.

17. David A. de Silva, *Honor, Patronage, Kinship, and Purity: Unlocking New Testament Culture* (Downers Grove, IL: InterVarsity Press, 2000), 276.

18. Pickup parses this distinction out by noting that "Matthew's Pharisees do not have table fellowship with nonobservant Jews. But this does not seem to mean that they would be opposed to associating with non-Pharisees as long as ritual purity at table was maintained" ("Matthew's and Mark's Pharisees," 109). In my view, Jesus would fit in the category of non-Pharisaic *and* Torah observant. As such, he would not have an issue eating with non-observant Jews.

19. Brown and Roberts, *Matthew*, 511.

20. de Silva, *Honor, Patronage, Kinship, and Purity*, 275n62. Levine helpfully puts ritual impurity in context: "Uncleanness is not a disease, and it implies no moral censure; it is a ritual state in which both

These observations fit with Matthew's consistent portrayal of Jesus as carefully Torah observant and as one who teaches his followers to do the same (Matt 5:17–20; 12:7; 15:3–9; 17:24–27; 19:16–19; 21:28–32; 23:23). This is a Jewish man who wears the required tassels (κράσπεδον; *kraspedon*) on the hem of his cloak (Matt 9:20; cf. Num 15:38) and who in no way disregards Sabbath observance but claims instead that he and his disciples have interpreted the Scriptures (Matt 12:3–6) about the Sabbath accurately and so are "innocent" of breaking it (ἀναίτιος, *anaitios*; 12:7).[21]

The second conflict over purity between Pharisees and Jesus during his Galilean ministry occurs at Matt 15:1–20. This text provides corroborative evidence for Neusner's reconstruction of Pharisees as committed to eating meals in a heightened state of purity, to approximate priestly requirements. Pharisees "who had come from Jerusalem" (Matt 15:1) express concern that Jesus's disciples are not following the handwashings prescribed by "the tradition of the elders" (15:2). The Torah provided certain handwashing stipulations for priests as they ministered in the temple and before the altar.

> Then the LORD said to Moses, "Make a bronze basin, with its bronze stand, for washing. Place it between the tent of meeting and the altar, and put water in it. Aaron and his sons are to wash their hands and feet with water from it. Whenever they enter the tent of meeting, they shall wash with water so that they will not die. Also, when they approach the altar to minister by presenting a food offering to the LORD, they shall wash their hands and feet so that they will not die. This is to be a lasting ordinance for Aaron and his descendants for the generations to come." (Exod 30:17–21)

Handwashing was tied particularly to the priestly service of "presenting a food offering to the Lord" (Exod 30:20). This connection of purity concerns for handwashing with eating fits both the Pharisees' interest expressed in Matthew 15:1–2 and their earlier concern over Jesus eating with those who could affect his state of ritual purity (Matt 9:9–13). Matthew portrays these Jerusalem Pharisees as interested in the relevance of these priestly (food) regulations for Jews beyond the priestly circle, for themselves as well as for Jesus and his disciples.[22]

---

men and women likely found themselves most of the time" ("Discharging Responsibility: Matthean Jesus, Biblical Law, Hemorrhaging Woman," 387).

21. The contest between Jesus and Pharisees over Sabbath observance (Matt 12:1–14) also fits a recurring topic of the rabbinic material; Jacob Neusner, "The Pharisaic Agenda: Laws Attributed in the Mishnah and the Tosefta to Pre-70 Pharisees," in Neusner and Chilton, *In Quest of the Historical Pharisees*, 313.

22. See m. Yad. 1:1–2:4; and Nolland's excursus on ritual handwashing (*Gospel of Matthew*, 611–15).

Matthew's conclusion to this pericope differs from Mark's (7:1–23), both in his additional final statement (Matt 15:20b) and in the omission of Mark's (authorial and parenthetical) comment from 7:19: "(Thus he declared all foods ritually clean)" (CJB). By this omission and his added conclusion—"to eat with unpurified hands does not defile a person" (Matt 15:20b)—Matthew highlights that Jesus's answer should be connected to the initial Pharisaic concern for handwashing (15:1–2) and not read as a summary dismissal of Jewish purity regulations.

In addition to these conflicts over eating practices, Matthew includes a passage on tithing that provides another window into purity disagreements between Jesus and the Pharisees. In Matthew 23:23–24, Jesus both affirms the Pharisees' tithing practices and critiques their inordinate focus on such tithing.

> How dire it will be for you, scribes and Pharisees, you hypocrites! For you tithe mint, dill, and cumin, but you neglect the weightier matters of the law: justice and mercy and loyalty. These you should have done, without neglecting the others. You are blind guides, who strain out a gnat yet swallow a camel!

It is important to note that Matthew's Jesus does not disdain the Pharisaic concern for tithing even the smallest of plants, in line with the Torah, where "a tithe of everything from the land" is required (Lev 27:30). Instead, he calls for greater integrity in loyalty to the whole Torah: "These you should have done, without neglecting the others" (Matt 23:23b). While the connection between tithing and purity may not be immediately obvious to the contemporary reader, tithing was in fact closely associated with purity through its impact on Jewish eating practices.[23] As Neusner clarifies,

> Since food that had not been properly grown or tithed could not be eaten, and since the staple of the diet was agricultural products and not meat, the centrality of the agricultural rules in no small degree is on account of precisely the same consideration: What may one eat, and under what circumstances?[24]

As we have seen thus far, purity concerns and practices, as they are worked out in relationship to determinations about one's meal companions (i.e., *who might a Jew eat with?*), appear across Matthew's narrative (Matt 9:9–13; 11:19;

---

23. Jacob Neusner, "The Rabbinic Traditions about the Pharisees before 70 CE: An Overview," in Neusner and Chilton, *In Quest of the Historical Pharisees*, 309.

24. Neusner, "Pharisaic Agenda," 317.

15:1–20; and 23:23). In each case, Pharisees and Jesus disagree on these practices in one way or another. Yet at no point does Matthew characterize Jesus as
denigrating or ignoring purity commandments. Instead, Matthew portrays Jesus
prioritizing other Torah commandments or scriptural mandates (e.g., from the
prophets) over purity regulations, without losing sight of the latter.

This motif of prioritization of some biblical teachings over others runs across
the First Gospel. In Jesus's response to the Pharisaic critique of eating with
"tax collectors and sinners" (Matt 9:13), he quotes Hosea 6:6, "I desire mercy
not sacrifice." In Hosea, this divine sentiment prioritizes actions of mercy over
cultic offerings rather than negating the latter. As James Limburg notes, "The
prophets do not advocate doing away with the machinery of the cult, and Jesus
does not call for abolishing the law. Instead both the prophets and Jesus call for
reform" (via reprioritization).[25] This same refrain from Hosea recurs in Matthew
12:7, in the context of a Sabbath dispute, where Jesus's use of Hosea 6:6 implies
that Pharisees would be able to apply rightly the Sabbath commandment if
they prioritized mercy in their hermeneutic. This coheres with what we have
already seen in Matthew 23:23, where Jesus prioritizes "the weightier matters of
the law: justice and mercy and loyalty."[26] Jesus also identifies the two greatest
commandments as love of God and love of neighbor (Matt 22:34–40), another
moment of prioritization in Matthew's narrative.[27] A similar kind of prioritization
is also evident in the Mishnah. For example, in Avot 2:1 we hear of "light" and
"weighty" commandments. As Gary Burge paraphrases it, "Surely not all laws
could be equally important: some might be 'weighty,' others 'light.'"[28] What we
see Matthew's Jesus doing in this regard fits a Jewish pattern and therefore makes
historical sense.

I have given considerable attention to the topic of purity for illuminating the
conflict between Matthew's Pharisees and Matthew's Jesus for two reasons. First,
purity practices form an important *intersection of emphasis* between the rabbinic
traditions and the First Gospel, suggesting a fruitful area from which to consider
the historical Pharisees. According to Neusner, "approximately 67 percent of
all legal pericopes [from pre-70 CE authorities] deal with dietary laws: ritual
purity for meals and agricultural rules governing the fitness of food for Pharisaic

---

25. James Limburg, *Hosea–Micah*, IBC (Louisville: Westminster John Knox, 1988), 30; cf. 1 Sam 15:22: "to obey is better than sacrifice."

26. Matthew 23:23 alludes to Mic 6:8, with its call to "doing justice and loving mercy and being ready to walk with the Lord your God" (i.e., being loyal to God; LXX, my translation).

27. Also compare Matt 15:1–9, for Jesus's critique of Pharisees for neglecting the priority of honoring parents by focusing on "your traditions" (15:3, 6).

28. Gary M. Burge, "Commandment," in *Dictionary of Jesus and the Gospels*, 2nd ed., ed. Joel B. Green, Jeannine K. Brown, and Nicholas Perrin (Downers Grove, IL: InterVarsity Press, 2013), 151.

consumption."[29] Matthew's focus on purity as a significant area of disagreement between Pharisees and Jesus coheres with the rabbinic portrait, providing multi-source attestation.[30]

Second, I have focused on purity conflicts between Jesus and Pharisees because of frequent misperceptions in gospel studies regarding the role of purity in first-century Judaism and so potentially for understanding the intentions and practices of Pharisees.[31] It is not the Pharisees' commitment to the Torah's purity commandments that provide the impetus for Jesus's criticisms. Instead, it is their prioritizing of these commands over the Torah's "weightier matters" that warrants his critique in Matthew. Additionally, the aim of Pharisees to maintain a stricter level of purity to approximate priestly behavior led to exclusionary practices at meals, which we see Jesus disavowing in his own ministry.

This significant point of contention between Jesus and Pharisees fits plausibly in the first *Sitz im Leben* and suggests the viability of drawing on Matthew's portrait of Pharisees in this area of purity debates for a reconstruction of the historical Pharisees.

Social Roles and Positions

The window Matthew provides into this probable historical conflict between the Pharisees and Jesus over the centrality of purity raises questions regarding *the social position* of Pharisees relative to that of Jesus. On the narrative face of the Gospel, the Pharisees and Jesus seem to be in comparable positions in relation to the Jewish people, who are portrayed as receptive to both. Matthew implicitly acknowledges the receptivity of the crowd and even Jesus's disciples to the Pharisees at a number of points (e.g., 5:20; 16:5–13; 23:1–7), and this portrait fits Josephus's report that the Pharisees have the people "on their side" (at least during the time of the Hasmoneans; see *Ant.* 13.298).[32] As Saldarini suggests about Matthew's portrait, "The opposition of the scribes and Pharisees to Jesus is

---

29. Neusner, "Rabbinic Traditions," 299. Neusner's method involves identifying within the Mishnah and Tosefta "the names of rabbinic sages presumed to have lived before 70, or the Houses of Shammai and Hillel, two such masters" and isolating the associated traditions for analysis (297).

30. We might also note that some of the Matthean material on purity is already attested in both Mark (e.g., Matt 15:1–20) and Q (e.g., Matt 23:23).

31. See Levine's important critiques in "Discharging Responsibility"; idem, *The Misunderstood Jew: The Church and the Scandal of the Jewish Jesus* (San Francisco: HarperSanFrancisco, 2006); and idem, "Jesus in Jewish-Christian Dialogue," in *Soundings in the Religion of Jesus: Perspectives and Methods in Jewish and Christian Scholarship*, ed. Bruce Chilton, Anthony Le Donne, and Jacob Neusner (Minneapolis: Fortress, 2012), 175–88.

32. Mason describes Josephus's Pharisees as "a nonaristocratic group with enormous popular support" ("Josephus' Pharisees," 37). Dunn suggests that the Pharisees had significant influence on the people, because they were motivated by purity not just for themselves but for the whole of Israel (*Ant.* 13.297–298); see James D. G. Dunn, *Jesus Remembered*, vol. 1 of *Christianity in the Making* (Grand Rapids: Eerdmans, 2003), 268–69.

reasonable and expected, for they and the Jesus movement were leadership forces trying to shape Jewish life and piety and trying to defend Jewish society from the many non-Jewish political and social pressures which surrounded it."[33] We can add to this the set of shared assumptions between Jesus and the Pharisees in their disputes over Torah. As Anders Runesson notes, "The critique against the Pharisees, the very force of the arguments used by the Matthean Jesus, depends on this shared foundation."[34]

Saldarini, from his substantive work on Pharisees, has suggested the label of "retainers" for them, that is, "most Pharisees were subordinate officials, bureaucrats, judges and educators."[35] As retainers, they functioned between the governing class and the populace and enacted social change not directly but through influence on both the elite patrons they served and the people who looked up to them. Jesus, on the other hand, was of the artisan class, whose popular support and role as a teacher seems to have propelled him into direct comparison and interaction with the Pharisees (e.g., Matt 9:11; 12:38; 22:16, 36; cf. 19:16).[36]

In spite of their differences in social standing, Matthew portrays the Pharisees as the group most closely corresponding to Jesus in his teaching role, especially as they both enjoyed popular support and were both focused on Torah interpretation, with purity being an important area of contention.[37] In the essentials of this portrait, Matthew illumines a plausible, even likely, relational framework for understanding the historical Pharisees vis à vis Jesus.

---

33. Saldarini, *Pharisees, Scribes, and Sadducees*, 173. This fits Ilan's suggestion that the "Pharisees were an opposition party during most of the Second Temple period"; Tal Ilan, *Integrating Women into Second Temple History*, TSAJ 76 (Peabody, MA: Hendrickson, 2001), 37. Saldarini notes more broadly that the "social positions and functions assigned to the scribes and Pharisees, and also the Sadducees, chief priests and elders, are sociologically probable and fit first century Jewish society as we know it from Josephus, other New Testament books and later rabbinic sources" (*Pharisees, Scribes, and Sadducees*, 172).

34. Anders Runesson, "Behind the Gospel of Matthew: Radical Pharisees in Post-War Galilee?," *CurTM* 37 (2010): 467.

35. Saldarini, *Pharisees, Scribes, and Sadducees*, 284.

36. Saldarini identifies Jesus as from "a lower class artisan family" (*Pharisees, Scribes, and Sadducees*, 151).

37. Pickup distinguishes scribes from Pharisees by the formal teaching role of the former (cf. Matt 7:28–29), although he also acknowledges overlap between the two groups (see Mark 2:16). Pharisees taught "in an informal and secondary capacity" ("Matthew's and Mark's Pharisees," 111). Commenting on Matthew's regular pairing of the two groups (e.g., Matt 5:20; 12:38; 15:1; 23:2, 13, 15, 23, 25, 27, 29), Pickup suggests that the Matthean phrase "scribes and Pharisees" illumines Matthew's recognition both that scribes "are the formal and primary teachers of the Law" (via their placement at the front of the pairing, 103) and "that the Pharisees served a highly influential, albeit secondary teaching role alongside the scribes" (104). Saldarini (*Pharisees, Scribes, and Sadducees*, 274) concludes that most scribes were "middle level officials and that their position gave them some power and influence, but they were subordinate to and dependent on the priests and leading families in Jerusalem and Herod Antipas in Galilee during the time of Jesus."

The Particular Case of Matthew 23

Even if we are able to draw on Matthew's sketch of the relationship between Jesus and the Pharisees for a reconstruction of the Pharisees, Matthew 23 is routinely problematized for Matthew's historical veracity. David Garland expresses the issue acutely when he writes that chapter 23 should be understood as

> a Matthean composition whereby Matthew has taken up traditions and interpreted them through alterations and rearrangements to express his own theology. Therefore, Matthew's intention may express something quite opposite to Jesus' intention in the original setting.[38]

Certainly, the polemic of the traditions included in Matthew 23:13–39 has been intensified through Matthew's arrangement of these "woes" into seven carefully plotted castigations of "scribes and Pharisees," involving three "woe" pairs, followed by a climactic seventh "woe" (vv. 13–15, 16–23, 25–28, capped by 29–36).[39] When compared to Luke 11:42–52 (both drawn from Q material), Matthew's seven-fold invective against Pharisees reads more harshly.[40] Indeed, the placement of Matthew 23 as the climax of the confrontation between the Jerusalem leadership and Jesus lends further weight to these "woes" (Matt 21–23). Coupled with Matthew's omission of any positive characterization of Pharisees, we might be justified in agreeing with Saldarini that "little reliable historical information can be gleaned" from Matthew 23.[41]

Since the goal of this chapter is to discern historical possibilities for the historical Pharisees from Matthew's Gospel, I do not attempt a thoroughgoing historical analysis of Matthew 23 to determine which of its parts might go back to the historical Jesus and which stem from Matthew's redaction. Instead, I suggest three ways Matthew 23 might authentically reflect historical Pharisees.

First, Matthew 23 begins with a seemingly out-of-place affirmation of the Pharisees for the evangelist.

---

38. David E. Garland, *The Intention of Matthew 23*, NovTSup 52 (Leiden: Brill, 1979), 65.

39. Brown and Roberts, *Matthew*, 208–9.

40. Although Luke's stylized balance of three "woes" aimed at Pharisees and three at "experts in the law" (νομικός, *nomikos*) certainly involves strong rhetoric.

41. Saldarini, *Pharisees, Scribes, and Sadducees*, 165. Offering an opposing view, Casey provides a reconstruction of an Aramaic Q behind parts of Matthew 23 (and Luke 11), and concludes from his reconstruction that "behind the vigorous editing of Matthew and Luke, we have a source whose contents are genuine" (Maurice Casey, *An Aramaic Approach to Q Sources for the Gospels of Matthew and Luke*, SNTSMS 122 [Cambridge: Cambridge University Press, 2002], 103).

Then Jesus spoke to the crowds and to his disciples: "The scribes and Pharisees sit in Moses' seat. So practice and obey whatever they tell you to do." (Matt 23:1–3a).

Though the exact import of the Pharisees "sit[ting] in Moses' seat" is debated, Jesus clearly affirms something about their role in relation to the Jewish populace. Mark Allan Powell suggests that Jesus refers not to the teaching authority of the Pharisees (which is hard to square with the rest of Matthew; cf. 16:12) but to their role in reading out the Scriptures in synagogues. Through this function, they provided *access* to the Scripture for the Jewish people, who should practice the commands from God that the Pharisees communicate in these readings.[42] Alternately, Matthew's Jesus might be distinguishing between the teaching role of the Pharisees and their misapplication of the Torah. Pickup suggests that Jesus is saying "the people should follow the scribes and Pharisees' teaching of the Scriptures, but just not their behavior or the halakha of their oral traditions."[43] This fits with the refrain of Matthew's Jesus that the Pharisees, rather than being exemplars of Torah obedience, are "deficient in Torah observance."[44] This assessment bears an affinity with the Qumran critique of "those who seek smooth things" (e.g., CD 1.18; 1QH^a X, 32), usually identified with Pharisees, and potentially focused on finding ways to bypass complete obedience ("finding 'loopholes'").[45] Whatever the meaning of 23:2–3a, it is likely that this uniquely positive framing of the Pharisaic role is a tradition that Matthew has inherited and conserved.[46]

Second, the structuring of Matthew 23:13–39 is important as it relates to historical Pharisees. I have noted that there are seven "woes" that frame this part of Matthew 23. The term οὐαί (*ouai*) has traditionally been rendered "woe," but it can also be translated, "how dire it will be." In other words, this interjection can be used as an expression of displeasure (BDAG 734), which approximates a word of judgment,[47] or as an announcement of impending calamity, as in Matthew 24:19. In the latter text, the sense of judgment seems irrelevant and

---

42. Mark A. Powell, "Do and Keep What Moses Says (Matthew 23:2–7)," *JBL* 114 (1995): 431–32; Lynn Cohick, "Pharisees," in *Dictionary of Jesus and the Gospels*, 2nd ed., 674.

43. Pickup, "Matthew's and Mark's Pharisees," 106. He goes on to clarify: "Matthew's Jesus castigates the scribes and Pharisees for failing in their public life to offer an adequate example of how to live so as to fulfill the Torah" (107).

44. Runesson, "Behind the Gospel of Matthew," 466.

45. Green, "What Do We Really Know about the Pharisees," 411; see also James C. VanderKam, "The Pharisees and the Dead Sea Scrolls," in Neusner and Chilton, *In Quest of the Historical Pharisees*, 225–36.

46. Saldarini, *Pharisees, Scribes, and Sadducees*, 165.

47. Garland concludes from his look at Matthew and the Old Testament that *ouai* in Matthew 23 "connotes a powerful and denunciatory judgment akin to a curse" (*Intention of Matthew 23*, 87).

even inappropriate: "οὐαί to pregnant and nursing mothers." Garland argues, "This statement represents . . . a compassionate concern for the necessity of flight for those whose physical condition makes flight less than propitious."[48] Reading *ouai* in Matthew 23 as Jesus's announcement of impending calamity coheres well with the broader Matthean portrait of Jesus's prophetic role in warning about (though not enacting) judgment. Judgment, a significant Matthean motif, is not part of the present arrival of the kingdom but is deferred for the final day when God (and the Son) will right all wrongs (e.g., Matthew's coupling of "end of the age" language with final-day judgment at 13:39–40, 49; see also 10:15; 11:22, 24; 12:36, 41–42; 25:31–33).[49] In this reading of Matthew 23,

> Jesus [is] announcing prophetic judgment on these leaders for their actions and their hypocrisy that together work against the kingdom. Jesus himself does not enact this judgment in the present; instead, he speaks of future judgment for actions done (cf. 16:27).[50]

And, as Garland emphasizes, these words are pointed to a narrative audience of the crowds and disciples as a warning to consider their own hypocritical behavior (23:1).[51]

Finally, Matthew 23—however carefully arranged by the evangelist, with its heightened polemic—does address a number of topics fitting the interests of first-century Pharisees, as reconstructed from rabbinic material. Neusner notes that "the topics of the rabbinic traditions attributed to pre-70 Pharisees compared closely with the agenda of Matthew 23:1–33 . . . in the woe sayings that pertain to the Pharisees . . ."[52] I have already examined Jesus's warnings in 23:23–24 and 23:25–28, with their attention to purity-related matters, and have suggested that the purity themes in Matthew's Gospel are consistent with the rabbinic portrait of Pharisees.

The third "woe" (Matt 23:16–22) addresses the making of vows, which Neusner includes in his list of topics of concern to the historical Pharisees: Matthew's Pharisees "are much like those of the rabbis; they belong in the Roman period,

---

48. Garland, *Intention of Matthew 23*, 68. He understands *ouai* to have two different connotations here and in Matthew 23.

49. It is also suggestive that John the Baptist's original vision for Jesus's ministry involving judgment (Matt 3:13) seems to be challenged by Jesus's ministry of mercy (11:2–6). Whatever John's vision for "the Messiah's deeds" (11:2), Matthew's vision is focused on Jesus's merciful actions of healing and preaching the kingdom to the poor (11:3–5).

50. Brown and Roberts, *Matthew*, 209.

51. Garland, *Intention of Matthew 23*, 214–15.

52. Neusner, "Rabbinic Traditions," 298.

and their legal agendas are virtually identical: tithing, purity laws, Sabbath observance, vows, and the like."[53] It is also the case that Jesus's critique of the manner in which the scribes and Pharisees enact their vows accords well with the Jewish context described by Philo, writing in the first century, who identifies some of his fellow Jews who "swear at length and make whole speeches consisting of a string of oaths and thus, by their misuse of the many forms of the divine name in places where they ought not to do so, show their impiety" (*Decalogue* 94). Earlier, Jesus has taught his followers to keep their word without resorting to thoughtless vows—"but let your word stand as either 'Yes' or 'No'" (Matt 5:37; cf. Philo, *Decalogue* 92). This teaching is expanded and extended in Matthew 23:16–22 to emphasize that "taking an oath before God is a serious action and may not be negated by elaborate circumlocutions."[54] This sensibility expressed by Matthew's Jesus coheres with the early first-century Jewish context, as illumined by Philo.[55]

We have seen that Matthew's portrait in chapter 23 affirms some important facets of Pharisaic aims and practices suggested in other contemporaneous sources.[56] Yet Matthew 23 does heighten the polemic against Pharisees to a higher register by his gathering of "woes" into seven perfective, dire warnings.[57] Coupled with this rhetorical intensification is the evangelist's omission of any examples of Pharisees responding positively to Jesus. In other words, while Matthew does illumine some important aspects of the historical Pharisees, he does not provide the whole picture. If we only had Matthew and not Luke-Acts, for example, we would not know of Pharisees who act benevolently toward Jesus or even join his movement (e.g., Luke 13:31; Acts 15:5; 23:9). Therefore, the portrait of the Pharisees in Matthew should be read judiciously and sensitively for understanding the historical Pharisees.

> [Matthew's] selectivity of narrative calls for circumspection. We ought to
> be careful in using any portrayal to characterize adequately the historical

---

53. Neusner, "Rabbinic Traditions," 301.

54. Brown and Roberts, *Matthew*, 210.

55. Belkin suggests that Philo (and Josephus; see *Ant.* 5.169) supports Jesus's view of oaths against the Pharisees in Matt 15:5–6, in which Jesus (as Philo) is opposed to the fulfillment of an "anti-social" oath (Samuel Belkin, "Dissolution of Vows and the Problem of Anti-Social Oaths in the Gospels and Contemporary Jewish Literature," *JBL* 55 [1936]: 227–34).

56. For an argument that Matt 23:15—the second "woe"—is authentic to Jesus and reflects a situation in which (some) Pharisees attempted to recruit gentile sympathizers to join them in military resistance against Rome, see Michael F. Bird, "The Case of the Proselytizing Pharisees?—Matt 23.15," *JSHJ* 2 (2004): 117–37. See discussion below on the political aims of Pharisees.

57. For the role of Matt 23:37–39 in mitigating the tone of Matthew 23, see W. D. Davies and Dale C. Allison, *A Critical and Exegetical Commentary on the Gospel According to Saint Matthew*, 3 vols., ICC (London: T&T Clark, 1988–1997), 3:319–25.

group in question. A reading that assumes such a direct correspondence is particularly troubling when the relative power differentials between the emerging entities of Judaism and Christianity in the centuries following the time of Jesus shifted so dramatically.[58]

Issue of the Political Aims of the Pharisees in Matthew

Frequently at issue in discussions of the historical Pharisees is the question of their political interests and goals. Neusner, for example, notes that Josephus's portrayal of Pharisees as influential in the political sphere has no parallel in the rabbinic material and sees the Gospels as more congruent with the latter than the former.[59] Steve Mason summarizes (though does not commend) a common view that Josephus portrays a Pharisaic movement away from politics during the early part of the first century CE: "the Pharisees attained some power under Alexandra, then faded from political life under Herod (or earlier), to resurface only on the eve of the revolt in 66."[60] From this perspective the Gospels, and Matthew specifically, characterize the Pharisees as essentially non-political. The question I address in this final section of the chapter involves the political interests of Matthew's Pharisees and how they might map onto the historical terrain.

It is first important to address the reading of Josephus that arrives at a reconstruction of the Pharisees as ebbing and flowing in their political aims (or simply ebbing after the time of the Hasmoneans). Mason argues that the Pharisees are much more incidental to Josephus's interests than has often been acknowledged, so that we cannot sketch with confidence any kind of trajectory from political engagement to disengagement.[61] Mason summarizes the narrative portrait of the Pharisees in Josephus as follows:

> Pharisees appear as an occasional aggravation to the elite. They are a nonaristocratic group with enormous popular support and a perverse willingness to use that support demagogically, even on a whim, to stir up the masses against duly constituted authority—Hasmonean, Herodian, or Josephan.[62]

---

58. Brown and Roberts, *Matthew*, 514. For other historical considerations in Matthew's portrayal of the Pharisees, see ch. 21 of that volume.

59. Neusner, "Rabbinic Traditions," 310–11.

60. Mason, "Josephus' Pharisees," 38. For a full-blown argument that the Pharisees move away from political interests to internal concerns around purity, see Jacob Neusner, *From Politics to Piety: The Emergence of Pharisaic Judaism* (Englewood Cliffs, NJ: Prentice-Hall, 1972).

61. Mason, "Josephus' Pharisees," 37–40.

62. Mason, "Josephus' Pharisees," 37–38.

Similarly, E. P. Sanders describes Pharisees as *standing for dissent* during both the Herodian and Roman years. "They were not in power, nor were they close to those who were. Yet when the time looked ripe, they offered resistance or even engaged in insurrection."[63] And Wright, drawing on the range of sources for the Pharisees, suggests an overarching thesis that makes a great deal of sense:

> Faced with social, political, and cultural "pollution" at the level of national life as a whole, one natural reaction . . . was to concentrate on personal cleanness, to cleanse and purify an area over which one did have control as compensation for the impossibility of cleansing or purifying an area—the outward and visible political one—over which one had none. The intensifying of the biblical purity regulations within Pharisaism may well therefore invite the explanation that they are the individual analogue to the national fear of, and/or resistance to, contamination from, or oppression by, Gentiles. Ceremonial purity functions almost as a displacement activity when faced with the apparent impossibility of national purity.[64]

With this potential reconstruction from Josephus (and incorporating the rabbinic material) in view, we can turn to Matthew and the specific text that most readily addresses the question of Pharisaic political interests. Matthew 22:15–22 narrates some disciples of the Pharisees, along with Herodians, coming to test Jesus once he arrives in Jerusalem.[65] The test involves the question of paying the imperial tax (κῆνσος, *kēnsos*; 22:15–17). The intended trap centers on the apparent lose-lose scenario in answering the question. Responding that paying the tax is lawful or appropriate would risk alienating those who see Rome's occupation as an affront (e.g., zealots and their sympathizers). Yet to answer the opposite could be taken as a threat to Rome itself.[66]

Matthew's alignment of Herodians with Pharisees in this passage (inherited from Mark) is suggestive.[67] Helen Bond argues that Herodians are most likely loyalists or supporters of Herod Antipas.[68] If so, they would seem to sit on the

---

63. E. P. Sanders, *Judaism: Practice and Belief, 63 BCE–66 CE* (Minneapolis: Fortress, 2016), 610.

64. Wright, *New Testament and the People of God*, 187–8.

65. Matthew's Pharisees appear in Jerusalem more frequently than they do in Mark and Luke (see Matt 21:45; 22:34, 41; 27:62). As Saldarini notes (*Pharisees, Scribes, and Sadducees*, 173), "Josephus places the Pharisees in Jerusalem, so their presence is not improbable."

66. Brown and Roberts, *Matthew*, 486.

67. Pickup ("Matthew's and Mark's Pharisees," 93) finds it curious that Matthew retains the reference to Herodians here while omitting Mark's earlier references to them (Mark 3:6; cf. Mark 8:15). If Matthew is careful to retain his source against a thematic interest in Matt 22:15–16, this might illumine historical material.

68. Though not a formal party (Helen K. Bond, "Herodian Dynasty," in *Dictionary of Jesus and the Gospels*, 2nd ed., 382).

opposite pole from at least some Pharisees, who may have had little sympathy for Rome (as in the sketch above). Matthew (and Mark before him) appears to narrate an unusual alliance focused on tripping up this messianic claimant over a political question.[69] Especially given this unusual pairing across a political spectrum, it seems that Matthew is portraying Pharisees as having political aims and interests, but without the institutional authority to enact their desires on their own.[70]

Jesus's answer also suggests interpreting this passage as thoroughly political and not just incidentally so (as if the question were merely a ruse). We see this in Jesus's cryptic, riddle-like answer. He first asks for the coin used to pay the tax. The denarius provided would have had the inscription "Tiberius Caesar Augustus, son of the Divine Augustus" on one side and "High Priest" on the other. Such an absolute claim to divine authority (both religious and political)[71] surely countered Jewish monotheistic faith and loyalty (e.g., an understanding that everything belongs to Israel's God; e.g., Pss 24:1–2; 50:9–12). Thus, it seems accurate to understand Jesus's concluding words as a riddle, "So give to Caesar what belongs to Caesar and to God what belongs to God" (Matt 22:21).[72] Through the riddle,

> Jesus can implicitly assert Yahweh's universal rule in the face of Rome's claims to sovereignty, yet avoid falling into his opponents' trap of directly eschewing payment of the imperial tax. It is no wonder that his opponents are amazed at his response (22:22).[73]

In my reading, Matthew 22:15–22 portrays both Jesus and the Pharisees as having political aims, not only religious ones. The characterization of the Pharisees from this pericope seems to fit with constructions of Pharisees as politically motivated, but as those without direct institutional power to enact

---

69. While the question is more than a political one, it is certainly not less than political, as seen by Jesus's answer to it.

70. Wright suggests that "[t]hey only obtained power if they colluded with or influenced another group who already possessed it," as with the Herodians described in this pericope (*New Testament and the People of God*, 189). If this assessment is correct, it might help explain the various collations of Jewish groups across Matthew. One that has been questioned in terms of historical veracity is Matthew's reference to "the Pharisees and Sadducees" at 3:7 and 16:1, 6, 11–12. Yet according to Saldarini, "it is possible and even probable that the Pharisees and Sadducees, as interest groups within Judaism, might have common interests in how Judaism was lived and might unite against a new faction centered around Jesus" (*Pharisees, Scribes, and Sadducees*, 167).

71. Nicholas Perrin illuminates these claims well in *Jesus the Priest* (London: SPCK, 2018).

72. Ben Witherington III, *Matthew*, SHBC 19 (Macon, GA: Smyth & Helwys, 2006), 413. For other riddles of Jesus in Matthew, see 10:34; 12:39–40; 22:41–46.

73. Brown and Roberts, *Matthew*, 203.

change. Matthew's Pharisees are portrayed, not as central officials of Judaism, but in ancillary relation to other groups who hold institutional power.[74]

CONCLUSION

The purpose of this analysis has been to explore facets of Matthew's portrait of the Pharisees that might find historical resonance with portraits of Pharisees from other sources. Historically plausible contours of the Matthean Pharisees include their aims and practices related to purity regulations that exceed what was expected of non-priestly Jews and the related interest in eating meals in this state of purity (Matt 9:9–13). Some of the relevant purity practices included handwashing (15:1–9) and the tithing of food-related items (23:23). Matthew's reference to Pharisaic interest in elaborate oaths (23:16–22) fits with Philo's description of some of his contemporaries. And whatever Matthew's Jesus means to affirm about the role or authority of Pharisees in Matthew 23:2–3b, this saying appears to reflect an inherited tradition, which does not fit Matthew's interests particularly well, and so may shed light on historical realities. Finally, Matthew 22:15–22, which affirms the political interests of at least some Pharisees, coheres with their characterization in Josephus that they are more than an internally focused sect concerned solely with purity and table fellowship.

While it is certainly the case that Matthew shapes his portrait of the Pharisees (as he does his portrait of Jesus) to address his own context and audience, the historical plausibility of a number of facets of Matthew's Pharisees suggests arguments that the evangelist is simply or even primarily reflecting controversies between his community and their contemporary Jewish antagonists might be overdrawn.[75] While Matthew's own interests ought to remain a matter of interpretive focus, the First Gospel offers its own contributions to knowledge of the historical Pharisees.

---

74. Pickup, "Matthew's and Mark's Pharisees," 108.
75. Pickup draws a similar conclusion ("Matthew's and Mark's Pharisees," 110–12).

CHAPTER 8

Alternate History and the Sermon on the Mount: New Trajectories for Research

BETH M. SHEPPARD

Analyzing the Sermon on the Mount (Matt 5:3–7:27) provides as many questions as answers when it comes to what might be known about the historical Jesus. Is the Sermon a composite of several of Jesus's teachings or an address originally given in a single sitting? What is its relationship to Luke's Sermon on the Plain (6:20–49)? Has the Sermon on the Mount been redacted by Matthew, and if so, how much liberty might he have taken with it? What was the original occasion or impetus for the homily? Where was it actually delivered and to whom was it addressed (the disciples or a larger crowd)? How might Moses typology impact the accuracy or originality of the speech?

Over twenty years ago Warren Carter provided an overview of some the various hypotheses that scholars have advanced about these and other questions. He concluded that there was no particular consensus for the core issue of whether the words originated with Jesus. At most, the majority of scholars propose that Matthew "creatively shapes and interprets material passed on to him by early Christian communities."[1] In his study, Carter indicated that there were some outliers, however, who maintained that Matthew wrote the Sermon while constructing his Gospel. There are still others who assert the exact opposite— that Jesus's address as recorded by the evangelist is essentially a transcript of the Savior's actual words. No matter the criteria we apply to the biblical text to try to determine what actually happened or what Jesus said, we will likely never know the definitive answers to our questions about the Sermon. The lack of absolute knowledge, though, is not a problem unique to our field. Uncertainty is inherent in the discipline of history in general. As historians Martha Howell and Walter Prevenier put it, there is a central paradox of the profession that "historians

---

1. Warren Carter, *What are They Saying about Matthew's Sermon on the Mount?* (Mahwah, NJ: Paulist, 1994), 9.

are prisoners of sources that can never be made fully reliable."[2] Yet Howell and Prevenier offer hope that if historians "are skilled readers of sources and always mindful of their captivity, they can make their sources yield meaningful stories about a past and our relationship to it."[3]

In this hopeful vein, it is proposed that an approach to episodes in Jesus's ministry like the Sermon on the Mount that combines the two methods of cultural history and alternate history may ultimately yield new insights about the historical Jesus. While the bulk of this essay covers theoretical and methodological concerns, focus falls on the crowds present in the setting provided in Matthew's account of the Sermon (4:25–7:1 and 7:28) as well. The object will not be to provide answers to questions that have been raised about the Sermon but to suggest some different trajectories for research concerning that pericope. First, though, it is necessary to set the stage.

SETTING THE STAGE: CULTURAL HISTORY HOLDS A KEY

Careful historical research is necessary for theater troops when they are working with a script in the genre of naturalism. In that style of drama, playwrights seek to portray the lives of everyday people in ordinary situations, warts and all. When performed, a play in this mode requires accuracy in every last detail. A realistic set, period costumes, and appropriate props that don't detract from the realism of the scene serve as vital ingredients in the production.[4] They aren't merely background but help to fill in the blanks between the lines of the script and the full dramatic moment, resulting in a believable performance that is true to life. In other words, it is a host of minutiae that assists with transporting the audience back to the place and time in which the action is set.

Similar to how musing on small details helps to achieve a high level of verisimilitude in drama, focus on what may at first glance appear incidental will likely work to help flesh out a plausible portrait of Jesus and the world in which he lived and moved. This is where cultural history comes in. It is a method of

---

2. Martha Howell and Walter Prevenier, *From Reliable Sources: An Introduction to Historical Methods* (Ithaca, NY: Cornell University Press, 2001), 3.

3. Howell and Prevenier, *From Reliable Sources*, 3.

4. Katie Turner acknowledges that period costumes are not always completely historical because in addition to providing details of the period, "costume is used to evoke emotions that enhance the narrative, and thus designers will diverge from accurate recreations in order to achieve this." Still, she writes, "Whatever the end result, all successful period costuming begins the same way: with a strong foundation in history. Creative decisions are made *after* academic research" (Katie Turner, "'The Shoe is the Sign!' Costuming Brian and Dressing the First Century," in *Jesus and Brian: Exploring the Historical Jesus and His Times via Monty Python's Life of Brian*, ed. Joan E. Taylor (London: Bloomsbury, 2015), 221–37 (here 221, 224; emphasis original).

investigating the past that became fashionable in history departments in the mid-1960s. By that time, as historiographer Lynn Hunt observed, almost a third of the articles in the leading journal *Annales* engaged cultural rather than social, economic, political, or demographic history.[5] Cultural history is still a staple in the discipline, as demonstrated by the fact that undergraduate history students at Yale may elect to take courses focused on this method in addition to tracks related to other modes of analysis, such as those concerned with social change, economics, or politics, to name a few.[6]

There are two main characteristics of cultural history. The first is a willingness to consider different sources, even those that were previously underrepresented in investigations, and the second is a tendency to value all aspects of everyday life as worthy of study, no matter how commonplace. A prime example of a recent Bible-based project focused on cultural history is the four volume *Dictionary of Daily Life in Biblical and Post-Biblical Antiquity*, edited by Edwin M. Yamauchi and Marvin R. Wilson. Yamauchi reveals his attention to cultural history's primary markers in the introduction to that work. He states that the project is an attempt to "systematically and comparatively survey different aspects of culture, whether they were highlighted in the Bible or not."[7] At the same time, he indicates that those writing entries would be digging into extrabiblical texts when hunting sources of information.

For anyone interested in the very broad method of cultural history, where unlikely sources prove illuminating and any aspect of a historical event is worthy of study, the fact that a strand of historical Jesus research is tremendously reliant on the Gospels as source material and pays specific attention to the actions and teachings of Jesus might seem a tightly circumscribed project. This stance is apparently shared by others such as Morna Hooker. She writes, "It would seem that those who have pursued the *ipissimi verba Jesu* in the belief that this would take them to the historical Jesus have in fact succeeded only in shunting themselves into a siding."[8] The fact of the matter is that in any well-rounded biography about a real person, just as with a play that is a piece of fiction, there is much

---

5. Lynn Hunt, "French History in the Last Twenty Years: The Rise and Fall of the Annales Paradigm," *Journal of Contemporary History* 21 (1986): 209–24 (here 216).

6. https://history.yale.edu/academics/undergraduate-program/regions-and-pathways/cultural-history. For a broader overview of cultural history and description of how it has been used by E. P. Sanders, see Beth M. Sheppard, *The Craft of History and the Study of the New Testament*, RBS 60 (Atlanta: Society of Biblical Literature, 2012), 159–64.

7. Edwin M. Yamauchi and Marvin R. Wilson, eds., *Dictionary of Daily Life in Biblical and Post-Biblical Antiquity*, 4 vols. (Peabody, MA: Hendrickson, 2015), 1.

8. Morna D. Hooker, "Foreword: Forty Years On," in *Jesus, Criteria, and the Demise of Authenticity*, ed. Chris Keith and Anthony Le Donne (New York: T&T Clark, 2012), xiii–xvii (here xvi).

more to consider than what the main protagonist said and did.[9] For instance, when considering the historicity of a spectacle like the Sermon on the Mount, there are always questions regarding the logistics of pulling something like that off, including the first century participants' access to resources or venues, how word spread to potential audiences, not to mention possible concerns about inclement weather, transportation, security, sanitation (or perhaps lack thereof), and a host of other details. Surely these elements were a part of the everyday life of the historical Jesus.

Authors of the essays contained in *The World of the New Testament: Cultural, Social, and Historical Contexts*, edited by Joel B. Green and Lee Martin McDonald (Baker Academic, 2013), or even Samuel L. Adams's *Social and Economic Life in Second Temple Judea* (Westminster John Knox, 2014) already explore what various elements of living in the first century might have been like. Such social-science based studies foreshadow models that might be used in exploring nuances in what is recorded about Jesus of Nazareth. Adams illustrates this point beautifully. He comments that the use of the word "debts" in Matthew's Sermon on the Mount (6:12) assumes, "an established system of borrowing and lending, with the possibility of heavy interest payments and eventual debt slavery."[10] He also sketches out general practices related to lending and liabilities within the culture based on his research. It is beyond the scope of Adams's project, however, to speculate on how Jesus financed his ministry. Yet, his observations raise a host of very real questions: To what degree did itinerant teachers and even carpenters typically go into hock during their lives? At what stages of a craftsman or teacher's career might borrowing have been necessary? What were the logistics of getting payment to the lender (how often, where was payment made, were agents used)? All of these issues might be explored with an eye toward tendering a plausible hypothesis about Jesus's own financial resources and activities.

Here is the main point: when we as historians set our sights almost exclusively on determining the authenticity of Jesus's miracles, individual sayings, theology, or the content of his message, as worthy as these tasks are, we might miss other information that may enable us to deduce details about the historical Jesus. Yamauchi himself provides an example. After reading Marvin R. Wilson's entry on "Barbers & Beards" in the *Dictionary of Daily Life*, he writes, "We can conclude

---

9. The focus on the words of Jesus is a situation likely exacerbated by the convention of red letter editions of the New Testament, which were first published at the turn of the twentieth century by Louis Klopsch, and the more recent work of the Jesus Seminar. Charles M. Pepper, *Life-Work of Louis Klopsch: Romance of a Modern Knight of Mercy* (New York: Christian Herald, 1910), 324–25.

10. Samuel L. Adams, *Social and Economic Life in Second Temple Judea* (Louisville: Westminster John Knox, 2014), 113.

with almost certainty that Jesus had a beard."[11] Jesus's facial hair, however, is never explicitly mentioned in Matthew, Mark, Luke, or John. Artwork, archaeological finds in ancient barbershops, classical writings that mention grooming practices, along with texts by the rabbis that include a few comments about hirsute features are all indirect sources, which contribute to this conclusion about Jesus's appearance.[12]

THE LIMITS OF CRITERIA

As the example from Yamauchi above illustrates, the almost paralyzing conundrum of the inadequacy of the Gospels to provide a definitive, complete portrait of Jesus based only on his words or miracles can be somewhat alleviated by asking new questions and looking at indirect sources. At the same time, it is important to acknowledge that all historians, both those using the methods of cultural history and others using more traditional methods of investigating the past, need and use criteria to evaluate the information from which they are drawing their conclusions. This is true whether they are looking at primary, secondary, or perhaps even tertiary witnesses like the Gospels or indirect sources of information drawn from the Greco-Roman and Jewish worlds. Undeniably, triangulating various resources and methods to support a theory is always a best practice, since doing so only strengthens an argument. As Jerry Toner cautions, however, cultural historians who use indirect evidence can run into problems not only due to the random nature of some of the evidence that has survived but also the temptation to lump together a wide range of sources while ignoring "differences in time, geography, context and register" that require sources be interpreted on an individual basis.[13] He suggests three elements to keep in mind when developing models based on indirect sources:

1. Awareness of the dangers of using disparate sources, which attunes the researcher to "avoid using the 'exceptional' elements within the evidence as indicators of what is ordinary."
2. Use of a broad array of resources in ways that result in models that are internally consistent with the social context in which people lived.

---

11. Edwin M. Yamauchi, "Introduction," in *Dictionary of Daily Life in Biblical and Post-Biblical Antiquity*, 2.

12. The bibliography for Wilson's entry includes only studies on the topic, which in turn assess the primary sources. Wilson, "Barbers & Beards," *Dictionary of Daily Life in Biblical and Post-Biblical Antiquity*, 144–45.

13. Jerry Toner, "Barbers, Barbershops and Searching for Roman Popular Culture," *Papers of the British School at Rome* 83 (2015): 91–109 (here 93).

3. Drawing on the disparate resources to provide "a benchmark against which local nuance may be applied."[14]

Any resulting model for a given historical event doesn't claim to be 100 percent accurate in every detail, but at least offers a plausible conjecture. Toner concedes that for many of his classicist colleagues, "this approach is too speculative."[15] Presumably, the same sentiment will be shared by biblical historians when applying cultural history to Jesus research. Even so, the traditional criteria that our own field developed for working with the most direct sources we have (the Gospels) along with our tried and true methods like source, genre, redaction, and other criticisms are not perfect either. Darrell L. Bock, for instance, lists ten yardsticks of best practice for analyzing source material on the historical Jesus in a little book he wrote in 2012.[16] While Bock paints with a broad brush and his general conclusions are sound, there is always the danger that for less-experienced investigators, the overenthusiastic application of this criteria to historical Jesus sources might potentially yield inaccurate results. Let me be more specific.

A good practice in historical research is to look for many sources attesting to the same "fact," sometimes called the principle of multiple attestation. Bock himself observes this guideline with some success when he chooses essentially to steer clear of the Gospel of John in discussing what might be known about Jesus.[17] Granted, the Gospel identified with the Beloved Disciple differs substantially in content from the Synoptics and contains anecdotes that cannot be corroborated. Further, the broad brush with which Bock paints his portrait is plausible without it. Nevertheless, one must be careful not to make the leap that John's unique material is somehow flawed simply because it is distinctive. After all, the principle of multiple attestation itself does not work in the case of rumors or gossip. Consider the situation of Samuel Clemens, aka Mark Twain,

---

14. Toner, "Barbers, Barbershops," 93

15. Toner, "Barbers, Barbershops," 92.

16. Darrell L. Bock lists ten rules in his text *Who is Jesus: Linking the Historical Jesus with the Christ of Faith* (New York: Howard Books, 2012), 16–24. Devising criteria to evaluate sources, however, is a practice that stretches back to E. Bernheim (1889). He was followed by Charles Langlois along with Charles Seignobos (1898). For a summary, see Howell and Prevenier, *From Reliable Sources*, 70. The Langlois and Seignobos book was translated into English by George G. Berry in 1904 (New York: Holt & Company, 1904) and is available on the Project Gutenberg site.

17. Bock, *Who is Jesus?*, 12. Bock does treat the material from John extensively in his earlier work, *Jesus according to Scripture: Restoring the Portrait from the Gospels* (Grand Rapids: Baker Academic, 2002). For his part, Richard Bauckham argues that the Beloved Disciple may indeed be the author of the Fourth Gospel and an eyewitness to events, which for those who value first-person accounts over derivative ones, would lend a certain weight to the Fourth Gospel. See Richard Bauckham, *Jesus and the Eyewitnesses: The Gospels as Eyewitness Testimony* (Grand Rapids: Eerdmans, 2006), 384.

about whom in 1897 there were reports in multiple circles of his death that were clearly an exaggeration. Clemens did not meet his maker until 1910.[18] Concerning uniqueness, just because an event has only a single witness that cannot be corroborated, this does not necessarily mean that its historicity is dubious. In fact, William the Conqueror's Doomsday book includes information about families and holdings for which there is no other evidence but for which there is no real reason to doubt they existed. Why couldn't the same be true for some of the anecdotes in the Fourth Gospel? In short, multiple attestation does not equate to empirical verification, and the premise that no statements are true unless they are empirically shown to be true is itself unverifiable. So, this criterion is not infallible, even though it does generally contribute to the reasonableness of a historian's rendition of the past.[19]

In addition, Tobias Hägerland points out that even a newer, less traditional criterion, known as recurring attestation, where scholars hunt for repeated patterns within the body of material we have about Jesus, also has a weakness because it "misses those singular, unrepeatable major events in Jesus' life which by definition cannot be recurrently attested, yet were crucial to the shaping and outcome of his career."[20] In short, no rule for analyzing the Gospels works perfectly all the time. So, why not throw off the traces and dabble in some cultural history using indirect sources? After all, according to Howell and Prevenier, regardless of what records of the past are available, they will not be good enough to allow for absolute precision. All sources, even primary ones, are invariably biased and not ideal. Regardless, historians are still forced to rely on the sources they have in hand or can uncover through hunting in archives, digging in the dirt, or interviewing stakeholders.[21] As the prior observation about a bearded Jesus shows, the Gospels are not the exclusive sources by which something might plausibly be known about Jesus. Like the cultural historians who are investigating

---

18. Twain's response to the rumors was published in the June 2, 1897 edition of *The New York Journal* and reads, "The report of my death was an exaggeration." The misquote, "the reports of my death are grossly exaggerated," seems to stem from the Twain biography by Albert Bigelow Paine, *Mark Twain: A Biography: The Personal and Literary Life of Samuel Langhorne Clemens*, vol. 3 (New York: Harper & Brothers, 1912), 1039.

19. Mark Goodacre, in a thought experiment, imagined the impact on New Testament scholarship had Mark never been written. He notes that while 90 percent of Mark is reproduced in the other Gospels, there is 10 percent that is not. Yet, that 10 percent is vital for theories such as Wrede's messianic secret or Mark's portrait of the contentious disciples that provides evidence for power struggles in the early church (Mark Goodacre, "A World without Mark," unpublished manuscript presented at the conference "Erasure History: Approaching the Missing Sources of Antiquity," University of Toronto, November 11, 2011, pp. 7–8). I am grateful that Goodacre was willing to share the manuscript with me.

20. Tobias Hägerland, "The Future of Criteria in Historical Jesus Research," *JSHJ* 13 (2015): 43–65 (here 54).

21. Howell and Prevenier, *From Reliable Sources*, 80–81.

other topics and periods of history, we simply need to be willing to widen the aperture of our search for the historical Jesus beyond his actions and words.

CANONS OF SOURCES

It is interesting to observe that when one considers the lights or sources that scholars of the historical Jesus shine on the past, it becomes apparent that there is a canon—a stock collection of resources that those interested in the historical Jesus regularly consult. Mark Allan Powell provides a summary that includes material remains, Roman sources, Jewish sources, the epistles, the canonical Gospels (and their own hypothetical/reconstructed sources), and apocryphal gospels and writings.[22] What is particularly odd is that the treatment of Greco-Roman materials is rather limited. He includes only those authors who make (or may make, given the possibility of interpolations in some cases) explicit reference to Jesus, such as Josephus, Tacitus, and a few others.

Powell's formulation, which represents the tried and true canon of sources that frequently appear in historical Jesus studies, masks an emerging tendency to consider a broader array of Greco-Roman sources. This development is driven by the recognition that in addition to Second Temple Judaism, or Hellenism, Roman contexts also have a part to play in understanding the historical Jesus.[23] For instance, Keith and Le Donne's *Jesus, Criteria, and the Demise of Authenticity*, though not a biography about Jesus, includes a reference to a passage in Seneca.[24] For his part, Sean Freyne, while liberally diving into Josephus in the study he produces on the life of Jesus, also mentions other works by classical authors.[25] Gerhard Lohfink likewise references Josephus a handful of times, but also gives a nod to Seneca in his *Jesus of Nazareth*.[26] Craig Keener provides a feast of references to Greco-Roman literature in his work, as indicated by an

---

22. Mark Allan Powell, *Jesus as a Figure in History: How Modern Historians View the Man from Galilee*, 2nd ed. (Louisville: Westminster John Knox, 2013), 34–59.

23. See the comments by Joel B. Green and Lee Martin McDonald, "Introduction," in *The World of the New Testament: Cultural, Social, and Historical Contexts* (Grand Rapids: Baker Academic, 2013), 5. For his part, Craig Evans distinguishes between two classes of Greco-Roman sources—those that reference Jesus and/or early Christianity and those that may be plumbed for background of the New Testament. See Craig E. Evans, *Ancient Texts for New Testament Studies: A Guide to the Background Literature* (Grand Rapids: Baker Academic, 2005), 287–300. For an example of research that focuses on the Jewish context, see James H. Charlesworth, *Jesus within Judaism: New Light from Exciting Archaeological Discoveries* (New York: Doubleday, 1988).

24. Keith and Le Donne, *Jesus, Criteria, and the Demise of Authenticity*, 226.

25. Sean Freyne, *Jesus, A Jewish Galilean: A New Reading of the Jesus-Story* (New York: T&T Clark, 2004), 203–4. Classical works other than Josephus are mentioned six times in his two hundred page text on Jesus. He also takes the presence of heavily Romanized cities in the Galilee region like Sepphoris and Tiberius quite seriously (16).

26. Gerhard Lohfink, *Jesus of Nazareth*, trans. Linda M. Maloney (Collegeville, MN: Liturgical Press, 2012). Lohfink's index included only an "Index of Biblical Citations." A count of classical materials was

index to "Other Greco-Roman Sources" that is just over twenty-nine pages in length.[27] Even Robert Geis, who specifies in his account of Jesus's ministry that the source material is the canonical New Testament, goes on a few pages later to acknowledge that he has used the Loeb Classical Library editions for other works by Jesus's rough contemporaries.[28] In any event, to a cultural historian extensively exploring Greek and Latin sources in addition to Jewish sources is natural, given that Palestine was part of the Roman Empire and there was likely some degree of Romanization. After all, Jesus suffered his death at the hands of a Roman procurator, and in the gospel texts there are occasionally nods to Roman soldiers, officials, and others.[29] Even when focusing on Galilee, it is hard to sidestep the fact that the thoroughly Roman capital city, Tiberias, is just a few miles around the shore from Jesus's hometown of Capernaum.[30]

So, consulting a wide variety of writings from the Greco-Roman side of the library in order to reconstruct aspects of the life of the historical Jesus from the perspective of cultural history is a logical next step.[31] Although rabbinic writings and the Dead Sea Scrolls have been rightly prominent in studies that address Jewish aspects of the historical Jesus for quite some time, there is much yet with regard to the Roman cultural context that has yet to be thoroughly explored. When we finally do get to our speculation about the Sermon on the Mount, toward the end of this essay, that will be the focus. In the meantime, let's turn to two short examples.

SAMPLING CULTURAL HISTORY, ROMAN CONTEXTS, AND THE HISTORICAL JESUS

Martial, the Roman poet who was actively writing at the end of the first century, has an epigram in which he mentions that the lavish feasts enjoyed by

---

the result of analyzing his endnotes and being attentive to his use of the names of classical authors in the body of his text. In addition to Seneca, he also references Plato and Homer.

27. Craig Keener, *The Historical Jesus of the Gospels* (Grand Rapids: Eerdmans, 2009). Unfortunately, Keener's stature in some quarters of the academy is diminished, according to Powell, by a reputation for being selective in his use of these sources to achieve specific results and the perception that he is "engaged in apologetics rather than a quest to determine what can be regarded as historical" (Powell, *Jesus as a Figure in History*, 260).

28. Robert Geis, *Life of Christ* (Lanham, MD: University Press of America, 2013), viii and xi.

29. In Matthew see 8:5–13; 27:27–30; 27:62–66.

30. Margaret Davies remarks, with some surprise, that although Matthew sets Jesus's public ministry primarily in Galilee, neither Sepphoris nor Tiberias, Herod Antipas's old capital and his newer one, are mentioned in the Gospel. Margaret Davies, *Matthew*, Readings: A New Biblical Commentary (Sheffield: JSOT Press, 1993), 19.

31. Bock himself references a number of Roman authors, from Dio Cassius to Florus, when discussing the phenomenon of legitimizing miracles done by leaders in the Greco-Roman world (Bock *Who is Jesus?*, 71–72 and 221n18).

the wealthy elite end up destined the next day for the *infelix damnate spongea virgae*,[32] or sad, doomed, sponge on a stick. This epigram, when combined with a reference in Seneca the Younger about a suicidal gladiator seeking the privacy of a bathroom and ramming a toilet sponge down his own throat (*Letters* 70.20–21), seems to indicate that Greco-Roman personal hygiene involved some sort of loofahs, rather than toilet paper.[33] Such information, when brought to bear on Matthew 27:48 (cf. Mark 15:36; John 19:29, 30), where we read that wine was administered to Jesus on a sponge that was attached to a reed (*kalamos*) in his final moments, lends a certain color to that action, turning it from an odd anecdote to an example of tasteless toilet humor that functions as a scathing insult to the condemned man.[34] In this context, we are reminded that a full portrait of the past isn't just about what happened but about what an action may have meant within its wider cultural milieu.[35]

Speaking of scatological issues, Craig Evans analyzes a Roman source that doesn't make Powell's list, namely, the graffiti in Pompeii and Herculaneum, to explore the question of Jesus's likely level of literacy. Given that at least a third of the inscriptions in the town deal with issues related to defecation, and still others are peppered with misspelling and grammatical errors, Evans observes that in the Roman world there is at least "a crude literacy that reaches all levels of society."[36] This evidence, combined with other information about the ubiquity of inscriptions, graffiti, and other text remains lead Evans to conclude, "what strikes me as most logical inference . . . (is) that Jesus was literate to some degree."[37]

ALTERNATE HISTORY: A KEY TO FINDING TOPICS

While these two examples regarding Jesus's crucifixion and his level of literacy made use of Roman sources that might not necessarily be on the typical "go to"

---

32. Martial *Epigr.* 12.48.7 Ann Olga Koloski-Ostrow renders this and prefers, "the unhappy sponge on the doomed mop stick," implying excrement gets mopped up from the floor (*The Archaeology of Sanitation in Roman Italy: Toilets, Sewers and Water Systems* [Chapel Hill: University of North Carolina Press, 2015], 228).

33. Paul Roberts, *Life and Death in Pompeii and Herculaneum* (London: British Museum, 2013), 264.

34. There would be a difference between toilet humor/mockery and a perception of ritual uncleanliness. Jodi Magness asserts that while the Qumran community viewed urination and defecation as unclean, that was not necessarily the case with some of the rabbis. In addition, she interprets Jesus's comments in Mark 7:1–16 (cf. Matt 15:11) about handwashing to indicate that Jesus did not necessarily think that excrement was impure (Jodi Magness, *Stone and Dung, Oil and Spit: Jewish Daily Life in the Time of Jesus* [Grand Rapids: Eerdmans, 2011], 137 and 142).

35. It would be most interesting to follow up on this idea and determine whether or not there are any classical studies related to insults, bathroom humor, and the like that might be studied for insight into the life of Jesus.

36. Craig A. Evans, *Jesus and the Remains of His Day: Studies in Jesus and the Evidence of Material Culture* (Peabody, MA: Hendrickson, 2015), 82.

37. Evans, *Jesus and the Remains of His Day*, 86.

reading lists of those involved in past quests for the historical Jesus, the topics involve aspects of everyday life. Therefore, they are within the purview of cultural history. Diving into the texts of the Gospels themselves, one may discover all sorts of other elements that might be of interest in exploring the life of Jesus beyond his teachings and miracles. For instance, one might investigate what Jesus likely wore and where he may have gotten his clothes; what specific roads he might have taken to travel from city to city and how many miles a traveler like Jesus might log in a day; whether he used messengers or how he might have gotten news of what was going on in Jerusalem when he was in Galilee, just to name a few.

A thought technique used by historians that is variously called speculative history, virtual history, imaginative history, or alternative history may be called into service to provide new questions for historians to investigate about the life of Jesus. In the process of creating an alternate (imagined) scenario about the past, which sometimes uses counterfactuals and at others a fictional parallel anecdote, one may be forced to fill in details about which props were likely available, consider logistics of first-century life, and think carefully about cause/effect factors that might be at play when drafting any scene featuring Jesus or his immediate contemporaries. In short, virtual history complements cultural history.

There is little objectionable in using a bit of imagination to provide leads for new subjects of study with an eye toward fleshing out the bare bones of what is known about an actual event or person in the past. Imaginative scenarios assist historians to think outside of the box, draw attention to weaknesses in the existing body of scholarship or its sources, allow investigators to question causal relationships that are taken for granted, or highlight mistaken or biased assumptions about a topic. Alternate history is a heuristic technique. Think of it as the historian's version of profiling with the goal of assisting the historian to catch a glimpse of the more elusive elements of the past.

Imaginative histories, particularly in the form of counterfactual ponderings, crop up in treatments of modern history when historians ponder the question, "What if . . . ?" Certainly, posing hypothetical scenarios about the past can seem like little more than the creation of historical fiction. Historian Niall Ferguson boldly states one of the main objections to the method: "Why concern ourselves with what didn't happen? Just as there is no use crying over spilt milk, . . . so there is no use in wondering how the spillage might have been averted."[38] Ferguson is not daunted by this critique, however. He goes on to remark that

38. Niall Ferguson, ed., *Virtual History: Alternatives and Counterfactuals* (New York: Basic Books, 1999), 1.

imagining alternate scenarios "is a vital part of the way in which we learn."[39] This makes sense. Almost everyone asks themselves questions like "What if I had not turned in my assignment late?" or "What if I had answered that question during the last job interview differently?" Reflections like these encourage the sort of thoughts that tell us something about ourselves, our actions, and our motivations. Sometimes the conclusions that are drawn affect our future choices and behaviors. While Richard Evans and Jeremy Black are correct that in the hands of unscrupulous or at least incautious authors it is possible to rewrite history to serve modern biases or political agendas, we shouldn't throw the baby out with the bathwater.[40] Even Evans concedes that alternate history is sometimes useful. This depends on factors such as:

1. The degree to which the historian's intentions relate to illuminating the past, creating something for entertainment, or reacting to his/her contemporary context.
2. The scope of the historian's knowledge base and the level of research undertaken.
3. The extent to which the imaginative scenario is fettered to what is known about the past or roams completely free.[41]

Keeping in mind these three factors and the idea that thought experiments are tools rather than ends in and of themselves, there should be little objection in using alternate history to help uncover new topics that cultural historians might investigate with regard to the historical Jesus.

EXAMPLES OF NEW TESTAMENT IMAGINATIVE HISTORY

Although full-length imaginative histories in the field of New Testament studies are not particularly plentiful, there are a few. Bruce Longenecker's *The Lost Letters of Pergamum* is not focused explicitly on the life of Jesus at the outset but is intended to portray late first-century life in Asia Minor.[42] Nonetheless, it does

---

39. Ferguson, *Virtual History*, 2.

40. See Jeremy Black, *Other Pasts, Different Presents, Alternative Futures* (Bloomington: Indiana University Press, 2015), 67, and Richard J. Evans, *Altered Pasts: Counterfactuals in History* (Waltham, MA: Brandeis University Press, 2013), 78–79. For instance, Evans links the popularity of Robert Harris's historical novel about Nazi Germany entitled *Fatherland* to its ability to play on British fears concerning German reunification and the European Union.

41. Evans, *Altered Pasts*, 124–25.

42. Bruce W. Longenecker, *The Lost Letters of Pergamum: A Story from the New Testament World*, 2nd ed. (Grand Rapids: Baker Academic, 2016).

reach a climax when one of the main characters begins to correspond with Luke (the author of the Gospel and Acts) and discusses details from that account of Jesus's life. *The Lost Letters* is well researched and, though fictional, received positive reviews from those who recognized the pedagogical value of the work.[43]

In *The Shadow of the Galilean*, another imaginative account of the life of Jesus, Gerd Theissen sketches out the state of scholarly research about the historical Jesus in a way that is accessible to readers.[44] During the course of this particular alternate history, it so happens that a fictional character explicitly references the Sermon on the Mount. The plot centers on a character named Andreas, a wealthy merchant who hails from Sepphoris and is mistakenly swept up and jailed with protestors who were demonstrating in Jerusalem against Pilate. In exchange for his freedom, Pilate blackmails Andreas into spying on Jesus in Galilee to determine whether or not Jesus was contributing to political instability. Once in Nazareth, Jesus's hometown, Andreas speaks with a couple whose son was so enthralled after hearing the beatitudes that the young man abandons this family to follow Jesus. The couple observes that many sons and other young, impoverished people in the region were forsaking their familial obligations to follow idealistic dreams of ending injustices related to social, economic, and political oppression.[45] The portrait painted assumes that those who made up the bulk of the crowds that followed Jesus and were susceptible to his message were young (probably male) and from lower economic strata. They were essentially zealots in the making. Later, Theissen expands his portrait of Jesus's followers to include the poor or destitute who throng to Jesus for free handouts of food along with a small percentage of wealthy.[46]

A slightly more cosmopolitan audience than that imagined by Theissen is present in the version of the Sermon on the Mount portrayed in the film *Monty Python's Life of Brian*. Carl Dyke summarizes the scene overall in which "a reverently performed, quietly charismatic Jesus" can be heard at a distance. Meanwhile the camera's focus is on Brian and the "characters at the fringes of the audience straining to make out his words across great distance and accumulated

---

43. For instance, Joseph Fantin, in his review of the text writes, "This book is not simply historical fiction with the late first century as a backdrop for the events of the narrative. It is a well-crafted description of the context in which some of the early Christians lived. It is a book on New Testament history and culture in narrative form (Joseph D. Fantin, "Review of *The Lost Letters of Pergamum: A Story from the New Testament World*," *Bibliotheca sacra* 163.649 (2006): 123.

44. Gerd Theissen, *The Shadow of the Galilean: The Quest of the Historical Jesus in Narrative Form* (Philadelphia: Fortress, 1987), 1.

45. Theissen, *Shadow of the Galilean*, 70–72.

46. Theissen, *Shadow of the Galilean*, 112, 121. Later in the story Levi, a publican, is mentioned as one of Jesus's followers, 146.

crowd sounds."[47] This audience includes men and women. In addition, those in expensive clothing and jewels rub shoulders with those costumed humbly. And looming over all are a handful of dispassionate Roman soldiers, who were presumably there to ensure that peace was kept. The diverse nature of those gathered to hear Jesus likely reflects Matthew 4:25, which mentions that those who thronged to Jesus included not only locals from Galilee but also visitors from the Decapolis (the city of Hippos is almost directly across the lake from Tiberias), Jerusalem, Judea at large, and the area beyond the Jordan.

Although the writers of the film script were not biblical scholars and their primary goal was to entertain audiences (with a secondary one of commenting on how the church interprets the Bible), their parallel history was nonetheless extraordinarily well researched.[48] Not only did the writers read the Gospels multiple times as they began the project, but during their weeks researching the background of the Gospels they dove into other materials, such as the Dead Sea Scrolls.[49] Philip Davies even finds episodes in the film that reflect familiarity with Josephus and rabbinic literature. He also maintains that the wordplay during Jesus's mountaintop oration in which "peacemakers" is misheard by those in the back as "cheesemakers" is a clever reference to the Tyropoean Valley in Jerusalem, a name that can indeed be translated as Valley of the Cheesemakers.[50]

As well researched as the satire might be, there are some flaws. For instance, if the Sermon (or a sermon) was delivered to a crowd in Galilee by Jesus during the first half of the first century, it is unlikely Roman soldiers would have been present to keep the peace. Granted, the irony of Jesus referring to blessings for peacemakers in the presence of soldiers who are part of the *Pax Romana* is part of the humor of the scene. Yet, Galilee was administered by Herod Antipas who, according to E. P. Sanders, was an ally of Rome. This means that it was not an occupied territory. Antipas governed with Jewish administrators, not Roman.[51]

---

47. Carl Dyke, "Learning from *The Life of Brian*: Saviors for Seminars," in *Screening Scripture: Intertextual Connections Between Scripture and Film*, ed. George Aichele and Richard Walsh (Harrisburg, PA: Trinity Press International, 2002), 229–50 (here 237).

48. On the aims of the piece, see the comments by Graham Chapman, et al., *The Pythons Autobiography* (New York: St. Martins, 2003), 281, 287.

49. Chapman et al., *Pythons Autobiography*, 279.

50. Philip R. Davies, "Life of Brian Research," in *Biblical Studies/Cultural Studies: The Third Sheffield Colloquium*, ed. J. Cheryl Exum and Stephen D. Moore, LHBOTS 266, JSOTSup 266 (New York: T&T Clark, 1998), 400–414 (here 404). For his part, James Crossley asserts that even historical Jesus research itself influenced the film. He identifies several reconstructions of Jesus that were produced in earlier generations of biblical scholars in the characterization of Brian (James G. Crossley, "Life of Brian or Life of Jesus? Uses of Critical Biblical Scholarship and Non-Orthodox Views of Jesus in Monty Python's *Life of Brian*," *Relegere: Studies in Religion and Reception* 1.1 (2011): 93–114 (here 109, 113).

51. E. P. Sanders, "Jesus' Relation to Sepphoris," in *Sepphoris in Galilee: Crosscurrents of Culture*, ed. Rebecca Martin Nagy, Carol L. Meyers, Eric M. Meyers, and Zeev Weiss (Raleigh: North Carolina Museum of Art, 1996), 75–79 (here 76).

That non-Jews (including Roman soldiers) were not present in significant numbers in Galilee during the life of Jesus is confirmed by archaeological evidence. Specifically, the garbage dump at Sepphoris does not include pig bones in the pre-70 CE strata, reflecting Jewish dietary proscriptions. It is only following the Jewish revolt that porcine bones comprise 30 percent of all animal remains, indicating a Roman presence after the war.[52] Still, as Joan E. Taylor puts it, the aim is not "to determine whether the Pythons got anything right, but how the scene asks us to reflect on the biblical texts."[53]

Taylor's own goal in studying Monty Python's work is to discover the ancient ordinary residents in first-century Galilee who are missing from elite histories by employing reception exegesis of the film. That is a hair's breadth difference from what is being proposed in this essay—that biblical scholars themselves begin creating imaginative artifacts like the film and other imaginative histories for use as a point of departure to investigate the past in new ways. Given the word count imposed on this essay, the works of Theissen and the Pythons serve as substitutes to creating a new virtual history of Jesus. We will use these two existing works to demonstrate how imagining alternate versions of past events is an exercise that prompts one to think of details in the everyday culture of the time that are likely part of the life of the historical Jesus.

VIRTUAL HISTORY, CULTURAL HISTORY, AND THE SERMON ON THE MOUNT

When it comes to the Sermon on the Mount, determining Jesus's exact words may be an impossible feat. Classicists note that even Cicero, who published his own orations after delivering them, did not produce a transcript of what he actually uttered. Instead, he modified his original words for consumption in print format.[54] If even the remarks from the famed orator's own mouth didn't match those of his pen, it is difficult to assume any record of a mountaintop address delivered by Jesus, written after the fact and filtered through sources and witnesses, would do much more than genuinely represent the themes and character of Jesus's message to his audience. Yet, the alternate histories sketched by the Pythons and by Theissen challenge us to think about the logistics involved when

---

52. Craig A. Evans, *Jesus and His World: The Archaeological Evidence* (Louisville: Westminster John Knox, 2012), 24.

53. Joan E. Taylor, "The Historical Brian: Reception Exegesis in Practice," in Taylor, *Jesus and Brian*, 96.

54. Robert Morstein-Marx, *Mass Oratory and Political Power in the Late Roman Empire* (Cambridge: Cambridge University Press, 2004), 25–27.

large gatherings were present to hear discourses and might point the way toward at least filling in that aspect of the picture of the historical Jesus.

The fact that Jesus drew crowds (variously designated ὄχλος, πλῆθος, πολλοί, and λαός in the Gospels) when he appeared, did miracles, and spoke is a historical detail that is confirmed by multiple attestation. In his study of Matthew, J. R. C. Cousland attributes a few instances of the "crowds" in that Gospel to the evangelist's sources Mark and Q. Cousland is, however, reticent to ascribe Matthew's copious use of the crowd elsewhere to M.[55] Instead, he identifies most of the other thirty occurrences of the word "crowd" (crowds) as a result of editorial activity.[56] The fact that there are so many of these unique Matthean mentions of audiences, though, makes the presence of large groups a theme in the evangelist's work. Further, it is one that is not unique to Matthew. Luke and John also indicate that crowds are present during Jesus's public ministry. Whether or not John and Luke, like Matthew, might characterize the crowds in ways that serve their specific narrative agendas, this common theme in their portraits implies that the presence of crowds was plausible. Combined with the mentions in Mark and Q, the presence of crowds during Jesus's ministry is likely rooted in historical fact.[57]

When substantial crowds gather, however, there are always issues related to logistics. The Monty Python skit, for instance, raises questions about acoustics. In an age without microphones or bullhorns, how was it possible for people to hear Jesus when he delivered discourses? The scene in *Life of Brian* also prompts one to think about whether the gathered crowds stood, as the Pythons portrayed it, or sat, given that Matthew references Jesus himself sitting down (Matt 5:1). For his part, Theissen stumbles on another problem in his own imaginative history: how potential audience members become aware that they should assemble when and where Jesus planned to be without radio announcements and newspaper advertising. In fact, Theissen's main character, Andreas, doesn't ever figure this out. He wanders throughout Galilee only catching glimpses of Jesus's shadow, commenting, "Although we asked about Jesus everywhere, we never met him.

---

55. J. R. C. Cousland, *Crowds in the Gospel of Matthew*, NovTSup 102 (Leiden: Brill, 2002), 32–34.

56. Cousland, *Crowds in the Gospel of Matthew*, 34.

57. On characterization of the crowd in Luke, see Mbengu D. Nyiawung and Ernst van Eck, "Characters and Ambivalence in Luke: An Emic Reading of Luke's Gospel, Focusing on the Jewish Peasantry," *HvTSt* 68.1 (2012), 1–12; Richard S. Ascough, "Narrative Technique and Generic Designation: Crowd Scenes in Luke-Acts and in Chariton," *CBQ* 58 (1996): 69–81. For a character analysis of the crowds in John, see Cornelius Bennema, "The Crowd: A Faceless, Divided Mass," in *Character Studies in the Fourth Gospel*, ed. Steven A. Hunt, D. Francois Tolmie, and Ruben Zimmermann, WUNT 314 (Tübingen: Mohr Siebeck, 2013), 345–55. Bennema is more interested in how the depiction of the crowd furthers John's plot than he is in the existence of crowds as a historical fact.

We did not find him either on the road to Bethsaida or on the way back when we went along the Sea of Galilee to Tiberias. Everyone had heard about him and many people had seen him . . ."[58]

Of course, it is possible to ascribe supernatural solutions to these puzzles—that as God's son, Jesus's voice miraculously projected; he inherently knew the topography of the land and had an innate ability to maximize audience sight-lines and acoustics at events that took place in the countryside at ad hoc venues; and significant numbers of individuals, by serendipity, never had work or family obligations of their own and thus always just happened to be nearby in rural Galilee at any occasion when Jesus was healing or speaking, forming massive, ready-made crowds. These solutions presuppose a divine Christ who mysteriously drew followers to himself.[59] But one must take care not to put all the weight on this view at the expense of the full incarnation. Acknowledging the human Jesus has its place. Cultural history, which focuses on the ordinary, helps to keep theology grounded. It reminds us that there was also a human side of the Messiah, who likely had to deal at least at some level with the practical aspects of crowd management.

First, let's tackle the idea of ancient advertising. Some level of publicity may have been necessary if, as W. F Albright and C. S. Mann maintain, it is unlikely that a large entourage constantly accompanied Jesus.[60] There are three possibilities for how individuals in the classical world learned that an event was about to occur. One involved using written notices. During the late Republic, for example, this method of communication was employed in the marketplaces of Rome to notify Roman citizens that a *contio*, or formal assembly preceding a legislative vote, would be convening in the Forum.[61] At both Pompeii and Herculaneum, painted notices and graffiti helped to spread the word of upcoming sporting events.[62] Another method used to publicize impending happenings involved advertising through interest groups, specifically the *Collegia* or trade guilds.[63] Matthew, for his part, intimates that the synagogues played a role in

58. Theissen, *Shadow of the Galilean*, 119. Clearly, this also serves as a device to remind readers that Christians today have no direct access to Jesus but can only catch glimpses through the sources.

59. Another assumption is that rural Galilee was a fairly populous region where crowds of significant size could be gathered on short order. How likely this might have been is subject to debate. Fergus Millar remarks that even in Italy, distance affected participation in events in Rome and that "for most of Italy, there was no likelihood that peasants would come from the fields for a day to go to market and participate in political decisions." Instead, most attendees at unscheduled functions would have been idle observers or casual passersby who happened to be in the Forum already (Fergus Millar *The Crowd in Rome in the Late Republic* [Ann Arbor: University of Michigan Press, 2002], 28, 33).

60. W. F. Albright and C. S. Mann, *Matthew*, AB 26 (New York: Doubleday, 1971), lxxv.

61. Morstein-Marx, *Mass Oratory and Political Power*, 8.

62. Roberts, *Life and Death in Pompeii and Herculaneum*, 29–30.

63. Morstein-Marx, *Mass Oratory and Political Power*, 133.

promoting Jesus during the early phase of his ministry (4:23), so it is logical that this particular strategy was at work in facilitating the gathering of crowds throughout Jesus's ministry.[64] It might, however, be possible to take this a step further. Since Jesus is identified as a carpenter and some of his disciples were fishermen, might these networks of professional colleagues and tradesmen have been mobilized to spread the word throughout the countryside when Jesus was slated to teach or appear? Finally, heralds were engaged in the ancient world to announce activities of interest to the public. If cultural historians are able to demonstrate that the practice of using heralds was in place in first-century Galilee, this may also have been an option for promoting Jesus's orations. Thucydides mentions that in ancient Greece heralds were active as ambassadors during wartime. In Rome, the *Fetiales* were an order of priests who were charged with making proclamations of war, peace, and official announcements.[65] Along similar lines, when it came to snap meetings of assemblies related to the work of the Roman Senate, it was the case that "the magistrate simply had his herald first make the announcement from the Rostra (or another templum), then sent him to do the same throughout the city, perhaps following the line of the city walls."[66] One might wonder whether Jesus's disciples fulfilled a heraldic function. If they did, it wouldn't seem to be a great leap for them to go from announcing Jesus's upcoming orations and lectures to participating in the Great Commission. They would have been accustomed to spreading word about Jesus and the kingdom of God. A good study of ancient advertising in first-century Galilee would be welcome and would assist in exploring evidence of the likelihood of these and other issues with regard to the historical Jesus.

In addition to advertising, appropriate speaking venues are an important consideration if crowds were gathering in great numbers to hear Jesus. The traditional site of the Sermon on the Mount as depicted in Matthew (with the provisos that it actually may or may not have been a single, unified discourse and that there may be some relationship with Luke's Sermon on the Plain) is a small hill just to the northwest of Capernaum; though, in the words of Daniel J. Harrington, "attempts to determine the exact site are useless."[67] Yet that has not stopped scholars from speculating on everything, from whether the use of

---

64. There are differing views on when this sermon was preached, whether it was early in Jesus's career or later, when his career was at its height. See the discussion by Dan Lioy, *The Decalogue in the Sermon on the Mount*, StBibLit 66 (New York: Lang, 2004), 89. For Jesus's activity in synagogues during his public ministry see also Mark 1:38, Luke 4:14–15, John 18:20.

65. Donald Lateiner, "Heralds and Corpses in Thucydides," *CW* 71 (1977): 97–106 (here 99).

66. Morstein-Marx, *Mass Oratory and Political Power*, 39.

67. Daniel J. Harrington, *The Gospel of Matthew*, SP 1 (Collegeville, MN: Michael Glazier, 2007), 78.

"mountain" in Matthew 5:1 serves a merely idiomatic function, to the presence of that word in the text indicating that the discourse took place on a landmark known to the local inhabitants of the region, like the Horns of Hattin. Others simply assert that the speech was delivered on a hill near the lake.[68] None of the proposed solutions, however, really dig into the issue of how the problems with acoustics might have been solved (unless the site was on a hill sloped to naturally amplify sounds), let alone issues regarding sight-lines (the ability to see the speaker from the back of those gathered around). A solution that has not been the source of speculation is whether Jesus may have spoken in a theater.

One might dare to suggest four reasons for this lack:

1. The Gospels don't ever present Jesus speaking in a theater.
2. Matthew does not specifically place Jesus in any Galilean city where theaters exist (Sepphoris, Tiberias) and in fact seems to posit a rural rather than urban Galilean ministry.
3. Scholars are exercising appropriate caution about the dating of the extant theaters, which may not have been constructed during Jesus's lifetime.
4. It is assumed that theaters are venues for mimes and popular entertainment, which are different sorts of spectacles altogether from serious religious discourse.

Even though these reasons at first glance seem to preclude the possibly that theaters played any role in Jesus's ministry, it is possible that a good study of ancient speaking venues used by crowds would still be worthwhile. After all, our primary sources, the Gospels, present representative scenes from the life of Jesus rather than a full record, which the Fourth Evangelist is quick to point out (John 20:30, 21:25). It seems premature to rule out the idea that Jesus did not speak in a variety of larger venues beyond the synagogues mentioned in Matthew 4:23–24. Synagogues could not accommodate massive crowds, as Jordan J. Ryan observes. In fact, Ryan estimates that the synagogue at Magdala included benches that would only seat one hundred twenty to two hundred people.[69] Second, although the gospel authors do not explicitly locate Jesus in either Sepphoris or Tiberius, if these written witnesses to his life received their final form after the Jewish revolt, then it is possible the authors and editors might have wished to downplay

---

68. See the survey of possibilities in Thomas Tehan and David Abernathy, *An Exegetical Summary of the Sermon on the Mount*, 2nd ed. (Dallas, TX: SIL International, 2008), 12.

69. Jordan J. Ryan, *The Role of the Synagogue in the Aims of Jesus* (Minneapolis: Fortress, 2017), 57–58, 64.

any association with these locations. After all, the first city, the City of Peace, essentially opted out of the Jewish War. The second surrendered, was quite near the site that hosted Vespasian's camp (*J.W.* 4.1.3), and ultimately was the site of the massacre of one thousand two hundred prisoners of war from Tarichaea. Linking Jesus too closely with either of these cities in the aftermath of the Revolt might not have been viewed as the best strategy for persuading those with Jewish backgrounds or sympathies that Jesus was the Messiah. The Fourth Evangelist seems to be the one most open to Tiberias, mentioning in passing that some boats had originated from there (John 6:23) and referring to the lake as the Sea of Tiberias (John 6:1, 21:1).

The issue of dating the theaters of Sepphoris and Tiberias, both of which incidentally are associated with hills or mountains (the one at Sepphoris follows the slope of the acropolis, and the venue excavated in Tiberius abutted the base of what is now known as Mt. Berenice) is another point that is not as cut-and-dried as one might think. While E. P Sanders states that the theater at Sepphoris was not built until fifty years after Jesus's crucifixion, agreeing with Zeev Weiss and Ehud Netzer on the age of that structure, excavations by the University of South Florida "credit Antipas the most likely builder" and note that the venue was enlarged in the second century CE.[70] One imagines, then, that the original theater may have been completed at the time of Jesus. James F. Strange is also of the opinion that Herod Antipas likely built the theatre at Tiberius, so if that public space was not completed during Jesus's lifetime, it may have at least been under construction.

Just because there is the possibility that theaters that could accommodate significant crowds (the one at Tiberius had a capacity for five thousand to six thousand, and the Sepphoris structure could seat about four thousand five hundred) existed, does not necessarily mean that orations took place on theater stages. In fact, it is sometimes hard to imagine that anything other than plays or mimes were staged in those venues. Still, it is important not to overlook the fact that the author of Acts describes the theater of Ephesus as the setting for an impromptu assembly of all of the people of Ephesus on an occasion when the silversmiths became concerned about their livelihood (Acts 19:23–41). It is hard to imagine that a generously sized public space like a theatre would have

---

70. The earlier dating was reported by James F. Strange, "Sepphoris: The Jewel of the Galilee," in *Galilee in the Late Second Temple and Mishnaic Periods: The Archaeological Record from Cities, Towns, and Villages*, vol. 2, ed. David A. Fiensy and James Riley Strange (Minneapolis: Fortress, 2015), 22–38 (here 27). Craig A. Evans sides with this earlier dating (Evans, *Jesus and His World*, 23). On the later date, see Sanders, "Jesus' Relation to Sepphoris," 76; and Zeev Weis with Ehud Netzer, "Hellenistic and Roman Sepphoris: The Archaeological Evidence," in Nagy, Meyers, Meyers, and Weiss, *Sepphoris in Galilee*, 75–80 (see figure 9).

been empty except when there were religious festivals or scheduled theatrical entertainments. One might conjecture that a theater would be a logical choice of venue if anticipated audiences exceeded the size of a local synagogue or bouleuterion for virtually any public event. An in-depth treatment of the use of theaters in Greco-Roman Palestine or at least the Greek East is needed and would hopefully include other details, such as how such spaces were reserved by entertainers, speakers, or those calling meetings. According to Acts 19:35, a γραμματεύς was responsible for crowd control and the presence of the assembly in the space. This raises the question of whether Jesus or his disciples might have coordinated with these sorts of functionaries during Jesus's ministry.

Positing the potential use of a theatre by Jesus in circumstances when a large audience convened would also clear up questions regarding not only crowd capacity but also questions about acoustics and sightlines. If Jesus sat while addressing groups, which Dan Lioy is quick to point out was the standard teaching position of rabbis, then delivering a sermon in a space like a theater would solve those issues.[71] Further, use of a large public outdoor auditorium would answer the question of whether a sizable crowd gathered to hear Jesus would have stood or sat during the oration. Cicero himself seemed to differentiate between seated Greek audiences and Roman onlookers, who heard orations while on their feet (Cicero, *Flac.* 15–16).[72]

Given that seats were assigned to audience members in ancient theatres based on local class system structures, and that therefore the wealthiest would have had the best seats, Jesus's words during the Sermon on the Mount announcing blessings for those less fortunate would have certainly been ironic if delivered in such a setting.

CONCLUSION

Although what has been offered here isn't proof of any particular aspect of the Sermon on the Mount, hopefully it is a sketch that points out some avenues for further research. The Quest for the historical Jesus has not run its course. Instead, alternate histories, such as the Pythons' *Life of Brian* or Theissen's *The Shadow of the Galilean* may be used to inject new life into the biblical historian's project. When contrary-to-fact histories, parallel scenarios, or other fanciful

---

71. Lioy, *Decalogue in the Sermon on the Mount*, 89.

72. Morstein-Marx, *Mass Oratory and Political Power*, 36–37. Of course, this does assume that envisioning a seated Jesus was not an editorial decision designed to highlight the fact that Jesus was the ultimate authority at the gathering, since in the Roman forum the practice was for the convening magistrate to be the lone figure seated on a *tribunician* bench or a curile chair. See Morstein-Marx, *Mass Oratory and Political Power*, 40.

imaginings are executed with a high level of research and linked to what is known about Jesus, the results may be surprising. Such exercises may be useful in discovering new avenues of inquiry about the historical Jesus and the world in which he lived. Some of these new investigative projects will undoubtedly go beyond an interest in Jesus's words and deeds to focus on subject matter that piques the curiosity of biblical cultural historians. There is still much to discover about Jesus, if we are willing to engage models that draw on knowledge of everyday life at the time of Jesus and support our conjectures with indirect evidence. Ultimately such an approach will expand what may be plausible about the historical Jesus, fleshing out our portraits of the first-century Galilean in new and refreshing ways.

CHAPTER 9

A Test Case: Jesus's Remarks before the Sanhedrin: Blasphemy or Hope of Exaltation?

DARRELL L. BOCK

The recent book, *Jesus, Criteria, and the Demise of Authenticity*, edited by Chris Keith and Anthony Le Donne, has been trumpeted as the "epitaph of the criteria-movement in historical Jesus research."[1] As fine as the collection of scholars is that the book assembled, as good as the points are on the limits of a strictly criteria-based approach to such study, and as complex as the limits and obstacles of the task of doing ancient historical reconstruction are, it still begs the question: How will we assess the Jesus material whose character is doubted by so many? One has the sense that the answer of at least some of their scholars is to let the case be made for the general direction of the sources as we have them, run some series of critical tests (what those are was less than clear), and look for the narrative flow of what we possess. The question remains, is that workable and enough? The angel may well be in the details. So I propose to examine one text on the Jewish examination of Jesus before he was taken to Pilate and show how working with a combination of criteria and background can be of help.[2]

Before looking at the event, a few things need to be said about the critical method that the Keith/Le Donne book critiques, since the volume does firmly call into question the historiographical presuppositions behind these criteria

---

1. Alan Kirk's endorsement for the book, *Jesus, Criteria, and the Demise of Authenticity*, ed. Chris Keith and Anthony Le Donne (London: T&T Clark, 2012).

2. I have two major studies of this event. The first looks at the background to it, as well as making an initial case for the event's core authenticity: Darrell L. Bock, *Blasphemy and Exaltation in Judaism and the Final Examination of Jesus*, WUNT 2/106 (Tübingen: Mohr Siebeck, 1998). The second is a detailed examination of the case for the core authenticity of this event: idem, "Blasphemy and the Jewish Examination of Jesus," in *Key Events in the Life of the Historical Jesus: A Collaborative Exploration of Context and Coherence*, ed. Darrell L. Bock and Robert L. Webb, WUNT 247 (Tübingen: Mohr Siebeck, 2009), 589–667. Much in this essay about the event will be summarized from points made in far more detail in these two works.

and the ways they have been used. Let it be said at the start that the criterion of dissimilarity in its strictest form is an example of the criteria approach gone wrong, being too excessive in what it excludes and how it sees a culturally rooted historical process. However, the use of the roots argument that the criteria are deep-seated in a flawed form criticism fails. To point out a flawed origin still does not remove the goal that such a project has, namely, providing an approach to the Gospel sources that argues that one has to make a case for their credibility. So my sense is that the Keith/Le Donne volume is guilty of overkill in the other direction. What is needed is finding a balance between what tools like criteria can and cannot do for us. Another question is what else is needed to help us adjudicate the skepticism and doubt with which many approach Gospel sources.

A word is also needed on how "authenticity" is assessed. Authenticity and historicity are not just about what happened but also about how what happened came to be seen. There are many ways to affirm the "authentic" historical impact of a past event. Historical significance is not static and frozen. Historical authenticity has depth; some of it emerges over time. Historical significance impacts lives as it emerges in light of subsequent events and connects to things that follow. Significance can reside in what is implicit, and a writer can be historical and make that implicit element explicit in his reporting. This is certainly how the Gospels work. They are written with an awareness of the larger story and series of events that are brought into play in their narrative. This is why a narrative dimension has to be a part of historical Gospel reflection. Still, something like the criteria can help us get a handle on the core direction of events. It is this more limited use for which I shall argue.

One final point about criteria and authenticity assessment needs to be made. The bar of the criteria can be compared to the kinds of standards we see in assessing court cases before a jury. Getting over the bar measures whether one can have some confidence about what is being assessed, but failure to reach the bar cannot yield a firm conclusion about a text's failure. This is not special pleading. It is a recognition that we are working with limited evidence and standards that, when met, tell us much, but when they are not leave us practically where we were. My example is the differing standard used in American courts. When the standard for O. J. Simpson's trial was "beyond a reasonable doubt," a standard that requires a very high level of corroboration for a charge, Simpson was found "innocent," not because people thought he had not committed murder but because the evidence could not meet the high standard the law required to convict him of murder. When the burden shifted to civil court and a "preponderance of the evidence," a decidedly lower standard, he was found "guilty" and was required to pay a fine. This example illustrates a key point about the corroboration standard of the historical study of Jesus. People may be working with different proof standards and may also be forgetting what failure to gain them may or may not say about the kind of judgment being made.

My position is that a criteria-like approach is not the be-all and end-all for Jesus studies, but that it is an important and useful component in such a study. The criteria may work better for sorting out the general character of events and themes than for proving the exact wording of particular sayings. However, even this much is a step in a helpful direction for material that is questioned and contended over as much as the Jesus material. So, let's take a test case of a potentially significant event and see what combination of assessments can help us decide if the account is anything close to an account that can be accepted as reflective of what took place.

THE BROAD SCENE AND THE CRITERIA

The scene in its broadest terms, that the Jewish leadership had a role in Jesus's death, has wide attestation. Not only do the Gospels reflect this in agreement with Markan tradition, but Josephus notes this in *Jewish Antiquities* 18.63–64, as we detail below. The Gospel of Thomas (saying 66) speaks of the stone the builders rejected. The Gospel of Peter speaks of the Jews not washing their hands of Jesus's death, unlike Pilate.[3] This could simply be an expansion based on Matthew and so is of limited value. The Gospel of Nicodemus portrays some Jewish leaders bringing Jesus to Pilate.

The idea that something like this examination took place is multiply attested within the Gospels and alongside the testimony of Josephus.[4] Not only do we have the material in Mark 14:53–65, Matt 26:57–68, and Luke 22:54, 66–71 but also a brief note in John 18:13–14, 19–23 to a general examination, but with no detail. There also is a remark by Josephus that some of the leadership and Pilate were responsible for Jesus's death. *Jewish Antiquities* 18.64 in part reads,

---

3. Helmut Koester, *Ancient Christian Gospels: Their History and Development* (London: SCM, 1990), 216–20, sees the *Gospel of Peter* using independent tradition. If so, then this is another source attesting the connection.

4. As is well known, the Josephus text is controversial, having been preserved in a form that shows the presence of Christian influence. Still, most scholars and classicists see a portion of that text as authentic, including the portion tied to the involvement of Jewish leaders. See Robert Webb's analysis, "The Roman Examination and Crucifixion of Jesus: Their Historicity and Implications," in Bock and Webb, *Key Events in the Life of the Historical Jesus*, 669–773 (here 685–87).

"And when Pilate, at the suggestion of the principal men amongst us, had condemned him to the cross, those that loved him at first did not forsake him" (Whiston). Obviously the "principal men among us" refers to those who were leaders. The Johannine remark simply has Jesus defend the public nature of his ministry and suggests injustice that the Jewish leaders are examining him. It is very brief, so it does not help us consider what caused the leadership to examine Jesus nor does it fit the criteria in any of its specifics beyond saying such an event took place. So, even if we could verify John's scene specifically according to the criteria, it would not help us other than to confirm such an examination happened. This means we are left with what Mark, Matthew, and Luke tell us, and yet none of this multiple attestation to this broad theme helps us with the details of the examination scene.

Also testifying to some type of examination are other texts from the New Testament. Acts 4:23–26 alludes to such a role, and 1 Thess 2:14–15 offers a generic charge against the Jews who killed Jesus and the prophets. This linkage of Jesus to the rejection of the prophets is something that appears in one of the most important of Jesus's parables, the Parable of the Wicked Tenants (Matt 21:33–45 = Mark 12:1–12 = Luke 20:9–19). This parable is an allegory about Israel's history of unfaithfulness that Jesus told during his last week in the midst of the key confrontations that took place at that time. He was warning them about their rejection of him and that it fit a historical pattern, alluding to Psalm 118 and the rejection of the keystone. The linking of Jesus's treatment to past rejection of the prophets also appears in Stephen's speech in Acts 7. The idea of official Jewish opposition is multiply attested, both in sources and in forms, but none of this helps us with the details of the examination itself.

A second criterion also is of help. This is one John Meier argues for, the criterion of rejection and execution. Rome had no reason to take the initiative against Jesus. He had no army. His movement was religious. As long as it was nonviolent and caused no major stir, he might be watched but need not be stopped. These criteria of multiple attestation and rejection point to the authenticity of the general event but cannot in themselves suggest anything about the specifics.

When it comes to the specifics of the scene, we are left with the Synoptic Gospels. As we shall see, they exhibit a gist with variation pattern common in the Gospels. The core event and sayings are similar, but there is variation in how it is told. Here we need to distinguish between having the very words of the scene versus hearing its general voice, its gist. The latter is important and still testifies to a core historicity. It is that level of specificity we pursue.

THE CULTURAL BACKDROP, HISTORICAL
PLAUSIBILITY, AND OTHER CRITERIA

It is here also that features beyond the criteria are of help as we consider the historical context for the debate between the new movement around Jesus and the Jewish leadership. One such category is the cultural background to the events tied to Jesus's death and the polemics surrounding it. With an event as important as this, there was likely some oral tradition circulating, not only in the church but also in official Jewish circles, about what had taken place. How we got to Jesus being crucified would have been a topic of public debate and knowledge. Each side would have made its version of the events known to those in Jerusalem, a city whose population at the time was not so large, roughly twenty-five thousand to seventy-five thousand. In the case of the church's view, the core features of this memory are very similar in the Gospels. They needed to be reasonably accurate to retain any credibility in the subsequent public debate about Jesus. In other words, the public nature and significance of this dispute operated as a kind of constraint over how such a meeting was reported and circulated in the early tradition.

The core of the scene in the three Gospels is similar. All three have Jesus queried on whether he is the Christ. Mark 14:61 has the question in a more explicitly sensitive Jewish form, "Are you the Christ, the Son of the Blessed?" This roundabout way of saying "Son of God" reflects Jewish respect for speaking about God in formal settings. Matthew 26:63 says it more directly, "I charge you under oath by the living God, tell us if you are the Messiah, the Son of God." Luke 22:67 has, "If you are the Messiah, tell us." The point is the same, while the variation reflects what is common in renderings rooted in oral tradition. The key query shared in all versions is that Jesus was asked if he was the Christ, the Messiah.

Jesus responds by citing Psalm 110:1 in all three Gospels, affirming that the Son of Man will be seen at God's right hand. Jesus both claims and predicts that God will accept and vindicate the Son of Man, who is Jesus, since "Son of Man" is Jesus's favorite way to refer to himself. Matthew and Mark also have this Son of Man figure riding the clouds, an allusion to Daniel 7:13–14. In Daniel, the Son of Man receives dominion from the Ancient of Days, who pictures God. Matthew and Mark note that Jesus's reply brought an assessment from the leadership that Jesus had blasphemed against God, illustrated by the tearing of their robes. Luke simply notes that what Jesus said resulted in him being taken to Pilate.

When it comes to the details, we need to consider the objections and issues they raise. Most important here is to focus on the judgment that what Jesus said was seen as blasphemous by the leadership. Something like this can explain how Jesus ended up before Pilate. What we are showing is that at least in this case, beyond any criteria, which only bring us into the field of play for the discussion, the cultural and historical background yields far more detail.

When one steps away from the criteria as any kind of positive guide, the result is often the raising of objections as to why we cannot trust the sources we have. Such objections are also used to trump any claims one might make through the application of the criteria. So it is time to consider such objections to this event. Three core objections exist. After that we will consider two more questions: (1) an alternative explanation of the scene as a creation by Mark or the early church, and (2) whether Jesus would have said something like he is portrayed to have said.

First, it is argued that the charge of blasphemy at the examination does not fit the Jewish definition of that term according to which one has to use the divine name in order for blasphemy to be present (m. Sanh. 7:5). In addition, there is the objection that making a messianic claim in itself was not blasphemous. So the question becomes, does the account give indication of a potential act or utterance that would have been understood as blasphemous?

In fact, it does. Contrary to common popular opinion, the blasphemy was not the claim to be Messiah. There are records of numerous other messianic-like figures in the first century, none of whom was accused of blasphemy.[5] Josephus notes several figures who raised hopes of the arrival of the end, and none of them was accused of blasphemy (*Ant.* 18.85–87, 97–98; 20.167–88). Some of these figures had names or nicknames, such as the Samaritan, Theudas, and the Egyptian, while other texts just refer to unnamed prophetic figures. So what is blasphemy? What did the leadership see in what Jesus said?

Blasphemy is a speech or act that shows intense disrespect for God—what one might call slander. Blasphemous speech could take many forms. To use the divine Name in an inappropriate way is certainly blasphemy and is punishable by death (Lev 24:10–16; m. Sanh. 6:4; 7:5; Philo, *Moses* 2.203–6). At the base of these ideas about blasphemy lies the command of Exodus 22:28 not to revile God or the leaders he appointed for the nation.

Acts of blasphemy concentrate on idolatry, a show of arrogant disrespect toward God, or the insulting of his chosen leaders. Often those who blasphemed verbally acted on their feelings. God manages to judge such offenses. Examples in

---

5. Correctly E. P. Sanders, *Jesus and Judaism* (Philadelphia: Fortress, 1985), 298.

Jewish exposition are Sisera (Judg 4:3 and Num. Rab. 10.2; disrespect toward God's people), Goliath (1 Sam 17 and Josephus, *Ant.* 6.183; disrespect toward God's people and worship of Dagon), Sennacherib (2 Kgs 18–19; cf. Isa 37:6, 23; disrespect for God's power), Belshazzar (Dan 3:29 in Theodotion's version and Josephus, *Ant.* 10.233, 242, disrespect for God's presence in the use of temple utensils at a party), Manasseh (acting against the Torah; Sifre §112), and the Roman general Titus (b. Git. 56b and 'Abot R. Nat. B 7; entering, defaming the temple, slicing open the curtain, and taking the utensils away).[6] Acting against the temple is also blasphemous (1 Macc 2:6; Josephus, *Ant.* 12.406). Significantly, comparing oneself to God is also blasphemous, reflecting arrogance according to Philo (*Dreams* 2.130–31; *Decalogue* 13–14.61–64). At Qumran, unfaithfulness in moral action by those who pretend to lead the people (CD 5.12) and the act of speaking against God's people (1QpHab 10.13) are blasphemous. Within Israel, the outstanding example is the golden calf incident (Philo, *Moses* 2.159–66).

So let's define blasphemy. When applied to God as object, blasphemy represents an offense against God and a violation of a fundamental principle of the faith that gives glory to him. Attacking God's people verbally is a second class of blasphemy (Sennacherib; Goliath). Those who challenge the leadership God has put in place for his people can also be seen as attacking God himself. So blasphemy refers to a wide range of insulting speech or activity. This is crucial background to how blasphemy might relate to Jesus in the leadership's view. Behind all of this is the idea that God's glory and honor are unique and should be protected and preserved.

In the text as it stands in all the versions of this event that we have, at least with regard to the use of Psalm 110:1, when Jesus claims God will bring him as Son of Man into his presence and either seat him at his right hand (alluding to Ps 110:1) and/or have him ride the clouds (alluding to Dan 7:13–14), this was heard by the leadership as robbing God of his unique honor and glory. They saw this as blasphemous, even though, as we are about to see, Jews at that time debated the idea of someone being able to sit with God.

How might Jesus's claim to sit at God's side have been heard in Judaism? It depended on who was hearing it. In some wings of Judaism, such an idea could be entertained for a great leader like Moses or a future figure like the Son of Man in 1 Enoch 37–71.[7] But other Jews objected to such ideas. In 3 Enoch, the angel

---

6. Numbers Rabbah, Sifre, and Avot of Rabbi Nathan are later Jewish expositions of the Hebrew Bible that see these biblical figures as having blasphemed.

7. In the second century BCE Jewish text of the Exagoge of Ezekiel, Moses has a dream and is told to sit on God's thrones. In the Hebrew Bible, only in Dan 7:9 is God's throne described in the plural. This text probably elaborates Exod 7:1. There, God promises Moses, "I will make you God to Pharaoh." It pictures

Metatron claims to be the "Lesser Yahweh" and is punished by God for having the nerve to make such a comparison.[8] There also is a well-known tradition repeated more than once involving Rabbi Akiba. In this account, Akiba suggests that David can sit next to God in heaven. However, the other rabbis object, rebuking him and saying, "How long will you profane the Shekinah (i.e., the glory of God)?"[9] They are reminding him that he is blaspheming in their view.

Now the bulk of the Jewish leadership at the time of Jesus was made up of the Sadducean party. They were traditional conservatives who focused on what the Torah or first five books of their Scripture taught. They disliked additions to the tradition like those reflected in Exagoge or 1 Enoch. They would have found it hard to believe that this Galilean teacher could share God's direct presence in the manner he was suggesting. Jesus's remarks qualify as blasphemy in that cultural context, given the leadership's rejection of those remarks. The treatment of this objection shows what good cultural work can do to sort out a dispute about the text. At the least, one can argue that the story fits the cultural setting. This invokes another criterion that Theissen and Winter are known for, "Plausibility of Historical Context."[10] So here we see the coexistence of cultural argumentation with a criterion that reflects the working in detail with the context of Jesus's ministry. The case here is not airtight, but it does at least show that Jesus's claims and the reaction to it fit the cultural setting.

Second, the scene is said to be unrealistic since the leaders are seen running around to set up a meeting with Pilate during a high feast time, holding a trial that could not be held on a feast day or holiday.[11] Some argue that what is taking place here is a projection back of later apologetic concerns to blame Jewish leaders for Rome's act. A variation on this objection argues that this cannot be a trial since Jews could not execute anyone, only Rome could. As we shall see, two responses can quickly deal with this challenge. First, the text does not portray the Jews as having the right to execute. They are preparing a case to take to Rome, who can and does make the final decision. Thus second, this is not a trial at all, but more like a grand jury or prosecutorial inquiry to see if charges can be sustained in another venue.

It is fallacious to claim that the presence of apologetic erases the presence of

---

an incredible authority that includes judgment. In 1 Enoch, the Son of Man is described as a future figure who sits next to God and judges, a figure later named as Enoch. In both cases we have greats of Hebrew lore who are considered perhaps to be worthy of such an honor.

8. This Jewish work comes from the second century CE.

9. The story is in the Babylonian Talmud, b. Hag. 14a, 14b; b. San. 38b.

10. Dagmar Winter, "Saving the Quest for Authenticity from the Criterion of Dissimilarity: History and Plausibility," in Keith and Le Donne, *Jesus, Criteria, and the Demise of Authenticity*, 115–31, esp. 127–28.

11. This objection belongs to Sanders, *Jesus and Judaism*, 298.

historical detail. The debate of the community with Jews who did not believe would have inevitably been contentious and apologetic from the moment there was a rejection of Jesus's challenge to the Jewish community. Jesus had asked the community to turn to God and presented his authoritative role in that claim. Thus the presence of an apologetic element involving Jesus in the material is not an automatic reason to reject the historicity of the presence of such elements of debate.

A more substantial objection is the issue of scrambling to get Jesus to Rome during a feast time. What is not relevant is the appeal to a trial that cannot be held during a feast or a holiday since, as has just been mentioned, the questioning might not have been considered a trial at all. It may have been a mere examination to see if the charges could be taken to Pilate. This is why we have called the scene an *examination*. So could an examination have been held at this time?

Again the historical context gives us help. This was a special situation. The leaders had Jesus in their hands. The opportunity to pass him on to Rome and get a quick judgment from the prefect was subject to Pilate's presence in Jerusalem. Time was of the essence, and striking while the opportunity existed important. So the special circumstances made it convenient to expedite matters. Pilate was already in town, but he would head home to Caesarea Maritima soon. The less time Jesus was held, the better, because of his popularity with some. There are later texts about deceivers of the people that allow both for exceptional examinations and for a quick resolution of the deceiver's fate if the judgment is that he is guilty.[12] Jesus's situation fits into this kind of special scenario. Charges of Jesus being seen as a deceiver by opponents are multiply attested, including a later Jewish source (Luke 23:2; Matt 27:63–64; John 7:12, 47; b. Sanh. 43a).[13] Again historical and cultural background and plausibility help us see a fit with this event.

The third objection is, from where did the witnesses for this scene come since no disciples were present? At best, according to the sources, Peter and John were outside, but were they within earshot (John 18:15)?

Actually, there are several candidates for potential witnesses. The rise of a community of Jewish followers of Jesus in Jerusalem after his death is a historical

---

12. August Strobel, *Die Stunde der Wahrheit: Untersuchungen zum Strafverfahren gegen Jesus* [ET: The Hour of Truth: Investigations of the Criminal Proceedings against Jesus], WUNT 21 (Tübingen: Mohr Siebeck, 1980), 85, notes texts from the Mishnah (m. Sanh. 11:3–4) and the later Tosefta (t. Sanh. 7:11; 10:11).

13. What the fifth-century Talmud attests is seen in other texts of the first and second centuries as well. Cf. David Neale, "Was Jesus a Mesith?," *TynBul* 44 (1993): 89–101; Graham Stanton, "Jesus of Nazareth: A Magician and a False Prophet Who Deceived God's People?," in *Jesus of Nazareth: Lord and Christ: Essays on the Historical Jesus and New Testament Christology*, ed. Joel B. Green and Max Turner (Grand Rapids: Eerdmans, 1994), 164–80; N. T. Wright, *Jesus and the Victory of God*, vol. 2 of *Christian Origins and the Question of God* (Minneapolis: Fortress, 1996), 439–42.

given that virtually no one doubts. This community would have immediately been in running public debate with other Jews and the official Jewish leadership. We know this because three decades later a descendant of the high priestly family of Annas and Caiaphas, Annas II, is responsible for the death of James, a member of Jesus's family. Caiaphas was the high priest during Jesus's life and would have been the high priest during the time of any examination of Jesus. Annas was the patriarch of the family and was the father-in-law of Caiaphas. Once one realizes these family connections in the leadership of both sides of this religious dispute, then one can see that a family feud existed in Jerusalem for a long period consisting of three decades. During this time, each side would have made its case for or against Jesus in the running debate. The official position regarding Jesus would have been publicly known in a city that was not that large. This kind of public and official conversation would have fed the core tradition. The public nature of the debate and its long-standing duration over several decades preserved each side's official position and protected it from the influence of rumors or speculation about the events.

More than this, some members of the leadership appear to have had sympathetic relations with the new believers. Here figures like Nicodemus and Joseph of Arimathea can be mentioned. They would have known and could well have related what took place at the examination. In addition a figure like Saul (Paul), as a previous persecutor of the church, would have known the official Jewish position against Jesus.[14] We also could mention the potential presence of servants around these events who may have known what took place. Any or all of these could have served as potential sources for an act that is likely to have been a topic of public debate, given the rapid rise of the new movement soon after Jesus's death. Again, wrestling with the cultural and historical setting can help us consider how the report of the event might have emerged.

THE SAYING ITSELF: ALTERNATIVE TAKES ON THE EVENT AND THE USE OF CRITERIA

Another issue to examine is the alternative model for how we got our text. It is the claim that Mark or the early church formed our text to present Jesus as an

---

14. On the possibility of access to records of trials, one can consider that Josephus had access to information about trials and deliberations, if his summary of the situation of James is any indication of his access to sources. And there are examples of letters having been sent with those under custody that gave official indication of the charges (Acts 23:26–30). This means there could have been types of official records somewhere. If there had been access, information could have been obtained. Someone like Paul could have had such access to official Jewish information.

example about how to face suffering and persecution. Thus, the event is created with words placed in Jesus's mouth. So our questions revolve around whether this is a better alternative explanation.

In sum, this is not a very compelling argument. Jesus's defense here is unique and tells the disciples nothing about how to stand up for Jesus. Jesus's reply is about himself. The only things Jesus models are courage in the face of questioning and the willingness to suffer and die for seeing himself as the Christ, the Son of God. But there is nothing particularly instructive in how Jesus goes about this. Other than giving confidence to stand and suffer, which the scene does show, the account does little more in this regard. So this explanation cannot be the rationale for the full scene.

Finally, we come to a key question to pursue. Would Jesus have said something like what he is portrayed to have said in this scene? This possibility is also challenged in three ways. The first challenge claims that Jesus had previously never presented himself in such terms. He focused on the kingdom, not himself. More than that, he showed hesitation, at least in public, to use key titles like Christ and Son of God.[15] As we shall show, this claim may come down to what one does with the title Son of Man. The second challenge claims that Jesus did not use Scripture in the way he is portrayed to have done here.[16] This kind of scriptural reflection is the product of the early church looking back at Jesus. The third challenge claims that Jesus may have said something like this and may have even used one of the two passages alluded to, but he did not use both of them together.[17] In this version of the argument, unlike the first above, Jesus did refer to himself as Son of Man and predict a divine vindication, but he did not appeal to sitting at God's right hand from Psalm 110. That is the early church talking.

It is important to note that in this third version the core authenticity for the scene is still affirmed, even if that does not come with the embrace of every core element in the scene. So it is important to note a key difference between the third form of this argument and the first two. In the first two forms of the objection, Jesus did not say anything like what he is claimed to have said. We are not in touch with the historical Jesus at all. In the third version, Jesus did make a claim and even one that caused the offense of blasphemy. He just did

---

15. Sanders, *Jesus and Judaism*, 297 (first objection). He argues that nothing in the public teaching of Jesus would have led to the question being asked to begin with, much less getting an answer from it.

16. Norman Perrin, "Mark XIV.62: The End Product of a Christian Pesher Tradition," *NTS* 12 (1966): 150–55; Eugene Boring, *Mark: A Commentary*, NTL (Louisville: Westminster John Knox, 2006), 413–14.

17. James D. G. Dunn, *Jesus Remembered*, vol. 1 of *Christianity in the Making* (Grand Rapids: Eerdmans, 2003), 749–54.

not say as much as the text has him saying. So we have a point of contact with the historical Jesus, but one that the early church amplifies.

So, did Jesus refer to himself as a key figure in God's program?

First, our look at other previous events would show that Jesus making a self-reference in God's program is not merely a matter of what Jesus said, but what he *did*. Claims of authority in action stand at the center of God's promise of kingdom through several public events. Jesus talked less about who he was and chose instead to highlight his role through what he did.[18]

Second, it can be argued that Jesus came to Jerusalem and became more public once he got there. This represented a change from his previous strategy.

Third, Jesus did consistently point to his status—though rarely referring to himself as Messiah and Son of God because of how those terms could be misunderstood. His title of choice was Son of Man—and even when confessed as Christ, Jesus spoke of the Son of Man. This requires a closer look at the Son of Man title than we have taken until now, for in this examination scene Jesus responds to questions about who he is with the title Son of Man.

Remember that the expression Son of Man has two roots. On the one hand, in Aramaic it is an idiom referring to a human being. Just as the son of David is David's son or son of Sarah is Sarah's son, so son of man is the son of a human being. Put simply, it means a person. The second root comes from the expression "one like a Son of Man" in Daniel 7:13. Here the expression is not a title but a description of a figure who rides the clouds and comes to the Ancient of Days to receive dominion from God. What is interesting is that although the everyday idiom points to a human being, the use in Daniel 7 points to a transcendent figure, since in the Hebrew Bible the only beings who ride the clouds are either God or the gods (Exod 14:20; 34:5; Num 10:34; Ps 104:3; Isa 19:1). Heaven and earth meet in this description. The expression was not a formal title at the time, although its use in 1 Enoch 37–71 at about this time shows that some Jews were beginning to think in such terms.

More interesting is the usage of the general expression in the New Testament. Son of Man appears eighty-two times in the Gospels, and in every case but one

---

18. To argue this is the burden of the entire 850-plus page study presented in Bock and Webb, *Key Events in the Life of the Historical Jesus*. Here, using common historical-critical rules and historical-cultural backdrop as done in this essay, a full sequence of twelve events is presented and defended in detail to make this point. James Charlesworth of Princeton Seminary in reviewing our book noted that "Bock, Webb and their collaborators are to be lauded for this list; but it is only a beginning" (James Charlesworth, "A Review of Darrell L. Bock and Robert L. Webb [eds.] *Key Events in the Life of the Historical Jesus*," *JSHJ* 13 [2013]: 220). Fair enough, but what is here shows that Jesus presented himself as central to the kingdom and that the kingdom was central to his preaching. Some of the argumentation that follows reflects points made and substantiated in the larger volume.

(John 12:34) it is used by Jesus. The one exception describes someone reflecting on what Jesus has said, so it is not really an exception either. This is not a term the church or people use to describe Jesus. It is a term he uses about himself. It is consistently rendered as "*the* Son of the Man" in its Greek. This means that it is not a generic use in this rendering.

An even closer look at the term shows that there are about fifty-one sayings involved in this usage once one excludes overlaps that reflect parallel uses between the Gospels. Fourteen of these are in Markan sources, while ten reflect Q. The rest are divided between material unique to Matthew (eight sayings), Luke (seven sayings), and John (thirteen sayings). In other words, this use is deeply multiply attested. Here is another key detail where the application of the criteria shows their potential value. It is a title rooted across the entire tradition that recalls how Jesus spoke about himself. Numbers here are not precise ("about fifty-one sayings") because one can place certain sayings in more than one category and whether in certain cases one has a parallel or not is debated, impacting the final numbers. The distribution across the sources is deep enough that this number difference does not impact the key point about the presence of multiple attestation. In fact, scholars like to divide these sayings into three types. Some sayings describe what Jesus does in his earthly ministry. Other sayings deal with Jesus's suffering. The final class speaks of the Son of Man's authority at the end of time or in judgment. This last class is called the apocalyptic Son of Man sayings. Jesus's reply here about seeing the Son of Man on the clouds and seated at God's right hand is an apocalyptic saying. This class of sayings is also multiply attested. Mark has three such sayings in 8:38, 13:26, and 14:62. This last case is what is used in the event in question.

The claim that this Son of Man idea is a product of the church faces two questions. First, how is it that this title appears only on Jesus's lips at different levels of tradition if it is the product of the early church? In other words, who made up the rule that the different strands of tradition reflect that this title would only be placed on the lips of Jesus? And second, if this major title for Jesus is a creation of the early church, why do our materials outside the Gospels show so little use of it? Why do they show not a single use of it as a confessional title for Jesus? There are only four uses outside the Gospels (Acts 7:56; Heb 2:6; Rev 1:13; 14:14). This is unlike other titles, like Christ or Son of God, which show up often in the epistles and Acts as well as in the Gospels.

All of this makes it far more likely that Jesus referred to himself with this title than that the church created it for him. Its use at his examination fits the thrust of his ministry disclosure patterns and his use of this title. A point like this suggests that at least in a case of such widespread multiple attestation, the plausibility lies on the side of Jesus's use. The value of the criterion in this example shows its potential value for some arguments.

What about the objection that Jesus did not use Scripture in this manner? This is a variation on the previous objection that argues that this kind of complex allusion to texts from the Jewish Bible, called a *pesher*, comes from the early church and not from Jesus. Much of what we have already said applies to this objection. It is simply unreasonable that Jesus did not reflect on Scripture about his mission, especially when he saw that mission as tied to God's plan. So it is difficult to justify a rule against historicity that says if a passage refers to Scripture in a reflective way, it must be the early church's invention. Jesus's ministry claimed that God had promised things that were now being realized. Where would those promises be but in the sacred texts of the community?

There is nothing in the evidence of the use and availability of Psalm 110:1 or Daniel 7:13 that demands a use limited to the post-Easter period. Daniel 7 imagery especially was circulating in Jewish texts like 1 Enoch 37–71.[19] Jesus shows signs of using Daniel 7 in the discourse on the end that appears in Mark 13, Matthew 24, and Luke 21. Psalm 110:1 appears very ambiguously in Mark 12:35–37 (cf. Matt 22:41–46; Luke 20:41–44), where Jesus uses the text not to refer to himself directly but simply to ask why David referred to the one to come as Lord rather than son. The cultural tension in Jesus's question thus stands: how does the ancestor in a patriarchal society show such respect to a descendant that he gives his far younger relative the title "my Lord"? The question is left unanswered in Mark 12, which leaves the reader with something to ponder. The text has that inherent ambiguity that supports historicity.[20] Here is another important detail potentially supported by a criterion. The use in Mark 14 picks up the issue of the meaning of Psalm 110.

These two Hebrew Bible texts (Ps 110:1 and Dan 7:13–14) did make a deep

---

19. For a defense of an early provenance for this text before the time of Jesus and possibly even in Galilee, see Darrell L. Bock and James H. Charlesworth, eds., *Parables of Enoch: A Paradigm Shift*, JCTCRS 11 (London: Bloomsbury, 2013).

20. There is a technical debate over whether Jesus would have said Ps 110:1 in a way that reflects what we have here. The debate has to do with three issues: (1) the use and difference between the Psalm in Hebrew and its Greek rendering, (2) whether Jesus spoke in Hebrew, Aramaic, or even in Greek here, and (3) the theological possibilities that the differences of the Greek text introduced. Of course, If Jesus spoke Greek, then the changes came with the use of that language, but behind it would still stand this custom of respect for the use of the divine name. Either way, the background for the move is clear and culturally plausible. The disputed line rendered carefully from the Hebrew reads, "Yahweh said to my Lord, 'Sit at my right hand . . .'" The challenge is that only in Greek do we get the ambiguity of the text as we have it, "The Lord said to my Lord." If Jesus, following Jewish custom, was careful about not pronouncing the divine name, since out of respect the name Yahweh was often avoided in formal public discussion, then this custom would have resulted in a reading, "The Lord said to my Lord." This is exactly what the texts in Mark 12 and 14 have.

impact on the early church, being their most cited texts. Some suggest that this wide use points to the likelihood that the church inserted the references here for apologetic reasons. However, the profound influence of these passages suggests rather that they had been emphasized by the community's founder. One need not choose between apologetics and history or between Christology and history. These categories in the early church were not either-or categories, but both-and.[21]

Both Hebrew Bible passages were available for Jesus to use at his examination. Nothing Jesus does or says at the trial represents a stretch for his usage of these sources, even read critically by the criteria. If Jesus used either Psalm 110 or Daniel 7 at this scene, then the point of offense was made. His opponents would have seen the use of either text claiming God's defense and vindication of the Son of Man as a blasphemous claim of close association with God's glory. If Jesus claimed either that he as Son of Man was to be seated in God's presence as a result of divine activity, or that he would ride the clouds to receive authority, then the claim of sharing divine glory was made and the reaction of his opponents rejecting the claim would have followed. If either text was used, then the core historicity of the event stands. This leaves us with one final objection, our third query about whether Jesus would have said this. Can one make the case that Jesus used both texts?

In this objection, Jesus alludes to Daniel 7, since the evidence for his use of Daniel 7 is so extensive, but he does not use Psalm 110. The key to this objection is the idea that Jesus rejected the messianic title for himself, so the use of Psalm 110:1 reflects the early church and not Jesus. To a significant degree one can address this issue in discussing Jesus's declaration at Caesarea Philippi—Jesus gave the title *Christ* a qualified acceptance in terms of popular understanding, recasting the term for his followers.[22]

Yet another factor here is the variations in Jesus's replies at the examination in Matthew, Mark, and Luke. When asked if he is the Christ, Jesus says in Matthew 26:64, "You have said so." The same question in Mark 14:61–62 yields the reply, "I am." Luke 22:67–68 has Jesus respond that if he says yes they will not believe and if he asks them they will not answer. Is Jesus reluctant to answer, does he affirm the title, or does he qualify the question? The ambivalent response in two of the versions indicates that the question is formed in a way that Jesus does not entirely accept. His answer in all three accounts suggests that being the Messiah alone does not say enough. In other words, in all versions he trumps

---

21. But Boring, *Mark*, 414, argues for a choice between the categories.
22. This is the burden of the essay by Michael Wilkins, "Peter's Declaration concerning Jesus' Identity in Caesarea Philippi," in Bock and Webb, *Key Events in the Life of the Historical Jesus*, 293–381.

the question. They want to know about Messiah, but he responds with a full divine vindication. However, this is not a rejection of the title. It simply points out that what it means is far more than was realized. In that sense, Mark's crisp "I am" affirms what is accepted. Jesus is the anointed one of God in terms of authority and rule.

That Jesus rejected the title of Christ, as some claim, faces a major hurdle, much like the discussion on the Son of Man—but in reverse. Where Son of Man had a restricted use, the title of Christ was widely used, and so the depth of its presence in the early church needs to be explained if Jesus actually had rejected its use. It is clear that the early community accepted this title for him, so much so that Christ became a key part of his name in all of the earliest materials we have. If Jesus had rejected this title, it is hard to know why the church would have ever affirmed this, given that such a claim of kingship created so many problems for them in terms of both persecution and social acceptance. The criterion of embarrassment applies here. Once again, asking a question that reflects the kind of issue a criterion raises may well apply to another key detail. Why create a title that brings with it problems? The better explanation is that Jesus accepted the title, although the handling of the sources shows he did so with some qualification.

Dunn argues that at his examination, and in his ministry as a whole, Jesus answered this question about being the Messiah with a "qualified no."[23] So Jesus did not use Psalm 110:1. My position is one step over. I think he answered the messianic question with a qualified yes. Dunn claims Jesus never uses the title of himself, never unequivocally welcomes its application to him by others, and refuses the dominant royal militaristic association. Dunn is right about a militaristic understanding; however, some scenes argue for some acceptance of the title. These scenes include the healing of the blind man who cries for help from the Son of David, parallels with David in discussing the Sabbath, and the meeting involving the Samaritan woman. They show Jesus responding positively on these occasions to this association—a multiply attested theme! (Bartimaeus: Mark 10:46–51 = Matt 20:29–34, with two blind men in Luke 18:35–42; David and the Sabbath: Mark 2:23–27 = Matt 12:1–8 = Luke 6:1–5; Samaritan woman: John 4). The same conclusion also emerged from the Caesarea Philippi scene. For me, the apocalyptic Son of Man pictures the authority to rule and judge that the royal militaristic messiah ultimately is said to possess. In this scene, Jesus used both ideas together with the title Son of Man and the citation of a royal psalm (110:1).

---

23. Dunn, *Jesus Remembered*, 652–53. This issue is very complex. For a full discussion of a response, see my essay in *Key Events in the Life of the Historical Jesus*. I make only a few remarks here.

Despite the challenges, this scene has a coherence that can be understood through a combination of cultural and historical analysis and the application of authenticity criteria. None of the objections block our path to understand that what actually took place is in fact in general agreement with the sources. Jesus made a remark that his opponents rejected. When Jesus claimed that the divine presence was on his side and that he shared a place with that authority, his opponents thought he had affirmed that he was the anointed one of God and that his exalted claim had offended the unique honor due to God in the process. What they saw religiously as blasphemy, they translated into a political charge to take to Pilate. On the other hand, Jesus made a claim to divine vindication and exaltation. In the end, the dispute about Jesus revolved around these conflicting claims. Ultimately, Jesus gave the word himself that led to his death—and to the debate about the world-changing events that followed it.

CONCLUSION

Now my question is, how could one even have this discussion and assessment without at least considering how some of the criteria might apply? Granted, cultural and historical backgrounds bear the major burden in this discussion about the potential authenticity of this event. Nevertheless, here and there, and often at key points, it is the criteria that lead into questions that point to observations that allow an assessment of the text and its historical probability. Granted also, these arguments are not airtight. There are retorts to some of the points I have raised. However, the key observation to make is that one of the ways to make a case of assessment involves a proper kind of circumspect appeal to the criteria. They may not be the be-all and end-all of historical Jesus study. They may be flawed, but they still have value. Calls for their demise may be premature, even if those calls should be heeded to a degree to put them in a more appropriate place.

CHAPTER 10

The John, Jesus, and History Project and a Fourth Quest for Jesus

PAUL N. ANDERSON

Over the last two centuries, the *Historical Quest of Jesus* has taken many a turn, depending on understandings of history, gospel traditions, ancient worldviews and contexts, literary relationships between gospel traditions, and contemporary modern or postmodern inclinations. In that sense, the fascination with this subject is not unlike the patristic focus on what might be called the *Theological Quest of Christ* from the third through the fifth centuries CE. And, in a very real sense, both quests have been engaging an overlapping set of issues within the biblical texts, albeit applying the best methodological tools available at the time for addressing the Johannine riddles—theological, historical, and literary.[1]

While the first four church councils from Nicea (325 CE) to Constantinople (451 CE) involved an intra-faith set of discussions, the Jesus debates from Reimarus to the present have engaged all input—from religious to antireligious approaches—seeking to ascertain the truth with the best tools available in the Scientific Era. After all, Jesus of Nazareth is arguably the single most important figure in human history, so the stakes are high indeed, within Christianity and beyond. As a result, the intensity of debate surrounding the relationships between the Jesus of history, the Christ of faith, and the Gospel of John have been unsurpassed in critical biblical scholarship within the modern era.[2] How-

---

1. For overviews of how John's Christology contributed to theological debates in the early church, see T. E. Pollard, *Johannine Christology and the Early Church*, SNTSMS 13 (Cambridge: Cambridge University Press, 1970) and Maurice F. Wiles, *The Spiritual Gospel: The Interpretation of John in the Early Church* (Cambridge: Cambridge University Press, 1959). For epistemological analyses of John's christological tensions and of three dozen leading riddles—theological, historical, and literary—see Paul N. Anderson, *The Christology of the Fourth Gospel: Its Unity and Disunity in the Light of John 6*, WUNT 2/78, 3rd ed. (Eugene, OR: Cascade Books, 2010 [1996]) and idem, *The Riddles of the Fourth Gospel: An Introduction to John* (Minneapolis: Fortress, 2011), 157–72.

2. The tensions between history and theology in the nineteenth century Germany quests of Jesus are featured in Albert Schweitzer's overview of the first century or more of Jesus research: *The Quest of the Historical Jesus: A Critical Study of Its Progress from Reimarus to Wrede*, trans. W. Montgomery (London:

ever, the twenty-first century has evidenced a shift in critical analysis, and the formerly established paradigm excluding the Fourth Gospel from the historical quest of Jesus is now challenged by a more inclusive paradigm, which calls for new approaches to the modern Quest.

Of course, there are good reasons for excluding John's highly theological presentation of Jesus as the Christ in the conducting of historiographic inquiry. First, John is very different from the Synoptics, despite overall similarities. John's Jesus speaks in the language of the evangelist, and 85 percent of the material in John is *not* found in the Synoptics. So, if such features represent the historical ministry of Jesus, how could they only be reported in John? Second, John omits many of the features of Jesus's ministry central to portrayals of Jesus in the Synoptics. If Jesus spoke in parables about the kingdom of God, cast out demons, and dined with sinners, how could such features *not* have been reported by a trustworthy eyewitness? Third, given John's highly theological thrust, beginning with a confessional hymn to the eternal *Logos* and presenting Jesus as having divine sway over persons and events, how could such a rendering represent a disinterested and objective historical account rather than an invested and embellished one? If positivistic historical inquiry endeavors to minimize error, one can understand why it has seemed safest to many a critical scholar to simply leave John out.

Then again, the Fourth Gospel also possesses more mundane, topographical, and archaeologically attested material than all the other Gospels combined—canonical and otherwise.[3] How could such content be a part of John's story of Jesus if it were devoid of historical knowledge altogether? Given the likelihood that John's Prologue was added to the narrative later, its opening to the story of Jesus, like Mark's, begins with the ministry of John the Baptist, rather than a hymnic confession. Second, given that Mathew and Luke made use of Mark, the primary contrast is between John and Mark, although the distinctive material in Matthew and Luke also supports Mark's overall presentation. Thus, rather

---

Black, 2010 [original Eng. ed. 1910]); and, when a closer look is taken, many of these debates center on the Gospel of John. Regarding the most intense of the debates—between Schleiermacher and Strauss—see Paul N. Anderson, "The Jesus of History, the Christ of Faith, and the Gospel of John," in vol. 2 of *The Gospels, History and Christology: The Search of Joseph Ratzinger-Benedict XVI*, ed. Bernardo Estrada, Ermenegildo Manicardi, Armand Puig i Tàrrech (Rome: Libreria Editrice Vaticana, 2013),

    63–81.

    3. Interestingly, in the most exhaustive treatment of the subject, over half of the essays on archaeology and Jesus focus on features in the Gospel of John: *Jesus and Archaeology*, ed. James H. Charlesworth (Grand Rapids: Eerdmans, 2006). In particular, see Urban C. von Wahlde, "Archaeology and Topography in the Gospel of John," 523–86, and Paul N. Anderson, "Aspects of Historicity in the Gospel of John: Implications for Investigations of Jesus and Archaeology," 587–613. On "John, the Mundane Gospel," see Paul N. Anderson, "Juan. El Evangelio Terrenal y la Arqueología," *Arqueología e Historia* 18 (April 2018): 39–45.

than a 3:1 tally, with John's being a losing minority report, it might be better
to see John and Mark as two distinct perspectives on Jesus and his ministry—a
bi-optic presentation.[4] If John's story of Jesus was constructed with at least Mark
in mind, it is well seen as a complement to Mark—adding early material and the
Judean ministry of Jesus as a means of filling out the picture.[5] Third, much in
John seems more historically plausible than the Synoptic presentations. John's
two- or three-year ministry and multiple visits to Jerusalem are more plausible
than a one-year ministry with a single trip to Jerusalem in the Synoptics, the
last supper was more likely on the eve of the Passover rather than being a Passover meal, and the ministry of Jesus overlapping with the ministry of John the
Baptist rather than the Synoptic sequential presentation all seem more likely.
Further, John's presentation of women playing leading roles in the ministry of
Jesus, its more informal and egalitarian view of church organization, and insights
into religious and political tensions seem more primitive and realistic than do
Synoptic presentations of the same.

For these and other reasons, many a scholar has found the historical disparaging of John's presentation of Jesus to be critically insufficient, despite the very
real problems of including it in the Quest. And yet, the very importance of the
venture requires the use of all worthy sources, difficult or not. This is especially
the case if the material deemed historically worthy is used to compose a portrait
of what Jesus of Nazareth and his ministry might have been like. As Marcus
Borg reflected, following the Jesus Seminar's elimination of 82 percent of gospel
material as unworthy historically, a positive way of describing the parsimonious
and safe approach is to say, "at least" 18 percent of the Gospels' material can
be used to help us recover a picture of what Jesus was saying and doing.[6] However, while a selection of 18 percent of gospel material might be fairly reliable,

---

4. This is the conclusion of an extensive analysis of all the similarities and differences between John 6
and Mark 6 and 8, performed in Anderson, *Christology of the Fourth Gospel*, 72–251. Thus, John and Mark
reflect two distinctive perspectives from the earliest stages of gospel traditions' development, representing
bi-optic perspectives on Jesus and his ministry. See Paul N. Anderson, "Mark and John—The Bi-Optic
Gospels," in *Jesus in Johannine Tradition*, ed. Robert T. Fortna and Tom Thatcher (Louisville: Westminster
John Knox, 2001), 175–88; idem, "Mark, John, and Answerability: Interfluentiality and Dialectic between
the Second and Fourth Gospels," *Liber Annuus* 63 (2013): 197–245.

5. Compelling on the view that the Johannine evangelist may have been familiar with Mark are the
contributions of Richard Bauckham, "John for Readers of Mark," in *The Gospel for All Christians: Rethinking
the Gospel Audience*, ed. Richard Bauckham (Grand Rapids: Eerdmans, 1998), 147–71; and Ian D. Mackay,
John's Relationship with Mark: An Analysis of John 6 in the Light of Mark 6–8, WUNT 2/182 (Tübingen: Mohr
Siebeck, 2004). Familiarity, however, does not imply literary dependence.

6. See my *Quaker Religious Thought* dialogue with Marcus Borg along these lines, beginning with Paul
Anderson, "On Jesus: Quests for Historicity, and the History of Recent Quests," *Quaker Religious Thought*
94 (2000): 5–39; answered by Marcus Borg, "The Jesus Seminar from the Inside," *Quaker Religious Thought*
98 (2002): 21–27; followed by my response to his and other essays in that issue: "Jesus Matters: A Response
to Professors Borg, Powell, and Kinkel," *Quaker Religious Thought* 98 (2002): 43–54.

final portraits using only that material are bound to be distortive, especially if other worthy material (such as most of John's presentation) is programmatically excluded from the database.[7]

Put otherwise, if a selection of "certain" material involves parts of an ear, the nose, and the chin, those features might represent parts of a face accurately, but the partial portrait would not look like a real face. Worse, it would be distortive. In historiographic portraiture, a larger field of elements with more varying degrees of plausibility would represent a closer similitude, impressionistically, than a limited inclusion of fewer features—though accurate. Thus, a more textured approach to ways Jesus was remembered within gospel traditions and beyond will be more realistic than limiting the database to a smaller number of "certain" inferences.[8] This is where adding the Gospel of John—and all other worthy material—to the historical Quest of Jesus becomes a required move if a realistic impression of his ministry is desired. The question is how to go about it. That is what the John, Jesus, and History Project has sought to explore and what the Fourth Quest of Jesus advances.[9]

THE HISTORICAL QUESTS FOR JESUS— THE RENEWED QUEST AND BEYOND

While Dale Allison has rightly criticized the division of Jesus Research into periods,[10] research and trends tend to move in chapters or seasons. The thrust of nineteenth-century German scholarship on Jesus saw movement from Friedrich Schleiermacher's belief that the Gospel of John was the closest among the Gospels to the Jesus of Nazareth to David F. Strauss's total disparaging of

---

7. Along these lines, see my analyses of the twelfth plank in the platforms involving the dehistoricization of John and the de-Johannification of Jesus: Paul N. Anderson, *The Fourth Gospel and the Quest for Jesus: Modern Foundations Reconsidered*, LNTS 321 (London: T&T Clark, 2006), 43–99, published also as idem, "Why This Study Is Needed, and Why It Is Needed Now," in *Critical Appraisals of Critical Views*, ed. Paul N. Anderson, Felix Just, SJ, and Tom Thatcher, vol. 1 of *John, Jesus, and History*, SymS 44 (Atlanta: SBL Press, 2007), 13–70.

8. This is where the more nuanced approach to Jesus research as put forward by James D. G. Dunn is most helpful; see his *Jesus Remembered*, vol. 1 of *Christianity in the Making* (Grand Rapids: Eerdmans, 2003).

9. For earlier reports on the John, Jesus, and History Project, see Paul N. Anderson, "Das John, Jesus, and History Projekt—Neue Beobachtungen zu Jesus und eine Bi-optische Hypothese," *ZNW* 23 (2009): 12–26; a revised and expanded edition was published as idem, "The John, Jesus, and History Project—New Glimpses of Jesus and a Bi-Optic Hypothesis," in *The Bible and Interpretation* (February 2010): n.p. Online: www.bibleinterp.com/articles/john1357917.shtml.

10. Allison points out that nearly two books on Jesus were produced per year during what is called "the No Quest" period (between the publication of Schweitzer's book in 1906 and the publication of Käsemann's essay in 1954—ninety books in forty-eight years). See Dale C. Allison Jr., "The Secularizing of the Historical Jesus," *PRSt* 27 (2000): 135–51. Nonetheless, Gerd Theissen and Annette Merz rightly describe this period as "the collapse of the quest" (*The Historical Jesus: A Comprehensive Guide*, trans. John Bowden [Minneapolis: Augsburg Fortress, 1998], 5–7).

John for historical purposes. Schleiermacher favored John over Matthew and the Synoptics because of its intimate familiarity with the subject; Strauss rejected John for historical purposes because of its theological thrust.[11] Alongside those discussions, the Gospel of Mark came to be seen, rightly, as the first of the Gospels to be written, but following William Wrede's questioning of Mark's historicity, the nineteenth-century Continental Quest of Jesus came to an abrupt halt. Albert Schweitzer's 1906 book on the subject certainly caused a pause within the venture, concluding that Jesus "came to us as one unknown"—calling for the historical Jesus to be found in the lives of his followers, seeking to follow him faithfully.[12]

Given Rudolf Bultmann's conviction that virtually nothing can be known of the Historical Jesus,[13] a good deal of New Testament scholarship over the next half century or so went in the direction of recovering the history of gospel traditions and their relations to each other, rather than the historical quest of Jesus. Henry Cadbury, however, criticized the interest of Reimarus (seeking the "goal" of Jesus) as *The Peril of Modernizing Jesus.*[14] He later described the "No Quest" chapter as *The Eclipse of the Historical Jesus*, although he also did a fair amount of writing on Jesus of Nazareth, himself.[15] The corner was decisively turned, however, when Ernst Käsemann addressed the subject of "The Problem of the Historical Jesus" for the Old Marburgers' gathering in October of 1953.[16] In that address, he pointed out that in the light of the World Wars, the Jewishness

---

11. Friedrich Schleiermacher argues that John's intimate presentation of Jesus reflects firsthand knowledge of the subject over and against more fragmented Matthean (Synoptic) portrayals (*The Life of Jesus*, ed. Jack Verheyden, trans. S. MacLean Gilmour [Philadelphia: Fortress, 1975]). David F. Strauss did everything he could to overturn Schleiermacher's approach (*The Christ of Faith and the Jesus of History: A Critique of Schleiermacher's The Life of Jesus*, ed., trans. Leander E. Keck [Philadelphia: Fortress, 1977]). On the critical frailty of Strauss's approach, see Anderson, "Jesus of History, the Christ of Faith, and the Gospel of John," 63–81.

12. William Wrede, *The Messianic Secret*, trans. J. C. G. Greig (Cambridge: Clarke, 1971). With these words, Schweitzer closes his classic treatment of the subject in *Quest of the Historical Jesus*, 403, following his own advice by later becoming a medical missionary to Africa.

13. Rudolf Bultmann, *Jesus and the Word* (New York: Scribners, 1934), opens his book on Jesus, claiming that virtually nothing can be known about the historical Jesus, only suppositions about him.

14. Henry J. Cadbury, *The Peril of Modernizing Jesus*, 2nd ed. (Eugene, OR: Wipf & Stock, 2007 [1937]); Cadbury also contributed a cautionary parallel: idem, "The Peril of Archaizing Ourselves," *Interpretation* 3 (1949): 331–38.

15. In addition to his first book on Jesus, Cadbury wrote a second book a decade later—as well as half a dozen other essays on Jesus—a notable exception to the "No Quest" era: Henry J. Cadbury, *Jesus: What Manner of Man*, 2nd ed. (Eugene, OR: Wipf & Stock, 2008 [1947]). See also Cadbury, "Jesus and the Prophets," *JR* 5 (1925): 607–22; idem, "Jesus and John the Baptist," *JQR* 23 (1933): 373–76; idem, "Intimations of Immortality in the Thought of Jesus," *HTR* 53 (1960): 1–26; idem, *Jesus and Judaism*, Shrewsbury Lecture (Indianapolis: John Woolman, 1962); and idem, *The Emphasis of Jesus*, Shrewsbury Lecture (Indianapolis: John Woolman, 1962).

16. Ernst Käsemann, "The Problem of the Historical Jesus," in *Essays on New Testament Themes*, trans. S. J. Montague, SBT 41 (London: SCM, 1964), 15–47; first published as "Das Problem des historischen Jesus," *ZTK* 51 (1954): 125–53.

of Jesus can no longer be ignored; the Jesus of history must be investigated, albeit with some restrictions. Those restrictions, of course, involved setting up positivistic criteria designed to distinguish the Jesus of history from the Christ of faith, and this was done largely at the expense of the Fourth Gospel. His work was followed by Günther Bornkamm, Martin Dibelius, and others, and to use James Robinson's language, *the New Quest of Jesus* had thus begun.[17]

Over the next several decades, new methodologies came to be used in the Quest of Jesus—especially social-science methodologies and interdisciplinary approaches to historical inquiry regarding Jesus. Kenneth Bailey, John Pilch, Bruce Malina, Richard Rohrbaugh, and others developed social-sciences criticism as an approach to biblical studies, applying social and economic systems in Mediterranean culture to studies of Jesus and the Gospels.[18] Likewise, John Riches, Marcus Borg, and others applied religious anthropology theory, including the works of Mary Douglas, to Jesus research, and Geza Vermes and Ed Sanders illuminated centrally the Jewishness of Jesus.[19] Given the freshness of these new disciplinary approaches to Jesus research, N. T. Wright punctuated the movement with a name in the early 1980s: *the Third Quest of Jesus*.[20] Nonetheless, Third Questers continued to play it safe regarding the Gospel of John. They worked primarily with the Synoptics, and thus the Fourth Gospel continued to be excluded from Historical Jesus inquiry despite being included in some of the research.[21]

Alongside these developments, Robert Funk, Marcus Borg, John Dominic Crossan, and others launched the Jesus Seminar in 1985.[22] While some

---

17. James M. Robinson, *The New Quest of the Historical Jesus* (London: SCM, 1959). Also furthering the New Quest was the earlier work of Martin Dibelius, *Jesus*, trans. Charles B. Hedrick and Frederick C. Grant (Philadelphia: Westminster, 1949); as well as those of Günther Bornkamm, *Jesus of Nazareth* (New York: Harper & Row, 1960 [1956 German]); and Ernst Fuchs, *Studies of the Historical Jesus*, trans. Andrew Scobie, SBT 42 (London: SCM, 1964). The positivistic skepticism of the New Quest was furthered in America by such scholars as Norman Perrin, who counseled, "When in doubt, leave it out" (*Rediscovering the Teachings of Jesus* [New York: Harper & Row, 1976]).

18. Kenneth E. Bailey, *Poet & Peasant* and *Through Peasant Eyes: A Literary-Cultural Approach to the Parables of Luke*, combined ed. (Grand Rapids: Eerdmans, 1983 [1976, 1980]); John J. Pilch, *The Cultural World of Jesus: Sunday by Sunday* (Collegeville, MN: Liturgical Press, 1996); Bruce J. Malina, *The Social World of Jesus and the Gospels* (London: Routledge, 1996); Bruce J. Malina and Richard L. Rohrbaugh, *Social-Science Commentary on the Synoptic Gospels* (Minneapolis: Fortress, 1993); and idem, *Social-Science Commentary on the Gospel of John* (Minneapolis: Fortress, 1998).

19. John K. Riches, *Jesus and the Transformation of Judaism* (London: Darton, Longman & Todd, 1980); Geza Vermes, *Jesus the Jew: A Historian's Reading of the Gospels* (Minneapolis: Augsburg Fortress, 1981); Marcus J. Borg, *Conflict, Holiness, and Politics in the Teachings of Jesus*, 2nd ed. (New York: Contiuum, 1998 [1984]); E. P. Sanders, *Jesus and Judaism* (Minneapolis: Fortress, 1985).

20. N. T. Wright, "Towards a Third Quest? Jesus Then and Now," ARC: *The Journal of the Faculty of Religious Studies, McGill University, Montreal, Canada* 10 (1982): 20–27.

21. See the overview by Ben Witherington III, *The Jesus Quest: The Third Search for the Jew of Nazareth*, 2nd ed. (Downers Grove, IL: InterVarsity Press, 1997 [1995]).

22. Their primary works include: Robert W. Funk, Roy W. Hoover, and the Jesus Seminar, *The Five*

Third Questers were involved in this project, Crossan saw himself as a New Quester, and the project was sometimes referred to as *the Renewed Quest*.[23] As an extension of the positivistic skepticism of the New Quest, the Jesus Seminar sought to demarcate the overall judgments of critical biblical scholarship in determining hard categories of certainty regarding all the sayings and actions of Jesus by means of assigning papers and having the members vote by the casting of marbles. No sitting on the fence! The marbles were weighted as a means of measuring the scholars' historicity judgments.[24] The results were then tabulated and documented in two books, documenting the judgments of the seminarians, who overall followed the two dichotomies of Strauss (1865): if it is theological, it can't be historical; and, if the choice is between the Synoptics and John, the Synoptics win, hands down; John loses.[25] Again, among the seven pillars of scholarly wisdom laid out by Robert Funk, the Gospel of John and even similarities to John in the Synoptics were eliminated categorically from historical consideration, assuming a priori Johannine ahistoricity.[26] Oddly enough, given that the Gospel of Thomas has some form-critical similarities with the Q tradition (material shared by Matthew and Luke but not found in Mark) as primarily a sayings tradition, the Jesus Seminar hailed Thomas as "the Fifth Gospel," and it received more pink and red designations than any of the other

---

Gospels: The Search for the Authentic Words of Jesus (New York: Polebridge, 1993); and Robert W. Funk and the Jesus Seminar, *The Acts of Jesus: The Search for the Authentic Deeds of Jesus* (San Francisco: HarperSanFrancisco, 1998).

23. John Dominic Crossan, *The Historical Jesus: The Life of a Mediterranean Jewish Peasant* (New York: HarperCollins, 1991); and idem, *Jesus: A Revolutionary Biography* (New York: HarperCollins, 1994). See also W. Barnes Tatum, *In Quest of Jesus*, rev. and enlarged (Nashville: Abingdon, 1999 [1982]), 102–7; Robert W. Funk, "Milestones in the Quest for the Historical Jesus," *The Fourth R* 14.4 (2001).

24. The statistical probabilities with which the Jesus Seminar defined their judgments are as follows: "There's been some mistake" (black)—.0000 to .2500; "Well, maybe" (grey)—.2501 to .5000; "Sure sounds like Jesus" (pink)—.5001–.7500; "That's Jesus!" (red)—.7501 and up. Funk et al., *Five Gospels*, 37.

25. Funk et al., *Five Gospels*, 3, describes these two dichotomies as "the two pillars of modern biblical scholarship." Thus, it is little surprise that in both of their volumes there was virtually nothing regarding the sayings or acts of Jesus in John that possessed any semblance of historicity, and Funk's description of the Seminarians' operations in *Acts of Jesus*, 10, is as follows: "The first step is to understand the diminished role the Gospel of John plays in the search for the Jesus of history. The two pictures painted by John and the Synoptics cannot be both historically accurate. . . . The differences between the two portraits of Jesus show up in a dramatic way in the evaluation, by the Jesus Seminar, of the words attributed to Jesus in the Gospel of John. The Fellows of the Seminar were unable to find a single saying they could with certainty trace back to the historical Jesus."

26. Thus, the "bolt out of the Johannine blue" in Matthew 11:27 and Luke 10:22, and even in Thomas 61:3 is excluded from historical possibility (and thus is judged black, when the preceding verse is judged grey) simply because it is reminiscent of John 3:35; 7:29; and 13:3 (Funk et al, *Five Gospels*, 182). According to Robert Funk, in his *Honest to Jesus: Jesus for a New Millennium* (San Francisco: HarperSanFrancisco, 1996), 127, the bases for these judgments are as follows: "In the Gospel of John, Jesus is a self-confessing Messiah rather than a self-effacing sage. In John, Jesus seems to have little concern for the impoverished, the disabled, and the religious outcasts. Although John preserves the illusion of combining a real Jesus with the mythic Christ, the human side of Jesus is in fact diminished. For all these reasons, the current quest for the historical Jesus makes little use of the heavily interpreted data found in the Gospel of John."

Gospels, including Mark. While claiming to *not* be theological in its interest—only historical—the Seminar's understandings of Jesus and his ministry had extensive theological implications.[27]

To some degree, the programmatic omission of the one Gospel claiming firsthand knowledge of Jesus and his ministry by the first three Quests, bolstered by the fact that the media covered the Jesus Seminar's findings extensively, caused serious New Testament scholars to question the bases for and operations of excluding the Gospel of John from Jesus research altogether. For one thing, the posteriority of John could not simply be assumed, and ignoring features of its primitivity seemed intellectually irresponsible.[28] Thus, John A. T. Robinson, Peter Hofrichter, and Klaus Berger had wondered if John might have been the first of the Gospels to be composed, although Hofrichter saw John as the first and last of the Gospels.[29] Second, leading Johannine scholars internationally did not see its tradition as being derivative from alien sources or the Synoptics, but had come to see it as a self-standing autonomous tradition with its own story to tell.[30] Rudolf Schnackenburg, Raymond Brown, Barnabas Lindars, Moody Smith, Craig Keener, and others viewed John's as an independent tradition developing in its own distinctive ways.[31] Even some Jesus scholars had come to see John as

---

27. Gary Kinkel cried foul along these lines, while also critiquing the operative expansion of the canon without going through a proper canonization process ("Jesus Projects: A Theological Critique," *Quaker Religious Thought* 98 [2002]: 35–42). Kinkel then goes on to note that while the Jesus Seminar argued its interests were historical and not theological, their members then went on to speculate on the theological implications of the Jesus exposed by their non-theological—and even anti-theological—methodologies.

28. Aspects of John's primitivity had been rather clearly established by several scholars earlier: Erwin R. Goodenough, "John: A Primitive Gospel," *JBL* 64 (1945): 145–82; Arthur C. Headlam, *The Fourth Gospel as History* (Oxford: Blackwell, 1948); William F. Albright, "Recent Discoveries in Palestine and the Gospel of St. John," in *The Background of the New Testament and its Eschatology: In Honour of Charles Harold Dodd*, ed. W. D. Davies and D. Daube (Cambridge: Cambridge University Press, 1956), 153–71; C. K. Barrett, "History," in *Essays on John* (London: SPCK, 1982), 116–31; Raymond E. Brown, "The Problem of Historicity in John," *CBQ* 24 (1962): 1–14, also published in his *New Testament Essays* (Garden City: Image, 1965), 187–217.

29. John A. T. Robinson, *The Priority of John*, ed. J. F. Coakley (London: SCM, 1985); followed by Peter L. Hofrichter, *Modell und Vorlage der Synoptiker: Das vorredaktionelle Johannesevangelium*, Theologische Texte und Studien 6 (Hildesheim: Olms, 1997); Klaus Berger, *Im Anfang war Johannes: Datierung und Theologie des vierten Evangeliums* (Stuttgart: Quell, 1997).

30. Establishing rather firmly a view of John's nondependence on the Synoptics are the works of P. Gardner-Smith, *Saint John and the Synoptic Gospels* (Cambridge: Cambridge University Press, 1938); C. H. Dodd, *Historical Tradition in the Fourth Gospel* (Cambridge: Cambridge University Press, 1963); and D. Moody Smith, *John among the Gospels*, 2nd ed. (Columbia: University of South Carolina Press, 2001 [1992]). This also is my conclusion, having conducted extensive evaluations of John 6 and 18–19 in relation to the Synoptics, the two Johannine passages most closely connected to Mark and the Synoptic Gospels (Anderson, *Christology of the Fourth Gospel*, 33–251; idem, "Aspects of Interfluentiality between John and the Synoptics: John 18–19 as a Case Study," in *The Death of Jesus in the Fourth Gospel: Colloquium Biblicum Lovaniense LIV, 2005*, ed. Gilbert Van Belle, BETL 200 (Leuven: Peeters, 2007), 711–28.

31. Leading critical commentaries seeing John's as an autonomous tradition include: Rudolf Schnackenburg, *The Gospel According to St. John*, 3 vols., trans. Kevin Smyth (London: Burns & Oates; New York: Seabury, 1968–1982); Raymond E. Brown, *The Gospel according to John*, 2 vols., AB 29–29A (Garden City, NY: Doubleday, 1966–1970); Barnabas Lindars, *The Gospel of John*, NCB (Grand Rapids: Eerdmans, 1972);

having more historically rooted material than had otherwise been imagined, even if the particulars were sketchy.[32] Further, if the Gospel of Thomas was to be included in the historical Quest of Jesus, ways ought to be found to make use of the Gospel of John, despite diversity of views on its origin, composition, authorship, and character. These matters are what set the stage for the John, Jesus, and History Project, which held the first of its first meetings in 2002.

THE JOHN, JESUS, AND HISTORY PROJECT—
AN INTERNATIONAL CONVERSATION

Given new reports that critical scholars had voted and determined that the Gospel of John had little or nothing historical to contribute to Jesus research,[33] several Johannine scholars wondered if it were time to take the issue on—full bore—to see what a sustained and focused inquiry might produce. So, at the 2000 Nashville SBL meetings, Tom Thatcher, Felix Just, Eldon Epp, and I met and sketched the outline of a consultation proposal that would examine the issues critically. Tom Thatcher drew up the proposal and presented it successfully to the program committee the following year. We then recruited top Johannine scholars Alan Culpepper, Moody Smith, Mary Coloe, and Jaime Clark-Soles to be on the steering committee. This led to the first consultation meeting of the John, Jesus, and History Project at the Toronto meetings in 2002, where we invited lead papers and responses along two lines: "The Dehistoricization of John" and "The De-Johannification of Jesus." Our goal was to state clearly and bluntly the two predominant critical views on the matter, including the bases for each, and then to subject them to critical evaluation in order to ascertain their strengths and weaknesses, including instances where planks in each critical platform are robust, and where they are frail.[34] Along these lines, Robert Kysar gave a thorough overview of the first issue, while Paula Fredriksen offered a case study, showing the weakness of the second platform.[35]

D. Moody Smith, *John*, ANTC (Nashville: Abingdon, 1999); Craig S. Keener, *The Gospel of John: A Commentary*, 2 vols. (Peabody, MA: Hendrickson, 2003).

32. See especially John P. Meier, *The Roots of the Problem and the Person*, vol. 1 of *A Marginal Jew: Rethinking the Historical Jesus*, ABRL (New York: Doubleday, 1991), and idem, *Mentor, Message and Miracles*, vol. 2 of *A Marginal Jew: Rethinking the Historical Jesus*, ABRL (New York: Doubleday, 1994); and Paula Fredriksen, *Jesus of Nazareth, King of the Jews* (New York: Knopf, 1999).

33. See, for instance, David Van Biema, "The Gospel Truth?," *Time* 147.15 (1996): 52–59; and Jeffrey Sheler, "In Search of Jesus," *U.S. News and World Report* (April 8, 1996): 47–48.

34. Thus, Anderson, "Why This Study Is Needed," 13–79.

35. Robert Kysar, "The Dehistoricizing of the Gospel of John," in Anderson, Just, and Thatcher, *Critical Appraisals*, 75–102; and Paula Fredriksen, "The Historical Jesus, the Scene in the Temple, and the Gospel of John," in Anderson, Just, and Thatcher, *Critical Appraisals*, 249–74 . Fredriksen's paper was responded

We had been assigned a room holding seventy attendees, but fifteen minutes before the session began, the room was totally filled. So, Felix Just identified an available large room down the hallway, to which we moved. It was a good thing we did, as there were over two hundred in attendance at that first meeting. This level of interest was sustained over the next fourteen years, as the attendance at our forty-four SBL sessions—featuring two hundred twenty-five presentations and responses from 2002 to 2016—averaged over a hundred, ranging between forty and three hundred.[36] We also collaborated with other groups, including the Johannine Literature, Historical Jesus, the Bible in Ancient and Modern Media, and the Synoptic Gospels Sections in order to create interdisciplinary engagement between various interests of scholarship. The next two years of our sessions (2003–2004), we continued to explore literature reviews and disciplinary approaches to these issues, which completed our tenure as a consultation.

In our steering committee meetings, one of our early questions was whether to establish a single methodology before proceeding. Wayne Meeks, however, gave us wise counsel. He'd been a part of another consultation years earlier, which sought to establish an agreed upon methodology before launching into a field of inquiry. The group spent several years on that question alone and could never come to agreement on a single methodological approach, and the overall project was eventually abandoned. Therefore, our committee decidedly adopted the opposite approach. First, we invited four additional literature reviews, posing strengths and weaknesses of previous approaches to the issues.[37] Second, we invited scholars to put forth their own methodological approaches, expecting things to sort themselves out in terms of viability in relation to the performance of the methodologies along particular lines.[38] Third, we also welcomed scholars

---

to by Mark Allen Powell, "On Deal-Breakers and Disturbances, in Anderson, Just, and Thatcher, *Critical Appraisals*, 277–82.

36. We also organized three separate conferences before the Atlanta 2011 and 2015 meetings and before the Baltimore 2013 meetings, which became or engaged separate book-length projects. The papers presented at each of those sessions numbered 39, for a total of 264 papers overall, delivered by over 200 scholars from multiple countries and perspectives, within our fifteen years of meetings. In that sense, the John, Jesus, and History Project is one of the most extensive and sustained Jesus research endeavors in recent history.

37. Marianne Meye Thompson, "The 'Spiritual Gospel': How John the Theologian Writes History," in Anderson, Just, and Thatcher, *Critical Appraisals*, 103–7; Jack Verheyden, "The De-Johannification of Jesus: The Revisionist Contribution of Some Nineteenth-Century German Scholarship," in Anderson, Just, and Thatcher, *Critical Appraisals*, 109–20; Mark Allan Powell, "The De-Johannification of Jesus: The Twentieth Century and Beyond," in Anderson, Just, and Thatcher, *Critical Appraisals*, 121–32; and D. A. Carson, "The Challenge of the Balkanization of Johannine Studies," in Anderson, Just, and Thatcher, *Critical Appraisals*, 133–59.

38. The methodological papers included (all found in Anderson, Just, and Thatcher, *Critical Appraisals*): D. Moody Smith, "John: A Source for Jesus Research?," 165–78; Andrew L. Lincoln, "'We Know That His Testimony Is True': Johannine Truth Claims and Historicity," 179–97; Colleen M. Conway, "New Historicism and the Historical Jesus in John: Friends or Foes?," 199–215; Gilbert Van Belle with Sydney Palmer, "John's

to argue any case they wished—for or against historicity in John, spelling out resultant implications for Jesus research—but to marshal their assertions with compelling evidence and reason. Fourth, we then sought to test the durability of modern critical platforms regarding the dehistoricization of John and the de-Johannification of Jesus, seeing if new critical platforms were required. Fifth, we also asked for papers to be submitted before the conference meetings so that they could be e-mailed to scholars on our e-list (soon numbering over five hundred scholars internationally); this allowed for summaries of the papers at the meetings, with a good 30–45 minutes of discussion to follow.[39]

These approaches created a great synergy of interdisciplinary engagement, the sharing of diverse perspectives, and the sorting through of a variety of issues within an open and robust international academic community of inquiry. Thus, our first triennium as a consultation allowed us to conduct *critical appraisals of critical views*, and these presentations were gathered into the first of our John, Jesus, and History volumes.

Following our consultation triennium (2002–2004), our project was approved for two further triennia as a group within the national Society of Biblical Literature meetings. This meant that we were allowed to schedule between two and four sessions per year, provided the papers and presenters were strong. What we proposed was to extend further our critical analyses of the two predominant modern critical platforms. Therefore, we engaged "Aspects of Historicity in the Gospel of John" as a means of testing the *dehistoricization of John* platform (2005–2007). We then engaged "Glimpses of Jesus through the Johannine Lens" as a means of testing the *de-Johannification of Jesus* platform (2008–2010). As a means of charting the second triennium, Alan Culpepper suggested we break the Fourth Gospel up into three sections, inviting papers and responses each year to aspects of historicity in John 1–4 (2005), John 5–12 (2006), and John 13–21 (2007). As a means of charting the third triennium, we moved from the most certain to the least certain: glimpses of Jesus in the Johannine passion narrative (2008), the works of Jesus in John (2009), and the words of Jesus in John (2010). These papers and responses were then gathered into the second and third central volumes of the John, Jesus, and History Project.[40]

Literary Unity and the Problem of Historicity," 217–28; and John Painter, "Memory Holds the Key: The Transformation of Memory in the Interface of History and Theology in John," 229–45.

39. Great appreciation is due to Tom Thatcher, who faithfully sent these papers out to our e-list of scholars several weeks before the meetings. Tom served as our first chair (2002–2004), followed by Tom Thatcher and Paul Anderson as co-chairs (2005–2007), Paul Anderson and Jaime Clark-Soles as co-chairs (2008–2010), Jaime Clark-Soles and Craig Koester as co-chairs (2011–2013), and Craig Koester and Catrin Williams as co-chairs (2014–2016).

40. These papers and responses were then published as the second and third volumes in our central

In addition to our central agenda, however, it became apparent that additional issues needed to be addressed related to the subjects of "John," "Jesus," and "History"—the inclusion of the Oxford comma, here, was intentional. First, our group was approached by the SBL leadership, asking if we would host a session celebrating sixty years of the discovery of the Dead Sea Scrolls at the 2007 San Diego meetings. We agreed and organized such a session; Tom Thatcher and Mary Coloe then edited the essays into a state-of-the-art book on the subject.[41] In addition, Tom Thatcher had been working on a project for some time, which invited eighteen leading Johannine scholars to contribute essays along the lines of "What We Have Heard From the Beginning," followed by responses from emerging scholars.[42] This book also appeared in 2007, so in addition to the two sessions on "Aspects of Historicity in John 13–21," the John, Jesus, and History Group hosted an extra session on "John and Qumran: Sixty Years of Discovery and Dialogue," and three sessions on "The Past, Present, and Future of Johannine Studies." Among our two hundred and sixty-four papers and responses over our five triennia, forty-eight were presented in our six sessions hosted in 2007. Given that we were also celebrating the publication of our first volume, that was a big year for the John, Jesus, and History Project!

By the end of our second triennium, it was becoming apparent to us that we needed to address a number of further issues in addition to our central program. Therefore, we organized a book review session (2008),[43] the first of two methodological sessions on criteria for determining Johannine historicity (2009 and 2014), and three sessions on archaeology and the Fourth Gospel (2010, 2011, 2012).[44] Thus, the old paradigm, which programmatically excluded the Gospel of John from Jesus Research, was being replaced by a new paradigm, which included the Fourth Gospel in the Historical Quest of Jesus. Two formidable Jesus scholars, Mark Allan Powell and James Charlesworth, had published essays to that effect

series: Paul N. Anderson, Felix Just, SJ, and Tom Thatcher, eds., *Aspects of Historicity in the Fourth Gospel*, vol. 2 of *John, Jesus, and History*, ECL 2 (Atlanta: SBL Press, 2009); and idem, *Glimpses of Jesus through the Johannine Lens*, vol. 3 of *John, Jesus, and History*, ECL 18 (Atlanta: SBL Press, 2016).

41. Mary L. Coloe and Tom Thatcher, eds., *Qumran and the Dead Sea Scrolls: Sixty Years of Discovery and Debate*, EJL 32 (Atlanta: SBL Press 2011).

42. Tom Thatcher, ed., *What We Have Heard from the Beginning: The Past, Present and Future of Johannine Studies* (Waco, TX: Baylor University Press, 2007).

43. The books reviewed by Judith Lieu, Amy-Jill Levine, and Andreas Köstenberger were Paul N. Anderson, *Fourth Gospel and the Quest for Jesus*; Richard J. Bauckham, *The Testimony of the Beloved Disciple: Narrative, History, and Theology in the Gospel of John* (Grand Rapids: Baker Academic, 2007); and D. Moody Smith, *The Fourth Gospel in Four Dimensions: Judaism and Jesus, the Gospels and Scripture* (Columbia: University of South Carolina Press, 2008).

44. Our plans are to publish these two volumes in the future, envisioned as: *Archaeology and the Fourth Gospel: John, Material Culture, and Jesus*; and *John, Jesus, and History, Volume 6: Methodologies for Determining Johannine Historicity*.

in 2009 and 2010, and within the new millennium, a Fourth Quest of Jesus had indeed begun.[45] This led us to organize a joint session with the Historical Jesus Section at the 2010 meetings, which was hosted by Greg Sterling, the chair of that section.

The completion of our third triennium wrapped up successfully our critical appraisals of critical views. In light of multiple aspects of historicity in John and a robust array of glimpses of Jesus through the Johannine lens, the two predominant critical platforms have failed to withstand sustained tests of critical scrutiny. Thus, *the dehistoricization of John* and *the de-Johannification of Jesus* are critically flawed platforms, which must be replaced by more nuanced approaches to the issues. Indeed, considerable problems still remain related to John, Jesus, and history, but the question is *how* to address them, not *whether* to do so. That being the case, two further sets of issues presented themselves as needing to be addressed: first, history of John's composition and relation to Synoptic traditions; second, the history of the Johannine situation with relation to John's story of Jesus. In addressing these issues of John's tradition-history and situation-history, we adopted James Dunn's more generous approach to historical Jesus studies: *Jesus remembered*.[46] Therefore, what we set out to accomplish in proposing our fourth and fifth triennia was slated as investigating "Jesus Remembered in the Johannine Tradition" and "Jesus Remembered in the Johannine Situation."

Our application to continue as an SBL group for six more years was successful, and the conducting of these two trajectories developed as follows. First, in discerning what could be known regarding how Jesus was remembered within the Johannine tradition, we recruited sets of papers focused on *intratraditional* developments. We began with memory theory and the movement from orality to the written preservation of memory, featuring two sessions organized by Tom Thatcher and his colleagues in the Ancient and Modern Media Section (2011). Additional open joint sessions with the Johannine Literature Section were also held as a means of drawing in unsolicited papers on the subject (2011, 2012), and a further session on Jesus Remembered within the Johannine Tradition was

---

45. Mark Allen Powell, "'Things That Matter': Historical Jesus Studies in the New Millennium," *WW* 29.2 (2009): 121–28; James H. Charlesworth, "The Historical Jesus in the Fourth Gospel: A Paradigm Shift?," *JSHJ* 8 (2010): 3–46.

46. The title of Dunn's first volume in his *Christianity in the Making* series. See also his important essay, idem, "Let John Be John: A Gospel for Its Time," in *Das Evangelium und die Evangelien*, ed. Peter Stuhlmacher, WUNT 28 (Tübingen: Mohr Siebeck, 1983), 309–39. On the subject of memory and its function within gospel traditions, however, see the Cognitive-Critical analyses of Franz Mussner, *The Historical Jesus in the Gospel of St John*, QD 19 (Freiburg: Herder & Herder, 1967); and Paul N. Anderson, "The Origin and Development of the Johannine *Egō Eimi* Sayings in Cognitive-Critical Perspective," *JSHJ* 9 (2011): 139–206; and idem, "The Cognitive Origins of John's Christological Unity and Disunity," *HBT* 17 (1995): 1–24.

organized for 2013. We also reflected upon relations between the Johannine Gospel and Epistles, including the possibility of multiple editions within the Johannine tradition's development. These considerations led directly to two further inquiries. As Urban von Wahlde's three-volume commentary on the Gospel and Letters of John had just come out, we organized a review session for the 2011 meetings.[47] Then, as a means of engaging the Johannine Epistles, we organized a pre-conference on the Johannine Epistles at the McAfee School of Theology before the SBL meetings in 2010. These essays were then published in 2014.[48]

We further embarked upon comparisons and contrasts between John and each of the Synoptic Gospels (including the hypothetical Q tradition) to discern how Johannine-Synoptic similarities and differences might convey something of Jesus remembered *intertraditionally*—between John and other gospel traditions— whatever such contacts might or might not have been. Respondents were also organized to engage the papers in each of these sessions, which began with com-paring/contrasting John with Mark (2012), followed by similar analyses with Luke (2013), Matthew (2014), and Q (2016). An earlier session had also been organized to consider Jesus remembered in the Fourth Gospel and within second-century traditions (2012). Given that the fiftieth and sixtieth anniversaries of C. H. Dodd's *magna opera* were coming up in 2013, Tom Thatcher and Catrin Williams were commissioned to gather essays celebrating Dodd's legacy along these lines, and a pre-conference honoring the contributions of Dodd and Raymond Brown was held at Saint Mary's Seminary in Baltimore before the SBL meetings in 2013, hosted by Michael Gorman.[49]

Following the contributions of J. Louis Martyn and Raymond E. Brown, taking note of Jesus remembered within the Johannine situation also required attention, considering the two (or more) levels of history within the development of the Johannine tradition. Like our other sessions, we organized four papers and a response, followed by a sustained discussion for sessions within our fourth and fifth triennia. Our first set of papers (2013) explored Jesus remembered in the Palestine-connected Johannine situation (30–70 CE). Our second session focused on Jesus Remembered in the first diaspora phase of the Johannine community's development—engaging especially Jewish and Roman elements within that

---

47. Urban C. von Wahlde, *The Gospel and Letters of John*, 3 vols., ECC (Grand Rapids: Eerdmans, 2010); reviewed by Paul Anderson, Alicia Myers, and Craig Koester.

48. Published as Paul N. Anderson and R. Alan Culpepper, eds., *Communities in Dispute: Current Scholarship on the Johannine Epistles*, ECL 13 (Atlanta: SBL Press, 2014).

49. Published as Tom Thatcher and Catrin H. Williams, eds., *Engaging with C. H. Dodd on the Gospel of John: Sixty Years of Tradition and Interpretation* (Cambridge: Cambridge University Press, 2013).

situation (2014). Papers are still being gathered for the second diaspora phase of the Johannine situation—engaging other Christian communities and traveling (docetizing) ministers in the later Johannine situation. The multiplicity of issues related to *Jesus Remembered in the Johannine Tradition* and *Jesus Remembered in the Johannine Situation* are intended to comprise volumes 4 and 5 in our central series.[50] Along these lines, Alan Culpepper and I organized a second McAfee School of Theology pre-conference on John and Judaism before the SBL meetings in 2015, and the collected essays were published in 2017 as a state-of-the-art collection on the subject.[51]

A final subject of inquiry takes further some of the analysis conducted back in the second year of our meetings (2003). In that session, I had critiqued the six planks in each of the platforms regarding the dehistoricization of John and the de-Johannification of Jesus, noting that among the five portraitures of Jesus featured in Marcus Borg's and Bart Ehrman's analyses of recent Jesus research, each of these portraitures is also distinctively discernible within the Gospel of John.[52] Thus, images of Jesus as a Jewish prophet, a wisdom-sage, an institution-challenging cynic, a holy person, and an apocalyptic figure are not only discernible within the Fourth Gospel, but their presentations are at times clearer in John than they are in the Synoptic Gospels or Thomas. Therefore, Craig Koester was commissioned to draw together three sessions of papers (2013, 2015, 2016), which have now been published as a stand-alone book.[53] During our final two years of our fifth triennia, Helen Bond and Catrin Williams drew together responses to the John, Jesus, and History Project, and those sessions led to further reflections on advances achieved and work yet to be done.

Given the 2016 publication of volume 3 in the *John, Jesus, and History* central series, in addition to noting the advances of the two earlier central volumes in contributing to Johannine and Jesus studies alike, a review session was organized for the 2015 meetings. Prepublication versions of the essays were sent to the reviewers, and in addition to appreciating the overall contribution of the Project, several questions were raised. First, Jan van der Watt questioned the openness to diverse methodologies rather than seeking to establish

---

50. Forthcoming as *John, Jesus, and History, Volume 4: Jesus Remembered in the Johannine Tradition*; and *John, Jesus, and History, Volume: 5 Jesus Remembered in the Johannine Situation*.

51. R. Alan Culpepper and Paul N. Anderson, eds., *John and Judaism: A Contested Relationship in Context*, RBS 87 (Atlanta: SBL Press, 2017).

52. Marcus J. Borg, *Jesus in Contemporary Scholarship* (Valley Forge, PA: Trinity Press International, 1994); Bart D. Ehrman, *Jesus: Apocalyptic Prophet of the New Millennium* (Oxford: Oxford University Press, 2001).

53. Published as Craig Koester, ed., *Portraits of Jesus in the Gospel of John*, LNTS 589 (London: Bloomsbury, 2018).

methodological unity at the outset. This was not by accident, however, as it was felt that inviting diverse approaches to the issues would allow methodologies and their applications to establish themselves (or not) along the way.[54] Second, several scholars raised questions regarding the relation between John and the Synoptics. Mark Goodacre engaged my Bi-Optic Hypothesis, appreciating John's augmentation of and plausible correction of Mark, as well as some presence of "interfluentiality" between various stages of the traditions.[55] He took issue, however, with my following Lamar Cribbs in seeing Luke as being influenced by John's formative tradition, given Luke's departures from Mark in Johannine directions, preferring a view of John's dependence on Luke. In addition, a full session on Johannine-Synoptic relations was organized for the 2016 meetings so as to focus more extensively on this complex set of issues. A third focus of the 2015 session addressed the issue of what is meant by "history." Pushing back against objectivist perspectives on memory and historiography, Andrew Lincoln asserted the importance of allowing John's theologically influenced perspective to be regarded in its own right rather than forcing it into a synoptic mold. And, if theological expansions upon elements in the Johannine narrative are a given, such might also have transpired if John knew the Synoptics.[56] A second set of papers involving methodologies for determining Johannine historicity had been organized for 2014, and a further set of papers on the character of Johannine historiography was organized for 2016.

In reflecting on the five triennia of the John, Jesus, and History Project, the steering committee (now consisting of Craig Koester, Alan Culpepper, Helen Bond, Catrin Williams, Tom Thatcher, and myself) decided to conclude the project on a high note, having completed our basic goals. As of 2019, we have published eight volumes, with four more volumes to be edited and finalized.[57] Over 200 top scholars internationally have presented in our sessions, from a variety of diverse methodological and theoretical perspectives, and the following advances are well established, requiring further inquiry.

---

54. These issues had been addressed in vol. 1 of the John, Jesus, and History Project, *Critical Assessments*.

55. Of course, even though this reflects my best thought on how to approach the Johannine riddles, it is not expected that other members of the steering committee will have considered or agreed with it; we all have our own ways of addressing the issues involved. We have invited all approaches to the Johannine riddles, by the best scholars worldwide, welcoming a diversity of approaches and critical theories.

56. This perspective was addressed effectively in Wendy Sproston North's essay, "Points and Stars: John and the Synoptics," in Anderson, Just, and Thatcher, *Glimpses of Jesus*, 119–31. In Tom Thatcher's response (158), however, he concludes that "North's analysis of John 12 and 20 . . . does not demonstrate John's dependence on Mark and Luke, but rather simply assumes such dependence."

57. Again, the volumes yet to be finalized include as of now: *John, Jesus, and Archaeology*; *Jesus Remembered in the Johannine Situation*; *Jesus Remembered in the Johannine Tradition*; and *Methodologies for Conducting Johannine Historiography*.

Advances Contributed by the John, Jesus, and History Project:

1. Historical Jesus research and Johannine tradition research comprise two of the most intensive and extensive fields of inquiry within modern biblical scholarship, and until now there has been little sustained inter-disciplinary critical engagement between these two related fields—to the detriment of each.

2. The dehistoricization of John is critically flawed, as multiple aspects of historicity abound within the Fourth Gospel—including mundane, topographical, spatial, contextual, and linguistic features, as well as archaeologically attested details.

3. The de-Johannification of Jesus is also critically flawed, as many features of the Fourth Gospel offer glimpses into the historical ministry of Jesus, providing valuable insights for understanding Jesus of Nazareth—despite John's theological interests and thrust.

4. Because criteria for determining Jesus research historicity have been programmatically designed to exclude Johannine content from the historical Quest of Jesus, new criteria are required within an inclusive and more adequate historiographic quest.

5. The development of the Johannine tradition shows evidence of reflective dialectic between memory, perception, and experience—leading to inferences of meaning and the discernment of significance between earlier and later stages of its development.

6. As a tradition developing parallel to those of the Synoptic Gospels, some intertraditional engagement with other gospel traditions is discernible, but the autonomy of John's tradition overall suggests that it may well serve as an independent source for corroborating, augmenting, and perhaps even correcting Synoptic renderings of Jesus's ministry—just as Synoptic elements pose a tether for evaluating some of John's features. Detailed analyses of John's relations with each of the other traditions are thus essential for discerning the particulars of John's intertraditional engagements.

7. Given the fact that the Johannine Epistles inform the situation in which John's story of Jesus developed, considering a history-and-theology analysis of the narrator's engagement with a multiplicity of contextual issues informs a more textured understanding of why John is different from the other Gospels. As an emerging consensus is coming to see the Epistles as having been written between the early and final stages of the Gospel's formation, some of the issues addressed in the Epistles illuminate

a contextual appreciation for ways John's story of Jesus was crafted as a means of conveying earlier memories with the needs of later audiences.

8. Finally, the issue of "history" itself must be reconsidered, as new understandings of memory theory, media studies, cognitive analysis, and meta-history have caused modern historiographers to rethink what is meant by "history," and perhaps more importantly, to challenge simplistic assertions of what is not.

While a good number of New Testament scholars were resistant to even the idea of the John, Jesus, and History Project, questioning its motives and operations, its agenda and interest has been totally critical and analytical. First, while a parsimonious quest for Jesus of Nazareth might be simpler and easier, adding John to the mix makes things far more complex and difficult. However, scholarly ease is not the interest; addressing a troubling lacuna in modern scholarship is the overriding critical concern. Second, if restoring a greater sense of Johannine historicity makes an impact upon Jesus research, the identification of John's historical reliability over and against one or more of the Synoptic Gospels may well pose a challenge to traditional views rather than bolstering them. Assuming John's differences from the Synoptics reflect "the theological interests of the evangelist" might be easier for conservatives to accept than to imagine that Mark (followed by Matthew and Luke) might have gotten it wrong here and there. Therefore, if John's memory of Jesus is accorded historical weight, this might pose a scandal to traditionalist scholars as well as being a nuisance to historical-critical scholars. Third, the modern myth of objectivism as the measure of historical truth is also brought into question, as more generous views of historical memory have come to include paraphrastic adaptation, rhetorical design, contextual delivery, and narrative selectivity. These must also be seen as features of historical tradition. In these and other ways, the new millennium has called for a new and inclusive stage in critical Jesus research, and that has led to a *Renewed Look at John* and a *Fourth Quest of Jesus.*

THE RENEWED LOOK AT JOHN—THE TURNING OF THE NEW MILLENNIUM

In 1957 at an Oxford conference on "The Four Gospels," John A. T. Robinson presented a paper on "The New Look on the Fourth Gospel."[58] In this important

---

58. John A. T. Robinson, "The New Look at the Fourth Gospel," *TU* 73 (1959): 338–50 (reprinted in *Twelve New Testament Studies* [London: SCM, 1962], 94–106).

essay, Robinson outlines five features of the "Old Look" on John, favored by what he calls "Critical Orthodoxy," which demands dogmatic allegiance of would-be reasoned biblical scholars and theologians. The elements of the "Old Look" included: (a) John's use of the Synoptics as sources, (b) John's reflecting diaspora (post-70 CE non-Palestine) perspectives, (c) the Johannine evangelist's not knowing Jesus, (d) John's theology reflecting later theological developments, and (e) the Fourth Evangelist's certainly not being John the Apostle. Conversely, in light of recent research, the "New Look" on John infers: (a) John's use of independent traditions, (b) John's reflecting pre-70 CE Palestine-rooted perspectives, (c) the possibility of the Johannine evangelist having known Jesus, (d) John's theology reflecting early and later developments, and (e) taking the work of the Fourth Evangelist seriously, whether or not he was John the Apostle, although such a view cannot be ruled out entirely. Of course, Robinson was building a case for John's priority versus its posteriority, on which he expanded later with a formidable monograph.[59]

Robinson's work was highlighted a decade or so later, when Archibald Hunter's 1968 book on John featured "the New Look on John," in which the author argues for a renewed appreciation for its historicity.[60] In this work, Hunter carried the basis for Robinson's earlier thesis further, citing as evidence for the "New Look" the works of P. Gardner-Smith, Eduard Schweizer, E. C. Hoskins, Rudolf Bultmann, C. H. Dodd, C. K. Barrett, Victor Martin, and Raymond Brown in showing a renewed interest in John's historicity. Given John's autonomous tradition having originated in Palestine, even if finalized in a Diaspora setting, the case seemed strong for seeing John as an independent Jesus tradition with its own perspectives on Jesus and his ministry conveyed. As John's narrative clearly shows signs of being an independent tradition, featuring Hebrew and Aramaic features in rather simple Greek, covering the early Galilean and the non-Galilean ministry of Jesus in authentic ways, it is puzzling that Robinson's

---

59. See Robinson, *Priority of John*. His 1985 work was engaged critically at the Salzburg 2000 Symposium on John and the Synoptics, resulting in the collection of essays edited by Peter Hofrichter, *Für und wider die Priorität des Johannesevangeliums*, Theologische Texte und Studien 9 (Hildesheim: Olms, 2002). While nearly all scholars infer early and distinctive material within the Johannine tradition, the fact of its connections with the Johannine Epistles and Apocalypse, as well as some of its highly developed features, lead most scholars (rightly, I believe) to place its finalization around the turn of the first century CE, despite possessing primitive material and memory.

60. Archibald M. Hunter, *The Gospel of John: The New Look at the Fourth Gospel* (Philadelphia: Westminster, 1968). Especially suggestive are his treatments of topography and the course of Jesus's ministry in John (49–65) and the parables and sayings of Jesus in John (78–102). On the latter, see the groundbreaking book of Ruben Zimmermann, *Puzzling the Parables of Jesus: Methods and Interpretation* (Minneapolis: Fortress, 2015), especially 333–60.

(and Hunter's) signaling the "New Look" did not entirely win the day critically. A number of factors may have been involved.

Over three decades later, Robinson's influence was analyzed in the light of "New Currents" at work in Johannine global studies. Tom Thatcher notes that rather than apply new disciplines and explore new vistas onto the Johannine riddles, Robinson simply offers new evidence to address old issues: *line* and *author*. First, on the line, rather than move from Jesus → tradition → Synoptics → John, Robinson simply reverses the order of the final two elements: Jesus → tradition → John → Synoptics. Thus, any evidence pointing toward the lateness of John or John's engagement of Synoptic traditions would overturn the program. A second set of issues involves the fact that John's authorial riddles are terribly hard to solve, and during the interim, Johannine scholarship had moved from "line and author" to "*text* and *reader*." Therefore, in addition to the use of *newer methodologies*, the "New Currents" in Johannine interpretation has shown evidence of *new perspectives*, including a *global diversity of voices*, which continue to shape the ways scholars understand and address history, theology, and biblical texts.[61]

Other factors involving the Dodd-Robinson-Hunter paradigm's being eclipsed, or perhaps circumvented, point to other good work emerging, disciplinarily.[62] On one hand, the "New Look" on John was followed by several commentators, and some scholars explored the historical reliability of John's narrative, while others dismissed it categorically.[63] Three particular developments detracted somewhat from that thrust. First, J. Louis Martyn's 1968 book on *History and Theology in the Fourth Gospel* piqued the interest of New Testament scholars in the history of the Johannine situation—the second level of history, somewhat eclipsing the historicity of its tradition.[64] Thus, interests of Johannine scholars shifted

---

61. See also the incisive analysis of the tension between the older "New Look" and the intervening New Critical Orthodoxy by Tom Thatcher, "The New Current through John: The Old 'New Look' and the New Critical Orthodoxy," in *New Currents through John's Thought: A Global Perspective*, ed. Francisco Lozada Jr. and Tom Thatcher, RBS 54 (Atlanta: SBL Press, 2006), 1–26.

62. See, for instance, reviews of recent Johannine research: Harold W. Attridge, "Genre Bending in the Fourth Gospel," *JBL* 121 (2002): 3–21; and Paul N. Anderson, "Beyond the Shade of the Oak Tree: Recent Growth in Johannine Studies," *ExpTim* 119 (2008): 365–73.

63. In addition to Brown's commentary, see those of Lindars (1972), Schnackenburg (in English 1968–1982), Smith (1999), and Keener (2003), as well as the conservative-though-analytical commentaries of D. A. Carson, *The Gospel According to John*, Pillar New Testament Commentary (Grand Rapids: Eerdmans, 1991); Andreas Köstenberger, *John*, BECNT (Grand Rapids: Baker, 2004); and Ramsey Michaels, *The Gospel of John*, NICNT (Grand Rapids: Eerdmans, 2010). As examples of polar opposite approaches to Johannine historicity, see Maurice Casey, *Is John's Gospel True?* (London: Routledge, 1996); and Craig L. Blomberg, *The Historical Reliability of John's Gospel: Issues & Commentary* (Downers Grove, IL: IVP Academic, 2001).

64. J. Louis Martyn, *History and Theology in the Fourth Gospel*, 3rd ed. (Louisville: Westminster John Knox, 2003 [1968]); see also idem, *The Gospel of John in Christian History: Seven Glimpses into the Johannine Community*, rev. and expanded ed., ed. Paul N. Anderson, Johannine Monograph Series 8 (Eugene, OR: Wipf & Stock, 2019 [1978]). Martyn's work on the Johannine situation was also bolstered and expanded by Raymond E. Brown, *The Community of the Beloved Disciple* (Mahwah, NJ: Paulist, 1979). On the dialectical

from John's traditional material to its rhetorical use. Second, as Barrett's commentary and the Leuven School argued for seeing John's spiritualizing thrust as expanding upon Synoptic material, the autonomy of John's tradition was somewhat displaced.[65] Along these lines, Moody Smith noted some moving away from the advances of Gardner-Smith and Dodd to some of the conjectures of Streeter regarding John's spiritualization of Synoptic traditions.[66] Third, with Alan Culpepper's groundbreaking 1983 book on *The Anatomy of the Fourth Gospel* (Fortress) creating a wave of interest in the literary and rhetorical features of John's story of Jesus, literary interests among Johannine scholars have featured more prominently among Johannine scholars than historical interests. Thus the shift from John's *line and author* to John's *text and reader*, as described in the "New Currents" analysis.

Nonetheless, these interruptions to the "New Look" have not totally overturned its thrust, but what has emerged is something of a multidisciplinary set of studies forming something of what might be called a "Renewed Look" at John. First, while fascination for the later stage(s) of Johannine history has captivated the interest of many Johannine scholars, the basis for Martyn's paradigm itself has largely collapsed. Martyn built his paradigm upon the inference of a Signs Gospel underlying John's story of Jesus, allowing him to focus upon what the evangelist did with the material. However, diachronic theories imagining alien sources underlying the Johannine narrative have fallen on hard times, and there is absolutely no evidence for any of the three major and several minor sources supposedly employed by the evangelist within Bultmann's paradigm; nor is there any compelling evidence to support Robert Fortna's inference of a Signs Gospel (Fortna did his doctorate on this subject under Martyn).[67] Thus, the

---

Johannine situation, see also Wayne A. Meeks, "Man from Heaven in Johannine Sectarianism," *JBL* 91 (1972): 44–72; and D. Moody Smith, *Johannine Christianity: Essays on its Setting, Sources, and Theology* (Columbia: University of South Carolina Press, 1984).

65. C. K. Barrett, *The Gospel According to St. John*, 2nd ed. (London: SPCK, 1978 [1955]). See also Thomas L. Brodie, *The Quest for the Origin of John's Gospel: A Source-Oriented Approach* (Oxford: Oxford University Press, 1993); Frans Neirynck, "John and the Synoptics," in *L'évangile de Jean: Sources, rédaction, théologie*, ed. Marinus de Jonge, BETL 44 (Leuven: University Press, 1977): 73–106.

66. B. H. Streeter, *The Four Gospels: A Study of Origins* (London: Macmillan, 1924); see the critique of such movement by Smith, *John among the Gospels*.

67. Robert T. Fortna, *The Gospel of Signs: A Reconstruction of the Narrative Source Underlying the Fourth Gospel*, SNTSMS 11 (Cambridge: Cambridge University Press, 1970). Fortna then builds a case for the theological tension as rooted in the evangelist's dialogue with his imagined source: idem, *The Fourth Gospel and Its Predecessor: From Narrative Source to Present Gospel* (Philadelphia: Fortress, 1988). However, in light of the analyses of D. Moody Smith, *The Composition and Order of the Fourth Gospel*, 2nd ed., Johannine Monograph Series 2 (Eugene, OR: Wipf & Stock, 2015 [1965]); Gilbert Van Belle, *The Signs Source in the Fourth Gospel: Historical Survey and Critical Evaluation of the Semeia Hypothesis*, BETL 116 (Leuven: Peeters, 1994); and Anderson, *The Christology of the Fourth Gospel*, the evidentiary case for alien sources underlying the Johannine narrative has been virtually decimated.

early tradition underlying John's story of Jesus cannot be considered non-Johannine. Second, even if Johannine "independence" has given way to John's "autonomy," as John's familiarity with Mark has garnered greater acceptance among scholars, familiarity does not imply dependence. If John was produced for hearers and readers of Mark,[68] it reflects an augmentation, and to some degree a correction, of the first Gospel. Further, as Lamar Cribbs argued for Luke's access to John's tradition, several scholars have found that thesis plausible.[69] Therefore, simplistic views of the relation between the Synoptics and John reflecting a "one-way street"—thereby discounting John's story of Jesus as having no historical purchase—are critically unsustainable. Third, while analyses of the literary and rhetorical design of the Fourth Gospel have received extensive attention for several decades, this does not discount its historical origin and character.[70] After all, there is no such thing as non-rhetorical history, so the fact of John's literary design does not preclude the possibility of its reflecting historical memory, however and wherefrom it may have developed.[71] Thus, while the "New Look" ironically had been either discounted or obscured following Hunter's heralding its advance, what might be called an interdisciplinary and globally perspectival "Renewed Look" on John has nevertheless arisen in the twenty-first century.

In light of these developments, James Charlesworth concluded in 2010 that the Fourth Gospel can no longer be excluded from Jesus research and that ways must be found to explore its historically significant content in the light of other traditional sources. Charlesworth outlined the previous consensus regarding John's disuse by Jesus scholars as represented by such scholars as Bornkamm, Sanders, Crossan, Wright, and Vermes.[72] After citing ten reasons why John's presentation of Jesus's ministry should not be considered historically inferior

68. With Mackay, *John's Relationship with Mark*, and Bauckham, "John for Readers of Mark."

69. F. Lamar Cribbs, "St. Luke and the Johannine Tradition," *JBL* 90 (1971): 422–50; idem, "A Study of the Contacts that Exist between St. Luke and St. John," SBLSP 12.1 (Cambridge: SBL, 1973), 1–93; and idem, "The Agreements that Exist between Luke and John," SBLSP 18 (Missoula, MT: Scholars Press, 1979), 215–61. See also Mark Matson, *In Dialogue with Another Gospel? The Influence of the Fourth Gospel on the Passion Narrative of the Gospel of Luke*, SBLDS 178 (Atlanta: Society of Biblical Literature, 2001); Barbara Shellard, "The Relationship of Luke and John: A Fresh Look at an Old Problem," *Journal of Theological Studies* 46.1 (1995): 71–98; idem, *New Light on Luke: Its Purpose, Sources and Literary Context*, JSNTSup 215 (London: Sheffield Academic Press, 2002); and Paul N. Anderson, "Acts 4:19–20—An Overlooked First-Century Clue to Johannine Authorship and Luke's Dependence upon the Johannine Tradition," *The Bible and Interpretation* (Sept 2010): n.p. Online: www.bibleinterp.com/opeds/acts 357920.shtml.

70. Margaret Davies, *Rhetoric and Reference in the Fourth Gospel*, JSNT 69 (London: Sheffield Academic Press, 1992).

71. See, for instance, D. Moody Smith's analysis of John's presentation as *metahistorical* ("The Presentation of Jesus in the Fourth Gospel," *Interpretation* 31 [1977]: 367–78).

72. Charlesworth, "Historical Jesus in the Fourth Gospel," 4–13.

to those of the Synoptics, he lists five influential opinions supporting a new paradigm that includes the Fourth Gospel in Jesus research, including the works of John Meier, Gerd Theissen and Annette Merz, Richard Bauckham, Paul Anderson, and Moody Smith.[73] He then goes on to cite the value of recent archaeological work in connection with the historical *realia* of the Johannine narrative, and he notes the contribution of the John, Jesus, and History Project within this new paradigm.[74] Just a year earlier, Mark Allan Powell, who had chaired the Historical Jesus Section of the Society of Biblical Literature for several years, had also declared that the Gospel of John could no longer be ignored in the historical Quest of Jesus.[75]

In addition to the John, Jesus, and History Project, two other international ventures have also developed in the new millennium. First, in 2016, the Enoch Seminar hosted a special conference on "John the Jew: Reading the Gospel of John's Christology as a Form of Jewish Messianism" as the sixth conference in the series of Nangeroni Meetings, held in Camaldoli, Italy. In this conference, it became unquestionably clear that even some of the leading themes of Johannine Christology (the Son as equal to the Father, uncreated, christological titles, etc.) are by no means exceptional within Second Temple Jewish literature. Therefore, their origin was as likely to be Jewish as it was Hellenistic.[76] That same year, a third conference in the Princeton-Prague Symposium on the Historical Jesus emphasized "Illustrating How to Use the Gospel of John in Jesus Research." In those sessions held at Princeton Theological Seminary, top Johannine and Jesus scholars explored the reasons why the Fourth Gospel is fundamental to Jesus Research. Again, while views differed on John's relation to parallel traditions, the consensus was that John was doing something different—rooted in historical memory—while also contributing an autonomous understanding of the Jesus of history, not simply the Christ of faith.[77] Thus, a Fourth Quest for Jesus is not only called for in the new millennium; indeed, it is already well underway.

---

73. Charlesworth, "Historical Jesus in the Fourth Gospel," 34–39.

74. Charlesworth, "Historical Jesus in the Fourth Gospel," 13–34.

75. Powell, "'Things That Matter.'"

76. These essays are published in Benjamin E. Reynolds and Gabriele Boccaccini, eds., *Reading the Gospel of John's Christology as Jewish Messianism: Royal, Prophetic, and Divine Messiahs* (Leiden: Brill, 2018); my essay in that collection is Paul N. Anderson, "Jesus, the Eschatological Prophet in the Fourth Gospel: A Case Study in Dialectical Tensions," 271–99.

77. These essays are published in James H. Charlesworth, ed., *Jesus Research: The Gospel of John in Historical Inquiry*, Jewish and Christian Texts 26 (London: T&T Clark, 2019); my essay in that collection is Paul N. Anderson, "Why the Gospel of John is Fundamental to Jesus Research," 7–46.

A FOURTH QUEST FOR JESUS—AN INCLUSIVE APPROACH

After a century and a half of programmatically excluding the Gospel of John from Jesus research by critical scholars, the dehistoricization of John and the de-Johannification of Jesus can no longer be seen as critically viable. The Synoptics are theologically oriented as is John; John contains a good deal of mundane and history-congruent material not found in the Synoptics; and John and Mark clearly reflect two independent perspectives on the ministry of Jesus that may inform each other if compared to each other. Therefore, to some degree, the contest is between Markan and Johannine perspectives on Jesus, although the distinctive material in Matthew and Luke also corroborates Mark's presentation overall. Nonetheless, if all worthy resources are to be included in twenty-first century Jesus research, the Gospel of John can no longer be ignored in critically serviceable quests. The question is how to go about including John. That being the case, several advances in the quest deserve consideration.[78]

Inclusive Criteria for Determining Gospel Historicity

Rather than using criteria designed to favor Synoptic features over and against Johannine ones, new criteria for determining gospel historicity are required. Further, even though criteria of authenticity may point to some solid inferences, the material rejected is not necessarily inauthentic. The epistemological character of its origin must still be considered, and that might yet have implications for gospel historiography. With Morna Hooker's critique of Perrin's naïve assumptions along these lines nearly a half-century ago, because Jesus was a Jew, and because his followers sought to preserve what he taught, those two categories might well point *toward* historical memory of Jesus rather than away

---

78. It is worth noting that modern gospel-historians have not yet caught up with twentieth-century historiography and its post-structuralist developments, let alone become able to move into the twenty-first century, disciplinarily. A mere overview of the last half century or more of leading critical theory on historiography will sober one's romanticized estimations of von Ranke's nineteenth-century dictum, *wie es eigentlich gewesen* ("how things actually were"). See, for instance, Marc Bloch, *The Historian's Craft* (New York: Vintage Books, 1953); Ernst Breisach, *Historiography: Ancient, Medieval, and Modern*, 3rd ed. (Chicago: University of Chicago Press, 2007 [1983]); E. H. Carr, *What Is History?* (Cambridge: Cambridge University Press, 1961); John Lewis Gaddis, *The Landscape of History: How Historians Map the Past* (Oxford: Oxford University Press, 2002); Gina Hens-Piazza, *The New Historicism* (Minneapolis: Fortress, 2002); Georg G. Iggers, *Historiography in the Twentieth Century: From Scientific Objectivity to the Postmodern Challenge* (Middletown, CT: Wesleyan University Press, 1997); Martha C. Howell and Walter Prevenier, *Reliable Sources: An Introduction to Historical Methods* (Ithaca, NY: Cornell University Press, 2001); Keith Jenkins, *Re-Thinking History* (London: Routledge, 1991); Karl Popper, *The Poverty of Historicism* (London: Routledge, 1957); Aram H. Veeser, ed., *The New Historicism* (London: Routledge, 1989); Hayden White, *Metahistory: The Historical Imagination in Nineteenth-Century Europe* (Baltimore: Johns Hopkins University Press, 1973). Methodologies for determining Johannine historicity, alongside that of the Synoptics, deserve to benefit from the best of critical theory, not simply its earlier forerunners.

from it. Thus, the criteria of *dissimilarity* and *embarrassment* are flawed from the start.[79] While they may indeed help us identify material unlikely to be concocted, they may also function to eliminate a good deal of worthy historical material not measuring up to what might be called "criteria of idiosyncrasy."

Likewise, if *multiple attestation* functions to eliminate all distinctive content in Matthew and Luke, let alone John—even if it reflects historical memory, that criterion is likewise flawed. Sometimes (most often?) a distinctive report or pericope is included because of historical interest, not simply as a factor of theological investment. Thus, the leading criteria emerging from the New Quest deserve critical scrutiny themselves,[80] and the volume gathered by Chris Keith and Anthony Le Donne performs a set of incisive analyses regarding the strengths and weaknesses of what have come to be standard criteria.[81] Further, because *naturalism* is itself a subjective category, and because *coherence* is finally a circular inference, the leading four or five criteria for determining gospel historicity are largely flawed, especially if they are used to eliminate material from the quest, based upon such a rhetorically constructed sieve. If the Fourth Gospel were

---

79. Morna D. Hooker, "Christology and Methodology," *NTS* 17 (1970): 480–87; and idem, "On Using the Wrong Tool," *Theology* (1972): 570–81. See also idem, "Foreword," in *Jesus, Criteria, and the Demise of Authenticity*, ed. Chris Keith and Anthony Le Donne (London: T&T Clark, 2012), xiii–xvii. To paraphrase Hooker, sometimes a paraphrase, even if it is not a direct citation, may be more representative of historical authenticity than a verbatim quotation, if the latter is taken out of its larger context.

80. See, for instance, the work of Edward T. Wright, "On the Historical Reliability of Ancient Biographies: A Thorough Examination of Xenophon's *Agesilaus*, Cornelius Nepos's *Atticus*, Tacitus's *Agricola*, and The Gospel According to John" (PhD diss., Asbury Theological Seminary, 2019) where between 70–80 percent of their material is singularly attested. This does not prove, however, that none of that material is confirmedly ahistorical. With Anthony Le Donne, "The Rise of the Quest for an Authentic Jesus: An Introduction to the Crumbling Foundations of Jesus Research," in Keith and Le Donne, *Jesus, Criteria, and the Demise of Authenticity*, 3–21, one of the cardinal flaws of modern biblical criticism is its striking negligence regarding self-criticism. The way that I put that concern is to call for *second criticality*. Ricoeur's *second naïveté* is not the end of dialectical thinking; analytical thought must also criticize criticism as well as tradition. If criticality fails to criticize criticism, it cannot bear the esteemed mantle of critical authority. Thus, being mindful of strengths and weaknesses of one's own views, in addition to those of others (both traditional and critical), is required of worthy academe. See Paul N. Anderson, "Second Criticality—An Interdisciplinary Approach to the New Testament," in *From Crisis to Christ: A Contextual Introduction to the New Testament* (Nashville: Abingdon, 2014), x–xii.

81. In this important volume, Keith and Le Donne, *Jesus, Criteria, and the Demise of Authenticity*, valuable critiques of the leading criteria for determining historicity within the New Quest are posed. In addition to Chris Keith's challenging of *form-critical methodologies* (25–48), Jens Schröter's critique of *authenticity criteria* for determining historicity (49–70), and Loren Stuckenbruck's analysis of the use of Hebraic/Aramaic features for determining primitivity (73–94), the criterion of *coherence* is critiqued by Le Donne (95–114), the criterion of *dissimilarity* is critiqued by Dagmar Winter (115–31), the criterion of *embarrassment* is critiqued by Rafael Rodríguez (132–51), and the criterion of *multiple attestation* is critiqued by Mark Goodacre (152–69). In the concluding essays by Dale Allison (186–99) and Chris Keith (205), the way forward is projected in two ways. First, criteria for eliminating material from banks of historical data should themselves be marginalized; inauthenticity criteria cannot establish what they claim. Second, gospel-historiography should move toward memory analysis, as tradents were humans—feeling, thinking, perceiving, remembering, recasting, delivering, writing, editing beings—requiring inquiry into cognitive-critical analyses along the way.

seen to be in play within the larger venture, however, several inclusive criteria for determining gospel historicity are as follows:[82]

- *Corroborative Impression Versus Multiple Attestation.* A significant problem with the criterion of multiple attestation is that by definition it excludes everything that might be added to Mark's account of Jesus's ministry by other gospel traditions and writers. Further, if Mark was used by Matthew and Luke, then triple-tradition material may simply denote their uses of Mark rather than reflecting independent attestations of a historical memory or event. And, if anything within John—or for that matter, in Matthew or Luke—is intended to augment or correct Mark, it is automatically excluded from consideration, even if the basis for such a judgment is flawed. A more adequate approach looks for corroborative sets of impressions, wherein paraphrases, alternative ways of putting something, or distinctive renderings of a similar feature inform a fuller understanding of the ministry of Jesus. Such an approach would thus include the Johannine witness rather than excluding it programmatically.

- *Primitivity Versus Dissimiliarity or Embarrassment.* While the criteria of dissimilarity and embarrassment might keep one from mistaking later Christian views for earlier ones going back to Jesus, they also tend to distort the historiographic process itself. What if apostolic Christians and their successors *actually did get something right* in their memories of Jesus? Or, what if Jesus of Nazareth *actually did teach conventional Jewish views* during his ministry? The criterion of dissimilarity would thereby exclude such features from historical consideration, allowing only the odd or embarrassing features to be built upon. Even if such data are unlikely to be concocted, to exclude other material from the database of material creates an odd assortment of portraiture material, which if used would create a distortive image of Jesus. And, while embarrassing features might be less likely to have been concocted, does a collage of unseemliness really represent a subject better than an assortment of honorable and less honorable features? A more adequate way forward is to identify primitive material, seeking to distinguish it from its more developed counterparts. This may include Palestine-familiarity features, Aramaic and Hebraic

---

82. These criteria were presented at the 2009 SBL meetings in our methodology session in my paper, Paul N. Anderson, "Dialectical History and the Fourth Gospel." They were later summarized in *From Crisis to Christ* (175–76), and Paul N. Anderson and Jaime Clark-Soles, "Introduction and Overview," in Anderson, Just, and Thatcher, *Glimpses of Jesus*, 1–25, adapted here from pages 18–19.

terms, primitive institutional developments, and other undeveloped material less influenced by the later mission to the gentiles.

- *Critical Realism Versus Dogmatic Naturalism or Supranaturalism.* Just as dogmatic supranaturalism is an affront to historical inquiry, so is dogmatic naturalism—especially when it functions to exclude anything that might approximate perceptions of the wondrous in gospel narratives. John's prologue was probably added to a later or final edition of the Gospel, so its cosmic perspective should not eclipse or distort the more conventional features of John's narrative, just as the birth narratives of Matthew and Luke should not eclipse their more mundane features. Rather, political realism, religious anthropology, and social-sciences analyses should provide helpful lenses for understanding the perception of Jesus as a Galilean prophetic figure in all four gospel traditions. After all, John's narrative begins in ways similar to Mark's, launched by the association of Jesus with John the Baptist (John 1:6–8, 15, 19–42—likely the original beginning of John's narrative), and it concludes with his arrest, trials, and death in Jerusalem at the hand of the Romans. Therefore, historical and critical realism acknowledges the historical problem of wondrous claims, but it also considers cognitive, religious, political, and societal aspects of realism that might account for such impressions.

- *Open Coherence Versus Closed Portraiture.* Two central flaws in coherence-oriented criteria for determining historicity in the quest for Jesus include the circularity of the approach and the closed character of its portraiture. On one hand, the Gospels form the primary database for determining a coherent impression of Jesus of Nazareth; on the other, those same Gospels are evaluated on the basis of information contained within them. Further, scholars too easily form a view of what cannot represent a feature of Jesus's ministry based upon the narrowing down of what he must have done and said. Therefore, an open approach to coherence, including possible and plausible features (not just likely or certain features) provides a more textured approach to the subject.

In addition to these proposed methodologies, other criteria for determining historicity may also be serviceable, and scholars are encouraged to develop their own criteria for conducting gospel historiography with John in the mix. For instance, within John's composition history and situation history, emerging insights from particular engagements with other traditions or issues in the audience may be profitable for understanding how Jesus was remembered within John's story of Jesus. Whatever the case, scholars must be mindful of the assumptions upon which a judgment is based, qualifying the outcomes of their inquiries on the basis of those givens. The Jesus Seminar did this quite clearly, although many of their assumptions were wrong at the outset, as their criteria had been crafted in order to further an explicitly anti-Johannine bias.[83] Within an inclusive quest, however, the playing field is leveled, and John thus becomes a resource for confirming and also challenging perspectives in other gospel traditions, as well as vice versa.

Gradations of Certainty

A second plank in the Fourth Quest's platform involves a more nuanced approach to gradations of certainty. While the Jesus Seminar sought to drive an either/or wedge between the opinions of scholars on the question of historicity, such an approach fails to allow a potential middle ground, given that some issues are terribly difficult to decide based on the available evidence. Within the John, Jesus, and History Project, the editors did not stipulate how our authors should approach their subjects; we simply asked them to perform their analyses of Johannine themes and texts and to describe any implications that might follow regarding the historical Jesus. Therefore, whether a detail or feature of the Johannine text advances or does not advance knowledge of the historical Jesus, we asked each of our authors to describe their degree of certainty regarding each judgment, including its critical basis. We thus encouraged our authors to locate their various judgments along the following grid and to say why they did so.

- Certainly not (1–14%)
- Unlikely (15–29%)
- Questionable (30–44%)
- Possible (45–54%)
- Plausible (55–69%)
- Likely (70–84%)
- Certain (85–99%)

An important advantage of allowing a larger middle area is that both positive and negative certainties are extremely elusive within any history-adducing

---

83. Benefitting from the critiques of Hooker, Keith, and Le Donne, these new criteria are designed not to eliminate material; they are primarily designed to discern plausible material worthy of including Jesus research. See Gerd Theissen and Dagmar Winter, *The Quest for the Plausible Jesus: The Question of Criteria* (Louisville: Westminster John Knox, 2002).

venture, especially the quest for Jesus. On this matter, *positivism*—if it is employed in any approach to ancient historiography—must be plied with reference to *falsification* as well as *verification*. Too often calls for positivistic judgments are levied only in one direction: challenging historical claims yet failing to establish inferred falsification. While claiming certainty that something happened is an elusive matter, so is claiming that something cannot have happened, or did not happen—an error that positivist scholars too easily commit.

Additionally, a fallacious tendency within modern critical studies involves moving facilely from "not certain" to "certainly not." Therefore, sound judgments must be more measured in their analyses, and more nuanced gradations of certainty deserve to be employed by gospel historians. An "unlikely" appraisal of certainty need not be jammed into a "certainly not" category, when proving such a thesis lacks a compelling basis. Likewise, an inference might not fall into categories of "certain" or "likely," but it might simply be "plausible"—posing at least some service to the historical quest for Jesus in corroborative ways. Likewise, a feature might not be "unlikely," but it may simply be problematic or "questionable," or even "possible." So, including "plausible," "possible," and "questionable" as workable measures increases the middle ground within Jesus research in that it allows more nuanced approaches to the issues rather than forcing either-or judgments.[84] And of course, no space is allotted either for 0 percent impossibility or 100 percent certainty, as total certainty in ancient historiography is impossible to decide. Historical agnosticism must thus remain an element within honest inquiry, rather than forcing a judgment pro or con in all cases. Whatever gradations of certainty scholars may choose, however, they should articulate *why* they make such a judgment, which then invites other scholars to engage meaningfully their judgments, bases, and implications.

The Dialogical Autonomy of the Fourth Gospel

The overall appraisal of Johannine composition over the last several decades has seen a movement away from being a derivative composition. Given sustained analyses of Bultmann's highly diachronic approach, few scholars today imagine John's use of alien sources or traditions.[85] There is absolutely no evidence of such, and when all of Bultmann's criteria for identifying underlying and overlaying sources are applied to John 6—the place where four of the five sources should

---

84. With Theissen and Winter, *Quest for the Plausible Jesus*.

85. Thus, Kysar reports a change of mind regarding John's use of sources: Robert Kysar, "Review of *The Christology of the Fourth Gospel* by Paul N. Anderson," *RBL* 1 (1999): 38–42.

be showcased—the distribution is random.[86] Smith and van Belle, however, embraced different approaches to John's tradition, which are currently followed by various Johannine scholars. Representing the majority view, Smith follows Gardner-Smith, Dodd, Brown, and others in seeing John's tradition as an autonomous Jesus tradition, perhaps with some Synoptic contact but not dependent on the Synoptics. Van Belle and the Leuven School, along with some followers of Barrett, infer that if the Fourth Evangelist expanded theologically upon elements within his own story of Jesus (which he does), he plausibly expanded upon synoptic stories of Jesus, which might account for similarities and differences between the Synoptics and John. The problem with such a view, however, is that 85 percent of John has no parallel with or connection to the Synoptics, and every instance in which there is a connection fails to show a verbatim or exact similarity for more than a word or two. Thus, contact or similarity cannot imply literary dependence, as Matthew clearly depended on Mark.[87] Rather, John's tradition appears to be a self-standing tradition, which likely had some contact with other traditions, the details of which must be sorted out with particularity.

While John's narrative holds together as a unit, it does reflect stages of development and a final editorial process, at least. Scholars have come to appreciate the overall unity of John's narrative since the influential work of Alan Culpepper was published in 1983,[88] yet it still has several perplexities that are best explained by the inference of a final editor adding some material to an earlier stage of its composition. These include the Prologue (John 1:1–18) and chapters 6, 15–17, and 21 (as well as 19:34–35) as the most plausible inferences regarding later material added by the final editor to the earlier work of the Beloved Disciple (according to John 21:23–24).[89]

Therefore, building on the works of Brown, Lindars, Smith, and others, the Johannine tradition enjoyed several decades of oral delivery (probably in Galilee and Judea), and after a move to a Hellenistic setting (traditionally Asia Minor) the material was gathered into written units—likely having some familiarity with Mark's rendering. According to Ian Mackay, the evangelist plausibly heard

---

86. Anderson, *Christology of the Fourth Gospel*, 70–166.

87. Anderson, *Christology of the Fourth Gospel*, 97–104. In Barrett's view, John had either read or become familiar with Mark's content in some way, although "it is certain that John did not 'use' Mark as Matthew did" (C. K. Barrett, *The Gospel According to St. John: An Introduction with Commentary and Notes, Second Edition* [Louisville: Westminster John Knox, 1978], 45).

88. R. Alan Culpepper, *Anatomy of the Fourth Gospel: A Study in Literary Design: Foundations and Facets* (Philadelphia: Fortress, 1983).

89. So argues Lindars, *Gospel of John*, who is followed by John Ashton, *Understanding the Fourth Gospel* (Oxford: Clarendon, 1991), and myself independently, in seeing his basic two-edition approach to John's composition as the most plausible means of dealing with John's literary riddles and aporias.

Mark's narrative performed among the churches and produced something similar but different, as an alternative to Mark.[90] Thus, the first edition or written stage of John's story of Jesus likely came together between 80 and 85 CE. With Brown, however, the Beloved Disciple probably continued preaching, teaching, and perhaps writing until his death around 100 CE, and the final editor, who likely was the author of the Epistles, finalized the Johannine Gospel and circulated it among the churches after his death.[91] This modest two-edition approach to John's composition deals with the most difficult perplexities in the most efficient ways, accounting for the development of the Johannine tradition in light of other materials, including other Gospels and other Johannine writings.

John among the Gospels—Not Exactly a One-Way Street(er)!

When considered among the Gospels, the likelihood of John's being the last Gospel to be written, however, has led to several flawed inferences. First, the precedent of Matthew's and Luke's uses of Mark does not imply that John used Mark or any of the other Gospels as sources, even if there were Johannine familiarity with one or more of these traditions. If the Fourth Evangelist had his own story to tell, he might have worked off of Mark's pattern, but if familiarity is inferred, his operation would thus have been augmentive and corrective, producing an alternative view. After all, the five signs in John's first edition (as referenced above) are precisely the ones *not* included in Mark. Second, rather than having access to Mark as a written source, John's familiarity with Mark appears to have been oral-aural in its contacts, perhaps involving more than one form and stage of intertraditional contact. Further, if Luke had heard some of John's material being delivered, this might account for the fact that Luke departs from Mark at least six dozen times in ways that cohere with John; most of Luke's typical characteristics are not found in John, but several of John's features are indeed found in Luke. Thus, most Johannine-Synoptic relations appear to have originated from oral-tradition engagements, or even secondary orality, rather than the working off of written texts directly. Third, even though John was likely finalized last, this does not imply that Johannine-Synoptic contacts reflect the Synoptics' influence upon John. John's oral tradition may well have been one of Luke's sources (see Luke 1:2), and John's traditional contacts with early Markan and later Matthean traditions may well have gone both ways, especially

---

90. Mackay, *John's Relationship with Mark*.

91. See Paul N. Anderson, "On 'Seamless Robes' and 'Leftover Fragments'—A Theory of Johannine Composition," in *The Origins of John's Gospel*, ed. Stanley E. Porter and Hughson Ong, Johannine Studies 2 (Leiden: Brill, 2015), 169–218.

if they took place in the oral stages of tradition.[92] Therefore, in contrast to B. H. Streeter's view that Johannine-Synoptic contacts reflect the Synoptics' influences upon John, "interfluence" is the more plausible inference, as it cannot be assumed that the impact went only in one direction.[93]

The value of viewing John's story of Jesus within an overall bi-optic hypothesis is that it helps one understand why John might be similar and dissimilar from the Synoptics. If the Prologue was indeed added to an earlier stage of John's composition, John's story of Jesus appears to have originally begun, like Mark, with the ministry of John the Baptist. And, if the feeding and sea-crossing narratives in John 6 were added later, as well as the great catch of fish in John 21, the five signs in John's first edition appear to have augmented Mark as an apologetic presentation of Jesus as the Jewish Messiah. Thus, John's narrative appears to augment Mark in terms of the chronological (first and second signs of Jesus—John 2:11; 4:54) and geographical elements of Jesus's ministry (three signs in Judea). It also appears that John's later material may have functioned to harmonize John's story of Jesus with those of the Synoptics, and yet the first and final endings of John's narrative (John 20:30–31; 21:25) both appear to defend its distinctive presentation over and against otherwise known renderings—implicitly Mark first and then the other Gospels later. John's distinctive I-Am sayings and presentation of a Jesus who speaks in the language of the evangelist, however, reflects the evangelist's paraphrastic rendering of Jesus and his teachings in his own words, and by the time the Johannine oral tradition is rendered in written form, John's presentation of Jesus must be seen as highly interpretive, even if it represents a recasting of historical memory in Johannine terms.

---

92. A "Bi-Optic Hypothesis," outlining particular relations between the Johannine tradition and each of the Synoptic traditions, is spelled out in Anderson, *Fourth Gospel and the Quest for Jesus*, 101–26, and elsewhere.

93. Streeter, *Four Gospels*. For instance, with Raymond Brown (*An Introduction to the Gospel of John*, ed. Francis J. Moloney [New York: Doubleday, 2003], 102–4), if the oral-tradition preachers underlying Mark and John may have traveled together in ministry (cf. Acts 8), this might account for buzz-words sticking between the Markan and Johannine traditions that were not furthered in Matthew's and Luke's incorporations of written Mark. And, if the traditions were still in their informal stages, it is impossible to know if the influence went in one direction or another. Thus, cross-influence (Brown), or interfluence (Anderson) is the most plausible means of accounting for common details shared distinctively between Mark and John. Likewise, later engagements between Matthean and Johannine traditions regarding ecclesiology and leadership may also reflect some degree of interfluentiality. Further, given the facts that Mark and Matthew reference details found only in John (Mark 14:58; 15:29 ← John 2:19; Matt 21:14 ← John 5:1–15; 9:1–7), and that Luke departs from Mark over six dozen times in ways that coincide with John, and that even the Q tradition preserves a remarkably Johannine saying (Matt 11:27; Luke 10:22 ← John 3:35; 7:27–28; 10:14–15; 13:3–4; 17:1–3, 22–25), it cannot be naively assumed that intertraditional movement was only a "one-way street," even if John was finalized last among the Gospels.

A Synchronicity of Tradition: A Diachronicity of Situation

Given John's synchronicity of tradition, even if more than one authorial or editorial hand was involved, its presentation of Jesus still hangs together in unity, and it deserves to be interpreted as a whole. As Barrett often pointed out, after all John's narrative at least made sense to *someone*, and it deserves to be interpreted that way by modern scholars, as well. On the other hand, no other corpus of multi-formal writings in the New Testament is as corroborative of a contextual situation in early Christianity as the Johannine writings, and what the Epistles and Apocalypse contribute to a reading of the Gospel is an appreciation for the setting(s) in which John's story of Jesus developed and was delivered. The Johannine situational context thus also goes some distance in accounting for how John is different from Mark and the Synoptics, and why. If the development of the Johannine situation can be seen in three phases (the first in Palestine; the second and third in a post-70 CE Diaspora setting), the Epistles and Apocalypse illuminate the later two phases, and evidence within the Gospel itself illuminates the first, in addition to the second and third phases. Upon closer scrutiny, there appear to be at least two crises, or contextual engagements, within each of these three phases—crises that are largely sequential but somewhat overlapping.

In the first phase (30–70 CE), tensions are clear between *the Galilean Jesus and the Judean religious authorities*. John's author is familiar with Galilee, Samaria, and Judea, and he endeavors to show how Jesus and his prophetic agency from the Father was embraced by many but ironically rejected by the Judean leaders, who were blind to continuing revelation because of their fixed religious convictions. The Johannine evangelist endeavors to show that Jesus fulfilled the role of the Mosaic prophet (Deut 18:15–22), and yet his rejection by the Judean authorities can only be explained on the basis of the blind and miscomprehending audiences predicted by Isaiah (Isa 6:9–10).[94] A second set of engagements with *followers of John the Baptist* is palpable in presenting him as testifying of Jesus (*not* himself) as the one in whom people should trust. That being the case, the Johannine presentation of John the Baptist is not simply the lead witness to Jesus's messiahship, but he also points Baptist adherents in later generations and further regions to Jesus as the anticipated Jewish Messiah.[95] These two apologetic interests appear to

---

94. Paul N. Anderson, "The Having-Sent-Me Father—Aspects of Agency, Encounter, and Irony in the Johannine Father-Son Relationship," in *Semeia 85: God the Father in the Gospel of John*, ed. Adele Reinhartz (Atlanta: SBL Press, 2001): 33–57.

95. On the history of the Johannine situation, see Paul N. Anderson, "The *Sitz im Leben* of the Johannine Bread of Life Discourse and its Evolving Context," in *Critical Readings of John 6*, ed. Alan Culpepper, BibInt 22 (Leiden: Brill, 1997), 1–59; and idem, "Bakhtin's Dialogism and the Corrective Rhetoric of the Johannine Misunderstanding Dialogue: Exposing Seven Crises in the Johannine Situation," in *Bakhtin and Genre Theory in Biblical Studies*, ed. Roland Boer, SemeiaSt 63 (Atlanta: SBL Press, 2007), 133–59. Raymond

have developed within the early stages of the Johannine tradition, and they also account to some degree for the selection of material included in the narrative.

In the second phase (70–85 CE), the Johannine evangelist and others moving to a setting within the Pauline mission continue to be engaged with *the Jewish communities of Ephesus or some other area* (with Brown, there is no superior site than the unanimous second-century memory of John residing in Ephesus), but they also encounter gentile believers and are forced to straddle both communities. Here the identification of Jesus as fulfilling the typologies of Moses and Elijah continues to develop, bolstered by attestations from Jewish Scripture, and the first edition of John's narrative is formed, attesting the five signs of Jesus (assuming John 6 and 21 were added later) as a parallel to the five books of Moses. In answering monotheistic appeals to Moses and the Shema (Deut 6:1–9), the Johannine evangelist appealed to the prophetic agency of Moses and his prophecy that God would raise up a prophet who would not speak his own words but only God's words—attested by their having come true on multiple occasions (Deut 18:15–22). The acute Jewish-Johannine crisis now is with the local synagogue in Asia Minor. The inclusion of "Nazoreans" in the Birkat ha-Minim (a curse against the heretics) added to the twelfth of eighteen benedictions within synagogue-worship liturgies around that time functioned to discipline perceived ditheism among Jesus adherents. It may have resulted, though, in alienating some Johannine believers, who felt excluded from synagogue fellowship (John 9:22; 12:42; 16:2). It could also be that the Johannine schism referenced in 1 John 2:18–25 reflects some Jewish adherents to "the Father" departing from the Johannine community, having been proselytized back into the local synagogue by friends and family. To reject the Son is to forfeit the Father. A second crisis during this phase is also evident within the first edition material: Jesus is presented as the divine Son as an affront and challenge to *the imposition of emperor worship, required during the reign of Domitian* (81–96 CE). Thus, the ironic presentation of Pilate as the "impotent potentate" and the climactic confession of Thomas, "My Lord and my God!" (John 20:28) furthered the Johannine apologetic thrust in the face of imperial hegemony. Not only is Jesus the Prophet like Moses—fulfilling Jewish Scripture, but he also is the

---

Brown includes four or five of these six dialectical tensions in his overall Johannine theory (*Introduction to the Gospel of John*, 151–88); for an engagement of the Roman imperial backdrop, see Richard J. Cassidy, *John's Gospel in New Perspective: Christology and the Realities of Roman Power*, Johannine Monograph Series 3 (Eugene, OR: Wipf & Stock, 2015 [1992]). See also Paul N. Anderson, "The Community that Raymond Brown Left Behind—Reflections on the Dialectical Johannine Situation," in *Communities in Dispute: Current Scholarship on the Johannine Epistles*, ed. Paul N. Anderson and R. Alan Culpepper, ECL 13 (Atlanta: SBL Press, 2014), 47–93.

divine Son—putting Roman emperor-worship hegemony in its place. Likewise, the last verse of 1 John (5:21) reflects the overall concern in living under empire: "Dear children, keep yourselves from idols!"

The third phase (85–100 CE) involved an expansion of the Johannine community into several communities within the larger Jesus-adherent situation, which included other Jewish and gentile believers in Jesus as the Christ. Thus, Johannine "Christianity" has not yet individuated totally from its parental Judaism and is not sectarian, but is cosmopolitan, which is why it faces a number of crises and tensions in seeking to maintain its Jewish ethos and corporate unity. An emerging crisis within this phase of the Johannine situation involved *gentile Christian docetizing teachers and traveling ministers,* who appear to have been teaching doctrines of cultural assimilation—believing in Jesus as the Jewish Messiah but not expecting his followers to embrace outward signs or practices of Judaism (1 John 4:1–3). They appear to have been willing to embrace some aspects of emperor worship and/or related pagan festivities (1 John 2:15–17; 5:16–21), heralding a non-suffering Jesus as a legitimation. Thus, the Docetists in the Johannine situation were not Gnostics; those developments happened later. Rather, docetic Christology legitimated cheap grace and easy discipleship, and most of the incarnational thrust of the Johannine narrative can be found in the later material (John 1:14; 6:51–58; 19:34–35; 21:18–23). A second challenge within this phase is evidenced by *tensions with the primacy-loving Diotrephes and his kin* (3 John 9–10), which the Elder as the final editor addresses in gathering and circulating the testimony of the Beloved Disciple. Thus, the later material in John's story of Jesus pointedly asserts the leadership of Christ (rather than Peter, John 6:68–69), leading all believers through the present work of the Holy Spirit (the *paraklētos,* John 15–16), and the priestly prayer of Jesus implores unity within the community of believers, who are in the world but not of the world (John 17).

These developments in the Johannine situation therefore go some distance toward accounting for the contextual thrust of John's witness to Jesus as the Messiah/Christ in ways that are distinctive from Mark, but which are also crafted to target the evangelist's *apologetic interests* (especially in the first edition—leading people to believe in Jesus as the Jewish Messiah/Christ), while also serving a needed *pastoral function* (especially in the later material—calling for believers to abide/remain in Christ and his fellowship) against centrifugal tensions within the later Johannine situation. John's story of Jesus thus appears to be rooted in historical memory, even going back to the ministry of Jesus in Galilee, Samaria, and Judea, but it also has been rendered in the paraphrastic language of the evangelist and is crafted to meet the needs of later audiences along the way. This accounts for the fact of John's primitive topographical and mundane features, as well as its interpretive renderings and expansions upon incidents and details. It should not, however, be seen as an expansion upon the Prologue; rather, the Christ-hymn of John 1:1–5, 9–14, and 16–18 (like 1 John 1:1–3) should be seen first as a community's confessional reflection upon John's story of Jesus, delivered and received within a Hellenistic setting.

As John's story of Jesus probably began with references to the Baptist's pointing to Jesus (John 1:6–8, 15, 19–42), echoing Mark's opening sections, the community's Christ-hymn (plausibly developing in ways similar to Phil 2:5–11; Col 1:15–20; Heb 1:1–4) appears to have been added to the narrative as an engaging introduction to the final edition of the Fourth Gospel, performing also a function similar to the birth narratives of Matthew and Luke.[96] Thus, the high-christological thrust of the Johannine Prologue should *not* be seen as "the first stroke of the Johannine quill," eclipsing all mundane and earth-bound content, projecting an image of "God striding over the earth" over the following narrative, as earlier scholars had assumed. No. The Prologue also emphasizes the Word-become-flesh (John 1:14), whereby audiences claimed to have encountered the Johannine dialectical presentation of Jesus as Christ, presented in both fleshly and glorious terms. In that sense, the effect of the Johannine narrative is bolstered by an experientially engaging introduction, and the worship hymn of the community is then grounded by the Johannine narrative, presenting an alternative story of Jesus, connecting Jesus remembered with later audiences.

VENTURING INTO THE FOURTH QUEST: A PRELIMINARY SKETCH

In my best judgment as a Johannine scholar, the above approaches to the Johannine riddles (theological, historical, and literary) account most effectively for John's distinctive presentation of Jesus as the Christ. In that sense, the epistemological origins of John's *theological tensions* are factors of: a) a dialectical thinker, presenting many an issue in both-and ways, reflecting on earlier perceptions and their adjustments in the light of later experiences and understandings; b) a Prophet-Like-Moses agency schema rooted in Deuteronomy 18:15–22, whereby

---

96. On the origin and function of the Johannine Prologue, see Paul N. Anderson, "On Guessing Points and Naming Stars—The Epistemological Origins of John's Christological Tensions," in *The Gospel of St. John and Christian Theology*, ed. Richard Bauckham and Carl Mosser (Grand Rapids: Eerdmans, 2007), 311–45; and idem, "The Johannine *Logos*-Hymn: A Cross-Cultural Celebration of God's Creative-Redemptive Work," in *Creation Stories in Dialogue: The Bible, Science, and Folk Traditions*, Radboud Prestige Lecture Series, ed. R. Alan Culpepper and Jan van der Watt, BibInt 139 (Leiden: Brill, 2016), 219–42.

the Son represents the Father authentically; c) the dialectical Johannine situation calls for emphasizing the divine agency of Jesus as the Christ when apologetic interests are at hand, while emphasizing the human and suffering Jesus when countering docetizing tendencies in the later Johannine situation; and d) the rhetorical crafting of the narrative employs irony, repetition, and characterization as a means of engaging later audiences with John's story of Jesus.[97]

John's *historical riddles*, however, are explicable epistemologically as factors of: a) a dialectical thinker with his own story of Jesus to tell—emphasizing some features in his own paraphrastic language—making connections between earlier perceptions and later understandings intratraditionally; b) presenting an individuated memory of Jesus as an alternative to Mark, augmenting the first circulated gospel narrative chronologically and geographically, and setting some of Mark's presentation straight as the "second" gospel; c) continuing to translate the Palestine-rooted ministry of Jesus for later Jewish and Hellenistic audiences—explaining customs and preserving Aramaic and Hebrew features of early memory while also expanding upon their later relevance; d) harmonizing the later features of John's presentation of Jesus with the fuller Synoptic record—adding the feeding and sea-crossing narratives, the ambivalent restoration of Peter, and a worship hymn, while also augmenting the Synoptic view—emphasizing a more primitive and familial ecclesiology including the role of women, a suffering Jesus, and appealing to the Beloved Disciple's memory as an authoritative traditional source.

Finally, John's *literary perplexities* are best accounted for on the bases that, while we have an overall synchronicity of tradition, there is something of a diachronicity of situation and development within John's story of Jesus. Thus, a) movement from oral tradition to written tradition accounts for some of the aporias and sequence oddities in the narrative, as what had been previously narrated is either reflected upon or anticipated in written form; b) repetitions and variations reflect the narrator's emphases rather than the adding of extraneous material; c) later material does appear to be added to an earlier stage of the material, and it is more than plausible that the author of the Johannine Epistles sought to preserve the work of the evangelist by adding the John 1:1–18 and John 21 as well as chapters 6 and 15–17 and a few other features (such as 19:34–35); d) the final compiler attests to the veracity of the Beloved Disciple's testimony and circulates it as a compelling memory of Jesus and his ministry around the turn of the century, defending its distinctive selection of material among the other

---

97. Anderson, *Christology of the Fourth Gospel*, 137–69, 252–65.

Gospels as an alternative Jesus tradition worthy of consideration and embrace (John 21:23–25).

Thus, in light of John's dialogical autonomy, the origins and character of its theological, historical, and literary riddles are more fully understood, and when making use of the revised criteria for determining Jesus-research historicity, a sketch of what may result in further Jesus research is as follows.[98]

1. Jesus in Primitive Memory

While the Fourth Gospel was likely finalized last among the Gospels (ca. 100 CE), it conveys a number of features regarding the ministry and intentionality of Jesus that reflect more primitive understandings than those conveyed in the Synoptics and other New Testament literature. When primitive understandings of Jesus are sought in bi-optic perspective, the following features emerge:

- *Jesus as a Jewish rabbi teaching his band of followers*—this feature comes through in all four Gospels, and John's Hebrew and Aramaic language, in addition to its familiarity with regional Jewish customs, corroborates the Synoptic witness significantly.
- *Jesus and the privileging of women*—along these lines, John's narrative restores primitive and distinctive accounts of Jesus and his inclusive ministry, posing something of a corrective to the emergence of male leadership in the second and third generations of the movement.
- A *non-ritualizing religious leader*—John's innocence regarding baptismal and eucharistic rites reflects a more primitive memory of Jesus and his ministry, to some degree pushing back against cultic developments while still adhering to earlier transformational and martyrological associations with such themes.
- *Informal views of the church and its leadership*—the juxtaposition of Peter and the Beloved Disciple poses an alternative apostolic vision as something of a corrective to the emergence of Ignatian hierarchical leadership, emphasizing egalitarian access to the Holy Spirit's leadership and the leadership of Christ being rooted in truth rather than force.
- *Transformative encounters and their impressions*—especially in the Markan and Johannine traditions, diverse instances of transformative encounters

---

98. Putting into play the inclusive criteria for determining historicity within a bi-optic approach to Jesus research, the following outlines reflect my own approach to the subject in a forthcoming book with Eerdmans: Paul N. Anderson, *Jesus in Johannine Perspective: A Fourth Quest for Jesus* (Grand Rapids: Eerdmans, forthcoming).

with Jesus are recorded, suggesting differing understandings of Jesus and his ministry from the earliest stages of traditional memory; thus, cognitive-reflective factors in traditional origins and developments must be considered in interdisciplinary Jesus research.

2. Jesus and Corroborative Impressions

Given that corroborative impression offers a more generous perspective on the ministry of Jesus, the Johannine tradition poses an invaluable source of independent attestation regarding features that are similar-yet-different between the bi-optic presentations of Jesus and his ministry. Some of these features are as follows:

- *John the Baptist and Jesus, challenging ritual means of purity*—in both the Synoptics and John, the baptizer is presented as challenging ritual means of purification by immersing people in the free-flowing Jordan and other pools in the wilderness rather than designated bathing pools (*mikva'ot*), calling for moral repentance, justice, and resistance to compliance with the Romans, challenging leaders who were perceived as betraying the Jewish populace and its ideals.

- *The callings of disciples*—preceding a rather abrupt calling of the Twelve in Mark 3, the presentation of the baptizer's followers leaving him and becoming followers of Jesus in John 1 contributes a more informal and realistic understanding of how the ministries of the baptizer and Jesus were connected early on. This also accounts for a multiplicity of calling narratives in the Synoptic Gospels, suggesting a more extensive set of connections between the ministries of Jesus and John, which then accounts for their later associations with one another.

- A *prophetic temple incident*—when John's and Mark's presentations of the temple incident are viewed together, they corroborate an impression of a prophetic demonstration. Thus the incident appears not as a loss of temper, but as a provocative action performed with intentionality (in Mark Jesus looked around and came back the next day; in John the event was an inaugural prophetic sign), which also supports the provocative character of Jesus's ministry—following directly on the prophetic ministry of John the Baptist. If it occurred at the launching of his public ministry, this explains why Jewish leaders from Jerusalem came to Galilee seeking Jesus in Mark 7 and why they wanted to kill Jesus already in John 5.

- *Healings on the Sabbath*—nearly all the healings in the Synoptics and John occur on the Sabbath, and viewing Jesus in bi-optic perspective suggests a key factor in his healing ministry was the creation of cognitive dissonance, so as to suggest the redemptive and salutary function of Sabbath observance over and against legalistic regards. Especially if the sick and the marginalized would have gathered near synagogue and temple areas, the corroborative impression between John and the Synoptics lends valuable insights into the social concerns behind the healing ministries of Jesus.
- *Jesus as the Eschatological Prophet*—in the Synoptics and John Jesus is presented as claiming to have been sent from the Father with a sense of prophetic agency. His self-references as the Son of Man and the Mosaic Prophet come through in a variety of ways, creating resistance from societal and institutional leaders.

3. Jesus and Critical Realism

In terms of critical realism, viewing Jesus in bi-optic perspective contributes a more textured set of political, economic, and societal understandings of Jesus and his ministry. The Johannine presentation of multiple trips to Jerusalem is not only more realistic than the Markan presentation of a single trip; it also accounts more effectively for the events during the final days of Jesus, including his trials and execution by the Romans in Jerusalem.

- *The Galilean prophet and his ambivalent receptions in Judea*—especially graphic in John are the engagements between Jesus and the Judean religious leaders. Palpable in bi-optic perspective are diverse messianic understandings among the Judean, Samaritan, and Galilean populaces—negotiated by Jesus and his followers. The challenge this non-credentialed charismatic leader from the northern periphery posed to the centralizing religious leaders in Jerusalem and the south is especially pointed in John.
- *Roman occupation and its consequences*—palpable also among the Gospels, and especially in John, is the fact of Roman occupation and its perceived strengths and vulnerabilities. Relations between the priestly class and the Roman officials are more fully understood in bi-optic perspective, as the religious leaders both fear and manipulate Roman officials, while the Roman officials both assert their prowess and simultaneously expose their sense of tenuousness before the masses.

- *Popularism and its liabilities*—Jewish zealotry and the desire to overthrow the Romans by force is identifiable in bi-optic perspective, as the Synoptic Jesus is followed by Simon the Zealot, the feeding is presented as a revolt in the desert in John and Mark, and messianic secrecy is exhorted by Jesus so as to not encourage nationalistic popularism. In John 6, even some of his disciples abandon him, he flees a hasty coronation by the crowd at the feeding, and he disparages the sensationalism of signs-faith.

- *The Last Supper as a common meal*—here the sacramentally innocent presentation of the Last Supper in John smacks of greater critical realism over and against the more cultic institution of a meal of remembrance in the Synoptics and Paul. No doubt the development of a Christian alternative to the Jewish Passover meal developed in the early Christian movement, but even in Mark Jesus is not killed on the Passover, so John's presentation of the meal on the day before the Passover is more historically plausible than the Markan presentation of the event as a Passover meal.

- *The crucifixion and the last days of Jesus*—understanding of the events surrounding the last days of Jesus is greatly enhanced by viewing them in bi-optic perspective. John's archaeological and topographical details bolster events reported around the arrest of Jesus, his trials, and his crucifixion with nails—including the breaking of the legs of other crucifixion victims—as well as details related to the burial of Jesus.

4. Jesus in Open Coherence

When Jesus is viewed in bi-optic perspective, a number of features emerge, which are bolstered by John's independent witness to the presentation of Jesus and his ministry in the Synoptics. While many of the particulars differ, rather than a historical weakness, this actually presents a more textured understanding. Thus, a greater sense of open coherence emerges from considering similar-yet-different features of Jesus and his ministry among the inclusive witness to Jesus and his ministry, attested by multiple impressions and memories of his ministry.

- *Jesus and parabolic instruction about the leadership of God*—while the parables of the kingdom in the Synoptics capture more realistically the teaching language and content of Jesus of Nazareth, a somewhat different version of his parabolic instruction about the leadership of God is availed in the Gospel of John. In bi-optic perspective, the hiddenness of God's working, conveyed by metaphoric imagery and associations, is described paradoxically in ways that cohere between the Johannine and Synoptic Gospels.

- *Jesus and the gifting of the Spirit*—in the Synoptic Gospels and John alike, Jesus promises to empower and guide his followers by means of the Holy Spirit, especially during times of trial. While the Johannine rendering of this theme reflects its emerging understanding within the developing Johannine situation, the theme is also sounded within the Synoptic traditions and the Acts of the Apostles. This overall theme coheres in a number of corroborative ways.

- *Embracing the neglected and the marginalized*—while many of the particulars vary between the Synoptic and Johannine Gospels, Jesus is nonetheless presented as extending grace and healing to children, "sinners," lepers, and tax collectors (the Synoptics), while in John, Jesus reaches out to Samaritans, the family of the royal official, and the grieving family of Lazarus (John). In bi-optic perspective, Jesus reaches out to fishermen and laborers, to women with special needs, to the ill and the dejected, and to the poor of the land—extending divine grace and inclusive welcome.

- *Rejecting violence as the way of the kingdom*—in all four Gospels, Jesus commands his followers to put away the sword, and in the Q tradition, he instructs his followers to love their enemies in creative ways. In John, Jesus declares that he *is* a king, but his kingdom is one of truth, which is why his disciples cannot fight to further it. In these ways, Jesus is presented in bi-optic perspective as rejecting the "fourth philosophy" of the Zealots and calling for alternatives to violence in engaging the Roman presence with creative possibilities.

- *The love commands as radical faithfulness to the ways of God*—in the Synoptic and Johannine Gospels alike, Jesus calls his followers to love as a means of fulfilling the commandments of God. In the Synoptics, Jesus summarizes the Ten Commandments by going to the heart of the matter—loving God and loving neighbor. The Johannine Jesus (as remembered also in 1 John) further commands his followers to love one another; if one claims to love God but does not love one's fellow community members, such attestations ring hollow.

While the particulars of the above outlines must be developed further, there is enough here in this preliminary sketch to suggest some of the values that an inclusive quest for Jesus of Nazareth might contribute. Of course, these are only a few of the trajectories that invite development, and many others may also emerge as scholars extend beyond the canonical Gospels to include Jesus tradition within the writings of Paul, the General Epistles, the Acts of the Apostles, the Gospel of Thomas, and other noncanonical writings. In some ways, the modern rejection of the Fourth Gospel from historicity interests reflects a delayed reaction against its theological impact during the fourth through fifth centuries of the patristic era, but such a perspective fails to "let John be John" as a late first-century account of Jesus remembered. Further, there is no part of the New Testament more attested and affirmed in the second and third century Christian writings than the Gospel of John, and most of those references relate to John's distinctive story of Jesus, spiritualized though it may be. So, the conversation continues, and perhaps a Fourth Quest for Jesus can help us sort out more authentically matters related to the Jesus of history rather than allowing interests in the Christ of faith to eclipse or distort such a worthy endeavor.

CONCLUSION

When Marcus Borg and I did a series of presentations together on "Jesus in Bi-Optic Perspective: Latest Scholarship on the Synoptics and John" at Reed-wood's Center for Christian Studies in 2010,[99] Marcus asked me at the end of our first session, "Okay, Paul, what if it is determined that the Gospel of John is the only Gospel representing an eyewitness memory of Jesus and his ministry; what difference would that make? Would it simply inform us of multiple trips to Jerusalem and a few other features, or would it contribute anything really new to our understanding of Jesus?" Shocked by his mere allowance of such a possibility, I responded, "Thanks, Marcus, but first, I really am not much interested in what such a consideration might produce; I'm more concerned with rectifying a flawed approach. If John represents an authentic and self-standing Jesus tradition in some way, it ought to be included somehow in the mix, no matter what comes of the quest." I then continued, "Then again, if John's narrative really does contribute to a fuller understanding of Jesus and his ministry, the elevated place of women around Jesus, a familial and egalitarian ecclesiology, a concern for authentic spirituality, and a view of continuing revelation might make an extremely important set of contributions to twenty-first century Jesus research, and I suppose that's why a Fourth Quest is needed."

Upon reflection, the John, Jesus, and History Project has not only suggested that a Fourth Quest of Jesus is needed; in many ways and on many levels, what it confirms is that such a quest is already well underway.

---

99. Paul N. Anderson, "A Fourth Quest for Jesus . . . So What, and How So?," *The Bible and Interpretation* (July 2010): n.p. Online: www.bibleinterp.com/opeds/fourth357921.shtml.

APPENDIX 1

Volumes Emerging Directly from the John, Jesus, and History Project

ALREADY PUBLISHED

- *John, Jesus, and History, Vol. 1: Critical Appraisals of Critical Views.* Edited by Paul N. Anderson, Felix Just SJ, and Tom Thatcher. SBL Symposium Series 44. Atlanta: SBL Press, 2007.
- *John, Jesus, and History, Vol. 2: Aspects of History in the Fourth Gospel.* Edited by Paul N. Anderson, Felix Just SJ, and Tom Thatcher. ECL 2. Atlanta: SBL Press, 2009.
- *Qumran and the Dead Sea Scrolls: Sixty Years of Discovery and Debate.* Edited by Mary Coloe PBVM and Tom Thatcher. Early Judaism and its Literature 32. Atlanta: SBL Press 2011.
- *Engaging with C. H. Dodd on the Gospel of John: Sixty Years of Tradition and Interpretation.* Edited by Tom Thatcher and Catrin H. Williams. Cambridge: Cambridge University Press, 2013.
- *Communities in Dispute: Current Scholarship on the Johannine Epistles.* Edited by Paul N. Anderson and R. Alan Culpepper. ECL 13. Atlanta: SBL Press, 2014.
- *John, Jesus, and History, Vol. 3: Glimpses of Jesus through the Johannine Lens.* Edited by Paul N. Anderson, Felix Just SJ, and Tom Thatcher. ECL 18. Atlanta: SBL Press, 2016.
- *John and Judaism: A Contested Relationship in Context.* Edited by R. Alan Culpepper and Paul N. Anderson. Resources for Biblical Study 87. Atlanta: SBL Press, 2017.
- *Portraits of Jesus in the Gospel of John.* Edited by Craig Koester. LNTS 589. London: Bloomsbury, 2018.

PROJECTED BOOK-LENGTH PROJECTS

- *Archaeology and the Fourth Gospel: John, Material Culture, and Jesus.*
- *John, Jesus, and History, Vol. 4: Jesus Remembered in the Johannine Situation.*
- *John, Jesus, and History, Vol. 5: Jesus Remembered in the Johannine Tradition.*
- *John, Jesus, and History, Vol. 6: Methodologies for Determining Johannine Historicity.*

APPENDIX 2

Jesus in Bi-Optic Perspective

Despite arguing for the incorporation of the Fourth Gospel as a legitimate source for Jesus research, this does not mean that all of John is of historical value, or that John is to be preferred over and against the Synoptics. By and large, the Synoptic view of Jesus is to be preferred over the Johannine, historically, corroborated by elements of the Matthean and Lukan traditions (and the hypothetical Q tradition) that cohere with the Markan perspective. Nonetheless, as a preliminary projection as to what a view of Jesus in bi-optic perspective might look like, below is the outline of Part IV of *The Fourth Gospel and the Quest for Jesus* (127–73), worth building upon in the Fourth Quest.

A. *Dual Attestation*—Jesus Impressions Corroborated by John and the Synoptics:
  • Jesus's Association with John the Baptist and the Beginning of his Public Ministry
  • Jesus's Calling of Disciples as a Corporate Venture
  • A Revolt in the Desert (the feeding, sea crossing, discussion, and Peter's confession)?
  • Jesus as a Healer—Healing on the Sabbath
  • Jesus's Sense of Prophetic Agency from the Father and Religious Resistance
  • Jesus's Cleansing of the Temple
  • The Culmination of Jesus's Ministry—His Arrest, Trials and Death in Jerusalem
  • Attestations to Appearances and the Beginning of the Jesus Movement
B. *Synoptic Contributions* to the Quest for the Jesus of History:
  • Jesus's Teachings about the Kingdom of God in Parables and in Short, Pithy Sayings
  • The Messianic Secret and the Hiddenness of the Kingdom
  • Jesus's Healing and Exorcizing Ministries

- Jesus Sends out his Disciples to Further the Work of the Kingdom
- Jesus Dines with "Sinners" and Provocations toward Renewal
- Jesus Cleanses the Temple as an Intentional Challenge to the Restriction of Access to God
- Jesus's Teaching on the Heart of the Law—The Love of God and Humanity
- Jesus's Apocalyptic Mission

C. *Johannine Contributions* to the Quest for the Jesus of History:
- Jesus's Simultaneous Ministry alongside John the Baptizer and the Prolific Availability of Purifying Power
- Jesus's Temple Cleansing as an Inaugural Prophetic Sign
- Jesus's Travel to and from Jerusalem and his Multi-Year Ministry
- Early Events in the Public Ministry of Jesus
- Favorable Receptions in Galilee among Samaritans, Women, and Gentiles
- Jesus's Judean Ministry and Archaeological Realism
- The Last Supper as a Common Meal and Its Proper Dating

CHAPTER 11

Jesus's Burial: Archaeology, Authenticity, and History

CRAIG A. EVANS AND GREG MONETTE

INTRODUCTION

The purpose of this chapter is to show that the burial of Jesus as an event in history is highly probable. This chapter will make use of two of the criteria of authenticity: multiple attestation and embarrassment. We will show that these criteria are not useless, as some contend, but are effective when used properly. We will also employ the use of a third criterion, namely the criterion of verisimilitude. The evidence of archaeology and its relevance in the study of the burial of Jesus narratives will also come into play.

It is important to make clear that the historicity of the burial of Jesus does not require that every detail be established before accepting the event itself as historical. Embellishments, vagaries, and even minor discrepancies do not in themselves negate the burial story or other stories in the Gospels. Historians recognize that we often work with incomplete and even contradictory data. This reality does not make the historian's job futile. Robert McIver explains that

> While it may not be possible to identify the up to 20 percent of the details of the gospel traditions that may not exactly represent what happened, these details would be consistent with the general trend of what did happen. It could therefore be argued that the Gospel accounts preserve at least a first-order faithfulness to the actual deeds and teachings of Jesus, and that this first-order faithfulness is based on the fact that the majority of the details provided in the description of events recorded in the Gospels are indeed factual. It might be concluded, then, that a case can be built to support the

assertion that the gospel traditions may be used to form a well-informed broad picture of what Jesus did and said.[1]

THE CRITERIA OF AUTHENTICITY IN CONTEMPORARY DEBATE

In *Jesus, Criteria, and the Demise of Authenticity* (henceforth referred to as JCDA),[2] editors Chris Keith and Anthony Le Donne, along with their contributors, have raised a number of questions with regard to the methods used to determine historically authentic New Testament narratives and traditions. They observe that for a century the gospel tradition has been critically sifted in the light of the proposed criteria of authenticity (such as Semitic influence/interference, coherence, dissimilarity, embarrassment, and multiple attestation). Yet few think that the use of these criteria, in the words of Morna Hooker, really provide "a way of establishing 'assured results.'"[3] The criteria offer no guarantees as to what comes from Jesus. They merely act as common sense guides toward reducing subjectivity (not eliminating it). Very little is "confirmed"; there are few "assured results." But this hardly means that tools such as the proposed criteria should be abandoned. What the criteria are and how they should be employed is the key.

Dale Allison rightly comments that "tools do not dictate how they are used; the hands that hold them do that."[4] The criteria are tools that are handled by scholars to help them in their detective work. In and of themselves the criteria do nothing. When building a home, it is required that builders receive permits based on the quality of their workmanship before the home can be inhabited. The tools do not construct the home. The builder does. The quality of the home is not based on the tools but on how they are used. The reason why the scholarly guild exists is to act as a peer-review check on the sometimes-fertile imaginations of the person putting forth a novel hypothesis. Nobody believes that the criteria provide a shortcut for the historical quest. However, they do act as a guide and

---

1. Robert K. McIver, "Eyewitnesses as Guarantors of the Accuracy of the Gospel Traditions in the Light of Psychological Research," *JBL* 131 (2012): 529–46, here 546. See also the helpful discussion of the accuracy of memory recall of ancient and medieval rabbis in Armin D. Baum, *Der mündliche Faktor und die synoptische Frage: Analogien aus der antiken Literatur, der Experimentalpsychologie, der Oral Poetry-Forschung und dem rabbinischen Traditionswesen,* TANZ 49 (Tübingen: Francke, 2008), 404–5.

2. Chris Keith and Anthony Le Donne, eds., *Jesus, Criteria, and the Demise of Authenticity* (London: T&T Clark, 2012).

3. Morna D. Hooker, "Foreword: Forty Years On," in Keith and Le Donne, *Jesus, Criteria, and the Demise of Authenticity,* xiii–xvii (here xiii). See also M. D. Hooker, "On Using the Wrong Tool," *Theology* 75 (1972): 570–81. This study did not receive the attention it deserved when it was published.

4. Dale C. Allison Jr., "It Don't Come Easy: A History of Disillusionment," in Keith and Le Donne, *Jesus, Criteria, and the Demise of Authenticity,* 186–99 (here 197).

provide a rationale behind making historical claims regarding events described in ancient texts.

More importantly and more basically, the criteria aid the historian in assessing and evaluating the sources themselves—not only the pieces and parts of the sources—but the sources as a whole. Even Keith, Le Donne, and company appeal to the New Testament Gospels—not apocryphal texts—in their respective discussions of the Jesus of history.[5] Archaeologists regularly make use of the four New Testament Gospels, the book of Acts, and Josephus; they do not make use of second-century Gospels and gnostic writings.[6] Why not? They rightly and sensibly employ criteria that help identify and evaluate sources useful for historical (and archaeological) research. Sources that exhibit verisimilitude (culturally, linguistically, topographically, and the like), appear not to be heavily influenced by ancient editorial bias, and contain data that appear in other independent sources are the kind of sources responsible historians utilize. This is what critical scholars, historians, and archaeologists find in the New Testament Gospels; so (not surprisingly) they use them.

This is not the place for an in-depth review of Keith and Le Donne's book.[7] However, a few comments are necessary. In his introduction to the book, Le Donne affirms his belief that the traditional "authenticity criteria" are outmoded

---

5. We see this in Chris Keith, *Jesus against the Scribal Elite: The Origins of the Conflict* (Grand Rapids: Baker Academic, 2014). After his critical assessment of Gospel material concerned with Jesus's controversies with Jewish scribes, Keith concludes that "one can trace the conflict plausibly to Jesus's ministry and, indeed, to Jesus himself. This argument stands in direct contrast to the theory that the controversy narratives are the fabrications of early Christians . . ." (p. 156). Keith is surely correct. He arrives at this sensible conclusion because he relies heavily on the first-century Gospels of Matthew, Mark, Luke, and John—not the later gnostic and apocryphal gospels (see the index on pp. 176–79) and because he follows widely recognized criteria, even though he distances himself from the traditional nomenclature of these criteria and their all too frequent scholarly misuse (see pp. 73–84). Keith's principal criterion is what he calls the "memory approach" (p. 83). Judging from his discussion of Jesus and his scribal encounters, Keith also regards broadly attested tradition and plausible social settings as indicators of authentic tradition. Here we have forms of the criteria of multiple attestation and verisimilitude. Both Keith and his colleague Le Donne are deeply indebted to the work of James D. G. Dunn, *Jesus Remembered* (Grand Rapids: Eerdmans, 2003). See Anthony Le Donne, *The Historiographical Jesus: Memory, Typology, and the Son of David* (Waco, TX: Baylor University Press, 2009), 11, and passim.

6. One will do well to look at James H. Charlesworth, ed., *Jesus and Archaeology* (Grand Rapids: Eerdmans, 2006). Examination of the index of the ancient texts that are cited in this book will reveal more than a thousand citations of the New Testament Gospels. Not one of the thirty-one contributors to this scholarly collection found it necessary to appeal to apocryphal or gnostic Gospels for information about the Jesus of history.

7. See the review by Craig A. Evans in *EvQ* 85 (2013): 364–65. Other reviewers point out that apparently no scholar who held to more positive views of the value of the traditional criteria was invited to contribute to *Jesus, Criteria, and the Demise of Authenticity*. This is the principal flaw of an otherwise rich and insightful collection of studies. We hear of what is wrong with the criteria—at least with some of them—but not what is right and useful about them and why criteria are in fact necessary if we are going to engage in critical historiography.

and that therefore the "entire 'criteria approach' is bankrupt."[8] He believes the traditional criteria are hopeless because they were birthed in the context of historical positivism.[9] Is this true?

The critique of the traditional authenticity criteria offered by Keith, Le Donne, and their several contributors is on the whole justified. Le Donne is surely correct to say that "it is the *conventional use* of the criteria that must be replaced by a more sophisticated historiography."[10] Furthermore, no one will dispute that most of the traditional criteria came to expression in a time when historical positivism was in vogue. The positivist backdrop explains the black-and-white dogmatic tone in the employment of the authenticity criteria in the first six decades of the twentieth century. But most scholars have moved on. One of the hallmarks of the Third Quest of the 1980s and 1990s was its critique of the misuse of the criteria, especially the criterion of double dissimilarity, the most egregious criterion of them all.

Many scholars concerned with the historical Jesus—with perhaps the notable exception of several associated with the Jesus Seminar—continue to make use of the traditional criteria but at the same time have taken a greater interest in the social, religious, and political context of Jesus and his contemporaries. Study of the land of Israel, including its topographical and social geography, and above all the evidence of archaeology, have yielded much more promising fruit. The rich trove of material from the region of the Dead Sea, as well as related texts that at one time circulated at the turn of the era, have made it possible for scholars to appreciate with much greater precision and nuance the meaning of Jesus's teachings and activities and how they compare with those of other teachers in his time.

But in making use of the new data made available thanks to the discoveries of archaeology and new texts from antiquity, scholars continue to make use of criteria. This is necessary if they are to be historians in the critical sense. Historians, if they really are historians, must critically sift their sources. As a general rule they prefer older sources, that is, sources close to the events. They feel more confident when they have two or more independent sources that cover the same ground. Trained historians look for verisimilitude and, if possible, archaeological confirmation.

None of this is new, of course; nor is it peculiar to the work of New Testament

---

8. Anthony Le Donne, "The Rise of the Quest for an Authentic Jesus: An Introduction to the Crumbling Foundations of Jesus Research," in Keith and Le Donne, *Jesus, Criteria, and the Demise of Authenticity*, 3–21 (here 3, 5).

9. Le Donne, "Rise of the Quest for an Authentic Jesus," 5.

10. Le Donne, "Rise of the Quest for an Authentic Jesus," 4–5 (italics original).

scholars and their quest for the Jesus of history. Professional historians have been hard at it for some time. It may come as a surprise to some New Testament scholars that historians in fact do employ authenticity criteria, but usually in reference to the whole documents themselves. Louis Reichenthal Gottschalk (1899–1975), long-time distinguished professor of history at the University of Chicago, for years regarded as the doyen of American historians, penned an influential essay called "The Historian and the Historical Document."[11] Among the criteria that Gottschalk thinks are important are temporal proximity (that is, how close the document is to the events it describes), the purpose of the document (that is, its genre), the bias of the author, and the competence of the author.[12] Under the heading of "External Criticism" Gottschalk takes into account the authenticity of the document (and here he treats the subject of forgery and hoax), textual criticism, and interpretation.[13] Under the heading of "Internal Criticism," Gottschalk discusses "credibility," "verisimilitude," and "corroboration."[14]

Gottschalk's essay contains nothing new or surprising. It was a clear articulation of what most historians recognized as the proper and necessary assessment of documents. In greater detail and with far more examples we hear the same criteria and methodology outlined in Gilbert Garraghan's *A Guide to Historical Method*, published by Fordham University Press. This influential book remained in circulation for decades as a standard text for history.[15] Garraghan, the late research professor of history at Loyola University in Chicago, offers seven lengthy chapters under the heading "Appraising the Sources." These chapters consider the authenticity, analysis, integrity, and credibility of sources.[16] Among other things, Garraghan discusses credibility, verisimilitude, multiple attestation, corroboration, eyewitness testimony, and conflicting testimony.[17]

The difficulties of historiography are well appreciated by classical scholars. Yet these scholars, whose primary sources approximate the New Testament Gospels and Acts, assess their sources and wrestle with questions of authenticity by

---

11. Louis Gottschalk, "The Historian and the Historical Document," in *The Use of Personal Documents in History, Anthropology and Sociology*, ed. Louis Gottschalk, Clyde Kluckhohn, and Robert Angell, Bulletin 53 (New York: Social Science Research Council, 1945), 1–75.

12. Gottschalk, "Historian and the Historical Document," 16.

13. Gottschalk, "Historian and the Historical Document," 28–34.

14. Gottschalk, "Historian and the Historical Document," 35–47.

15. Gilbert J. Garraghan, *A Guide to Historical Method*, ed. Jean Delanglez (New York: Fordham University Press, 1946 [rev. ed., 1948; and 5th reprint 1957]).

16. Garraghan, *Guide to Historical Method*, 143–317.

17. Those interested in discussion of the critical evaluation of oral tradition, myth, and legend will want to review Garraghan, *Guide to Historical Method*, 259–77. For critical assessment of eyewitness testimony, see 282–317.

appealing to most of the criteria we think should be utilized: multiple sources, proximity to the events in question, verisimilitude, editorial bias, and the like. Classical historians have great appreciation for archaeology and the clarification and corroboration it can provide, for it is the correlation between text and artifact that gives historians confidence in the reliability of the text.[18]

Historians know, of course, that they cannot recover and reconstruct exactly what happened or what exactly was said. They know the past is lost. The historian's task, to the extent that it is possible, is to construct the most plausible portrait, using the extant literary and archaeological remnants left to us. The historian tries to piece together the "traces" that remain and from them construct a coherent, plausible account of what most likely was said or what most likely happened.[19] Fresh discoveries of either a literary or archaeological nature may well require a revision of that account. As it so happens, archaeology has provided significant aid in the interpretation of the New Testament accounts of the death and burial of Jesus.

MULTIPLE ATTESTATION AND THE BURIAL OF JESUS

Mark Goodacre's contribution to *JCDA* is focused on the usefulness of the criterion of multiple attestation. He concludes:

> Where the criterion of multiple attestation has value, it is in illustrating the historian's necessary preference for two sources rather than one, and for explaining the importance of independent witnesses to early traditions. Beyond the generality, though, it has the potential to be highly misleading, to encourage an unrealistic and old-fashioned expectation that the Gospels are made up of a variety of independent, self-contained sources that were collected together by docile redactors, or to hope that late, non-canonical sources embed early, independent sayings and traditions.[20]

---

18. It is to this correlation and confidence that Adrian Nicholas Sherwin-White (1911–1993) alludes, when he says: "The basic reason for this confidence is, if put summarily, the existence of external confirmations." See A. N. Sherwin-White, *Roman Society and Roman Law in the New Testament: The Sarum Lectures 1960–61* (Oxford: Oxford University Press, 1963; repr., Grand Rapids: Baker, 1994), 186–93, with quotation from 186–87.

19. For an excellent statement of the historian's task, especially with reference to Jesus research, see Robert L. Webb, "The Historical Enterprise and Historical Jesus Research," in *Key Events in the Life of the Historical Jesus: A Collaborative Exploration of Context and Coherence*, ed. Darrell L. Bock and Robert L. Webb, WUNT 247 (Tübingen: Mohr Siebeck, 2009), 9–93. The failure to engage Webb's learned essay is, in our view, a glaring weakness in *Jesus, Criteria, and the Demise of Authenticity*. Equally problematic is the failure to engage B. F. Meyer, *The Aims of Jesus* (London: SCM, 1979). Meyer severely criticizes German form critics and their ill-conceived criteria and misuse.

20. Mark Goodacre, "Criticizing the Criterion of Multiple Attestation: The Historical Jesus and the

Goodacre's main concern is not whether there is value for historians in looking for independently attested accounts involving historical figures, but in making sure that the accounts being used to argue for independent attestation are in fact so. Fair enough. One could debate the existence of Q[21] and the independence of John[22] from the Synoptics. But for the purpose of this essay it is unnecessary because we have independent tradition in the writings of Paul and the Gospel of Mark, which is probably the earliest written Gospel. And in any case, the hypothetical Q source does not contain a passion narrative and so is of no help for the present study.

The tradition that relates the burial of Jesus is the most primitive material in the New Testament pertaining to the historical Jesus.[23] The majority of scholars believe that our most ancient witness to Jesus's burial is found in Paul's first letter to the church in Corinth (i.e., 1 Cor 15:3–8).[24] Most date this letter to around 54–55 CE, thanks to the discovery of the Gallio inscription.[25] The passage reads:

For what I received I passed on to you as of first importance: that Christ died for our sins according to the Scriptures, that he was buried, that he was

---

Question of Sources," in Keith and Le Donne, *Jesus, Criteria, and the Demise of Authenticity,* 152–69 (here 169).

21. Goodacre, "Criticizing the Criterion," 154–61.

22. Goodacre, "Criticizing the Criterion," 164. Highly dubious is the multiplication of "independent" sources in John Dominic Crossan, *The Historical Jesus: The Life of a Mediterranean Jewish Peasant* (San Francisco: HarperCollins, 1991), 427–50. By hypothesizing various sources and layers, for which there really is no evidence whatsoever, Crossan is able to conjure up a host of independent sources. This then allows him to find a greater number of multiply attested units of Jesus tradition. Crossan does this because he relies heavily on the criterion of multiple attestation. Equally problematic are the surprisingly early dates he assigns to the extra-canonical Gospels and his hypothesized underlying sources. By dating the canonicals as late as possible and the extra-canonicals as early as possible, Crossan is able to blur the temporal boundaries between the earlier and better sources on the one hand and the later and more dubious sources on the other.

23. Of course, when we use the term "historical Jesus" we speak of the portrait, which modern historians attempt to reconstruct from the fragmentary data that survive from the ancient past. We can never have certainty that our scholarly reconstructions correspond to the "real" person who lived in first-century Roman Palestine. However, this does not mean that we cannot have confidence that our scholarly portrait *reflects* the historical Jesus. For more on this important distinction, see John P. Meier, *The Roots of the Problem and the Person,* vol. 1 of *A Marginal Jew: Rethinking the Historical Jesus,* ABRL (New York: Doubleday, 1991), 21–40; Webb, "Historical Enterprise and Historical Jesus Research," esp. 9–38.

24. The antiquity of this passage is discussed in detail in Martin Hengel, "Das Begräbnis Jesu bei Paulus," *Auferstehung—Resurrection,* ed. Friedrich Avemarie and Hermann Lichtenberger, WUNT 135 (Tübingen: Mohr Siebeck, 2001), 119–83, esp. 121, 129–38, 175–76.

25. While Paul was in Corinth the Jews brought him before Gallio, the one-time proconsul of Achaea (Acts 18:12–26). The discovery of the Gallio inscription at Delphi confirms that Gallio was proconsul in 51–52 CE, putting Paul in Corinth most likely from autumn of 50 CE to the early summer of 52 CE. For more on this, see Colin J. Hemer, "Observations on Pauline Chronology," in *Pauline Studies: Essays Presented to F. F. Bruce on His 70th Birthday,* ed. Donald A. Hagner and Murray J. Harris (Grand Rapids: Eerdmans, 1980), 3–18. For further discussion on the issue of dating 1 Corinthians, see Gordon D. Fee, *The First Epistle to the Corinthians,* NICNT (Grand Rapids: Eerdmans, 1987), 722–34; Anthony C. Thiselton, *The First Epistle to the Corinthians,* NIGTC (Grand Rapids: Eerdmans, 2000), 1186–97; and Joseph A. Fitzmyer, *First Corinthians,* AB 32 (New Haven: Yale University Press, 2009), 540–42.

raised on the third day according to the Scriptures, and that he appeared to Cephas, and then to the Twelve. After that, he appeared to more than five hundred of the brothers and sisters at the same time, most of whom are still living, though some have fallen asleep. Then he appeared to James, then to all the apostles, and last of all he appeared to me also, as to one abnormally born. (1 Cor 15:3–8)

John Dominic Crossan makes much of the qualifying phrases "according to the Scriptures" in vv. 3 and 4. In fact, he argues that most of the passion tradition, including the burial of Jesus, is "prophecy historicized" not "history remembered." He explains:

The individual units, general sequences, and overall frames of the passion-resurrection stories are so linked to prophetic fulfillment that the removal of such fulfillment leaves nothing but the barest facts, almost as in Josephus, Tacitus or the Apostles' Creed.[26]

It is true that two of the key elements of the early confession in 1 Corinthians 15:3–8, "Christ died for our sins" (v. 3) and "he was raised on the third day" (v. 4), are both said to be "according to the Scriptures." But does this hint at the invention of history, inspired by the Old Testament, or is it really a bold confession that the unexpected death and resurrection of Jesus—not really part of Jewish expectation—was nevertheless prophesied in the Old Testament? It is telling that the confession "he was buried" (ὅτι ἐτάφη) is not qualified with the phrase "according to the Scriptures." The non-appearance of this qualifying phrase in reference to the burial of Jesus undermines Crossan's theory that the New Testament passion traditions are more "prophecy historicized" than "history remembered." Better is Mark Goodacre's suggestion that we have "history scripturalized."[27]

It is difficult to know which of the words in 1 Corinthians 15:3–8 are Paul's, and what is tradition he received.[28] Clearly Paul did not create this material *ex*

---

26. John Dominic Crossan, *The Birth of Christianity: Discovering What Happened in the Years Immediately after The Execution of Jesus* (New York: HarperOne, 1998), 521. The idea of prophecy historicized is the major premise in Crossan's *Who Killed Jesus? Exposing the Roots of Anti-Semitism in the Gospel Story of the Death of Jesus* (San Francisco: HarperCollins, 1995).

27. Mark Goodacre, "Scripturalization in Mark's Crucifixion Narrative," in *The Trial and Death of Jesus: Essays on the Passion Narrative in Mark*, ed. Geert van Oyen and Tom Shepherd, CBET 45 (Leuven: Peeters, 2006), 33–47. See also the rebuttal of Crossan's thesis in Craig A. Evans, "The Passion of Jesus: History Remembered or Prophecy Historicized?," *BBR* 6 (1996): 159–65.

28. There are a number of *hapax legomena* in this passage: ἁμαρτιῶν, κατὰ τὰς γραφὰς, ἐγείρω (in the perfect,

nihilo. As we see elsewhere in his letters, Paul's tendency was not to rely on the testimony and experience of others (e.g., Gal 1:11–2:10); Paul gives priority to what he received directly from the risen Lord. In this case, he has received early tradition from the church.[29] And this early tradition speaks of burial of Jesus, not just his death and resurrection.

Paul also alludes to the burial of Jesus when he contrasts Jesus's burial with the baptism of the believer (Rom 6:1–11; Col 2:12). Everett Ferguson comments that "[t]he connection of Baptism with the death of Christ for human sins was part of the early Christian message, but Paul proceeds to deepen this association and carry it further by his distinctive thought of dying and rising with Christ."[30] In a spiritual sense, the believer participates in the death, burial, and resurrection of Jesus (Rom 6:5). Citing Ferguson once more:

> The death and resurrection of Christ belonged together in the early Christian proclamation, so a resurrection for the baptized is implicit here. The association, even identification, of the believer with Christ is shown by the quite striking number of words compounded with the preposition "with" (σὺν)—"buried with" (6:4), "united with" (6:5), "crucified with" (6:6), "died with and shall live with" (6:8) . . . The conclusion in verse 11, "So you also must consider yourselves dead to sin," reflects the association of baptism with forgiveness of sins. Even so, there is no participation in the death, burial, and resurrection of Christ without baptism.[31]

In light of this, we can confidently assert that Paul, and those who passed on the tradition (1 Cor 15:3–8; cf. Gal 1:18–20) to him, believed that the burial of

---

instead of the aorist), ὤφθη, and τοῖς δώδεκα. For discussion on this, see John Kloppenborg, "An Analysis of the Pre-Pauline Formula in 1 Cor 15:3b–5 in Light of Some Recent Literature," *CBQ* 40 (1978): 351–57. See also Jerome Murphy O'Connor, "Tradition and Redaction in 1 Cor 15:3–7," *CBQ* 43 (1981): 582–89. The tradition that Paul received may have been in Hebrew or Aramaic. On the possibility of a Semitic original of the tradition, see Joachim Jeremias, *The Eucharistic Words of Jesus* (Oxford: Blackwell, 1955), 127–32. Jeremias does not provide a Semitic equivalent for κατὰ τὰς γραφὰς ("according to the scriptures"). For objections, see Hans Conzelmann, "On the Analysis of the Confessional Formula in 1 Corinthians 15:3–5," *Interpretation* 20 (1966): 15–25. The original language of the confession sheds little light on when it was passed on or from whom. There were Aramaic-speaking followers of Jesus from the time of Jesus right up until the time Paul wrote 1 Corinthians (54–55 CE) and beyond. One must use caution when using Semitic interference as a criterion for establishing early layers of Jesus tradition. On this, see Loren T. Stuckenbruck, "Semitic Influence on Greek: An Authenticating Criterion in Jesus Research?," in Keith and Le Donne, *Jesus, Criteria, and the Demise of Authenticity*, 73–94.

29. Reginald H. Fuller, *The Formation of the Resurrection Narratives* (Philadelphia: Fortress, 1971), 10: "It is almost universally agreed today that Paul is here citing tradition"; and more recently, Dale C. Allison Jr., *Resurrecting Jesus: The Earliest Christian Tradition and Its Interpreters* (New York: T&T Clark, 2005), 233–34: "This overview of foundational events . . . as almost universally recognized, [is] a pre-Pauline formula."

30. Everett Ferguson, *Baptism in the Early Church: History, Theology, and Liturgy in the First Five Centuries* (Grand Rapids: Eerdmans, 2009), 155.

31. Ferguson, *Baptism in the Early Church*, 156–57.

Jesus was a real event in space and time. It would be ill-advised to place so much theological weight on an uncertain, unknown event. Paul's arguments, in part based on very early tradition, clearly presuppose the burial of Jesus, which in turn presupposes burial in a tomb. The resurrection implies a reversal of burial and the vacating of a tomb. John Granger Cook rightly argues that Paul's use of the terms ἀνίστημι and ἐγείρω in his description of the resurrection of Jesus in 1 Corinthians 15 strongly supports the probability that Jesus was buried and that Paul's understanding of Jesus's resurrection included an empty tomb.[32]

THE CRITERION OF EMBARRASSMENT AND THE BURIAL OF JESUS

John P. Meier explains that the criterion of embarrassment "focuses on actions or sayings of Jesus that would have embarrassed or created difficulty for the early Church."[33] The four canonical Gospels are unanimous that Joseph of Arimathea, who we are told was a member of the Jewish Sanhedrin, was responsible for burying Jesus in his own tomb.[34] It is not easy to see early Christians inventing a member of the Sanhedrin who does something noble, in view of the tradition that the Sanhedrin voted in favor of Jesus's execution.[35] This isn't surprising because a member of the Sanhedrin buried Jesus, as was expected based on ancient Jewish custom.[36] What is surprising is that Joseph used his own tomb to inter the body of Jesus. By placing the body of an executed man in his tomb, the tomb becomes a place of shame and dishonor. The tomb will no longer be of use to the family of Joseph. We should also be surprised by the positive language used to describe Joseph.[37] It is not easy to explain why early Christians would

---

32. John Granger Cook, "Resurrection in Paganism and the Question of an Empty Tomb in 1 Corinthians 15," *NTS* 63 (2017): 56–75.

33. Meier, *Roots of the Problem and the Person*, 168.

34. Mark 15:43–46; Matt 27:57–60; Luke 23:50–53; John 19:38–42. For more on this, see Greg Monette, *The Wrong Jesus: Fact, Belief, Legend, Truth . . . Making Sense of What You've Heard* (Carol Stream, IL: NavPress, 2014), 185–86.

35. William L. Craig, *Reasonable Faith: Christian Truth and Apologetics*, 3rd ed. (Wheaton: Crossway, 2008), 364: "Given his status as a Sanhedrist—all of whom, Mark reports, voted to condemn Jesus—Joseph is the last person one would expect to care properly for Jesus." Cf. Raymond E. Brown, *The Death of the Messiah: From Gethsemane to the Grave*, vol. 2 (New York: Doubleday, 1994), 1240: "That the burial was done by Joseph of Arimathea is very probable, since a Christian fictional creation from nothing of a Jewish Sanhedrist who does what is right is almost inexplicable when we consider the hostility in early Christian writings toward the Jewish authorities responsible for the death of Jesus."

36. It was the responsibility of the Sanhedrin to bury the corpses of the executed in and around Jerusalem in order to obey Deut 21:22–23. Although victims of execution were to be buried by the Sanhedrin, they were not to be buried in places of honor (like their family tombs). We see this in the writings of the rabbis. See: m. Sanh. 6:5, 6, and m. Sem. 13.7.

37. According to Mark 15:43, Joseph was "waiting for the kingdom." Matthew (27:57) states that he

have fabricated a positive narrative surrounding Joseph of Arimathea if there was nothing to it. The story of the mercy of Joseph, a member of the Sanhedrin and therefore a man who would have been known to many in Jerusalem, could have proven to be very embarrassing if the story was in fact complete fiction. It is better explained as historical.

Some suggest that the criterion of multiple attestation and the criterion of embarrassment cancel each other out, in that it seems unlikely that people would repeat an embarrassing story.[38] But this argument is not sound. It is often the case that in individual or group recollections of a past event, an embarrassing detail is the very first thing that is repeated because it is an important part of the story, an indelible part of memory. One should not assume that just because something is not likely to be invented, it is not likely to be passed around. The flight of the disciples when Jesus was arrested and their absence at the place of crucifixion illustrates this principle. This is hardly a story post-Easter Christians would invent, but its wide circulation (for it is in all four Gospels) does not really surprise. We might add that Paul was deeply ashamed of his violent persecution of the early church, yet he does not hesitate to discuss it in his letters (1 Cor 15:9; Gal 1:13, 23). The author of the book of Acts does not omit it, either (Acts 7:54–8:1; 9:1–5; 22:4; 26:8–12).

ARCHAEOLOGY AND THE BURIAL OF JESUS

Not discussed in *JCDA* is a criterion that is standard among historians but often overlooked by New Testament scholars. This is the criterion of verisimilitude. This criterion asks if the material reflects the realities of the time and place it alleges to depict. Does the source speak of real people, real places, and real events, as they are known from other sources, including the findings of archaeology? As mentioned already, archaeologists and historians make use of the New Testament Gospels because these sources exhibit verisimilitude. Archaeologists and historians do not make use of second and third century gnostic sources because they do not exhibit verisimilitude. New Testament scholars would do well to follow the lead of archaeologists and historians. New Testament scholars may have reasons for their fascination with the apocryphal gospels, but historical verisimilitude should not be one of them.

At one time no one argued that the bodies of Jesus and the two men who

---

became a "disciple of Jesus." Luke 23:50–51 adds that Joseph was a "good and upright man." John 19:38 coheres with Matthew by claiming that Joseph was a "disciple of Jesus."

38. Goodacre, "Criticizing the Criterion," 165–67.

were crucified with him were denied burial. But in an essay published in 1994 John Dominic Crossan argued that given Roman law, given the prophecy-based story of the passion, including the burial, and given the paucity of archaeological evidence for the burial of crucifixion victims, we should probably assume that Jesus was not buried. Rather, we should assume that in keeping with Roman practice, the bodies of Jesus and the two men crucified with him were left hanging on the cross or, at best, were cast into a nearby ditch where they were mauled and eaten by dogs.[39]

Comments found in Greco-Roman literature seem to support the claim that Jesus probably wasn't buried. Horace (ca. 25 BCE) speaks of "hanging on a cross to feed crows" (*Ep.* 1.16.48). Suetonius (ca. 110 CE) reports that an angry Octavian (ca. 42 BCE) assured a man about to be executed (probably by crucifixion) who had expressed concern about this burial, "The birds will soon settle the question" (*Aug.* 13. 2). Juvenal (ca. 125 CE) gives expression to gallows humor when he says, "The vulture hurries from dead cattle and dogs and crosses to bring some of the carrion to her offspring" (*Sat.* 14.77–78). A third-century text describes the crucifixion victim as "evil food for birds of prey and grim picking for dogs" (Ps. Manetho, *Apotelesmatica* 4.200). On a second-century epitaph the deceased declares that his murderer, a slave, was "crucified alive for the wild beasts and birds" (Amyzon, cave I). Many other texts spare readers such gruesome details, but do mention the denial of proper burial (e.g., Livy 29.9.10; 29.18.14).[40]

But Roman legal material explicitly states that the bodies of the executed, if request is made, can be taken down and given proper burial (*Digesta* 48.24.1, 3).[41] In any case, the Greco-Roman texts have nothing to do with law and custom in Israel in peacetime. Our surviving literary evidence suggests that the bodies of those who were executed in and around Jerusalem during peacetime were not only permitted to be buried but were expected to be buried before sundown the day of death. This was done in order to preserve the purity of the land, as outlined in Deuteronomy 21:22–23. Josephus, writing in the 70s, states that in

---

39. John Dominic Crossan, "The Dogs beneath the Cross," in *Jesus: A Revolutionary Biography* (San Francisco: HarperOne, 1994), 123–58; and idem, *Who Killed Jesus?*, 188. The only mainstream New Testament scholar of whom we are aware who follows Crossan is Bart D. Ehrman, *How Jesus Became God: The Exaltation of a Jewish Preacher from Galilee* (New York: HarperOne, 2014), 157, 377n8. We are not aware of any archaeologist or historian who accepts this quirky argument.

40. The classic survey of crucifixion in Roman late antiquity is Martin Hengel, *Crucifixion: In the Ancient World and the Folly of the Message of the Cross* (Philadelphia: Fortress, 1977). For a current and very learned assessment, see Gunnar Samuelson, *Crucifixion in Antiquity*, 2nd ed., WUNT 2/310 (Tübingen: Mohr Siebeck, 2013).

41. The *Digesta* was compiled in the sixth century by Emperor Justinian. It contains legal material from the first century BCE to the fourth century CE. Most of the material in book 48 is drawn from first- and second-century sources.

his time even the bodies of those "sentenced to crucifixion are taken down and buried before sunset" (*J.W.* 4.317). Because only Rome possessed capital power in Judea and Samaria in the time of Jesus (John 18:31),[42] this means that those crucified by *Roman authority* were, nevertheless, permitted burial according to Jewish law and custom. Those crucified or executed by other means were buried and, in fact, from the Jewish point of view *had* to be buried to prevent the defilement of the land. There is simply no chance that the bodies of Jesus and the two men crucified with him would have been left hanging on their respective crosses, just outside the walls of Jerusalem, on the eve of Passover, unburied and subject to scavenging birds and animals.

This did not mean, of course, that the executed were given honorable burial (which usually meant burial in a family tomb); rather, they only received proper burial before sundown. Rabbinical texts refer to this policy: "They [the Sanhedrin] did not bury [the executed person] in the burying-place of his fathers. But two burying-places were kept in readiness by the Sanhedrin, one for them that were beheaded or strangled, and one for them that were stoned or burnt" (m. Sanh. 6:5).[43]

In his discussion on the burial of Jesus by Joseph of Arimathea, archaeologist Shimon Gibson rightly states:

> Joseph's plea on religious grounds would not have been ignored by the Roman authorities. Josephus testifies to the fact that the Romans did not require their Jewish subjects to violate their religious laws (*Against Apion II.*73). I surmise he would have argued that respect be accorded to the executed man based on the prevalent Jewish custom of the time that dead bodies must not be left exposed to be eaten by wild animals and buzzards. It was vital that the body of Jesus be buried before sundown and the beginning of the Sabbath when burials were prohibited. Instructions are provided in Deuteronomy: "And if a man has committed a sin worthy of death, and he is to be put to death, and thou hang him on a tree: his body shall not remain all night upon the tree, but thou shalt in any wise bury him that day . . ." (21:22–23).[44]

---

42. Sherwin-White, *Roman Law and Roman Society*, 36. Josephus states that the Roman governor was "entrusted by Augustus with full powers, including the infliction of capital punishment" (*J.W.* 2.117). In 62 CE high priest Annas, son of Annas the Great, was removed from office by the Roman governor for convening the Sanhedrin without permission and then condemning James, the brother of Jesus, to death (Josephus, *Ant.* 20.197–203).

43. The one who dies by crucifixion would be considered "strangled."

44. Shimon Gibson, *The Final Days of Jesus: The Archaeological Evidence* (New York: HarperCollins, 2009), 131. For a study of the interpretation and application of Deut 21:22–23 in the first century, see Craig

The Roman administration was careful not to disturb Jewish sensitivities during peacetime.[45] Craig Evans explains:

> Every source we have indicates that this was the practice in Israel, especially in the vicinity of Jerusalem, in peacetime. War was another matter, of course. When Titus besieged Jerusalem from 69 to 70 CE, thousands of Jews were crucified and very few of them were buried. The whole point was to terrorize the resistance and bring the rebellion to an end (as recounted by Josephus, *Jewish War* 5.289, 449). This was the true "exception that proves the rule": Roman authority in Israel normally did permit burial of executed criminals, including those executed by crucifixion (as Josephus implies), but they did not during the rebellion of 66–70 CE.[46]

The written record is unified in stating or assuming that during peacetime in the land of Israel the executed were given proper burial. The archaeological evidence, so far as we have any, supports the written record. In 1968, in the northeastern part of Jerusalem in the town of Giv'at Ha-Mivtar, an ossuary was discovered containing the bones of a man in his twenties and those of a young child. The right heel of the man, whose name was Yehohanan, was transfixed by an 11.5 cm iron nail. Fragments of wood still clung to the nail, whose tip was bent back, making extraction impossible.[47] The crucified man was buried, along with the nail; and one year later, when his bones were gathered and placed in an ossuary (bone box), the nail remained in his heel.[48]

The skeletal remains of Yehohanan are not the only evidence for the proper burial of a victim of crucifixion. The remains of a man both crucified and beheaded were recovered from what is now called the Abba Cave, once again in the Jerusalem neighborhood of Giv'at Ha-Mivtar. Nails were recovered from the ossuary. One nail was still embedded in the man's hand. On an ornate inscription inside

---

A. Evans, *Jesus and the Remains of His Day: Studies in Jesus and the Evidence of Material Culture* (Peabody MA: Hendrickson, 2015), 109–30.

45. For further discussion, see Craig A. Evans, "Getting the Burial Traditions and Evidences Right," in *How God Became Jesus: The Real Origins of Belief in Jesus' Divine Nature—A Response to Bart Ehrman*, ed. Michael F. Bird (Grand Rapids: Zondervan, 2014), 71–93, 217–20.

46. Evans, "Getting the Burial Traditions and Evidences Right," 80.

47. For image, see Clyde E. Fant and Mitchell G. Reddish, *Lost Treasures of the Bible: Understanding the Bible through Archaeological Artifacts in World Museums* (Grand Rapids: Eerdmans, 2008), 319; Evans, *Jesus and the Remains of His Day*, 294 fig. 6.2. See also 297 fig. 7.5 for photo of iron nails recovered from the excavated ruins of a mansion near the Mount Zion Gate.

48. The authors have visited the Sackler Medical Center of the University of Tel Aviv in Israel in 2013 and 2015, where we were permitted to view the heel of Yehohanan, with its embedded iron nail, as well as the nails and skeletal remains of Antigonus. We are grateful to Professor Israel Hershkovitz for granting us this privilege and for taking the time to discuss several interesting aspects of crucifixion and osteology.

the cave, written in paleo-Hebrew, appears the name Mattathias son of Judah, or, in Greek, Antigonus son of Aristobulus II.[49] The identification has been confirmed in a recent study.[50] In addition to the discovery of two properly buried victims of crucifixion, we also have at least one properly buried victim of beheading.[51]

In view of the unified testimony of both written and archaeological evidence, there is no justification for the claim that the bodies of Jesus and the men crucified with him would not have been buried or that perhaps they would have been buried in an unknown place.[52]

CONCLUSION

In her recent statement on the question of the criteria used to identify authentic material, Morna Hooker states:

> My chief plea . . . is for less dogmatism in our conclusions, and the recognition that all our results are only tentative. We know too little to be dogmatic, and it is probable that any rigid division of material into "authentic" and "non-authentic" distorts the picture. All the material comes to us at the hands of the believing community, and probably it all bears its mark to a lesser or greater extent; to confine our picture of Jesus to material which passes all our tests for genuineness is too restricting.[53]

Professor Hooker's comments are prudent and justified. But avoiding dogmatism and rigid distinctions between authentic and inauthentic material does not mean that the criteria historians utilize are useless or that "authenticity" is

---

49. J. M. Grintz, "The Inscription from Giv'at ha-Mivtar: A Historical Interpretation," *Sinai* 75 (1974): 20–23; idem, "The Last Way of the Last Hasmonean," *Ha'Umma* 43 (1975): 256–69. These two studies are in modern Hebrew. Credit for the identification also goes to the late Nicu Haas.

50. Yoel Elitzur, "The Abba Cave: Unpublished Findings and a New Proposal Regarding Abba's Identity," *IEJ* 63 (2013): 83–102. One of the complicating factors in the identification of these skeletal remains as belonging to Antigonus are the apparently discrepant claims found in Josephus (*Ant.* 15.8–9) and Dio Cassius (*History* 22.6). According to the former, Antigonus was beheaded (also reported in Plutarch, *Ant.* 36.2), but according to the latter, he was crucified. Analysis of the remains shows that Antigonus was both crucified and beheaded. See the discussion in Evans, "Getting the Burial Traditions and Evidences Right," 85–86.

51. And once again in Giv'at ha-Mivtar; in this case the remains of a man in his 50s, whose head was taken off with two strokes. We again thank Professor Hershkovitz for allowing us to view these important artifacts of crucifixion.

52. Crossan will be remembered for asserting that "with regard to the body of Jesus, by Easter Sunday morning, those who cared did not know where it was, and those who knew did not care." See John Dominic Crossan, *Jesus: A Revolutionary Biography* (New York: HarperCollins, 1994), 158. For a more detailed treatment, see John Dominic Crossan, *Who Killed Jesus?* (New York: HarperCollins, 1996). For a more recent discussion in support of Crossan's theory, see chapters 4 and 5 in Bart D. Ehrman, *How Jesus Became God: The Exaltation of a Jewish Preacher from Galilee* (New York: HarperCollins, 2015).

53. Morna D. Hooker, "Christology and Methodology," *NTS* 17 (1971): 480–87 (here 485–86).

meaningless. We need to think more clearly about our criteria, what they are, and how to apply them properly. We must also be clear about what we mean when we speak of *authenticity*. A saying attributed to Jesus that is judged to be authentic does not mean we necessarily possess the *ipsissima verba*, the "very words." Just because we conclude that an event is authentic, this does not mean that we are aware of every detail.

In the case of the burial of Jesus, we have good reasons for believing that we have before us an authentic story. The burial narratives lack the sort of exaggerations we discover in the second-century apologetically driven passion narratives found in writings like the Gospel of Peter and the Acts of Pilate. The burial narratives of the canonical Gospels show restraint. They also exhibit verisimilitude and cohere with all known relevant sources.

In conclusion, it is worth observing that although Christianity had many critics in its early centuries, none of them raised doubts about the burial of Jesus. In the words of John Granger Cook, "the Platonist critics of Christianity (Celsus, Porphyry, Hierocles, Julian, and Macarius's anonymous pagan philosopher), while not accepting the resurrection of Christ, do not (according to the surviving evidence) reject the historicity of the burial."[54] The criticisms of these men were nasty and personal, and sometimes perceptive, but they never doubted that Jesus was a real person, that he died a real death, and that he was buried in a real tomb.

---

54. John Granger Cook, "Crucifixion and Burial," *NTS* 57 (2011): 193–213, here 213n88. This important point is pursued in greater detail in Margaret M. Mitchell, "Origen, Celsus and Lucian on the 'Dénouement of the Drama' of the Gospels," in *Reading Religions in the Ancient World: Essays Presented to Robert McQueen Grant on his 90th Birthday*, ed. David E. Aune and Robin Darling Young, NovTSup 125 (Leiden: Brill, 2007), 215–36.

CHAPTER 12

Jesus's Resurrection, Realism, and the Role of the Criteria of Authenticity

MICHAEL R. LICONA

G ary Habermas is the foremost authority on the historical evidence for the resurrection of Jesus. Having studied the subject for more than half a century, Habermas has compiled an impressive bibliography of more than three thousand five hundred academic journal articles and books written on the topic from 1975 to the present. That amounts to an average of more than eighty publications every year. Dale Allison asserts that, soon after Jesus's death by crucifixion, at least some of Jesus's disciples and the apostle Paul believed that he had returned to life supernaturally. But what led to their belief? Allison answers, "That question holds its proud place as the prize puzzle of New Testament research."[1]

There are three major challenges to answering that question. First, there is the question of whether historians have the proper tools to enable them to investigate an event that is miraculous in nature. The second pertains to the general ability of historians to learn about the past, given the many challenges they face with such an enterprise. And, finally, a few scholars have recently questioned the effectiveness of tools commonly employed by historians of Jesus known as the criteria of authenticity. This article will address all three of these challenges.

HISTORIANS AND MIRACLE CLAIMS

There are numerous reasons given for why historians are prohibited from adjudicating miracle claims. Although an extensive treatment cannot be conducted here, I will address what is perhaps the most common objection offered today:

---

1. Dale C. Allison, *Resurrecting Jesus: The Earliest Christian Tradition and Its Interpreters* (New York: T&T Clark, 2005), 200.

Historians must employ *methodological naturalism* (MN).[2] MN states that all scientific investigation must be conducted with only natural causes in mind. MN takes no position on whether supernatural causes are responsible for certain events. However, MN does not allow supernatural causes to be considered, since the tools of scientific investigation are incapable of identifying them. MN should not be confused with *metaphysical naturalism*, which holds that the natural realm is all that exists. Thus, *methodological naturalism* is a particular method, while *metaphysical naturalism* is a worldview.

MN is a generally accepted principle in scientific and historical investigation. Its purpose is to prevent scientists and historians from drawing conclusions that go beyond what the evidence can bear and from employing "god of the gaps" solutions; that is, appealing to a supernatural cause when the cause is unknown.

While we want to avoid the problems MN is designed to prevent, there are several problems with MN that should likewise be avoided. One problem is MN would actually prevent scientists and historians from discovering the true cause if the nature of the cause is supernatural. Molecular biologist Michael Behe illustrates this weakness in the following analogy:

> Imagine a room in which a body lies crushed, flat as a pancake. A dozen detectives crawl around, examining the floor with magnifying glasses for any clues to the identity of the perpetrator. In the middle of the room, next to the body, stands a large, grey elephant. The detectives carefully avoid bumping into the pachyderm's legs as they crawl, and never even glance at it. Over time the detectives get frustrated with their lack of progress but resolutely press on, looking even more closely at the floor. You see, textbooks say detectives must "get their man," so they never consider elephants.[3]

There is a solution that preserves the benefits of MN while eliminating its weakness. Historians may conclude that an event occurred while leaving its cause undetermined. For example, let us suppose that astronomers have been tracking a comet for more than a decade, announce the comet is on a collision course with our moon, and that the impact will occur on a specific day. When that day arrives, the Hubble Space Telescope and observatories all over the world aim at the moon and the event is televised live worldwide. The comet slams

2. I have provided a more extensive critique of methodological naturalism in Michael R. Licona, "Historians and Miracle Claims," *JSHJ* 12 (2014): 106–29, and a lengthy analysis of the major arguments against historians investigating miracle claims in Michael R. Licona, *The Resurrection of Jesus: A New Historiographical Approach* (Downers Grove, IL: IVP Academic, 2010), 133–98.

3. Michael J. Behe, *Darwin's Black Box* (New York: Free Press, 1996), 192.

into the moon, as predicted, and as the dust settles, the message "Jesus is Lord" appears on the lunar surface in both Hebrew and Greek. We will call this *Event C*. Scientists are baffled and can provide no natural explanation for the message. However, they would not be prohibited from rendering the conclusion that *Event C* had occurred, since the evidence for it would be undeniable. Scientists would acknowledge the occurrence of *Event C* but refrain from naming its cause. This form of MN would provide all of the benefits (i.e., prohibiting scientists from going beyond what the evidence can bear and from employing a "god of the gaps" solution) and is far less restrictive than what is typically employed.

One may take a similar approach with one of Jesus's miracles: his resurrection. If the resurrection hypothesis explains the data in a manner that is superior to competing hypotheses, a historian could conclude that Jesus had risen from the dead while reserving judgment on the cause of the event. Some historians might object that this would be an illegitimate approach for a historian, because Jesus's resurrection would require a supernatural cause, and that is beyond what a historian can investigate. However, in that case one would have to make a similar objection to *Event C*. But such would be silly in view of the evidence that *Event C* had occurred. If one replies that the evidence for Jesus's resurrection is not as strong as what is posited for *Event C*, this would shift the matter from whether historians can adjudicate on an event that seemingly requires a supernatural cause to whether there is sufficient evidence to justify the conclusion that the event had occurred. Accordingly, if there is sufficient data to justify the conclusion that a certain event has occurred, there should be no a priori reasons for prohibiting historians from concluding that it has in fact occurred, even if the cause of the event cannot be determined using the tools of historical investigation.

GENERAL CHALLENGES TO DISCOVERING THE PAST

A second major challenge to historical investigation is the general ability of historians to learn about the past, given the many challenges they face in such an enterprise. I teach a Philosophy of History course. I will often begin the course by showing a twelve-inch segment of rail from a railroad track, explaining that it comes from the now extinct B & O Railroad and that B & O passenger trains used to run over it. I then ask my students if they believe my story. At this point, I see a lot of blank stares, because the students are assessing whether I have just set them up for embarrassment. "Okay, I see that you don't want to answer that question just yet, because you don't have enough information."

I then produce a large envelope and direct their attention to the postmark, which reads "05/23/2009." I then remove a letter from the envelope and point to the letterhead, which says, "Baltimore & Ohio Railroad Museum." I then read the letter dated May 21, 2009:

> This section of rail was manufactured between 1923 and 1927 for use by the Baltimore & Ohio Railroad.
>
> It is 100 pound rail which translates to a weight of approximately 33 pounds for this 12 inch section.
>
> This section of rail came from behind the roundhouse by what is now Platform 2, where the train ride currently departs. This route is the location of the original first 1.5 miles of commercial track ever laid in this country.

I then summarize the evidence supporting the rail's authenticity. We have the rail segment. We have an eyewitness (i.e., me) who purchased the rail segment. I testify that I spoke with the manager in person while visiting the museum, when she agreed to have the segment cut and shipped to me. Although anonymous, we have an official letter from the museum providing information pertaining to the rail I received, which the manager later informed me she had written. The letter came in an envelope with an official seal that provides the date it was sent. These data amount to very strong historical evidence that the rail segment once belonged to a track actively used in the glory days of passenger train travel.

Despite this evidence, neither my students nor you, the reader, can have absolute certainty that this rail segment is all I have described. For I may have fabricated the story, the letter, and the envelope. But neither can I have absolute certainty, since the museum manager may have deceived me and cut a segment from a rail that was never used in that specific capacity. Moreover, even if the museum manager and I intended to be truthful, the welder she contracted to cut the rail segment may have unintentionally, or even intentionally, cut it from the wrong track, and the museum manager may have never discovered it. So, apart from further investigation, neither my students nor you, the reader, nor I will ever have complete certainty that the rail segment I own is what I had requested and what was represented to me. For the possibility exists that it is not. However, the evidence is strong enough to justify having reasonable confidence that the rail segment is precisely what I had requested and what was represented to me.

This story illustrates many of the challenges involved in historical investigation and the nature of historical knowledge. Professional historians who specialize in matters pertaining to the philosophy of history devote a lot of time, even a career, to discussing them. Many readers may now be thinking, "Those people need to get a life! Historians must already lead a boring life. And you're saying there are some who specialize in discussing how to define history, what historians are actually trying to discover, and how they should go about doing it? And I thought watching golf was boring!"

Studying the philosophy of history is actually a lot more interesting than one might initially think. I began my doctoral research by reading more than one hundred books and journal articles written by philosophers of history. I read much that had been written during the hot debate over the nature of history that had occurred from the 1960s to the end of the twentieth century, a debate in which postmodernist historians were appealing to challenges to our ability to know what happened in the past, with many concluding that the past is unknowable and some even predicting the end of history.

After all, the past survives only in fragments preserved in texts, artifacts, and the effects of past causes. The documents were written by biased authors who had an agenda, who were shaped by the cultures in which they lived and are often foreign to us, who had access to a cache of incomplete information that varied in its accuracy, and who selected from that cache only information relevant to their purpose in writing, who often suppressed details when including them would complicate their literary portrait, who varied in the accuracy of their memories and the degree of their commitment to reporting in a manner we would regard as accurate by today's standards. Accordingly, all sources, including modern ones, must be studied with great care within a historical investigation.

While postmodernists did not introduce these challenges to the debate, they reiterated them.[4] But most philosophers of history believe postmodern approaches go too far in their skepticism about our ability to know about the past. By the end of the twentieth century, even some leading lights of the post-modernist movement in the discipline of history were hinting at defeat in the decades-long debate. Keith Jenkins, one of those leading lights, confessed that "most historians—and certainly most of those who might be termed 'academic' or professional 'proper' historians—have been resistant to that postmodernism which has affected so many of their colleagues in adjacent discourses."[5]

---

4. See Hayden White, *Tropics of Discourse: Essays in Cultural Criticism* (Baltimore: Johns Hopkins University Press, 1978), 82.

5. Keith Jenkins, "Introduction: On Being Open about Our Closures," in *The Postmodern History Reader*, ed. Keith Jenkins (New York: Routledge, 1997), 1; cf. 9. See also Richard Evans, "Review: From Historicism to Postmodernism Historiography in the Twentieth Century," *HistTh* 41 (2002): 79–87, 81; Georg G. Iggers, *Historiography in the Twentieth Century: From Scientific Objectivity to the Postmodern Challenge,*

Postmodernist David Roberts admits that Ernst Breisach may be right that postmodernism has come and gone among historians.[6] Realist historian Brian Fay comments,

> Except for some interesting exceptions at the margins of the discipline, historical practice is pretty much the same in 1997 as it was in 1967: historians seek to describe accurately and to explain cogently how and why a certain event or situation occurred. . . . For all the talk of narrativism, presentism, postmodernism, and deconstruction, historians write pretty much the same way as they always have . . . [7]

In his response to the postmodern challenge, Behan McCullagh writes, "I know of no practicing historians who admit that they cannot discover anything true about the past. They may admit to being fallible, but they do not deny that a lot of the basic facts they present are very probably true."[8] Therefore, the prediction that postmodernism would bring about the end of history was a failed prophecy.[9] Today, a chastened realism remains on the throne.[10]

Unfortunately, most biblical scholars are unaware of the lengthy debate over the postmodern challenge that has taken place among philosophers of history, because they do not read the literature in that field. So, some New Testament scholars believe they are making contributions to the discipline when in reality the party is over and they missed it! As a result, they are doomed to hack away at the thick brush with their machetes, clear a path they will one day pave, and when they arrive at the end of their new road, find the rubbish from others who camped there years ago, extinguished their fires, scattered the ashes, and returned home to a cautious realism. My hope is that the number of New Testament scholars who follow this course will be limited.

2nd ed. (Middletown, CT: Wesleyan University Press, 2005), 133, 145, 150; Nancy F. Partner, "Historicity in an Age of Reality-Fictions," in *A New Philosophy of History*, ed. Frank Ankersmit and Hans Kellner (Chicago: University of Chicago Press, 1995), 21–39; John Tosh, *The Pursuit of History: Aims, Methods, and New Directions in the Study of Modern History*, rev. 3rd ed. (Essex: Longman, 2002), 194–200; Perez Zagorin, "History, the Referent, and Narrative: Reflections on Postmodernism Now," *HistTh* 38 (1999): 1, 3, 9; John Zammito, "Ankersmit and Historical Representation," *HistTh* 44 (2005): 161, 163.

   6. David D. Roberts, "Postmodernism and History: Missing the Missed Connections," *HistTh* 44 (2005): 252.

   7. Brian Fay, "Nothing But History," *HistTh* 37 (1998): 83. See also Mark T. Gilderhus, *History and Historians: A Historiographical Introduction*, 6th ed. (Upper Saddle River, NJ: Prentice Hall, 2007), 124.

   8. C. Behan McCullagh, *The Truth of History* (New York: Routledge, 1998), 15.

   9. Jens Bruun Kofoed, *Text and History: Historiography and the Study of the Biblical Text* (Winona Lake, IN: Eisenbrauns, 2005), 16.

   10. Two of the finest book-length critiques of postmodernist approaches to history are McCullagh, *Truth of History*, and Richard. J. Evans, *In Defense of History* (New York: Norton, 1999).

If one major lesson can be learned from the debate among philosophers of history over the nature of history, it is that we should avoid extreme positions on either end. The time has passed in which a historian of antiquity is free to say we can have historical certainty that *Event X* occurred in the manner precisely described by a source. For, in light of the multiple challenges to learning about the past, the only way to have such certainty would be to use a time machine and view the event taking place. Of course, similar challenges exist for archaeologists, geologists, and evolutionary biologists, who often work with such a paucity of data that it makes them envious of all that historians often possess.

On the other hand, the multiple challenges to discovering the past often do not leave historians without the ability to have reasonable assurance not only that *Event X* occurred, but also that it occurred in a manner quite similar to the way it is described by an ancient source. Students of the historical Jesus face most if not all of the challenges mentioned above when reading the Gospels. In each of the four canonical Gospels, the entire life of Jesus has been summarized in less than twenty-five thousand words. Like everyone who has ever lived, the evangelists and their sources had imperfect memories.[11] The evangelists were biased. Their agenda was to provide us with a literary portrait of Jesus in which certain aspects of Jesus's character and roles were emphasized. Therefore, each evangelist selected certain stories and teachings of Jesus to include in their narrative that would assist him in completing his portrait. As with every person who has ever lived, the evangelists were influenced by the cultures in which they lived, cultures now quite foreign to us. Occasionally, the evangelists suppressed details when it would complicate the portrait of their subject. One sees this most clearly in John's presentation of Jesus in Gethsemane and on the cross where, unlike in the Synoptics, little space is devoted to Jesus agonizing over what is to come and there is no cry of anguish from him on the cross over being forsaken by God. Plutarch, who wrote biographies around the same time, had a similar practice.[12]

The Gospels are not entirely portraits. Neither are they entirely photographs. They contain elements of both photograph and portrait. Perhaps it would be

---

11. Since we are here approaching the Gospels as historians, no assumptions of divine inspiration can be made. Whether the imperfect memories of the evangelists and/or their sources impacted the Gospels they wrote is not an issue I am here addressing.

12. For example, in his *Life of Brutus* (*Brut.*, 33), Plutarch reports that Brutus discovered and executed Theodotus, who had counseled the Egyptian king Ptolemy to kill Pompey. However, in his *Life of Pompey* (*Pomp.*, 80), Plutarch reports that Brutus put Theodotus to death with every possible torture. Since Brutus was, in general, a moderate and gentle person, Plutarch apparently did not wish to include this detail in his *Life of Brutus* and complicate his portrait of him. However, a portrait of Brutus was not Plutarch's concern when writing his *Life of Pompey*.

more accurate to think of them as hybrids. Ancient biographers sometimes altered their photographic snapshots in order to bring greater illumination to their readers. One may think of a photographer who takes a photograph of a couple walking hand in hand through a meadow of flowers on a sunny day. In order to emphasize the romantic element of the moment, the photographer may use editing software and add a slight blur to the photograph. The true character of the scene is preserved, even clarified, while its photographic accuracy is slightly diminished.

Another analogy may be helpful. When creating an English translation of the Bible, translation committees must first decide on the type of translation they wish to create. A literal translation, such as the NASB, ESV, NRSV, and KJV, attempts to provide a translation that is word-for-word as much as possible. A dynamic-equivalent translation, such as the NIV and NLT, are more interested in providing a thought-for-thought translation. Of course, thought-for-thought translations should not be judged for accuracy according to word-for-word standards. To do so would be to miss the objective of the translation. Optimal-equivalent translations, such as the NET and CSB, attempt to be hybrids of literal and dynamic translations. Paraphrases, such as the Message, are not translations in a technical sense. Instead, the objective of a paraphrase is to capture the main thought in a text while presenting it in a clear and readable manner.

I view the Synoptic Gospels as using an optimal-equivalent model of reporting the teachings and acts of Jesus, while John is our dynamic-equivalent. At times, John is even closer to a paraphrase while at other times he goes even further, especially with the discourses. And yet, when we read some pericopes in John that also appear in the Synoptics, such as the feeding of the five thousand, we can observe that John did not always employ portrait elements. He just employed them more often and more freely than the Synoptics. One may debate the historical reliability of the Gospels. However, the standard challenges to historical knowledge noted by postmodern historians do not prevent historians from adjudicating on the historicity of miracles in general and the resurrection of Jesus in particular.

CRITERIA

In 2012, Chris Keith and Anthony Le Donne served as coeditors for a volume that included essays from a group of respected scholars who question, to varying degrees, the value of using the criteria of authenticity in historical Jesus research.[13] Because the philosophy of history is often neglected in New Testament studies, the conversations in *Jesus, Criteria, and the Demise of Authenticity* are both thoughtful and useful (hereafter *JCDA*). The contributors do not form a single voice when it comes to answering the question of whether the criteria can still play a useful role in historical Jesus research. While some regard the criteria as useless and wish to jettison them altogether, others see value in most of the criteria once they are refined and the expectations of what they can provide are lowered.[14]

Several of the contributors remind us of the challenges involved in obtaining accurate historical knowledge and the tentativeness of our historical conclusions. Jen Schröter reiterates what we discussed in the previous section.[15] Winter informs readers that we can no longer say, as was once thought, that if historical inquiry is properly conducted, it will always result in accurate conclusions and that historians can be entirely objective while examining bare facts.[16] Instead, historical conclusions conducted with great integrity will sometimes be erroneous, and we can only speak in terms of degrees of probability.[17]

Le Donne contends that the criterion of double dissimilarity should be abandoned.[18] And he is probably correct. Dagmar Winter suggests it should be replaced by the criterion of historical plausibility.[19] Raphael Rodriguez argues the criterion of embarrassment cannot yield much about Jesus.[20] Loren Stuckenbruck contends that an early dating of a tradition does not require that it originated with Jesus.[21] He also argues that the presence of Semitisms does not automatically mean the tradition is early. However, his essay does not lead us to conclude that the presence of Semitisms is a useless criterion. Rather, it informs

---

13. Chris Keith and Anthony Le Donne, eds. *Jesus, Criteria, and the Demise of Authenticity* (London: T&T Clark, 2012).

14. Elsewhere I have provided a lengthy review of *Jesus, Criteria, and the Demise of Authenticity*. See Michael R. Licona, "Is the Sky Falling in the World of Historical Jesus Research?," *BBR* 26 (2016): 353–68.

15. Jens Schröter, "The Criteria of Authenticity in Jesus Research and Historiographical Method," in Keith and Le Donne, *Jesus, Criteria, and the Demise of Authenticity*, 49–70.

16. Dagmar Winter, "Saving the Quest for Authenticity from the Criterion of Dissimilarity: History and Plausibility" in Keith and Le Donne, *Jesus, Criteria, and the Demise of Authenticity*, 115–31 (see 115).

17. Winter, "Saving the Quest for Authenticity," 116, 125.

18. Anthony Le Donne, "The Criterion of Coherence: Its Development, Inevitability, and Historiographical Limitations" in Keith and Le Donne, *Jesus, Criteria, and the Demise of Authenticity* , 94–114 (see 108). See also Gerd Theissen and Dagmar Winter, *The Quest for the Plausible Jesus: The Question of Criteria*, trans. M. Eugene Boring (Louisville: Westminster John Knox, 2002). See especially the concluding remarks on 167–71.

19. Winter, "Saving the Quest for Authenticity," 126.

20. Raphael Rodriguez, "The Embarrassing Truth About Jesus: The Criterion of Embarrassment and the Failure of Historical Authenticity," in Keith and Le Donne, *Jesus, Criteria, and the Demise of Authenticity*, 132–51.

21. Loren T. Stuckenbruck, "'Semitic Influence on Greek': An Authenticating Criterion in Jesus Research?," in Keith and Le Donne, *Jesus, Criteria, and the Demise of Authenticity*, 73–94 (see 74n2).

us that it is not one of the strongest criteria and should be used alongside other criteria. Mark Goodacre and Winter acknowledge the value of the criterion of multiple independent sources.[22] However, Goodacre questions whether this criterion can be applied to the Gospels, since he rejects the idea of a Q source and has reservations pertaining to John's independence from the Synoptics.[23] Schröter and Allison observe that the criteria have not overcome subjectivity or led to a consensus among scholars about Jesus.[24]

Unfortunately, many of the contributors resort to the challenges offered by postmodernists, contending that those challenges justify pessimism over ever arriving at a historical Jesus.[25] In my opinion this pessimism goes beyond what is justified. Consider the following by Schröter:

> One must take into account that a historical inquiry is always an enterprise in which the historian studies historical data to develop an idea of what might have happened. Thereby, the remains from the past must not be confused with the events themselves. Rather, the historical sources are selective and often subjective recollections and interpretations of events from which the historian attempts to recover the events themselves. On the other hand, "memory" is by itself a problematic historical category. It does not lead automatically to a more adequate picture of the past, but, to the contrary, can be affected by misperception, wrong information, oblivion, and projection.[26]

He continues, contending that as research on the Gospels at the turn of the twentieth century pointed out, even the Gospel of Mark, as the earliest story about Jesus, cannot be regarded as a reliable biographical account. Rather, it has its own theological agenda in presenting Jesus as the representative of God's kingdom (which is growing secretly), who will return as the Son of Man at

---

22. Winter, "Saving the Quest for Authenticity," 127; Mark Goodacre, "Criticizing the Criterion of Multiple Attestation: The Historical Jesus and the Question of Sources" in Keith and Le Donne, *Jesus, Criteria, and the Demise of Authenticity,* 152–69, esp. 168–69.

23. Goodacre, "Criticizing the Criterion of Multiple Attestation," 162–64.

24. Schröter, "Criteria of Authenticity in Jesus Research and Historiographical Method," 58; Dale C. Allison Jr., "It Don't Come Easy: A History of Disillusionment," in Keith and Le Donne, *Jesus, Criteria, and the Demise of Authenticity,* 186–99, esp. 195, 197. Scot McKnight also notes that the criteria have not led to a consensus but is not skeptical concerning the use of the Gospels to construct a historical Jesus, although he regards historical Jesus studies as being "theologically useless" to the church, with the exception of its use in apologetics. See Scot McKnight, "Why the Authentic Jesus Is of No Use for the Church," in Keith and Le Donne, *Jesus, Criteria, and the Demise of Authenticity* , 173–85 (see 175, 179n16, 181, 183).

25. By "historical Jesus" I mean the Jesus composed solely of those elements about him that can be established with reasonable historical certainty and apart from faith. Of course, the "real Jesus" was much more than the "historical Jesus."

26. Schröter, "Criteria of Authenticity in Jesus Research," 51.

the end of time. It would be inappropriate, therefore, to apply the designation "historical Jesus" to the gospel accounts.[27]

Schröter's opinion is shared by many. However, I do not understand why Mark's theological agenda would disqualify his life of Jesus as a reliable portrait from which historians may construct a historical Jesus. Plutarch certainly has a moral agenda when writing his *Lives*. Notwithstanding, that does not lead classicists to think Plutarch's *Lives* cannot be regarded as reliable biographical accounts and that it is inappropriate to think historians can find a historical Cicero or a historical Caesar or a historical Cato Uticensis in his biographies of them. Of course, scholars mean different things by the term "reliable." If Schröter means that Mark is not a precise and exhaustive report of what we would have seen if we had been there and one that is free of authorial interpretation, this can be granted. But the same can be said of all ancient *and modern* biographies. Yet, this does not prevent historians from finding historical kernels in them in order to reconstruct portraits of the main characters that are essentially true or "true enough."[28]

A Life of Josh

In March 2014, I was a speaker at a conference in Ft. Wayne, Indiana. While there, I had lunch with a college senior who was majoring in philosophy named Josh. He was uncertain where he wanted to do graduate work and what he wanted to study. Yet, he impressed me as being intelligent and pleasant.

When I returned to Atlanta, I reflected on my encounter with Josh. You might say that I was able to construct an idea of Josh in my mind. This idea of Josh was based on my interpretation of him after meeting him, an interpretation that could very well have been mistaken in some ways, given the possibility of wrong impressions and inaccurate memory. Moreover, the Josh I experienced that weekend may have been quite different from the Josh as experienced by his parents, his girlfriend, his siblings, his closest friends, or his classmates, since Josh relates to all of them in different ways. Furthermore, no one but Josh will ever know and understand in precise terms how he relates to himself. No one is fully aware of his deepest inner reflections, thoughts, and feelings about himself. In fact, what is true of most of us is almost certainly true of Josh: there are things about himself he does not entirely comprehend.

---

27. Schröter, "Criteria of Authenticity in Jesus Research," 53.
28. The term "true enough" is from Christopher Pelling, *Plutarch and History: Eighteen Studies* (Swansea: Classical Press of Wales, 2002), 160.

So, let us slightly alter the above words of Schröter to articulate the challenge of finding a historical Josh.

> One must take into account that inquiry about Josh is always an enterprise in which one studies historical data to develop an idea of what might have happened thus far in the life of Josh. Thereby, the remains from the past must not be confused with the events themselves. Rather, the sources who know Josh, including Josh himself, are selective and often subjective in their recollections and interpretations of events in the life of Josh from which they attempt to recover the events when describing them. On the other hand, "memory" is by itself a problematic historical category. It does not lead automatically to a more adequate picture of past events in the life of Josh. To the contrary, it can be affected by misperception, wrong information, oblivion, and projection.

We could continue the parallel further:

> Although quite early and in fact written while its main character was still alive, a *Life of Josh* could not be regarded as a reliable biographical account. Rather, it would have its own historiographical agenda in presenting Josh as a historical figure about which we can know a considerable amount with a reasonable amount of certainty. It would be inappropriate, therefore, to apply the designation "historical Josh" to the *Life of Josh*.

In the strictest sense, the *real Josh* is unknowable. And the same may be said of the *real Jens Schröter* and the *real Michael Licona*. Are we then to regard any rendition of the *historical Josh* as being hopelessly inadequate? How am I to learn about Josh? One may reasonably suggest that I interview those who know him best. His family members, close friends, and colleagues would be primary sources, the most valuable places to begin. Perhaps I can also find an unsympathetic source, a person who does not like Josh. Memories of his childhood shared by his parents would be valuable, although they would be recalling events that occurred more than two decades ago.

The *historical Josh*, constructed on elements about him and established with a high degree of certainty, will not be exhaustive. Nor will it be entirely accurate, since memories are imperfect. There will also probably be items that are skewed due to bias. Josh's mother may selectively remember him as being a better child than he actually was, while one of his sisters may recall him as being a worse brother than he actually was. Nevertheless, we would probably have a fairly accurate portrait of Josh before us. We would trust eyewitness testimony, especially when provided close to the events (criterion of eyewitness/early sources). We would trust information about Josh provided by two or more independent witnesses (criterion of multiple attestation), especially if one of the witnesses was someone who does not like Josh (criterion of unsympathetic sources). And we would trust data provided by a relative who loves him and who relayed an event involving Josh that is embarrassing to him or to them as a family (criterion of embarrassment).

Although the challenges of knowing the past are very real, they are often not of such a nature that they prevent historians from obtaining knowledge of people, events, conditions, and states of affairs that are largely true. As I read the historical Jesus literature, what stands out to me is not the lack of data (although we wish we had more) nor the inadequacy of our methods (although they are by no means fullproof), but the observation that the horizons of historians are often the guiding force of their investigations. We are all influenced by our race, gender, nationality, ethics, our political, philosophical, and religious convictions, the way we were raised, the academic institutions we attended, and the group of people whose acceptance and respect we desire. There is no way around it. The horizons of historians often compromise the integrity of their historical investigations. Moreover, data is pliable. And not even the best methods can prevent an irresponsible handling of the texts. As Allison himself writes, "Tools do not dictate how they are used; the hands that hold them do that."[29]

While it is true that the criteria have not led historians of Jesus to a consensus, it can likewise be observed that scientific method has failed to lead scientists to a consensus in many matters. Scientists are encamped on different sides of numerous issues. And scientists have been known to fudge the data.[30] When we permit our horizons to guide how we employ the tools of our historical trade, the conclusions are often going to be skewed. Thus, a significant responsibility of the problem, perhaps the bulk of it, must be attributed to the historian. So, rather than point an accusing finger at the criteria and blame them for failing to provide a "consensus historical Jesus," we should instead take a deep look at ourselves.

Rather than jettisoning the criteria, a better route may be to admit that

---

29. Allison, "It Don't Come Easy," esp. 197.

30. See Scott O. Lilienfeld, "Fudge Factor: A Look at a Harvard Science Fraud Case," *Scientific American* (November 1, 2010): n.p. Online: www.scientificamerican.com/article/fudge-factor/. Scientists operate with their horizons as much as historians do. This can lead to the misuse of method. See "How Many Scientists Fabricate and Falsify Research?," n.p. Online: http://phys.org/news162795064.html.

one's expectations of the criteria have been idealistic and then revise those expectations accordingly. We want the criteria to work like a calculator. We enter the data, press the "Enter" button, and receive assured results. Calculators do not make errors. However, statisticians can use them in an improper manner to get the numbers to say what they want. So, even if the application of the criteria was similar to using a calculator, flawless results would not be assured.

But the criteria do not function like a calculator. And there are better analogies to describe their role. Physicians employ certain criteria when diagnosing a patient's symptoms. Highly gifted and experienced physicians will accurately diagnose their patients more often than their colleagues. Still, they will misdiagnose a patient occasionally or be left without an answer, due to human error or a paucity of data. Occasionally, this will result in tragic consequences to the patient. Yet, we do not encourage physicians to jettison their criteria for making diagnoses. Juries consider the data and sometimes arrive at wrong judgments, resulting in the guilty going unpunished and the innocent being unjustly punished. Sometimes the jury is incompetent. But there have been plenty of occasions when the jury applied the rules correctly and the available data led them to the wrong conclusion. Yet, we do not view our legal system with the pessimism modeled by many of JCDA's contributors.

The bottom line is the historian's use of the criteria should be viewed in a manner similar to those employed by physicians and juries. Some physicians, jurists, and historians are more proficient than many of their colleagues. However, no one is perfect and incorrect conclusions are inevitable in all human pursuits. And yet imperfection does not justify the pessimism often observed by some JCDA contributors.

Criteria and the Resurrection of Jesus

I now wish to take a look at two matters in historical Jesus research related to Jesus's fate, specifically his death and resurrection, and assess the role the criteria of authenticity play. There is nearly a universal consensus among historians of Jesus that he was executed via crucifixion and died as a result, and that shortly thereafter a number of his disciples had experiences they believed were of the risen Jesus appearing to them. What data have led to a consensus opinion pertaining to these facts?

Space limitations prohibit an extensive answer.[31] So, I will offer three brief reasons for concluding that Jesus died by crucifixion and three for concluding

---

31. For an extensive treatment on Jesus's death by crucifixion, see Licona, *Resurrection of Jesus*, 303–18.

that the disciples believed the risen Jesus had appeared to them. First, Jesus's death by crucifixion is multiply attested by a fair number of ancient sources, Christian and non-Christian alike. It is very probable that Josephus reported the event in his original version of *Antiquities* 18.3.[32] Tacitus, Lucian, and Mara bar Serapion are all aware of the event.[33] Lucian adds that Jesus's crucifixion took place in Palestine.[34] In Christian sources, Jesus's execution is widely reported, with and without specifying the mode of crucifixion. All four canonical Gospels report Jesus's death by crucifixion, as does much of the New Testament, which refers to it regularly.[35] Jesus's death and/or crucifixion are also abundantly mentioned in the non-canonical Christian literature.[36]

Second, some of the reports of Jesus's death by crucifixion are very early. Paul mentions Jesus's death by crucifixion no later than 55 CE (Gal 2:20–21) and said he preached the same to those in Corinth around 51 CE, no more than twenty-one years after Jesus's crucifixion (1 Cor. 15:1–11). Jesus's death appears numerous times in the *kerygma* of the oral formulas. The earliest report of Jesus's death is found in the tradition in 1 Corinthians 15:3. Virtually all scholars who have written on the subject hold that Paul here provides tradition about Jesus he had received from leaders in the Jerusalem church. There is likewise widespread agreement that this tradition was composed very early, reflected

---

32. Much literature has been written on the authenticity of this text, with a majority of scholars concluding that Josephus mentions Jesus's death while also granting that a Christian editor redacted and added a number of elements in the text. See Licona, *Resurrection of Jesus*, 235–42.

33. Tacitus does not specifically name crucifixion as the mode of Jesus's execution, but instead reports that Jesus suffered "the most extreme penalty" (*Ann.* 15.44). Mara bar Serapion does not mention the mode of execution. Although of questionable historical value, the Talmud also reports the event, but uses the term "hanged" (b. Sanh. 43a).

34. Lucian, *Peregrine*, 11.

35. Mark 15:24–37; Matt 27:35–50; Luke 23:33–46; John 19:16–37. Before the canonical Gospels were written, the death of Jesus is reported abundantly throughout the Pauline corpus and in all of Paul's undisputed letters except Philemon (Rom 1:4; 4:24; 5:6, 8, 10; 6:3, 4, 5, 8, 9, 10; 7:4; 8:11 [twice], 34; 10:9; 11:26; 14:9, 15; 1 Cor 8:11; 15:3, 12, 13, 15, 16, 20; 2 Cor 5:14, 15; Gal 1:1; 2:21; Phil 2:8; 3:10, 18; Col 1:18, 20; 2:12, 14, 20; 1 Thess 1:10; 4:14; 5:10; 2 Tim 2:8, 11. Crucifixion of Christ [crucifixion, cross]: 1 Cor 1:17, 18, 23; 2:2, 8; 2 Cor 13:4; Gal 2:20; 3:1; 6:12, 14; Eph 1:20; 2:16). We find Jesus's death also attested in Hebrews and 1 Peter (Heb 2:9, 14; 9:15–10:14; 12:2; 13:20; 1 Pet 1:3, 21; 2:24; 3:18). Both were certainly written in the first century and may pre-date the canonical Gospels (L. T. Johnson, *The Real Jesus: The Misguided Quest for the Historical Jesus and the Truth of the Traditional Gospels* [San Francisco: HarperSanFrancisco, 1996], 151, 164).

36. Ign. *Eph.* 16:2; Ign. *Trall.* 9:1; Ign. *Rom.* 7:2; Ign. *Barn.* 7:9; 12:1; Ign. *Mart. Pol.* 17:2. The Gospel of Peter (Gos. Pet. 10, 18) and the Epistle of the Apostles (Ep. Apos. 9) report Jesus's death by crucifixion. The Gospel of the Hebrews mentions Jesus's death by implication of his bodily resurrection. The Gospel of Mary and the Gospel of Truth likewise mention Jesus's death. Jesus's crucifixion—without mentioning whether he died—is mentioned in the Gospel of the Savior (91–92, 100–108). Jesus is crucified and dies in the Coptic Apocalypse of Peter and The Second Treatise of the Great Seth, gnostic writings dated to the third century. The Gospel of Thomas (Gos. Thom. 65) and the Gospel of Judas (Gos. Judas 57) probably refer to the death of Jesus in Thomas's version of Jesus's parable of the vineyard and the wicked tenants, and in Judas's mentioning of Jesus's betrayal, resulting in the sacrifice of Jesus's body.

what the Jerusalem apostles were teaching, and is the oldest extant tradition pertaining to the resurrection of Jesus.[37]

A third evidence for Jesus's death by crucifixion is that the passion narratives appear largely credible, given their often-embarrassing nature. While a number of accounts existed of Jewish martyrs who had acted bravely under circumstances of extreme torture and execution, reports of Jesus's arrest and martyrdom show a far less valiant Jesus.[38] In the former, the martyrs are strong, bold, and courageous throughout their ordeals. When we come to the passion narratives in the canonical Gospels, we find a number of the positive traits exhibited by Jesus shared by Jewish martyrs. Like the others, once arrested, Jesus stands boldly in his convictions. In all, there are moments of great composure during their painful ordeals. Jesus prays, as do Eleazar, Stephen, Polycarp, and Rabbi Akiba. Even Jesus's enemies are impressed with his behavior while under great duress, as are those witnessing the martyrdoms of the seven brothers, Eleazar, Polycarp, Rabbi Akiba, and Rabbi Hanina ben Taradion.[39]

However, the accounts of Jesus's martyrdom differ significantly from the others. Whereas a number of the other martyrdom reports seem constructed to provide encouragement to others who may face similar situations, the passion narratives of Jesus provide no such encouragement. Jesus anguishes over his impending treatment and wants to avoid it if at all possible.[40] This would certainly not have inspired those whom he had instructed to take up their own crosses and follow him if they wanted to be his disciples.[41] Jesus's request that God remove the cup from him if possible stands in contrast to the defiant words of the martyrs who in essence say, "Bring it on!" and "Racks and stones may break my bones, but resurrection awaits me!" Rather than proclaiming that he will not forsake God or his law, as did many of the Jewish martyrs, Jesus instead cries out, asking God why he has forsaken him.[42] Given the likely embarrassing nature of these comments of despair to the early church, they are unlikely to have been invented.[43]

---

37. See Licona, *Resurrection of Jesus*, 223–35, 318–29.

38. 2 Macc 7; 4 Macc 6:1–30; y. Ber. 14b; b. Ber. 61b; b. Abod. Zar. 18a; compare also accounts of early Christian martyrs (Acts 6:8–7:60; Ign., *Mart. Pol.* 7:1–16:1).

39. Mark 15:4–5, 39; Matt 27:54; Luke 23:39–42, 47; John 19:7–12.

40. Mark 14:32–42; Matt 26:36–46; Luke 22:39–46.

41. Mark 8:34; Matt 16:24; Luke 9:23.

42. Mark 15:34; Matt 27:46.

43. Differing from Rodriguez's reservations pertaining to the criterion of embarrassment, many scholars recognize value in its use. See Louis H. Feldman, "Introduction," in *Josephus, Judaism, and Christianity*, ed. Louis H. Feldman and Gohei Hata (Detroit: Wayne State University Press, 1987), 42; Robert H. Gundry, *Mark: A Commentary on His Apology for the Cross*, 2 vols. (Grand Rapids: Eerdmans, 1993), 965–66; Craig S. Keener, *A Commentary on the Gospel of Matthew* (Grand Rapids: Eerdmans, 1999), 682; Geza Vermes, *The Passion: The Story of an Event That Changed Human History* (New York: Penguin, 2006), 122.

For this reason, we get a sense that in the canonical Gospels we are reading authentic reports of Jesus's arrest and death, even if a cleanup or omission may have occurred with some of those embarrassing details by Luke and of almost all of them by John. Accordingly, the embarrassing elements in the passion narratives weigh in favor of the presence of historical kernels.

While open to possibilities, historians must be guided by probabilities. Thus, given the strong evidence for Jesus's crucifixion, without good evidence to the contrary the historian must conclude that the process killed him. This conclusion is shared by virtually all scholars who have studied the subject.

In summary, the historical evidence is very strong that Jesus died by crucifixion. The event is multiply attested by a number of ancient sources, some of which are unsympathetic, even hostile, to the Christian view. They even appear in multiple literary forms, being found in annals, historiographies, biographies, letters, and tradition in the form of creeds, oral formulas, and hymns. Some of the reports are very early and can reasonably be traced to the Jerusalem apostles. And the passion narratives appear credible, given the embarrassing elements in them. For those who would call for the abandonment of the criteria or regard them as having little value, I would want to hear from them whether they think Jesus died by crucifixion and, if so, on what basis they have arrived at this conclusion.

We will now look at some data supporting the fact that Jesus's disciples had experiences they interpreted as the risen Jesus appearing to them. Jesus's resurrection and appearances are mentioned in the oral tradition in 1 Corinthians 15:3–7. As mentioned above, the content of this tradition, though not necessarily its form, can be traced to Jesus's disciples with a high degree of confidence, rendering it very early. In 1 Corinthians 15:8, Paul claims to have been an eyewitness of the risen Jesus who had appeared to him. The appearances are multiply attested in the kerygma of 1 Corinthians 15:3–7, the speeches in Acts (2, 10, 13), which most scholars agree contain summaries of apostolic teachings, the four canonical Gospels, Acts (9, 22, 26), 1 Clement, which may have been written by a follower of Peter, and possibly Josephus (unsympathetic).[44]

Therefore, the appearance reports are early, attested by multiple independent sources, at least one of which claims to have been an eyewitness, and possibly attested by an unsympathetic source. There is a nearly universal agreement among scholars who study the topic that the apostles proclaimed and believed Jesus had been raised and had appeared to them.[45] So, again, I would want to

---

44. 1 Clem. 42:3; Josephus *Ant.* 18:3.

45. For an extensive treatment, see Licona, *Resurrection of Jesus*, 318–461.

hear from those who would call for the abandonment of the criteria or regard them as having little value, (1) whether they think many of Jesus's disciples and Paul had experiences they interpreted as the risen Jesus appearing to them and, if so, (2) on what basis they arrive at this conclusion. Although the criteria of authenticity have limitations and do not guarantee accurate results, they are useful tools that assist historians in the quest to discover the past. They use them when considering the individual logia and acts of the characters being considered (atomism). Yet, historians should go beyond the criteria and also consider the entire portrait of those characters presented (holism).[46] Although they may have a preference between atomism and holism, there is nothing requiring them to focus on one to the exclusion of the other.

Historians should give primary consideration to those facts that are virtually certain, followed by others for which historical confidence is still good. And when all is done and historians have reached a conclusion, they hold it provisionally, understanding that disconfirming data may surface in the future or someone may make an important observation previously overlooked, either of which would justify the abandonment of the conclusion they now hold. Since consensus often eludes us, the best historians will occasionally arrive at conclusions that differ from those of the majority. They will sometimes be mistaken. But they are more likely correct than not.

CONCLUSION

The question "Did Jesus rise from the dead?" is one of the most important questions one may ask and has garnered an extraordinary amount of interest from New Testament scholars. In this essay, I have considered three major contemporary challenges to investigating the question. Some question whether historians have the proper tools to enable them to investigate an event that is miraculous in nature. Others question the general ability of historians to learn about the past, given the many challenges they face with such an enterprise. Still others have recently questioned the effectiveness of the criteria of authenticity. We have seen that these three challenges are not nearly as difficult to overcome as those who posit them imagine. In fact, in this essay I have contended that none of them prohibit historians from conducting a sound investigation into the question, "Did Jesus rise from the dead?"

---

46. See Winter, "Saving the Quest for Authenticity," 117; Allison, "It Don't Come Easy," 198.

Part Three

. . .

The Book of Acts and
Christian Origins

CHAPTER 13

Social Memory in Acts

MICHAEL F. BIRD AND BEN SUTTON

H istorical Jesus research has recently been confronted with the suggestion that the criteria of authenticity, normally used to distinguish "authentic" from "inauthentic" materials in the Gospels, are incapable of actually identifying authentic Jesus material as originally proposed by form critics.[1] But it is not just historical Jesus research that has been shaped by form criticism and its derivative methodologies; the study of Acts—specifically its history—has also been subject to a similar methodological approach that separates history from layers of interpretation. Our proposal is that social memory theory, with a particular nod to Chris Keith's Jesus-memory approach, represents not only a viable replacement of form-critical approaches but provides a framework for how a historian can work toward a plausible historical construction of the early church. It can accomplish this without questing in vain for a naive positivistic retrieval of the past nor settling for purely synchronic analyses of the Lucan narrative. In both historical Jesus research and Acts studies, the common link is an epistemological assumption about how close the historian can get to an "actual past."

This essay will, therefore, suggest Acts-memory as an analogous methodology and cover the following areas: the correspondence of epistemological foundations between historical Jesus and Acts research rooted in form-critical assumptions, and the importance of a renewed historiography informed by social memory theory and media studies. We will then make some brief observations for Acts research based on our proposal.

---

1. Chris Keith, "The Indebtedness of the Criteria Approach to Form Criticism and Recent Attempts to Rehabilitate the Search for an Authentic Jesus," in *Jesus, Criteria, and the Demise of Authenticity*, ed. Anthony Le Donne and Chris Keith (London: T&T Clark, 2012), 25–48. On the failure of form criticism, see Michael F. Bird, *The Gospel of the Lord: How the Early Church Wrote the Story of Jesus* (Grand Rapids: Eerdmans, 2014), 113–24.

OBSERVATIONS FROM HISTORICAL JESUS RESEARCH REGARDING THE CRITERIA OF AUTHENTICITY

In historical Jesus research there has been a blossoming conversation about the value of searching for the "past actuality" of Jesus through various criteria of authenticity (e.g., dissimilarity, multiple attestation, embarrassment, etc.).[2] The various criteria, issued by form critics, imply that the pursuit of the historical Jesus is umbilically tied to the assumptions that authentic traditions can be identified once we deconstruct the text—eliminating any later additions— and then using the remaining authentic materials to reconstruct the historical Jesus.[3] Chris Keith observes the distinction between deconstruction and reconstruction, notably expressed in the approach of the late Ernst Käsemann. Käsemann proposed the application of the various criteria to individual units in order to reconstruct a picture of Jesus *after* the sifting of inauthentic material achieved through form criticism. Keith writes, "Notable in Käsemann's statement, however, is that he expresses the new element in his enquiry—finding the 'genuineness' of an individual unit of tradition—as that which occurs only once form criticism has finished its task of identifying traditions for which the *Sitz im Leben* is responsible."[4] This reconstruction on the basis of deconstruction bears a strong resemblance to the quest for authentic traditions and episodes in Acts scholarship, which operated on the same set of assumptions for the most part. Furthermore, the separation of "past" and "early Christian theological interpretation" is called by Keith the "heart of form criticism,"[5] and this too is the common ancestor of Acts research and usually inveighs against Luke's reliability as a historian.

OBSERVATIONS FROM ACTS RESEARCH REGARDING HISTORICAL RELIABILITY OF LUKE'S HISTORY

One of the strongest and most enduring influences in Acts research has been F. C. Baur, who proposed an examination of Luke's work via *Tendenzkritik*. This was developed from several premises that Baur accepted, especially a sharp

---

2. See Stanley E. Porter, *The Criteria for Authenticity in Historical-Jesus Research: Previous Discussion and New Proposals*, JSNTSup 191 (Sheffield: Sheffield Academic Press, 2000).

3. Keith, "Indebtedness," 31. See also Anthony Le Donne, "The Rise of the Quest for an Authentic Jesus: An Introduction to the Crumbling Foundations of Jesus Research," in Keith and Le Donne, *Jesus, Criteria, and the Demise of Authenticity*, 3–21 (see 10, 16–17).

4. Keith, "Indebtedness," 31.

5. Keith, "Indebtedness," 32.

divide among New Testament documents and their variegated portrayal of Paul.[6] Baur found, on the one hand, representations of a Petrine school in some New Testament literature, on the other hand New Testament writings deriving from Pauline churches—with Acts representing an attempt to synthesize and cover over the earlier divide. Luke's attempt at providing a reconciled picture between the Pauline and Petrine factions further proved to Baur that it was a late writing and therefore sufficiently removed from the events to add suspicion to the reliability of its claims.[7] Baur commented on the picture of Paul that Luke gives by saying:

> The Acts of the Apostles . . . remains a highly-important source of the history of the Apostolic Age. It is, however, a source which needs strict historical criticism before it can be held to yield a trustworthy historical picture of the persons and circumstances which it treats.[8]

Due to the alleged intramural conflict within the early church between Petrine and Paulinist elements, Baur's goal was to identify the tendencies of the authors (*Tendenz*) and how they related to this division.[9] Additionally, Baur's commitment to a thoroughly idealist philosophy (Hegelian) resulted in the most sincere skepticism of historicity, while still pursuing history as an objective thing to be retrieved beyond authorial tendencies and through the various layers of tradition.[10] Jens Schröter acknowledges the serious flaw in this separation of fact

---

6. See Craig S. Keener, *Acts: An Exegetical Commentary*, 4 vols. (Grand Rapids: Baker Academic, 2012–2015), 1:197.

7. W. Ward Gasque, *A History of Interpretation of the Acts of the Apostles* (Peabody, MA: Hendrickson, 1989), 28.

8. F. C. Baur, *Paul, the Apostle of Jesus Christ: His Life and Work, His Epistles and His Doctrine*, 2nd rev. ed., ed. Allan Menzies, trans. Eduard Zeller (London: Williams & Norgate, 1876), 1:13.

9. Something Baur also applied to the Gospels, resulting in the very influential conclusion that the Synoptics provide a more reliable historical account than John. See James D. G. Dunn, *Jesus Remembered*, vol. 1 of *Christianity in the Making* (Grand Rapids: Eerdmans, 2003), 40–41.

10. This distinction between history and historicity is made in numerous locations; see esp., Joseph B. Tyson, "From History to Rhetoric and Back: Assessing New Trends in Acts Studies," in *Contextualizing Acts: Lukan Narrative and Greco-Roman Discourse*, ed. Todd Penner and Caroline Vander Stichele, SymS 18 (Atlanta: SBL Press, 2001), 23–42 (here 27–28). See also Horton Harris, *The Tübingen School: A Historical and Theological Investigation of the School of F. C. Baur* (Leicester: Apollos, 1990), viii–ix; Robert Yarbrough, *The Salvation Historical Fallacy?: Reassessing the History of New Testament Theology* (Leiden: Deo, 2004), 24–26; James D. G. Dunn, *Beginning from Jerusalem*, vol. 2 of *Christianity in the Making* (Grand Rapids: Eerdmans, 2009), 34; though Dunn goes on to acknowledge (35–36) the importance of Baur's initial observation that Christianity was not as unified as is simply portrayed in Acts. See also Roger E. Olson, *The Journey of Modern Theology* (Downers Grove, IL: InterVarsity Press, 2013), 94, who mirrors Dunn's comments about history without philosophy for Baur, when he writes of Hegel, "What is the point of all this speculative thinking? Just this: only by supposing reality to be this way [panentheistic 'Absolute Spirit'] is knowledge of ultimate reality possible, and philosophy and religion, Hegel believed, are worthless without this pursuit." Cf. Osvaldo Padilla, who notes Baur's reliance on Leopold von Ranke in addition to Hegel, in *The Speeches*

and value, while still appreciating Baur as a pioneer for the way to do history in a manner concerned with the whole picture of history and not just the details.[11] Nonetheless, Schröter is perhaps too kind, given that Baur was still making the distinction between authentic material and later additions, something that Schröter himself has shown to be totally inadequate for a responsible historiography. The influence of Baur on the development of form criticism—with its desire to identify authentic materials—has been keenly felt in the subsequent history of the interpretation of Acts, and within innumerable studies ever since.[12]

The subsequent focus of historical inquiry in Acts has been primarily directed toward the speeches which comprise nearly 30 percent of Luke's total work. The two primary avenues of investigation into the speeches have been source criticism and narrative criticism—with an accompanying conversation surrounding Luke's place among ancient historians.[13] In general, the source critics have tended to be optimistic in Luke's use of traditional material, while still recognizing his literary freedom.[14] On the other hand, the narrative critics and their forebears emphasized the creative freedom of Luke in comparison with the ancient historians who mixed literary artistry with rhetorical flair. This freedom released the narrative critics from historical concerns until the literary artistry had been examined. This latter method is Martin Dibelius's stated aim and also his legacy in Acts research.

It is obvious that Dibelius was concerned to distance his approach from the source critics who look for sections that could be isolated and as having come from specific sources.[15] That does not mean that Dibelius saw in Luke an absence

of *Outsiders in Acts: Poetics, Theology and Historiography*, SNTSMS 144 (Cambridge: Cambridge University Press, 2008), 17.

11. Jens Schröter, *From Jesus to the New Testament: Early Christian Theology and the Origin of the New Testament Canon*, ed. and trans. Wayne M. Coppins, BMSSEC (Waco, TX: Baylor University Press, 2013), 16. See also the excellent analysis in Tyson, "From History to Rhetoric and Back," 25–29.

12. Martin Dibelius, *Studies in the Acts of the Apostles*, ed. Heinrich Greeven (London: SCM, 1956), 132, 174; Henry J. Cadbury, *The Making of Luke-Acts* (Peabody, MA: Hendrickson, 1999 [1932]), 39; Carl N. Toney, "Paul in Acts: The Prophetic Portrait of Paul," in *Issues in Luke-Acts: Selected Essays*, ed. Sean A. Adams and Michael Pahl (Piscataway, NJ: Gorgias, 2012), 239–62 (here 240–41).

13. Tyson notes that rhetorical criticism falls as a subcategory of literary or narrative criticism ("From History to Rhetoric and Back," 30).

14. Notably, F. F. Bruce, "The Speeches in Acts—Thirty Years After," in *Reconciliation and Hope: New Testament Essays on Atonement and Eschatology*, ed. Robert Banks (Exeter: Paternoster, 1974), 53–68. Specifically, Bruce identifies two sources that he feels add weight to the argument of Luke recording actual events: an Aramaic presence, and a supposed "testimony" source. While Dibelius is consciously opposed to the efforts of the source critics, Bruce does not shy away from the probability of sources when the evidence suggests it. Bruce accepts the literary skill of Luke, but still finds the speeches to contain material that is in conflict with what is obviously Luke's position (esp. on the temple in Stephen's speech). If Luke was composing his own speeches and situating them for his own purposes *without* regard for a historical situation, Bruce argues that it would not be expected to find these alternative positions. Once again this goes against the work of Dibelius.

15. Referring to the section of Acts 6:1–13:3 Dibelius states, "The complicated nature of this section of

of sources, only that it was much harder to precisely identify his sources. This, together with the limitations of applying form criticism to Acts, led to Dibelius's pursuit of the author's style.[16] Finding a certain style or quality allowed Dibelius to separate tradition from Luke's literary creations, though Dibelius admitted that this is not always straightforward or conclusive.[17]

The emphasis on literary structures also pushed interests of historical authenticity in the speeches to the side. Padilla makes the astute observation that because Dibelius views historians as free to create, he is willing to grant Luke the title of historian *until* he uses that creativity to *preach*.[18] This, Padilla argues, contributes to a separation of theology and history (even creative history) that continues past Dibelius but is based on Baur's similar separation between history and historicity.

Joseph Tyson locates himself in this trajectory of Acts research inclined toward literary analysis when he says:

> The intellectual and cultural patterns of the late twentieth century . . . have set the historical context for biblical studies generally and for the study of Acts specifically. It is no coincidence that many of us began to turn toward literary studies of Acts within a context of diminishing confidence in historical study and that, as a result, methodological proliferation was encouraged. We began to experiment with narrative, reader-response, genre, and rhetorical criticism. It is plausible to suggest that literary and rhetorical critics of the New Testament expressed a sense of freedom from the domination of historical criticism.[19]

Representing this freedom are scholars such as Luke Timothy Johnson, Steve Mason, and Todd Penner, who are all concerned almost exclusively with Luke's

---

Acts illustrates the fact that the whole book cannot be traced entirely to a few sources; nor can the author's own contribution be worked out evenly and according to a uniform principle in all parts of the work" (Martin Dibelius, "Style Criticism of the Book of Acts," in *Studies in the Acts of the Apostles*, ed. Heinrich Greeven, trans. Mary Ling [London: SCM, 1956], 11). See also the extensive survey of the source critics in Ernst Haenchen, *The Acts of the Apostles*, trans. Bernard Noble and Gerald Shinn, rev. R. McL. Wilson (Oxford: Blackwell, 1971), 24–34.

16. The style of the narrative units is identified by "their inner rhythm, their pathos and their ethos, to discover what is their individual quality" (Dibelius, "Style Criticism of the Book of Acts," 24).

17. Dibelius, "Style Criticism of the Book of Acts," 11. In the end, Dibelius is still looking for divergence from form(al) "style" unique to the larger literary forms (legend, speech, summary, etc.) as opposed to the smaller forms.

18. Padilla, *Speeches of Outsiders in Acts*, 30. This is highly ironic since Dibelius notes elsewhere that the ancient historians were using their creative liberties to *encourage* certain political ideals, regimes, etc. It is certainly not that far to stretch such creative encouragement to include preaching. See also, Gasque, *History of Interpretation of the Acts of the Apostles*, 233–34.

19. See Tyson, "From History to Rhetoric and Back," 30–31.

literary artistry. As Mason observes, after the shift in research on the speeches moved toward literary analysis, there has been "an even greater focus on whole narratives as internally referential systems, replacing earlier preoccupations with the underlying events, sources, or other external referents."[20] While Mason is still interested in many of the same external sources, his focus is especially on the rhetorical conventions inherent in speeches.

Despite this dedicated shift away from history toward narrative analysis, there is a group of scholars who resisted the urge to separate history from the narrative. Even in the same period as Dibelius, Henry Cadbury arrived at some of the same positions, but with a less skeptical view of Luke's historical utility.[21] In support of Luke's literary creativity, Cadbury identified similar Scripture citations and phrases that appear in several different speeches attributed to various characters.[22] While these similarities led Baur and Schneckenburger to conclude Luke's unifying revision, Cadbury shows that there is a correspondence between language used for Peter's speeches in the epistles to the Hebrews, Philippians, Galatians, Ephesians, and several sayings of Jesus. This phenomenon is found in the speeches of other speakers in Acts as well. This led Cadbury to conclude, against the positions of the Tübingen *Schule*, that "a more satisfactory modern view . . . will incline rather to see in all the coincidences listed not so much personal influence or identity of origin, but a common Christianity mediated by the historian [Luke] and shared by others, or even commonplaces of vocabulary or expression more general than any religious boundary."[23]

Continuing Cadbury's blend of source and narrative criticism of Acts speeches, Conrad Gempf makes great strides in understanding the ancient historians by showing that "the write-up of a speech in an ancient history *does call for rhetorical skill simply because the author must, while being faithful to the main lines of the historical 'speech-event', adapt the speech to make it 'speak*

---

20. Steve Mason, "Speech-Making in Ancient Rhetoric, Josephus, and Acts: Messages and Playfulness, Part I," *Early Christianity* 2 (2011): 1–23 (448). Mason goes on to note that "with a larger academic constituency, Acts has been subjected to many newer kinds of rhetorical, reader-response, and also narratological analysis" (449).

21. Henry J. Cadbury et al., "The Greek and Jewish Traditions of Writing History," in *Prolegomena II Criticism*, vol. 2 of *The Beginnings of Christianity, Part I The Acts of the Apostles*, ed. F. J. Foakes Jackson and Kirsopp Lake (London: Macmillan, 1922), 7–29.

22. Henry J. Cadbury, "The Speeches in Acts," in *Additional Notes to the Commentary*, vol. 5 of *The Beginnings of Christianity, Part I The Acts of the Apostles*, ed. F. J. Foakes Jackson and Kirsopp Lake (London: Macmillan, 1922), 392–427 (see 407).

23. Cadbury, "Speeches in Acts," 415. A similar view is taken by C. H. Dodd: "The first four speeches of Peter cover substantially the same ground. The phraseology and the order of presentation vary slightly, but there is no essential advance from one to another. They supplement one another, and taken together they afford a comprehensive view of the content of the early *kerygma*" (C. H. Dodd, *The Apostolic Preaching and Its Developments* [London: Hodder & Stoughton, 1956 (1936)], 21).

to' a new audience in a different situation."[24] Craig Keener elaborates this point by noting, "Ancient historiography . . . employed speeches in a manner different from modern usage; although the event of the speech might be historical, the degree to which the content of a speech conformed to the actual speech delivered on that occasion varied according to the writer, his sources, and the extent to which any accurate memory of a speech existed."[25] This is due to the situation of ancient history writers and their audiences, who expected "elaboration" as well as a cohesive and unified narrative.[26]

Cadbury began a trek for a third way for Acts research to approach the literary and historical intersection of Acts. As evinced by several scholars since his publications, there is a growing recognition that there is no necessary separation between history and literary creation, but this must be understood within Luke's own context—a context that is more complex than ancient rhetoric alone and thereby resists the *purely* rhetorical, literary, and source-critical interests.[27]And while the location of meaning for the speeches (as a part of historiography) is gaining momentum in its recognition of an intersection of history and literary writing, no thorough epistemology has been adopted to explain methodological decisions. The remainder of this essay will set out a recommendation for such an epistemology and accompanying methodology.

Historiography Remix: A New Foundation for Acts Research

Underlying all critical methodologies is an epistemological assumption about the access a historian has to the content of analysis. Inherent to the form-critical epistemology influencing research in the Gospels and Acts is the assumption that there is an accessible authentic core that can be uncovered. Recognition of

---

24. Conrad Gempf, "Public Speaking and Published Accounts," in *The Book of Acts in Its Ancient Literary Setting*, vol. 1 of *The Book of Acts in Its Ancient Literary Context*, ed. Bruce W. Winter and Andrew D. Clarke (Grand Rapids: Eerdmans, 1993), 259–303 (here 264). See also Eckhard Schnabel who writes, "Speeches in historical narrative rarely reproduce the actual words that were spoken. However, the speeches were not free inventions but provided an approximation of what was said, even if sometimes imaginative reconstruction was necessary" (*Acts*, ZECNT [Grand Rapids: Zondervan, 2012], 35).

25. Keener, *Acts*, 1:271.

26. "Historians writing for more elite audiences would be evaluated by both how plausible and how rhetorically sensitive their speeches were to both the speakers and situations that they depicted" (Keener, *Acts*, 1:271).

27. Robert Tannehill represents one of the significant narrative critics who also recognizes the importance of a more than strictly narrative approach ("The Function of Peter's Mission Speeches in the Narrative of Acts," *NTS* 37 [1991]: 400–414). The basic method of Tannehill is to bracket off historical questions in order to focus on the narrative (cf. Dibelius). However, Tannehill is much more accepting of the importance that historical studies bring to studying narrative, even going as far as saying that "study of first-century Mediterranean literature and society may illuminate unspoken assumptions behind the narrative and may also suggest specific reasons for emphases in the text" (Robert C. Tannehill, *The Narrative Unity of Luke-Acts*, 2 vols. [Minneapolis: Fortress, 1989, 1994], 2:5).

the insufficiency of the criteria of authenticity in Gospels research to actually achieve this retrieval has brought with it a replacement epistemology, coined as Jesus-memory by Chris Keith, based on social memory theory and influenced especially by Jens Schröter's "theory-of-history."[28] Foundational to this episte-mology is that the past-as-it-happened is impossible to recover. Instead, the only remains of events in the past are necessarily interpretations from the start— interpretations that are formed in communities with certain languages, customs, media, and identity-forming commemorative narratives. As Schröter writes: "[C]entral to current Jesus research is the methodology-of-history insight that *every* appropriation of the past rests on a combination of event and narrative."[29]

Social memory theory is the approach that best comprehends the combina-tion of event and narrative to which Schröter refers.[30] Social memory concerns the dynamic relationship between the past (collective/cultural memory) and the present (individual/collected memory) within a specific generation (communi-cative memory). Keith explains:

> By focusing upon the *social* formation of memory in the present, whether that means autobiographical memory that is socially formed or cultural memory that is autobiographically appropriated, the primary task of social memory theory is to conceptualize and explain the various manners in which cultures (and individuals as culture-members) appropriate the past in light of, in terms of, and on behalf of the present.[31]

It is the inherent interpretation of all memory that renders the pursuit of authentic tradition untainted by interpretation as incoherent. However, Schröter doesn't fault the form critics and other early historians for the conclusions they came to but rather observes that every period of historical investigation and history writing can only utilize the concepts of memory and knowledge of which they were aware in their own time. Instead he says,

---

28. As Schröter puts it, "The hermeneutical and epistemological framework is formed by engagement with the science of history" (Jens Schröter, "Preface to the English Edition," in *From Jesus to the New Testament*, n.p.). The list of influential studies utilizing social memory is pages long and is therefore absent, but see at least Alan Kirk and Tom Thatcher, eds., *Memory, Tradition, and Text: Uses of the Past in Early Christianity* (Atlanta: SBL Press, 2005).

29. Schröter, *From Jesus to the New Testament*, 130 (italics original).

30. Defending this definition based on the suggestions of Sandra Hübenthal, while possible, is outside the scope of this project, but see her essay, "Social and Cultural Memory in Biblical Exegesis: The Quest for an Adequate Application," in *Cultural Memory in Biblical Exegesis*, ed. Pernille Carstens, Trine Bjørnung Hasselbalch, and Niels Peter Lemche, PHSC 17 (Piscataway, NJ: Gorgias, 2012), 175–99.

31. Chris Keith, *Jesus' Literacy: Scribal Culture and the Teacher from Galilee*, LNTS 413 (London: T&T Clark, 2011), 56.

The intellectual-historical presuppositions upon which [New Testament science] is based have taken form—at least for the European and North American cultural sphere—since the late eighteenth century, thus in a period that was decisively shaped by enlightenment, idealism, and histor- icism. The historical-critical consciousness, which emerged as part of these developments, was then—at the latest since Max Weber—itself subjected to critical reflection.[32]

The process of coming to terms with the enlightenment historicism has brought a better understanding of the access which historians have to "history." Historians must responsibly move on from assumptions that we can get back to "what actually happened"—without denying that something did in fact happen.

Congruent with the approach above, Schröter insists that we now understand "history" as being the structuring of historical data into a coherent picture of what *could have* happened.[33] This leads Schröter to use the term "falsifiable" because he recognizes that as new information comes to the awareness of histo- rians (or philosophers of history), that the "(hi)story" may need to be amended.[34] "Thus," he says "the result of such an approach cannot be the reconstruction of a past reality behind the texts . . . we are dealing with conceptualizations of the historical imagination that are accountable to the sources and that interpret the historical material from the perspective of the respective present."[35]

Schröter's observation highlights exactly what Keith and Le Donne are proposing with the Jesus-memory approach. Because historians of Jesus must move beyond the quest for past actuality, there must be a reformulation of his- torical research. This doesn't deny the valuable historiographical *intent* behind some traditional criteria or other historical-critical methodologies. Many of the same historical, political, and literary questions need to be asked. What the

---

32. Schröter, *From Jesus to the New Testament*, 9.

33. This accords with several contemporary New Testament historians who acknowledge that the historical artifacts leave the historian with "data" which must be pieced together in order to create "facts" and (hi)story. See especially Dunn, *Jesus Remembered*; Michael R. Licona, *The Resurrection of Jesus: A New Historiographical Approach* (Downers Grove, IL: InterVarsity Press, 2011), 27–132; and Robert L. Webb, "The Historical Enterprise and Historical Jesus Research," in *The Key Events in the Life of the Historical Jesus*, ed. Darrell L. Bock and Robert L. Webb (Grand Rapids: Eerdmans, 2010), 9–94.

34. Schröter, *From Jesus to the New Testament*, 23. In another essay Schröter writes, "History, as image of the past, is always due to revisions and modifications. When the image of the past changes, so does our perception. It is therefore possible to transform or to correct the historian's pictures of Jesus by referring to sources, not noticed or not known so far, or to confront the familiar material with new insights" (Jens Schröter, "Remarks on James D. G. Dunn's Approach to Jesus Research," in *Memories of Jesus: A Critical Appraisal of James D. G. Dunn's Jesus Remembered*, ed. Robert B. Stewart and Gary R. Habermas [Nashville: B&H Academic, 2010], 129–43 [131]).

35. Schröter, *From Jesus to the New Testament*, 19.

Jesus-memory approach to history does is place the historian on a better *epistemological* foundation that recognizes what is actually possible when doing historical research. Schröter elaborates this process: "The goal of history writing is thus not *reconstruction of the past* but *construction of history*: it constructs a picture of the past that has relative validity, determined by the state of knowledge of the researchers, and determined by the view that the interpreter sets forth with the aid of the known material."[36]

What does this new methodology contribute to studies in the Acts of the Apostles? As briefly examined in the section on Acts, the previous two centuries of research into the speeches have failed to propose an adequate or appropriate *epistemology* to account for the complex situation of Luke's composition of Acts, given ancient rhetorical conventions and media. In sum, the approach to the Acts of the Apostles needs to apply the observations from the Jesus-memory approach. The resulting nomenclature for Acts research could be termed "Acts-memory" to show the reliance on the same epistemological principles. Namely, that epistemologically the historian (ancient and modern) is interpreting the *record* of an already-interpreted event/experience/source/witness in an attempt *not* of re-creation of the actual past but of a historically plausible construction facilitated by historical, cultural, philological, social, and religious-critical analysis.

Because we are no longer separating the tradition from its inception, or ignoring history to elevate Luke's unhindered literary imagination, where should we begin? The answer is in the historical artifact as cultural memory. As Pieter Botha notes, "to the degree that our goal is to understand these ancient documents in historical contexts, it is essential to understand the medium in which they originated. Historical interpretation requires an effort to experience the tradition in its intended medium."[37]

Astrid Erll employs the term "cultural memory," which can be used in two ways: (1) cultural memory as a metonymy ("cultural" memory)—resulting in "collected-memory" at the individual level; and (2) cultural memory as a metaphor (cultural "memory")—resulting in "collective-memory" at the group level.[38] He explains, "[I]n speaking of 'cultural memory' we are only sometimes dealing with metaphors proper, but always with tropes, that is, with expressions that have

---

36. Schröter, *From Jesus to the New Testament*, 35.

37. Pieter J. J. Botha, *Orality and Literacy in Early Christianity*, BPC 5 (Eugene, OR: Cascade, 2012), 9.

38. The importance of this distinction is reflected in various disciplines. One example is the lamentation of Anthony Le Donne in his work on historiography, where he cites the categories as "memory" and "commemoration" before going on to state that "social memory theorists often confuse literal memory with memory as a metaphor for tradition" (Anthony Le Donne, *The Historiographical Jesus: Memory, Typology, and the Son of David* [Waco, TX: Baylor University Press, 2009], 60).

a figurative meaning."[39] The figurative meaning is designated by Erll through the use of single quotation marks for the figurative aspect of cultural memory. For 'cultural' memory the figurative aspect is 'cultural' by which is reflected the socio-cultural influence upon organic or individual memory. That is why she can use the expression "cultural memory as a metonymy," since the memory is truly memory of an individual.[40] The opposite designator makes the distinction clearer: For cultural 'memory,' the 'memory' is the figurative element that reflects the fact that memory in this case is a metaphor for a memory artifact—in Erll's words the, "symbolic order, media and institutions through which social groups and societies establish their knowledge systems and versions of the past (their 'memory')."[41] In this case, "cultural memory as a metaphor" signals the fact that the reference to memory is not to organic memory (of an individual), but to an established or crystallized *external* medium for remembering.

As historians, it is this *external* media artifact that we have access to. However, for the culture of origin, the external media has connection to numerous networks of information. This is the information that the Jesus- and Acts-memory historian is working to understand before making judgments about the meaning of a text. In a complex media culture (combining literate, illiterate, and textual faculties), the historians' understanding of the artifacts must include the respective media culture. This is reflected in the descriptive phrase "texts with roots in oral tradition," which enhances the oft-cited term "oral-derived text," employed by John Miles Foley.[42] Both expressions are used to refer to *written* texts as we have them, which contain elements previously existing in an *oral* medium.[43]

OBSERVATIONS FOR FUTURE ACTS RESEARCH

Framing historical investigation in terms of studying oral cultures in light of extant texts, Rafael Rodriguez astutely observes that "the interest in oral

---

39. Astrid Erll, *Memory in Culture*, trans. Sara B. Young, PMMS (New York: Palgrave Macmillan, 2011), 96–97.

40. The memory of an individual will also be referred to as *organic memory* and *biological memory*. Metonymy is defined as the figure of speech (trope) where one name, object, or concept is put in the place of a related or identical name, object, or concept. In this case Erll is suggesting that cultural memory used as metonymy is in the place of the individual's memory which has been shaped by culture, hence 'cultural' memory.

41. Erll, *Memory in Culture*, 99, figure IV.1.

42. John Miles Foley, *Immanent Art: From Structure to Meaning in Traditional Oral Epic* (Bloomington: Indiana University Press, 1991), 15.

43. Rafael Rodríguez, *Oral Tradition: A Guide for the Perplexed*, Guides for the Perplexed (London: T&T Clark, 2014), 70; and the chart on 83: "Oral-derived texts are not necessarily composed orally (though they could be), nor are they necessarily transcriptions of an actual oral performance (though again, they might be)."

tradition certainly opens up fresh perspectives on the written texts of early Christianity. But it never opens up access to actual oral tradition."[44] Instead, we are pushing, with Rodriguez, toward comprehending "the function of written texts in (oral)-traditional contexts."[45] The texts in question are the speeches in Acts, which imply an oral event. While many may doubt the actuality of an oral event behind the speeches in historical works, as a function of rhetoric the use of speeches signifies at least that in the first century world speeches were an important vehicle for communication (even if their representations were not "recordings"). Furthermore, the first-century media culture for followers of Jesus entailed the propagation of a message—the gospel. When *communicating* a certain message is at the center of a group's identity, the appearance of "speeches" begs to be approached not strictly in rhetorical terms but also in terms of the *content* rhetorically communicated.

The work of John Miles Foley provides the concepts and terminology to appreciate the complex presentation of speeches in Luke's Acts of the Apostles. Foley pioneers the idea that the meaning of any given media must first be approached with the question of "how" a text communicates meaning, before the question of "what it means" is answered. This places media studies as the important first step after an epistemologically responsible historiography is established.

So, what does "how" look like for the speeches in Acts? (Keeping in mind that the speeches in a written medium are relatively removed from whatever environment in which they would have originally been heard). In order to suitably pursue "how" an oral-derived text communicates meaning, there are three components within the communicative act which allow access to a text's meaning: (1) performance arena, (2) register, and (3) communicative economy. These three components combine to create "word-power," which has meaning because of its relationship to tradition.[46] Tradition here signifies the commemorative narratives used in a community to identify itself.

First, *performance arena* refers to the context of a performance. For oral cultures this could be a specific location whose significance is based on its relevance to the traditions of a community.[47] As with the "cultural memory" or "master commemorative narrative," the stories that define a group or culture can be

---

44. Rodríguez, *Oral Tradition*, 118.

45. Rodríguez, *Oral Tradition*, 118.

46. This relationship is given the title *traditional referentiality* by Foley, *Immanent Art*, 6–7.

47. Or, as Foley remarks: the "locus in which some specialized form of communication is uniquely licensed to take place" (John Miles Foley, *The Singer of Tales in Performance* [Bloomington: Indiana University Press, 1995], 8).

effective particularly because of *shared* experiences, thereby creating frames. Physical locations are especially suitable to this end.

However, once you move out of the strictly oral context, the performance arena must be introduced to the audience through the text. The performance arena must be re-created and "summoned . . . by textual signals."[48] Only after the text signals the performance arena via introductory formula, geographical or spatial settings, etc. can the audience be prepared to respond appropriately since—in an oral-derived setting—they may no longer be prepared simply by being in the right location. Foley notes,

> Within this situating frame [i.e., performance arena] the performer and audience adopt a language and behavior uniquely suited (because specifically dedicated) to a certain channel of communication . . . What is more, the familiarity of the performance arena—all that is prescribed about the present transaction in terms of earlier transactions—places the audience in a position to bridge the gaps of indeterminacy that are the natural partners to the (now recognizable) meaning-laden signals.[49]

This explanation of the performance arena's significance highlights the next two terms that combined create "word-power."

Second, if performance arena is the location (textual or otherwise), *register* is the "idiomatic version of the language" used within that arena.[50] The register is a way of speaking that takes on extra meaning *only* when used within a specific performance arena. While that may sound exclusive, the evocation of a performance arena can happen rapidly and for any length of time. As soon as a performance arena is "entered," the author and audience are expecting the words to have special significance.[51]

---

48. Foley, *Singer of Tales in Performance*, 80.

49. Foley, *Singer of Tales in Performance*, 47–49.

50. Foley, *Singer of Tales in Performance*, 15.

51. As Foley puts it, the register invokes "contextually appropriate signals for institutionalized meanings" (Foley, *Singer of Tales in Performance*, 50). Foley goes on to identify several possible features of a register: archaisms, parallelism, figurative language, special formulas including direct reference to traditional material, nontextual features that may be reproduced in a performance or signaled in the margin of a text being read, recurring themes, and structural clues (chiasm, etc.). All of these features of the register are *a part of the tradition*, regardless of the medium (textual or oral) (Foley, *Singer of Tales in Performance*, 82–93). On the permanence of tradition, which gives a reference point to the *register* words, Foley notes: "Because so much of what a register 'means' depends crucially on what is understood of its context as brought into play by the event of performance and the referent of tradition, the individual integers can indeed portray a continuing reality. That is, the world to which they provide access is not simply inaugurated ex nihilo with each instance of sounding, but must be understood as ever present to the always vocable code and therefore present to anyone who can use that code properly" (Foley, *Singer of Tales in Performance*, 55–56).

Third, once the performance arena is entered and the appropriate register is used, the success of the communication (performance, text, etc.) is termed *communicative economy*. Foley's summary of communicative economy aptly distills the process of meaning conveyance. If both participants are in the performance arena—having the proper mnemonic frameworks, context, etc.—they will be able to use the meaning-freighted register, whereby "signals are decoded and gaps [in the performance] are bridged with extraordinary fluency, that is, economy . . . Once those signals are deployed . . . the work issues forth with surpassing communicative economy, as the way of speaking becomes a way of meaning."[52]

CONCLUSION

The separation of Acts's material into the categories of *either* historical actuality *or* literary verisimilitude/fabrication owes much to the form-critical assumptions that were absorbed into the study of Acts across the twentieth century. Based on the wrong assumptions about epistemology, the form critics employed authenticity criteria to facilitate the separation of the Acts material. They assumed that separation was possible provided one had the right methods, like knowing the oral forms and their social settings or identifying each book by where it fell in the intramural Peter vs. Paul ecclesiastical civil war. However, it seems clear now that not only were these the wrong tools for the job but the tools were also not particularly effective and never delivered what they were supposed to.

Employing media studies in order to understand ancient texts involves the cooperation of numerous lines of research, including ancient rhetoric, cultural norms (such as levels of literacy or class structure), comparison with other ancient documents of the period, and political structures and rulers, as well as literary techniques. All of these elements are vital for the meaning of a text to be communicated. However, none of them can be effective without an epistemology that reflects our distance from past events. Acts research has drawn largely from the same well as Gospels research and is therefore similarly in need of moving on. The speeches in Acts, because they evince first-century media assumptions, provide the opportune location to begin testing the value of the Acts-memory approach for history construction.

In contrast to form criticism, social memory theory, with advances in our understanding of ancient media, provides a better way of understanding Luke's narrative. It should be noted that a memory approach is not an apologetic strategy

---

52. Foley, *Singer of Tales in Performance*, 53–54.

to prove the history of Acts, nor is it the study of "tradition" simply rebranded as "memory" with a view to stressing the distortion of collective memory in Luke's retelling. Rather, Acts-memory is a mixture of epistemology, hermeneutics, and media that proposes that event and interpretation are inherent to all memory and transmission of a memorial narrative. Event and interpretation cannot be separated in Acts any more than one can separate blue and red from purple. We know both are there, so we must simply appreciate the artifact—in this case Luke's narrative—with its characteristics and referents.

CHAPTER 14

Acts: History or Fiction?

CRAIG S. KEENER

The question of Luke's accuracy in the Gospel is connected, at least to some degree, with his accuracy in his second volume, the book of Acts, which a strong majority of Acts scholars regard as a historical monograph. And if Luke is interested in accurate history, presumably he had good reason to trust the accuracy of his sources in the Gospel, which include Mark and material that also appears in Matthew. Those sources were recent for Luke, so he was in a much better position to evaluate them directly than are we.

If Luke in fact traveled with Paul in the "we" material of Acts 20–28, as he apparently claims, he spent up to two years in Judea and had access to eyewitness material for the Gospels. Even for those skeptical that Luke traveled with Paul, Acts offers further opportunities to test Luke's historiographic practice against outside sources (such as Paul's letters and externally documented ancient events). If Luke proves a careful historian in Acts, we may expect no less careful an approach to the events surrounding Jesus in his first volume.

In this essay, I argue for Luke's reliability as an ancient historian. In the brief space available here I cannot address all the arguments of Luke's critics, but I do respond to them in detail in my four-volume commentary on Acts. Lest such critics suppose, as they sometimes suggest, that Luke's defenders are unfamiliar with the force of critics' arguments, I am quite familiar with their arguments. My commentary cites more than ten thousand secondary sources and roughly forty-five thousand extrabiblical ancient references.[1] Here, however, I offer a bird's-eye view of Luke's method, which shows consistent dependence on available information.

---

1. Craig S. Keener, *Acts: An Exegetical Commentary*, 4 vols. (Grand Rapids: Baker Academic, 2012–2015).

LUKE TRAVELED WITH PAUL

Acts often uses the first-person plural ("we"), including in nearly the entire final quarter of the book. Although opinion is not unanimous, a majority of scholars think that the "we" material in Acts stems from an eyewitness.[2] This explains why it constitutes the most detailed material in Acts. On the most common critical dating of Luke-Acts (70–90 CE), most of Luke's narrative belongs to the period of living memory (often estimated at roughly sixty to eighty years). The "we" material could be earlier, but if it was written at the same time as the rest of Acts (which I believe), most of it stems from just about ten to thirty years after the final events.[3]

There is good reason to believe that Luke himself authored this material.[4] Some doubt that a traveling companion of Paul wrote Acts, noting that the author's thinking differs from Paul's. Yet one must expect their thinking to differ: no one supposes that *Paul* wrote Acts. Moreover, the largest contrasts are between not Luke and Paul, but between Luke and some earlier scholars' anti-Jewish understanding of Paul.[5] Pauline studies today recognize a much more Jewish Paul,[6] undercutting a major objection to Luke's "Jewish" depiction of Paul.

A minority of scholars suggest that Luke's "we" is merely a fictitious literary device. Yet such a "literary device" is unattested elsewhere! Fictitious first-person claims appear in some novels, but not in historical works.[7] Moreover, when they appear in novels, they appear throughout the story, but Luke's appears first in Acts 16:10, leaves off in Philippi (16:17), and picks up again years later in

---

2. As conceded even by leading detractors, e.g., William Sanger Campbell, "The Narrator as 'He,' 'Me,' and 'We': Grammatical Person in Ancient Histories and in the Acts of the Apostles," *JBL* 129 (2010): 385–407, here 386.

3. On my own estimated dating (*Acts*, 1:383–401), about fifteen years after the events depicted in the final quarter of Acts. For those who date Acts in the early sixties, it could be less than three years. Richard I. Pervo, *Dating Acts: Between the Evangelists and the Apologists* (Santa Rosa, CA: Polebridge, 2006), 359–63, holds a second-century date but lists thirty-one scholars advocating a date in the 60s; forty-eight in the 70s–80s; twenty in the 90s; and eleven for ca. 100 CE or afterward.

4. See fuller discussion and sources in Keener, *Acts*, 3:2350–74.

5. Challenging here esp. Philipp Vielhauer, "On the 'Paulinism' of Acts," in *Studies in Luke-Acts: Essays in Honor of Paul Schubert*, ed. Leander E. Keck and J. Louis Martyn (Nashville: Abingdon, 1966), 33–50. See critiques in e.g., Peder Borgen, "From Paul to Luke: Observations toward Clarification of the Theology of Luke-Acts," *CBQ* 31 (1969): 168–82; Stanley E. Porter, *Paul in Acts* (Peabody, MA: Hendrickson, 2001; reprint of *The Paul of Acts: Essays in Literary Criticism, Rhetoric, and Theology*, WUNT 115 [Tübingen: Mohr Siebeck, 1999]), 189–206; Karl P. Donfried, *Paul, Thessalonica, and Early Christianity* (Grand Rapids: Eerdmans, 2002), 90–96; Darrell L. Bock, *Acts*, BECNT (Grand Rapids: Baker Academic, 2007), 15–19.

6. From varying angles, see e.g., E. P. Sanders, *Paul and Palestinian Judaism: A Comparison of Patterns of Religion* (Philadelphia: Fortress, 1977); idem, *Paul: The Apostle's Life, Letters, and Thought* (Minneapolis: Fortress, 2015); Mark D. Nanos and Magnus Zetterholm, eds., *Paul within Judaism: Restoring the First-Century Context to the Apostle* (Minneapolis: Fortress, 2015).

7. See Arthur Darby Nock, *Essays on Religion and the Ancient World*, 2 vols., ed. Zeph Stewart (Cambridge: Harvard University Press, 1972), 828; Campbell, "Narrator as 'He,' 'Me,' and 'We,'" 388.

Philippi, where the narrator had remained (20:5–6). A false eyewitness might claim to witness the empty tomb, or Pentecost, but Luke's "we" appears only inconspicuously, mostly on voyages, keeping the focus on Paul.

Some have argued for a specific sort of fictitious "we," in sea-voyage narratives. Again, we lack such a device in ancient literature,[8] nor is Luke's "we" always limited to sea voyages.

More plausibly, some suggest that Luke's detail in the "we" material shows that he uses a travel journal as a source. But whose travel journal would it have been? Luke had access to many possible sources for parts of Luke-Acts (Luke 1:1–2), including from eyewitnesses (1:2), yet he nowhere else leaves an "I" or "we" except in this particular "source." Why would Luke become an inept editor of his material and leave a "we" that does not include himself only here? Much likelier, the "we" includes the first-person author of Luke 1:3.

In other words, Luke was Paul's traveling companion (cf. Col 4:14). This was also the unanimous tradition of ancient Christians, who had no reason to attribute the book to such a minor character (as opposed to, say, a leading apostle) if they did not have reason to believe that it was true.[9] If this "we" appeared anywhere else in ancient historical literature *outside* the New Testament, scholars would take for granted that the author included himself in the "we." Why NT scholars often approach the New Testament with greater skepticism than they do noncanonical documents is a question for a different day.

THE GENRE(S) OF LUKE-ACTS

Luke is self-evidently a Gospel, and most scholars consider the Gospels to be biographies. Contrary to the assumptions of some scholars who have limited familiarity with ancient biographies, biographic genre does have implications for historical reliability. Granted, ancient biographers and historians were not bound to modern narrative conventions for these genres, but neither did their readers expect them to invent events.

As I and others have shown elsewhere, the early Roman Empire was the peak period of historical influence in ancient biography, full-scale ancient biographies of public figures (as opposed to lives of the poets) normally rested on substantial information, and biographies of recent figures were normally quite accurate. Comparison among such biographic works demonstrates clearly that these

8. Susan Marie Praeder, "The Problem of First Person Narration in Acts," *NovT* 29 (1987): 193–218, esp. 210–14, 217–18.

9. See further discussion in Keener, *Acts*, 1:402–22.

biographers conceived their projects as historical and depended on substantial historical information.[10]

Scholars divide as to whether Luke's Gospel and Acts share the same genre. Because biography was a subtype of historiography, the genres are closely related in any case. Thus some scholars find historiographic elements in the Gospel and biographic elements in Acts. Especially in the early empire, biographers wrote in a historiographic way, whereas historiography often focused on major characters, in biographic fashion.

A strong majority of scholars see Acts as a historical monograph;[11] the second most common view, which is significantly less common, views Acts as a biographic succession narrative involving Jesus's successors (such as Peter and Paul). Claims that Acts was a "prose epic" (a virtually nonexistent genre, as epics were normally poetic) or a novel represent the least common views. Again, biography was a primarily historical genre and treating Acts as either biography or history means that Luke based his narrative on prior information.

Of course, both novels and histories are narrative sorts of works, so novels, like histories, remain useful for literary comparisons. But Acts is not a novel. In his final published works, Richard Pervo, most often associated with the view that Acts is a novel, concurred that Acts is ancient historiography rather than a novel per se.[12] Unfortunately, he stretched the definition of history to include historical novels. Even this broadening of historical boundaries would not, however, justify treating Acts as novelistic. Most novels were romances, which Acts (and the Gospels) conspicuously are not. A few novels about historical characters existed, but none are about recent characters. No novels included the massive amounts of prior information obviously displayed in the Gospels (obvious by comparing them in a synopsis) and Acts (obvious by comparing it with external history; see discussion below).[13]

If Acts is a work of historiography, then Luke's biographic first volume may be understood as a biographic volume in a two-volume work of history. It would thus be comparable, say, to Diodorus Siculus's treatment of Alexander of Macedon,

---

10. See esp. my *Christobiography: Memories, History, and the Reliability of the Gospels* (Grand Rapids: Eerdmans, 2019).

11. See e.g., Henry J. Cadbury, *The Book of Acts in History* (London: Black, 1955); Martin Dibelius, *Studies in the Acts of the Apostles*, ed. H. Greeven, trans. M. Ling (New York: Scribner's, 1956), 123–37; Luke Timothy Johnson, "Luke-Acts, Book of," *ABD* 4:403–20 (here 406); Gregory E. Sterling, *Historiography and Self-Definition: Josephus, Luke-Acts, and Apologetic Historiography*, NovTSup 64 (Leiden: Brill, 1992); Keener, *Acts*, 1:51–257.

12. Richard I. Pervo, *Acts: A Commentary* (Minneapolis: Fortress, 2009), 15.

13. See further Keener, *Acts*, 1:63–83, esp. 77–80.

which comprises an entire book in Diodorus's multivolume history. By connecting Jesus's biography with history, Luke makes even more clear that the form of biography he writes is from the most historiographic side of biography.

LUKE'S PREFACE (LUKE 1:1–4)

The preface for Luke-Acts addresses a historical topic (*the things that have been fulfilled among us*, Luke 1:1). This preface also uses much vocabulary that is commonly found in the prefaces of other ancient histories. Luke therefore invites his audience to expect a historical treatment of the subject.[14] One scholar has also compared the preface with ancient scientific treatises, contending that Luke writes on the more technical (and thus more precise) side of historiography rather than the more rhetorical side.[15]

Luke notes that *many* have written about these events before him (1:1); he undoubtedly includes among these sources Mark and the other material where Luke overlaps with Matthew.[16] Luke distinguishes his work from that of his predecessors, not in terms of the reliability of their information but in terms of writing style (1:3).[17] Luke notes that his material ultimately goes back to eyewitnesses (1:2) and that he can certify the truth of this material (1:3).

How can Luke attest this material? He may *have carefully investigated everything* (1:3), but the wording that he uses might imply something even more than investigation. Historians sometimes used the term here translated as *investigated* for thorough personal familiarity with a subject, especially when they participated in some of the events that they narrate.[18]

This language would fit Luke's use of "we" later in his narrative (Acts 16:10–17; 20:5–21:18; 27:1–28:16). Unless Luke left Paul after reaching Jerusalem and then just happened to return before his departure, Luke appears to have remained near Paul in Judea for up to two years (Acts 24:27). This would certainly allow Luke plenty of time to speak with Judean members of Jesus's movement who had been around since the movement's early days (cf. e.g., Acts 21:8–9, 16–18).

---

14. See e.g., Terrance Callan, "The Preface of Luke-Acts and Historiography," *NTS* 31 (1985): 576–81; David Paul Moessner, *Luke the Historian of Israel's Legacy, Theologian of Israel's 'Christ': A New Reading of the 'Gospel Acts' of Luke*, BZNW 182 (Berlin: de Gruyter, 2016), 67–123.

15. Loveday C. A. Alexander, *Acts in Its Ancient Literary Context: A Classicist Looks at the Acts of the Apostles*, LNTS 298 (London: T&T Clark, 2005), 12–13, 16, 41–42.

16. I do accept the Q hypothesis, but nothing in this essay depends on that premise.

17. For the range of treatments of predecessors in ancient prefaces, see Keener, *Acts*, 1:658–60; not all were critical (see e.g., Valerius Maximus 1.pref.; Pliny *Nat.* 3.1.1–2).

18. Moessner, *Luke the Historian of Israel's Legacy, Theologian of Israel's 'Christ'*, 68–107, esp. 106–7, 328.

Historians often used the term that is translated *carefully* in Luke 1:3 to affirm their attention to accuracy in detail.[19]

Can we be confident that Luke does in fact report accurately, as he claims? That Luke is not freely inventing material is clear. First, where we can check him against his sources, he tells the same essential story that they do, despite the sort of omissions and variation in detail characteristic of all ancient biographies and histories. Second, Luke describes his mission as *confirming* what Theophilus has already learned (Luke 1:4). Luke would not dare make such a claim if he diverged significantly from the information about Jesus and his movement already widely circulated by his day.

If we wanted to investigate history within living memory today, we would consult eyewitnesses or those who heard the story from them. We cannot do this for history two thousand years ago, but in Luke-Acts we have at our fingertips the record of someone who did precisely that. It is true that Luke's interests may differ from ours and he leaves out much information that would interest historians today. Nevertheless, what Luke does give us provides us a secure window into the life of Jesus and his movement, and we should be grateful. Most figures of antiquity lacked such capable biographers from within living memory.[20]

THE CHARACTER OF ANCIENT HISTORIOGRAPHY

Ancient historians and biographers regularly reworded their sources. Ancient elite readers would have actually looked down on Matthew and Luke for following the wording of Mark as closely and often as they do.[21] Biographers also freely rearranged events, often topically;[22] historians were not normally as free with sequence, but when they lacked access to public records, they could not always provide precise chronology.

Biographers tended to focus on their subjects' character, memorializing the person and using their behavior and (in the case of sages) teaching as a model to

---

19. See e.g., Eve-Marie Becker, *The Birth of Christian History: Memory and Time from Mark to Luke-Acts* (New Haven: Yale University Press, 2017), 103–4; cf. e.g., Diodorus Siculus 1.6.2; Josephus *Ant.* 1.17, 82; *War* 1.2, 6, 9, 22; *Life* 358, 360, 365, 412; *Ag. Ap.* 1.18.

20. For the usual accuracy of information within living memory as opposed to later, see e.g., Jan Vansina, *Oral Tradition as History* (Madison: University of Wisconsin Press, 1985), 173, 192–93, 197; Craig S. Keener, "Bart Ehrman and Robert McIver on Oral Tradition," in *Treasures New and Old: Essays in Honor of Donald A. Hagner*, ed. Carl S. Sweatman and Clifford B. Kvidahl (Wilmore, KY: GlossaHouse, 2017), 271–318.

21. See e.g., John S. Kloppenborg, "Variation in the Reproduction of the Double Tradition and an Oral Q?," *ETL* 83 (2007): 53–80, here 63–74, esp. 63.

22. See e.g., Arnaldo Momigliano, *The Development of Greek Biography: Four Lectures* (Cambridge: Harvard University Press, 1971), 13–14, 86.

follow or (in negative instances) to avoid. Historians tended to focus on public events that had wider impact.[23] Luke, of course, has interest in both.

One cannot write history without perspectives. One cannot even merely list some key events without deciding which events are "key." Modern historians often express interest in particular aspects of history—for example women's history, military history, or church history. Ancient historians also had interests and perspectives that shaped their writing.

Some of these perspectives were overt. For example, historians themselves frequently noted that they recorded the events of the past as examples for life in the present.[24] (In Scripture, cf. e.g., 1 Cor 10:11.) Such examples could provide sound military and political strategies. They could be used to support patriotic or political agendas. Quite often they were used to reward good behavior with honor and to provide moral examples to follow. Historians also spoke freely about the role of providence in human affairs, how God or the gods avenged their honor, and so forth.[25] Historians and biographers liked some figures about whom they wrote and disliked others.

Modern historians can mine ancient historical works for their information even when they disagree with their perspectives. We simply take those perspectives into account. Christian interpreters will naturally resonate with the theological perspectives of Luke-Acts, but historians, whether Christian or not, can derive information from this work regardless of whether they share Luke's views.

Historians regularly claimed that they had to stick to facts.[26] Lest we suppose them too biased to report their agendas correctly, many other ancient writers who were not historians themselves (such as Aristotle, Pliny, or Lucian) likewise expected historians to stick to facts.[27] Of course there were some bad historians, but they risked severe denunciation by their peers.[28] They do not, then, represent the standard that we would ordinarily expect.

---

23. Tomas Hägg, *The Art of Biography in Antiquity* (Cambridge: Cambridge University Press, 2012), 273.

24. See e.g., Herodotus 1.1 pref.; Polybius 1.1.1; 7.12; Diodorus Siculus 10.3.1; 11.11.2, 6; 11.38.6; 15.1.1; 17.38.4; Dionysius of Halicarnassus *Ant. rom.* 1.2.1; Tacitus *Agr.* 1; *Ann.* 3.65; Lucian *Hist.* 59; Colin J. Hemer, *The Book of Acts in the Setting of Hellenistic History*, ed. Conrad H. Gempf, WUNT 49 (Tübingen: Mohr Siebeck, 1989), 79–85; Samuel Byrskog, *Story as History—History as Story: The Gospel Tradition in the Context of Ancient Oral History*, WUNT 123 (Tübingen: Mohr Siebeck, 2000; repr., Boston: Brill, 2002), 256–65; Keener, *Acts*, 1:148–65.

25. See e.g., Polybius 31.9.1–4; 32.15.13; Diodorus Siculus 14.63.1; 14.69.4; 14.76.3; 27.4.3; 28.3.1; Cornelius Nepos 17.4.8; Livy 42.28.12; Valerius Maximus 1.1. ext. 3–5; 1.1.18–21; Josephus *J.W.* 4.622; *Ant.* 17.353; Pausanias 9.25.10; 3.23.3–5; 9.33.6; 9.39.12; Appian *Hist. rom.* 3.12.1–2; John T. Squires, *The Plan of God in Luke-Acts*, SNTSMS 76 (Cambridge: Cambridge University Press, 1993), 15–20, 38–51.

26. Polybius 2.56.11; 12.4c.4–5; 34.4.2–3; Josephus *Ag. Ap.* 1.26; *Ant.* 8.56; 20.156–57; Tacitus *Ann.* 4.11; cf. Dionysius of Halicarnassus *Thuc.* 8, 19, 55.

27. Aristotle *Poet.* 9.2, 1451b; Pliny *Ep.* 7.17.3; 8.4.1; Pausanias 1.3.3; Lucian *Hist.* 7–9, 24–25.

28. E.g., Thucydides 1.20.3; Polybius 2.56.1–3, 7, 10; 3.38.3; 12.3.1–12.15.12; 15.34.1; Diodorus Siculus

Ancient readers expected narratives, whether novels or history and biography, to be engaging and enjoyable,[29] but they expected a factual basis for history and biography, in contrast to novels. Some historians also took more storytelling or stylistic liberties than others in how they recounted their material; historians differed among themselves about how much was permitted. Because history was a narrative genre, historians could also flesh out scenes and speeches to portray them as close as possible to what the writers believed would have happened.

Such detailed descriptions are rare in Luke-Acts, not least due to space limitations. Acts includes many speeches, but they are summaries rather than fleshed out, full speeches (Acts 2:40). Ancient biographers and historians exercised varying ranges of literary flexibility in how they framed their material; by any standard, Luke, where we can test his use of Mark, avails himself of this flexibility less than most of his peers.

In any case, such flexibility was a matter of detail, not events. Ancient writers seem fairly unanimous that historians were not supposed to invent events. If they recounted an incident, it was normally because they had found it in their sources. Over the course of centuries, legends could arise, but studies of oral tradition suggest that the gist of a story usually remains substantially accurate within the shorter period of living memory. Luke-Acts recounts events mostly within living memory. All such factors incline us to expect Luke-Acts to inform us about genuine historical events.

EVALUATING DEGREES OF HISTORICAL RELIABILITY

Science, historiography, journalism, and other methods of investigation use somewhat different methods appropriate to their own spheres. Historical methodology is limited in its ability to evaluate events of the past. One cannot, for example, experiment regarding a historical figure's death by killing him or her again. Historiography deals with probabilities, not the level of certainty possible in, say, mathematics. Nevertheless, when independent, reliable sources agree on information, the degree of probability can sometimes be, for ordinary purposes, beyond reasonable doubt.

1.37.4, 6; 21.17.1; Velleius Paterculus 2.53.4; Josephus *Life* 336–39; *War* 1.7; Plutarch *Mal. Hdt.* 3–7, *Mor.* 855C–856B; Arrian *Ind.* 7.1; Lucian *Hist.* 24–25, 39–40; Dio Cassius 1.1.1–2.

29. Cf. 2 Macc 2:24–25; Tacitus *Ann.* 4.32–33; Maximus of Tyre 22.5; Dio Cassius 1.1.1–2; C. W. Fornara, *The Nature of History in Ancient Greece and Rome* (Berkeley: University of California Press, 1983), 120–33; Richard A. Burridge, *What Are the Gospels? A Comparison with Graeco-Roman Biography*, 2nd ed. (Grand Rapids: Eerdmans, 2004), 146, 181–82, 237–38; Catharine Edwards, "Introduction," in *Suetonius: Lives of the Caesars* (New York: Oxford University Press, 2000), vii–xxx (here xii–xiii).

As already noted, historians who were not eyewitnesses used sources.[30] They normally favored sources closest to the original events, and were more confident when the events were recent than when they belonged to the distant past. Some historians cited other sources by name only when they found conflicting reports, usually about the more distant past.[31] Luke does not name his sources, though he leaves no doubt that sources were available to him (Luke 1:1). Luke writes about events in living memory, when accounts of events had likely not diverged significantly. In Acts, as noted, Luke appears to be directly acquainted with events himself.

Three criteria are particularly helpful for evaluating particular historical claims. First, how close is the historian or his sources to the original event? Second, how carefully does he handle his sources? Where we can evaluate Luke, he meets both criteria better than most ancient historians did. Again, Luke's use of Mark is quite conservative by ancient standards.

Third, the extent to which independent sources support or challenge an author's claims also helps us to evaluate the author's reliability. Of course, the author could be more correct than the independent source, or (quite often) may speak to a different situation than the closest available source. Sources that are genuinely independent will normally omit much that another source includes. Nevertheless, this criterion is helpful in Luke-Acts. For the Gospel, we are mostly limited to sources regarding Judea and Galilee (regarding Herod Antipas, Pilate, etc.). By contrast, Acts provides a vast range of parallels with external sources, addressed at greater length below.

When historians compare the limited extant ancient sources, they raise questions, sometimes insoluble, for some claims found in any ancient historian. The strongest questions that scholars raise about Luke-Acts (see discussion below) address points peripheral to the narrative. Yet these questions are far outweighed by the many points at which independent, external data support Luke's claims. Even given the limitations of historical method, Luke fares quite well.

While these three criteria help us to assess given historical claims, a fourth criterion helps shape our expectation for claims that we cannot so readily test. Ancient historians normally had far more sources for their narratives than have survived to the present, and it goes without saying that they could not know which sources would survive to the present. If a historian typically follows his

---

30. See further R. A. Derrenbacker Jr., *Ancient Compositional Practices and the Synoptic Problem*, BETL 186 (Leuven: Leuven University Press, 2005), 52; Keener, *Acts*, 1:170–76; esp. Chris Alfred, "Source Valuation in Greek and Roman Biography: From Xenophon to Suetonius," in *Biographies and Jesus: What Does It Mean for the Gospels to be Biographies?*, ed. Craig S. Keener and Edward T. Wright (Lexington, KY: Emeth, 2016), 77–102.

31. See e.g., Valerius Maximus 5.7.ext. 1; 6.8.3; Tacitus *Ann.* 2.73, 88; 4.57; 13.20; Philostratus *Vit. soph.* 2.4.570.

sources where we can test him (i.e., where we have the source or information available), we should assume that his method where we cannot test him remains fairly consistent. To argue otherwise is simply to speculate, to argue from some cases of silence against the preponderance of the evidence that we have. Thus, we have strong reason historically to trust Luke's picture of events.

ACCURATE LOCAL COLOR

Accurate portrayal of locales does not demonstrate reliability of the accounts that occur there, but it does confirm that the author had a source of information. As two classicists note, "It is the accuracy over quite obscure details which is striking."[32] Even though no handbook for local titles of officials existed, for example, Luke always gets correct the titles for officials in different locales, for example politarchs (NIV: *city officials*) in Thessalonica and the *city clerk* in Ephesus (Acts 17:6–8; 19:35).[33] Either Luke or his source must have traveled to these locations, and if Luke reports Paul's travel there, why should we *not* think his source was Paul?

Luke also displays accurate information about Ephesus (Acts 19:1–41): Ephesians used a unique title for Artemis, sometimes defended her cult, were sensitive at precisely this time concerning the economics of Artemis worship, could have unscheduled meetings in the theater near the crowded market, and countless other details. Luke seems acquainted both with Ephesus and with a riot that took place there.[34] External evidence does not prove that the riot involved Paul, but why would Luke, who spends the final quarter of Acts defending Paul against the charge of causing public disorder (Acts 24:5), *invent* a riot concerning Paul?[35]

More important are the many correspondences in detail for Paul's ministry in the interior of Asia Minor, including the narrative's routes, sites, and characteristics (Acts 13–14).[36] While many people traveled to Ephesus, few people traveled to the rugged interior of Asia Minor.

Although further examples could be multiplied, I conclude this section with Luke's "we" narrative about the sea voyage (Acts 27:1–28:15). Even minor details of the account match what we know of weather conditions and the sailors'

---

32. Richard Wallace and Wynne Williams, *The Acts of the Apostles: A Companion* (Bristol: Bristol Classical, 1993), 27.
33. Cadbury, *Acts in History*, 40–41.
34. See further Paul R. Trebilco, *The Early Christians in Ephesus from Paul to Ignatius* (Grand Rapids: Eerdmans, 2007), 104–7; Keener, *Acts*, 3:2869–71.
35. See Craig S. Keener, "Paul and Sedition: Pauline Apologetic in Acts," *BBR* 22 (2012): 201–24.
36. See e.g., Keener, *Acts*, 2:1976–77.

actions.[37] Already in the nineteenth century, a mariner showed how the seasonal storm conditions, direction and timing of the ship's drift, and other details precisely fit Mediterranean conditions.[38] More recent meteorological studies offer further confirmation.[39]

Luke or his source was clearly aboard a ship in these conditions. Skeptics suggest that perhaps Luke simply added the mentions of Paul to the existing narrative, but if Luke describes the conditions accurately, is it not simpler to assume that he was also present with Paul, as he claims?

EVENTS IN ACTS

Often in Acts, and especially once the narrative stretches beyond Judea, we have sources available that can confirm Luke's reports about persons or events. Luke does not frame these events precisely the way that other sources do—independent writers rarely do—but we can attest many of the persons and sorts of events to which he refers.

For example, the depictions of Herod Agrippa I, Agrippa II, Felix, and Festus (Acts 12:1–23; 23:24–26:32) resemble what we know of these figures from Josephus, even though Josephus personally favors Herod Agrippa I more than does Luke.[40] More directly,[41] both Josephus and Luke report the occasion of Agrippa's death; that both report incidental details omitted by the other source suggests independent accounts about the same event, confirming the overlapping features.[42]

Josephus *Ant.* 19.343–50	Acts 12:19–23
Agrippa was in Caesarea at this time (19.343)	Agrippa was in Caesarea at this time (12:19)
Public setting (19.343–44)	Public setting (12:21)
Agrippa's glorious robe (19.344)	Agrippa's royal apparel (12:21)

---

37. See Hemer, *Book of Acts in the Setting of Hellenistic History*, 132–56.

38. James Smith, *The Voyage and Shipwreck of St. Paul (with Dissertations on the Life and Writings of St. Luke, and the Ships and Navigation of the Ancients)*, rev. Walter E. Smith, 4th ed. (London: Longmans, Green, 1880).

39. R. W. White, "A Meteorological Appraisal of Acts 27:5–26," *ExpTim* 113 (2002): 403–7.

40. See e.g., Keener, *Acts*, 2:1867–68, 1873–78, passim; 3:3328–31; 4:3422–24, 3433, 3436, 3441–42, 3450–60, 3473–79, 3495–96, 3548.

41. See Keener, *Acts*, 2:1965–68, including for the following chart.

42. C. K. Barrett, *A Critical and Exegetical Commentary on the Acts of the Apostles*, 2 vols. (Edinburgh: T&T Clark, 1994–98), 589, is probably also correct to find in Luke's curious mention of "Blastus" Luke's abridgement of a source other than Josephus.

Josephus *Ant.* 19.343–50	Acts 12:19–23
Flatterers hail Agrippa as divine (19.344–45)	Flatterers hail Agrippa as divine (12:22)
Agrippa suffers divine judgment immediately afterward (19.346–48)	Agrippa suffers divine judgment immediately afterward (12:23)
Because of the flatterers' blasphemy (19.346–47)	Because he did not defer the praise to God (12:23)
He suffered for five days from stomach pains (19.348–50)	He was eaten by worms (12:23)
He died (19.350)	He died (12:23)

The potential list of correspondences could extend to more than one hundred pages, as it does in one monograph by Colin Hemer,[43] including (here is a small sampling of his examples):

- Attestation of the Sergii Paulii (Acts 13:7) and their family connections to the region where Paul next journeyed, including Pisidian Antioch and Iconium (Acts 13:14, 51)[44]
- Although Paul never flaunted his Roman citizenship, his name strongly supports the likelihood that he was in fact a Roman citizen (Acts 16:37)[45]
- The Roman road from Philippi to Thessalonica would include stops in Amphipolis and Apollonia (Acts 17:1)
- The quotations in Acts 17:28 probably derive from authors that fit Paul's background in Tarsus (a quotation from Aratus) and his mention of an "unknown deity" (a quotation from Epimenides), perhaps suggesting that the report in Acts 17 condenses a lengthier original message by Paul
- A Roman historian attests the expulsion noted in Acts 18:2, probably at the time noted there
- An inscription attests that Gallio was in Corinth the very year that Paul appeared before him there in Acts 18:12

---

43. Hemer, *Acts*, 108–220, especially 108–58. I condense here my sample list from Keener, *Acts*, 1:204–6.

44. See esp. Stephen Mitchell, *Anatolia: Land, Men, and Gods in Asia Minor*, 2 vols. (Oxford: Clarendon, 1993), 2:6–7.

45. See Keener, *Acts*, 3:2517–27. Critics who claim that practicing Jews would not have been Roman citizens are poorly informed about ancient sources, as Martin Hengel, *The Pre-Christian Paul* (Valley Forge, PA: Trinity Press International, 1991), 11–14, rightly observes.

- The travels and their durations in Acts 20:13–17 and 21:1–8 match what is known
- The one speech to believers in Acts (20:18–35), notably in the "we" material, is full of the language Paul used in his letters to believers[46]
- Other sources also attest the death penalty for gentiles entering the temple (Acts 21:28)
- A Roman cohort in the Fortress Antonia watched for unrest in the temple that needed to be quieted (Acts 21:31)
- Josephus also notes the staircase by which the soldiers stationed in the Fortress Antonia descended into the temple in Acts 21:32, 35, 40[47]
- An Egyptian Jewish false prophet had recently gathered a following in the wilderness (Acts 21:38)
- Lysias's adopted Roman name "Claudius" (Acts 23:26) suggests that he had gained citizenship under Claudius, who frequently sold the franchise (and more cheaply as years passed; cf. Acts 22:28)
- Ananias is the correct name for the high priest at the time of Acts 23:2
- Felix was the governor at the time of Acts 23:24
- Archaeology confirms that Antipatris was the appropriate stop on the road from Jerusalem to Caesarea, and the terrain and ethnic demography show that it was the safest place to relieve the infantry (Acts 23:31)
- By asking Paul's province, Felix may have planned to refer Paul's case to a different governor, but Paul is from Cilicia, which in precisely this period was under his own superior (Acts 23:34)
- Although Felix was married three times, Drusilla was his wife at precisely the time in Acts 24:24
- Porcius Festus succeeded Felix as governor (Acts 24:27) at precisely this time
- Bernice was married before and after this time, but at precisely this time she was staying with her brother Agrippa II (Acts 25:13)

We know of no ancient novels that researched to produce such correspondences. Even if one is so skeptical as to doubt Paul's presence in the final quarter of Acts, it is difficult to doubt the presence of Luke or his source!

---

46. See esp. Steve Walton, *Leadership and Lifestyle: The Portrait of Paul in the Miletus Speech and 1 Thessalonians*, SNTSMS 108 (Cambridge: Cambridge University Press, 2000).

47. Josephus *War* 5.243–244.

COMPARING EVENTS IN ACTS AND PAUL'S LETTERS

One external source for Acts appears in the New Testament itself: Paul's letters. These letters address local situations. Paul's interests therefore differ from Luke's, so either set of sources naturally omits much of what the other includes. Nevertheless, the degree of overlap is comparable to what we find when we compare biographies of various figures with the letters those figures wrote.[48]

For example, Paul expected trouble in Judea (Rom 15:31), and what is probably his next set of letters depict him in Roman custody (e.g., Phil 1:13; Phlm 1:9).

Well over a century ago, Adolf von Harnack, a noted liberal historian of early Christianity, noted that Luke is accurate where we can check his claims with Paul. He noted thirty-nine specific cases. I list just a few here:

- Jesus's movement was large, even before the apostolic preaching in Jerusalem (Acts 1:15; 1 Cor 15:6)
- The Jesus movement expanded from Jerusalem, rather than Galilee (Rom 15:19, 26–27)
- The movement expanded elsewhere in Judea (1 Thess 2:14; Gal 1:22; Acts 9:31)
- The Judean churches faced persecution (Acts 7–8; 1 Thess 2:14), especially by Paul (Acts 8:1–3; 9:1–2; Gal 1:13–14; 1 Cor 15:9; Phil 3:6)
- Many Judean believers followed the law (Acts 15:5; 21:20; Gal 2:4, 12), and not all were pleased with Paul (Rom 15:31; Acts 21:21)
- The Twelve led the church in Jerusalem (Acts 1:13; 6:2; Gal 1:17; 1 Cor 15:5)
- Among the Twelve, Peter was the most significant leader, apparently followed by John (Acts 2:37; 3:1; 8:14, 17; 1 Cor 15:5; Gal 1:18; 2:9)
- Although not among the Twelve, Barnabas was also an apostle (Acts 14:4, 14; 1 Cor 9:5–6; 15:7) who had ties to the Jerusalem church (Acts 4:36–37; 11:22; Gal 2:13) and worked closely with Paul (Acts 11:25; 13–14; 1 Cor 9:6; Gal 2:1, 9)
- Another group of leaders was comprised of the Lord's brothers (Acts 1:14; 1 Cor 9:5), headed by James, who came to exercise authority no less than that of Peter and John (Acts 12:17; 15:13, 19; 21:18; 1 Cor 15:7; Gal 2:9, 12)
- Mark has close ties with Barnabas (Acts 15:37; Col 4:10)

---

48. See T. Hillard, A. Nobbs, and B. Winter, "Acts and the Pauline Corpus, I: Ancient Literary Parallels," in *The Book of Acts in Its Ancient Literary Setting*, ed. Bruce W. Winter and Andrew D. Clarke, vol. 1 of *The Book of Acts in Its First Century Setting* (Grand Rapids: Eerdmans, 1993), 183–213.

- Paul's subsequent companions included Silas and, in a subordinate role, Timothy (Acts 15:40; 16:1–3; 2 Cor 1:19; 1 Thess 1:1)
- A revelation of Jesus converted Paul near Damascus (Acts 9:3–6; Gal 1:12, 17; 1 Cor 15:8)
- Paul escaped his opponents in Damascus by being lowered from the wall in a basket (Acts 9:25; 2 Cor 11:32–33)
- Paul traveled to Jerusalem afterward (Acts 9:26; Gal 1:18–19) and preached there (Acts 9:28–29; 23:11; Rom 15:19)

Paul's letters also provide a partial itinerary for his years of ministry, which overlaps significantly with Acts.[49]

- Paul was persecuting believers (Gal 1:13–14; Acts 8:1–3)
- Paul was converted near Damascus (Gal 1:15–17a; Acts 9:3–9)
- Paul journeyed to Jerusalem (Gal 1:18–19; Acts 9:26)
- He went to Syria and Cilicia (Gal 1:21; Acts 9:30; 11:25–26)
- He and Barnabas returned to Jerusalem to resolve an issue (Gal 2:1–10; Acts 15:1–2)
- They returned to Antioch (Gal 2:11; Acts 15:30–35)[50]
- Paul and Silas preached in Philippi (1 Thess 1:1; 2:1–2; Phil 4:15–16; Acts 16:12–40)
- They preached in Thessalonica (1 Thess 2:1–2; Phil 4:15–16; Acts 17:1–9)
- Paul stayed in Athens (1 Thess 3:1–3; cf. Acts 17:16–34)
- Paul preached in Corinth (1 Cor 2:1–5; Acts 18:1–18)
- Then in Ephesus (1 Cor 16:8–9; Acts 19:1–41)
- Then in Macedonia (2 Cor 2:13; 8–9; cf. Acts 20:1–2)
- Then in Corinth (2 Cor 9:4; 7:5; Acts 20:2–3)
- Then to Jerusalem (Rom 15:22–25; Acts 21:15–19)
- Then to Rome (Rom 15:22–25; Acts 28:14–31)

Paul was publicly shamed in Philippi (1 Thess 2:2; Acts 16:22–23) and then faced severe hostility in Thessalonica, which also continued after Paul left (Acts 17:13; 1 Thess 1:6; 2:2). One scholar even contends that nearly three-quarters of

---

49. I adapt here Keener, *Acts*, 1:239–40. See Thomas H. Campbell, "Paul's 'Missionary Journeys' as Reflected in His Letters," *JBL* 74 (1955): 80–87, here 81–84; Charles H. Talbert, *Reading Luke-Acts in Its Mediterranean Milieu*, NovTSup 107 (Leiden: Brill, 2003), 203–4.

50. With a majority of scholars, I find numerous correlations between Gal 2:1–10 and Acts 15:6–22 (see Keener, *Acts*, 3:2195–2206; idem, *Galatians* [New York: Cambridge, 2018], 4–7; I also treat here the alleged incongruities), but a significant minority correlate Gal 2:1–10 instead with Acts 11:30.

Luke's details about Paul's stay in Thessalonica "are either directly or indirectly confirmed by 1 Thessalonians."[51]

Paul's letters also independently confirm many points about Paul's mission in Corinth.[52] Acts and Paul's letters depict Paul as the founder of the church in Corinth (1 Cor 3:6; 4:15).[53]

- Aquila and Priscilla minister together as a married couple (Acts 18:2, 26; Rom 16:3)
- They are known in Corinth and use their homes for God's work (Acts 18:3; Rom 16:5; 1 Cor 16:19)
- They have ties to Rome (Acts 18:2; Rom 16:3) and Ephesus (Acts 18:18–19; 2 Tim 4:19)
- Paul initially worked a trade to support himself in Corinth (Acts 18:3; 1 Cor 4:12; 9:6)
- Crispus is converted and baptized (Acts 18:8; 1 Cor 1:14)
- Timothy participates (Acts 18:5; 1 Cor 4:17; 16:10–11; 2 Cor 1:19)
- Silas participates (Acts 18:5; 2 Cor 1:19)
- Paul began ministry in Corinth before the arrival of Silas and Timothy (Acts 18:1–4; 1 Thess 3:6)
- Paul spent time in Athens en route (Acts 17:15–34; 1 Thess 3:1)
- Sosthenes, probably the same one, appears in Corinth (Acts 18:17; 1 Cor 1:1)
- The Corinthian believers are apparently familiar with Judaism (Acts 18:4–7; 1 Cor 1:22–24; 9:20; 10:32; 12:13; 2 Cor 11:22)
- The Corinthian believers know Apollos as a significant preacher, and he is associated at some point with Ephesus and with Paul (Acts 18:24–28; 1 Cor 3:5–6; 16:8, 12)
- Paul subsequently visits Ephesus at length (Acts 18:19; 19:8–10; 1 Cor 15:32; 16:8; cf. 2 Cor 1:8)

Paul continued to write letters before his journey to Jerusalem, and again later from Roman custody (on the most common dating of his letters). This allows some further comparisons, such as the following:

---

51. Rainer Riesner, *Paul's Early Period: Chronology, Mission Strategy, Theology*, trans. Doug Stott (Grand Rapids: Eerdmans, 1998), 366–67.

52. For the majority view that Acts is independent of most of Paul's letters, see C. K. Barrett, "Acts and the Pauline Corpus," *ExpTim* 88 (1976): 2–5; Walton, *Leadership and Lifestyle*, 14–17; Keener, *Acts*, 1:233–37.

53. Ben Witherington III, *The Acts of the Apostles: A Socio-Rhetorical Commentary* (Grand Rapids: Eerdmans, 1998), 537 (adapted in Keener, *Acts*, 3:2682–83).

- As in Acts 19:21, Paul plans to visit Macedonia (1 Cor 16:5), then Achaia (1 Cor 16:5–6; cf. 4:18–21), then Judea (Rom 15:25; 2 Cor 1:16), and finally Rome (Rom 1:11–13; 15:23–25)
- As in Acts 19:21–22, Paul sends Timothy from Ephesus ahead of himself (1 Cor 4:17; 16:8, 10); they later reunite (Acts 20:4; Rom 16:21)
- Paul visits Macedonia (Acts 20:1–2; 2 Cor 2:13; 7:5)
- As planned (2 Cor 13:1), Paul visits Achaia (Acts 20:2–3) and is soon accompanied by traveling companions from elsewhere (Acts 20:4; 2 Cor 9:4)
- After Macedonia and Achaia (Rom 15:26), Paul plans to visit Jerusalem (Rom 15:25; Acts 21:17) to bring an offering (Acts 24:17; Rom 15:25–26, 31)

Although we lack letters from Paul's trip to Jerusalem, his letters are consistent with what we see in the final quarter of Acts, a period when Luke traveled with him:

Paul anticipated danger from unbelievers in Jerusalem (Rom 15:31)	Paul encounters mob violence in Jerusalem (Acts 21:27–31)
Paul writes his next extant letters (including at least Philippians and Philemon, according to the most common chronology) in Roman custody	Roman soldiers detain Paul and hold him in custody (Acts 22:24–23:30)
Although Paul had presumably planned to reach Rome voluntarily (Rom 15:23–24) we next hear from him in Roman custody there (Phil 4:22, according to the most common interpretation)	Paul uses his Roman citizenship to get his case transferred to Rome (Acts 25:10–12)

OBJECTIONS SOMETIMES RAISED

Some argue against Acts's congruity with other sources by pointing to places where it differs from such sources. Most of these differences prove to be simply a case of one source reporting something that another source does not, an argument from silence that could be used to discredit any independent sources. What distinguishes ancient historical works from novels is not that any historical work was comprehensive; this would require what no source provides, namely, the inclusion of all possible information. What distinguishes them is that historical works depend on prior information, which we can sometimes attest by comparing other sources, whereas novelists could compose freely.

We do see differences of emphasis, showing different writers' different interests. For example, Luke emphasizes Jewish opposition more than does Paul, though it appears in Paul's letters as well (2 Cor 11:24; 1 Thess 2:14); Luke emphasizes Paul's own Jewishness often, though this appears in Paul's letters as well (Rom 9:2–3; 11:1). Luke and Paul write at different times addressing different issues, but this does not count against the accuracy of either.

At some points, however, differences appear that conflict with other sources. This is true for all ancient historians and biographers (except in the rarer cases where we lack sources with which to compare them).[54] Where conflicts occur, scholars often differ as to which source is more accurate (Josephus, for example, often contradicts himself on details, though in the case of Acts 5:36–37 scholars more often follow Josephus than Luke). Following are some of the major examples of such conflicts that scholars often highlight. (I omit here cases, which I address elsewhere, where critics of Luke appear simply historically misinformed,[55] or where objections are based simply on the critic's worldview rather than on historical information,[56] or cases of plausibility assessments without supporting external data.)[57]

- Acts 5:36–37: Josephus dates Theudas's revolt roughly ten years *after* this speech by Gamaliel
- Acts 15:4–29: scholars identify what they believe are tensions between this account and Paul's account in Galatians
- Acts 17:15–16: Paul sends Timothy from Athens in 1 Thess 3:1–2, suggesting that Luke has condensed and simplified his account[58]

---

54. For samples of the overlap and differences among ancient historians and biographers, see Michael R. Licona, *Why Are There Differences in the Gospels? What We Can Learn from Ancient Biography* (New York: Oxford University Press, 2017); Craig S. Keener, "Otho: A Targeted Comparison of Suetonius' Biography and Tacitus' History, with Implications for the Gospels' Historical Reliability," *BBR* 21 (2011): 331–55.

55. See examples in Craig S. Keener, "Note on Athens: Do 1 Corinthians 16.15 and Acts 17.34 Conflict?," *JGRChJ* 7 (2010): 137–39; idem, "Acts 10: Were Troops Stationed in Caesarea During Agrippa's Rule?," *JGRChJ* 7 (2010): 164–76.

56. See Craig S. Keener, *Miracles: The Credibility of the New Testament Accounts*, 2 vols. (Grand Rapids: Baker Academic, 2011); idem, "A Reassessment of Hume's Case against Miracles in Light of Testimony from the Majority World Today," *PRSt* 38 (2011): 289–310; idem, "Miracle Reports: Perspectives, Analogies, Explanations," in *Hermeneutik der frühchristlichen Wundererzählungen: Historiche, literarische und rezeptionsästhetische Aspekte*, ed. Bernd Kollmann and Ruben Zimmermann, WUNT 339 (Tübingen: Mohr Siebeck, 2014), 53–65; idem, "'The Dead are Raised' (Matthew 11:5//Luke 7:22): Resuscitation Accounts in the Gospels and Eyewitness Testimony," *BBR* 25 (2015): 55–79.

57. See Craig S. Keener, "Novels' 'Exotic' Places and Luke's African Official (Acts 8:27)," *AUSS* 46 (2008): 5–20; idem, "The Plausibility of Luke's Growth Figures in Acts 2.41; 4.4; 21.20," *JGRChJ* 7 (2010): 140–63.

58. See Keener, *Acts*, 3:2570–72; Hans Conzelmann, *A Commentary on the Acts of the Apostles*, ed. Eldon Jay Epp with Christopher R. Matthews, trans. James Limburg, A. Thomas Kraabel, and Donald H. Juel (Philadelphia: Fortress, 1987), 136. Such simplification appears regularly in ancient biography and historiography; see F. Gerald Downing, "Redaction Criticism: Josephus' *Antiquities* and the Synoptic Gospels (I)," *JSNT* 8 (1980): 46–65, here 57; Brian McGing, "Philo's Adaptation of the Bible in His *Life of Moses*," in *The Limits of Ancient Biography*, ed. Brian McGing and Judith Mossman (Swansea: Classical Press of Wales,

- Acts 21:38: Josephus treats the "terrorists" separately from the Egyptian and offers conflicting estimates of numbers

Scholars offer various explanations for these differences. In some cases, such as the alleged conflict in Acts 21:38, the apparent conflicts are easily explained: the term translated "terrorists" did have a wider usage, and Luke's numbers seem more plausible than Josephus's.[59] The differences in Acts 15 are far less striking than the similarities and are mostly a matter of one narrative omitting what the other includes.[60] In others, such as Acts 5:36, the debate is more heated.[61]

We should note, however, that even in a case such as Acts 5:36, if the conflict appeared in another ancient historian, no one would count this against the historian's overall reliability. Acts 5:36–37 appears in the speech behind closed doors, the very sort of setting from which scholars today expect the least from ancient historians. Even 21:38 is not an assertion by Luke himself, but the speech of someone whom the narrative presents as already misled by conflicting information (Acts 21:34). All these examples reflect peripheral detail rather than the main story. Even on the least supportive reading of Acts, then, these challenges do not undermine Luke's credibility as an ancient historian.

CONCLUSION

In this essay, I have highlighted merely a sample of the correlations between Acts and external evidence. Far from writing with the creative freedom of a novelist, Luke writes his work based on historical information available to him. External correspondences make this dependence clear in Acts just as his use of Mark makes it clear in his Gospel. We should therefore approach Luke's historical work with great confidence.

Of course, Luke, like other ancient historians, was interested not only in information about the past for curiosity's sake. He was interested in how the past instructs us to live in the present. For Christians, this means that we hear in Luke not simply voices from ages past, but the voice of one who speaks today.

2006), 117–40 (here 131–33); Maarten De Pourcq and Geert Roskam, "Mirroring Virtues in Plutarch's Lives of Agis, Cleomenes and the Gracchi," in *Writing Biography in Greece and Rome: Narrative Technique and Fictionalization*, ed. Koen De Temmerman and Kristoffel Demoen (Cambridge: Cambridge University Press, 2016), 163–80 (here 176); Licona, *Why Are There Differences in the Gospels?*, 20, 42, 46–48, 50–52, 56, 72, 75, 77, 80, 83, 95, 97, 100, 108–9; Keener, *Acts*, 1:143–47.

59. See Keener, *Acts*, 3:3172–77; Mark Andrew Brighton, *The Sicarii in Josephus's Judean War: Rhetorical Analysis and Historical Observations*, EJL 27 (Atlanta: Society of Biblical Literature, 2009).

60. As noted, see discussion in Keener, *Acts*, 3:2195–2206; idem, *Galatians*, 4–7.

61. See partial discussion in Keener, *Acts*, 2:1230–37.

Part Four

• • •

Responses and
Reflections

A Response by Larry W. Hurtado

LARRY W. HURTADO

T he four Gospels and the book of Acts portray individuals and events
as real, in our terms, as "historical." In the case of the Gospels, all four
purport to present an account of Jesus's ministry, and all four set it (with considerable detail) in early first-century Galilee and Judaea. But, from the second
century onward, the evident differences among the Gospels have proven to be a
difficulty for many Christians (such as Tatian), and have provided ammunition
for non-Christian opponents (such as Celsus).[1] Indeed, ironically, it is the existence of these multiple accounts of Jesus, all from roughly the same time, that
enables critical study of them and the Jesus tradition and makes evident their
individual emphases. Had we only one such account, our historical and critical
task would be much more difficult.

For, despite valiant efforts to do so, it is evident that the Gospels cannot
readily be harmonized into one flat and fully cohesive historical account. In
addition, it is clear, again most readily by comparing them with one another,
that they are by no means dispassionate historical accounts but, instead, are
thoroughly based on, and in various ways shaped by, faith in Jesus as God's
unique agent of salvation. The Gospels do not simply recount Jesus's career;
they commend him in the strongest terms to the believers for whom the authors
wrote. The traditions about Jesus were not preserved for antiquarian purposes
but to promote faith in him. These things being so, how are the Gospels to be
treated in critical historical inquiries about Jesus? In response to this question,
various criteria of authenticity were developed and deployed, and have come in
for criticism.

As for the differences among the gospel accounts, these extend beyond simply
what the individual authors chose to include. The more difficult matters are

---

1. Oscar Cullmann, "The Plurality of the Gospels as a Theological Problem in Antiquity," in *The Early
Church: Studies in Early Christian History and Theology*, ed. A. J. B. Higgins (London: SCM; Philadelphia:
Westminster, 1956), 39–54.

differences in the way the same incident or teaching of Jesus is reported.[2] As is well-known among scholars, these differences often align with other indications of the emphases of the individual Gospels authors. This is most evident in the Gospel of John, in which it is often difficult to distinguish what the author presents as words of Jesus from the author's own discourse. Of course, actually, each of the four Gospels gives an interpreted account of Jesus. I have likened this to the phenomenon of various renditions of a musical composition (suggesting, in this model, that the Gospel of John could be thought of as the jazz rendition!).[3] And, as for Acts, although we have only this one narrative of earliest Christianity, it, too, seems to combine historical reportage with (and shaped by) the particular emphases and aims of the author.

But the four Gospels and their focus on Jesus have always been the main object of the most intense scholarly concern and analysis. For nothing in the scholarly study of Christian origins, theologically or historically, compares with the energies given to questions about the figure of Jesus. Indeed, the resources and efforts brought to bear in composing the four Gospels attest that, well before the subsequent scholarly efforts to address these questions, there was a concern to underscore the importance of Jesus as a real, historical personage. I have argued that it was precisely the emphasis on Jesus's resurrection in earliest Christian faith that helped to generate this earliest historical concern for the figure of Jesus.[4]

For all of the Gospels exhibit a strong placement of Jesus in early first-century Galilee and Judaea, with copious references to cultural, geographical, political, institutional, and religious specifics of that time and those locales.[5]

In short, this all amounts to a shared programmatic effort to locate Jesus in a specific historical, geographical, and cultural setting. It represents an insistence that the Jesus whom the writers and intended readers of these Gospels revered (who include Gentile and Jewish believers in various locations in the Roman world), and were to see as linked with God's purposes in a unique way, is quite definitely *Jesus of Nazareth*. He is not some timeless symbol, not a mythical figure of a "once upon a time," but instead very specifically a Jew

---

2. Cf. e.g., the two accounts of the divorce question in Mark 10:1–12 and Matt 19:3–12; or the two accounts of the sea miracle in Mark 4:35–41 and Matt 14:22–33.

3. Larry W. Hurtado, *Lord Jesus Christ: Devotion to Jesus in Earliest Christianity* (Grand Rapids: Eerdmans, 2003), 283–347. And see pp. 349–407 for my discussion of the rendition of Jesus in the Gospel of John.

4. Larry W. Hurtado, "Resurrection-Faith and the 'Historical' Jesus," *JSHJ* 11 (2013): 35–52.

5. See my discussion of specifics in *Lord Jesus Christ*, 262–70.

whose life and activities are geographically and chronologically located in a particular place and period of Jewish history in Roman Judea.[6]

That is, with all due allowance for the evident differences among them, the four Gospels share a concern to affirm a strong link between the *Kyrios* Jesus, exalted by God to heavenly glory and rightful recipient of cultic devotion in early Christian circles, and the historical figure, Jesus of Nazareth, the Jewish male from Galilee.[7] This is true of the Gospel of John as much as it is of any of the Synoptic Gospels. Indeed, as Udo Schnelle observed, the shared choice of the genre of narrative gospel, not a collection of sayings (cf. the Gospel of Thomas) or a revelatory discourse (cf. the Gospel of Truth), but "a genre whose character requires a description of the life and work of the historical Jesus of Nazareth from a post-Easter perspective," shows that "the *vita Jesu* is of fundamental importance" already in all four of the Gospels.[8]

As is commonly known, however, the modern form of "quests" for a "historical" Jesus emerged with force beginning in the eighteenth century, especially in the deist aim to challenge the cultural authority of traditional Christianity in Europe. That is, the project was never simply pursued in the interest of historical knowledge, but always with additional motives, and by scholars who happen to align themselves with some form of Christian faith or (for various reasons) do not do so. And for scholars of both kinds of stance, historical Jesus work is not innocent of personal concerns. Anyone doing historical Jesus work who claims to have no such motive or concern is either deceitful or charmingly self-deceiving. Instead, those who pursue historical investigation of the figure of Jesus should openly acknowledge their own stakes in the matter, by the practice of good scholarly discipline try to avoid overdetermining the results, and then submit their results to critical examination by other scholars, including those with different concerns, who may be best perceptive in spotting tendentiousness and special pleading. Others can spot the mote in our eye better than we can!

But, to return to the early deist-inspired efforts, applying a clever adaptation of the Protestant critique of the Roman Catholic Church, in which church tradition was distinguished from, and assessed critically in contrast to, the New Testament, this deist project involved distinguishing and judging even the New

---

6. Hurtado, *Lord Jesus Christ*, 266.

7. Udo Schnelle argued that the Gospel of John in particular was written to correct docetic tendencies in a "Johannine community" (*Antidocetic Christology in the Gospel of John* [Minneapolis: Fortress, 1992]). Whatever the merits of that specific claim, he rightly points to the emphasis on the historical figure of Jesus shared by the Gospel of John and the other Gospels.

8. Schnelle, *Antidocetic Christology*, 229.

Testament writings in contrast to Jesus. In short, if for traditional Protestants the rot set in after the New Testament, for deists the rot began in the period after Jesus's crucifixion and is evident already in the Gospels, reaching its zenith in the doctrine of the Trinity.[9] So, to cite one well-known example, Thomas Jefferson produced (initially for himself) by hand a small book that distinguished between the authentic words of Jesus and what Jefferson saw as a supernaturalist corruption evident already in the gospel accounts.[10]

This sort of project, by Jefferson or anyone else, however, presupposed that it was fully possible to get behind the Gospels and their objectionable miraculous elements and proceed directly to a historically authentic Jesus, who for deists such as Jefferson was simply a respected teacher of morals. But, as the classic study by Albert Schweitzer so colourfully showed, efforts along these lines from Reimarus to Wrede only revealed how difficult this project was, and how varied were the results.[11]

Contributors to the present volume repeatedly indicate that they are responding to another multiauthor volume edited by Chris Keith and Anthony Le Donne.[12] In that volume, the contributors (though not entirely of one mind) tended to call into question the usefulness of an approach to the historical Jesus that rests heavily on a set of criteria for distinguishing what in the Gospels is historically authentic information about Jesus from early Christian interpretation of him and his significance. The now-classic example of a strict criteria-based approach is Norman Perrin's book, *Rediscovering the Teaching of Jesus*.[13] More specifically, after insisting that "the burden of proof will be upon the claim to authenticity," Perrin then declared that "the fundamental criterion for authenticity upon which all reconstuctions of the teaching of Jesus must be built" is

---

9. J. Z. Smith, *Drudgery Divine: On the Comparison of Early Christianities and the Religions of Late Antiquity* (Chicago: University of Chicago Press, 1990), 1–35, discusses some key figures and developments. His book is focused on the origins of comparative studies of early Christianity and its religious environment, but he provides some material relevant to this matter I discuss here.

10. Thomas Jefferson, *The Life and Morals of Jesus of Nazareth* (unpublished manuscript, 1820). A facsimile edition is available: *The Jefferson Bible, Smithsonian Edition: The Life and Morals of Jesus of Nazareth* (Washington, DC: Smithsonian, 2011). There are various published editions, e.g., *The Jefferson Bible: Life and Morals of Jesus of Nazareth* (Washington, DC: Smithsonian, 2011).

11. Albert Schweitzer, *Von Reimarus zu Wrede: Eine Geschichte der Leben-Jesu-Forschung* (Tübingen: Mohr, 1906); English translation: *The Quest of the Historical Jesus: A Critical Study of its Progress from Reimarus to Wrede*, trans. W. Montgomery (London: Macmillan, 1910). A more recent translation of the 1913 second edition comprises a work of some 300 more pages: Albert Schweitzer, *The Quest of the Historical Jesus, First Complete Edition*, trans. John Bowden (London: SCM, 2000).

12. Chris Keith and Anthony Le Donne, eds., *Jesus, Criteria, and the Demise of Authenticity* (London: T&T Clark, 2012).

13. Norman Perrin, *Rediscovering the Teaching of Jesus* (New York: Harper & Row, 1967; London: SCM, 1967). Cf., e.g., the extended (and in my view incisive) review by Werner Georg Kümmel, "Norman Perrin's 'Rediscovering the Teaching of Jesus,'" *JR* 49 (1969): 59–66.

what he called "the criterion of dissimilarity."[14] His aim (stated in rather positivist terms) was to identify "an irreducible minimum of historical knowledge available to us at the present time" about Jesus.[15] His results were a handful of sayings out of the entirety of the Gospels. It was Perrin's book in particular that prompted the oft-cited critique of this criterion of dissimilarity by Morna Hooker.[16]

But, in addition to Hooker's cogent critique of such heavy dependence on this criterion, we should also note that Perrin's study was shaped by certain theological and hermeneutical commitments. This book reflected Perrin's shift from his earlier alignment with his doctoral supervisor, Joachim Jeremias, to what he termed a "more sceptical" view that was heavily influenced by Bultmann's works, especially Bultmann's form-critical analysis of the history of the Synoptic tradition.[17] As evidenced by the title of his book and its exclusive concern with authentic *sayings* of Jesus, Perrin was also obviously influenced by Bultmann's hermeneutical and existentialist emphasis on the *words* of Jesus as the key data, on the view that the person of Jesus is found especially in his sayings.[18]

Indeed, in Perrin's work (and that of a goodly number of others of that day), there was an almost *exclusive* emphasis on the words/sayings of Jesus, with far less attention given to the *actions* of Jesus depicted in the Gospels. This should seem rather strange, given that all four of the crucial writings for historical Jesus research are *narratives*, not sayings collections. That is, the sayings ascribed to Jesus are all set within a narrative framework, a narrative "world" of Jesus's activity that actually serves to give them their meaning. As noted earlier, this seems to have been an intentional choice for the authors of the Gospels, and is of considerable significance in the literary history of early Christianity and in christological implications.[19] It is one of the several strengths of E. P. Sanders's book on Jesus that he focused on events, which he termed "*facts* about Jesus, his career, and its consequences," as the basis for his noteworthy portrait of Jesus.[20] Among the foregoing essays in this volume, those by Evans, Licona, and Bock,

---

14. Perrin, *Rediscovering*, 39.

15. Perrin, *Rediscovering*, 12.

16. Morna D. Hooker, "On Using the Wrong Tool," *Theology* 75 (1972): 570–81; also idem, "Christology and Methodology," *NTS* 17 (1970–71): 480–87.

17. Perrin, *Rediscovering*, 12; Rudolf Bultmann, *The History of the Synoptic Tradition*, 2nd ed., trans. John Marsh (Oxford: Basil Blackwell, 1968; German, Vandenhoeck & Ruprecht, 1921).

18. Rudolf Bultmann, *Jesus and the Word* (New York: Charles Scribner's Sons, 1958; German, 1934).

19. Hurtado, *Lord Jesus Christ*, 262–77, esp. 274; and also Richard A. Burridge, "Gospel Genre, Christological Controversy and the Absence of Rabbinic Biography: Some Implications of the Biographical Hypothesis," in *Christology, Controversy and Community: New Testament Essays in Honour of David R. Catchpole*, ed. David G. Horrell and Christopher M. Tuckett, NovTSup 99 (Leiden: Brill, 2000), 137–56.

20. E. P. Sanders, *Jesus and Judaism* (London: SCM, 1985), 5 (emphasis his), and his brief summary list of "the things best known about Jesus" (321). Note also his candid declaration of his own personal religious stance, and his effort to avoid it determining his results (334).

in particular, address in various ways certain events or actions narrated in the Gospels, a commendable widening of the scope of investigation beyond the sayings material.

The volume edited by Keith and Le Donne that prompted the present volume includes some strong statements about the limitations of criteria-based attempts to do historical Jesus work. Indeed, some of them (cited by various contributors to this volume) are even rather dramatic in force. But, even for advocates such as Perrin, the strict application of the widely used criteria of authenticity could obtain only a supposedly bare *minimum* body of material that could pass the tests. If the aim was simply to assure ourselves that there was such a minimum, in other words, that there was some *irreducible body* of material that made it practically inescapable that there really was a historical figure, Jesus, then I suppose that one could argue that the use of these criteria had some limited use. But if the aim was to obtain a *representative and adequate* body of material on the basis of which to produce a historical portrait of Jesus, then I think that the critics of the criteria are correct in judging that they do not achieve this.

The broad effect of the preceding essays in the present volume is to urge that the Gospels do provide us with a basis for forming a portrait of the historical Jesus of Nazareth, and I agree. But it seems to me that the contributors to the Keith/Le Donne volume agree with this also. They simply doubt that the traditional authenticity criteria are the best way to do this. The Gospels preserve and deploy in various ways a "remembered Jesus," and these memories both were adapted variously to serve the needs of the early Jesus movement (that became Christianity) and yet also often maintained a historical connection to the originating figure, Jesus, and his impact. Indeed, it seems to me that the Gospels even exhibit what we may call a deliberate archaizing effort evident in some things, for example, preserving conflicts between Jesus and religious opponents over hand-washing, details of Sabbath observance, divorce, Roman taxation, and other matters that were scarcely of major concern in the late first-century (and dominantly gentile) circles for which these texts were written. But these things were preserved deliberately, *as part of the presentation of Jesus's significance* for the original readers of the Gospels, not for antiquarian purposes.

To cite another example of this, there is the curious and consistent use of the expression "the son of man" (ὁ υἱὸς τοῦ ἀνθρώπου), which does not feature as a christological title in the evidence of earliest Christian confession.[21]

---

21. Nor, despite the many claims to the contrary, does this expression function as a known/fixed title in Second Temple Jewish texts. There is no evidence in support of the claim that "the son of man" was a recognized title for an eschatological figure. There were expectations for eschatological figures, but they

Instead, I judge that in the Gospel narratives the term is preserved and deployed simply as Jesus's preferred self-designation (in linguistic terms, a feature of Jesus's idiolect), and because *that was how it was remembered*. So the expression appears in these narratives (consistently and only on the lips of Jesus) as a key part of the authors' efforts to convey something of the "voice" of Jesus of Nazareth, as one means of respecting and expressing his historical specificity.[22]

But, to return to the question of authenticity criteria, the contributors to this volume (as I read them) basically contend that, despite the problems, they remain of some significant use in conducting a legitimately critical analysis of the "remembered Jesus" in the Gospels. I wonder, however, if the contributors to this volume have noted with sufficient care the distinction posited in the Keith/Le Donne volume between *criteria used to isolate "authentic" material, i.e., material that has supposedly not been affected by the transmission of it*, and *critical principles that can be used in assessing historical claims about Jesus*. The Keith/Le Donne contributors (and certainly Keith himself) are critical of the former, but not the latter.[23] For they judge the underlying assumption of the familiar authenticity criteria used in gospel studies to be fallacious: that the Gospels contain material from Jesus along with fictive material generated in the tradition-process, and that the criteria can identify that "authentic" or unrefracted material. So, in their view, critical historiography should, instead, proceed by recognizing that all Gospel material comes via the "remembrance" and traditioning process, and that even material that is technically fictive or legend may still preserve something of the historical effects and nature of Jesus's ministry.

In his most recent book on the historical Jesus, Dale Allison (a noteworthy contributor to the Keith/Le Donne volume) expresses a preference for aiming to capture what we may call the gist of Jesus's preaching and activities, granting

---

are never designated by this term. See, e.g., Maurice Casey, *Son of Man: The Interpretation and Influence of Daniel 7* (London: SPCK, 1979).

22. See my discussion in *Lord Jesus Christ*, 290–306; and my concluding essay in *Who is This Son of Man? The Latest Scholarship on a Puzzling Expression of the Historical Jesus*, ed. Larry W. Hurtado and Paul L. Owen, LNTS 390 (London: Bloomsbury T&T Clark, 2011), 159–77. The definite form of the expression "the son of man" likely translates an equivalent particularizing Aramaic form (*bar enasha*), which is otherwise difficult to find in Aramaic sources of Jesus's time. As Jesus's preferred self-designation, it suggests that he thought of himself as having a special identity and role, which is, of course, confirmed in the larger pattern of his sayings and actions.

23. E.g., in a contribution to the volume Keith emphasizes that the criteria of authenticity all were conceptually based on the form-critical assumption (as advocated by Bultmann, et al.) that the Gospels contained a mixture of material that came from the historical Jesus and other material that came from early Christian circles, and that the key task was to isolate the former ("The Indebtedness of the Criteria Approach to Form Criticism and Recent Attempts to Rehabilitate the Search for an Authentic Jesus," in *Jesus, Criteria, and the Demise of Authenticity*, ed. Chris Keith and Anthony Le Donne [London: T&T Clark, 2012], 25–48; and in the same volume note a similar analysis by Jens Schröter, "The Criteria of Authenticity in Jesus Research and Historiographical Method," 49–70).

that the Jesus conveyed in the Gospels comes to us only via the remembrances of his followers in the decades between Jesus and the composition of these writings.[24] So, instead of trying to establish a list of individual sayings and actions that incontrovertibly pass the tests of the familiar criteria, that is, sayings and actions that have somehow supposedly escaped the effects of being transmitted in early Christian circles, Allison argues that we can identify more broadly what were the characteristic things Jesus likely taught and did. The results of this professedly modest approach are, however, actually substantial (462 pages) and robustly stated. Note, for example, Allison's concluding remarks in his chapter, "The Christology of Jesus":

> The main thesis of the present chapter offers an explanation for both the great age of this Christology and its prevalence in our sources: Jesus himself already promoted a version of it, so it was there from the beginning. . . . .
>
> Jesus did not envisage a "brokerless kingdom." Nor did he proclaim a "kingless kingdom." Rather, when he looked into the future, he saw thrones, including one for himseslf. . . . We should hold a funeral for the view that Jesus entertained no exalted thoughts about himself.[25]

I rather suspect that the contributors to this volume would agree with the thrust of Allison's book, although he joined in a critique of reliance upon authenticity criteria in the Keith/Le Donne volume.[26]

In the preparation of my response to the essays in this volume, I read again Nils Dahl's discussion of the historical Jesus that originated in the early 1950s, an exercise that I recommend to all.[27] As with anything else I have read by Dahl,

---

24. Dale C. Allison, *Constructing Jesus: Memory, Imagination, and History* (Grand Rapids: Baker Academic, 2010).

25. Allison, *Constructing Jesus*, 303, 304. The phrases that Allison quotes (and rejects) here derive respectively from John Dominic Crossan, *The Historical Jesus: The Life of a Mediterranean Jewish Peasant* (San Francisco: HarperSanFrancisco, 1991), 225; and Richard A. Horsley and Neil Asher Silberman, *The Message and the Kingdom: How Jesus and Paul Ignited a Revolution and Transformed the Ancient World* (New York: Grosset/Putnam, 1997), 73. The title of Allison's chapter echoes the title of an often-overlooked book by Ben Witherington, *The Christology of Jesus* (Minneapolis: Fortress, 1990). But Witherington's stated aim differs from Allison's in attempting to portray Jesus's "self-understanding," although these statements by Allison seem to me to come pretty close to positing something of Jesus's thoughts about himself.

26. E.g., McIver's discussion of "Collective Memory and the Reliability of the Gospels' Traditions" seems to me to come down not far from where Allison stands on the matter.

27. The essay is now most readily accessible in Nils Alstrup Dahl, *Jesus the Christ: The Historical Origins of Christological Doctrine*, ed. Donald H. Juel (Minneapolis: Fortress, 1991), 81–111, "The Problem of the Historical Jesus," which I cite here. It appeared also in an earlier collection of Dahl's essays, *The Crucified Messiah and Other Essays* (Minneapolis: Augsburg, 1974), 48–89; and in *Kerygma and History*, ed. Carl E. Braaten and Roy A. Harrisville (Nashville: Abingdon, 1962), 21–49. It originated, however, in a collection of lectures published in 1953 (Oslo).

it remains instructive, and even anticipates where a good many historical Jesus scholars subsequently have wound up. For example, Dahl observed astutely, "The interest of faith in the tradition about Jesus served not only to shape but also to preserve the tradition."[28] Or how about this judgment: "We do not escape the fact that we know Jesus only as the disciples remembered him."[29] Or this one (which seems to me to anticipate remarkably the sort of stance that Allision espouses more recently): "Even without a clear differentiation between pure history and later theology, the gospel tradition permits us to draw a very clear picture of what was *typical and characteristic* of Jesus."[30]

As to method in historical Jesus study, consider these comments by Dahl, which offer what we might call a crucifixion-test for historical Jesus research.

> One point in the life of Jesus is unconditionally established: his death. A historically tenable description of the life of Jesus would be possible only in the form of a description of his death, its historical presuppositions, and the events preceding and following it.
>
> In any case, it is clear that what we know with certainty about the life of Jesus is that it ended on the cross. That end must be kept in mind in the attempt to understand the preaching and teaching of Jesus. An obvious weakness of many descriptions of Jesus—as a very pious, very humane, and somewhat harmless teacher—lies in the fact that it is not understood why high priests and Romans had any interest in the execution of this man.
>
> Accordingly, no one can maintain that historical research has access only to the preaching of Jesus and not to his life. Rather, we must state that a historical understanding of his preaching can be attained only when it is seen in connection with his life, namely, with the life that ended on the cross.[31]

This crucifixion-test does not function as the more well-known authenticity criteria criticized in the Keith/Le Donne volume, however. Those criteria are used to try to sort out at the micro-level authentic individual sayings and, occasionally, authentic events, and those who formulated and classically applied these authenticity criteria did so on the premise that the Gospels have so distorted the historical figure of Jesus that it is necessary to subject them to a putative

---

28. Dahl, *Jesus the Christ*, 93.

29. Dahl, *Jesus the Christ*, 94.

30. Dahl, *Jesus the Christ*, 95 (emphasis added).

31. Dahl, *Jesus the Christ*, 98, 99. I point also to my discussion in *Lord Jesus Christ*, 53–64, esp. 56–60, in which I engage proposals by Geza Vermes and J. D. Crossan that Jesus's execution was simply some kind of misguided police-action.

acid bath of criteria. But what Dahl proposes is effectively a criterion or test to be applied at the macro-level, to judge whether a given historical Jesus portrait can convincingly account for his crucifixion. To put it in simple terms, you have to offer a historical Jesus who, in light of his religious and political setting, generated both a devoted following and mortal opposition, culminating in a state execution by crucifixion.

I will add one other macro-level criterion as well, this one proffered as crucial by Sanders.[32] Another of the facts that we must recognize is that Jesus generated a following during his ministry, and, importantly, there was a sectarian movement devoted to him in the aftermath of his execution. That is, in this movement the person of Jesus was central and the defining factor in what was held to be a valid relationship with God. I agree with Sanders that "a hypothesis which does offer a reasonable and well-grounded connection between Jesus and the Christian movement is better than one which offers no connection."[33] In my view, the most logical reason for the prominence of Jesus in the post-crucifixion movement of his followers is that during his ministry he had already become the polarizing issue, both for his followers and his opponents.[34] Again, this does not serve for assessing individual sayings or events in the Gospel narratives. Instead, it acts as a test for a given finished portrait of the historical Jesus: Our portrait should be adequate to help account for the movement in his name that continued, and even took on a more vigorous life following his death.

I conclude this response to the preceding essays by expressing my gratitude for having the opportunity to read them in advance of publication. I found some more congenial than others, but that, of course, says as much about me as it does about them. The broad line taken in this volume, however, that the historical figure of Jesus matters, both for scholarship and for Christian faith, and that for critical scholarship there will continue to be a need for ways of making judgments about what is narrated in the Gospels and Acts, seems to me valid. But on this matter I do not think that the contributions in this book are actually at loggerheads with those in the Keith/Le Donne volume.[35]

---

32. Sanders, _Jesus and Judaism_, e.g., 18–22.

33. Sanders, _Jesus and Judaism_, 22.

34. In proposing the "forces and factors" that shaped and drove earliest Jesus-devotion in the post-crucifixion period, I posit Jesus himself, more specifically the impact he had upon his contemporaries (both followers and opponents) in his own ministry, as best accounting for his centrality (_Lord Jesus Christ_, 53–64).

35. The exception might be the stance of Scot McKnight, "Why the Authentic Jesus is of No Use for the Church," 173–85. He is correct that Christian faith cannot wait for historical Jesus scholars to agree on one portrait. But, in a contemporary world in which even the historical existence of Jesus is called into question (and with surprisingly widespread effect), the agreement of scholars that there _is_ a historical figure to try to describe is arguably meaningful for Christians.

CHAPTER 16

The Historical Jesus and Witness:
The Problem Is Not Method but Results

Scot McKnight

This optimistic and apologetically oriented collection of essays by notable evangelical scholars, some of whom are my friends, demonstrates yet one more time that the records about Jesus and the early church can pass muster when it comes to the methods of historians. If only the world of scholarship were as simple as that, if only the world of scholarship could agree, not only on method but also on the implications of those methods when applied to the records about Jesus, then we could all agree. But one scholar's sharp conclusions based on highly regarded methods—say, the criteria for assessing the gospel records about Jesus—is another scholar's opportunity to doubt either method or inference drawn from the evidence-extruded-through-method yielding yet another depiction of Jesus or the early church. I'm not cynical so much as honest about three decades of reading deeply into this conversation. What I've learned is that tallying up impressive lists of recent scholarship concluding the historicity of sayings or events is a Pyrrhic victory announced by an advocate to his or her friends who already knew the substance of the announcement before the announcement was even made. Such lists play well in an echo chamber. The other side is also only listening to itself. Dan Wallace's comment about George Tyrrell, that Harnack's Jesus was but "the reflection of a Liberal Protestant face, seen at the bottom of a deep well" describes even more today the faces of historical Jesus scholarship than it did in Tyrrell's day.[1]

IF ONLY THE METHODS WERE APPLIED CONSISTENTLY

One theme running through this book is that if the historian will simply apply the methods consistently, the Gospels and Acts will pop up with glorious

---

1. See Wallace's essay in the present volume (p. 93).

reliability or at least be shown to be essentially historical. I was once convinced of this approach, but time among historical Jesus scholars has convinced me this approach simply won't work. In fact, the argument reminds of the creationists, not least of whom are the intelligent-design folks, contending if science is done right it will prove that Genesis 1–2 is, after all, scientifically prescient. Both are big asks. Too big, in fact. Just as the scientists are not listening to the intelligent-design crowd, so the historical Jesus scholars of the academy are not giving much attention to evangelicals who think their approach is the most consistent to the methods. My first serious encounter with a powerful book contending for reliability is a book not read much anymore, but it is deserving of reading still. It was by E. C. Hoskyns and N. Davey, a breathtaking and beautifully styled case for reliability.[2] Then came I. Howard Marshall's study of Luke, which quickly but intelligently presented short cases for the reliability of most everything in Luke.[3] In those days a Roman Catholic, B. F. Meyer, impacted historical Jesus scholarship with his appeal to critical realism and turned the "criteria" into "indices" of reliability.[4] Those more convinced of the reliability of the Gospels jumped on the critical-realism bandwagon, but his approach did not convince the other side. About the same time an evangelical, Royce Gordon Gruenler, pressed a similar case for philosophical rigor and his approach was made all the more compelling because he had himself written a far more skeptical volume earlier.[5] I will skip ahead to the massive volume envisioned and edited by Darrell Bock and Robert Webb, yet another intelligent volume seeking to show that events in the life of Jesus can be shown by historical methods to be reliable.[6] I have read these volumes; I am impressed by each one; and I am convinced by the substance of each. But those of us in the conservative ledger on these issues are the ones convinced and, truth be told, in most cases we were convinced before we began.

Which leads to what I think is the most significant element in all discussions of historiography about Jesus, the apostles, and the early church: *witness*. This stuff gets personal fast. What N. T. Wright thinks is authentic is not what Marc Borg thinks is authentic is not what John Dominic Crossan thinks is authentic is not what Paul Fredriksen thinks is authentic is not what Darrell Bock thinks is authentic is not what Amy Jill Levine thinks is authentic is not

2. E. C. Hoskyns and N. Davey, *The Riddle of the New Testament*, 3rd ed. (London: Faber and Faber, 1947).

3. I. Howard Marshall, *The Gospel of Luke*, NIGTC (Grand Rapids: Eerdmans, 1978).

4. Ben F. Meyer, *The Aims of Jesus*, Princeton Theological Monographs Series (repr., San Jose, CA: Wipf & Stock, 2002).

5. Royce Gordon Gruenler, *New Approaches to Jesus and the Gospels: A Phenomenological and Exegetical Study of Synoptic Christology* (Grand Rapids: Baker, 1982).

6. Darrell L. Bock and Robert L. Webb, eds., *Key Events in the Life of the Historical Jesus: A Collaborative Exploration of Context and Coherence*, WUNT 247 (Tübingen: Mohr Siebeck, 2009).

what Dale Allison thinks is authentic is not what Richard Bauckham thinks is authentic. And so on. Whom, then, can we trust? Whom are we to believe? Which historian has the best method and the most consistent implications from that method? Our choice remains our choice and our choice drives us back to the same issue of witness. The conclusions of each are too close to the theological starting point of each. The close relationship between what one believes and where one stands on a variety of spectrums matters more than we care to admit. I admitted this some time ago and gave up the game of historical Jesus studies.

"USELESS FOR THE CHURCH"?

The opening essay of this volume begins by quoting me and my so-called "provocative" approach, and I have not changed my mind: "historical Jesus studies are useless for the church." Those are words of mine the authors of the opening essay, Robert Bowman Jr. and J. Ed Komoszewski, quote. I don't believe enough evangelical scholars have read enough historical Jesus scholars or sat at the table with the other side to know what historical Jesus scholarship really is. So, I will say it one more time: historical Jesus scholarship, and I mean the multitude of studies beginning at least with Hermann Samuel Reimarus through Albert Schweitzer and Rudolf Bultmann and Ernst Käsemann through E. P. Sanders and J. P. Meier:

(1) examines the Gospels and other ancient sources
(2) on the basis of the methods of sophisticated historiography tailored for Jesus studies in order
(3) to determine what is authentic from what is not
(4) so that the historian can gather the reliable evidence and then propose a portrait of Jesus that is
(5) distinguishable from the church's canonical Gospels (Matthew, Mark, Luke, John) and
(6) from the creedal presentation of Jesus (Trinitarian theology).[7]

This is what historical criticism does when it touches the Gospels, and it is what this line of scholarship has always done. Much confusion arises when it comes to what "historical Jesus" means, and for some in this volume it

---

7. Notice from this volume the definition of Michael Licona: "the Jesus composed solely of those elements about him that can be established with reasonable historical certainty and apart from faith" (294n25). He says the "real" Jesus is not the same and was much more than the "historical" Jesus. Indeed.

unsurprisingly means showing the historical and social context of the Gospels or some teaching of Jesus. Some, for instance, show what "kingdom" meant in the Jewish world of Jesus and then "contextualize" Matthew 4:17 ("the kingdom of heaven has come near"). But that is not historical Jesus scholarship as practiced since the days of Reimarus. Rather, the six elements stated above are what is meant when one does historical Jesus scholarship. To baptize the Jesus of Mark into his Jewish context is not historical Jesus scholarship but instead contextual exegesis of Mark. Historical Jesus scholarship has one goal since the day of Reimarus's postmortem publication: to correct the church's mistaken beliefs about Jesus and more or less take away his deity and make him a Jewish human again. Remove evangelical scholarship from the historical Jesus expression, and you will find nothing but those six elements at work in each scholar. As one very well-known historical Jesus scholar once said to me after I had tried to prove that the "historical Jesus" believed his death was atoning.[8] "That's not historical Jesus scholarship. Why? Because the historical Jesus couldn't be that theological." That same scholar also once told me that if the conclusions of historical work lined up with Christian orthodoxy, it was no longer historical Jesus scholarship!

I sat for more than five years at each Society of Biblical Literature on the advisory committee for the Historical Jesus Seminar in its heyday and I heard these six elements time and time again. I'm not so much criticizing historical Jesus scholars as I am those who think "historical Jesus" can be naively applied to much of what evangelicals are doing today. I contend that (1) what evangelicals are doing is an echo chamber of evangelicals who think historical Jesus scholarship can more or less confirm the canonical Jesus or the creedal Jesus on the basis of a rigorous method applied consistently; (2) that the methods we use will never get us to a full embrace of the canonical Jesus or the creedal Jesus—you can't prove by history that Jesus died for our sins or was raised for our justification; and (3) that we evangelicals are surrendering ourselves to skeptical methods when we enter into the historical Jesus enterprise. If we want to play this game, we have to play it all the way down, and when we do we will not have the Jesus of the Gospels or the Creed.

WITNESS IS THE WORD IN HISTORY

The fourth point above ("and then propose a portrait of Jesus") deserves some fleshing out. Historical Jesus scholarship, as it has been practiced by the majority

---

8. Scot McKnight, *Jesus and His Death: Historiography, the Historical Jesus, and Atonement Theory* (Waco, TX: Baylor University Press, 2005).

of its practitioners, has always been about composing a more accurate view of Jesus. Think of Albert Schweitzer's eschatological or apocalyptic Jesus, or Adolf Harnack's liberal Protestant Jesus, or Bultmann's existential Jesus, or Geza Vermes's Jewish Jesus, or Crossan's countercultural Jesus, or Marc Borg's religious-genius Jesus, or N. T. Wright's return-from-exile-to-the-temple Jesus, or James D. G. Dunn's Jesus as he was remembered. This is what this kind of scholarship is all about: some are much closer to the Gospels themselves (Wright, Dunn), while others are quite skeptical of the Gospels (Bultmann, Crossan). My point is this: *the aim of these scholars is to offer to their readers and to themselves a Jesus that corrects the church or lay folks or other scholars or the church's tradition about Jesus.* They are not just asking, "What happened?" No, they push forward to create a new narrative about Jesus, a portrait that improves what is believed by others today. My experience with these scholars is that these reconstructions of Jesus are identical to the Jesus they actually believe in.

Put differently, this work of framing Jesus is all about witness, and the witness of the church is that the canonical Jesus and the creedal Jesus are the church's Jesus, and historical Jesuses are an attempt to replace the church's Jesus with the historian's Jesus. Scholars who do this work become their own witness to who Jesus was and who he is for us today. It's not that I'm skeptical of doing history or even of historical methods, and I'll get to a larger point soon, but for now I put it this way:

> I believe history matters. Our faith is a faith rooted in actual events and persons.
> I believe the historical methods can reasonably establish certain facts.
> I believe history can be used to defend our faith.
> I know historical Jesus studies are designed to do something else.
> I believe the witness of the Gospels, reframed centuries later into the Creed, is the Jesus we Christians believe in.

I believe that Jesus can be defended apologetically by the historical undertaking, but that is not what historical Jesus scholars are doing. They operate on the basis of either the church getting him wrong or part of him wrong, or on the basis of an individual person's own judgment about the data to determine what that individual person will believe about Jesus.

It sounds harsh, but this is what I believe: if we trust the historian's methods, then Sunday morning must await the historian's judgment before the worship service can begin. It took me a long time to admit that and to surrender historical

Jesus scholarship. Once again, these terms matter, and I have an angle to argue. Robert M. Bowman Jr. and J. Ed Komoszewski contend the "historical Jesus" is the "real" Jesus (32f.), the one who lived in Galilee and told parables and all that, and they want us to be wary of calling the historical Jesus only the "historian's" Jesus. They know that others think the historical Jesus is a methodologically induced presentation of Jesus by a historian, and they point to both Leander Keck and Marianne Meye Thompson. I want to accept their points except for the reality that "historical Jesus" is an enterprise as outlined above. This changes the rules by which the game is being played. Bowman and Komoszewski, then, in essence are saying the game played today by the vast majority of historical Jesus scholars is the "reconstructed" Jesus, but not the historical or real Jesus. I can agree with that, as long as one admits that this is the game that is being played today (they do on p. 36).[9]

Now, let me address the most significant reason for my skepticism about this scholarship.

WHAT IS HISTORY?

What is history? I offer this description, one that flows through the six points above about historical Jesus scholarship:

> A historian (witness) examines evidence (texts, archaeological record, etc.) to ascertain facts in order to construct a reasonable hypothesis of what happened and frames what happened in a meaning-oriented narrative.

There is no such thing as uninterpreted history, whether we are talking studies of Julius Caesar, Nero, Augustine, Calvin, or the great revivals of the United States. Each historian gathers the facts into a bundle of interpretation. There is then no such thing as an uninterpreted Jesus. The witness called historian thus constructs a narrative about Jesus that interprets him.

Furthermore, there is no access to the "real" Jesus apart from the constructions called Matthew, Mark, Luke, and John and other narratives about Jesus from the ancient world. The Gospels are interpretations of Jesus, not simply records of facts about him. Matthew's opening genealogy is a hermeneutical move that connects Jesus to Abraham and David and the exile and then interprets him

---

9. Their contention that the methods of historical Jesus scholarship's "methodological naturalism" (p. 39) is just wrong if taken generally. For some, yes, but not for all. E. P. Sanders, and many more, accept some of the miracles as reliable.

as "God with us" (1:23), and John opens by calling Jesus nothing less than God (1:1). That's interpretation, and I contend those interpretations of our canonical Gospels are the *church's Jesus*. Any other Jesus, no matter how circumspectly examined and profiled, is not the church's Jesus. The Gospel writers, then, are doing what the historical Jesus scholars are doing: presenting a portrait of Jesus. It's all about witness, and I am asking that we choose which will be our authoritative witness.

Yes, these methods work, but we must ask what we hope to accomplish. The so-called criteria, mentioned and explained and scrutinized with sophistication in this book, work. They yield results. Historians discover data and sort out the facts from the data, but to find the facts, they have to assess the data's reliability the way judges and juries determine who's telling the truth. The methods Gospel scholars use are the methods applied to other figures like Robin Hood. Different scholars sort out the facts and often put them into a list, beginning with Bultmann, but we find one here in Bowman and Komoszewski's list of events, sayings, and teachings (pp. 22–23). The methods have to be scrutinized, and in this volume there is a fair amount of such scrutiny, and I'm thinking of Michael Metts's analysis of form criticism and the criteria, of Dan Wallace's angle on the criterion of embarrassment, or Robert McIver's and Michael Bird and Ben Sutton's collective-memory and social-memory approaches, of Paul Anderson's enthusiasm of recent scholarship on the Gospel of John, of Michael Licona's expertise on the reliability of the resurrection accounts, and also of Craig Keener's extraordinary prospectus on the historical value of the Acts of the Apostles. These scholars prove that the methods of the historians can be used to yield results that confirm the reliability of the Gospels and Acts.

However, methods aren't filters in an objective world, and so methods break down, because different historians weigh them differently. What Keener finds in Acts is not at all what Ernst Haenchen, J. A. Fitzmyer, C. K. Barrett, or Richard Pervo conclude. I appeal yet again to the importance of witness. And I want to contend that absenting this discussion from witness and turning to the historical methods crafted over a long time by intelligent historians leads scholarship into what I have in another location called Erastianism scholarship.

ERASTIANISM

Erastianism is a church-state political theory and may be defined as the church protected by a state yet with the state exercising final, if not absolute, authority. In other words, Erastianism makes the church answer to the state. I contend, then, that determining whether we believe the gospel accounts about Jesus on the basis of historians is *historiographical, if not epistemological, Erastianism* in that the faith of the church must answer to the supposed impartiality and disinterested research of the historians. Erastian historiography then is when someone else—someone not in the circle of faith—determines the rules.

I do not doubt the erudition of historians nor the ability of a historian to probe to the point of proving. Nor do I doubt the value of this kind of historical effort for Christian apologetics and the value that such work has for helping some to construct their faith.[10] What I do doubt is the *value of historical proof for constructing the Christian faith itself.* In the simplest of terms, the Christian faith—Christian orthodoxy—the faith of our fathers, whatever one wants to call it, is something that was constructed between one thousand five hundred and two thousand years ago and not something continually in construction. For those with a traditional view of Scripture, that narrative interpretation of Jesus and the labels given to him were *inspired by the Spirit* for the church to record. This, I repeat, is not historical Jesus work but orthodox faith at work.

So to return to the Erastian way of thinking, if the faith we believe *is reliant upon the research of the historian,* three things happen.

First, we must await each generation's or scholar's latest discoveries in order to know what to believe. Should we choose our favorite historian (N. T. Wright, James D. G. Dunn, D. C. Allison, Craig Keener)—and will that choice not already be based on preconceived postures in the faith?—or shall we choose a representative or the vote of the university professors (the famous Jesus Seminar approach)?

Second, if we choose to believe on the basis of the historians, then we must live with what the historians conclude. One cannot say, "OK, I now see that most historians do not think Jesus walked on water, that it is a myth, so I will accept that. But, when it comes to the resurrection, I cannot accept what most historians say because they are tampering now with the centrality of the faith itself." Put differently, *if you want to go with the historians, you must go all the way down with the historian.* Erastian historiography is absolute.

Third, our faith becomes a flux. What if, for instance, the latest historians conclude that *not only is Jesus not the Jewish Messiah but neither is he the Son of God or the Lord of lords or the King of kings but is instead a misguided Jewish prophet?*

---

10. A good example of which is Craig L. Blomberg, "The Historical Reliability of John: Rushing in Where Angels Fear to Tread?," in *Jesus in the Johannine Tradition*, ed. R.T. Fortna and Tom Thatcher (Louisville: Westminster John Knox, 2001), 71–82. For a thorough study, again Craig S. Keener, *Miracles: The Credibility of the New Testament Accounts*, 2 vols. (Grand Rapids: Baker Academic, 2011).

Or at least a very powerful prophet but far less than the church's Jesus? Or a profound teacher of morality? Are we to revise our creed and our confession on the basis of these sorts of conclusions by historians?

Erastianism is not the approach of Jesus or the apostles; it was not the approach of Christian orthodoxy or the Reformers. They did not cede the gospel to authorities who could determine what was to be believed or not. They knew where they stood. The faith in which we believe is ordered from the very beginning by the gospel lines now found in 1 Corinthians 15:3–8. If we wait for the most recent discoveries and articulations of historians, then we will not know what to believe until those articulations have been integrated into the churches through the proper intellectual challenges. Whose Jesus, we must ask, will we believe? Will it be the Jesus of Reimarus? Strauss? Thomas Jefferson? Albert Schweitzer? Bultmann? B. F. Meyer? Sanders? Crossan? Dale Allison Jr.? N. T. Wright? Or the one presented annually on CNN and Fox News? Or, will it be the church's Jesus?[11] It's all about the witness, and the church's witness is the Gospels and its message as developed in the Creed.

HISTORIOGRAPHY AND APOLOGETICS

I've been hard on historians and historiography because the aim of historical Jesus scholars is to reconstruct Jesus. But the methods do work if we recognize their limitations. One can prove that the tomb was empty with reason; one can prove that Jesus died; one can prove that events happened around Jesus for which there was no natural explanation. What one can't prove on the basis of historical method is that Jesus's death was atoning; that his resurrection ushers into us new life that lasts for eternity; that miracles are a reasonable explanation for things done by Jesus and that God was behind it all. One simply can't prove these things as a historian; historical methods run out once the evidence is determined. The framing is an interpretation, and that takes us to the next point.

No one has done better work demonstrating the viability of miracles than Craig Keener and Graham Twelftree. Neither of them is out to reconstruct Jesus. Rather, both examine the Gospels framed by their orthodox faith and conclude both that the Gospel miracles are reliable reports and that miracles are possible

---

11. This section is a slightly reworked section from my essay, "The Misguided Quest for the Nature Miracles," in *The Nature Miracles of Jesus: Problems, Perspectives, and Prospects*, ed. Graham H. Twelftree (Eugene, OR: Cascade, 2017), 174–91 (taken from pp. 188–89). In important ways, this was the question of Martin Kähler's response to the rise of the historical-critical method in Germany and its implications for theology, his discipline! See Martin Kähler, *So-Called Historical Jesus and the Historic, Biblical Christ*, trans. Carl E. Braaten, rev. ed. (Philadelphia: Fortress, 1964).

today. Craig Evans, also an author in this book, has had a career of defending the historical veracity of New Testament claims without attempting to reconstruct a new Jesus for us. N. T. Wright, who is a bridge between classic historical Jesus studies and the church, time and time again offers his readers credible and engaging accounts of the Gospels and Jesus framed by Israel's story while also offering, indirectly, assurance to believers that the Gospels are reliable. This kind of history is apologetics. History and historical method, then, is eminently useful and necessary for the church in its apologetics and defense of the truth claims it makes in the gospel.

In the end, for the church the historical Jesus must give way to the church's canonical and Creed-al Jesus. The Gospels, the Creed, and the church is our witness.

CHAPTER 17

Jesus, Skepticism, and the Problem of History: The Conversation Continues

Nicholas Perrin

In the academic guild—the arena where scholars mull over such things as Jesus, skepticism, and the problem of history—the more important conversations take time to unfold. This is one of those conversations. Though the point is never stated outright, the compilation of essays presented in this book is essentially a collective response to an earlier collected volume, Chris Keith and Anthony Le Donne's *Jesus, Criteria, and the Demise of Authenticity* (hereafter *JCDA*), published just over six years ago.[1] While similar concerns have been mooted in the past (here one thinks especially of an important 1972 essay by Morna Hooker), Keith and Le Donne's publication poses a head-on challenge to the *status quo* by calling on Jesus scholars to break up with the methodological principles we have come to know and love—or to know and eschew, as the case may be—as the criteria of authenticity.[2] For the chorus of voices behind *JCDA*, it's not enough to influence today's Jesus scholars to ply the standard criteria with more care, nothing less than a cease and desist order will do. And even if none of the individual essays contained in Keith and Le Donne's project are what one might consider groundbreaking, the volume as a whole has proved to be greater than the sum of its individual parts. *JCDA* has marked a clear turning point in the dialogue. Whether we know it or not, whether we like it or not, the conversation has changed. Enter the present collection of essays.

Like its predecessor, the present set of contributions approaches the problem of Jesus and history from different angles. Taken together, the essays offer not so much a compilation of tit-for-tat responses to discrete arguments, but a

---

1. *Jesus, Criteria, and the Demise of Authenticity* (London: T&T Clark, 2012). Since I will be limiting my remarks to essays handling the Jesus traditions, I must regretfully forego interaction with the pieces on Acts by Craig Keener, as well as by Michael Bird and Ben Sutton, and beg these authors' forgiveness.

2. Cf. Morna Hooker, "On Using the Wrong Tool," *Theology* 75 (1972): 570–81.

kaleidoscopic vision of the historical task that chastenedly acknowledges the limitations of the criteria, while also reasserting their usefulness in a qualified sense. According to Michael Metts ("Neglected Discontinuity between Early Form Criticism and the New Quest with Reference to the Last Supper"), for example, "Keith is correct in some of the methodological affirmations he predicates of New Quest criteriology" (67), providing research with "a helpful corrective" (69). For Darrell Bock, even if the Keith/Le Donne volume is "guilty of overkill," it has successfully identified the flawed origins of the criteria (206). As Paul Anderson ("The John, Jesus, and History Project and a Fourth Quest for Jesus") sees it, "the leading criteria emerging from the New Quest deserve critical scrutiny themselves, and the volume gathered by Chris Keith and Anthony Le Donne performs a set of incisive analyses regarding the[ir] strengths and weaknesses" (230). In fact, I suspect that most if not all of the contributors here would agree with Craig Blomberg and Darlene Seal ("The Historical Jesus in Recent Evangelical Scholarship") when they maintain that the Keith/Le Donne volume has helped bring us to a place where "the quest is not dead but simply needs to take on different contours" (62). As such, the present volume, precisely as a response to the *JCDA*, takes on a decided "Yes, but . . ." quality—an encouraging sign that the conversation is progressing rather than stalling.

IN DEFENSE OF THE CRITERIA OF AUTHENTICITY

Still, the "but"—rather the "buts"—are neither unimportant nor insubstantial. In this connection, I might mention Daniel Wallace's fascinating essay "Textual Criticism and the Criterion of Embarrassment." Written in response to Rafael Rodriguez's critique of the criterion of embarrassment (the principle that reported actions or sayings of Jesus, which are liable to embarrass the church are unlikely to have been invented by the church), Wallace's argument is simple and straightforward.[3] If text-critical comparison of manuscripts show that scribes sometimes emended texts due to their embarrassment over the received contents, which is patently the case (103–22), this suggests that the evangelists/early communities were not immune to the same editorializing tendencies (124). Accordingly, on this criterion, material potentially embarrassing to the ecclesial agenda *a priori* stands in good stead as authentic. Wallace's argument is generally persuasive. However, I do think he could have registered the point more forcefully, especially

---

3. "The Embarrassing Truth about Jesus: The Criterion of Embarrassment and the Failure of Historical Authenticity," in Keith and Le Donne, *Jesus, Criteria, and the Demise of Authenticity*, 132–51.

as (1) the criterion of embarrassment is often regarded as one of the strongest of the criteria; and (2) the argument lodged by Rodriquez, though winsomely written, is largely made to ride on outlier (and generally unconvincing) scholarly pronouncements bearing on texts classically associated with the criterion.

Darrell Bock likewise makes a convincing case, first by issuing a few salutary introductory remarks (205–7), and then by offering a test case in Jesus's confession before the high priest, all to show how the criteria can in fact be useful in authenticating dominical events and/or words. Bock's initial remarks consist of three brief strokes. The second and third of these are trenchant; the first, I fear, is less so, simply because here he gives the appearance of speaking past his interlocutors. Bock writes that the Keith/Le Donne volume fails to convince insofar as it insists that "the criteria are deep-seated in a flawed form criticism," for "a flawed origin still does not remove the goal that such a project has, namely, providing an approach to the Gospel sources that argues that one has to make a case for their credibility" (206). Granted, but it *may* require—as Keith, Le Donne, and company would want to insist—that we go about thinking about credibility in a different way, more exactly, that we reorient our inquiry to a set of realities different from that which the traditional criteria were designed to recover. (As the point stands, Bock seems to assume that the authors of *JCDA* are disinterested in making a case for the Gospels' credibility, when in fact, as far as we know, they are only interested in redefining what "credibility" really looks like.) Meanwhile, Bock's second and third remarks are incisive, not least when he writes that the Gospels "are written with an awareness of the larger story and series of events that are brought into play in their narrative" (206). I take this to mean (and if so, I fully agree) that responsible interpretation must begin not with an atomistic approach to the pericopae, as so much twentieth-century gospel research has proceeded, but with due appreciation of the given textual unit within a larger compositional unity.[4] Bock's final remark focuses on the bar of evidence: "People may be working with different proof standards and may also be forgetting what failure to gain them may or may not say about the kind of judgment being made" (207). This is an extremely important point and one that bears restating: just where the burden of proof lies in any given instance depends

---

4. This point is regularly made—as well as regularly unheeded—in the scholarship; see, for example, the *a propos* comments of Brant Pitre (*Jesus and the Last Supper* [Grand Rapids: Eerdmans, 2015]: 51): "Many Jesus scholars will reject a particular episode from the Gospels as unhistorical or implausible *before they have even interpreted the evidence in its context*. In this way, historical conclusions are drawn based on presuppositions and prejudgments that are often unstated, apart from any detailed analysis of the passage in question. This is . . . one of the most serious weaknesses of many scholarly works on Jesus" (emphasis original).

on whose version of "true north" you're depending on. This is a big problem in need of better resolution.

In his treatment of Mark 14:53–65, Bock makes a compelling case for the authenticity of Jesus's trial, as well as Jesus's recorded words as part of that event. It is at least compelling enough. Does multiple attestation help secure Jesus's trial within history? I think so. Does the (oddly named) criterion of rejection and execution? Again, yes. Do either of these *prove* the trial as historical fact? No. Nor does Bock pretend as much. Instead, our author modestly intends to show that the criteria *can* have some evidentiary weight, even if they by themselves fall short of being probative. For this reason (and this I think is his overall point), it would only be overreactive thinking that requires us to make the jump from earlier misapplications of the criteria to the conclusion that the criteria themselves are *ipso facto* illegitimate.

Craig Evans and Greg Monette ("Jesus's Burial: Archaeology, Authenticity, and History") also make effective use of the criteria of multiple attestation and embarrassment in their discussion of Jesus's interment, showing "that the burial of Jesus as an event in history is highly probable" (269). Their larger point is not so much to secure the event's historicity but to show that the recently posed objections to the criteria "are not nearly as difficult to overcome as those who posit them imagine" (302). Along the way, as a kind of "toss in," the two authors further observe that the criteria used by Jesus scholars are not unique to this particular field of research but are akin to procedures regularly used in other areas of historical investigation. All to say, it is not just (allegedly) outmoded Jesus scholars who take an interest in "credibility, verisimilitude, multiple attestation, corroboration, eyewitness testimony" (273); historians of various research interests have long seen evidentiary value in such things. This poses a stiff rejoinder to one of Keith and Le Donne's basic claims, namely, that the criteria of authenticity must be written off as the bastard children of an ill-conceived union between positivism and form criticism. Again, although the positivist spirit dominating so much of twentieth-century research severely qualifies the trustworthiness of conclusions drawn from the same uncritically prosecuted investigations, this by itself is no grounds for claiming that the basic principles undergirding the criteria are intrinsically—always and everywhere—faulty.

Along these lines, there is a certain irony in the fact that whereas Morna Hooker, with an eye to the New Quest, makes a plea "for less dogmatism in our conclusions" (283), many of those who have carried forward her cause have proven to be far more dogmatic in their methodological conclusions than their targeted heirs of the New Quest.[5] Here one may be forgiven for wondering whether many of the historiographical postmodernists among us are, in fact, responding to a palpable problem without reflecting the awareness that their solution to that problem is no less enthralled by the same—finally unwarranted—Kantian anxieties. One sometimes gets the sense that the criteria's fiercest detractors are those who, not unlike Dickens's Miss Havisham, have been jilted by "recoverable facts" and then continue to live in the Enlightenment past by refusing to shed the now-fading wedding dress of empirical purity, which forces us to choose between utter certainty and utter skepticism. At a foundational level, postmodern skepticism (insisting we *can't* be certain of anything) is far more similar to modern positivism (insisting we *can* be certain of anything) than it is different.

While Evans and Monette are concerned with Jesus's burial, Michael Licona ("Jesus's Resurrection, Realism, and the Role of the Criteria of Authenticity") takes up events reported on either side of this event: Jesus's death by crucifixion and resurrection. Like Craig and Monette, Licona also appeals to the criteria of multiple attestation and embarrassment. Here I appreciate the author's common-sense-realism approach, personalized by his account of his experience of his friend Josh. Yet there is also an edginess to Licona's argument. "So, again, I would want to hear from those who would call for the abandonment of the criteria or regard them as having little value," he writes, throwing down the gauntlet (301–2). Like other contributors to this volume, he advocates for a holistic approach to the Gospels.

The most strenuous objection to the rumored demise of the criteria seems to hail from Michael Metts, who argues that historically the New Quest was not a continuation of classic form criticism but an attempt to repeal certain of its key tenets. Thus, Metts argues, the attempt to discredit the criteria by virtue of their historical indebtedness to form criticism at worst runs afoul of the genetic fallacy, or at best fails to appreciate the extent to which the New Quest was truly a revolt against classic form criticism. There are strengths and weaknesses to this piece. On the one hand, Metts very helpfully provides us with a succinct review of the New Quest, even as he reminds us of the movement's historical situatedness. (Scholarly movements never arise in a vacuum, and the New Quest is no exception, seeking to respond to Bultmann on his own terms.) On the other hand, I sense that Metts's argument (not unlike Bock's leading introductory remark discussed above) fails to engage Keith's essential point, not least the latter's principle objection to—what he sees as the—methodically unwarranted

---

5. Cited in Morna D. Hooker, "Christology and Methodology," *NTS* 17 (1971): 480–87 (485).

bifurcation of "authentic" and "inauthentic" material, based on a philosophical objection to separating fact from interpretation. I suspect that Keith would agree with Metts that the New Quest was essentially a repudiative project: Keith would only add that the repudiation did not go far or deep enough.

BEYOND THE CRITERIA

In collective dialogue with *JCDA*, a number of essays here seek to resituate the criteria alongside a broader array of historiographical approaches. Beth Sheppard's piece ("Alternate History and the Sermon on the Mount: New Trajectories for Research") is a case in point. While I find myself unpersuaded by Sheppard's specific proposal that Jesus delivered his Sermon on the Mount in a theater (197–203), her broader observations on historical method are worth the price of admission. Sheppard writes that "when we as historians set our sights almost exclusively on determining the authenticity of Jesus's miracles, individual sayings, theology, or the content of his message, as worthy as these tasks are, we might miss other information that may enable us to deduce details about the historical Jesus" (186). Though the limitations of the current *modus operandi* are palpable, "the almost paralyzing conundrum of the inadequacy of the Gospels to provide a definitive, complete portrait of Jesus based only on his words or miracles can be somewhat alleviated by asking new questions and looking at indirect sources" (187). After all, "no rule for analyzing the gospels works perfectly all the time" (189). It's hard to argue with sentiments like these. Moreover, who can fail to resonate when Sheppard invites the guild of Jesus researchers to approach its task with greater flexibility and indeed (dare I say it?) imagination?[6]

Answering the call, Jeannine Brown's "Reconstructing the Historical Pharisees: Does Matthew's Gospel Have Anything to Contribute?" seems to deliver exactly the kind of fresh scholarship Sheppard is hoping for. In this essay, focusing on "the contribution from Matthew's portrait for a historical understanding of the Pharisees in the early part of the first century CE" (166), I am struck by how greater attentiveness to the coherence between the evangelist's text and early first-century historical realities (verisimilitude) promises not only to shed light on the quality of the Gospel writer's historiography but also, by extension, to enhance our ability to accurately assign discrete *Sitze im Leben*. Whereas the more directly polemical portions of Matthew have been normally deemed

---

6. I register a similar plea in *Jesus the Priest* (London: SPCK; Grand Rapids: Baker Academic: 2018), 11–15.

"ecclesial creation" or "redactional" (on the assumption that Jesus's "anti-Jewish" rhetoric is more likely a reflection of a post-parting-of-the-ways situation than anything resembling his own day), Brown's triangulation of these same passages against the relevant sources outside the Gospels reveals that this standard maneuver has been repeated with far too little critical reflection. If there is an implicit criterion of *in*authenticity in play when it comes to these kinds of materials (i.e., anything smacking of anti-Semitism is most likely non-dominical), Brown's essay is a salutary warning against hasty inferences.

Paul Anderson ("The John, Jesus, and History Project and a Fourth Quest for Jesus") rehearses the efforts of what has become for him a decades-long undertaking, dedicated to evaluating the evidentiary merits of the Gospel of John in historical Jesus research. In his assessment of the criteria, Anderson is far closer to the Keith/Le Donne approach than his co-essayists; he is generally in favor of dispensing with the criteria as we know them, not least because they are "designed to favor Synoptic features over and against Johannine ones" (245). (Apart from the criteria of multiple attestation, I am not sure why Anderson thinks this to be the case.) I trust that most readers of this piece will quickly realize historical Jesus scholarship's indebtedness to Anderson not only for his efforts in rehabilitating John but also for clarifying why such a retrieval is long overdue.

At the same time, I found the contribution puzzling in several respects. First, on the face of it, it is difficult to reconcile the jarring inconsistency between Anderson's Keith/Le Donne-esque critique of the criteria, on the one side, and his reiteration of Raymond Brown's compositional hypothesis (involving the heavily positivist move of positing multiple layers of redaction across the text on the basis of mirror readings), on the other. This seems a little like having your methodological cake and eating it too. Second, given Anderson's interest in recovering impressions rather than facts, one wonders, first, whether the bullet-point payoffs he lists (257–64) are so generalized that they actually add relatively little to the historical Jesus of Synoptic portraiture, and, second, whether a number of these "impressions" cannot be fully laid at the feet of late redactors. For example, if John's "juxtaposition of Peter and the Beloved Disciple poses an alternative apostolic vision as something of a corrective to the emergence of Ignatian hierarchical leadership," on what basis can it also be claimed that this reflects a "more primitive understanding[s] than those conveyed in the Synoptics" (259)? Frankly, I find myself confused at this juncture.

Robert McIver ("Collective Memory and the Reliability of the Gospels' Traditions") and Paul Eddy ("The Historicity of the Early Oral Jesus Tradition:

Reflections on the 'Reliability Wars'") provide excellent treatments to two very critical questions: (1) what is the overall probability that the Jesus traditions were faithfully remembered by those closest to him and (2) what kind of community controls were likely in place in the first-century transmission of Jesus traditions? Together the two pieces inject a clarifying dose of reality into a discussion burdened by unbridled imaginations fancying that, by the time the Gospels were written, the public words and deeds of Jesus either fell into historical oblivion or were so fundamentally mutated in the retelling that there's no telling what Jesus did and didn't do. At the same time, the paired essays are, if nothing else, a symbolic reminder that the guild has never settled whether the trajectory from the real Jesus to the Synoptic records is best explicated with recourse to memory research or the study of orality. Clarifying the interrelationship between authorized eyewitnesses and community traditioning processes remains a *desideratum*.

WHITHER THE CRITERIA OF AUTHENTICITY, JESUS, AND HISTORY

The essays gathered here are concerned with not just the nitty-gritty details of method but also the larger, ongoing conversation relating to faith and history. Blomberg and Seal provide an overview of Jesus studies in recent years, with particular attention to the evangelical contribution, not without some prescriptions going forward. They note "some very large anthologies of historical Jesus research within the past decade that combine together disparate perspectives in a way that was much rarer a generation ago" (48). Although the perspectival variation they have in mind is mainly theological in nature (a sign that evangelical Jesus scholars have in fact now earned a place at the table), it is equally true that we are—for better or worse—witnessing a burgeoning methodological diversity. For this reason, I confess a certain disappointment in the authors' closing discussion "Future Prospects for Historical Jesus Research," where they envision the possibility of a second volume of *Key Events in the Life of the Historical Jesus*, "tackling another ten to twelve pericopae with perhaps slightly less solid corroborating evidence via the standard criteria of authenticity" (62), even as they advocate for the application of the criteria to the Gospel of John (63). As vitally important as such projects may be, the proposed vision, as it is laid out, strikes me as slightly pedestrian, unnecessarily tied down to a set of tools that must now in fact—as some of the other essayists in this volume remind us—interface with other kinds of queries, giving way to a creative but coherent convergence of methods.

Finally, coming full circle to the volume's opening essay ("The Historical Jesus and the Biblical Church: Why the Quest Matters"), we find Robert Bowman and Ed Komoszewski (re)asserting the importance of history in Jesus studies—here I take the authors to mean not just a history of impressions but factual history. In this connection, Bowman and Komoszewski find themselves roiled by Scot McKnight's contribution to *JCDA* on two counts.[7] They object not only to McKnight's statement that "historical Jesus studies are useless for the church" but also to the claim that there are many Jesuses (a Jewish Jesus, a canonical Jesus, an orthodox Jesus, etc.). Against this second assertion (which is of course related to the first), our two authors insist along with Lesslie Newbigin that "there is only one Jesus, and there is only one history" (21).

In this back-and-forth between Bowman and Komoszewski on the one side, and McKnight on the other, it would be all too easy to draw unnecessary inferences and overinterpret one's interlocutor, so we must be careful. On one level, McKnight is assuredly correct about the existence of many Jesuses. Matthew, Mark, Luke, and John each have their own Jesus; even as the compilers behind the Gospel of Thomas have theirs. The canonical Jesus comes to us on different terms than the Jesus formulated by Nicaea; even as the Jesus emerging from the "assured results" of critical research is different from both of these. Here the distinctions between all of these Jesuses have to do with discrete universes of discourse. To make the same point in Wittgensteinian terms, it is virtually inevitable that the concept of "Jesus" acquire different significances within different social contexts, different language games, even as these different "games" are governed by different grammars, goals, and expectations. To this extent McKnight is quite correct: there are different Jesuses.

At the same time, as Bowman and Komoszewski seem to recognize, there are clearly certain theological dangers inherent in the predication of multiple Jesuses, the same danger that ultimately led Käsemann to pronounce Bultmann's project a failure. For this part, Bultmann not only drew a sharp distinction between the Jesus of history and the Christ of faith but also implicitly applauds the early church for (allegedly) having done so. There was certainly some theological convenience in this historical judgment. Only by positing the primitive church's disinterest in the historical facts of Jesus can we credibly suppose that the same church undertook the kind of demythologizing program now recommended by Bultmann. Of course, as Käsemann pointed out almost seventy years ago, Bultmann's project was essentially a resuscitation of primitive docetism.

---

7. "Why the Authentic Jesus Is of No Use for the Church," in Keith and Le Donne, *Jesus, Criteria, and the Demise of Authenticity*, 173–85.

Docetism certainly has its own set of attractions. Once Jesus has been abstracted from historically embedded flesh and refashioned to suit the contemporary context, humanity is once again where it wants to be, in that all-too convenient (not to mention all-too familiar) position where it may, as Calvin puts it, "imagine god according to its own capacity, as . . . it conceives an unreality and an empty appearance as God" (*Inst.* 1.11.8). By the same token, if by the phrase "many Jesuses" we mean to imply that we are renouncing the quest of reconstructing the real Jesus through rigorously informed and critically responsible imagination, then we have essentially already given away the store of the incarnation and defaulted to a gnostic position. In his time, Irenaeus insisted on the necessity of four Gospels, even as he equally insisted on the existence of one gospel undergirding all four. By analogy, Jesus scholars who operate from within a confessional framework, at least if they are to be consistent, ultimately have no choice but to insist that the many Jesuses of our ecclesial and academic discourses be finally tethered to a real Jesus who lived in history. If we choose to believe that this real Jesus is for all intents and purposes nonexistent (like a noiseless tree falling in the forest), it only means that we have allowed our foundational commitments to take a back seat to still-fashionable Enlightenment epistemologies.

Even so, epistemology shapes culture, which should in turn shape the nature of our arguments. If the perceived usefulness of our business-as-usual approach to the historical Jesus has been steadily eroding, losing ground in what Jeffrey Stout might call the "logical space of normative discourse," perhaps it *is* time we mend our ways.[8] Perhaps the moral of the story, at least at this point, is that the Jesus guild must be more tentative in applying its one-size-fits-all methods while providing more space for fresh arguments proceeding along different axes, involving a variety of disciplines and criteria. This need not spell the end of the criteria of authenticity. After all, in the final analysis, the criteria are nothing more and nothing less than certain kinds of arguments that, having been given birth in a particular context and deployed for specific purposes, have been cryogenically frozen in the form of a method, only then to be relentlessly reapplied with varying results. Some awareness that the criteria of authenticity have been applied in a pseudoscientific manner does not in principle invalidate the kinds of arguments which gave rise to the criteria, but it should certainly make us pause before drawing far-reaching conclusions on sometimes narrow grounds. Still, that the criteria of authenticity can and do provide grounds is indubitable. The reports of their deaths have been grossly exaggerated.

---

8. Jeffrey Stout, *Ethics after Babel: The Languages of Morals and Their Discontents* (Boston: Beacon, 1988), 28.

About the Editors

Darrell L. Bock (PhD, University of Aberdeen; Humboldt Scholar, Tübingen University) is Senior Research Professor of New Testament Studies at Dallas Theological Seminary. Bock is the author of over thirty books, including well-regarded commentaries on Luke and Acts and several books on historical Jesus studies, such as *Who Is Jesus? Linking the Historical Jesus with the Christ of Faith*.

J. Ed Komoszewski (ThM, Dallas Theological Seminary) is a freelance researcher and writer living in Texas. In addition to his previous work in the pastorate, Ed taught biblical and theological studies at the University of Northwestern—St. Paul and Bethlehem College & Seminary. He is the coauthor of *Reinventing Jesus: How Contemporary Skeptics Miss the Real Jesus and Mislead Popular Culture* and *Putting Jesus in His Place: The Case for the Deity of Christ*.

Contributors

Paul N. Anderson (PhD, University of Glasgow) is professor of biblical and Quaker studies at George Fox University (Newberg, Oregon). He is the author of *The Fourth Gospel and the Quest for Jesus* and the coeditor of the three-volume series *John, Jesus, and History*.

Michael F. Bird (PhD, University of Queensland) is academic dean and lecturer in theology and New Testament at Ridley College (Melbourne, Australia). He is the author of *The Gospel of the Lord: How the Early Church Wrote the Story of Jesus*.

Craig L. Blomberg (PhD, University of Aberdeen) is distinguished professor of New Testament at Denver Seminary. He is the author of *The Historical Reliability of the New Testament, Interpreting the Parables*, and *Jesus and the Gospels: An Introduction and Survey*.

Darrell L. Bock (PhD, University of Aberdeen) is senior research professor of New Testament at Dallas Theological Seminary. He is the author of *Studying the Historical Jesus: A Guide to Sources and Methods* and coeditor of *Key Events in the Life of the Historical Jesus*.

Robert M. Bowman Jr. (PhD, South African Theological Seminary) lectures annually at New Orleans Baptist Theological Seminary and is an independent scholar in Rockford, Michigan. He is the coauthor of *Putting Jesus in His Place*.

Jeannine K. Brown (PhD, Luther Seminary) is professor of New Testament and director of online programs at Bethel Seminary. She is the author of *Matthew* (Teach the Text Commentary) and associate editor of *Dictionary of Jesus and the Gospels* (2nd ed.).

Paul Rhodes Eddy (PhD, Marquette University) is professor of biblical and theological studies at Bethel University. He is the coauthor of *The Jesus Legend: A Case for the Historical Reliability of the Synoptic Jesus Tradition* and coeditor of *The Historical Jesus: Five Views*.

Craig A. Evans (PhD, Claremont Graduate University) is John Bisagno Distinguished Professor of Christian Origins at Houston Baptist University. He is the author of *Jesus and the Remains of His Day* and editor of *The Routledge Encyclopedia of the Historical Jesus*.

Larry W. Hurtado (PhD, Case Western Reserve University) is emeritus professor of New Testament language, literature, and theology at the University of Edinburgh. He is the author of *Lord Jesus Christ: Devotion to Jesus in Earliest Christianity* and *Mark* (New International Biblical Commentary).

Craig S. Keener (PhD, Duke University) is the F. M. and Ada Thompson Professor of Biblical Studies at Asbury Theological Seminary. He is the author of *The Historical Jesus of the Gospels* and *Christobiography: Memories, History, and the Reliability of the Gospels*.

J. Ed Komoszewski (ThM, Dallas Theological Seminary) formerly taught biblical and theological studies at the University of Northwestern—St. Paul and Bethlehem College and Seminary. He is the coauthor of *Reinventing Jesus* and *Putting Jesus in His Place*.

Michael R. Licona (PhD, University of Pretoria) is associate professor of theology at Houston Baptist University. He is the author of *The Resurrection of Jesus: A New Historiographical Approach* and *Why Are There Differences in the Gospels? What We Can Learn from Ancient Biography*.

Robert McIver (PhD, Andrews University) is senior lecturer in biblical studies and head of the School of Ministry and Theology, Avondale College, Australia. He is the author of *Mainstream or Marginal? The Matthean Community in Early Christianity* and *Memory, Jesus, and the Synoptic Gospels*.

Scot McKnight (PhD, University of Nottingham) is Julius R. Mantey Chair of New Testament at Northern Seminary. He is the author of *Jesus and His Death:*

Historiography, the Historical Jesus, and Atonement Theory and coeditor of *The Historical Jesus in Recent Research*.

Michael B. Metts (MA, Criswell College; MDiv, Southwestern Baptist Theological Seminary) is a PhD candidate in New Testament at the University of Aberdeen under Tomas Bokedal, specializing in historical Jesus studies.

Greg Monette (MA, MDiv, Acadia University; PhD cand., University of Bristol, Trinity College) is adjunct lecturer in biblical studies at Acadia Divinity College. He is the author of *The Wrong Jesus: Fact, Belief, Legend, Truth . . . Making Sense of What You've Heard*.

Nicholas Perrin (PhD, Marquette University) is the president of Trinity International University in Deerfield, Illinois. He is the author of *Jesus the Temple, Jesus the Priest*, and associate editor of *Dictionary of Jesus and the Gospels* (2nd ed.).

Darlene M. Seal (MA, Denver Seminary; PhD student, McMaster Divinity College) is the author of "The Form Criticism of Vincent Taylor," in *Pillars in the History of Biblical Interpretation*, vol. 3 (forthcoming).

Beth M. Sheppard (PhD, University of Sheffield) is dean of libraries and professor at the University of West Georgia. She is the author of *The Craft of History and the Study of the New Testament*.

Ben Sutton (PhD, Ridley College) is an ethicist at a healthcare nonprofit and an independent scholar researching the function of memory in culture.

Daniel B. Wallace (PhD, Dallas Theological Seminary) is senior research professor of New Testament at Dallas Theological Seminary and executive director of the Center for the Study of New Testament Manuscripts. He is the coauthor of *Reinventing Jesus* and *Dethroning Jesus*.

Scripture Index

Subject Index

379

Author Index